CRESCENT AND STAR

CRESCENT AND STAR

ARAB & ISRAELI PERSPECTIVES ON THE MIDDLE EAST CONFLICT

Edited by
YONAH ALEXANDER
&
NICHOLAS N. KITTRIE

AMS PRESS, INC.
New York & Toronto

Yonah Alexander is Professor of International Studies at the College at Oneonta of the State University of New York and is Senior Fellow at the Institute of International Law and Policy at The American University.

Nicholas N. Kittrie is Professor of Comparative Law and Director of the Institute of International Law and Policy at the American University.

Library of Congress Cataloging in Publication Data

Alexander, Yonah, comp.
    Crescent and star.

    Bibliography: p.
    1. Jewish-Arab relations—Addresses, essays, lectures
I. Kittrie, Nicholas N., 1928-   joint comp.
II. Title.
DS119.7.A642   301.29'17'492705694   72-5797
ISBN 0-404-10522-X
ISBN 0-404-10523-8 (pbk.)

Manufactured in the United States of America.

Second Printing, 1973

CONTENTS

Preface   xi

I. Nationalism and Statehood   3
  the arab rights
    F. Yahia: The Palestine People and International Law   6
    Y. Harkabi: The Arab Slogan of a Democratic State   28
  the israeli rights
    Bhim Singh and Angelina Helou: An Examination of
       Documents on Which the State of Israel is Based   52
    Zvi Ankori: The Continuing Zionist Revolution   66

II. Religious and Ethnical Conflicts   99
    Khalid Kishtainy: The Anti-Semitism Blackmail   101
    Jibran Majdalany: On the Necessity for an Anti-
       Racialist Solution to the Palestine Conflict   109
    Dafna Dan: Education in Hatred   118
    Ministry of Foreign Affairs (Jerusalem): On Arab
       Anti-Semitism   125

III. Minority and Human Rights   131
  arabs in israel
    Sabri Jiryis: The Arabs in Israel   134
    Ministry of Foreign Affairs (Jerusalem): The Arabs of
       Israel   151
  arabs in the 1967 occupied territories
    Palestine Research Center: Reign of Terror   162

Ministry of Foreign Affairs (Jerusalem): Israel in the Administered Areas 174

jews in the arab countries
Dafna Dan: Jews in Arab Countries 187

IV. **Arab Refugees** 197
Sami Hadawi: The Arab Refugees 199
Michael Comay: The Arab Refugees 205

V. **Expansionism and Boundary Conflicts** 217
Sami Hadawi: Israeli Expansionism 219
Ministry of Foreign Affairs (Jerusalem): The Provisional Nature of the 1949 Armistice Lines 228

VI. **The Status of Jerusalem** 236
Rouhi Al-Khatib: The Judaization of Jerusalem 238
Yosef Takoah: Barbed Wire Shall Not Return to Jerusalem 259

VII. **The Jordan River** 278
Omar Z. Ghobashy: The Development of the Jordan River 279
Ministry of Foreign Affairs (Jerusalem): The Arab Plan to Divert the Headwaters of the River Jordan 286

VIII. **Freedom of Navigation** 292
the gulf of aqaba
Institute for Palestine Studies: The Gulf of Aqaba and the Straits of Tiran 294
Ministry of Foreign Affairs (Jerusalem): Egypt's Unlawful Blockade of the Gulf of Aqaba 303
the suez canal
C. Bassiouni: Navigation Rights in the Suez Canal 309
Ministry of Foreign Affairs (Jerusalem): Israel and the Suez Canal 315

IX. **Aggression and Self-Defense** 318
Ibrahim Al-Abid: Palestine: Questions and Answers 320
Abba Eban: Israel's Action in Sinai and From a State of War to a State of Peace 324

X. **Economic Warfare** 328
Marwan Iskandar: The Arab Boycott in International Law 330
N. I. Dajani: Economic Impact of the Israeli Aggression 334
Abba Eban: Economic Effects 337
Ministry of Foreign Affairs (Jerusalem): Arab Boycott 339

XI. Guerrilla Activities   341
    Ezzeldin Foda: The Legitimacy of Resistance and Human Rights in the Occupied Territory   343
    Ministry of Foreign Affairs (Jerusalem): War by Terror   355

XII. The Role of the U. N. and the Big Powers   372
    Arab League: The Jarring Mission   374
    Ministry of Foreign Affairs (Jerusalem): International Guarantees and International Police Forces   391

XIII. Negotiations and Peace   398
    Ibrahim Al-Abid: Israel and Negotiations   399
    Association for Peace: Solutions to the Palestinian Problem   402

Multilateral, Bilateral, Unilateral Documents   407
    Convention between Great Britain, Germany, Austria-Hungary, Spain, France, Italy, The Netherlands, Russia, and Turkey Respecting the Free Navigation of the Suez Canal, 29 October 1888   409
    League of Nations Mandate for Palestine, 24 July 1922   413
    United Nations Resolution 181 (II) of 29 November 1947 — Partition of Palestine   420
    Resolution Adopted by the General Assembly, 11 December 1948   422
    Resolution Adopted by the UN Security Council, 1 September 1951   425
    Arab Summit Conference in Khartoum, 29 August to 1 September 1967   427
    United Nations Security Council Resolution of 22 November 1967   430
    The Husayn-McMahon Correspondence, 14 July 1915 — 10 March 1916   432
    Arab-Jewish Agreements Relative to Palestine, 3 January 1919 to 5 March 1919   437
    Israel-Lebanese General Armistice Agreement, 23 March 1949   441
    The Balfour Declaration, 2 November 1917   446
    The Palestine National Charter, 1 July to 17 July 1968   447
    Declaration of the Establishment of the State of Israel, 14 May 1948   452
    Law of Return, 5 July 1950   455

Maps   457
    1921 British Mandate over Palestine   459
    1922 Partition of Palestine by Great Britain   460

1947 U. N. Partition of Palestine   461
1949 Armistice Agreements Boundaries   462
1967 Cease-Fire Lines   463
Israel and the Arab States: Area and Population   464-5

Selected Bibiliography   467

For the Grandparents,
And the Grandchildren:
Daphne, Dean, Norda, Orde and Zachary —

With the hope that in their lifetimes
Swords may be beaten into plowshares

PREFACE

> By three things is the world
> sustained — justice, truth, and peace.
> — AVOT 1:17
> (Mishna, 220 A.D.)

> Do not commit treachery, nor
> depart from the right path. You
> must not mutilate, neither kill a
> child or aged man or woman. Do
> not destroy a palm tree, nor burn
> it with fire and do not cut any
> fruitful tree.
> — Abu Bakr
> (The First Caliph, 632 - 634 A.D.)

By the time this volume reaches its readers, the Middle East conflict will have made new headlines in the world press. War begets war and cruelty begets cruelty. Whether it is the massacre at the Munich Olympics or the Israeli army's retaliation against guerrilla bases and their neighboring villages — it has become almost irrelevant as to who was the first or last to strike its adversary.

And since keeping up-to-date with the Arab-Israeli vengeance is a futile effort, detailing one series of recent hostilities will serve sufficiently to illustrate the depth of the schism. The major question is how the circle of violence is to be broken.

On May 30, 1972, Air France Flight #132 from Paris via Rome reached Lod International Airport in Israel at 10:25 p.m. with 122 passengers, including returning residents, foreign tourists, and three young Japanese travelers. Moments after they and the crew passed the passport control station, the Japanese trio pulled out Czech-made automatic rifles and grenades concealed in their suitcases and started firing and hurling grenades into the crowd of several hundred men, women, and children gathered in the terminal. After the surprise attack, which lasted four minutes, the floors of the area were splattered with blood. Twenty-seven dead were counted, and some eighty people were wounded, many critically. Included in the dead were sixteen Christian Puerto Rican pilgrims. Two of the Japanese murderers were killed in battle — one blowing himself up accidentally with a grenade — and the other shot by bullets fired by his comrade. The third was captured alive by an airport employee.

Within hours of the incident, the Popular Front for the Liberation of Palestine (P.F.L.P.), the Marxist Palestinian Arab guerrilla group based in Beirut, Lebanon, announced its responsibility for the killings. The Front asserted that the "brave operation" was carried out by the "squad of Patrick Arguello," a group named in memory of Nicaraguan volunteer of P.F.L.P., who was killed in an abortive attempt to hijack an EL-AL plane the previous year. The Front also claimed that the incident was made in revenge for Jewish atrocities going back to April 9, 1948 when members of the Jewish terrorist organizations, the "Irgun Zvai Leumi" and the "Stern Gang," had massacred 254 men, women, and children at Deir Yassin, an Arab village in the western suburbs of Jerusalem. That massacre had caused a panic among the Arab population and a flight of Arab refugees from Jerusalem.

Concerning the three murderers, the P.F.L.P. stated that "those three heroes came thousands of miles to take part with the Palestinian people in their struggle against the forces of Zionism and imperialism." Mr. Bassam Zayed, the P.F.L.P. spokesman in Beirut, stated that the "revolutionary answer" given by the Japanese agents was aimed at raising "the temperature of the Arab-Israeli hostility" and at cutting "the enemies communications arteries." When he was asked if his organization had any moral misgivings about the massacre of innocent civilians, he replied: "None at all." All the bystanders at the airport, including the foreign Christian visitors, he contended, were "guilty" if only because they had not "raised a finger for the Palestinians." Besides, "the Palestinian Resistance had warned tourists who visited Israel that it is not responsible for their safety in a land which we consider the field of a continuing battle."

Cairo's semi-official daily, AL AHRAM, characterized the operation as "the peak of success." The Lod incident showed "that Israel could not immune herself against the renewal of commando operations. Every Israeli action aimed at undermining the resistance movement will be met with vengeance with whatever available means to prove that blind force and tyranny can be checked." Speaking in the same vein, Aziz Sidky, Egypt's Prime Minister, asserted that the "courageous action" exposed the Israeli myth that "it has no equal in the world for brilliance, genius, organization, and invincibility," and therefore "proves" that the Arabs are indeed capable of achieving an ultimate victory over Zionism and its state. Support for the exploit was also given by Egyptian President Anwar Sadat who said that it was ironic for the Israeli "murderers and terrorists" to pretend to mourn over the killings in the belief that the record of their crimes against the Arabs in the occupied territories had been lost.

The Lebanese government's attitude was more moderate, stating that it "condemns any action of whatever kind, and whatever source, which aims to harm innocent civilians and strangers to the conflict." President Suelliman Franjien also observed that the "repression" in the occupied territories captured by Israel in June 1967 "inexorably" brings extreme reactions.

Jordan's King Hussein, an avowed foe of P.F.L.P., was the only Arab leader to denounce the incident. He called it "a sick crime, committed by sick people, and planned by sick minds as well."

Israel condemned the "premeditated and wanton murder" at Lod. Referring to the massacre sponsored by P.F.L.P. as "liberation by proxy," Israel's Prime Minister Golda Meir also laid the blame on the Government of Lebanon which enabled P.F.L.P. to plot this and similar acts of political warfare. It is in Beirut, she claimed, that the headquarters of the P.F.L.P., as well as other Palestinian Arab organizations, are located and where "travel documents are prepared, and the arms, sabotage material and operational commands are issued. Training for terrorist operations abroad are also carried out on Lebanese soil." The connivance of the Egyptian government was also stressed. Cairo, she stated is the location for most meetings of the terror organizations and "is a prime source of their instruction." Also, Egypt "grants the major moral and political backing" to Palestinian Arab "exploirts."

Several days later Israel Galili, Minister Without Portfolio in Mrs. Meir's Cabinet, vowed that the deaths at Lod "will be avenged, but not rashly and not in disregard of the principles upheld by Israel."

In addition to the misery of the injured victims and the families of the wounded and dead, the tragedy produced several other results. There has been an escalation of Israeli suspicion, bitterness, and hatred towards the Arabs and an intensification of the propaganda war between the antagonists. Massive troop movements in Israeli settlements along the Lebanese-Israeli armistice lines have caused increased Arab anxiety over the possibility of Israeli military retaliation. The Arab Palestinian guerrillas in Lebanon, anticipating an Israeli attack, once again evacuated women and children from several Arab refugee camps in Southern Lebanon. And even in far away Puerto Rico, the repercussions have produced threats of retaliation against innocent Japanese and Arabs living and working there.

Munich, Lod and Deir Yassin are only a few in a long series of acts of violence that for half a century have plagued the people of the Middle East, frequently affecting also the lives and interests of other peoples and nations. While recent months have seen several attempts to reduce global tensions through accommodations between the Western democracies and Communism in both Europe and the Far East, the Middle East dispute not only continues smoldering, but constantly threatens to erupt again into major warfare which could engulf the region and possibly the entire world.

Numerous volumes have been written about the Middle East conflict. Yet new fact-finding missions continue making their pilgrimages to this little sliver of land on the eastern Mediterranean, to seek out the roots of the controversy. There have been British and American commissions, United Nations missions, and, most recently, a very prestigious delegation of heads of African states.

Despite all the attention which has centered on the Middle East, there has been no document generally available which directly presents the major issues of the conflict from the viewpoints of the main contenders, the Arabs and the Israelis. Believing that an open forum and an opportunity to present conflicting grievances are first steps towards a mutual appreciation of the interests involved, as well as towards any search for a just solution, we have sought in this volume to set the stage for a verbal confrontation between the antagonists.

We hope that this unique volume will furnish a large number of interested American and other readers with the unadorned background information from which they may make their own informed decisions regarding the justice of the

Arab and Israeli causes. It is hoped further, that additional insights into the mutual claims, fears, anxieties and gropings for a solution might help the antagonists themselves in relinquishing heroic despair in favor of a search for compromise and hope.

In preparing this volume, the editors are indebted to the various offices of information of the Arab States in the United States; the Arab League Office in London; Jordan's Ministry of Culture and Information; the Palestine Liberation Organization Research Center, the Institute for Palestine Studies, and the Fifth of June Society, Beirut; the Consulate General of Israel in New York; the Embassy of Israel in Washington, D. C.; Israel's Ministry of Foreign Affairs in Jerusalem; Israel Academic Committee on the Middle East in Jerusalem; and the Association for Peace in Tel-Aviv.

Some of the materials in this volume were collected as a by-product of a research project on the role of communication in the Middle East conflict, conducted by the Graduate School of Journalism, Columbia University, with the support of the Institute of International Order. Professor Alexander wishes to thank the Graduate School of Journalism and the Institute for their part in making this book possible.

Finally, some mention should be made about the editorial preparation of the selections which appear in this book. Some of the selections may be labeled "propaganda," and yet they are significant if only because they reflect the real or imaginary grievances and attitudes of the parties. Some of the documents in the book were originally issued on mimeograph sheets and in other forms of rapid printing. Often the material was obviously not edited carefully. To provide the reader with the general impression of the original documents, we have, with a few exceptions of obvious error, reproduced the documents as they were originally printed with inconsistent spelling, and awkward grammar. The inevitable repetitions in a number of instances and the awkwardness and differences in expression serve to confirm the vehemence of the antagonists, which has erupted so often on the intertwining issues of the Middle East.

Yonah Alexander
Nicholas N. Kittrie

Bethesda, Maryland
June 5, 1972

CRESCENT AND STAR

1. Nationalism and Statehood

INTRODUCTION

The Arab-Israeli conflict is known through its many consequences — military, political, economic and humanitarian. Its impact is felt regionally, as well as globally. Yet at the core there is one unmistakable cause: the ideological confrontation between Arab nationalism and Jewish nationalism, or Zionism. Highly charged with intense emotional and psychological implications, these ideologies are often misunderstood and misinterpreted. Any meaningful discussion of the problems of the Middle East, therefore, must consider the underlying assumption of the two antagonistic nationalisms.

The Arabs, until the end of the First World War, had long lived in a multi-national state, the Ottoman Empire, where Turks, Armenians, Greeks, and many other people of diverse races and religions resided side by side. Arab nationalism began with the intellectual awakening and cultural revival of the Arabs, mostly in the Eastern Mediterranean, at the end of the nineteenth century. The Ottoman decline, manifested by bureaucratic inefficiency and the abuse of minorities, gave the movement for Arab self-determination greater momentum in the early part of the twentieth century. World War I, however, failed to fulfill the Arab expectations for independence, and it was not until the post-World War II period that Arab nationalism reached its peak with the termination of British and French rule and the creation of several independent Arab states.

Arab nationalism has long been dominated by the "Pan-Arab" idea. This notion of homogeneity emphasizes the mission of uniting all the Arab-speaking peoples, Moslems and Christians, Semitic and others, from Baghdad to the Atlantic, under one flag. Yet in reality, this desire for solidarity and harmony, nourished by a consciousness of a common historical legacy going back to the Caliphates' rule which flourished after Prophet Muhammad, as well as a cultural and language unity, has been blocked by opposing trends of separatism and parochialism. As a result of territorial, dynastic, ideological, and personal rivalries, the Arab World is now fragmented into eighteen independent states striving to maintain their sovereignty.

Despite this manifestation of divisive forces in Arab nationalism, Arab leaders are convinced that the final amalgamation of their peoples is impossible without the removal of "the last vestiges of imperialism" in the Middle East. Accordingly, in Arab eyes, the battle over the control of Palestine is part of a continuing struggle against foreign domination of the area. More specifically, the state of Israel with its Jewish and European originated population is regarded as a colonial state, as well as a human and geographic base for continuing Western

Imperialism. Arab nationalism therefore seeks the destruction of the Zionist entity and the establishment of Arab rule over Palestine.

Yet the tactical approaches to achieve these aims have been a source of intra-Arab controversy. The most important issue relates to the role of the Palestinian Arabs themselves. Although in the earlier part of this century they constituted the main force resisting Jewish settlement in Palestine, their active role was greatly diminished by the intervention of the Arab states after the 1948 establishment of Israel. But the June, 1967 defeat of Egypt, Jordan and Syria made the Palestinians realize that the success of their struggle against the Zionist State would depend, in large measure, on their own efforts. In recent years they therefore sought to assert their legitimacy as the major Arab party in the conflict. In the face of this development one must consider whether the Palestinian Arabs have indeed a distinct national origin and a united purpose to establish a separate Arab state in the territory over which the Israelis now exert control, and to what extent their interests coincide with those of the neighboring Arab countries.

Zionism, or Jewish nationalism, views the creation of the State of Israel as its highest attainment. Influenced by the growth of modern nationalism in Europe during the last century, Zionism was spurred by the cataclysmic Nazi holocaust, which took the lives of one third of the world's Jewry. Zionism emphasizes the national as well as the religious and cultural affinity of the Jews and views the Jewish state as both a haven for the prosecuted and a nursery for national revival. Ideologically, Zionism is based on the denial of the "Galut" (diaspora) and the striving for "Geullah" (redemption). The first points to the problem of the homelessness of the Jews since their expulsion from the Holy Land after the Roman destruction, while the latter emphasizes the crystallization of Jewish national consciousness and the restoration of the exiled and dispersed people to their ancestral "Promised Land."

Zionism claims a coherent connection between the Jewish people, Judaism (as a religion and culture), the Hebrew language, and the Land of Zion. It also focuses on world sympathy for the rights of the Jewish people to reconstitute their homeland. Committed to a national state, where the Jews would avoid prosecution by constituting themselves a majority, the Zionist insistence upon Israel as a potential haven for all Jews arouses deepening Arab hostility and suspicions. But the Zionists who see their ideology as reasonable, uniquely humane, and even messianic, assert that there are no inherent and objective reasons for conflict between them and the Arabs. Indeed, they urge that the aspirations and interests of both peoples are complementary, and that long-range Arab interests in social and economic development would be furthered by Israel's enterprise. From the Israeli viewpoint the key issue, therefore, is Arab willingness to accept Israeli and Arab coexistence in the Middle East.

The following chapter deals with the conflicting Arab Palestinian and Israeli views, respectively, on questions of nationalism and statehood. The first effort to assess Arab nationalism is excerpted from F. Yahia's book, THE PALESTINE QUESTION AND INTERNATIONAL LAW, published by the Palestine Liberation Organization Research Center in Beirut (N. D.). Yahia deals with the status of Palestinian Resistance, with the external proposals for a solution of the "Palestine Question," and with the Palestinian people's prescription for the problem. The Israeli view on the Arab Palestinian issue is expressed by a Hebrew University lecturer, Dr. Y. Harkabi, who analyzes the meaning of the "Arab Slogan of a Democratic State." Dr. Harkabi undertakes to "unmask" this idea of the slogan as understood by the Arab Palestinian organizations. The selection is a revised text of articles that appeared in the Israel newspaper, MA'ARIV in 1970.

The Zionist national rights are dealt with in two selections. The Arab view is presented in an excerpt from Palestine Monograph No. 76 published by the Palestine Liberation Organization Center in September, 1970. The authors, Bhim Singh and Angelina Helou, examine the diverse elements of Israel's statehood and the legal instruments on which the Jewish claims are based. In particular, the authors analyze the Basel Program of 1897, the Balfour Declaration of 1917, the Mandate over Palestine, and the United Nations General Assembly Resolution of November 29, 1947. The second selection, which presents the Jewish view on Zionism and Israeli statehood, is Professor Avi Ankori's reply to an Arab scholar on the subject. It was originally published by the Israel Academic Committee on the Middle East. Professor Ankori is an Israeli historian currently teaching at Columbia University.

THE PALESTINE PEOPLE
AND
INTERNATIONAL LAW

F. Yahia

Recent years have seen two very significant factors in the Palestine situation. The first is the emergence and rapid growth of the Palestinian Resistance, which has given the Palestinian people a recognized national personality which cannot be disregarded by the international community. The second factor is the effort being exerted by external forces to impose a compromise solution and prevent the situation from becoming increasingly violent. These two factors are in fundamental contradiction to each other, and the future stability or devastation of the Middle East will depend on which of these two factors prevails over the other.

The Palestinian Resistance maintains that it is illusory to expect any peace in the Middle East until the factors that disturbed the peace, namely the racially-exclusive Israeli State and the denial of Palestinian self-determination, have been eliminated. The external forces, represented by the "Big Four" powers, the United Nations and certain Arab quarters which accept their formulae, believe that the first priority is to "stop the shooting at all costs," and to maintain a sort of permanent cease-fire based on a partial correction of the situation which would nevertheless leave intact some of the factors that have caused three wars in two decades. It is important to examine which solution proposed accords more with international law.

The growth of the Palestinian Resistance had begun before the June war. Armed struggle was launched on 1 January 1965, with the first operation by al-Asifah, the military wing of the Palestinian National Liberation Movement (Fateh)(1). The Palestine Liberation Organization, which was to become the political framework within which the movement for liberation as a whole would be coordinated, had been founded in 1964. Other groups were formed, sometimes reflecting trends of various political parties, and the public wish to see a closer unity of Palestinian forces was expressed with increasing strength. The result has been the Palestinian Armed Struggle Command, which by autumn 1969 had come to coordinate seven commando organizations representing an estimated 95 per cent of the total Palestinian fighting forces. One or two smaller groups, the best-known of which is the Popular Front for the Liberation of

Palestine, had not joined the Armed Struggle Command up to the time of writing. On the political level, the Palestinian National Council, containing representatives of various groups, and independents, provides the forum for debate and political decisions. The Palestinian Resistance thus has the character of a broad united front containing several political tendencies working together for a common national aim.

The status of the Resistance in international law merits consideration. Then it is proposed to examine the solutions proposed for the Palestine question, both by external forces and by the Palestinians themselves, in the light of international legal principles.

STATUS OF THE RESISTANCE

An important question of international law arising from the Palestine problem is the right of a people to resist the invasion and seizure of their land. Basically, it can be posed in these terms: does international law recognize a people's right to resist an alien invasion and occupation? What should be the attitude of states whose territories are partly occupied, or of neighbouring states, to the occupation and the resistance? Does the occupying power have any right to retaliate against the people of the occupied territories or of neighbouring states on the grounds that the latter's support of the resistance endangers the occupying power's security?

When international law was in a relatively primitive stage of development, the laws of war were considered to govern only the belligerent relations between regular armies of states. At that time, resistance movements had no recognized legal status, as they were irregular forces. Even though they might be allied to a state, or even owe allegiance to one, they were not considered as part of the forces under its regular military command. The enemy consequently often regarded them as persons unprotected by international law, and shot them out of hand. In the Franco-Prussian war, for example, the Prussians used to execute the *francs-tireurs*, an irregular French citizen militia(2). Such barbarities led to a realization that the deficiency in the law must be remedied, and the first attempt to do so came in the 1899 Hague Regulations on the Laws and Customs of War on Land. Article 1 of these gave recognition to the status and rights of irregular forces subject to four criteria of combatant status which had been drawn up by the 1874 Brussels Conference. These criteria were to be embodied in the 1949 Geneva Conventions. They were that such forces should be under a responsible command, wear a distinctive sign, carry arms openly and themselves observe the laws and customs of war.

The process of recognizing the right of resistance to enemy occupation advanced considerably during the Second World War. The Nazi occupation of many countries such as France, Norway, Holland, Yugoslavia and Greece led to the rise of a number of resistance movements in those countries. These movements gained world-wide admiration and recognition of their legal status as combatants by several governments, as well as support and encouragement. Thus the British Government encouraged the Yugoslavians to carry on resistance by guerrilla tactics from the mountains after the Nazi invasion of their country(3). So also, the British Government extended recognition to the French Committee of National Liberation on 26 August 1943(4). In June 1944 the Allies gave official recognition to the French Maquis (armed resistance fighters) as the French Forces of the Interior. These Forces were recognized by the Supreme Commander of the Allied Expeditionary Forces as an integral part of the troops commanded by him and a formal announcement to that effect was made(5). The anti-fascist Partisans in Italy were given a form of recognition in an international document. The 1947 Peace Treaty between the Allies and Italy referred to the "Resistance Movement which took an active part in the war against Germany."

These situations all created precedents which were to be strengthened by the growth of national liberation movements throughout the Afro-Asian world in ensuing years. At present therefore, there is wide recognition of the right of a people under occupation to form resistance movements and take up arms against the occupying power.

The legal belligerent status of resistance movements was given full and unequivocal recognition in the 1949 Geneva Conventions. The Third Convention, in Article 4, declared that captured combatants entitled to Prisoner of War status include:

> Members of other militias and members of other volunteer corps, including those of organized resistance movements, belonging to a Party to the conflict and operating in or outside their own territory, even if this territory is occupied, provided that such militias or volunteer corps, including such organized resistance movements, fulfil the following conditions:
> (a) that of being commanded by a person responsible for his subordinates;
> (b) that of having a fixed distinctive sign recognizable at a distance;
> (c) that of carrying arms openly;
> (d) that of conducting their operations in accordance with the laws and customs of war.

These conditions are clearly fulfilled by the Palestinian Resistance organized within the Armed Struggle Command. Apart from the Command itself, each component movement has its own command responsible for its members, its own insignia, its arms are carried openly, and the Resistance as a whole has announced publicly that it adheres to the Geneva Conventions(6).

During the Second World War, Nazi conduct was contrary to the laws and customs of war in many respects. As a result of a Nazi refusal to respect the status of resistance movements, "conflicts of view arose as to the status of persons or groups who continued to resist locally throughout the remaining years of general hostilities elsewhere. Most of this guerrilla activity was directed against the Axis occupation forces, and Germany . . . treated guerrillas as illegitimate combatants." In the closing stages of the Second World War, Nazi broadcasts went so far as to proclaim that "all the rules of warfare are obsolete and must be thrown overboard"(7).

The adoption of the 1949 Geneva Conventions was a final rejection by the world community of the Nazi interpretations of the laws of war. In theory the Israelis, as signatories of the Geneva Conventions, are supposed to abide by the high principles in them. The actual position is otherwise, for we find that the Israelis have revived the Nazi theory that it is unlawful to resist occupation, that guerrillas are "illegitimate combatants" and that rules of warfare can be declared obsolete and thrown overboard if adherence to them is inconvenient. Thus, they refuse to recognize the prisoner of war status to which resistance fighters are entitled when captured. This is a clear Israeli violation of Article 4 of the Third Geneva Convention. The illegality of this attitude was confirmed by the adoption of a resolution calling for recognition of Palestinian commandos' prisoner of war status at the Istanbul Conference of the International Red Cross and Red Crescent Societies in September 1969(8).

There is some doubt as to the international legal status of private individuals who carry out acts of resistance on their own initiative without being members of an established resistance organization. In the Nazi-held territories of Europe, it became quite a common practice for ordinary citizens to seize any opportunity they could to damage the occupant, even if they did not belong to the official resistance. Since they are not subject to organizational discipline and do not wear insignia, they do not fulfil all the criteria laid down in Article 4 of the Third Geneva Convention. The Conference which adopted the four Geneva Conventions decided against conferring the right to prisoner of war status on civilian individuals not in organized resistance movements, unless they take part in a *levée en masse* begun before the invader occupies their territory(9).

While individual, unorganized resisters are not granted prisoner of war status in international law, the Fourth Geneva Convention does lay down a certain minimum of protection for them on which there is no dispute. Article 5 requires that persons engaged in or suspected of activities hostile to the occupying power's security, as well as persons detained as spies or saboteurs, shall nevertheless be treated with humanity, and in case of trial shall not be deprived of tho rights of fair and regular trial prescribed by the Convention. This demonstrates that even persons who are not members of established resistance organizations are nevertheless entitled to basic human rights under international law.

The use of torture, now a widespread practice in Israel as has been seen from various reports, is a clear violation of the Third Geneva Convention on treatment of prisoners of war (in cases of members of resistance organizations) and of the Fourth Convention on treatment of civilians (in cases of unorganized resisters or suspects). Also to be counted as violations are prolonged detention or other punishments applied in penal institutions against those entitled to prisoner of war status, or without fair trial and humane treatment against any other persons detained by the occupation. One form of punishment frequently practised, as has been observed, is demoltion by the Israeli authorities of houses where one of the dwellers is suspected of connection with the Resistance. These demolitions are carried out on the orders of the Israeli Defence Minister (General Dayan), summarily and without any trial to verify whether the suspicion is true, and no provision is made for alternative accommodation. Article 6 of the Charter of the Nuremberg International War Crimes Tribunal declared the "wanton destruction of cities, towns or villages or devastation not justified by military necessity" to be a war crime. The Tribunal judged the German Chief of Staff, General Jodl, to be a war criminal for having ordered the evacuation of inhabitants and destruction of houses in certain provinces of Norway(10). As is the case with General Dayan, General Jodl was motivated by a desire to combat resistance of the inhabitants to occupation.

The resistance of the Palestinian people to Israeli occupation is therefore recognized by international law as legitimate. Furthermore, the Israelis' occupation of territory in their hands at present arose out of their acts of launching aggressive war in 1948 and 1967. This was defined by the Nuremberg Tribunal as the supreme international crime. It is a basic precept of law that legal rights cannot be acquired by the commission of an illegal act. From this it follows, accordingly, that the Israelis have not acquired legal rights from their acts of aggressive war and the subsequent occupation. In view of the illegal character of their occupation, they cannot lawfully claim even those rights to take measures for protecting the security of their occupation forces; rights which international law grants to an occupying power which has not gone to war

9

illegally. The Israelis persist, nevertheless, in claiming such rights and more for themselves both by their suppression of the population of the occupied territories, and by the allegations that neighbouring states are responsible for acts of resistance carried out in the occupied territories.

There is no legal basis for such an allegation. For one thing, the Palestinian Resistance has demonstrated very clearly, in both words and actions, that it is entirely responsible for everything it does and is not answerable to any government. It arises from the Palestinian people and their national aspirations, and the Palestinian people are the sole authority which controls it. Furthermore, the Arab States, as their own spokesmen have often declared, are not responsible for ensuring the protection of Israeli forces engaged in illegal occupation. Even in the case of a legal occupation, international law does not grant the occupying power legitimate sovereignty, but considers it to be temporarily in administration in occupied territory, and consequently responsible for maintaining its own security there. If, due to opposition of the territory's rightful inhabitants, it is unable to maintain security for its own presence there (in this case illegal anyway), it has no legal ground for blaming other states for its incapacity.

Other states, if they wish, have the right to extend aid to resistance movements. For instance, the Allies during the Second World War gave help to the resistance movement in countries like France, Norway, Yugoslavia or Greece. The legality of such aid is not questioned. If Hitler had alleged that the Allies had a duty to refuse aid to those resisting Nazi occupation, the Allies would doubtless have treated such an allegation with the contempt which it deserved. The parallel between Palestinian resistance to Israeli occupation and European resistance to Nazi occupation was well illustrated by Lady Fisher of Lambeth(11), who wrote:

> When French men and women formed themselves into resistance groups to embarrass and resist the German forces occupying their land, we hailed them (quite rightly, I believe) as heroes and heroines. Why therefore must Arabs, who try to do the same thing against enemy forces occupying their land, be referred to as 'terrorists' and 'saboteurs'? Surely they are only doing what brave men always do, whose country lies under the heel of a conqueror?

Lady Fisher's words emphasize an important aspect of international law: that its principles must be universally and equitably applied. The principles of international law which have evolved regarding the right of resistance were not tailor-made to fit only the cases of European countries under Nazi occupation; they are applicable to every country in the world that has been subjected to such an occupation. Many of them, indeed, such as those in the 1949 Geneva Conventions, were enunciated after the Second World War to demonstrate humanity's total rejection of the sort of acts committed by the Nazis, and desire that such acts should never be repeated by anyone.

The universally-applicable right of resistance renders it illegal for an occupying power to attempt to counter such resistance by reprisals against civilians either in the occupied territories or in neighbouring states. Article 33 of the Fourth Geneva Convention specifically prohibits reprisals against civilians and their property in occupied territories. Attacks on civilians in neighbouring countries, apart from the fact that they are directed against persons not responsible for resistance in the occupied area and are therefore ineffective, are also clear acts of aggression. They cannot be classed as legally justifiable

10

reprisals, since acts of resistance to armed occupation are not illegal; on the contrary, it is the Israeli occupation which is illegal, since it arises from acts of aggressive war. In the present context, such Israeli attacks constitute violations of the armistice and cease-fire agreements. They have been carried out on many occasions, for example against Salt, Irbid, Kafr Asad and Ain Hazzir in Jordan, Al Hamma and Maysaloun in Syria, and several villages in Southern Lebanon. The casualties in these attacks have been almost entirely civilians.

The Israelis have attempted to justify these violations by claiming that acts of resistance are also violations of the cease-fire agreements. This logic is totally false. The Israeli violations are acts by a government which is a party to the cease-fire, whereas the acts of resistance are a spontaneous and natural response of any people under occupation, and an exercise of a legally-recognized right, by the Palestinians who are not a party to the cease-fire. The argument which equates the war crimes of the aggressor with the legitimate self-defence measures of his victim strikes at the very foundation of international law. It is an argument which all who uphold international law will reject, as they would have rejected any attempt to equate the acts of the Nazi occupation with the lawful struggle of, say, the French Maquis or the Yugoslav Partisans.

The Israeli maintenance of the Nazi doctrine that resistance must be crushed no matter what violations of international law this involves, will inevitably lead to further bloodshed. How this bloodshed may be finally ended, through a solution that brings justice and accords with international law, will be considered in the remaining sections of this chapter.

EXTERNAL PROPOSALS FOR A SOLUTION

Following the war of June 1967, the United Nations continued to act in much the same way as it had since 1947. For several months, sterile debates were accompanied by a total failure to condemn the aggressor or to lay down principles that accorded fully with justice(12). Some mild resolutions were passed: one by the Security Council, calling for respect for the safety, welfare and security of the inhabitants of areas where military operations had taken place, and the return of the displaced persons to their homes(13), and two by the General Assembly calling on the Israelis to desist from any action to change the status of Jerusalem(14). All these three resolutions were disregarded by the Israelis, and no effective enforcement action was taken. In particular, the United Nations failed to live up to its avowed principles in this essential point: namely, that on the basic legal and moral issue of the Israeli launching of a war of aggression and seizure of large areas from the territories of U. N. Member States, the United Nations debates were sterile and failed to face up courageously to the fact that aggression had been committed. A Special Session of the General Assembly failed to adopt a resolution, and the 23rd Ordinary Session of the Assembly referred the matter to the Security Council.

> From the minute the issue came before the Security Council, the representative of the United States of America stiffened the already hard attitude he had maintained during the debates in the General Assembly, for no other reason than to support Israel by means of clever, lucid, camouflaged phrases(15).

The chances of the Security Council adopting any constructive attitude, in view of this stand by at least one of its permanent members, were thus virtually non-existent from the start.

11

Neither a draft resolution proposed by Mali, Nigeria and India, nor an alternative one proposed by the United States, secured adoption. After lengthy debating, a resolution proposed by the United Kingdom was unanimously adopted by the Council on 22 November 1967(16). Essentially, this resolution, in one interpretation or another, was to form the basis of the various plans put forward by outside parties since then, for a so-called "peace settlement" of the Palestinian question. It is necessary, therefore, to examine this resolution in detail in order to understand the whole matter of the legality or otherwise of "peaceful solutions" which outside parties are endeavoring to impose on the Palestinian people.

By the 22 November Resolution, the Security Council paid lip service to certain principles: "The inadmissibility of the acquisition of territory by war and the need to work for a just and lasting peace, . . . and that all Member States in the acceptance of the Charter of the United Nations, have undertaken a commitment to act in accordance with Article 2 of the Charter." This Article specified that U.N. members should settle disputes by peaceful means and refrain from the threat or use of force against the territorial integrity or political independence of any state. While the reaffirmation of such principles by the Security Council sounded pleasant, it was meaningless, since the Council took no decision to condemn the Israelis for violating these principles, or to ensure respect for them in the future.

On the contrary, the whole basis of this Resolution was that the aggressor should not be condemned for his acts of aggression, but should, rather, be allowed to commit these acts with impunity. This attitude of the Security Council is clear from the fact that the wording of its Resolution draws no moral distinction between aggressor and victim. Thus, in operative paragraph 1 of the Resolution, the Council "affirms that the fulfilment of Charter principles requires the establishment of a just and lasting peace in the Middle East which should include the application of both the following principles:

(I) Withdrawal of Israeli armed forces from territories occupied in the recent conflict;

(II) Termination of all claims or states of belligerency and respect for and acknowledgement of the sovereignty, territorial integrity and political independence of every State in the area and their right to live in peace within secure and recognized boundaries free from threats or acts of force."

Operative paragraph two demonstrates the same moral myopia, for in it the Council "affirms further the necessity:

(A) For guaranteeing freedom of navigation through international waterways in the area;

(B) For achieving a just settlement of the refugee problem;

(C) For guaranteeing the territorial inviolability and political independence of every State in the area, through measures including the establishment of demilitarized zones."

In the third operative paragraph, the Council requested the Secretary General "to designate a special representative to proceed to the Middle East to establish and maintain contacts with the States concerned in order to promote agreement and assist efforts to achieve a peaceful and accepted settlement in accordance with the provisions and principles in this resolution." The fourth operative paragraph required the Secretary General to report progress to the Council.

The first and second operative paragraphs purport to outline the terms of the peace settlement, rather than generalities or procedural matters, and so it is these two paragraphs that require the most serious attention. They are characterized by the distorted logic so prevalent in U.N. circles, namely that the way to solve a conflict between justice and injustice is to try to take a "neutral" position of compromising between them. Invariably, in any such compromise, it is justice which is sacrificed, because justice is an absolute. It is impossible to reach a compromise which is "somewhat unjust," and at the same time maintain that justice has been upheld.

Yet this is precisely what the Security Council's Resolution 242 tries to do. It is allegedly in favour of "a just and lasting peace;" it seeks to correct one injustice by calling in vague terms for "withdrawal of Israeli armed forces from territories occupied in the recent conflict;" but in the same breath calls for the perpetuation of an even more glaring injustice, the situation arising from the Israeli war of aggression of 1947-48. There is little doubt as to the real meaning of the second part of operative paragraph one; behind its fine-sounding verbal camouflage of sovereignty, territorial integrity, political independence or "right to live in peace" it is an attempt to coerce the Arab States into surrendering the rights of the Palestinian people, in exchange for evacuation from territories seized by the Israelis in June 1967. By calling on the Arab States to end the state of belligerency, to acknowledge the racialist Israeli State's "sovereignty, territorial integrity, political independence and right to live in peace" on land to which it has no title, the Security Council struck a serious blow against several principles of international law. For, by voting for the legitimization of the Israeli State and its pre-1967 territorial seizures, the Security Council was declaring that might is right, and that international law should be waived before the violence of a conqueror. It was also maintaining that the right of a dispossessed people to self-determination in their ancestral homeland should be disregarded, and a state based on racial discrimination should be tolerated. All these attitudes expressed by the Security Council in this Resolution are diametrically opposed to international law as it has developed in our present age. By hiding this illegality behind legal phrases like sovereignty, territorial integrity and political independence, the Security Council hoped that the world would be deceived into accepting it as legal. Even so might the appeasers of 1938 have pleaded for acknowledgement of the Nazi State's sovereignty, territorial integrity and political independence and its right to "live in peace" within the "secure and recognized boundaries" of Austria and Czechoslovakia.

Both these two operative paragraphs implicitly base their logic on the theory that aggressors should be appeased rather than condemned or punished for their crimes. It has been noted above that the June war, whose resultant crisis the Security Council was called to resolve, was an aggressive war launched by the Israelis. Far from condemning or imposing sanctions on the Israelis for their aggression, which would have been the Council's proper course according to its responsibilities under Chapter VII of the Charter, the Council in this Resolution proposed to reward them by calling on the victims to make concessions.

In addition to the Security Council's call for the renunciation of the Palestinians' inalienable rights, the Resolution also instructed the Arab States to reward the aggressor with other concessions. Thus, in operative paragraph two, the Council completely accepted the aggressor's tendentious interpretations on the navigation question, and told the Arab States to yield their legally-defensible rights on this issue. In order to guarantee "the territorial inviolability and political independence" of states, the Council proposed "measures including the establishment of demilitarized zones." It should be pointed out that the Arab States have posed no threat to any State's "territorial inviolability and political independence" (legally-acquired or otherwise), but on three occasions have had to fight defensively against Israeli aggressive wars. The last occasion resulted in severe Israeli encroachments on the territorial inviolability of Arab States — encroachments which still continue without any serious move by the Security Council to fulfil its responsibilities. On whose territory, it may be asked, are such demilitarized zones to be established? And what guarantee, if any, does the Council envisage to prevent Israeli encroachment and assertion of sovereignty over these zones, as happened with such zones on the Syrian, Jordanian and Egyptian Demarcation Lines from 1948 to 1967?

In the light of all this whittling away of the basic principles of international law, the call in operative paragraph two for "a just settlement of the refugee problem" is clearly revealed as simply another verbal deception, a smokescreen behind which the Council hoped the Palestinian people's legitimate rights could be liquidated with impunity. The Resolution, very discreetly, does not define what such a just settlement could be, for the obvious reason that, if it is to be really just, it would be diametrically incompatible with the other provisions of the Resolution. A just settlement of the refugee problem involves not only the Palestinians' inalienable right of return, as affirmed by the General Assembly in Resolution 194 and subsequent resolutions, but also their right to self-determination, in accordance with the U.N. Charter, in the whole of their historic homeland, and to live under a system free from racial discrimination, in accordance with the principles in the Universal Declaration of Human Rights, the Genocide Convention, the Convention for the Elimination of All Forms of Racial Discrimination, and other international instruments including U.N. resolutions condemning racialism.

No such just settlement is envisaged in Security Council Resolution 242. Quite the reverse: the Resolution envisages the perpetuation of the racialist Israeli State on Palestinian territory, and its strengthening with a form of recognition extorted from Arab States. Under such terms, a just settlement of the refugee problem, or indeed any other problem arising from Zionist aggression, is manifestly unattainable. This supposed guarantee of refugee rights in the Security Council's Resolution is as meaningless as the guarantee of "civil and religious rights" in the Balfour Declaration. Both the Security Council Resolution and the Balfour Declaration were documents drafted by the British Government with the aim of deceiving public opinion, while the people of Palestine were to be despoiled of their rights in accordance with the interests of the imperial powers and their Zionist allies.

A further deception was perpetrated in this Resolution, which has apparently escaped the attention of those Arab circles who claim the Resolution offers a chance of a "reasonable settlement." It is argued by some quarters that although the Resolution is in many ways inadequate, it should be accepted because it offers the Arab States a chance of "liquidating the consequences of aggression," that is, of recovering the territories the Israelis seized from them in June 1967. How realistic is this attitude? It has probably been put in its best perspective by a political journal from Britain, the country sponsoring the Resolution, thus: "On the central issue of Israel's withdrawal it compromises between the vagueness of the American resolution and the precision of the Afro-Asian one. The resolution calls for the withdrawal of Israeli armed forces from territories occupied in the recent conflict. Lord Caradon's last-ditch battle was his successful rejection of a Russian effort to insert 'all the' before the word 'territories.' With the Egyptians signifying assent, the Russians then voted the straight Caradon line. The Indian delegate had made the point that by withdrawal he understood 'total' withdrawal. Lord Caradon did not agree."(17). Thus, from Lord Caradon, the distinguished representative of the United Kingdom who proposed the Resolution, we have the admission that the Israeli withdrawal clause is nothing more than a confidence trick.

By its failure to condemn aggression, and its call to the victims to appease the aggressor by concessions, the Security Council fell lamentably short of the standards enunciated in the words of the U.N. Secretary General. After the June war, U Thant declared:

> There is the immediate and urgently challenging issue of the withdrawal of the armed forces of Israel from the territory of neighbouring Arab States occupied during the recent war. There is near unanimity on this issue, in principle, because everyone agrees that there should be no territorial gains by military conquest. It would, in my view, lead to disastrous consequences if the United Nations were to abandon or compromise this fundamental principle . . . It is indispensible to our international community of States — if it is not to follow the law of the jungle — that the territorial integrity of every State be respected, and the occupation by military force of the territory of one State by another cannot be condoned(18).

By adopting that Resolution on 22 November 1967, the U.N. Security Council turned its back on respect for basic principles of international law, and in fact adopted a position of compromise between international law and the international crime of launching aggressive war. No legal body can long maintain its authority if it compromises between law and crime, and it is actions such as the Security Council's adoption of Resolution 242 that have seriously undermined what moral and legal authority the United Nations once possessed.

It has been argued that, since the Security Council is a supreme authority, it is not subject to the rule of law, but is itself vested with the powers to make or change the law. Thus we find it argued that, whereas under the League of Nations, power was theoretically subject to the rule of law, "in the Charter of the United Nations we now find the opposite principle, that law is subordinate to power. Insofar as the five principal States can agree among themselves they are not limited by law in anything which they may decide to do, and the rest of the world is pledged to obey"(19). The theory that international law should be governed not by the democratic principle but by a despotic oligarchy has on occasions found support in the attitudes and actions of the Security Council's permanent members. However, the limitless application of this theory is highly questionable, even according to international law as it is at present constituted.

Where a system of law is regulated by a constitution, any authority of that system, whether legislative, executive or judicial, has power to act according to the terms of that constitution. If it exceeds the terms of the constitution, it may be said to have acted illegally. There is no absolute authority in any constitutional legal system, since the function of a constitution is to define the limits of an authority's powers.

The constitution of the United Nations legal system is the U.N. Charter. The Security Council, like other organs of the United Nations, has powers to act according to the functions granted to it in the Charter. These powers are certainly very wide (excessively so, in the view of many writers), but they are not unlimited. Thus, U.N. members "confer on the Security Council primary responsibility for the maintenance of international peace and security," in which

15

it "acts on their behalf," and indeed must "act in accordance with the Purposes and Principles of the United Nations." (Article 24). Members "agree to accept and carry out the decisions of the Security Council in accordance with the present Charter," (Article 25) with the implication that members are not so bound where a Council decision does not accord with the Charter.

Chapter VI of the Charter authorizes the Council to call upon parties to a dispute to settle it, to investigate such a dispute, and make recommendations as to a settlement. Chapter VII gives it wider powers, but at the same time, more detailed responsibilities, regarding any "threat to the peace, breach of the peace, or act of aggression." Its prime task, according to Article 39, is to "make recommendations, or decide what measure shall be taken in accordance with Articles 41 and 42, to maintain or restore international peace and security." Article 41 provides for "measures not involving the use of force" and Article 42 for forceful measures.

The Charter demonstrates that the Security Council's functions have two important characteristics. First, the Council must act according to the Purposes and Principles of the United Nations, since it acts on behalf of the Organization's members. Secondly, the Council has the prime responsibility for maintaining or restoring international peace and security.

Among the Purposes and Principles of the United Nations listed in Chapter I of the Charter are "to take effective collective measures for the prevention and removal of threats to the peace and for the suppression of acts of aggression or other breaches of the peace;" and "to develop friendly relations among nations based on respect for the principle of equal rights and self-determination of peoples." The Security Council's actions have not accorded with either of these two purposes. In the first place, the Israelis were guilty of a very clear act of aggression in invading and seizing the territories of Arab States in June 1967. At no time has the Security Council done anything effective to suppress that act of aggression, nor to counteract the continual threats to the peace that Israeli policies involve. Resolution 242, with its requirement that the Israeli State should be acknowledged within secure and recognized boundaries on territory to which it has no legal claim, is a clear violation of the U.N.'s principle of respect for self-determination of peoples, in this case the Palestinian people. To affirm a racialist state's so-called "right to live in peace" is manifestly contrary to the Preamble of the Charter, which reaffirms "faith in fundamental human rights, in the dignity and worth of the human person, in the equal rights of men and women and of nations large and small."

The fact that Resolution 242, far from suppressing aggression, actually encouraged it by awarding concessions to the aggressor, demonstrates that the Security Council did not live up to its responsibilities under Chapter VII of the Charter. Encouragement of aggression cannot by any stretch of the imagination be termed a good way of maintaining or restoring international peace and security; on the contrary, it is the surest method of ensuring that international peace and security suffer a total collapse.

By its adoption of Resolution 242 and by its other actions (or lack of them) following the June war, the Security Council has departed from the Purposes and Principles of the United Nations and has failed to discharge its task as the guardian of international peace and security. It is thus correct to maintain that it has acted illegally, or contrary to its constitution, the U.N. Charter, in regard to the Palestine question. The Palestinian people are therefore under no obligation to conform to its recommendations.

It is not proposed here to go into details of all the various "peace plans" based on Resolution 242 and put forward by various quarters. In the first place, these plans have been so numerous and verbose that they would fill a large volume by themselves. In the second place, since Resolution 242 rests on such an unsound legal basis, it follows that any plans founded on it can also make no claim to legality. It is, however, of some value to examine some of the moves made by certain quarters on an official level with a view to implementing the Resolution.

The Resolution itself provided, in operative paragraph three, for the appointment of a special representative of the Secretary General whose task, broadly, was to make contact with different parties in an effort to facilitate implementation. Dr. Gunnar Jarring, the Swedish Ambassador to the Soviet Union, was appointed for this purpose. The story of his long odyssey, in which he journeyed back and forth between Nicosia, Amman, Cairo, Jerusalem and New York, merely demonstrated how the talents of a diplomat of integrity can be wasted fruitlessly when he is given a hopeless mandate by the United Nations. Since the Resolution whose implementation he was to assist took no account of the Palestinians, who are primarily concerned in the matter, his mission was doomed to failure from the start, even though it was given the wholehearted cooperation of the Jordanian and U.A.R. Governments and the somewhat reluctant lip-service of the Israelis.

At the close of 1968, it became apparent that Dr. Jarring's mission was not producing concrete results(20). The idea of some type of intervention by the major powers to strengthen his mission came increasingly to the fore. Mr. Charles Yost, following the announcement of his appointment as United States representative at the U.N., called for joint collaboration between the Soviet Union and the United States to impose a settlement on the Middle East. He expressed the view that such a settlement should come through "a United Nations initiative supported by the Great Powers. The really vital interest of both the United States and Russia is to remove the grave threat to their own security which the present situation poses," Mr. Yost added(21). This was accompanied by hints of a new Soviet initiative, in accordance with the Security Council Resolution, to overcome the "deadlock"(22). Shortly afterwards, it was reported that a Soviet proposal for four-power talks on the Middle East was being considered by the United States, Britain and France, and the Soviet Ambassador in London handed the British Foreign Secretary a suggestion for a "stage by stage implementation of the Security Council Resolution"(23). The Soviet plan was stated to "envisage the sending of U.N. troops to the Middle East"(24). A French proposal for Big Four talks was subsequently accepted by the United States(25), and these talks were started officially with meetings of the Soviet, American, French and British Ambassadors at the U.N. These contacts were from time to time supplemented by Big Two discussions between the Soviet Union and the United States.

In view of the close secrecy which has surrounded these talks, the ground which has been covered, up to the time of writing, can only be a matter of speculation. All that is definite is that the major powers have been attempting to work out a formula on the basis of the Security Council Resolution. Apart from the Resolution's inadequacy as a basis for restoring peace in the Middle East, the competence of the Big Four to play the role of peacemakers needs to be seriously questioned. Let us examine their past records.

Britain, as is well known, was the imperial power whose leaders gave Zionism its first public endorsement in the Balfour Declaration. Throughout the Mandate

17

period, British rule in Palestine enabled Zionist colonizers to settle, arm themselves and establish a position of strength, without which it would have been impossible for them to found their racialist state. In ensuing years up to this day the British Government supplied arms to the Israelis, and joined them in the Tripartite invasion of Egypt in 1956. During the June war, the British Government gave full endorsement to the Israeli position over the navigation question and other issues. They have given no indication of any significant policy change since then.

The United States gave considerable support to Zionism during the closing years of the British Mandate, and played the leading part in pressing the Zionist case for partition at the U.N. in 1947. With the exception of a brief period following the Tripartite invasion of Egypt, the United States has given solid political support to the Israeli State, in particular after the June war. It has also consistently supplied the Israelis with arms, including napalm and, more recently, Phantom fighter-bombers, and has now replaced France as the main source of supply.

France, for a considerable period particularly during the Algerian war years, became known as Israel's close ally and main arms supplier. The Israeli atomic energy project is said to have been built up largely through French help, and the Mirage jet was the Israeli Air Force's most important aircraft during the June war. After that war, there was a significant shift in French policy, with President de Gaulle imposing a partial embargo on arms shipments to Israel, which was made total following the Israeli attack on Beirut airport. The reason for this shift was the perfectly correct assessment of the French Government that the Israelis were the aggressive party in the June war. It was nevertheless not accompanied by any awareness, on the governmental level, of the rights of the Palestinians or the illegal racialist character of the Israeli State, although such an awareness has begun to be felt among the more enlightened sections of French opinion. French official policy is still to maintain the so-called "right to exist" of the racialist State, but this is accompanied by a demand that it confine itself to its pre-1967 limits.

The Soviet Union has vacillated between two policies on the Middle East. Initially, in accordance with the teachings and internationalist spirit of Marx and Lenin, it opposed Zionism which it regarded as a reactionary chauvinistic force that divided Jewish workers from their Gentile fellows and removed them from the class struggle in their countries. Immediately after the Second World War, there was a tendency for Soviet policy in the Middle East to collaborate with the United States. This led to a joint campaign by the two powers to sponsor the Zionist case for partition at the U.N. The United States and the Soviet Union were the first two powers to recognize the Israeli State immediately after its establishment. The Soviet Union still has not withdrawn this recognition, despite its clear incompatibility with principles of egalitarianism and socialism on which Soviet policy is supposedly based. In the 1948 war, the United States and the Soviet Union, and Czechoslovakia with Soviet encouragement, were the principal sources of arms for the Israelis. After that war, the Soviet Union gradually shifted its position away from supporting the United States' ally Israel, as the cold war intensified. However, the basic Soviet policy of supporting the racialist state's "right to exist" and of disregarding the Palestinian people's rights to self-determination has remained unchanged, despite Soviet expressions of verbal support and supplies of arms to certain Arab Governments.

Since the time of the Cuban missile crisis, there has been a steady thaw in the cold war and an increasing rapprochement between the Soviet Union and the

United States in the framework of "peaceful coexistence." This has generally taken the form of tacit, unpublished "understandings" whereby each recognizes the other's sphere of influence — Latin America for the United States, Eastern Europe for the Soviet Union, for instance. This trend was less noticed in the Middle East than elsewhere, because spheres of influence were less clearly demarcated and, at least until after the June war, were still the subject for bargaining. A significant stage in U.S.-Soviet collaboration appears to have been the Glassboro Summit meeting of Mr. Johnson and Mr. Kosygin. No details are yet known of the secret agreement reached between these two statesmen on the destinies of the Middle East, without consulting the Arabs, except that they both agreed the racialist Israeli State should be preserved(26).

This Soviet attitude of accord with the United States, together with the failure to withdraw recognition of Israel or to acknowledge and support the Palestinians' legitimate resistance struggle, calls into question the verbal support of Soviet leaders for the Arab cause. Nor are arms supplies to the Arab States any proof of Soviet sincerity. Britain, and even the United States, have on occasions supplied arms to some Arab States, without following a policy of loyal support for Arab rights.

Thus, all the four major powers engaged in discussions to help implement the Security Council Resolution have played an important part in creating or strengthening the racialist Israeli State, and they are all agreed in their desire to preserve it. None of them have shown any readiness to accept the Palestinians' right of self-determination. Their talks have been carried on without consulting the Palestinians or considering their interests; although it is the Palestinians who are most concerned in the whole issue. It is, after all, they and their land whose future is at stake, and it is the denial of their rights in their land which lies at the root of the problem.

Apart from the fact that all the Big Four, because of their past records, are unfit to play any part in resolving this problem, their discussions and any decisions they may reach behind the Palestinians' backs are in no way binding. Indeed, this procedure of four major powers sitting in a secret cabal to settle the future of another nation without the latter's consent is reminiscent of another "Big Four" decision — reached at Munich on 29 and 30 September 1938, between Britain, France, Germany and Italy. Then, it was the fate of the Czechoslovak people and their homeland that was decided. "Nor were the Czechs themselves allowed to be present at the meetings. The Czech Government had been informed in bald terms on the evening of the 28th that a conference of the representatives of the four European Powers would take place the following day. Agreement was reached between 'the Big Four' with speed"(27). The result was the dismemberment of the Czechoslovakian homeland as a "peaceful settlement" of the problem posed in Europe by Nazi territorial expansionism.

Human memories are short. The shadow of Munich has faded behind more than three decades, and plausible-sounding arguments are advanced in favour of repeating its performance in the Middle East. We are told, for instance, that it is worth sacrificing the rights of the small, uninfluential Palestinian people as the price to avoid a third world war. Yet this "third world war" possibility, presumably to be fought out between the United States and the Soviet Union, is extremely far-fetched, as the two supposed antagonists, despite their past rivalry, are now on excellent terms with each other. They are coexisting peacefully together with great enthusiasm, and are in accord on their Middle East policies on such essentials as their desire to arrange their spheres of influence in the region, to preserve the Israeli State, and to deny Palestinian self-determination.

19

The chance of a U.S.-Soviet war now is about as great as would have been the likelihood of a Franco-British war immediately after signing of the Sykes-Picot Agreement.

Likewise, we are told that a "Big Four" guarantee is the only hope of preventing prolonged bloodshed in the Middle East. What happened to a similar guarantee, the 1950 Tripartite Declaration? Two of its signatories, Britain and France, helped Israel launch an invasion in 1956 against Egypt, and the third guarantor, the United States, has been the most persistent encourager of Israeli aggression, particularly during and since the June war. The Tripartite Declaration was not intended to guarantee peace, but only to protect the Israeli State's hold over territory it had then seized, for when it expanded beyond that territory, the tripartite "guarantee" of Middle East frontiers was quietly dropped. We hear the argument, however, that by adding the Soviet Union to the original signatories of the "guarantee," it can then be made watertight. Yet, even assuming the Soviet Union had honest intentions in signing such a guarantee, can we imagine it going to war, if necessary, to enforce it against the combined might of the Western imperial powers?

The Munich Agreement, it should not be forgotten, was also a "peaceful settlement," designed to prevent the outbreak of the Second World War. The "peace for our time" proclaimed by the British Prime Minister Chamberlain lasted for one year. To attain this, the rights of a small people in their ancestral homeland were sacrificed. The aggressor was appeased with territorial concessions. The Munich Agreement was a cast-iron guarantee of peace, underwritten by the four most powerful European States of that time. The adoption of a similar formula to solve the Palestine problem would produce similar interesting results.

THE PALESTINIAN PEOPLE'S SOLUTION

A European historian wrote of the 1930's: "The reign of international law was brought to an abrupt close. The prevailing fashion of the unilateral repudiation of treaties rode roughshod over the sanctity of covenanted agreements. From a dream of universal peace men suddenly awoke to the crude realities of naked aggression"(28). The cause of this development was a series of acts of appeasement towards aggressors, who were able to seize territory with impunity. The description could aptly be applied to the present.

The Munich Agreement was only one incident in this process of deterioration of international law, which also included such acts as the Japanese invasion of Manchuria, the Italian invasion of Abyssinia, and eventually the Nazi invasions of several European countries. Each time an act of aggression was committed with impunity, the aggressors were tempted to go further. Thus, the Nazi seizure of Czechoslovakia was only the preliminary phase of further expansion, destruction of populations of the seized territories, and the establishment of German settlers in their place. In Hitler's words: "The aim of National Socialism must be to secure for the German people an extension of the space in which our people must live"(29). The Israeli policy of territorial expansion, expulsion of the Arab population and establishment of Zionist settlers on their soil, is so close an imitation of Nazi policy, that the Palestinians, and Arabs in general, cannot afford to ignore the historical parallels of their situation with that of Europe in the 1930's. It is in the light of the lessons of history, therefore, that the Palestinian people's attitude to peace in the Middle East merits consideration.

The parallels must not, however, be oversimplified. There are differences between Czechoslovakia in 1938 and Palestine today. For one thing, the process in Palestine has gone further: the aggressor state is more firmly established, the rightful population is already largely dispossessed. This, if anything, renders the situation even more serious. Israel is not directly represented, as Germany was at Munich, at the Big Four talks, but only indirectly, through its principal ally and backer, the United States. Likewise, the Israeli State does not commit acts of aggression purely on its own account as Nazi Germany did at least initially, but as part of a world-wide pattern of imperial domination. The symbiotic relationship between Zionism and imperialism is the key to understanding this. The Israel-U.S. relationship also enables one to realize the truth behind the so-called Israeli "opposition" to the Big Four talks and apparently lukewarm attitude to the Security Council Resolution. Israeli declarations of opposition to "solutions imposed from outside the Middle East region" are too strident to be convincing. They are motivated by two considerations: first, the well-known technique of seeming intransigent in order to extract more advantageous terms (Hitler also used this immediately before Munich)(30); and secondly, in the hope of inducing a Pavlovian reaction of acceptance of a Big Four settlement on the Arab side, on the theory that "if the enemy is opposed to it, it must be a good thing." This psychiatric prediction applied only too accurately to the reaction of some Arab circles.

A further difference between the two situations is that the Palestinians are aware of the past lessons of history, and are mobilized in armed resistance. The Palestinian people's resistance and their attitude to peace are based on the same principle as that embraced by the European resistance movements which fought against Nazi occupation during the Second World War. This principle is that peace must be on a just and durable basis, and this can only be achieved by eradicating those factors which caused war. Aggression, in short, must be eliminated, not appeased.

The Palestinian people and their resistance organizations have rejected the Security Council Resolution and all plans inspired by it, because that Resolution and those plans represent an appeasement of aggression. In calling for an acknowledgement of the Israeli State within secure and recognised boundaries, the Resolution proposes awarding the aggressors the fruits at least of their 1947-48 aggression, if not all the fruits of the 1967 one. It must be stressed that the extent of territory concerned is not the essential fact, but the principle; for once the principle is accepted that aggression should be allowed, the aggressor, on that basis, will proceed to further conquests when he is ready. Hitler did not receive the whole of Czechoslovakia by the Munich Agreement, but once that Agreement established his "right" to seize other people's territory, he used it as his "legal" basis for further seizures. Theft is still theft, whether the sum involved is one dollar or a million. If the Israeli "right" to seize any part of Palestine, however small, is once admitted, this will herald a long period of Israeli territorial annexations in the Middle East, and will endanger the security of all Arab countries within reach of Israeli armed forces.

In the light of these facts, the Palestinian National Council has declared that "the Palestinian cause in the present phase is facing the dangers of being liquidated for the interests of Zionism and imperialism through the Security Council Resolution of 22 November 1967 and all so-called peaceful solutions and liquidation plans proposed, including the Soviet plan which aims at laying down a timetable for the implementation of the Security Council Resolution."

While exposing the illusory "peaceful solution" of Resolution 242, the Palestinian National Council, the most broadly representative body of the

Palestinian people, also laid down the criteria for the attainment of genuine peace. It declared:

> The Arab Palestinian people resolutely reject all liquidatory resolutions and plans including the Security Council Resolution of 22 November 1967 and the Soviet plan and any other plans. The Palestinian people, in their bitter struggle to liberate their homeland and return to it, aim only at the establishment of a free democratic society in Palestine for all Palestinians, Muslims, Christians and Jews, and the redemption of Palestine and her people from the domination of world Zionism, since that is a reactionary religio-racialist movement with fascist roots, organically linked to world imperialism(31).

Since a peace settlement based on appeasement would be unsatisfactory and short-lived, the Palestinian people, led by their Resistance, have resolved that the future peace of the Middle East must be a peace based on respect for the highest principles of international law. There is nothing at all ambiguous about this. The Palestinian Resistance has outlined in detail how true peace must be established, and the correct principles are clearly defined in numerous solemn international documents. Let us examine the Palestinian approach to peace in the light of the principles of international law.

In one of its early statements, Fateh, the largest commando organization, gave an indication of the peace programme of the Resistance. Referring to its conduct of armed struggle against occupation, Fateh declared:

> This undermining of the Israeli Zionist existence will conitnue until Palestine has been restored to its rightful owners, the Palestine Arabs, who have lived on this land alongside the Jewish minority uninterruptedly for 4,000 years.
>
> Al-Fateh, the Palestine National Liberation Movement, wishes to point out, however, that its operations — which today enjoy the support of the entire Palestinian people — are in no way aimed at the Jewish people as such with whom they lived in harmony in the past for so many centuries. Nor does it intend to 'push them into the sea.' This resistance and the liberation movement Al-Fateh is coordinating is aimed solely at the Zionist-military-fascist regime which has usurped our homeland and expelled and repressed our two million people, condemning them to a life of destitution and misery . . .
>
> The movement Al-Fateh is leading is the organized expression of this people's liberation struggle whose counterparts are to be found throughout the world, wherever fascist and imperialist aggression is being waged — in Vietnam, South Africa, Angola, Bolivia or elsewhere. In occupied Palestine as in these countries, the humble, ordinary subjugated people are taking up arms in self-defence and for the eventual liberation of their homeland . . .
>
> And they also know that on the day the flag of Palestine is hoisted over their freed, democratic, peaceful land, a new era will begin in which the Palestinian Jews will again live in harmony, side by side with the original owners of the land, the Arab Palestinians(32).

Subsequently, Fateh published this more detailed statement of its position:

> After being expelled from their homeland, and having lived for 20

years in camps in the most humiliating way, our people are now taking up arms to defend their interests. All political means have been exhausted. Although our rights have been recognized almost unanimously by the General Assembly of the United Nations, and on several occasions, Israel has refused to carry them out. No other way remains for us.

Peace is the final objective of our people. But this peace cannot be achieved unless our people are given back their legitimate rights:

— The unconditional right of return and national status for every Palestinian, when it pleases him to take it;

— The right of individuals to recover their properties seized by the enemy;

— The right to a democratic life in a democratic country, and consequently to measures of protection against any sort of aggressive hegemony;

— The stopping of Zionist immigration.

That is the minimum on which a peace in Palestine could possibly be conceived.

For the realization of these aims, our Palestinian people have organized themselves under the leadership of the Palestine National Liberation Movement, Al-Fateh.

Our people's struggle is therefore represented by Al-Fateh. It is thus independent from the actions or declarations of other interested parties. 'Israel' is now in conflict with the Arab countries. There should be no confusion between the two conflicts. There is the conflict over the 1967 act of aggression, and the main conflict over Palestine itself . . .

It is a question here of the existence of a people. Our people are not just defending a land by arms; they are not trying to recover a lost land for reasons of living space or vanity: it is a question that genocide has been committed against a society, a civilization, a complete organism of human society. It is in this case a problem of existence; liberation here takes on the meaning of a protective action of a social entity. In considering the Palestine problem, one should think of a social entity in danger and of a criminal action against it. The crime has been committed: but now it is a question of a people, who do not die(33).

The Palestinians, in formulating their doctrine on peace, have had to bear in mind that the Israeli State refuses to honour any U.N. resolutions which it considers disadvantageous to itself. These include Resolution 194 on the refugees' right of return, and other resolutions on reaffirmation of refugee rights, respect for Armistice Agreements, status of demilitarized zones and, since June 1967, the rights of newly displaced persons, the illegality of the annexation of Jerusalem and respect for the cease-fire. The Israelis and their supporters maintain that peace requires the Arab States to make concessions: to renounce the rights of the expelled Palestinians, give the Israeli State diplomatic recognition, forget Jerusalem's historic Arab character and allow the Israelis any territorial adjustments they need to place them in a strong strategic position for their next blitzkrieg. Other concessions might also be demanded, such as accepting Israeli economic domination of the Middle East (the Abba Eban plan). Failure to make such concessions will result in the Arabs being accused of intransigence, although the Israelis themselves are not prepared to make any concessions.

The Palestinian people, in rejecting any peace based on concessions to the aggressor or territorial adjustments, whether in the framework of the Security Council Resolution or any other plan, base themselves on the principle in the Atlantic Charter, that territorial changes should only come about in accordance with the freely-expressed wishes of the peoples concerned. This principle, enshrined in the U.N. Charter as the self-determination principle, was violated in 1948 with the establishment of the Israeli State. The Palestinian people are not prepared to tolerate a "peace settlement" based on the violation of so basic a principle of international law. It must be stressed here that the problem is not simply a refugee problem, nor is mere enforcement of Resolution 194 an adequate solution. The Palestinians have the right not only to return to live in Palestine, but also to be a sovereign people there, exercising their right of self-determination in the whole of their homeland.

The self-determination principle, as well as Article 2 of the U.N. Charter, established a rule that acquisition of territory by aggression is illegal. This had earlier been declared in the Kellogg-Briand Pact, on whose basis the Nuremberg Tribunal condemned the launching of aggressive war as "the supreme international crime."

Arising from the self-determination principle is the Palestinian view that peace cannot be restored until the racialist Israeli State is overthrown. There has been some confusion among the uninformed public abroad on this issue, due to Israeli propagandists' use of emotive phrases (also written into the Security Council Resolution) such as "right to exist" or "right to live in peace." Yet international law denies the right of any state based on racial discrimination to exist and to be allowed "peacefully" to trample on basic human rights. It has also become increasingly accepted in international law since World War Two that a racialist state by its very nature is a threat to the peace of the surrounding area. This finds expression, for instance, in a U.N. General Assembly resolution which notes with concern:

> That the Government of South Africa continues to intensify and extend beyond the borders of South Africa its inhuman and aggressive policies of apartheid and that these policies have led to a violent conflict, creating a situation in the whole of southern Africa which constitutes a grave threat to international peace and security.

The Assembly, in this Resolution, also considered:

> That effective action for a solution of the situation in South Africa is imperative in order to eliminate the grave threat to peace in southern Africa as a whole(34).

South Africa's racialist policies are undoubtedly a potential threat to peace in that they may at any time lead to the outbreak of a full-scale war although they have not yet done so. Israel's racialist policies, on the other hand, are a proven threat to peace as they have already caused three full-scale wars and may cause a fourth one in future.

Because it endangers peace as well as contravening basic human rights, racialism aroused these words from the U.N. General Assembly:

> That racism, Nazism and the ideology and policy of apartheid are incompatible with the objectives of the Charter of the United Nations and the Universal Declaration of Human Rights, the Convention on the

Prevention and Punishment of the Crime of Genocide, the United Nations Declaration on the Elimination of All Forms of Racial Discrimination, the International Convention on the Elimination of All Forms of Racial Discrimination and other international instruments.

In that Resolution, the Assembly:

> Calls upon all States and peoples, as well as national and international organizations, to strive for the eradication as soon as possible and once and for all, of racism, Nazism and similar ideologies and practices, including apartheid, which are based on racial intolerance and terror(35).

The solution put forward by the Palestinian Resistance fully accords with these principles, in that it envisages a democratic Palestinian State in which all its citizens, of whatever religion or ethnic origin, enjoy equal rights. The emergence of the Resistance which represents the Palestinian people now offers a solution to this problem where formerly there had been a void. Foreign observers interested in the Palestinian question used, quite legitimately, to pose the problem: if the Palestinians regain their homeland, what will happen to the Jewish settlers? Before the emergence of a Resistance genuinely representative of the Palestinians, there was nobody who could answer this authoritatively. The void was sometimes filled with the words of irresponsible demagogues who had no authority to speak for the Palestinian people. Now, the Palestinians, through their Resistance, have spoken in unmistakable terms: those Jews prepared to live on a basis of equality as Palestinian citizens will be welcome to do so. Nobody can reasonably ask for more than equality with his fellow men in basic human rights.

In this writer's view, only the Palestinian Resistance has put forward a programme for the restoration of peace and the solution of the Palestine problem which fully accords with the principles of international law as they have evolved today. The fact that the Palestinian people are compelled to take up arms in order that this programme of secure peace and racial equality can be implemented is due essentially to the lamentably irresponsible fashion in which the United Nations has acted throughout, and the sordid intrigues carried out by the major powers, the "Big Four."

To those who put forward the pacifist argument that any violence must be avoided at all costs, and that conciliation is the only way, through United Nations or big power mediation, an answer is required. This writer recognizes that where international disputes can be solved through compromise and conciliation, in a just and legal manner, this is infinitely preferable to the use of force. In civil law, the courts can often solve a dispute between citizens without them having to resort to the more primitive redress of a fistfight. However, there are occasions when law must be firm and uncompromising, when the issue is one of basic rights or the commission of a crime. If a civil court, as a compromise, allowed a thief to keep half of what he had stolen, or permitted a murderer to go unpunished, the result would not be social stability, but a total breakdown of the law. In the case of Palestine, the issue is not like a dispute over fishing rights or the delineation of a border. It concerns principles which lie at the heart of the entire concept of international order: the right of a people to live in their own land, to exercise self-determination, to live free from racial discrimination. It concerns also serious violations of international law, crimes against peace, war crimes and crimes against humanity committed by the Israeli State, crimes which, if they go unpunished, will threaten all the ideals on which civilization is based, as did the Nazi crimes. The Palestine question is one where international law must be firmly applied, and supported by all those who desire to prevent another lapse into barbarism.

These, then, are the issues at stake in the future of the Middle East. In pursuing their quest for a just and lasting peace, the Palestinian people must continue to be guided by their understanding that such a peace should be based on respect for the principles of international law. Only thus can the threat of war eventually be eliminated from this region of the world, and may peace once more prevail in the land of peace.

NOTES

(1) Military communique No. 1, published by Fateh.

(2) Cf. Oppenheim, op. cit., 7th ed., Vol. II, pp. 215-216 for details of how the Nazis also applied this practice in the 1941 Barbarossa Jurisdiction Order and the Wacht und Nebel decree. Acts carried out under this logic were judged to be war crimes by the Nuremberg Tribunal.

Cf.WAR CRIMES REPORTS, 12 (1949), p. 86; also section 37 of the British Military Manual, and U.S. War Department Rules of Land Warfare, 1940, No. 351.

(3) Winston S. Churchill, THE SECOND WORLD WAR (London, 1948), Vol. III, pp. 197-198.

(4) E. L. Woodward, BRITISH FOREIGN POLICY IN THE SECOND WORLD WAR (H.M.S.O., 1962), p. 224.

(5) THE TIMES, 17 July 1944; Oppenheim, op. cit., 7th ed., Vol. II, p. 574, note 2.

(6) AL DUSTUR newspaper (Amman), 9 May 1969, reported that the Palestinian Red Crescent informed the Swiss Foreign Minister of this intention.

(7) Stone, op. cit., p. 565 and note.

(8) AL DUSTUR, and other newspapers, 13 September 1969.

(9) Oppenheim, op. cit., 7th ed., Vol. II, p. 373, note 3.

(10) Ibid., Vol. II, p. 416.

(11) Letter to THE TIMES, 26 March 1968.

(12) For details of these debates, see Nasser, op. cit., pp. 30-45.

(13) Res. 237 (1967).

(14) Resolutions 2253 (ES-V) and 2254 (ES-V).

(15) Nasser, op. cit., p. 35.

(16) Res. 242 (1967).

(17) THE ECONOMIST, 25 November 1967.

(18) U.N. DOC. A/6701/ADD. 1, pp. 20-21.

(19) Smith, op. cit., p. 95.

(20) Cf. FINANCIAL TIMES, 12 November 1968, and editorial in WASHINGTON POST, 12 November 1968.

(21) ATLANTIC MONTHLY, January 1969.

(22) Cf. Tass Agency Report, 26 December 1968.

(23) THE OBSERVER, 5 January 1969.

(24) LE MONDE, 9 January 1969.

(25) THE DAILY TELEGRAPH, 6 February 1969.

(26) See account of Glassboro meeting and President Johnson's subsequent broadcast in KESSING'S CONTEMPORARY ARCHIVES, p. 22180, 29 July — 5 August 1967.

(27) Churchill, THE SECOND WORLD WAR, Vol. I, p. 285.

(28) E. Lipson, EUROPE 1914-1939 (London, 1945), p. 331.

(29) Quoted by Lipson, op. cit., p. 384.

(30) See Churchill, THE SECOND WORLD WAR, Vol. I, pp. 275-276.

(31) Council statement issued at Cairo Congress, 1-4 February 1969.

(32) Press Release No. 1, issued by Fateh Information Section, January 1968.

(33) VERS UNE PAIX EN PALESTINE, pamphlet of Fateh Information Section.

(34) Res. 2396 (XXIII) of 2 December 1968.

(35) Res. 2438 (XXIII).

Nationalism and Statehood
the arab rights

THE ARAB SLOGAN
OF A DEMOCRATIC STATE

Y. Harkabi

THE SLOGAN "DEMOCRATIC PALESTINIAN STATE"

The crux of the Arabs' position in their conflict with Israel has been the problem of safeguarding the Arab character of the country. To this end were aimed the demands that they made during the Mandate to prohibit sale of land to Jews and to stop Jewish immigration, to desist from altering the country's character with respect to its ethnic makeup and ownership of land. The problem which the Arabs faced during the Mandate of arresting the process of the country's judaization was compounded after the founding of the State of Israel because thenceforth it became one of turning back the wheel of history and annulling the Jewish State.

The problem of eliminating the Jewish State is enmeshed in the question of having to expunge a fact created in the course of time, namely, the presence of a considerable Jewish population. For the existence of a Jewish State depends upon a concentration of Jews, and therefore elimination of the State requires in principle "reduction" of the Jewish community. Hence the motifs of killing the Jews and of throwing them into the sea which were so often reiterated in Arab pronouncements. The Arab position, insofar as it was politicidal (i.e., calling for annihilation of a State), was bound to lead to a genocidal position, even had the Arabs not been bent upon revenge.

After the Six-Day War, when the Arabs became aware that by making extreme statements they had prejudiced their position in foreigners' eyes, they commenced to seek a way of evading the trap of politicide that entails genocide, that is, a way of lending a moderate tone to their position calling for the annihilation of Israel. Arab propagandists denied that they had used expressions advocating murder of the Jewish population, or they claimed that at most "Jewish provocations" aroused their anger and the extreme statements, which they allegedly did not intend. Ahmed Shukeiry exonerated himself by claiming that he never advocated throwing the Jews into the sea, that this was merely a Zionist libel. He explained that what was meant was that the Jews would return to their countries of origin by way of the sea: "They came by the sea and will return by the sea" (PALESTINE DOCUMENTS FOR 1967, p. 1084). Thus, from a means of annihilation the sea was metamorphosed into a simple means of transportation. Accordingly, the proportion between the Arab and Jewish populations will be restored not by violence but by an international project that will return Jews to their countries of origin.

Arab spokesmen began to brandish the slogan of "a Democratic Palestinian State in which Arabs and Jews will live in peace." Indeed, this slogan was well received among many circles in the world at large as evidence that the Arab position had become more moderate. Many people overlooked its ambiguity and disregarded the fact that it by no means contradicted the basic Arab position of the past, for the slogan may still mean that Jews would be reduced to an insignificant minority which would be permitted to live in peace. Once this slogan was unfurled, a debate concerning its significance arose among the Palestinian Arabs.

A revealing indication of the true intention of the slogan "Democratic Palestinian State," as understood by the Palestinian organizations, is found in a report to its members by the Popular Democratic Front for the Liberation of Palestine concerning deliberations at the Sixth Congress of the Palestinian National Council which met in Cairo in September 1969. The Popular Democratic Front is a fedayun organization headed by Na'if Hawatmeh, which broke away in February 1969 from Georges Habash's Popular Front for the Liberation of Palestine. A delegation of the Popular Democratic Front proposed to the Congress that "a progressive content" be given to the slogan "Democratic State." Their own interpretation of this slogan will be explained below. Deliberation over this subject was central in the Congress. The Congress rejected the proposal, claiming that the slogan "Democratic State" was merely a propaganda device. Moreover, it was stressed that adopting this slogan as a principle in the national programme would impair the Arab character of Palestine. Nevertheless, since the slogan had gained support abroad for the Arabs it was decided that it was worthwhile to maintain it.

Here follows the translation of a section of the report by the Popular Democratic Front, entitled "Internal Circular Concerning Debates and Results of the Sixth National Council":

> The slogan "The Democratic Palestinian State" has been raised for some time within the Palestinian context. Fatah was the first to adopt it. Since it was raised this slogan has been met with remarkable world response. Our delegation brought to the Congress a resolution proposal intended to elucidate the meaning of this slogan from a progressive point of departure, opposed in principle to the slogan of throwing the Jews into the sea, which had done grave damage to the Arab position in the past.
>
> When debate on this subject began, everyone thought that they were in agreement concerning it. But as the debate unfolded considerable opposition surfaced, and it became even more pronounced when our delegation raised its resolution proposal for debate. In the course of the discussion the following views came to light:
>
> 1. The view which maintains that the slogan of "The Democratic Palestinian State" is a tactical one which we brandish because it has been well received internationally.
>
> 2. Another view which maintains that we consider this slogan to be strategical, not tactical, but that it should remain a slogan and is not a basic principle. This position is identical with the previous one, with a mere attempt at word play.

29

3. The third view was more straightforward in rejecting the slogan and its progressive content proposed by our delegation. The position of this faction was based on the claim that the slogan contradicts the Arab character of Palestine and the principle of self-determination which was established in the National Covenant of the (Palestine) Liberation Organization, and it also advocates a peaceful settlement with the Jews of Palestine.

That is, if this slogan is taken literally, the Arab character that the country must have after its "liberation" will be undermined, for a large group of Jews would be permitted to remain. The Palestinian National Convention stipulated that only the Palestinian Arab people has the right of self-determination in the country, whereas the slogan "Democratic State" makes the Jews partners. Moreover, this slogan may imply reconciliation with the Jews rather than a war a l'outrance.

These were the contending views concerning the slogan of "The Democratic Palestinian State." We were able to arrive at a recommendation to continue in the adoption of the slogan with the proviso that the Executive Committee of the Liberation Organization undertake to study its meaning and present the results of its investigation to the National Council at its next session for debate.

There were also echoes of this debate in newspapers, as touching upon such a crucial issue for the Arab position, and from them as well one may learn about the mood of the Congress. AL-HURRIYYA (20 September 1969), the weekly of the Popular Democratic Front, stated: "Even general slogans like 'Democratic State,' which had won support of the Palestinian Right, were rejected by the Sixth National Council. There appeared among the rightist ranks on the Council manifest racist tendencies on the Israel question, as well as reactionary tendencies in the solutions that they proposed for this issue which were close to the well-known Shukeirian ones." (The Popular Democratic Front calls itself "The Left" while it considers most of the other groups "The Right," this label reserved especially for Fatah.)

AL-MUHARRIR of 9 September 1969, reported: "After a long debate on this point ("Democratic State"), the need was expressed to balance the propaganda slogans of the issue and necessary strategic aims. It was agreed that statements concerning the Democratic State be made only in the context of the principle of general liberation of Palestine and annihilation of the Israaeli entity, so that there be neither misunderstandings nor comparisons between the waves of European Jewish immigration to Palestine and the original sons of the country." That is, the slogan "Democratic State" equates the right of the Jewish immigrants who settled in the country and the Palestinian Arabs, whereas the official position had affirmed that only the Palestinians have the right of sovereignty over the country.

The Popular Democratic Front is the most leftist of the fedayun organizations. It lays claim to a Marxist-Leninist view and a class approach, representing the Palestinian workers and peasants. It appears to be riding a wave of leftist radicalism which is a conspicuous trend in most Arab countries.

Ahmad Hamrush, editor of the Egyptian weekly RUZ AL-YUSUF, indicates in his weekly, "One of the deepest and most palpable phenomena in the wake of the defeat is the trend toward the Left in the Arab Homeland" (8 December

1969). The leftist social content in the message of the Popular Democratic Front is more likely to attract Palestinian youth than Fatah, which postpones formulation of a social theory until after what it calls "the end of the stage of liberation." The Popular Democratic Front conducts extensive propaganda activity in the West and has connections with circles of the New Left. Among the Palestinian organizations, including Fatah, it may be estimated to be the one most acceptable to New Left circles.

The Popular Democratic Front, on its own testimony, prepared more conscientiously than the other participants for the Sixth Congress of the Palestinian National Council, the first at which it was represented. It formulated memoranda and draft resolutions. This material was collected in a book of 167 pages entitled THE PRESENT SITUATION OF THE PALESTINIAN RESIST-ANCE MOVEMENT: A CRITICAL STUDY (Beirut, 1969), for which Na'if Hawatmeh wrote an introduction. Here follows the formulation of the resolution proposed by the Popular Democratic Front to the Palestinian National Council concerning the Democratic State (p. 165):

The Palestinian National Council, in accordance with the Palestinian people's belief in democratic solutions for the Palestine question, resolves as follows:

1. To reject the chauvinist and reactionary Zionist-colonialist solutions advocating recognition of the State of Israel as one of the facts of the Middle East region, for these solutions contradict the right of the Palestinian people to self-determination in its country and they consecrate the expansionist Zionist entity which is linked to colonialism and hostile to the Palestinian and Arab national liberation movement and all forces of liberation and Socialism in the world.

2. To reject the Palestinian and Arab chauvinistic solutions, raised before and after June 1967, which advocate slaughter of the Jews and throwing them into the sea, and to reject the reactionary solutions which advocate the consolidation of the State of Israel within secure and recognized boundaries as expressed in the remembered-for-ill resolution of the Security Council. These solutions are at the expense of the right of the Palestinian people to self-determination in its country, and they plant in the Middle East region a racist-capitalist-expansionist State linked dialectically to international capitalism which is hostile to the Palestinian, Arab and world liberation movement and to all the forces of Socialism and progress in the world.

3. The struggle for a democratic popular solution of the Palestine question and the Israel question is based on the elimination of the Zionist entity represented in all institutions of the State (army, administration and police) and all chauvinist and Zionist political and cooperative institutions, and (it is based on) the establishment of a Democratic Popular Palestinian State in which Arabs and Jews will live without discrimination, a State opposed to all forms of class and national suppression, conferring the right on both Arabs and Jews to develop their own national (*wataniyya*) culture.

4. By virtue of the link of history and destiny between Palestine and the Arab nation, the Democratic Popular State of Palestine will be an organic part of an Arab federal State in this region, a State of democratic content, hostile to colonialism, imperialism, Zionism and Arab and Palestinian reaction.

31

"The democratic solution" is thus represented as a compromise between two chauvinistic solutions — a Jewish State and throwing the Jews into the sea — as though these were equivalent and symmetrical. Thus, this is supposedly a fair solution: the Arabs renounce killing the Jews, and the Jews renounce their State. The Palestinian State will become a popular democracy, but its Arab character will be preserved nonetheless by its being part of an Arab federation to which they also affix the label "democratic." The final article is intended to answer the claim that the Democratic Palestinian State will be an anomaly among the Arab States and thus difficult to digest within the context of Arab unity.

The pronouncements of the Democratic Front may be taken to imply that its intention is a bi-national State. In another place in the same book, it is stated (p. 136): "The Palestinian State, which will eliminate racial discrimination and national persecution, must be based on a democratic solution of the existing conflict resting on coexistence (ta'ayush) between the two peoples, Arab and Jewish." It should be noted that this recognition of "a Jewish people" is an innovation within the general Arab position which, for the most part, has been based on the claim that the Jews constitute only a religion and therefore do not deserve to have a national State. But this recognition of the Jews as a people is qualified, for they are a people which has no right to a State of its own but must settle for participation in a State whose nationality is Palestinian. The significance of their being a people is therefore cultural, not national-political. Hawatmeh tells Lufti al-Khuli, editor of AL-TALI'A: "We urged initiation of a dialogue with the Israeli Socialist organization Matzpen, which adopts a position based on an Arab-Jewish bi-national State. But we have not reached concrete results which might impel Matzpen to adopt a completely progressive, democratic stand on the Palestine question based on liquidation ("tasfiyya") of the Zionist entity and establishment of a democratic Palestinian State opposed to all kinds of class and national suppression" (AL-TALI'A, November, 1969, p. 106). That is, the proposal for a bi-national State is not sufficiently progressive for Hawatmeh because recognition of Jewish peoplehood implies for him the need to grant the Jews cultural autonomy.

This magnanimous concession is not new; Shukeiry was ready to do the same. One of the paradoxes of the Democratic Front is that, while the Popular Front for the Liberation of Palestine, from which the Democratic Front split because it was allegedly too far to the Right, does not participate in the institutions of the Palestine Liberation Organization, the Democratic Front is a member living under one roof with organizations much further to the Right than the Popular Front. To be accepted in the Command of Armed Struggle, an arm of the Palestine Liberation Organization, the Executive Committee of the Liberation Organization required the Democratic Front to declare itself "loyal to everything written in the National Covenant as the minimal programme for the relations in the Command of Armed Struggle" (Abu Iyad in a conversation with al Khuli, AL-TALI'A, June, 1969). The Democratic Front refers to the Covenant in the internal circular quoted above. It is amazing how its "democratic" proposals are compatible with the contents of the Palestinian National Covenant. In all its resolution proposals there is no suggestion to amend this Covenant, or at least Article 6 concerning the Jews who would be permitted to remain in the liberated State.

Thus, despite all the pretensions of the Popular Democratic Front, the difference between its position and that accepted by the other Palestinian organizations may be merely a matter of the size of the tolerated Jewish minority. A current notion among many Arab spokesmen is that a considerable number of Israelis are in the country against their will, and that, if Zionism were abolished, along with "the national coercion" that it imposes, they would abandon the country. European Jews would not wish to live in a Palestinian Arab State, preferring to emigrate, while Jews from Arab countries would "rejoice" at the opportunity afforded them to return to their countries of origin. These are very common themes in writing and speech. Contact with the Jewish community in Israel and the open bridges have not yet shaken these ideas. It seems that they have a vital role within the Arab position, making them less amenable to change. If self-reduction of the Jews is assured after the victory, why become involved in declarations to the effect that this reduction will be done violently? What does the Arab position lose if it declares that Palestinian citizenship will be given to all Israelis?

The Popular Democratic Front thus attempts to confer a humane guise on the Arab position by dissociating annihilation of the State of Israel from the necessity of having "to reduce" the number of its Jewish inhabitants. It should be noted that its position is basically neither moderate nor congenial. In the Arab-Israeli conflict, as a political conflict, the main question is the attitude to Israel as a State and to its sovereignty. The Popular Democratic Front's rejection of Israel as a State is intensified, as if indulgence toward Jews were counter-balanced by greater severity against their State. In the view of the Popular Democratic Front, Israel as a Jewish State is not an autonomous phenomenon with its own odious features; it is rather part of everything dark and inhuman in international life — imperialism, colonialism and capitalism — which must be fought to the bitter end. From the time of the First World War, Arabs insisted that Israel was established with the help of colonialism; or later that it persisted owing only to the aid of American imperialism. But within leftist trends the link between Israel and colonialism or imperialism is now viewed as organic — not simply as a supportive arrangement, and opposition to the existence of Israel is thus accentuated.

The Popular Democratic Front is absolute in its rejection of the possibility of a peaceful solution and of the Security Council resolution. In this, its stand is far more radical than that of some Arab States. Even the Khartoum Summit Conference resolutions are treason in its eyes: "This conference offered the Arab peoples hollow promises, 'no peace, no recognition, no negotiation with Israel,' as though the question on the agenda were that of negotiation and peace and not overcoming the aggression and annihilating its bases" (p. 85). Accepting the Security Council resolution is worse treason, for it implies recognition of Israel, even if Arab States excuse their acceptance as a tactical manoeuvre: "The contention that acceptance of the Security Council resolution is a tactical position, whose aim is 'elimination of the traces of the aggression,' in order to continue action for the liberation of Palestine, is a misleading, demagogic and fraudulent claim which only arouses loathing and nausea in the souls of Arab revolutionaries" (p. 88). The solution can only be by violence. In the resolution proposal offered by the Democratic Front to the National Council, it is stated with emphasis: "The national liberation movement will achieve a Democratic Popular Palestinian State only by armed struggle and a people's war of liberation against Zionism, imperialism and reaction, by destruction of the Israeli State and liberation of the Jews from the Zionist movement" (p. 167).

The radicalism in this position against Israel the State is expressed also in radicalism in the form of warfare. It is not accidental that leftist fedayun organizations in particular, like the Popular Front and the Democratic Front, see the struggle as world-embracing and advocate means such as attacking civilian

33

aeroplanes, while an organization like Fatah dissociates itself, at least by declaration, from these means.

In pronouncements of Fatah, though they are not always straightforward, there are glimpses of a genocidal position. For example, in Fatah's monthly, THE PALESTINIAN REVOLUTION, No. 7 (June, 1968), p. 38, it is explained why a conventional war does not suit the Palestinian goal: "For the aim of this war is not to impose our will on the enemy but to destroy him in order to take his place (ifna'uhu lil-hululi mahallahu) . . . In a conventional war there is no need to continue the war if the enemy submits to our will . . . while in a people's war there is no deterrent, for its aim is not to subjugate the enemy but to destroy (ifna') him. A conventional war has limited aims which cannot be transcended, for it is necessary to allow the enemy to exist in order to impose our will over him, while in a people's war destruction (ifna') of the enemy is the first and last duty." The expression, ifna', used here is extreme, its literal meaning being "reduction to absolute nothingness." This destruction does not refer to army units, as in military parlance, but to the enemy in order "to take his place."

In contrast to such expressions, even Fatah spokesmen adopt more moderate language, as well as the slogan "Democratic State." JEUNE AFRIQUE (3 March 1970) reports a change in the position of Fatah on the authority of articles published in Fatah's monthly:

> The (Palestinian) revolution (i.e. the position of the Palestinians, especially that represented by Fatah) rejects the thesis according to which only those Jews who lived in Israel before 1948 or before 1914 and their descendents will be accepted (i.e., as citizens. The article alludes to positions taken in the Palestinian National Covenant of 1964, which implies that only Jews who were in the country before 1948 would be recognized as Palestinians, or, in the amended version of 1968, in which this article was made more extreme, restricting this right to Jews who were in the country before "the Zionist invasion" in 1917.) After all, Dayan and Allon, who were born in Palestine before 1948, are racist Zionists who cannot pretend to Palestinian citizenship, while the new immigrants may be anti-Zionist and may contribute to the establishment of a new Palestine. One of the Fatah leaders, Abu Iyad, announced in a press conference that not only the progressive, anti-Zionist Jews but all Zionists who will be ready to abandon their racist ideology will be received with open arms as Palestinian citizens. The Palestinian revolution is convinced that all Israeli Jews will change their attitude and subscribe to the new Palestine, especially after the destruction of the political, economic and military structures of the present oligarchy.

Confusion on this issue within Fatah ranks is discernible in the fact that, when the Kuwait newspaper AL-SIYASA reproduced this statement from JEUNE AFRIQUE, the spokesmen of the central propaganda office of Fatah located in Damascus (Middle East News Agency, 15 March 1970) responded that the articles upon which JEUNE AFRIQUE relied, allegedly published in THE PALESTINIAN REVOLUTION, (which was the official publication in Arabic), never appeared there. Such articles were actually published in the English publication FATAH of 20 November 1969, 1 January and 19 January 1970. But one may assume that there were such pronouncements, and that JEUNE AFRIQUE relied upon them, though they were not published in the central organ of Fatah. For example, Salah Khalaf, called Abu-Iyad, whose position in Fatah is second to that of Arafat, made statements similar to the ones attributed to him here in an interview in AL-TALI'A, June 1969.

JEUNE AFRIQUE wishes to attribute a moderate position to Fatah before it crystallized and became accepted policy. However, it is likely that Fatah spokesmen will use more and more formulations similar to that of the Popular Democratic Front, if only for tactical purposes. The change in a propaganda formula will probably not seem a matter of principle to them. For Fatah anticipates, in any case, that terrorism will reduce the number of Jews. In a public statement issued on the fifth anniversary of the beginning of Fatah activity (1 January 1970), it is stated that guerrilla actions will spread to the heart of Israel's territory, and then the Israeli "will find himself isolated and defenseless against the Arab soldier in his house, on his land, on the road, in the café in the movie theatre, in army camps and everywhere, far from the area under control of the Israeli Air Force and mechanical equipment which assures him protection and security of life. These acts will force him to consider and compare the life of stability and repose that he enjoyed in his former country and the life of confusion and anxiety he finds in the land of Palestine. This is bound to motivate him towards reverse immigration" (THE PALESTINIAN REVOLUTION, No. 22, January 1970, p. 8).

The article in the Palestinian National Covenant which is so extreme regarding the Jews is becoming known in the world. A number of foreign journals recognized the importance of this document and reproduced the English translations of my article which explains the Covenant. There will most likely be pressure among the Palestinians to change the Covenant and make it more moderate and palatable.

The position which combined annihilation of the State with elimination of its inhabitants (politicide and genocide) was consistent, for this made possible the subsequent realization of the aim of establishing an Arab State. But the position which advocates annihilating the State without doing away with its inhabitants, the State nevertheless becoming Arab, is self-contradictory. The Arabs avoid this contradiction by clinging to the illusion that the Jews desire to emigrate and will reduce their community on their own, as well as by exaggerating the number of Palestinians. However, from a practical aspect, how can the Palestinians return to their fomer dwelling places if the Jews are not eliminated?

The Palestinians labour under another illusion concerning the power of "the resistance," as they euphemistically call guerrilla-type warfare against Israel. Guerrilla warfare, upon which the Popular Democratic Front and other Palestinian organizations rely, has a chance of success when it becomes an internal war, a citizen war, in which the population's support of authority is undermined. But fedayun actions are essentially an external war which cannot be turned into a people's war of the inhabitants of Israel against their Government. Israel's control of areas with an Arab population does not fundamentally change the picture. The model of internal war is more appropriate to what may happen in Arab countries, wreaking havoc within them but not between them and Israel.

The readiness expressed in the slogan "Democratic State" for declaratory recognition of partial rights for Israelis, though giving the Arabs a better base for propaganda and diplomacy, signifies a stage in the retreat in the Arab position. The contradictions contained in the slogan "Democratic State" will bring about many inner struggles, debates, forums and symposiums. This slogan will become another subject over which the Arabs will be divided. The Jewish community will increase and the possibilities of digesting it as a minority will become smaller. For some time now they have been non-existent. The retreat in the Arab position will continue, for the meaning of the Arab position is becoming more apparent, which the Arabs used to define their aims, is becoming restricted. The difficulties involved in a political position will become more obvious. From the Arab point of view, brandishing the slogan "Democratic State" creates more problems than it solves.

ARAB RECONSIDERATIONS POINTING TO A CHANGE?

In Arab journalism, particularly in periodicals, interesting articles and symposia are often published concerning social problems, self-criticism and the Arab-Israeli conflict. Israeli newspaper reporting usually skips over these articles because it is by its nature more concerned with political events, more with Arabs' actions and less with their ideas. Such journalistic portrayal of the Arab world becomes pallid because of the absence of the human-ideological dimension of events. Human beings not only operate; they also think about their actions. Furthermore, concerning ourselves with the opponent's reflection tends to humanize him by viewing him along with all his human problems. The Six-Day War and its aftermath raised questions for the Arabs and stimulated them to reassess their procedure in the conflict. They began to grapple with the question of their objective in the conflict. This wrestling is primarily concerned now with the slogan "Democratic Palestinian State."

Studying their deliberations over this question is important for us for three reasons:

1. It contributes to our understanding of the opponent's intention, however disconcerting this may be. The tension of involvement in the conflict has often engendered among Israelis a tendency toward self-deception and a desire to play down the severity of the Arab position. Arabs brandish the slogan of a democratic State as a means of psychological warfare against us, in order to weaken our determination, and we should be aware of this.

2. This issue provides an aperture through which we may witness the difficulties the Arabs confront because of their genocidal position toward Israel, and it shows why the ideological structure of the Arab position compels them to retreat from it. This may also herald a change in their position toward us.

3. The Arabs use the slogan of a Democratic State as a propaganda means in foreign countries. In order to discredit it, there is nothing better than to rely upon their own words, which disclose its underlying significance.

In the weekly supplement of the Beirut newspaper AL-ANWAR (8 March 1970), a long symposium was published concerning the meaning of the slogan "The Democratic State," in which the views of most of the prominent fedayun organizations were represented. A translation of extracts from this symposium is here presented, along with comments, signed Y. H., and a summary concerning its significance.

Moderator: The main objective of the symposium is to discuss all the solutions proposed by the various groups of the resistance movement under the slogan "The Democratic Palestinian State," particularly the proposals of Fatah and the Popular Democratic Front. I omit from the discussion those solutions which were hatched up apart from the groups of the resistance movement, whether openly or secretly. I refer particularly to the solution adopted by the

United States to establish a Palestinian State in the West Bank and the Gaza Strip, and France's proposals concerning the establishment of a Palestinian State to be connected with some Arab countries.

At the beginning of the symposium, I thus turned to the representative of the (Popular) Democratic Front for the Liberation of Palestine: I would like you to explain to us the Front's viewpoint concerning the Democratic Palestinian State on the basis of the resolution presented to the Sixth Congress of the Palestinian National Council which was convened last September.

Representative of the Democratic Front: . . . The adoption of a particular slogan, in our estimation, does not stem from a subjective position or a subjective desire but from a study and analysis of the evolution of the objective situation, the objective possibilities present in society and within history — moving forces, as well as the nature of the potential evolution of these forces in the future. . . .

Coexistence ("ta'ayush") with this entity (Israel) is impossible, not because of a national aim or national aspiration of the Arabs, but because the presence of this entity will determine this region's development in connection with world Imperialism, which follows from the objective link between it and Zionism. Thus, eradicating imperialist influence in the Middle East means eradicating the Israeli entity. This is something indispensable, not only from the aspect of the Palestinian people's right of self-determination, and in its homeland, but also from the aspect of protecting the Arab national liberation movement, and this objective also can only be achieved by means of armed struggle . . .

We believe that hypothetical questions such as, what will happen if the working class or the Communist Party takes over the Government in Israel? are irrelevant. For there are no signs indicating that the working class will be capable of taking over the Government in the near or distant future without armed struggle under the leadership of the Palestinian national liberation movement. Moreover, the status of the Israeli entity as a foreign colony implanted in the region impels the majority of the workers in the Zionist State to consolidate themselves around the ruling class, consequently obstructing the development of class war within Israel. This phenomenon is observable in the case of many colonialist settlements. This is observable in Algeria, where most of the sectors of the French colony that were Fascist and radically opposed to the Algerian revolution were from the petite bourgeoisie and the workers. Therefore, the liberation of Palestine is indissolubly linked with the victory of the Palestinian national liberation movement.

> The problem is: Israel as "reactionary" deserves to be attacked; but what will happen if Israel becomes Socialist and progressive? This possibility is summarily dismissed as out of the question. (Y. H.)

Farid al-Khatib: I don't consider my view to be identical with that of Fatah. I am a friend of Fatah, and my view is very close to its view . . .

The idea of coexistence in a Palestinian State is not new. This idea was first brought up officially by Yahya Hamuda (Chairman of the Palestinian National Council) . . . Then in October, 1967, I believe, Abu Iyad (a Fatah leader) announced, at a press conference held by the Beirut newspaper AL-YAWM, the adoption by Fatah of the idea of the Democratic Palestinian State as a solution for the Zionist contradiction presently found on Arab soil . . .

The Democratic Palestinian State, as conceived by Fatah, I believe, is as follows: There is a basic condition for establishing the Democratic Palestinian

State: the winning of victory. Otherwise it cannot be brought into effect. The slogan of the (Palestinian Democratic) State is one of struggle; it can in no way be isolated from the Palestinian national liberation movement . . .

In short, the Democratic State is linked to the Palestinian national liberation movement. I believe it is necessary to present the details of the Palestinian State gradually, for in presenting the idea Fatah wished to say to the world that the objective of the Palestinians and the Arabs is not to throw the Jews into the sea but to disband the Zionist State and establish a new one. What is sought is not the development of Israel into a form acceptable to the Arabs, as Member of Knesset Uri Avneri advocates; the objective is to disband the Zionist State and establish a new one, according to the will of the Palestinian national liberation movement and the will of the Jews who lived in Palestine originally, that is, before 1948, and those who came later . . .

> The Arab position rejects in principle the very existence of Israel; it is not critical of a certain kind of Israel, as some Israelis tend to think. It is true that Arabs usually express their principal opposition to the existence first and then go on to enumerate its sins: expansionism, aggression, and so on. This enumeration is intended to reinforce the basic denial of Israel's existence; it does not mean, as some may mistakenly suppose, that if Israel were without sin they would be reconciled to its existence. In this manner, the sins they ascribe to Israel are irrelevant to the judgment they impose upon it.
>
> Readiness to recognize the Jews who came after 1948 is meant to demonstrate to the world the humane character of the Palestinian revolution. (Y. H.)

There is no benefit in discussing details of the Democratic State at present, for the objective in presenting this slogan at the present stage is to leave a narrow opening for the Israeli enemy, while the resistance groups strike relentless blows at the enemy within Palestine, to the point that his military, economic and political forces are exhausted and he is sore pressed. Then the enemy will have no possibility but to look towards that narrow aperture, attempting to find an outlet. Then the Palestinian revolution can remove the veil, so that the Israeli enemy may find deliverance. Thus, it is not beneficial to remove the veil now . . .

The Representative of the Arab Liberation Front (a fedayun organization of Iraqi influence): There is no special (separate) solution for the Palestine issue. The solution must be within the framework of the Arab revolution, because the Palestine issue is not merely the paramount Arab issue but the substance and basic motivation of the Arab struggle. If the Arab nation suffers from backwardness, exploitation and disunity, these afflictions are much more severe in Palestine. That is, the Arab cause in the present historical stage is epitomized in the Palestine issue . . .

The liberation of Palestine will be the way for the Arabs to realize unity, not to set up regional State No. 15, which will only deepen disunity. The unified State will be the alternative to the Zionist entity, and it will be of necessity democratic, as long as we understand beforehand the dialectical connection between unity and Socialism. In the united Arab State all the minorities — denominational and others — will have equal rights . . .

> Thus, the intention is not to set up a Palestinian State as an independent unit, but to incorporate it within a unified Arab State, which will be

democratic because progressive, and which will grant minority rights. (Y. H.)

When this slogan was put forth, it was understood that it was intended to conciliate progressive public opinion and the world leftist movement, but this cannot be accomplished with impractical slogans. The tactical nature of this slogan cannot elude public opinion . . .

The Arab Liberation Front considers the slogan of the (Democratic) Palestinian State, whether tactical or strategic, as incorrect, especially in the present situation, in which the Israeli enemy enjoys political, economic and military superiority, and any settlement is liable to consecrate this superiority of the enemy . . .

The Liberation Front rejects the idea as a tactical step because if, let us assume, Israel agrees to it, the sponsors of the idea will have to accept it . . .

As I have already mentioned, the slogan of the Democratic State does not presently serve Arab interests. It is identical with what some regimes have proposed, that, since Israel has not accepted the Security Council resolution, we should accept this resolution, which consecrates Zionist presence on Arab land.

Shafiq al-Hut (A leader of the PLO and head of its Beirut office): . . . The Palestinian problem is that of a Zionist-colonialist invasion at the expense of a land and a people known for thirteen centuries as the Palestinian Arab people . . .

> This is an example of the tendency to depict the Palestinian people as though it existed from yore. This is intended to counter the claim that Zionism did not encounter a Palestinian people, and that it was colonialism that created the Palestinian people since the Mandate Powers delineated the national borders in the Middle East. Indeed, in the past describing Palestine as an independent unity was considered betrayal of Arab nationalism, and Palestinian Arab spokesmen even insisted at the beginning of the Mandatory period that they were Southern Syrian Arabs, not Palestinians.

I side with Farid al-Khatib in holding that there is no benefit in expatiating upon the slogan "Democratic Palestinian State." I hope the fedayun organizations will not do so, although I would encourage discussion of it by those who are not in responsible positions. Whatever discussion of it there is on the part of the fighting groups may cause a sense of helplessness, despair or weakness . . .

As far as concerns the human situation of the Jews, which Farid al-Khatib mentioned, we should expose the Zionist movement and say to the Jew: The Zionist movement which brought you to Palestine did not supply a solution to your problem as a Jew; therefore you must return whence you came to seek another way of striving for a solution for what is called "the problem of the persecuted Jew in the world." As Marx has said, he has no alternative but to be assimilated into his society . . .

Even if we wished, by force of circumstances, a Democratic Palestinian State "period," this would mean its being non-Arab. Let us face matters honestly. When we speak simply of a Democratic Palestinian State, this means we discard its Arab identity. I say that on this subject we cannot negotiate, even if we possess the political power to authorize this kind of decision, because we thereby disregard an historical truth, namely, that this land and those who dwell upon it belong to a certain environment and a certain region, to which we are linked as one nation, one heritage and one hope — Unity, Freedom and Socialism . . .

If the slogan of the Democratic State was intended only to counter the claim that we wish to throw the Jews into the sea, this is indeed an apt slogan and an effective political and propaganda blow. But if we wish to regard it as the ultimate strategy of the Palestinian and Arab liberation movement, then I believe it requires a long pause for reflection, for it bears upon our history, just as our present and certainly our future.

I conclude with a warning, that this may be the beginning of a long dispute resulting in a substitute for the basic objective of the Palestinian revolution, which is the liberation of the Palestinian land and individual in the national sector, to which the land and the Palestinian individual are related (i.e. the pan-Arab sphere).

Representative of as-Sa'iqa (A Syrian fedayun organization): I agree with Shafiq al-Hut that there is no group which may determine independently the meaning of this slogan, or consent to its implementation. This problem does not belong to the Palestinians alone, because the Zionist design threatens the Arab region and not only the Palestinians, and every Arab citizen has the right to express his opinion concerning presumed or proposed solutions. Neither the Palestinian alone, nor any of the resistance movements, has the right to hold an independent view concerning the destiny of Palestine regarding the procedure to be adopted after the revolution or its victory.

It seems that this slogan has been raised prematurely, and this may be one of the principal reasons for the divergence of views concerning it. Thus, there is no consensus concerning the distinct meaning of this slogan . . .

The Jews are human beings like all others. No man can bear to live forever in tension, a state of emergency and threat. Every man searches for stability. However, the people living today in Palestine, subjected to this predicament, cannot return to the countries from which they emigrated, nor can they find an alternative to bearing arms against the Arab revolution, which continues to mean for the Jews the pulverization and ultimate liquidation of the millions living in Palestine.

I think that when we propose to those Jews a substitute for their present life, for the threat of death, we can reap benefit for our cause and make great strides on the way to victory. We cannot overlook the fact that these Jews, the majority of whom were born in Palestine, know no other homeland . . .

I was among those who thought five years ago that we must slaughter the Jews. But now I cannot imagine that, if we win one night, it will be possible for us to slaughter them, or even one tenth of them. I cannot conceive of it, neither as a man, nor as an Arab.

If so, what do we wish to do with these Jews? This is a problem for which I do not claim to have a ready answer. It is a problem which every Arab and Palestinian citizen has an obligation to express his opinion about, because it is yet early for a final, ripe formulation to offer the world and those living in Palestine.

Thus, I think that among many Jews, those living in Palestine, especially the Arab Jews, there is a great desire to return to their countries of origin, since the Zionist efforts to transform them into a homogeneous, cohesive nation have failed. There is a well-known human feeling — yearning for one's homeland, one's birthplace. There are a number of known facts concerning the Jews living in Palestine today which clearly point to this feeling among them. They desire to

40

return to their countries of origin, especially Jews from the Arab region.

It should be made clear that the Arabs initially blocked the way for Jews to return to their countries. If the Arab Governments had treated these situations from the start, the problem would have "budged" by now. There are a number of known circumstances which point to this.

We have made the Jews think constantly for twenty years that the sea is before them and the enemy behind, and that there was no recourse but to fight to defend their lives . . .

For us, as the "Vanguards of the Popular War of Liberation," al Sa'iqa, the slogan is not tactical but strategic. And, as I have said, we cannot imagine how it is possible to solve the problem of these Jews without permitting them to dwell either in Palestine or in another homeland they choose. My estimation is that many of them will choose to live outside Palestine, for Palestine will not be able to absorb all the Palestinians, as well as the Jews living there.

Representative of the Democratic Front: . . . The organization mentioned above (Matzpen) advocates a Socialist Palestine, in which the Arabs and Jews will live in equality, that is, having equal rights and obligations, and that it be part of a federal union in the Middle East . . . It is hard to say that there is responsiveness in Israel to the idea of a Democratic State. Although the idea of Matzpen is more acceptable from the Arab viewpoint, even that of Arab nationalism, Matzpen merely expresses the view of the Left; in fact, an insignificant minority of what is called the Israeli Left. Although it is a vocal and noisy organization, it represents but a small fraction of the Israeli Left . . .

It may be assumed that the continuing generation process, imposed upon history but actually existing, of what is called Jewish nationalism in Palestine must be terminated. This is not to be by annihilation of this human group living there, because such a solution is not only inhuman, it is also impractical. It must be terminated by the victory of the Palestinian revolution. I agree with the representative of al-Sa'iqa that the slogan of the Palestinian State is not a tactical slogan in the Machiavellian sense. We adopt this slogan not simply in order to win world public opinion, or to deceive the Jews regarding their destiny. This slogan must be presented clearly and with intellectual honesty. It should be stated that Zionism must cease to exist in Palestine, but this does not necessitate the human liquidation of the Israeli community living in Palestine . . .

We do not adopt this slogan because we are weak, with the intention of changing it when we become strong. The matter must be explained otherwise. Our struggle must have a clear objective based on actual reality, not on our desires and wishful thinking . . .

As for the question concerning what will happen if Israel agrees to our impractical assumptions on which we base a political position, the answer is: Israel will not agree to this slogan, and it is impossible for Israel to agree, because it means elimination of the State of Israel and all the class interests on which Israel is based. There has never been in history a class, social, or political power which has consented to its own elimination . . .

Moderator: . . . Can we consider the Kurdish problem and the manner of its solution as similar to the Jewish problem and its solution under the heading of the slogan of one Democratic State? . . .

Representative of the Liberation Front: Our view of the subject of Kurdish national rights follows from objective and historical considerations which substantially contradict the nature and objectives of the Zionist movement. The Kurds comprise a nationality having a distinct, well-known historical, geographical and human dimension . . .

In this connection, we must not forget the historical, religious and social ties that have bound Kurdish-Arab brotherhood for centuries. Salah al-Din al-Ayyubi (who was a Kurd) was the one who led the struggle against the foreign presence in the Arab region a number of centuries ago.

Farid al-Khatib: I agree with the view of the representative of the Democratic Popular Front, namely, if a group of people lives together for a long time in a homeland, they become a nationality, as has happened in America. But it seems that calling the Jewish denomination a nationality is premature . . .

The Jews are a denomination associated with more than one people; the Arabs are a people which embraces more than one religion . . .

As far as the Arab character of the Democratic State is concerned, the Jews in Palestine have the right to express their view concerning the Arab character of the Democratic State in a democratic manner. And although it is possible to say that the Democratic State is Arab, and to say furthermore that it is a union, it is advisable to hold back additional information until the appropriate stages in the evolution of the resistance are reached. When the Zionist movement came to Palestine, it first sought a refuge, afterwards a homeland, and then a State; and now it is striving to build an empire within and outside Palestine (i.e. Zionism also disclosed its objectives in stages).

There is nothing to be gained by summoning the Jews in the Zionist State to join the national liberation movement, as Shafiq al-Hut proposed, when he advocated convening the unified State at once. This will not convince the Jews of the world and world public opinion.

As far as concerns the number of Palestinians, all those who emigrated to Latin America in the nineteenth century, and those who live in the desert, in exile, under conquest, or in prison, all are citizens in the State. For example: the number of Bethlehemite residents living in South America exceeds the number of those Bethlehemites living in occupied Palestine, and the combined total (of all Palestinians) is not less than that of the Jews not living in the Zionist State . . .

Shafiq al-Hut: First, how can Farid (al-Khatib) think that the Jews and Zionists who came to set up an empire in our country have the privilege to express their democratic right in the Palestinian State? Second, how can he claim that it is difficult to convince Jewish citizens to join the liberation movement?

Farid al-Khatib: I think that most of the Jews living in Palestine are groups of people who were deceived by the Zionist movement and the world imperialist movement. And the Jew, as a man, has the right to express his opinion in a democratic manner regarding his future life after the collapse of the Zionist State, which is opposed to the Democratic State insofar as it discriminates between the Eastern Jew and the Western Jew and the Circassian Jew.

The second point: The greatest ambition of the revolution is to polarize Jews of the Zionist State into the ranks of the resistance movement . . . But what I wanted to say is that it is difficult to persuade the Jews to join the resistance movement because its immediate objective is to dissolve the Zionist contradiction within the Zionist State . . .

Representative of the Democratic Front: It seems to me that many of the disagreements that exist concerning this idea can be traced to some manner of misunderstanding or lack of communication . . . This State is not bi-national in the sense that there would be two national States joined together in one form or another. This solution must be rejected, not only because it is inconsistent with our own desire, but also because it is not a true democratic solution. It is rather a solution that will represent the continuation of the national conflict which exists between the Jews and Arabs, not a solution of this conflict. It is impossible to speak of a democratic solution if it is powerless to eliminate the conflict between the different denominations and peoples within the Democratic State. When we speak of democracy it must be clear that we do not mean liberal democracy in the manner of "one man, one vote." We mean a people's democratic regime, which will put an end to the social basis upon which Zionism rests, and will consequently settle the class conflicts, and then those among the denominations and peoples.

> That is, not democracy expressed in elections, but democracy which allegedly represents the "true" will of the people, even without consulting them. Then, there is no reason to be apprehensive about the number of Jews, because the number will not determine policy. (Y. H.)

The Representative of al-Sa'iqa: The struggle is a protracted and very bitter one, and I think that adopting the slogan of the Democratic State at this early stage is premature, and that the Palestinian revolution should persevere in the way of the people's war of national liberation.

Shafiq al-Hut: I agree with the representative of al-Sa'iqa, and I believe we are on the same wave-length.

Representative of the Democratic Front: I support what the representative of al-Sa'iqa says.

Representative of the Liberal Front: I agree with what the brother says.

Farid al-Khatib: I also.

When considering the possibility of an ideological change, we generally look to factors in external reality which may cause it. Thus, in the contact between reality and ideology, reality prevails and ideology gives way, or is interpreted according to the exigencies of the time. But it seems that even the internal structure of a position and the content of an ideology may embody factors which necessitate a change: factors which condition the degree of receptivity to change, and others which condition its mode. For example, predicating the Arab position upon a rejection in principle of Israel's existence has made it less susceptible to gradual change and compromise of a quantitative modality, as in the case of a conflict between two States over a divisible portion of land. The Arab position has demanded elimination of Israel's sovereignty, not its partial elimination. The demand that "justice be done to the Palestinians" was defined as the restoration of sovereignty over the country to them, whereas a compromise settlement — "partial justice" — was rejected as perpetuating the injustice. As opposed to this principle of the Arab position, which has hindered the possibility of its change and a settlement, the content of the position — the call for politicide and the reduction of the Jewish community this entails — makes the position difficult to maintain and impels its change. We see signs of this in the debate on the subject of the Democratic State, for this slogan was adopted on account of the difficulty of adhering to the genocidal position of the previous formulation.

The representative of al-Sa'iqa declares that five years ago he contemplated slaughtering the Israelis, whereas now he cannot imagine such a deed. Has the trauma of the Six-Day War, the main event of the past five years, actually instilled in him moral refinement or compassion? It is more likely that the reason is rather that the Six-Day War and the events surrounding it revealed to him: 1. that the genocidal objective is impractical because the Israelis will not resign themselves to the slaughter; 2. the degree to which the Arabs lost world public opinion because of their barbaric statements concerning slaughter of the Jews. The change in position was probably influenced by these factors.

If the Arabs must drop the objective of slaughtering the Jews, the question naturally arises: What is to be done with these Jews? This is not a matter of assessing what the Arabs would actually do if they won. In this respect there is probably no change, and the last defeat possibly even increased the desire for revenge. The problem the Arabs confront is that of defining their objective in the conflict. The form of guerrilla warfare requires more indoctrination of the soldier than conventional warfare, in which the individual merges more with his unit. It is for this reason also that the participants in the symposium stress the need for a clearly defined objective.

If the number of Jews living in Israel is not reduced, then, on a national level their quantitative and qualitative weight will dilute the Arab character of the liberated State, and on a personal level there will be sufficient room for these Jews as well as for the Palestinians who supposedly all desire to return. In order to evade these difficulties, the spokesmen in the symposium try to breathe life into old ideas: that the Jews brought to the country were misguided by Zionist deceit (Zionism therefore not being a vital need), and that they remain by coercion (criticism by Israelis of themselves and their State, in a manner unknown in Arab countries, is interpreted as a sign of hatred for the State and a desire to emigrate). On these grounds it is believed that the Jews would rejoice at the opportunity to leave. An interesting element of self-deception is added, that the Jews from Arab countries wish to return to their countries of origin. One suspects that this illusion contains the psychological dimension of *amour-propre* and self-adulation: the Arabs are so good and were so kind to the Jews that it is inconceivable for the Jews not to desire ardently to return to live under their protection. However, along with these notions, there are signs of recognition that this is a false hope, and that the Jews have nowhere to return, especially those born in the country, who will soon become a majority of the Jewish community. Grappling with these contradictory notions is conspicuous in the case of the al-Sa'iqa representative, who maintains at one and the same time that most Jews have nowhere to emigrate, and yet that many will emigrate.

The spokesmen also try to evade this problem by claiming that the Jews are not a people. Their attachment to the country is therefore weak, and the hope that they will emigrate is reinforced. Moreover, in the clash between the Jewish group, whose cohesion is supposedly religious and not national, and the group whose cohesion is national, the latter will prevail, thereby determining the character of the country. Therefore, even if a considerable Jewish community remains, there will be no such thing as a partnership between two homogeneous groups, creating a bi-national State. The Democratic Front, which stresses the Palestinianism of the Democratic State more than its Arab character, also regards membership in an Arab federation as inherent in the very founding of this State, while the Iraqi organization rejects the very idea of the Palestinian State and regards it at best as a region within a unified State. (For this organization, the struggle in Palestine has the value of a catalyst for the rest of the changes in Arab countries, or a spark that will ignite a revolution that will spread to all of them.) Along with these hopes of reducing the number of Jews in the "Democratic State" there is the notion of tipping the population scales in the Arabs' favour by considering all Palestine Arabs, wherever they may live, as actual rather than potential citizens of the State according to an Arab Law of Return of sorts.

All the participants in the symposium agree that the Jews do not presently constitute a people. However, the recognition gnaws at some of them that nationalism is not something static but an evolution, and as time goes on the Jews in Israel will become consolidated into a people and a nation. Hence the conclusion that this process must be forestalled by the founding of a Palestinian State. The temporal factor thus works against the idea that the Israelis are not a people, and against the possibility of founding a Palestinian State. It is no accident that Shafiq al-Hut vigorously maintains the essential and permanent nature of the Jewish status as non-people and non-nation. According to the view presented by Arabs, only a people has the right of political self-determination and deserves a State of its own. If the Jews are indeed becoming a people, this means that they are in the process of acquiring these rights.

For most of the participants, the slogan "Democratic State" is merely tactical, the aim being to create a positive impression on the outside world and to enchant the Israelis who, as the speaker who describes Fatah's views says, will eventually discover its full meaning. For the Democratic Front this is presumably not merely a slogan, but a principle they sincerely hold as an implication of the progressivism they profess. However, even they wrestle with the slogan; they arm themselves with various qualifications: the State will be a member within an Arab federation, and the democracy will not be formal, nor expressed in numerical representation, but a "true" democracy of "the content" — that is, its policy will be fixed as proper, representing progress expressed in "the Palestinian revolution." The final qualification is their insistence upon the prior condition for establishing the Democratic State, that Israel be destroyed in a war à l'outrance.

For those who regard the slogan "Democratic State" as merely a tactic, the problem arises that it is impossible to lead the public only by tactical slogans; one must present the objectives of a national vision. While the slogan "Democratic State" may be helpful externally, it is quite destructive internally, impairs the State's Arabism and undermines confidence in the feasibility of "returning" to the country, since it would not be evacuated. Shafiq al-Hut states blatantly that acceptance of this slogan means abandoning the idea of Arabism. From the Arab aspect another question arises: if the Jews are a people, it is doubtful that they would consent to live in a non-Jewish State; hence the hope that they will emigrate; since the Palestinians are a people, they certainly will oppose returning to a State which is not Arab.

It appears that the Palestinians and Arabs are beginning to sense the predicament of their position. In the past they could be content with the formulations "restoration of rights" and "restoration of the homeland," which were restricted to the meaning of the objective as it had bearing upon what would be given to the Arabs, and the implication concerning what would be taken away from the Jews was overlooked. Arab spokesmen in foreign countries are still striving to focus on the need to rectify the injustice inflicted on the Palestinians, while evading the implication of this rectification for the Jews. The necessity of defining the position in all its aspects and the debate concerning the Democratic Palestinian State undermine the Arab position. The slogan of a Democratic State seemed to be an escape from a genocidal position, but it was revealed as the first step of retreat and the source of problems and bewilderment. I think it is no exaggeration to say that this slogan opened a Pandora's box for the Arab position in the conflict. Hence the deep apprehensions of all the participants in the discussion concerning this slogan, and the dramatic agreement of everyone at the end of it that the slogan "Democratic State" is premature, even though this contradicted the previous insistence by some on the need for a clear definition of the objective.

In the past the Arabs could distinguish between their internal and external positions. Today, the possibility of adhering to a genocidal position internally and brandishing the slogan "Democratic State" externally has become problematic. However, it is possible that an attempt at this kind of distinction was implicit in their refraining from publishing an official translation of the new version (1968) of the National Covenant into English (an official version of the previous version had been published). It was preserved as an internal document and source of inspiration, while externally at the same time they brandished the slogan of the "Democratic State."

It appears that those who formulated the Palestinian Covenant of 1968 sensed the difficulties inherent in the Arab position and wished to anticipate them by nailing down the qualification that only a small Jewish minority (the descendants of those who came to the country before 1917) would be given citizenship in "the liberated State," thus assuring the Arab character of the country. If there was excessive fanaticism in this stipulation, manifest extremism, the reason was probably the apprehension that otherwise the ground would begin sliding beneath the Arab position.

There are also difficulties on the practical level. The Palestinian leaders inflated hopes that salvation would come from fedayun activity. The gap between the pretensions and execution was bridged with false announcements in which the Popular Democratic Front, despite its progressivism, surpassed all others. (On 17 December 1969, it announced that its men attacked on a front the length of twelve Israeli settlements, and that Israel acknowledged this attack. Even the Command of the Armed Struggle was sceptical and as a result the Democratic Front froze its membership in the Command.)

An accepted rule of theoreticians of guerrilla warfare is that a condition for its success is its becoming an internal war of the people against the regime — in this case meaning the Jews against their Government. This problem also arises in the discussion: how to induce Israelis to join the Arab side. However, the prevailing view is quite pessimistic regarding Jewish participation in a direct struggle against their own State. Al-Hut feels, apparently, the significance of the Arabs' inability to influence Israelis to join them, and it is he, the Rightist among the participants, who resists this assessment.

Col. Qadhafi, the ruler of Libya, spoke bluntly to the Palestinian organizations in a recent speech (31 March 1970). He took note of their paltry accomplishments (they have not gone beyond external warfare and actions near the border) and said that they must turn their war into an internal one. If they cannot succeed, it would be better for them to disband and become a conventional army, more appropriate for external warfare in which the superiority of the Israelis has certainly been demonstrated. The fedayun organizations themselves have stressed many times that the Arabs have no chance of success in a conventional war. It is not surprising that Qadhafi's words aroused a storm and bitter reactions.

Peoples and public movements are prepared to acknowledge a certain failure or mistake, but they will not readily admit the failure of their entire orientation. And when success does not smile upon them, they are ready to struggle further. Public positions are pertinacious. The difficulties in the Arab position do not imply its change in the near future or readiness for a settlement with Israel. The Palestinian leaders are plagued by the apprehension that, when it becomes clear how they have failed, their world will collapse about them. It is hard to imagine what tragedy is awaiting them. The war the Arab States declared against Israel in the name of the Palestinians brought destruction upon them, and who knows whether or not they will eventually blame the Palestinians? The Palestinians will ultimately have to be satisfied with much less than their pretensions. However, sometimes, when a movement fails, its supporters do not give up it or its ideas, but become more devoted and fanatical, at least for a time (Professor Festinger, WHEN PROPHECY FAILS). Disappointment is liable to engender among some Palestinian circles an apocalyptic mood and desperate readiness for destruction, including self-destruction. They are liable to direct their anger inwards, against the Arab countries. Thus, the way to an end of the Arab-Israeli conflict is not bedecked with roses on any side. It appears that analysis of the Arab position, even on an abstract level, shows that its alteration is an internal necessity. The abstract and practical levels are certainly not identical, but neither are they altogether independent. Therefore, there is reason to assume that the change in the Arab position which appeared on the level of abstract analysis will eventually be reflected in changes in the world of deed.

THE LIBERATED STATE

The problem of the significance of the slogan brandished by Palestinian spokesmen that the objective they have before their eyes is to establish a Democratic Palestinian State in the place of Israel continues to occupy the Arab and Palestinian public. It was brought up for discussion by the Popular Democratic Front in the negotiations prior to the signing of an agreement by the fedayun organizations in Jordan on 6 May 1970.

According to this agreement, a "Central Committee" was set up which embraces all the fedayun organizations (except the Communist "Quwat al-Ansar"). The agreement constitutes an ideological and programmatic platform to all these groups and has made possible the participation of all of them in the seventh Assembly of the National Palestinian Council which met in Cairo from 30 May to 4 June 1970. Here is the report on the deliberations on the subject of the slogan of a Democratic State before the agreement was signed, as it appeared in the official organ of the Popular Democratic Front, the weekly AL HURRIYYA, which is published in Beirut (issue 515 of 18 May 1970). The report is highly condensed, but of great interest:

> At the last meeting, differences of opinion came to the fore on two inter-connected subjects: the first was that of the slogan of a Democratic Palestinian State which was part of the programme proposed. Four organizations came out in its defence: "Fatah," "Al-Tala'i," the "Democratic Front" and the "Popular Front — General Command." The other organizations negated it as exhibiting unacceptable tendencies.
>
> A tendency to compromise that hides beyond the traditional attitudes prevalent in the past and behind devotion to an issue which is *ab initio* not subject to discussion, namely the question of the Arabism or non-Arabism of Palestine; this tendency was represented by the "Organization of Arab Palestine" and the "Central Committee for the Liberation of Palestine," and a tendency to compromise hiding behind ambiguous words, such as the call for a democratic society; this tendency was represented by the "Popular Front," the "Front for Struggle" and the "Arab Liberation Front."
>
> The discussion on this subject was the background for the general formulation in the text of the communiqué on the agreement which said: 'The aim of the Palestinian struggle is the complete liberation of Palestine,

in which all citizens would coexist, having equal rights and obligations within the framework of the Arab nation's hopes for unity and progress.'

The second subject round which a clear dispute revolved conspicuously was that of the view of the resistance movement regarding the Israeli society. Here, again, those organizations were to the fore which maintained that the Jews living in Israel were all Zionists and should be viewed solely from that angle. By contrast, the four organizations ("Fatah," "Al-Tala'i," the "Democratic Front" and the "Popular Front — General Command"), though there were differences of opinion between them, saw in this attitude an unobjective position reflecting a chauvinist mentality. They emphasized the significance of the appearance in Israel of small leftist groups hostile to the existence of Israel as a State. They said that these small leftist groups were likely to grow in strength and to develop, parallel to the development of the progressive trend in the Palestinian resistance movement itself.

The discussion on this subject was the background for the formulation in the communiqué which says 'Israel personifies, in the nature of its being, a closed society in which the linked progressive forces cannot bring about any fundamental change.' And so we witness the fact that the modifications to the programme proposed were in the nature of a step backwards, in which a special role was played by the "Popular Front," the "Central Command," the "Organization of Arab Palestine" and the "Front for Struggle."

The report summarizes the division of the ten fedayun organizations, members of the "Central Committee" and of the "Palestine Liberation Organization," in respect of their stance towards the slogan of a Democratic State and their attitude towards the likelihood of finding allies among the Jews of Israel. The positions are identical with those that became perceptible in a symposium arranged by Al-Anwar (MA'ARIV, 17 April 1970): "Fatah," "Al-Sa'iqa[12] (or "al-Tala'i," the organization of the Syrian Ba'ath), the "Popular Democratic Front" (Naif Hawatma) and the "Popular Front — General Command" (its leader Ahmed Jibril, who broke away from the "Popular Front" of Dr. Habash) support the slogan of a Democratic State. At the same time, they do not group together all the Jews in Israel as Zionists who cannot be redeemed, but they envisage the possibility that there might emerge groups which would become the allies of the Palestinians in the goal of liquidating the Jewish statehood.

The "Organization of Arab Palestine" (its leader, Ahmed Zahrur, broke away from the "Popular Front" in April 1969) and the "Central Committee for the Liberation of Palestine" (its leader, Dr. 'Izam Al-Sartawi) demand that liberated Palestine should be Arab and not bi-national. This goal is, indeed, accepted by the other organizations, but these two fear that behind the slogan of a Democratic State there may be concealed a quest for Arab-Jewish partnership in the State. The equality of rights between Jews and Arabs should be not on a collective but only on a private level and even so within an all-embracing Arab framework.

The "Popular Front for the Liberation of Palestine" (Georges Habash), the "Front of the Palestinian Popular Struggle (Bahajat Abu Gharbiya — an organization of former Jerusalemites), and the "Arab Liberation Front" (organization of the Iraqi Ba'ath), reject the slogan of a Palestinian State, since they stress Pan-Arab union. The problem of the Jews will be solved by citizenship — again, all rights to the Jews as citizens, but none to them as a community.

The differences of opinion are not really major and, indeed, all the organizations were able to come to terms and to an agreement which embraced the following principles: 1. Liberation of the whole of Palestine; 2. Establishment of a progressive society which will not discriminate between its citizens; 3. This society will be Arab, not bi-national, and within the framework of the hopes of the Arab nation for unity and advancement. The "Democratic Front," though endorsing the formula, views it as a regression from the progressivism it advocates, as, in its views, a declaration should be made that national rights would be granted to the Jews, though the grant would be defined as a cultural autonomy. The step backwards, if indeed there is one, is infinitesimal.

It should be noted that the organizations could agree to this wording, because it limited itself to the mention of the liberation activities and made no mention at all of the fact that the intention was to set up a Palestinian State, as some of them feared that Palestine, as a State on its own, if a sizeable Jewish minority remained in it, would be different in character from the other Arab States and be a foreign body in the Arab union. The liberated State should, therefore, be like the other Arab States and the purpose of Article 6 of the Covenant was to ensure that.

The problem of the Democratic State is linked to that of Article 6. They represent the two sides of the same coin — the position of the Jews in the "liberated" Palestinian State. The intention lurking behind Article 6, which lays down that only Jews who lived in the country before 1917 would be granted Palestinian citizenship, is to reduce the number of the Jews, so that the country would become Arab and then it would also be possible to make it "democratic" and grant voting rights to all, without fearing the influence of Jewish votes. As against the claim that this provision exhibits extremism in relation to the Jews, the Arabs defend themselves by making use of the letter of Professor Sayigh printed in the London "Times" of 28 February 1970. This is the official line of the "Palestine Liberation Organization" and it is worthwhile our examining it. Here is the letter:

Sir:

Because the objective of a unitary, democratic state in Palestine is not easy to attack, we are now witnessing a concerted attempt by Israeli government spokesmen to cast doubt upon the sincerity of the Palestinian resistance movement's intentions.

Mr. Eitan Ruppin's letter to "The Times" of February 20 is to be seen in the context of this campaign. Like so many other Israeli propagandists recently, he cites the Charter of the Palestine Liberation Organization. Depending on universal ignorance of what this document contains, he asserts that it offers equal rights only to Jews who resided in Palestine prior to 1917. In fact, no date at all is mentioned in the charter with regard to Jewish citizenship. What it says is this: "Article 6: Jews living in Palestine before the time of the Zionist invasion are also considered as Palestinains."

What is significant, however, is that since the emergence of a militant resistance movement, after the June war, Palestinian attitudes towards Jews have become more, not less, liberal. Thus, in September, 1969, at the 6th National Assembly, the main commando groups (Fateh, P.D.F.L.P., and Saequa) [sic] submitted an amendment to Clause 6, with the intention of making it more clearly inclusive of all Jews, without any qualification at all, except that they should free themselves from colonialist attitudes and accept to live in peace with Muslims and Christian Palestinians. A subcommittee has been appointed to reword Clause 6 in this sense in preparation for the next General Assembly.

This open commitment to accept Jews as equal partners in a new society (not matched by a similar Zionist commitment towards Arabs) has been expressed by leaders of all the resistance groups, in hundreds of interviews, statements, and internal documents, in Arabic as well as in other languages. It is trading on prejudice to suggest that Palestinian leaders say one thing to foreigners, another to Arabs.

The example Mr. Ruppin gives, of an interview with Yasser Arafat, published in AL-ANWAR, on January 20, is a case not of Arab double-talk, but of Israeli misquotation. The passage in question (which, significantly, Mr. Ruppin does not quote in full) runs as follows: "The idea of the democratic state which the Palestinian Revolution has put forward has been subjected to a concentrated campaign, even by some Arab brothers. This idea, proposed by Fateh, follows the basic idea calling for the liberation of the land and the removal of the Zionist structure, and the setting up of the Arab democratic state on the ruins of this expansionist, criminal structure *thus enabling Palestinian Christians and Muslims to live with Jews, with equal rights and duties.*" [Mr. Ruppin omitted the italicized words]

Yours faithfully,
Yusif A. Sayigh, Director, Planning Centre
Palestine Liberation Organization,
Beirut, Lebanon, Feb. 23

The following should be noted: Professor Sayigh makes use of the formal claim that the date 1917 is not mentioned explicitly in Article 6 of the Covenant, but only before "the beginning of the Zionist invasion." It ignores, and certainly not by inadvertence, that the "Palestinian National Council," which modified the Covenant in July 1968, in the chapter of resolutions (p. 51 of the official report) defined the Zionist invasion as having begun in the year 1917. It is also no accident that in the English translation of the Article, Sayigh omits the word "beginning" in conjunction with the Zionist invasion, but adds the word "also" which is not to be found at all in the Arabic original.

This paragraph is also misrepresented by Professor Hisham Sharabi of Georgetown University, Washington, D. C. His version is: "Jews living in Palestine until the time of the Zionist occupation (1948) are also Palestinians" (Sharabi, PALESTINE AND ISRAEL: THE LETHAL DILEMMA, Pegasus, New York, 1969, p. 201). The original document reads, in Arabic: "Al-Yahud alladh'ina kanu yuquimuna iqamatan 'adiyatan fi Filastin hatta bad'i alghazu alzahiuni laha yu'tabrana filastiniyyin." Professor Sharabi replaces the term "invasion" with "occupation," and this too is done by no mere chance. It is disconcerting to note how these two renowned scholars resort to such distortions.

If 1917 is not intended, then why does not Professor Sayigh find it necessary to give his version as to the date determining the Zionist invasion? Sayigh does not mention that the declaration of Yasser Arafat emphasized that the Palestinian State would be Arab, in other words, the Jews would constitute a minority in it which will not affect its Arab character. Sayigh, apparently, sees it as self-evident. If there is nothing wrong in Article 6, why was it necessary to re-phrase it and why was a special committee appointed for that purpose?

In the meantime, the "Palestinian Council" to which the sub-committee for the rewording of Article 6 was to submit its recommendations was convened for its seventh session from 30 May to 4 June 1970. The meeting was extensively covered in the Arab press and many details of its deliberations were published. There was no mention whatsoever in any of the communiqués, articles and analyses that the Covenant was amended or Article 6 was altered. It cannot be assumed that this could have been done in secret, for the Covenant is an official document which must be before the eyes of the Palestinians and guide them in their path. As against this, announcements were repeatedly made from which it could be learnt that the Covenant remained in force: the "Popular Front for the Liberation of Palestine," on entering the "Palestinian Liberation Organization," affirmed its adherence to the Covenant through its representative Dr. Alyamani (AL—HAWADITH, 12 June 1970, p. 14). The Covenant is actually mentioned in the agreement of 6 May as a document binding on all the organizations. There is nothing, no hint, in the 6 May 1970 agreement, of an intention to amend it, or that it had been discussed. It is clearly said, though in relation to a proposal to accept Jordanians as members in the "Palestinian Liberation Organization" which would have made it necessary to change the Covenant, that "Fatah," "Al-Sa'iqa," and the "Democratic Front" demanded that the Covenant should not be altered (AL—HAWADITH, 12 June 1970, p. 13).

There is certainly much significance in the fact that three Palestinian National Assemblies have already been convened since it was drafted but no amendments made to it. The dispute among the Palestinians on the issue of the Democratic State sheds light on the reason why they find it difficult to arrive at a common formula in relation to the Jews in the "liberated" State, other than under the phrasing agreed upon on 6 May, which in no wise contradicts what is written in Article 6, but merely lends it support.

AN EXAMINATION OF DOCUMENTS
ON WHICH
THE STATE OF ISRAEL IS BASED

Bhim Singh
Angelina Helou

A brief survey of the essential elements of a state will prepare the ground for a political and legal definition of Israel. For it is this type of survey which points to the classical and general norms of statehood and by so doing clarifies the position of every state within the context of the law of nations.

ESSENTIAL ELEMENTS OF A STATE

A state, a representative in every way of what is called a subject of international law, i.e., a true international person, must have the following characteristics:

1. Territory
2. Population
3. Government
4. Independence or Sovereignty(1)

With regard to territorial sovereignty, two important factors must be considered:

A. The state's boundaries.
B. The nature of the state's right over the territory in question.

The extent of the territory subject to the jurisdiction of any state is determined by definite boundary lines, as in the case of domestic real property of any citizen.

But definite boundary lines are not only essential from a juridical viewpoint. They are also essential in creating effective citizenship or membership of a certain state.

It is the sharing of the same territory as defined by drawn boundaries which creates common interests and solidarity among the citizens.

It is also very important to point out the significance of a defined territory for a state, large or small, in view of the fact that this definition indicates the area within which its internal policies can be carried out and outside which its foreign policy will be conducted.

Accordingly, defined boundaries are an integral part of statehood especially denoting state jurisdiction, effective citizenship, and the nature of state authority and power.

When a state exercises authority over a certain territory, or in other words, when a state has sovereignty over a definite part of the surface of the earth, special reference is made to the nature of the rights over the territory in question.

(Territorial sovereignty bears an obvious resemblance to ownership in private law. As a result of this resemblance early international law borrowed the Roman concept for the acquisition of property and adapted it to the acquisition of territory. These rules are still the fundamentals of the law on the subject.)

Under the dictates of the modern body of rules of international law, state sovereignty — real state title — over a territory is acquired through the following means:

a. Occupation
b. Prescription
c. Cession
d. Conquest
e. Accretion(2)

Each of these means should exhibit certain required elements to be considered lawful, For example:

Occupation may be defined, here, as a means of acquiring territory not already forming a part of the domain of any state. Also, in order to create a title to territory, occupation must be "effective occupation," that is to say, it must be followed up by action which shows that the state not only desires to, but can and does control the territory claimed or occupied.

Title by prescription arises out of a long continued possession, where no original source of proprietary right can be shown to exist, or when possession in the first instance being wrongful, the legitimate proprietor has neglected to assert his right, or has been unable to do so. Long possession, in this case, must be continuous, public and peaceful in order to have the effect of extinguishing a prior title to sovereignty. In other words a continuous, public, and undisturbed exercise or display of state authority must be shown.

Cession is a form of transferring the title to territory from one state to another. It results sometimes from war, sometimes from peaceful negotiation; it may either be gratuitous or for some consideration.

Title through conquest, however, is rare because the annexation of territory after a war is generally carried out by a treaty of cession. Also conquest, the acquisition of the territory of an enemy by its complete and final subjugation and a declaration of the conquering state's intention to annex it, receives an obvious moral objection to its legality. In fact the coming into force of the United Nations Charter ended the legality of the acquisition of title to territory through conquest.

The Purposes of the United Nations are:

"1. To maintain international peace and security, and to that end to take effective collective measures for the prevention and removal of threats to the peace, and for the suppression of acts of aggression or other breaches of the peace, and to bring about by peaceful means, and in conformity with the principles of justice and international law, adjustment or settlement of international disputes or situations which might lead to a breach of the peace;

2. To develop friendly relations among nations based on respect for the principle of equal rights and self-determination of peoples, and to take other appropriate measures to strengthen universal peace;

3. To achieve international co-operation in solving international problems of an economic, social, cultural, or humanitarian character, and in promoting and encouraging respect for all without distinction as to race, sex, language, or religion; and

4. To be a centre for harmonizing the actions of nations in the attainment of these common ends."(3)

Title through accretion is the result of a natural operation, e.g., the addition of new territory to the existing territory of a state by the drying of a river.

This framework of definition of the legality of territorial claims, reflecting international law, provides very limited or no chances under which a state may speak in terms of a right to annex new territories. At the same time it reflects the international value of definite boundary lines of a state which conditions its jurisdiction and thereby its external policy and relations.

Territorial provisions affect the number of population in a state; also this number influences a state's territorial policies. The interaction of these two factors has been a major dynamic in statecraft. However, in the modern era, and with the above framework in mind, the starting point in a discussion on the population of a state is, generally, built on the assumption that territory is the constant factor.

An approach to the study of population as an element of a state, and an obvious element, involves the following considerations:

A. The size of population in relation to the land territory, i.e., the capacity of the land to maintain the population.
B. The economic conditions of the population.

The rate of population growth within the boundaries of a state is viewed in connection with the land resources available. Some states are sparsely populated, others are densely populated; some states put their land resources to maximum utilization with the use of modern methods and techniques, others have high resource potential awaiting development; also the relatively equilibrating movements of factors of production among the different states contribute to the problems of population pressure or scarcity. The size of population is thus actually viewed in relation to the means of sustenance and to the state of development of the means of production. Other or additional reflections on the problem vary according to different public policies and concerns.

State policies promoting unusual rates of increase in the size of population have been those inclined to do so for militaristic purposes or to put into use areas of unexploited territories. Otherwise, the size of population is ordinarily weighed with a desired standard of living for the masses.

The economic conditions of population are presumably related to its size and to the material resources of the state. Some states, due to their natural bounties, and regardless of the size of population may afford a comfortable living standard for the majority. This, however, may not always be the case.

Natural resources may be used for purposes other than the welfare of the masses. For example, they may be consumed by the needs of the military element of the nation; they may not be exploited at all and the masses kept within the vicious circle of poverty and want; and they may be scarce and yet, the population, relying on external opportunities and resources, may enjoy a decent level of living.

Thus the economic conditions of the people in a state are primarily related to natural wealth and secondly to public policies and the institutions of the state.

The composition of the population also contributes to its economic conditions, especially when the concept of unity is implied. It is national unity which leads to expediency in state welfare which is one in promoting the desired qualities of the citizens.

The availability of natural resources in a state and the institutional setup of the people tend to be the two major factors in upholding solidarity. (Solidarity, in this respect, implies a high degree of autonomy, the desired degree of individual welfare, and the necessary spirit of nationalism.)

Thus territory and people (the first factor being considered as constant) are found to their best advantage within a state when the institutional framework, at all levels, functions in a smooth manner of coordination for the general welfare.

At this point the third characteristic of a state comes into view. It is the operation of a government. Without this type of operation or institutional setup, there could be no assurance of internal stability and of the ability to fulfil international obligations.

According to the rule of law, a state needs an instrument for the exercise of its power. This instrument is its government. The inherent authority of a state (for every state has authority inherent in itself) is only exercised by the government as its agent.

By definition a government consists of all those persons, institutions, and agencies by which the will and policy of the state is expressed and carried out.

The basic fact of any government is that it acts for the whole community. This means, first, that the whole community will come under its control; no individual or group may claim the right to evade the operation of measures designed to apply to all.

It thus may be said that the government is the important indispensable machinery by means of which the state maintains its existence, carries on its functions, and realizes its policies and objectives. (The form of government varies with the purposes of the state.)

An overall picture of the entity of a state, however, could be seen through the concept of sovereignty or independence. Here all the state elements are viewed in a unified manner reflecting the ability of the state to regulate its internal affairs without outside interference or control.

Sovereignty, an essential characteristic of statehood, is very much dependent on the machinery of government, on the public policy, the size of the state, and on the economic conditions of the citizens.

Sovereignty also, in its internal manifestation and its external exercise, is restricted by international rules and regulations. This is the case especially in connection with external sovereignty. Just as the rules of local law limit the activities of individuals, so also does international law limit the conduct of states.

The preceding brief survey of the essential elements of the state — Territory,

Population, Government, Independence — form a sort of political and legal statement or a political and legal standard in the light of which some judgement may be passed concerning Israel as a state.

ESSENTIAL ELEMENTS OF ISRAEL

Since Israel is an expression of Zionism, it is discussed as a state in the light of the principles and objectives of this doctrine.

Dr. Nahum Goldmann, President of the World Zionist Organization, in his address celebrating the Seventh Anniversary of the Foundation of the Zionist Organization said:

> "Nations realize their ideal in our century through the forms of a state. The state was never the main objective of Zionism . . . The sovereign state of the nineteenth and the twentieth century is a modern invention, not a Jewish one. Its greatest protagonist was a great philosopher but a Prussian philosopher, Hegel. He conceived the idea that the sovereign state, towering over everything, which can afford to do anything, is the peak, the highest form of expression of human civilization. In my humble opinion, this is an absolutely barbaric idea . . . Some time will pass, and I will not live to see it, but I hope that my children will, until the sovereign state no longer exists . . . If we were only a movement for the founding of state, we would have achieved our aim marvellously and would be able to step down from the arena of Jewish history and world history with a great sense of triumph, with dignity. But when one knows that if this state (referring to Israel) becomes a state like all others, another Lebanon or another Syria, or perhaps even qualitatively a little better, then it will not be able to discharge its historical task, and that instead this state must be an instrument to realize the specific Jewish ideas from the prophets down to Ahad Ha'Am, Martin Buber and Gordon, to realize them and not only to preach them, when one knows all this, then one understands that the State of Israel and the Zionist movement, which is, as it were, its parent, still has vast tasks . . . "(4)

The above quotation reflects some reluctance in Zionism to accept the modern concept of state — subject of international law. In fact the same reluctance, on the part of Zionism, is true of its view of international law at large. Mr. Abba Eban, then Israeli Ambassador to the United States, on Edward Murrow's television program "Person to Person" on September 20, 1957, said: "International law is the law which the wicked do not obey and which the righteous do not enforce."

Bearing this in mind and with the derivative assumption that Israel, therefore, may be treated as an exception, a survey comparing the elements of this state with the norms of international law may help us to judge its nature.

THE TERRITORY OF ISRAEL

What is the territory of Israel? This shall always remain an open question as long as statehood is not the ultimate aim of Zionism. The final goal is the redemption of the Jewish people — the Ingathering of the Exiles in Israel — an area which is not defined.

Speaking about the Declaration of Independence, David Ben-Gurion stated:

> "The problem was whether to declare the State without specifying its

56

borders or to specify the borders as fixed by the United Nations. I was opposed to specifying the borders. I pointed out that no borders were named in the American Declaration of Independence and maintained that we were under no obligation to designate them."(5)

The declaration of the establishment of the State of Israel uses the United Nations' General Assembly resolution of November 1947 concerning the partitioning of Palestine as the immediate justification.(6)

"On the 29th November, 1947, the United Nations General Assembly passed a resolution calling for the establishment of a Jewish State in Eretz Israel; the General assembly required the inhabitants of Eretz Israel to take such steps as were necessary on their part for the implementation of that resolution. This recognition by the United Nations of the right of the Jewish people to establish their State is irrevocable."(7)

Did Israel keep within the territorial limits of the United Nations Resolution of November 1947?

The acceptance of this United Nations resolution by the Zionists is, in reality, a paradoxical acceptance. For the State of Israel did not keep within the limits of this resolution, nor did the Zionists acquire all the land for their state building in a manner compatible with the Charter of the United Nations.

The representative of the Jewish Agency for Palestine addressing the *ad hoc* Committee at the fourth meeting on October 2, 1947, showed dissatisfaction with the majority proposal for the partitioning of Palestine. He said:

"According to David Lloyd George, then British Prime Minister, the Balfour Declaration implied that the whole of Palestine, including Transjordan should ultimately become a Jewish state."(8)

Total Jewish ownership in Palestine by 1948 was roughly 1,971,014 dunums. This compared to the total area of Palestine — 27,027,023 dunums (including water area of 704,000 dunums) reflected the ratio of Jewish ownership to the total area of the land, viz., 7.6%.(9) When the State of Israel was declared, 80.5% of the land of Palestine was acquired. This means that 76.6% was at that time acquired by force or conquest.(10)

A. Title to the acquired land area of Palestine is here very much bound to the spirit of the Mandate over the country and to the power of the United Nations resolution of November 1947.

1. The 76.6% of the land area of Palestine represents the domain of the people of Palestine upon the termination of the Mandate. Therefore its occupation by a simple minority was illegal.(11)
2. The United Nations resolution of November 1947 was only a recommendation. This is because the United Nations, under its Charter, does not have the power to implement this type of resolution. In other words, it does not have the power to create states.

B. Nor could title be transferred to Israel over the territories it occupies through prescription. A title acquired through prescription is conditional to:

1. Absence or silence of original claim to the occupied land.

2. Possession of the territory be long, continuous, public and undisturbed.

The two million and a half Palestinians never gave up the call for the basic human right of a people to their homes and property. In addition to this, this right has been codified in the body of international law through the United Nations resolutions. For example, paragraph 11 of the General Assembly resolution 194 reads:

> "Resolves that the refugees wishing to return to their homes and live at peace with their neighbors should be permitted to do so at the earliest practicable date, and that compensation should be paid for the property of those choosing not to return and for loss of or damage to property which, under principles of international law or inequity, should be made good by the Government or authorities responsible.
> "Instructs the Conciliation Commission to facilitate the repatriation, resettlement and economic and social rehabilitation of the refugees and the payment of compensation, and to maintain close relations with the Director of the United Nations Relief for Palestine Refugees and, through him, with the appropriate organs and agencies of the United Nations."(12)

Though for the last twenty years Zionist occupation of Arab land may be viewed as relatively continuous and public, it cannot be defined as either long or undisturbed.

Even if the continuous state of war between Israel and the Arab countries is disregarded, the emergence of the Palestinian guerrilla forces and their activities have made the territorial occupation of the Zionists far from undisturbed.

C. Arab resistance does not allow Zionism to claim title to Palestine or any other occupied Arab territory through cession or through conquest. (Annexation of territories as a result of conquest is generally carried out by a treaty of cession. The Arabs have never been party to such a treaty.)

A new factor in this resistance is the rise and development of the different movements for the liberation of Palestine from Zionism. These forces reinforce Arab resistance and at the same time make it impossible, in the long run, for the Zionists to vindicate any claim to the Arab land.

The fact remains, however, that the Zionists are in Palestine and other Arab territories by conquest — a conquest which the Arabs chose to resist. A peace treaty in the area between Israel and the Arabs, which has been the official call of the Israeli Government since its inception, implies a treaty of cession. Some points of controversy arise here:

1. A peace treaty with the Arab States could not be binding on the Palestinians. But it may be interpreted that the Arab countries, by so signing, recognize the Zionist occupation of and claim to the territory of Palestine.
2. A peace treaty with the Arab States may be viewed as a treaty of cession because the Arab States have taken the role of legal sponsors of the people of Palestine. (It is not until the Palestinian people form a government of their own, in exile, that they can, in a legal sense and thus effectively, protect their rights from any treaty of this type.)

Thus the territorial claim of Zionism to the occupied Arab areas must be treated in an exceptional manner. And this is an instance of a theme of

58

exceptions which ushered in the development of political Zionism and its application.

It is of importance to mention at this point that the founder of political Zionism, Theodor Herzl, made the human element in the formation of the Jewish state of a greater significance than the territorial element. He said:

> "It is true that the Jewish state is conceived as a peculiarly modern structure on unspecified territory. But a state is formed, not by pieces of land, but rather by a number of men united under sovereign rule . . . Man is the human, land the objective, groundwork of a state; the human basis being the more important of the two."(13)

The significance of the so-called human element in statehood here, surpasses ordinary comprehension. Herzl introduced certain concepts to explain this:

1. The concept of a willing people. "The Jews wish for a state — they shall have it, and they shall earn it for themselves."(14)
2. The concept of a Gestor — "The director of affairs not strictly his own. He has received no warrant — that is no human warrant -- higher obligations authorize him to act."(15)

A human and a superhuman element becomes basic in the formation of a Jewish State. "As a matter of fact, a mixtuie of human and superhuman goes to the making of the state."(16) The human element being the people, and the superhuman, the directive force of the Gestor. (World Zionist Organization taking the role of the Gestor.)

Jewish state building, then, takes the form of two momentums: accumulation of willing people under the direction of a "state forming power," the Gestor, and the accumulation of the objective, the land — a never ending process.

Therefore the territorial element in Zionism, by the nature of the doctrine, is not a stable element within fixed boundary lines. It is always in a state of becoming.

While the declaration of the establishment of the state of Israel did not provide for fixed boundaries, it did provide for the Ingathering of the Exiles.

> "The State of Israel will be open for Jewish immigration and for the Ingathering of the Exiles . . . "(17)

The territory of the Jewish state is thus obviously made flexible to the demands of the waves of Jewish ingathering and to the requirements of the "state-forming power," the World Zionist Organization.

THE POPULATION OF ISRAEL

This is a case of different waves of immigrants from different parts of the world, united only in their Jewish religion, coming to settle on a land belonging to the Arabs.

The immigrants have expelled the Arabs, who had been peacefully settled in their own homes and on their own property, and in their place they have established a system of colonization.

It is strange to find out how Zionist leaders justify these acts of colonization. At one moment Dr. Nahum Goldmann, President of the World Zionist

Organization, refers to the Arabs as the Indians of America and almost in the same breath speaks of their history as the history of a great civilization:

> "When we appeared on the scene of history, most progressive groups in the world were our best friends. Many of them are no longer. But when these opponents argue that we did the Arabs wrong, that while we may not have expelled a large group, hundreds of thousands of people, we have brought it about that they are no longer masters of their land, when one asks 'why not give America back to the Indians,' the only answer to that is that we have a higher right on our side . . . We have the higher right for two simple reasons. One is what I would call a metaphysical, a religio-mystical reason, because Jewish history is unthinkable without the central position of Eretz Israel . . . However, in the totality of Arab history, the history of a great civilization, the centers are Damascus, Baghdad, Granada, Spain, but Palestine has played a very minor role . . .
>
> "And the second reason is the fact that for the Arabs who have large areas of land, which they will not have settled in a hundred years, Palestine, which is one or two percent of this area, does not play a decisive role . . . "(18)

The population element in the State of Israel is to be looked upon as the result of a process of transplanting people with all the consequences and influences that this involves.

The figures below reveal the growth in the Jewish population of Palestine. In 1882, the number of Jews living in Palestine approximated 24,000. The approximate numbers of Jews entering the country until the declaration of the information of the State of of Israel were: from 1883 to 1903: 25,000, from 1904 to 1914: 40,000, in 1918: 56,671, from 1919 to 1923: 36,000, from 1924 to 1931: 84,000, from 1932 to 1939: 265,000, from 1940 to 1948: 130,165.(19)

There was also the natural increase in Jewish population resident in Palestine and some emigration from Palestine. The total number of Jews in Palestine at the time of the proclamation of the state was 649,633.

At the beginning of 1967 Israel's Jewish population had reached 2,344,900. The following table gives some indication of natural increase since 1948 and that due to immigration.

Period (Beginning)	Natural Increase	Migration Balance	Total Increase	% of Migration Balance from Total Increase
1948—'51	88.4	+666.4	754.8	88.3
1952—'54	101.4	+ 20.2	121.6	16.6
1955—'57	100.7	+136.1	236.8	57.5
1958—'60	101.5	+ 46.9	148.4	31.6
1961—'64	134.2	+193.8	328.0	59.1
1961	32.7	+ 37.8	70.5	53.6
1962	32.2	+ 55.0	87.2	63.1
1963	33.7	+ 53.0	86.7	61.1
1964	35.6	+ 48.0	83.6	57.4
1965	37.0	+ 22.9	59.9	38.2
1966	37.5	+ 8.3	45.8	18.1(20)
1967	34.4	+ 4.3	38.7	11.1(21)

The average immigration balance from the total increase in population is 42% per year. Current figures of the recent number of immigrants to Israel roughly show the same average per year with a slightly positive rate of increase.

Unlimited immigration has always been the policy of the State of Israel. Consequently great efforts are made to encourage the incoming of more and more immigrants. Among the first laws issued by the state, for example, was the Law of Return which has conferred upon every Jew in every part of the world the right of "Aliyah" — (immigration) to Israel. This law starts with the following statement: "Every Jew has the right to come to this country as an oleh" —(22) (i.e., immigrant).

Addressing the conference of leaders of Jewish organizations, Mr. Eshkol, late prime minister, issued a strong appeal for Aliyah:

> "Will it be said, Heaven forbid, that this generation witnessed the new dawn of Jewish statehood and the sunset of the Jewish people."(23)

Rabbi Nissim reminded the delegates that "no Jew can be at peace with himself and with his people except in the Land of Israel." While speaking on the vital relationship between a nation and its land, he declared that "the hour of salvation would come when Diaspora Jews came to Israel."(24)

Thus the population element in the State of Israel is quite different from the population element of other states of the world. Here the state is regarded as an instrument to serve all the Jews all over the world; it is an instrument to ingather the exiles.

> "The purpose of the state is to secure the existence of the Jewish people. Not only of the two and a half million Jews who live in Israel today or the three or four millions of tomorrow. The purpose of Zionism is to safeguard the existence, the uniqueness and the identity of all Jews in the world, above all of those who can lead a full life in their own state, something which the Jews of the Golah cannot do. This is the greatest argument for aliya if one wishes to cooperate in building a future for the Jewish people. But the purpose is to use the instrument of the State, of the Jewish minority, of a country of one's own, a language of one's own, a culture of one's own, to secure the threatened existence of the nation."(25)

As the State of Israel is an instrument to serve the purpose of Zionism as quoted above from the words of the President of the World Zionist Organization, Dr. Nahum Goldmann, so it is an instrument to secure the land territory necessary for the increasing numbers. General Yitzhak Rabin declared:

> "I would venture to say that Israel's victory in the Six Day War was the greatest Jewish military achievement in the history of our people. It was the greatest of our wars, and its results have established the broadest boundaries that the history of the Jewish State in the Land of Israel has ever known."(26)

Israel, thus, in the form of a state, reflects a process of colonization seeking ultimate fulfillment in the consolidation of the Jewish nation — i.e., the ingathering of world Jewry in one area. And, this means that neither the territory nor the population of the State of Israel represent an actual state of affairs and therefore do not fall within the general standards of statehood. The two essential elements of the State of Israel represent then a very peculiar condition — a dangerous precedent for the formation of statehood.

GOVERNMENT AND SOVEREIGNTY

In terms of Zionist ideology, the government of Israel is also a potential government. The basic fact of all governments, as has been mentioned before, is that they act for the whole community.

In Zionism the whole community, being the total number of Jews all over the world, means that it is legally impossible for the government of Israel to be acting for the whole Jewish community. Accordingly there is a gap in the power of the Israeli government which is filled by the presence of the World Zionist Organization. If the Israeli government were the ultimate Israeli government in the view of Zionism, then there would be no need for maintaining the structure of the World Zionist Organization.

Thus the government of Israel is in an anomalous position:

A. It is expected to be acting for the whole Jewish community.

1. The presence of the World Zionist Organization as a public body does not make this fully possible.
2. Any claim it makes to authority over nationals of other countries, who have the Jewish faith, brings it into conflict with those countries.

B. By endorsing a policy of free immigration, the government of Israel is not fulfilling its full responsibilities to its own citizens. A few of the implications involved are:

1. The presence of an incoming group is always a factor affecting the distribution of the national wealth.
2. The receiving of immigrants on such a large scale unsettles the economy of the country and gives a feeling of instability and economical insecurity to the existing Israeli population.
3. A policy of free immigration has to be translated into a policy of expansionism since Israel does not own a land area sufficient to absorb the waves of immigrants. Heavy expenditure is needed for defence purposes.

   Thus the government of Israel, by encouraging and working for free immigration, simultaneously prepares a well-equipped army to secure the necessary land area.

   The open, free immigration policy creates even greater hostility from the Arabs who are aware that this will lead to expansion. This hostility finds its expression in Arab defence and desire to eliminate the dangers to them from this expansionist Zionist entity.

   Actually both viewpoints are quite logical. The truth of both stands clear. The result is a state of constant insecurity on the part of the average Israeli citizen.
4. Foreign and defence policies of the state take the predominant position making the life of the Israeli citizen largely dependent on outside relations and the power of the military.

The relation of the government of Israel with the World Zionist Organization, with world Jewry and its obligations to the average Israeli citizen certainly affect its characteristics as a government. It is the policy of unlimited immigration which renders the Israeli government a special character of its own — a character which puts it in a position which affects the fate of nationals of other countries and at the same time perpetuates conditions of discomfort inside the country itself.

The following words were said during the first few years of statehood, but still apply to Israel as long as its immigration policy remains the same:

> "With unlimited immigration on top of defence and development, it is miraculous that Israel continues to survive at all. No country has ever attempted such a policy before; no people other than the Jewish people, in Israel and the Diaspora, could have succeeded. But at what a cost in struggle and discomfort for everyone concerned — from immigrants themselves to the settled population and to the Government."(27)

The critical position of the government of Israel due to being an agent of a state with undefined boundaries and population, to its anomalous relationships with the World Zionist Organization, to its identification with world Zionism, and due to inadequacy in meeting the demands of the Israeli citizens and thus fulfilling the normal functions and duties of a state towards its own public — the multiplicity of all these factors reflect the contradictory position of the government in the State of Israel.

Sovereignty, the fourth essential characteristic of a state, is here, in the case of Israel, an impaired sovereignty.

A. The overall sovereignty of the State of Israel is to be related to the nature of the right this state has over the territory of Israel. It was mentioned previously that the legality of the right Israel has over the occupied territories is not confirmed. According to the laws of nations, Israel's ownership or exercise of power over occupied Palestine is not legal. Basically, therefore, Israel cannot exercise sovereignty over Palestine.

B. If the State of Israel is viewed as an instrument of Zionism, then it lacks independence.

C. If the State of Israel is responsible for the welfare of the Jews all over the world, then its sovereignty in relation to its own deemed territory is only partial.

D. The dependence of the State of Israel on world Jewry and Zionism to fulfil its own tasks cripples its sovereignty.

The sovereignty of Israel is, of its very nature, within the scope of a wider concept of sovereignty — Zionist sovereignty, a new concept understood only within the framework of Zionist action all over the world. How Zionist sovereignty stands in relation to international law, is a question which is not answered yet. The same question also arises in relation to the position of Israel as an instrument of Zionism. However, the World Zionist Organization has no international authority. But its control over the policies of Israel with regard to such Zionist concepts as the "Jewish people" which is basic to Zionism and the "Ingathering" policy in the State of Israel, bring Israel into conflict with other states. The U.S. Department of State commented on the "Jewish people" concept:

> "The Department of State recognizes the State of Israel as a sovereign

State and citizenship of the State of Israel. It recongnizes no other sovereignty or citizenship in connection therewith. It does not recognize a legal-political relationship based upon the religious identification of American citizens. It does not in any way discriminate among American citizens upon the basis of their religion.

Accordingly, it should be clear the the Department of State does not regard the 'Jewish people' concept as a concept of international law."(28)

The founder of political Zionism gave the World Zionist Organization the qualification of a "state forming power." However the State of Israel was formed and the World Zionist Organization is still in a process of development. Thus it could be concluded that the role of Zionism in state formation is incomplete. At least this is what the existence of the World Zionist Organization after the establishment of the State of Israel denotes.

Should judgement then be made on the State of Israel now or in the future when it is developed to the extent conceived in Zionism? What should be the position of international law regarding a process of state formation like that undertaken by the Zionist effort?

The State of Israel, as it has been defined by Zionist leaders, is an instrument of Zionism. Zionism is an ideology which finds its material realization in the World Zionist Organization. This organization, which has no international status, is the prime mover of Israel.

NOTES

(1) Gerhard Von Glahn, LAW AMONG NATIONS, (New York: The Macmillan Company, 1965), Chapters 6-12.

J. L. Brierly, THE LAW OF NATIONS, (Oxford: University Press, 1963), Chapter IV.

(2) Ibid. Gerhard Von Glahn, Chapter 16. J. L. Brierly, Chapter V.

(3) Charter of the United Nations, Chapter One, Article One.

(4) Organization Department, World Zionist Organization, BASLE 1897 — ISRAEL 1967, ASSEMBLY TO MARK THE SEVENTIETH ANNIVERSARY OF THE FOUNDATION OF THE ZIONIST ORGANIZATION AT THE FIRST ZIONIST CONGRESS, (Publishing Department of the Jewish Agency, 1967), pp. 25-36.

(5) David Ben-Gurion, ISRAEL: YEARS OF CHALLENGE, (New York: Holt, Rinehart and Winston, 1963), p. 40.

(6) A discussion of the legality of this resolution is presented in Chapter Two of AN EXAMINATION OF DOCUMENTS ON WHICH THE STATE OF ISRAEL IS BASED.

(7) Joseph Badi, editor, FUNDAMENTAL LAW OF ISRAEL, (New York: Twayne Publishers, 1961), p. 9.

(8) YEAR BOOK OF THE UNITED NATIONS 1947—1948, (New York: Department of Public Information — United Nations, 1949), p. 234.

(9) The above data have been compiled from Zionist sources. However, statistics of Mandatory Government (Village Statistics, March 1945) show that the share to Jews of land distribution was 1,491,700 dunums. Out of this share 175,000 dunums represented long-term land leases by the government. Thus Jewish ownership, in actuality, was then 1,316,700 dunums. Consideration should also be given to 100,928 dunums which were bought by Jews by that date but not registered. Thus the figure of Jewish land ownership rises to 1,417,628 dunums. Yusuf Sayegh, THE ISRAELI ECONOMY (Beirut: Research

Center — Palestine Liberation Organization, 1966), pp. 74;77.

(10) 3.9% represented land purchased by the Jewish National Fund during a period of 45 years. 76.6% captured land within a period of less than a year through the media of force. Angelina Helou, INTERACTION OF POLITICAL, MILITARY AND ECONOMIC FACTORS IN ISRAEL (Beirut: Palestine Research Center, 1969), p. 88.

(11) Article 22 of the Mandate provided that the object of the mandate system is to ensure the "well being and development" of the inhabitants of these territories, as a "sacred trust of civilization." The mandate is described as a "tutelage," exercised on behalf of the League and in its name. This notion of tutelage was borrowed from private law and was a novelty in international law. Yet the spirit of the mandate accordingly insures the concept of free self-determination.

(12) YEAR BOOK OF THE UNITED NATIONS 1948--1949, (New York: Department of Public Information — United Nations, 1950), p. 203.

(13) Theodor Herzl, THE JEWISH STATE, (New York: The Maccabaean Publishing Co., 1904), p. 98.

(14) Ibid., Author's Preface, p. xx.

(15) Ibid., p. 79

(16) Ibidem.

(17) Joseph Badi, editor, op. cit., p. 9.

(18) Organization Department, World Zionist Organization, BASLE 1897 — ISRAEL 1967, ASSEMBLY TO MARK THE SEVENTIETH ANNIVERSARY OF THE FOUNDATION OF THE ZIONIST ORGANIZATION AT THE FIRST ZIONIST CONGRESS, op. cit., pp. 27-28.

(19) The Central Bureau of Statistics, STATISTICAL ABSTRACT OF ISRAEL 1958—1959, (Jerusalem: the Government Printer, 1959), p. 7.

(20) The Central Bureau of Statistics, STATISTICAL ABSTRACT OF ISRAEL 1967, (Jerusalem: The Government Printer, 1967), p. 20. Figures in thousands.

(21) The Central Bureau of Statistics, STATISTICAL ABSTRACT OF ISRAEL 1968, (Jerusalem: The Government Printer, 1968), p. 18. Figures in thousands.

(22) Joseph Badi, editor, op. cit., p. 156.

(23) JERUSALEM POST, January 9, 1969, p. 8.

(24) Ibid.

(25) Organization Department, World Zionist Organization, BASLE 1897 — ISRAEL 1967, ASSEMBLY TO MARK THE SEVENTIETH ANNIVERSARY OF THE FOUNDATION OF THE ZIONIST ORGANIZATION AT THE FIRST ZIONIST CONGRESS, op. cit., p. 26.

(26) Ibid., p. 38.

(27) Edwin Samuel, PROBLEMS OF GOVERNMENT IN THE STATE OF ISRAEL, (Jerusalem: Rubin Mass, Publisher, 1959), p. 22.

(28) Letter from Assistant Secretary of State Talbot to Dr. Elmer Berger, Executive Vice-President of the American Council for Judaism. April 20, 1964, DIGEST OF INTERNATIONAL LAW 35 (1967).

THE CONTINUING
ZIONIST REVOLUTION

Zvi Ankori

The conflict between Israel and the Arabs of Palestine, thus opened Abu-Lughod his argument, began with "the Jewish Problem." That problem was a European phenomenon which had nothing to do with Palestine. The conflict erupted as a result of the action of Zionism which set about to solve the European Jewish problem by bringing in European Jewish settlers to Palestine and eventually creating there a Jewish state: Israel.

Dr. Abu-Lughod is right. Israel is indeed the product of Zionism; and Zionism did come to solve "the Jewish Problem" as it was known primarily in Europe in the eighteenth, the nineteenth, and, alas, also the twentieth centuries. But what was Zionism all about, and how did it propose to solve the "Jewish Problem" which Dr. Abu-Lughod mentions as a term only and never cares to explain?

ZIONISM: A NATIONAL LIBERATION MOVEMENT

Zionism was, and is, a modern national liberation movement, on a par with a host of other well-known modern national liberation movements of the nineteenth and twentieth centuries.

Like all other national liberation movements, Zionism was out to recapture for the Jewish people the independence and the sovereignty which are the right of every people and which are the condition — a better one has not been devised yet — for the free exercise of national will and action. The Jews lost that independence and sovereignty at a tragic juncture of their history two thousand years ago.

The nineteenth century, which saw Zionism assume shape and formulate its ideology as we know it today, witnessed the awakening and partial fulfillment of the national aspirations of a number of European peoples, just as our own generation will go down in history as the period of the awakening and liberation of peoples in Asia and Africa.

Not only did peoples with a relatively recent history of oppression begin clamoring for their national rights. Ancient peoples, too — some who had reached the peak of their historical and cultural achievements back in the classical period, when they were the contemporaries of the ancient Jewish commonwealth of Palestine — reasserted themselves anew and moved forcefully to gain a new lease on life. Such was, for instance, the nineteenth-century epic of the rebirth of Greece, whose struggle for independence from Muslim Turkish subjugation fired the imagination and enthusiasm of the best minds of Europe. Such was, further, the story of the renascence of Italy and of her final unification in 1870.

The symbolic message of these events was not lost on the Jews. History, as it were, set about to vindicate the creed of which they, in their endurance and martyrdom, had been a living expression for two millenia: the creed, that is, that a people's yearning for liberty knows no expiration date and that no statute of limitations does, or can, conceivably apply to a people's claim to sovereignty over the land in which its historical roots are firmly set.

Pondering over the lesson of his time, one of the great socialist Jewish theorists and an early ideologist of modern Zionism expressed this idea in his book ROME AND JERUSALEM in terms of historic justice: now that ancient Rome has regained her erstwhile role in renascent Italy, the time was ripe for Rome's surviving victim — Jewish Jerusalem — to be restored to her rightful place among nations.

Yet — and here we reach the crux of "the Jewish Problem" — while in its ultimate objective, that is, in the task of recovering Jewish sovereignty which was lost in the Judaeo-Roman War, Zionism was no different from other national liberation movements, past or present, it differed from them all in its points of departure. Whereas the other movements arose among peoples who, though oppressed and exploited, continued to live on their own land — so that their liberation task called merely for expelling the imperialistic intruders and restoring the people's mastery over its own home — Zionism had to cope with Jewry's unique position in the world: homelessness.

It is no coincidence that the Balfour Declaration of 1917 as well as other British Mandate and League of Nations documents spoke of a "Jewish National Home." I truly sympathized yesterday with Dr. Abu-Lughod when I saw him stumble on that peculiar terminology. Indeed, the designation has no peer in the annals of history and diplomacy. But, unique as it may be, it was neither a clever invention of Zionist negotiators nor a mere whim of the British chancellery. The term accurately conveyed the Jews' unique predicament.

For what the Jews were missing through the long course of their diasporic history was precisely that: a home. And it was the Jews' homelessness that cast the giant shadow which haunted them along the weary road leading to the very heart of the modern-day "Jewish Problem": the initial defeat; the ensuing exile from their ancestral homeland; the wandering and settlement in the lands of others who either tolerated the Jews as useful aliens or resented them as outright intruders; the centuries of medieval persecution, physical as well as religious, of segregation, and of legal and social discrimination; the frustrations, the short-lived illusory successes, and the final despair that lay in the path of the late eighteenth- and early nineteenth-century Emancipation movement (the Jewish Civil Rights movement, if you prefer a terminology to which our ears are better attuned today); the failure to win the social acceptance or integration of the Jew into European society, no matter how suicidally high was the price of his own identity that he was ready to pay in return; and finally, the emergence, in the nineteenth century, of modern European anti-Semitism, whose bitter fruit in our

67

own time can never be forgotten.

It was with the Jewish people's unique condition of homelessness that Zionism as a national liberation movement had to cope from the very start. The fact that such a task was unparalleled in the history of national liberations does not make Zionism any less legitimate or any less worthy a cause than any other "normal" liberation movement of the past century or of our own generation.

Zionism's point of departure could therefore not be the proclamation of a revolution in the conventional political sense — that is, as with other liberation movements, a revolution bent on seizing power and establishing institutions of sovereign rule — but the introduction of a fundamental change in the geo-demographic position of Jewry in the world. It meant the transfer of a whole people back to its home, to Palestine. Indeed, not to any other country but Palestine, which in spite of the millennial gap never ceased to be the Jews' home in their own eyes as well as in the eyes of the world.

Ever since our loss of independence, Palestine has been subjected to a succession of regimes of various hues which incorporated her as a province in one empire or another, but she has never been a state with a separate identity. That separate identity — shall I use Dr. Abu-Lughod's nomenclature? — that "Palestinian identity," lived only in the minds of the Jews, in their prayers, in their historical memory, in their hopes and national ideology. Even the short-lived Crusader kingdom, though animated by "Holy Land" ideology, was but an extension of West European Christendom *outremer*.

Nor, for that matter, has Palestine ever been an Arab state. Although the Arabs ruled the Middle East (including Palestine) for quite a long period and brought about far-reaching changes in the demographic makeup of the region, Palestine always remained a province of a larger Arab political unit: a province of the Umayyad Caliphate of Damascus, for instance, or of the Abbasid Caliphate of Baghdad, of the Fatimid Caliphate of Cairo, or of the later Ayyubid or Mamluk varieties of Egyptian sultanate — never an Arab nation with a separate state identity. The same holds true for the city of Jerusalem which never was the capital of any Arab kingdom, not even under her recent (Hashemite) masters.

It is we Jews, and we alone, who lent a special status and gave political, religious, and cultural identity to that land. And if that special status and that separate identity of Palestine have eventually become part and parcel also of Christian and Muslim lore, it is because we made them special and separate, and because we persisted in proclaiming them as such. If that land is holy, not only to Jews but to Christians and Muslims as well, it is because we were first to make it holy.

Hence, the recently fashionable learned advertisements and pronouncements of well-meaning academicians, debating with respectable gravity Israel's right or lack of right to one part or another of historical Palestine, are entirely irrelevant. Israel's recognition by the family of nations or Israel's victories on the battlefield, while extremely important in themselves, did not create the Jews' title to that land. They merely confirmed that title in terms of effective control over a territory of which we were robbed by the harsh decree of history two thousand years ago and which was cruelly assaulted twenty one years ago by the invading forces of non-Palestinian Arab states who defied the 1947 recommendation of the United Nations.

Our victory does not prove our right to Palestine, just as our defeat (had there been one) would not have proven the absence of that right. Our victory merely proves that we were ready to die in battle for what rightfully was — and in our minds, and hopes, and prayers has never ceased to be — ours.

Zionism was, then, and continues to be, a national liberation movement *par excellence*, a movement bent on reversing the course of Jewish history of the past two millenia by removing the diasporic disability imposed on Jewry from without. But, in order to succeed, Zionism, like all genuine national liberation movements of the nineteenth and, even more so, of the twentieth centuries, had to be also a revolutionary movement from within, and its vision of national redemption could never be divorced from far-reaching programs of reshaping Jewish society proper.

The fact that these revolutionary intra-Jewish aspects of Zionism are being perversely misrepresented these days by circles who so self-righteously dispense labels and grades and usurp monopoly over revolutionary wisdom is a sorry commentary on the intellectual integrity and political honesty of those circles. All I can say, conversely, for myself — and I am not the only one in my country who feels that way — is that, precisely from the vantage-point of Zionism, we, Israelis, follow with great interest and sympathy the true signs of social awakening and the constructive calls for social change in the Arab societies around us, so eloquently presented here yesterday by the other members of our panel. How wasteful it is that we are not allowed to share our experience with those who need it and how much poorer our region remains as result of the fact that we are not given the chance to work jointly with our neighbors for the upgrading of the quality of life in the region as a whole.

ZIONISM: A SOCIO-ECONOMIC REVOLUTION

Let me address myself to some of the intra-Jewish revolutionary elements which Zionism, from the very beginning, heralded as indispensable for Jewry's growth and maturation toward the ultimate goal of national liberation.

First and foremost among them was Zionism's call for restructuring the social and economic pattern of Jewish life. Zionism wanted not only to free Jewish society but to build it anew. It therefore asked for complete socio-economic transformation of the returning immigrants. Destitute shopkeepers and sweatshop-hands from the stifling ghettoes of Eastern Europe, people who never so much as sniffed the air of open spaces, were to raise themselves by their own bootstraps and turn into farmers, craftsmen, miners, scientists, fishermen, and, if need be, soldiers.

What Zionism demanded of the arriving settlers was to labor with their own hands: not bring in money and managerial skill and use the natives for menial jobs, as did European colonialists elsewhere, but learn to do every job by themselves and do it. Thus, the town-dwelling Jew, who for so many centuries and against his own will used to be identified in the Diaspora with petty commerce and money-lending, was called upon by Zionism to change his habits, even to forsake his innate thirst for learning, to interrupt his university studies (as did the first Zionist settlers in 1881 and generations of pioneers after them) and till the soil by the sweat of his brow and do all other work, however hard, by himself.

Of all the achievements of Zionism this socio-economic metamorphosis was the most revolutionary and demanded the greatest measure of personal dedication. In the long run, it was truly responsible for the emergence of "the Israeli prototype" as we know it today.

Visitors to Israel and students of Israeli society speak with admiration of the *kibbutzim*, and I should be the last to underrate the beauty and idealism of these workers' communes (I myself was a member of one back in my earlier years).

Yet the very creation of these kibbutzim would have been inconceivable without the revolutionized attitude to manual work — any work, but primarily that connected with agriculture — which Zionism consistently and most forcefully inculcated into Jewish youth.

Indeed, while in the early decades of this century a founding father of the first kibbutz in Palestine fired the zeal of young Zionist-Socialist pioneers with his preachment of "Religion of Labor" and was in his own way of life, despite advanced age, a living example of religious devotion to manual work, David Ben-Gurion, himself a farmhand many years ago and now a member of a kibbutz in the Negev Desert, recently suggested that the date of the establishment of the first Jewish agricultural school in Palestine (in 1870) be hailed as the true beginning of the Zionist era in Jewish history.

In brief, Dr. Abu-Lughod, it was neither a sense of "superiority" nor a tendency toward "exclusiveness' (the way you proclaimed here yesterday) that made Zionism insist on having all work in the newly established Jewish settlements performed by Jewish hands, and Jewish hands alone. A strange expression of superiority indeed — the backbreaking job of tilling the parched soil, pitching the manure, milking the cows, and digging irrigation ditches — and all this, mind you, by people whom you denounced as colonialists!

No, Dr. Abu-Lughod, the idea underlying Zionism's unparalleled attitude to manual work had nothing to do with excluding others. All it endeavored to do was to create for the first time a healthy worker class in Jewry. Indeed, much has been said and written about the achievements of Jewish labor in my country, achievements whose influence has transcended the boundaries of British Palestine and of Israel. The point I wish to stress here is that the Zionist ideology of labor revolutionized Jewry itself no less than it revolutionized the economy and the way of life of the Near East.

ZIONISM: A SECULARIST REVOLUTION

Secondly — and I shall be very brief on that, lest we are taken too far afield — Zionism was a secularist revolution in Jewry.

Although it was, to a very large extent, religious beliefs and practices which kept Jewish nationalism alive throughout the ages; though Jewish pilgrimage to the Holy Places and Jewish settlement in the ancient and venerated cities of Palestine never really ceased during the long centuries of Exile; and though a succession of messianic-activistic movements would sporadically flare up in various parts of Jewish Dispersion and thus help dramatize in religious terms the impatience of certain groups in Jewry with the diasporic way of life and with Jewry's oppressed status among nations — it was Zionism, as we know it from the late nineteenth century on, that for the first time translated these age-old yearnings and hopes into the modern secular idiom of national liberation. Naturally, the secular character of modern anti-Semitism added impetus to this development.

Leaving the language of prayer, of mystic expectation, and of Palestine-oriented religious devotion to the individual and his conscience, Zionism spoke to the world and to modern Jewry alike in the self-assertive vein of Jewish Power. While it addressed the world in terms of power of diplomacy, power of molding public opinion, and, eventually, power of international trust and alignments, it shook Jewry from within by making it rediscover its own power — in organization, in education, in self-defense.

Thus it applied the power of organized political action not only to lobbying for outside support, but to winning over the rank and file of the Jewish masses to the Zionist cause. It harnessed, further, the power of Jewish labor, science, and technology to compensate for the barrenness of the land and its centuries-long neglect. It pointed to the power that could be derived from marshalling the economic resources of the people and hailed the power of the people's unity as the instrument for putting these resources to work in well-planned and concerted action. Finally, it learned how to mobilize the power of the people's voluntary discipline and self-imposed sacrifice and how to use this power constructively under the leadership of democratically-elected autonomous institutions.

Most importantly: Zionism secularized the expression of Jewry's traditional attachment to Palestine. This it did in two ways. On the one hand, it made the modern Jew rediscover and proudly assert and emphasize the national component of his identity qua Jew — the national component, that is, which, though historically intertwined with the religious, has been deliberately muted, or denied outright, by some Emancipation-hungry (mainly Western) Jewish groups.

On the other hand, in terms of constructive action, it channelled the age-old messianic longings as well as the people's concrete needs for immediate alleviation of diasporic misery into five major endeavors; the organization of world-Jewish support for Zionist activities in and for Palestine; the acquisition of land in Palestine; immigration; settlement; and the establishment of Jewish self-governmental agencies (including that which was entrusted with the task of self-defense), groomed to take over, when the time for national liberation was ripe, all normal tasks of secular statehood.

To be sure, this process of intra-Jewish secularization is far from ended. On the contrary: the establishment of the Jewish State opened whole new areas of secular involvements, as anyone reading the papers must know. Indeed, the contest between traditional attitudes and secularism will, I predict, remain an important and turbulent part of the continuing Zionist revolution in Jewry.

ZIONISM: A LINGUISTIC REVOLUTION

Thirdly, Zionism called for a linguistic revolution in Jewry, for a renaissance of the ancient Hebrew tongue, once the living language of Jewish Palestine but long considered dead, or, at best, relegated to use in prayer, in study, or in purely literary creativity. Zionism expected that language to serve not merely as an educational instrument for the expansion of Jewish historical consciousness but as an effective vehicle for fusing together Jewry's scattered tribes who on their 2,000-year journey through alien nations and cultures borrowed the languages of their respective host-countries and molded them into jargons and dialects of their own.

Once alive on the lips of the returning people, the ancestral tongue was to recover its natural self-rejuvenating capacities and become a pliable and easily adaptable tool for modern living, as well as a powerful lever for the creation of a new culture of the highest order. Of all the successes of Zionism, the revival of Hebrew — first and foremost, as the spoken language of daily communication but, at the same time, as the language of sophisticated literary creativity of a quality that won a modern Israeli writer the Nobel Prize for Literature in 1966 — is, to my mind, the most tangible, the most complete, the most miraculous, and, so I wish to believe, of most far-reaching significance.

Consider what linguistic problems beset a number of newly liberated nations in our own generation: the linguistic difficulties of India, of Ceylon, of many an African state. Consider the tragic paradox that made liberated nations revert to the language of their erstwhile colonial oppressor as the only means of communication between their various tribes. Consider all that — and compare it with Hebrew reborn: a language as natural and playful on the kindergarten level as it is flexible and precise when used at the Institute of Technology or at a philosophy course in one of our universities; as fleshy and juicy and titillating in a folksong as it is rich and delicate and expressive in our modern poetry and prose.

It is, however, not enough to state that Zionism is perhaps the only modern national liberation movement which fully succeeded in solving the linguistic difficulties of the kind that confront emerging nations. It is important to add that it did so not without struggle and only after having successfully revolutionized the linguistic habits of Jewry.

That Palestinian Jewish settlers were in the forefront of this linguistic revolution and that they often had to turn their backs on some of their own diasporic leaders or supporters, goes without saying. Hebrew is alive today because those who rebelled against life in the Diaspora made the revival of the language a living part of their rebellion.

ZIONISM: A NEW BREED OF JEWS

Fourthly, Zionism meant self-liberation from ghetto mentality into new manhood; the creation of a new breed of Jews: proud, enterprising, efficient, ready to stand up for their rights, unafraid of adversity or of sacrifice.

And if to some outsiders that newly regained pride seems to border on cockiness, and the courage and readiness to fight are misread as aggressiveness, it is so, primarily, because they — the outsiders — have for so long been conditioned to a certain image of a "Jew," an image Zionism denounced and set about to erase as a sorry caricature, born of the incestuous union of Jewish misery and Gentile contempt.

So this is Zionism, my friends, as much a revolution from within as a liberation from outside oppression. Booted by the reactionary Right and the radical Left alike, in spite of Jewish contributions to the development of modern capitalism, on the one hand, and to modern social revolutionary movements, on the other; castigated for the Rothschilds, the Oppenheimers, the Morgenthaus, and other money potentates by some, and for the Karl Marxes, and Trotzkys, and Blums and, may I say, Marcuses by others — modern Jews, i.e., those who were molded by Zionist ideas, by Zionist self-discipline, and by Zionism's sober view of the world and as sober a view of themselves, straightened their backs and learned to look the world straight in the eye, without apology, without fear, with a new sense of self-respect and self-assertion.

Against bigots who would choose to fence us into ghetto reservations (ghettoes, incidentally, are not a novel twentieth-century experience; it is we, Jews, who were exposed to them first and forcibly locked up in them for many centuries, including the present one); against patronizing Gentile protagonists of civil rights for Jews, and against bootlicking Uncle Toms from within who would flip over these Gentiles' remark that some of their best friends are Jews, Zionism arose to speak with a new voice and to become -- how shall I put it to make you get the feel of it in terms of present-day realities with which you are better acquainted? — yes, to become the "Black Power" in Jewry, Black Power indeed, asserting the Jews' right to shape their own destiny, whatever the reaction of foe or friend.

It is this achievement in terms of psychology, in terms of new posture, of new style, new voice, that is, I believe, as important as all the other contributions of Zionism taken together.

ZIONISM: A REVOLUTIONARY MINORITY

God knows it wasn't simple. Like so many other revolutionary movements, Zionism was a minority viewpoint among the Jewish people: uncomfortable, disturbing, impatient. It aimed at the very heart of the diasporic status quo.

It was too vocal, argued some, while diasporic prudence should have taught us that a Jew better lie low. It was electrifying to the youth, while, at the same time, undermining the authority of the parents who were too busy eking out a miserable living or simply trying to survive. It was critical of the elders, a challenge to the traditional leadership of the diasporic community.

And so, contrary to your assertion, Dr. Abu-Lughod, many well-meaning Jews tried other remedies. Oh, how desperately they tried and how dismally they failed! Alas, most of them did not live to admit failure.

Today, when the memory of the most atrocious holocaust in history haunts us as a lesson in diasporic Jewish helplessness, while a strong and sovereign Jewish commonwealth is a 20-year reality; when (not unlike Black Power that eventually galvanized even the moderates in the Negro community) Israel came eventually to be viewed as the bulwark of Jewish survival and the rallying cry of Jewish identity also by Jews who never considered themselves Zionists nor intend to settle in the Jewish state — it is all too easy and convenient, Dr. Abu-Lughod, to harp on the "Zionization" of Jewry as if it were a case of innate Jewish intransigence and as if there were in the past hundred years no other, non-Zionist, attempts or proposals to cope with "the Jewish Problem."

Assimilation was one; Communism, another. There was also diasporic autonomism; cultural self-determination; etc., etc. Then there were the "territorialist" (meaning non-Palestinocentric) colonization efforts; settlement in Argentine; settlement in Soviet Birobidzhan; the futile suggestion of Madagascar, New Caledonia, Guyana; and so on, down the bitter road of dreams.

Even Zionists — indeed, some of the best minds among them — tried to dilute the classical formulations of Zionist goals, offering to reconcile themselves to half-measures, as long as the other side was willing to extend a friendly hand, and provided the desperate rescue needs were met with due haste. A bi-national state, suggested some; a federation of cantons along Swiss lines, proposed others; while yet another school of thought called for a non-state that would serve as a mere spiritual center. All of no avail! These are the hard facts, Dr. Abu-Lughod, and no amount of exercise in rewriting or erasing history nor any amount of dialectical gimmickry attuned to the radical jargon now in vogue will make a dent in them.

Remedies galore, indeed! Scores of them! But, whether of longer duration and actually put to test, or mere phantoms in a Kafka-esque world, each more ephemeral than the next, they all stare at us across the War and Holocaust years in graveyard silence — monuments of failure and mausoleums of frustration — for none of them had produced the one and only solution that was needed most: a sovereign home. Is it too far-fetched to speculate that, had the solution been available at the time, it might have made all the difference between life and death?

Yes, only the attainment of national sovereignty — the ultimate goal of all liberation movements and the ultimate goal of classical Zionism as well (alas, fully vindicated by the bitter course of contemporary Jewish history) — could provide the basis for the solution of Jewish "homelessness." True, several of the Zionist achievements within Jewish society would most probably have continued to mature and expand even without statehood. After all, the revival of Hebrew language and literature; the rise of a Jewish working class engaged in the primary stages of production; the development of Jewish agriculture; and the social experiment of the kibbutz (to cite some of the major revolutionary processes which Zionism introduced into Jewry) were set in motion prior and preparatory to the establishment of the State of Israel. Sure the vision of future statehood made their success possible, just as, conversely, their further development has been enhanced by the existence of the state. They nevertheless can hardly be defined as dependent, in the specific scope of their activity, on the sovereign status of the Jewish people in its national home.

Not so the supreme task of rescuing the people from the throes of genocide. The ways and means that a state has at its disposal in such a case, though not always adequate themselves, cannot possibly be matched by any private organization or group of individuals, however powerful and influential.

The gas chambers of World War II have taught us a lesson and we have vowed never to be weak again and never let the genocidal nightmare be repeated.

Indeed, not even Andrei Gromyko himself, the dour Soviet Foreign Minister and hardly a sentimentalist by anybody's description, could fail to see the crucial link between Jewry's clamor for sovereignty in Palestine and the unparalleled catastrophe that had befallen the Jews in the absence of the protective panoply of statehood. The man who, in the spring of 1967, laid the ground for the disastrous Soviet-Arab strategy that culminated in the Israel-Arab confrontation of June of the same year, had this to say to the Arabs twenty years previously, on November 26, 1947, three days before the recommendation for partitioning Palestine into a Jewish State and an Arab State was voted upon by the United Nations General Assembly:

> The representatives of the Arab States claim that the partition of Palestine would be an historic injustice. But this view is unacceptable if only because, after all, the Jewish people have been closely linked with Palestine for a considerable period in history.
>
> Apart from that, we must not overlook the position in which the Jewish people found themselves as a result of the recent World War. As a result of that war which was unleashed by Hitlerite Germany the Jews as a people have suffered more than any other people.

Hence, when in the tense days of spine-chilling anxiety in the latter part of May, 1967, President Nasser decided to flaunt at us the threat of "total war," we instantly comprehended the awesome message of that term and what its implementation might portend for our future.

And if nowadays some people, counting on the general fatigue with wars, deliberately choose to forget, and to make others forget as well, and slickly shrug off such bellicose pronouncements as innocently boisterous or boisterously innocent and at any rate a harmless case of the oriental knack for exaggeration, then, with all due respect, they cannot count on us to be partners in that collusion. We have not forgotten the recent past; we cannot and will not forget; and we shall make it our business to remind the world of the inherent dangers of the "Palestinian Revolution."

With the June War of 1967, we not only sprang to our own defense with an instinctive urge for self-preservation that was accompanied by a show a world Jewish unity unprecedented in the annals of our rather individualistically-minded people; but we also put our neighbors and the world on notice that, come what may, the fearsome shadow of Auschwitz would not darken our horizon again. That notice stands as long as we live — and, believe me, we say it in no sense of arrogance but out of anguish and the grim realization that no alternative is open to us.

And so, Dr. Abu-Lughod, we do not apologize for Zionism, we do not apologize for Israel strong and sovereign. We merely regret that the fulfillment of the Zionist dream came so late — too late, alas, to save the lives of millions of our brethren who needlessly perished in Nazi concentration camps.

Nor do we feel we ought to apologize for having introduced Western culture and Western scientific methods and technology in the service of the Middle East, for which we have been so vehemently denounced by Dr. Abu-Lughod. Indeed we have done it, and quite consciously so. Call it "bridgehead of Europe," if you will, or give it any other of those fashionable labels which, strangely enough for an intellectual community, claim immunity these days from rational analysis once they have been introduced into a discussion.

Yes, we have brought Europe to the Near East. But we have done so not in order "to denigrate the natives" (to quote from yesterday's presentation) because we thought the Arabs of the country were "barbarians," as Dr. Abu-Lughod's paranoid interpretation of Zionism would have it. We have done so because — well, let's face it, "unprogressive" though it may appear nowadays, when the "in" thing is to burn incense and practice yoga and be just plain "tired" of the West — Western civilization was indeed, in so many ways and in such variety of fields, superior to that which we found in the barren strip of territory called Palestine.

No, we are not ashamed of the fact that on our long trek through Europe, and along with the bitter suffering we were exposed to there, we kept our eyes and ears open and our minds alert to observe and study and absorb and benefit of the blessings of European learning and experience, and brought them along in our tool kit to be used in the task of rebuilding the country.

So we did irrigate the desert and, yes, we did drain the marshes with the most advanced devices of Western technology — if that is a sin — leaving behind the Arab *fellahin's* wooden plough, and the malaria, and trachoma, and the other diseases that plagued our country for centuries and decimated its inhabitants!

So we did build hospitals and child-care centers and institutions of learning and technology — if that is a sin — and we frankly fail to see why it should be considered an insult and "denigration of the natives" to state that these achievements benefited not only the Jewish population but also Israeli Arabs, giving them the lowest infant mortality and the highest life expectancy rate in the Arab world.

No, we truly and honestly do not apologise for our Western culture. But we categorically reject the simplistic and all too glib thesis that anything that has to do with the introduction of Western culture into the Middle East constitutes ipso facto colonialism.

For, unlike colonial accomplishments based on exploitation, which we abhor no less than Dr. Abu-Lughod and his compatriots do, all the above achievements came about through our own toil. Not by our acting as supervisors and skilled operators who command hosts of "native barbarians," but by imposing on our own society a process of occupational restructuring, retraining, and mobility, and by cultivating, in creed and deed alike, a brand of egalitarianism seldom found in other societies.

There is no doctrine of European superiority in Zionism, though quite naturally, borne as it has been primarily on the shoulders of people who hailed from Europe, the movement has been most appreciative of European technology and European political and institutional patterns and of what these could contribute to the upgrading of living conditions and to the improvement of the quality of life in the Middle East.

But with the maturation of the Zionist movement and its ever-greater assimilation into the region; with the rise of new Israeli-born generations, firmly rooted in the little Mediterranean corner which they, with pride and without being apologetic about it, call home; with the ever-increasing ratio of oriental immigrants in Israeli society and with our ever-growing understanding of our Arab neighbors living among us; finally, and no less importantly, with the expanding intellectual awareness among concerned people in Israel, no matter what their country of origin, of the intrinsic weight of Eastern values (some of them going back to our distant past in the Middle East) and of their potential contribution to the shaping and enrichment of our modern national culture — conscious and fairly successful steps are being taken to absorb the Eastern values as well.

Yet, I firmly reject Dr. Abu-Lughod's wholesale depreciation of Western values as well as his conveniently selective and vaguely generalized illustrations of his thesis. And I categorically reject Dr. Abu-Lughod's denunciation of Zionism as a carrier of these Western values, a denunciation which is automatically tantamount to an indictment of the gravest order. Not only do I refuse to subscribe to Dr. Abu-Lughod's judgment of Western values — and I say "values" deliberately, to distinguish from mere technology, which, after all, every Asian and African country is desperately trying to emulate — but I should like most emphatically to caution against blanket endorsement of the Eastern heritage.

Alas, no culture we know has an impeccable record of human decency and it would take very little effort to cite for each case of Western bestiality of man to his fellow man a matching example of Eastern tyranny and of wanton Eastern disregard for human life and dignity. Hence, while I should have had no difficulty in competing with my radical friend in the exposure of Western racism and colonial abuses (if only because we Jews were their victims more and longer than any other people), I consider it intellectually dishonest to select Europe's twentieth-century concentration camps as indicators of what Western civilization must inevitably lead to, as has been done here.

Now, I am sure you will all exempt me from stating how I feel about concentration camps and Nazi barbarism. But I truly wonder why some Eastern practices, such as the public spectacle of hanging, performed in the main squares of Baghdad and Damascus, should seem any less revolting — and I would have said the same even if no Jewish victims had been involved in any of these recent tragedies.

No, no civilization can honestly take out a claim to perfection. Consequently, the enumeration of human failings on either side will hardly contribute to our discussion.

There are so many Eastern traits which I should dread to see us adopt, just as I hope we are in the course of shedding a goodly number of European characteristics we could not help having acquired through the ages. But I do pray that we be granted the wisdom to blend in our emerging Israeli society and culture the very best and the most vital that both East and West can offer.

Whatever the Eastern and Western ingredients of that future synthesis, I further pray that, in the process, we shall never fail to espouse the one particular value we learned to cherish as a fundamental part of our Western upbringing (though its seed is already embedded in our biblical heritage) — the value which, regrettably, is ever less appreciated in the political climate of our times: democracy.

With the exception of Israel and Lebanon (the latter, indeed, the most "Western" and most "different" of all Arab states), democracy is to all intents and purposes nonexistent in the Middle East. I shall return to that point briefly a little later, when scrutinizing Dr. Abu-Lughod's own "vision" of a Palestinian state.

At this point let me merely say that, whether viewed from the vantage-point of intra-Jewish developments or in the social and political context of the whole region, the institution and effective pursuit of the democratic process within the Zionist movement, all through the five decades of the movement's existence prior to the establishment of the State, and the successful continuation of a democratic regime in the State of Israel ever since its inception in 1948, should justly be counted among the greatest and most durable achievements of Zionism.

In spite of wartime conditions, economic insecurity, and the explosive social pressures of mass immigration (including immigration from Arab and Communist territories where there had been little or no experience in democratic procedures), Israel stands out in the region and among the newly-liberated nations as a bulwark of true, Western-style democracy — democracy, that is, not for Jews alone but for all inhabitants of the State, whatever their national identity or religion.

And so, we do not apologize for our Western culture, no matter how you look at it: in terms of science, of technology, of democratic institutions, or of other values. We do admit having carried a branch of the tree of Western culture into the Palestinian wilderness.

But what is truly relevant here is that this branch has taken root in the Palestinian soil; that it is there now, not as a dried-up twig stuck in the sand, but as a living plant with prospects for further growth; that it constitutes an organic part of the new cultural enterprise which we have begun to build on the foundations of our ancient culture.

Moreover, in bringing the West to bear on the East we actually followed the normal pattern of Middle Eastern history — and I mean Islamic history, Dr. Abu-Lughod. You know as well as I do that in earlier ages, too, Western culture (or what at the time used to pass among the residents of the region for "Western culture") was ardently sought after and eventually absorbed and assimilated by none other than classical Islam.

That culture consisted basically of the treasured recollections of ancient Greek lore, in philosophy, in the sciences, in medicine, astronomy, and architecture, as interpreted and transmitted in the Middle Ages through Byzantine Greek channels. With the help of Arabic-speaking Greeks, Copts, Armenians, Jews, and a host of others, Islam successfully absorbed this tremendous body of Western learning, science, and experience and blended it with the Persian culture of the Sassanian Empire, which it had subdued militarily and converted. Thus was created in the long run a brilliant though eclectic civilization, unequalled so far in any subsequent chapter of Islamic history.

But Dr. Abu-Lughod has no use for history, not even for the historical lesson of his own civilization, just as he feels no need for demonstrating the supposedly detrimental effect of Western culture on the inhabitants of Palestine for which he takes us to task. Having bluntly accused us of two crimes — of being European intruders ourselves and of having subverted the country with an intruder-culture which we brought from the West — he finds us guilty on yet another count. Now that we have already settled in the Near East, he argues, why have we not "fused with the native population?"

Well, here again the technique remains the same: an accusation is made, and the sheer fact that it has been made is supposed to suffice as automatic confirmation of its substance. But does it really? Why, even such an apparently innocuous term as "native population," in which, without much ado, Dr. Abu-Lughod bundles together indiscriminately all the Arabs of Palestine while excluding the Jews as a matter of course, is not so self-evidently unequivocal.

Consecutive generations of Palestine-born Jews can be traced back at least as far as the eighteenth century, and even the Zionist immigration proper can boast of having produced some three generations of Palestinian Jewish natives. Conversely, a goodly number of Arabs, not excluding prominent families and vocal politicians, are relatively late arrivals; indeed, some do not antedate the British Mandate, having been attracted to Palestine by the economic opportunities resulting from Zionist immigration and settlement!

But, more importantly, even accepting Dr. Abu-Lughod's terminology, one would wish he had addressed himself first to the task of showing the intrinsic merit of the fusion he demands and demonstrating the Arabs' interest in seeing such fusion materialize, before hurling accusations at the Jewish immigrants for having failed to accomplish the task.

After all, the idea of fusion has serious and far-reaching implications: the deliberate dilution and eventual disappearance of the separate identities — national, ethnic, cultural, linguistic, religious, or any combination thereof — which distinguish the diverse groups of the Palestinian population from each other. Doesn't Dr. Abu-Lughod owe us first a discussion of whether such demand of fusion is right on principle, desirable as a long-range objective, or finally, attainable at all in the special socio-religious and ethnic-cultural climate of Palestine?

Even in the United States, the long-hailed example of the "melting pot," people are having second thoughts on whether the elements thrown together in the pot can, or indeed should, fuse completely. How much more so in Palestine, where each group represents and, yes, unlike America, insists on representing a separate national or religious ideal and is, so to speak, an outpost of hosts of people outside the country who pay allegiance to that ideal and who support the institutions entrusted with guarding and propagating it!

Take a walk in the Old City of Jerusalem, the area billed as the Arab city, and see for yourselves the bewildering conglomeration of ethnic neighborhoods, quarters based on countries of origin, religious groupings of diverse hues — partitions within partitions on top of yet other partitions — and ask yourselves: Have all these people fused? Can they ever? Indeed, should they? Why then are we Jews (and, so far as I understand Dr. Abu-Lughod, we alone), accused of not having reversed this historical trend and not having challenged the very grain of the Palestinian socio-religious and cultural pattern? Why should we, and we alone, have wanted to do so when, after all, the very idea of our return to our historic land was the result of recovered national awareness and when the express purpose of all our undertaking was to rebuild our separate national identity, not dilute it, to save it rather than make it disappear?

Conversely, I should have considered it outrageous if an Israeli leader or idologist insisted that the Arab minority in Israel "fuse" with us and lose its identity (and I do not envisage this ever happening). Loyalty as citizens of the State is one thing; fusion as a people is an entirely different matter.

Israel must, and indeed does, exercise every effort to let her Arab citizens feel that "Judaization," "Hebraization" (call it what you will; I have no word for it, since obviously the religious element must be left out of the discussion) is in no way the future she envisions for them. The contrary rather is the case, and quite rightly so. What Israel tells them and must never tire of telling them is that we respect and formally recognize their separate national identity. We must repeatedly assure them that we know they are part of a larger national, linguistic, and cultural unit, the "Arab World," and that we don't want them to detach themselves from it, just as we ourselves are and will always remain part and parcel of the broader "Jewish World." We must help them by whatever means necessary to cultivate their heritage, and must make a conscious effort to get to know this heritage, acquaint our children with it and teach them to respect it. By the same token, we must help the Arabs get acquainted with our Jewish heritage, and thus deepen and widen the areas of mutual understanding between our two peoples.

If obliterate we must, let us obliterate the gap between our respective standards of living, not the differences between our respective ways of life. If fuse we must, let us fuse our educational objectives and establish a common standard of education for Arab and Jew, while respecting the separate linguistic and cultural contents thereof. The future lies not in having the Jew and the Arab "fuse" and be neither Jew nor Arab, but in having both Jew and Arab learn to live together in mutual respect for, and recognition of, the ligitimacy of each other's right to separate identity and with appreciation for the blessings such a pluralistic approach can offer.

But Dr. Abu-Lughod does not pause to consider any of these problems. Obsessed by a phobia of the supposed Jewish sense of "superiority," which, we recall, he tried to read into a number of our activities and ideas, he views our non-fusion as a further manifestation of the same. The philosophic merits or demerits and the ethics of the very ideology of fusion are outside the pale of his interest. So is the discussion of the advisability, even from the Arab point of view, of such fusion in political and cultural terms; or the consideration of the practical difficulties in the way of such fusion and the price to be paid for it.

Let us, for the sake of argument, accept then Dr. Abu-Lughod's statement on his own terms and ask him simply how he expected us to go about the business of "fusion." What on earth should we have done?

Enter Arab villages and settle inside them? Would not he himself be standing at this rostrum and accuse us of expropriating the Arabs and trespassing on their land? Dr. Abu-Lughod knows Arab villages better than I do. He knows how closed, how clannish Arab rural society is (and I say this not by way of criticism but as a statement of fact). Will they want us? Will they accept us?

Or shall we penetrate their townships? We did — in Nazareth, for instance. Weren't we accused of expansionism? We are doing it now in Eastern Jerusalem, and some would wish to do the same in Hebron. Is it so simple?

Or should we perhaps intermarry to seal the "fusion?" Certain individuals did and, as with other cases in this category, some of these unions worked, others did not. But this is the private affair of individuals. So far as public policy and the attitude of the environment are concerned, you, Dr. Abu-Lughod, know as well as I do that the Arabs are opposed to such course of action on religious and other grounds no less than the Jews.

Yet, while fusion is not, and quite properly should not be the ultimate objective of our peoples, I am happy to say that much has been done to raze the walls of alienness that divide us. Paradoxically, the Six Day War served as the most effective catalyst in this process. Though hostilities did not cease, the sense of alienness did; and though the war is still going on, life is going on, too — life of Jews and Arabs together.

Frankly, I consider it the greatest privilege of my life to have lived to be present on June 29, 1967, less than three weeks after the ceasefire order, at what will one day be hailed as the dawn of a new era in the Middle East, notwithstanding the view to the contrary of scheming diplomats in the smoke-filled rooms of Moscow, Paris, London, Washington, and New York.

Dismantled were the barricades and the barbed wire that for so long tore and sliced and chopped the very heart of Jerusalem and the heart of her population. Filled in were the ditches and the trenches, cleared away were the heaps of debris and rubble and removed were the ugly anti-tank dragon's teeth that scarred the streets and the landscape of that beautiful city.

And two tremendous waves of humanity — Arabs from the old City and Jews from the new, who for the past twenty years were facing each other but could not see each other's face through the blank wall of indoctrination, hatred, and fear — streamed toward each other as if an act of spontaneous pilgrimmage to an invisible shrine of human hope and understanding. Sizing each other up with the wise and ageless eye of people who have seen a great deal on their journey through history; relearning to know each other; reviving old and never-really-forgotten acquaintances or eagerly making new ones; and practising on each other the rusty Hebrew and Arabic that had been stored away in hopeful abeyance for almost a generation — they finally became engulfed in each other with the kind of silent exhilaration, never-articulated disbelief, and exuberant sense of discovery that only great moments in history can evoke.

I cannot say that some of my best friends are Arabs; but I do have a number of Arab friends and I cherish their friendship, and I want to believe they, too, value me as a friend. I try to impart this feeling of brotherhood to my children, and even my youngest eight-year old daughter can guide you in the old City of Jerusalem with affection and an at-homeness that few of her Arab peers can match.

Ironically, indeed, never in the past twenty years has there been so much give-and-take — exchanging of goods, services, and ideas, and just plain meeting of Arab and Jew — in Palestine as since the Six Day War. Thousands of Arab students and non-students from all the surrounding countries are allowed each summer to visit Israel and hundreds of Arabs under Israeli rule cross the Jordan River daily to visit their families in Arab countries. Long lines of trucks roll every morning over the bridges, carrying the agricultural produce of the Arabs of the West Bank as far as Saudi Arabia and Kuwait, while West Bank Arab merchants traffic between Jerusalem and Amman using currency of both the Hashemite Kingdom and Israel.

Nothing even faintly approaching the dimensions of present-day Arab-Israel contacts (in terms of daily human activity, as distinct from the political, which monopolizes the headlines) has ever been recorded in the recent history of the two peoples or, for that matter, in the history of wars and military occupations in general. Indeed, just as some of the field operations of the Six Day War will enter the textbooks of military colleges for what they have contributed to the art of modern warfare, so will Israel's unprecedented "open bridges" experiment be studied as guideline for occupation procedures.

This policy which has no peer in human relations in time of war and which amazes every impartial observer and visitor, no matter how vocal or how slanderous the propaganda of the other side, was dictated, I suppose, by a number of political, economic, and psychological considerations. My point is, however, that it also mirrors the fundamental concept which stems from our Zionist upbringing and which I presented here in answer to Dr. Abu-Lughod's insistence on "fusion": our recognition of the cultural unity of the Arab world and our resolve not to force the Arabs under Israeli control to sever their links with their cultural and national hinterland even while Arab guns are firing, just as we on our part do not envisage ever tearing ourselves away from world Jewry. This is why no Israeli considers it a paradox that the same man who was the architect of Israeli victories over the Arabs in 1956 and 1967 also devised the "open bridges" policy. Indeed, that "archvillain" himself, Moshe Dayan, has repeatedly expounded this concept before Jewish and Arab audiences alike.

But Dr. Abu-Lughod claims to have detected another supposedly seamy side of Zionist ideology and, with the verve of one who uncovered a conspiracy, he summons none other but the Foreign Minister of Isreal himself to the witness stand. Mr. Abba Eban is quoted as having admitted that the sovereign State which we, Israelis, have built in Palestine was not meant to serve only the people who reside within its boundaries, but was established for the sake of Jewry everywhere.

Well, there really was no need to enlist the Foreign Minister for a statement of this kind and, even without the "supporting evidence" Dr. Abu-Lughod went to the trouble to produce, no one familiar with Zionist literature and thought would have denied the substance of it. Indeed, the point comes out clearly when our earlier analysis of the Zionist Revolution is pursued to its logical conclusion.

THE JEWISH STATE

In line with our initial stress, we recall, on Jewish homelessness as Zionism's unique point of departure, distinct from that of other national liberation movements, it obviously follows that the State of Israel, the ultimate goal of Zionism, was created (somewhat uniquely, too, to be sure) not solely for those Jews who already had the good fortune and wisdom to make it their home, but, primarily, for those who so far had not, yet are at present, or will be at some future juncture, in need of a haven from physical and/or spiritual persecution.

The tragedy of the Holocaust of the Second World War, which cost Jewry a price so enormous that it defies our grasp, lay precisely in the fact that there was no Israel to serve as refuge for Jews who weren't in Palestine yet, but needed it so desperately.

Now, this does not mean that a condition of actual persecution is a prerequisite for winning for the Jew his entry ticket to the free Jewish State. Israel arose in response to the Jewish need of, but also Jewish desire for, a national home. Hence, the state was built by and for those who either had to come, driven by anti-Semitism of whatever hue, or wanted to, driven by a quest of their own identity, searching for their historical roots and for a place of their own to live a full and creative Jewish life.

Thus (to follow up the example you mentioned yesterday, Dr. Abu-Lughod), if an American Jewish boy, instead of volunteering, say, for the Peace Corps in Guinea or in Cambodia, specifically prefers to perform some service in Israel — where, in the course of helping others, he furthers his own quest for self-understanding, is able to retrace his past, and recover the national and spiritual values of Judaism hitherto missing in his life — then, by all means, he is welcome. Indeed, many have come. But Israel will not fulfill her historic mission unless she remains open forever as a refuge for Jews fleeing persecution.

Alas, this task of rescue is far from done, despite the fact that a quarter of a century has gone by since "the moment of truth," when the appalling dimensions of the Hitlerite tragedy were discovered — a tragedy which, we recall, moved even a Gromyko to expressions of sympathy and desire to help heal the wounds.

Today, in Gromyko's own homeland (which itself was a victim of Hitler's cruelty), the old Czarist affliction, anti-Semitism, is raising its ugly head again, keeping in bondage a Jewish community of two to three million people. It will be a day of rejoicing and thanksgiving in all Jewry when this brutally (or, if you will, subtly) silenced branch of our people is permitted to determine its own future. Israel will receive with open arms all those who decide to be redeemed in their ancient homeland — and, to judge by the frequency of distress calls which even the powerful Soviet machine does not succeed in choking completely, they will be many.

Similarly, Israel is now engaged in the ingathering of thousands of Jewry's lost sons from other countries behind the Iron Curtain, survivors of Nazi cruelty, who on ideological grounds decided to fuse their own future with that of the East European peoples. After having jointly fought the German invader and jointly built the regime of their choice, they lived to see themselves rejected and denounced as "Zionists" by their former comrades-in-arms.

And, last but not least, we keep our gates and hearts open to receive, as we already have in the hundreds of thousands, our brethren whose life is in jeopardy in Arab countries.

Strangely, in his answer to a question yesterday concerning the motives for Jewish emigration from Arab lands, Dr. Abu-Lughod seemed to be unaware of the problem. It is to be regretted that he somehow failed to notice the total disappearance after 1948 of whole Jewries from Arab countries in the Middle East and North Africa, the existence of whose Jewish communities preceded by many centuries the advent of the Arab conquerors and the spread of Islam.

This self-admitted unfamiliarity of our Palestinian Arab colleague with the facts of the past two decades contrasts rather glaringly with the candid (or well-calculated) admission of Yassir Arafat, the Palestinian Arab al-Fatah leader whom we shall quote presently, that as many as a million and a quarter Arabic-speaking Jews (or "Arabs of Jewish faith," as he would have it) "live in what is now the State of Israel." Indeed, it has often been observed that, without it being formally planned, an actual exchange of population has taken place since 1948, with Israel absorbing as many Jewish refugees from Arab lands as there were Arabs who fled their homes in Palestine due to the 1948 hostilities.

It is equally regrettable that Dr. Abu-Lughod missed the sorry headlines in the international press reporting on the tragic conditions of the few thousand Jews who, willingly or not, have remained behind and are now held by certain Arab regimes as hostages in the Arab-Israeli feud. The State of Israel anxiously awaits the day when these unhappy remnants of once-glorious Jewries — innocent casualties of the vindictive reprisal policies of insecure dictatorships — will be set free and redeemed in their ancient homeland.

But let me return to Dr. Abu-Lughod's analysis of Zionism and Israel and to what, if I am not mistaken, was the last black mark he gave us on his grading sheet. The Jewish state, so he feels, is terribly "ghettoized" and cannot help being such. This, he tells us as a political scientist, runs counter to the trend prevailing today.

Frankly, I myself fail to discern, and Dr. Abu-Lughod did not mention, the criterion by which one state is judged to be a "ghetto" while another is not. Is it extent of territory, size of population, cultural vitality, or economic viability? Why should Israel — a country with two and a half million inhabitants and heading soon for the three-million mark — be considered a ghetto, while Lebanon, say, or Libya, or a host of other countries with similar populations are not? What makes Israel a ghetto but exempts, say, Jordan, with lesser resources and a smaller population, from being branded as such?

I am not a political scientist, but I can read, and do, and I observe carefully the international scene. Now, it is true that, ever since the end of the war, certain groups of countries, in Europe and elsewhere, succeeded in creating extremely promising international frameworks of economic and other cooperation, none however designed to replace the national sovereignty of states, be they as large as France or as small as Luxembourg.

It is exhilarating to observe the proliferation of liberated African and Asian nation-states in our generation, some of them so small that they have been dubbed "micro-states." Such states encounter special difficulties to be sure; and they cause difficulties as well. The U.N. has initiated special discussions regarding their seating in the international body, the service they need, etc., etc. In none of the discussions, however, has their supposedly "ghetto-like" character been mentioned, let alone invoked as an argument against their sovereignty.

No, I cannot see how in all earnestness Dr. Abu-Lughod expected us to take this kind of indictment of Israel at face value. Hasn't he, in fact, counted on terms like "ghetto" (or "colonialism" or "white superiority" or, conversely, "revolution") to conjure up in the minds of American listeners images which have nothing to do with the Middle Eastern situation, but, drawn from the charged atmosphere of the present-day social and racial strife in America, are sure to evoke instanteous response and sympathy?

Why should Israel be, by definition, a "ghetto," while, again by definition, her Palestinian Arab replacement proposed by al-Fatah in the same territory and with more or less the same amount of population is not, remains one of the mysteries of "revolutionary" dialectics. Such mysteries Dr. Abu-Lughod apparently feels need not be explained. It is sufficient, in his opinion, to include the "right" adjectives in the definition of the proposed Palestinian state and the rest will take care of itself. When, all that notwithstanding, "the rest" was not entirely clear to some in the audience yesterday and when, in a question from the floor, a passage was quoted from al-Fatah pronouncements which left Dr. Abu-Lughod's definition an empty shell, the answer was that the invoked quotation reflected an old position and was no longer valid. Rhetorical reformulations are, after all, a built-in component of modern revolutions.

So be it then. Let us by all means follow the authoritative and up-to-date texts only and find out exactly what al-Fatah has in store for us in the future. Such texts are not rare, to be sure. Public relations is another built-in component of contemporary radicalism, surely less costly and less exacting than performance in the field.

A full-page advertisement in the NEW YORK TIMES some time ago presented to the American public a carefully-worded explanation of what the al-Fatah concept of a Palestinian state was, using terms very similar to those which served as building blocks for Dr. Abu-Lughod's "vision": "a progressive, democratic, secular state of Jews, Christians, and Muslims" — in that order.

On first reading, one cannot help considering the text with blissful amazement: why, is that not what we all want? On second thought, the amazement turns into disbelief: isn't this what we actually have? Indeed there does exist a "progressive, democratic, secular state of Jews, Christians, and Muslims"; and it exists right now, not in a lecturer's "vision"; and it has a name: Israel! Then, on further thought, one remembers that in the Orwellian 1984-like macabre code of revolutionary dialectics words are used to obscure, not to clarify; carefully chosen and ordered, they serve as weapons for ideas and values entirely different from those which their overt meaning conveys.

"Progressive," sure. I join Dr. Abu-Lughod in despising the corrupt feudal Arab monarchies and, as I said earlier in this discussion, I congratulate him on linking his vision of his people's future to the idea of progress.

But what model of progress does he choose? Developing a cooperative movement? Organizing free workers' unions? Arab counterparts of kibbutzim? Modernization of methods of agriculture? Upgrading of education? Raising the status of the woman in Arab society? Medical and child care for all? In brief: socialism Israeli style? Or is the socialism he opts for patterned after that of the cruel, bloodthirsty, Syrian-Baathist, "progressive" military junta?

"Democratic," wonderful. But according to what model? We already mentioned above the fact that democratic institutions and procedures are practically nonexistent in the Arab Middle East (except for Lebanon), no matter how pompous the pronouncements.

I still have to see a Near Eastern nation conduct a full-scale, uninhibited election campaign, as we did last year under war conditions, and democratically elect a multi-party parliament, as we did, seating equally the elected representatives of minorities (one Arab, in our case, even became the Deputy-Speaker). I still have to find the Near Eastern country which conducts free elections for municipal and village offices as we do on all levels and for all segments of the population, and that has succeeded, as we have, to make the democratic ballot an integral part of the nation's way of life.

Indeed, hardly two years after the Six Day War, 8,000 East Jerusalem Arabs (out of 30,000 eligible) cast their vote along with their new Jewish neighbors, while in the previous municipal elections under Jordanian rule a mere 3,000 cared to exercise their democratic right. The Jerusalem case is even more instructive, considering the terrorist campaign of threats, bombings, and personal assaults which was conducted by the "revolutionary" exponents of "progress" and "democracy" and was designed to intimidate the Arab voters and keep them away from the polls. I leave it to this audience to ponder whether, of all people, the al-Fatah radicals, however effective their public relations, are qualified better than Israel to guide our country in the art of building a "progressive" and "democratic" state.

But there is a third adjective in the definition of the revolutionary Palestinian "vision" of a state: "secular." That adjective was even less innocently planted than the previous two. Just as the earlier-discussed indictment advanced the a priori assumption that Israel, simply by being a Jewish state, was ipso facto "ghettoized," so was also the "secular" slogan cleverly designed to stir up in Christian minds the age-old religious resentment (conscious or not) against a Jewish state for being, according to old preconceptions, a religious state, a "theocracy."

What is it that makes the Arabs supposedly better guardians of secularism than we are? Is it the fact that, on seizing control in 1948 of the ancient Jewish Quarter in the old city of Jerusalem, they wantonly blew up all the deserted Jewish synagogues? Or that they defiled our ancient burial ground on the Mount of Olives? Or that, in defiance of the armistice agreement, they never allowed the Jews access to the Western (Wailing) Wall? Do these great feats bestow on them the mantle of archsecularists?

Or is the Arabs' claim to secularism based on the fact that, all through the nineteen years of Jordanian rule, prestige mosques were erected opposite churches, as well as on the main squares of Christian townships and villages, and amplifiers were mounted on every minaret to blare Muslim prayers and sermons into captive ears, Muslim and non-Muslim alike? Or are, in the cynical mood of the present-day international game, the Arabs' calls for Pan-Islamic conferences and their threats of *jihad* (holy war) against us such signal achievements as to qualify the Arabs as standard-bearers of secular statehood in Palestine?

The brazen cynicism of the definition of the proposed Palestinian state reaches its peak in the clause stating that the future "secular" state is to consist "of Jews, Christians, and Muslims."

Now, by what curious twist of dialectics has the insistence on a secular state in Palestine been combined with the use of a religious criterion for defining the parties to the Palestine feud and to its solution — unless, that is, the combination was cleverly designed for hopefully receptive foreign ears? Wasn't it meant to be a paraphrase of the popular concept of America as the secular state of Protestants, Catholics, and Jews — a deliberately misleading paraphrase, to be sure, intended to bluff the American listeners who, since they could not be expected to grasp immediately the fundamental difference in goals and circumstances, would hardly object to an arrangement that proved constructive and just in their own society?

Dr. Abu-Lughod knows well that the two cases do not resemble each other. Those who eventually built America were fleeing religious persecution by European nation-states which insisted on conformity to state religion. Hence, the American pioneers consciously threw off their erstwhile national allegiance in order to mold a new nation with religious freedom for all. The clash in Palestine is of an utterly different nature: it is a clash of two peoples who insist on their respective national self-determination in that country.

There is no conflict in Palestine between the respective religious allegiances to the Jewish faith, to Christianity, or to Islam, which al-Fatah supposedly proposes to bring to an end through the creation of a secular state with freedom for all three faiths, but a conflict between two national allegiances: a conflict between Jews (in the national sense) and Arabs, the latter both Christian and Muslim. The particular conflict, the one that is truly reponsible for the suffering and despair of both sides, cannot be justly or practically solved except through freedom of national self-determination and the right to national sovereignty for both peoples; but al-Fatah rejects that solution. Rather, as we shall realize in a while, it intends to crush it, through the imposition of Arabism on all parties.

There is no religious war in Israel. Not even Dr. Abu-Lughod, bent as he was on expending his list of supposed Zionist evils, could or did claim there was one. Never has the Holy Land — a country with a long history of rather unholy religious strife — witnessed such full freedom for all creeds and such complete absence of interreligious tensions as in these recent post-Six Day War years. Not even the burning of the al-Aqsa Mosque in Jerusalem by a deranged Christian sectarian succeeded in stirring up a religious upheaval, though God knows what desperate attempts were made by certain circles to capitalize on the event.

To be sure, interreligious warfare is by no means unknown in this world of ours.

Blood is still sporadically being spilled, so we read in the papers, between Hindus and Muslims, though this, incidentally, prevents neither India nor Pakistan from self-righteously preaching to us how to conduct our relations with the Arabs. Blood is being spilled, so we see on television recently, between Protestant and Catholics in Northern Ireland. And religious strife is going on in Africa between Muslims and Christians or animist Negro tribes.

Closer home, tensions between Muslims and Christians mar the daily life of Lebanon, undermining the very foundations of the political structure of the country and greatly endangering the tenuous balance between the two major religious communities (and a number of lesser sects).

Against this general background of still more infrequent religious animosities, and especially against the background of the recent flare-up in Lebanon, which proved extremely dangerous despite the built-in political safeguards enjoyed there by each religious community, the peace prevailing between the different creeds in Israel stands out more prominently than ever. Conversely, the al-Fatah formula for Palestine, on the face of it somewhat reminiscent of the Lebanese arrangement yet failing even to recognize the need for incorporation of Lebanon-patterned political safeguards (for what little they're worth), will require a great deal of explaining before it can claim the serious attention of people who have some experience with inter-group relations in the region.

For what does al-Fatah's (and Dr. Abu-Lughod's) "vision" of a Palestinian state really mean, now that we have peeled off its assortment of enticing marketing labels? Since Dr. Abu-Lughod himself chose not to elaborate, yet bluntly rejected as obsolete and inaccurate an interpretative statement that was read to him yesterday by someone in the audience, we shall be well-advised to offer here another quote, one that will, I take it, win our colleague's *imprimatur*.

Well, Dr. Abu-Lughod will agree with me that Yassir Arafat is not *passé* yet and his dictum should carry some weight in the Palestinian Arab camp (though one never knows for sure how things stand at a given moment in revolutionary cabals). Let us therefore summon the leader himself and have him render an authoritative exposé of Palestinian Arab intentions.

In an interview reported in FREE PALESTINE, a publication of al-Fatah in Great Britain, Miss Salma al-Khalili posed to Yassir Arafat a number of leading questions, thus giving al-Fatah an opportunity to state precisely its position. Elated by what seemed to her Arafat's exceptional tolerance, she asked how he reconciled al-Fatah's offer to the Jews of Palestine of a "progressive, democratic state for all" with the al-Fatah slogan, "Long Live Palestine, Arab and Free." The following was his answer (part of which we have already mentioned above):

> The word 'Arab' implies a common culture, a common language, and a common background. The majority of the inhabitants of any future State of Palestine will be Arab, if we consider that there are at present 2,500,000 Palestinian Arabs of Muslim and Christian faiths and another 1,250,000 Arabs of the Jewish faith who live in what is now the state of Israel.

So here we finally have the answer, clear and precise. One may, of course, be less ecstatic than Miss al-Khalili in appraising the true quality and the dimensions of the "tolerance" which this definition supposedly reflects (I shall return to the ever more ubiquitous "Odes to Arab Tolerance").

For what about the 1,250,000 remaining Jews "who live in what is now the state of Israel" and cannot claim "a common culture, a common language, and a common background" with the Arab population? It seems that the interpretation read to Dr. Abu-Lughod yesterday from the floor was not obsolete and inaccurate after all and that little room, if any, was left in Fatahland for a "progressive and democratic and secular" self-expression of those others.

Similarly, one may entertain some doubt as to how sincere the exponents of this ideology were in the first place, for they certainly are not so foolish as to expect the 1,250,000 Jews who do meet the "common culture, common language, common background" prerequisite to have gone to the trouble of arranging a veritable exodus from the Arab lands of their birth at the cost of almost all their property and of their citizenship, of suffering and chicanery of all sorts — all that, mind you, for the dubious privilege of becoming "Arabs of Jewish faith" in "what is now the state of Israel" and will obviously cease to be what it "is now." Apparently, these, Jews, too — no "European intruders" even by al-Fatah standard — will have little choice but "love it or leave it."

THE AL-FATAH "VISION" — AN ARAB STATE

But whatever it really means, at least we have it now on good authority: the "progressive, democratic, secular state of Jews, Christians, and Muslims in Palestine" which Dr. Abu-Lughod offered here as his "vision" is an Arab state, pure and simple a state that mirrors Arab culture and is dedicated to its development, speaks the Arabic language and is rooted in the Arabs' historical background and heritage.

Not one of the attributes, so vocally heralded by Palestinian Arab protagonists and their Western cheerleaders as if they were a newly revealed gospel of the Brotherhood of Man, touches upon the essence of that state-to-be. These attributes — be they "coexistence" or even "cooperation of the three faiths," or "progressivism," or "democracy," or "secularism" — are all, at best, guidelines for the state's future political system; at their cynical worst, they are packaging gimmicks which any commission on truth in advertising would summarily throw out as fraud. Arabism, and Arabism alone, is by Yassir Arafat's own admission to be the basis of the state's formation; and the Palestinian Arabs' desire for a sovereign home of their own is the sole justification for wanting to establish it.

Then why not say so, openly, straightforwardly, with honesty and pride? This academic audience, and for that matter any audience, is entitled to have the plain truth and the motives behind it.

Yet, whenever we voice anxiety over the expected fate of those on whose very skin the Fatah formula for the "elimination" of the Jewish state and its replacement with a "Palestinian" (read: solely Arab) one would be written, Arab intellectuals and their zealous Western allies are up in arms: "Now really, how ungrateful can these Jews get? Haven't they taken notice of the fact that present-day Arab spokesmen have publicly dissociated themselves from the throat-slitting vocabulary of yesteryear?" Why, even old-guard Arab politicians have taken to denying they ever had any use for the notorious stock phrases of pre-1967-War Arab propaganda; at any rate, they claim, they never intended the threats to be understood literally. Doesn't such progress constitute sufficient cause for thanksgiving?

When, still unreassured, we keep on insisting that this is a mere change of rhetoric and not of objectives, and that no matter how "progressive" or "democratic" the process, its end result would be the same — the "elimination" of Israel — our argument is pooh-poohed with pious indignation as yet another proof of Jewish paranoia. For how on earth can any people be so insensitive as to overlook the truly gracious and the most reassuring of all guarantees: the Arabs' traditional tolerance?

Ah, Arab tolerance! Singing its praises to unsuspecting and guilt-ridden Western audiences on the campus-symposium circuit has become the daily bread of wandering troubadours who are betting heavily on the shameful neglect of medieval and Middle Eastern studies in our high schools and colleges.

Frequently, though perhaps unwittingly, the task of these Arab spokesmen is made easier by Western (also Jewish) intellectuals, who take masochistic delight in showing medieval Islam free of ghettoes, of racial prejudice and religious persecution, while these social ills continued to plague Christian Europe and eventually communicated themselves by inevitable contagion to the New World.

But even ignoring the fact that such enthusiastic comparisons paint an absurdly idealized picture of the past, omitting the seamy side which was present in medieval Islam as much as in any other society of men, one cannot help wondering at how ahistorical this approach is. For how can we be expected to accept without demurrer the simplistic equation of modern Arab nationalism with the cosmopolitan civilization that was medieval Islam: demographically multinational; culturally and socially pluralistic; richly diversified in the ways of life of its bearers; indeed, far from homogeneous even in matters of religion — a civilization, in brief, which, except for the common vehicle of the Arabic tongue, found itself not infrequently at odds with the narrow interests and objectives of Arabs and Arabism?

Furthermore, how can anyone be expected to take for granted that the medieval example — even if accurately described — be readily projected into our present situation as well?

But, if this idealistic concept of Arab tolerance, held by non-Arab liberals and scholars, provides yet another illustration of incorrigible Western gullibility, the "tolerance" bit sounds rather hollow on the lips of Arab exponents of "Continuing Palestinian Revolution" and their hero-worshipping radical Western allies. Tolerance, indeed! A strangely misplaced feather in the radicals' cap! Don't they under other circumstances choose to dismiss this rather rare commodity as so much "irrelevant" bunk and middle-class hypocrisy? Aren't their ideology and actions an undisguised show of contempt for tolerance?

Ah, but this one, mind you, is not just ordinary tolerance. It is Arab tolerance! Miss al-Khalili, the helpful lady who interviewed Mr. Arafat, was enraptured, we recall, by what seemed to her the Fatah leader's generous display of this quality. Dr. Abu-Lughod's "vision," too, expected us to take historic Arab tolerance for granted, as did another member of the panel, in his cryptic advice to historians to "go and learn more about it." Indeed, he singled out the Arabs as not merely tolerant but endowed (I believe I quote him verbatim) with "innate capacity for tolerance."

Well, I think our colleague's advice to historians is well taken, I would, however, be less than candid if I failed to admit that, precisely as historian, I am extremely wary of ascribing to a people — any people, my own not excluded — an innate capacity for tolerance or, for that matter, an innate capacity for any other specific attitude or behavior.

Innate or not, history is being invoked to prove the point: not merely to show "Arab tolerance" at work in the past, but to suggest on this basis a practical lesson for the present and future, "Let's go back to history," we are told, "back to the Golden Age of Arab-Jewish brotherly understanding." By all means, I say, let us go back to history. Let us, indeed, have a hard look at the historical pattern of Arab-Jewish relations since the rise of Islam and a hard look at "Arab tolerance" which is alleged to have underlain these enviable relations, "before Zionism destroyed it all."

Now, there is no need in this audience to dwell on the general significance of the Arab conquest made in the name of Islam some thirteen to twelve centuries ago, which proved to be a turning-point in the history of three continents. To the Jews, these conquests were a turning-point as well. For centuries, some eighty or perhaps as many as ninety per cent of the world-Jewish population lived in the vast territories which came under Arab dominion, from the eastern limits of Persia to the shores of the Atlantic Ocean.

The Arabs were pragmatic rulers. Like other warriors, past or present, they quickly learned that while it is sometimes easy to conquer, it is always a burden to govern. Having overrun tremendous tracts of well-populated land, they were faced with the onerous business of establishing in them patterns of — well, let's call a spade a spade — colonial rule that would serve the interests and the expansionist goals of the young Arab state and its state religion. (My apologies to the sensitive eardrums of our revolutionary colleagues who prefer to have the term "colonial" reserved for Western villains only.)

The military tasks confronting Arab colonialism were fairly simple to cope with. Not so the chores of government. The difficulties of co-ordinating and supervising the affairs of a host of subject peoples, ethnic groups, and religious communities who, in most cases, could boast greater experience in the complexities of statecraft than their conquerors, loomed ominously large, unfamiliar, and exacting. And the Arabs were not unaware of the fact that they had become heirs to civilizations older, richer, and more advanced by far than their own.

Unwilling to let their military expansion get bogged down in administrative, judicial, and fiscal matters for which they were utterly unprepared at the time, the Arab conquerors preferred to leave the existing administrative structure as intact as considerations of security and state interest allowed.

Given a theological rationale for viewing the recipients of pre-Islamic monotheistic revelation as the "Peoples of the Book" and therefore deserving "protection," it was especially easy for the Arabs to leave the affairs of these monotheistic non-Muslim minority groups entirely to the leadership of the groups themselves.

These "Peoples of the Book" — Jews, Copts, Nestorians, and other Eastern Church communities, whose loyalty to the new regime was unimpeded by debt of allegiance to the defeated formed power-structures in the region and whose conversion to Islam was not insisted upon on principle (as it was in the case of pagan "infidels") because they were already monotheists — were granted protection and self-government in an even larger measure than they had been used to under previous regimes.

To the Jews and to other "protected minorities" in the Muslim world, this autonomy was a burden, though a beneficial and welcome one. A burden, for its undisguised purpose was to leave to communal leadership the tasks of law enforcement and the collecting of taxes due to the realm from individual members of the communities. But welcome it was, because communal autonomy under Medieval Islam went far beyond our modern concept of "freedom of worship." Once the state, guided by its own self-interest and convenience, had turned the supreme Jewish institutions into semi-governmental agencies for tax collection and for the preservation of law and order, it could not help granting them, by the same token, full freedom of intra-communal action and the widest possible control over the members of the community in all fields of public and private activity.

Thus began for the Jews a period of unprecedented growth: in economic endeavor, in religious and cultural development, in building and fortifying a network of closely-knit communities led by state-recognized Jewish authorities. Yet, no matter how great and lasting its blessings, Jewish self-government under Islam was not grounded in any particular "tolerance" on the part of the Arab rulers. Rather, it serves as an illuminating example of how constructive and helpful to all parties is the happy coincidence of plain state interest and a community's potential contribution to it when that community is granted conditions conducive to free development and growth.

Now, I do not claim that such practical motivation makes the beneficial results of this governmental attitude any less important. All I say is we should not romanticize it and spread a myth of "innate Arab capacity for tolerance," when that capacity was neither "innate" — it clearly developed out of sober calculation of state interest — nor an expression of true "tolerance," surely not by present-day standards.

The truth of the matter is that there were two sides to the coin which Arab rulers handed out to their monotheistic, non-Muslim subject communities. While one side read "protection," the inscription on the other spelled "discrimination," and the latter had as strong a legal and theological rationale as the former.

Indeed, there was a clearly-marked price tag on "protection" — both in the literal sense of head-taxes and land-taxes and a goodly number of irregular pay-offs, and in terms of the motives behind such taxation. For while there was nothing intrinsically new in these tax categories, the novelty lay in the plainly discriminatory character of the levies. The new principle enunciated by the Arab rulers, in contradistinction to the previous regimes in the area, was that these taxes were to be levied on non-Muslims alone, precisely because they chose to remain non-Muslim.

Aside, then, from the financial disadvantage involved, these taxes were intentionally designed to segregate "believers" from "unbelievers," to stimulate and encourage conversion to Islam by offering practical advantages, and to serve as official marks of legal degradation, formally and boastfully stigmatizing the non-Muslims as second-rank subjects of the Muslim realm. The same idea expressed itself in the long list of social disabilities rehashed with delight by Arab historians and theologians. These included a number of obligatory outward signs of segregation such as special color of dress (serving eventually as model for the "Yellow Badge" which was later imposed on the Jews in Christian lands), the prohibition of carrying arms, etc.

True, compared with the sorry fate of Jewry under late-medieval Christendom or under modern anti-Semitism, the centuries of Jewish life under Islam present a picture of considerable peace and security. Not that cases of mob action, of physical persecution, or of religious constraint upon the non-Muslim subjects of the Islamic state were lacking. Jewish history and the history of Christian communities under Muslim dominion are replete with such instances, some mere local disturbances, others quite widespread, violent and of long duration. They all, however, can be explained away as exceptions rather than the rule — the rule, that is, of peaceful coexistence through the ages.

Yet, again, the built-in mechanism of that peaceful coexistence was not "Arab tolerance" which appears on closer scrutiny to have had very little of true tolerance in it and hardly deserves the name. What maintained the Arab-dominated coexistence of Muslims, Christians, and Jews was the non-Muslims' agreement to a status of "protected" inferiority, i.e., their conscious act of reconciling themselves, willingly or not, to the position of second-rate subjects, in return for undisturbed internal autonomy, and of relinquishing any political ambitions of their own or any vestige of desire for ethnic-national self-assertion. Only when reconciled to such a position could the Jew or the Christian under Arab domination enjoy the benefits of religious freedom and communal self-government and lead a life of relative security, even affluence, alongside his Arab neighbors.

90

Indeed, whenever the political interests or national aspirations of minority groups clashed with (or were suspected of potentially running counter to) the philosophy of Islamic superiority or the principle of Arabism as the dominant factor in the Arab state, the Arab government would move in swiftly, ruthlessly and unscrupulously, to crush in the bud any such attempts at self-assertion with all the means at their disposal. There was no trace of "tolerance" then, not even the faintest pretense of it — from Muhammand's blood-stained advance through the Arabian peninsula down to our times.

Such is the story of the expulsion of certain Jewish tribes from north Arabia, and the cruel extermination of another Jewish tribe in the same region, by Muhammad himself. Such, too, is the story of the expropriation of Jewish lands in Arab-conquered Palestine in the seventh century. And such is the story of the seizure, in the same century, of the Jews' most hallowed ground, the Temple Mount in Jerusalem, and its conversion by the Arabs, for political reasons and without any valid historical or religious basis, into a Muslim holy place.

In a similar category is Salah-a-Din's deliberate move, in the late twelfth century, to clutter the area facing the Western Wall with Muslim houses and to appropriate the Wall itself as a pious Muslim endowment (Waqf). Such was the political struggle waged against our freedom to worship at the Wall by the British administration in Palestine. Last but not least, such purely political motives were also behind the Jordanian policy of the past two decades which bluntly denied us access to this holiest relic of our past, in defiance of the armistice agreement.

All these examples, and many more that could be supplied from the past thirteen hundred years of history, of politically inspired actions in a domain which to the Western mind is clearly religious, suffice to unmask the farce, the perfidy, the brazen cynicism of invoking "Arab tolerance" as the constructive factor supposedly fostering a relationship of mutual respect and equality among the various population groups in our region.

The peoples who live in the Middle Eastern world know and understand this situation better than the well-meaning theoreticians of Western campuses. The Christian Maronites of Lebanon, to cite one example, do not rely on promises of "tolerance" but jealously guard their hard-won political rights. So do the other groups in Lebanese society. The Kurds, too, prefer to rely on the sword and on effective home-rule of their native area to force Iraqi Arab rulers to stand by their promises. The Druze in the southern mountain-range of Syria, the Negro tribes in southern Sudan, and the host of other ethnic and religious communities that make up the rich and colorful mosaic of Middle Eastern demography — all are on the alert to defend, and eventually expand, what little autonomous foothold they have succeeded in carving out for themselves during the centuries of Arab and Muslim rule in this region.

As has unfortunately been the case in other parts of Asia and Africa, colonial interests for too long a time conditioned the Western world to view the Middle East as a monolith — an Arab monolith, that is — so much so that even the present-day Big-Power policy planners also prefer to base their global strategies on the Middle East's supposed uniformity rather than its intrinsic diversity. While the fallacy of such an approach is being exposed daily by the irreconcilable divisions surfacing even within the Arab camp proper, too little attention is being paid as yet to the rumblings of national and ethnic awakening among the non-Arab and non-Muslim populations of the region. The yearning of these groups for greater freedom and self-assertion will, I predict, grow evermore intense and vocal as the example of restored Jewish statehood in the area and of the liberty and equality of opportunity enjoyed by minorities under Israeli rule spreads its influence.

For while all of the ethnic minorities in this part of the world have made dents of sorts in the thirteen-centuries-old structure of Arab domination, Zionism was the first to actually crack it beyond repair. In this sense, history will one day show, Zionism pioneered for the region as a whole.

ZIONISM: A DISSENT FROM "ARRANGEMENT"

Just as Zionism set about to reverse the 2,000-year-old diasporic course of Jewish history, it has also succeeded more than any other single factor in reversing the historical course of the Middle East set by Arab Islam in the seventh century.

To be sure, Zionism has never really been conscious of the broader role it was performing, nor has it ever deliberately acted, or planned to act, in a way that would go beyond the specific goal of Jewish national liberation. Yet, consciously or not, the Continuing Zionist Revolution shook and keeps on shaking the very foundations of the region as a whole, not merely the little corner of the Mediterranean we call Israel.

For Zionism is, in fact, the exact antithesis of the accommodating "arrangement" which, since the very beginning of Islamic expansion, has lulled the native ethnic groups in the area into accepting their subject status. Zionism did explode the myth of "Arab tolerance" which, while leaving the religio-communal self-government of minorities intact for practical reasons, robbed these minorities of something that transcends religion and community: the sense of peoplehood and of national belonging.

In diametrical opposition to medieval Jewry's conscious act of reconciling itself to second-rank status under Islam, Zionism proclaimed "new" Jewry's ringing triple dissent from the medieval "arrangement": refusing to accept the status of "protected" inferiority; refusing to relinquish political interest in, and claim to, the ancestral homeland; and refusing to forego ethnic-national self-assertion and the right to sovereignty any longer.

We do not sit in judgment over our fathers. Nor do we presume to know that under the circumstances prevailing in those early centuries we ourselves would have opted for another solution. Indeed, there is no telling whether another solution was at all available or whether our medieval ancestors had any other way open to them except to agree to a covenant of "protection." For all we know, through such agreement they may have saved Jewry and Judaism from the fate that befell a number of now-forgotten ethnic-national and religio-cultural groups which, in centuries past, led a life of their own in the Middle East and in North Africa. Bulldozed by the overwhelming onslaught of Islam, these groups eventually lost their separate identity and ceased to exist.

Moreover, our medieval forbears proved themselves quite capable of making the best of the given situation. They fortified and creatively expanded Judaism and the Jewish way of life from within, so that we here, a full thirteen hundred years later, could proceed from a position of inner strength to devise better patterns for our future. But more than this, they themselves became participants, as it were, in the Middle Eastern Arab way of life. Bowing to what seemed to them inevitable, and realistically assuming the low profile that their second-rate status called for, they eventually succeeded in promoting a mood of Arab-Jewish cooperation, useful to their masters and indispensable for their own survival.

No, indeed, we do not sit in judgment over our fathers. Yet, by the same token, we also do not feel bound today by solutions which our fathers found acceptable, perhaps inescapable, at the time. Nor must anyone consider such solutions irrevocably and irreversibly binding upon us.

To be sure, we would welcome a renewal of the spirit of Arab-Jewish co-operation in our lives and the lives of our neighbors. Bu such co-operation must, from now on, be based on a relationship other than the inequality epitomized by the medieval Islam-oriented "arrangement." We — as well as the Arabs — have broken out of the medieval framework in so many fields and in so many ways that there can be no question of "going back" to the concepts and practices of yesteryear. Make no mistake: those yesteryears which, in the eyes of some romantics, appear to have been a glorious era of internal growth and of brotherhood proved for the Jews to be, in fact, an era of inglorious degradation and of national, social, and legal inferiority, despite which, there was internal growth and brotherhood.

Moreover, not only was the historical pattern of Arab-Jewish relations considerably less idyliic than some would like us to believe and, indeed, hardly worthy of imitation, but the very "appeal to history" cannot help being in our case but an excercise in futility and self-deception.

History, like modern computers, cannot retrace, nor can it program for future reference, that which has not been fed into it by the course of time and by the succession of events, situation, and personalities. To appeal to the history of Muslim-Jewish relations in search of a constructive precedent to help us out of the present impasse is to appeal for goods which history simply cannot deliver. The truth of the matter is that history has no precedent for the situation we are in now.

The thirteen hundred years of our experience under Islam, from the rise of Muhammad and the successive Arab conquests after his death until as late as 1948, knew but one pattern of relationship between Arabs and Jews (or, later, Muslims and Jews): the relationship between rulers and subjects — Islamic rulers that is, and Jewish subjects. Whether the rulers were benevolent or not, generous or not, tolerant or not, did, of course, carry great weight at the time and continues to be of interest today as a matter of historical record; for the purpose of our present discussion it makes little difference. The one and only point of relevance in our context is that the rulers always were on the Islamic side of the fence; the Jews always remained subjects.

Never prior to 1948 had there been a confrontation of Muslim rulers and Jewish rulers, of sovereign Muslim Arab states and a sovereign Jewish state in their midst; and never had Arabs been subjected to Jewish rule, as has been the case since the establishment of the state of Israel. In brief: the situation created by Zionism is truly unparalleled in the annals of Arab-Jewish relations since Muhammad.

Hence, my friends, all the "Let's-go-back-to-history" pleas, even where motivated by genuine concern for the welfare and peace of the region (and I shall not be entirely wrong in suspecting that not all of them can be classified as such), are simply out of order. They prove how inadequately the effect of the Zionist Revolution on the Middle East as a whole and on the future general patterns of relations between Muslims and non-Muslims has been grasped, even by those with the best of intentions.

In fairness to the Muslim Arab leaders let it be said that they do read the signs correctly. The frantic calls for "de-Zionization" of the Middle East, repeatedly issued by those who form part of the Arab-dominated status quo or by outsiders who, because of vested interests of their own, are bent on preserving and exploiting this status quo, would not possibly have reached such a pitch had they been directed only against the two or three million Jews who stepped into the Arab beehive. The hysterically bellicose anti-Israeli posture of precisely the weakest — because the least homogeneous and internally the most insecure — Arab regimes clearly indicates their awareness of the fact that the impact of the Zionist Revolution travels far beyond the confines of Palestine proper. The writing on the wall cannot be mistaken. Zionism is not only a point of no return for the Jewish people. It also portends the irreversible process of decolonization of the Middle East as a whole — release, that is, from the Muslim Arab domination which imposed itself on the region thirteen centuries ago by way of military, religious, linguistic, and cultural conquest.

This decolonizing process must not, of course, be visualized as a blanket reversal of the region's history. No matter how arbitrary their initial conquest, Arabism and Islam have proved in the long run to be an extremely beneficial and enriching force in our part of the world and they are there to stay. And while for some ancient groups, already totally submerged by the all-engulfing wave of Islam, decolonization comes too late, new populations have arisen in the region through the years — the Palestinians are one such instance — who, precisely under the impact of Arabism and Islam, legitimately claim the right to full self-assertion and to national sovereignty of their own.

However one looks at it, the situation will never be the same again. Jewry will never be the same now that Jewish independence has been restored in the State of Israel. The Arab people can never be the same. Nor can the Middle East itself, or, for that matter, the world. Accustomed for so long to a certain image of the "Jew" and to certain preconceptions regarding Palestine and Jerusalem, the world will have to unlearn a great deal before it can reap the fruits of the new situation.

But what of now? Am I then saying that, with Palestine and the Middle East undergoing a total restructuring of their patterns of life and thought, there can be no immediate remedy to the woes caused by the Arab-Israel conflict?

In a way, this precisely is what I am saying. As in a Greek tragedy, both sides must play out their parts, and their clash is inevitable — inevitable, because it is a clash of two legitimate nationalisms over a country which each side legitimately cherishes as its own. They will both have to attain first that measure of inner strength and political self-assertion which may allow themselves to temper their self-centered aspirations and embrace a cause larger than themselves. That larger cause is there, waiting to be embraced: the cause of historic Palestine as a whole in which both our peoples will live alongside each other, combining their efforts and resources to build a better future.

There is nothing intrinsically wrong or illegitimate in the bona fide insistence of Palestinian Arabs on their right to national self-determination, and there is no need to hide this insistence under a heavy coat of fashionably radical makeup. That right was indeed recognized by the United Nations when on November 29, 1947, it recommended that an Arab state be created in Palestine, along with a Jewish state, following the expected termination of the British Mandate in May, 1948.

What is wrong and illegitimate is that this Arab insistence on the Palestinian Arab's right to statehood was blended with an insistence of another kind: the insistence that the prospective Arab state be the sole sovereign unit in Palestine and that, therefore, a Jewish state be denied the right to exist there. That other insistence, backed as it regrettably has been by twenty years of hostility and war, has hurt the Palestinians more than anyone else, indeed deprived them of statehood altogether. And that insistence is, as we have seen, still very much in evidence in the above-discussed al-Fatah formula, no matter how subtly it is phrased now and no matter how carefully it refrains from the crude slogans of yesteryear about throwing us into the sea.

For, truly, it was not the creation of Israel in 1948 that deprived the Palestinian Arabs of sovereignty by the armies of outside Arab states who, under the pretext of saving the country from "Zionist expansionism," encroached on the territory originally alloted to the Arab state-to-be and annexed it.

Take the case of the West Bank and Jerusalem. Indeed, one who listens these days to the chorus of indignant voices on campuses and in the august forums of the United Nations — including some very respectable voices which should know better — demanding that Israel return the West Bank and Jerusalem to Jordan, their supposedly "rightful" owner, cannot help pondering how conveniently short man's memory is. It is encouraging therefore to observe a Palestinian Arab perform a belated but honest post mortem, seeking to draw a lesson from past mistakes and present delusions and, first and foremost, to set the record straight.

> "It is astonishing," writes Aziz Shihadeh, a respected attorney from the city of Ramallah (north of Jerusalem), in the October, 1969, issue of the NEW MIDDLE EAST (London), "how historical facts have been distorted. It seems to be forgotten that when Jordan made an attempt to annex the Palestinian West Bank, she was threatened with expulsion from the Arab League. It was the subject of a heated controversy at the Arab League Council in April, 1950, which then took the following decisions: To reaffirm that the entry of the Arab armies into Palestine for the purpose of saving it should be of temporary measure, free from any characteristics of occupation and partition . . . "

The rest is fairly recent history which one would expect to be still fresh in the memory of people of my generation.

Jordan defiantly proceeded to annex the old City of Jerusalem and the rest of the West Bank, thus greatly enlarging the territorial extent of the then-newly-established Hashemite Kingdom and noticeably altering the character of its population. Yet the new state remained no less an artificial creation of British imperialism than had been the original Trans-Jordanian Emirate, itself a part of historical Palestine, arbitrarily severed by Britain from the more populous and advanced West Bank just a few years after the British wrested Palestine from the Turks.

The Hashemite annexation of territories which were designed by the 1947 resolution to be included in the Palestinian Arab state and in the international zone of Jerusalem was never recognized by any international body: neither by the United Nations, nor by the United States or the other great powers (except for Britain, of course), nor by the non-Arab Muslim states (with the exception of Pakistan), nor even by the Arab states themselves! The reluctantly "Jordanized" Palestinians, for their part, made the Palestinian half of the crown weigh heavily on the Hashemite king's brow.

All this, one would suppose, is common knowledge — or is it? For, lo and behold, no sooner had the Israelis seized the West Bank in the Six Day War, in response to Jordanian attack, when the Jordanian defiance of international resolutions and of intra-Arab agreements just described became the subject of an intriguing case of international amnesia.

Strange bedfellows pooled their resources and efforts to make everyone forget everything, to bully us into "returning" the territory to a nation which had had no business being in that territory in the first place and which had used it as a springboard for attacking our towns and villages. Self-anointed high priests of international justice and self-appointed policemen of world order — themselves holding on to territories captured as far back as a quarter of a century ago (and not from the German or Japanese aggressors alone) — began lecturing us that territorial adjustments must not reflect gains from military victories, even though, by international law, this rule does not obtain wherever such gains resulted from wars waged in self-defense and when the erstwhile possession of the territory by the defeated party was in itself unlawful.

Well, victories in general aren't the "in" thing these days, especially when even great powers find them hard to achieve. "Western" victories are so much less fashionable, even to Western eyes. Jewish victories are apparently the least palatable of all!

RETURN OF THE PALESTINIANS

Paradoxically, however, our June, 1967, victory not only brought territorial adjustment to us. It was also a great boon to the cause of Palestinian Arab national self-determination, which had been out of the hands of the Palestinians for twenty years.

In having brought to nought the results of the 1948 Arab invasions of Palestine, the Six Day War, a turning-point to so many parties on so many counts, resuscitated the independent spirit of the Palestinians. Tired of being browbeaten by their own brethren and used by them as pawns in a cruel game of international politics, the Palestinian Arabs reasserted themselves with a vigor which the neighboring Arab states, even more than the Israelis, can hardly afford to overlook.

Indeed, against the Israeli defense system the Palestinian Arab militants have so far had a limited effect, amounting to no more than nuisance value, notwithstanding their hasty promotion by a generous international press to the rank of "commandos." They have surely failed to achieve inside Israel what must be their primary aim as a guerrilla organization: the stirring up of a popular uprising. Their actual successes have been confined to sporadic acts of terror against the civilian population (mostly Arab), and even their spectacular attacks on international airways, though endangering many innocent lives, can in no sense be interpreted as military victories. The stunts hit the headlines of news magazines, not the defense lines of Israel and Zionism.

Ironically, then, it is in the Arab states proper, not in Israel, that the political and military presence of the Palestinians had become a dominant, inescapable fact of life, casting a dark and ever-lengthening shadow on Arab establishments, the "progressive" ones not excluded. This "Palestinian presence" surely will have to be taken into account as a weighty factor — eventually, I believe, as a constructive force — in any future plan for our region. I say this despite the fact that, for the time being, regrettably, those who pass for Palestinian spokesmen still cling, even more tenaciously than the older leaders, to anti-Israeli ideologies which are bound to prove as disastrous as those of the past.

ISRAEL: THE PALESTINIANS' NATURAL ALLY

Consequently, I for one, exercising my democratic right to differ with the official position of the Israeli government, despite my deep appreciation of the tactical prudence and the short-range political advantage inherent in the government's position, welcome the revitalized presence of Palestinian Arabs on the Middle Eastern scene and sincerely hope that a meaningful dialogue can and will before long be initiated between them and ourselves.

True, they must not hope to set back the clock of history. History is a stern teacher. In irrevocably turning present into past, history, as it were, puts us on notice that matters of war and peace are a deadly serious business, not a game that can be started all over again at will, when, contrary to expectations, a previous exercise has misfired. There is no "going back" — neither to the terms of the 1947 solution, torpedoed by the Arabs themselves in 1948, nor to the situation of June 4, 1967, no matter how violently the Arabs and their Soviet patrons insist upon it.

But while the circumstances and the exact conditions of the opportunity for Palestinian Arab statehood that was wasted in 1948 cannot be duplicated, the validity of the Palestinian Arab claim to sovereignty has not expired. Indeed, it is my considered judgment that, however explosive the post-Six Day War situation has been made by the dangerous meddling of outside powers, it is definitely auspicious for a new Palestinian Arab start — provided the Palestinians want it to be really new, free at last of the bear's hug of the neighboring Arab states, and provided they are ready to turn boldly to the one and only natural ally they have in the field: the Israelis.

A PLEA FOR A PALESTINIAN ARAB SISTER-STATE

Yes, now that Jewry's centuries-old hope and struggle for restoration of its sovereignty in Palestine had been achieved and Israel exists as the viable framework for Jewish national self-assertion and creativity, the cause of peace in Palestine — hence also the cause of the Jewish state in Palestine which needs that peace and wants it desperately — will best be served by our helping the Palestinian Arabs to emerge from their sorry plight into a position of sovereign statehood.

The Palestinian Arab state-to-be cannot and should not come in lieu of Israel, as Dr. Abu-Lughod and his friends would like it, clearving as they still do to an idea which for twenty years has caused futile bloodshed and suffering to all sides and which remains as unjust and unattainable now as it ever was. The Palestinian Arab state should rise and live and flourish alongside the State of Israel, cooperating with Israel for the progress and welfare of both peoples.

Most important: the Palestinian Arab sister-state could ally with Israel in a supreme effort to remove the Near East — an age-old victim of clashes between world empires — from the firing-line of Big-Power confrontation and save the region and the world from the inevitably devastating consequences of such a clash.

THERE IS A PALESTINIAN ARAB STATE NOW

The attainment of that state in the historical march of our two Palestinian peoples toward their respective sovereign future alongside each other is not as distant or as fantastic as it might seem. There is indeed a Palestinian Arab state in existence right now: the so-called "Kingdom of Jordan" — so-called, I say, for never in history has there been a state or nation by that name.

Now, what is "Jordan?"

Her territory, we recall, is part and parcel of historical Palestine. The majority of her inhabitants are Palestinians. Her economy, her educational system, and institutions, along with a great deal of her political life (an exception being the king's Bedouin army) are dominated by Palestinian talent, money, and personnel. What is more, al-Fatah and the other Palestinian Arab militant organizations do as they please on Jordanian territory, having in fact virtually created a state within the state.

No matter what name they give the new state structure on the East Bank, let the Palestinians assert themselves therein and assume responsibility in all domains of fullfledged statehood, independent of the surrounding Arab states; let them take upon themselves the duties along with the liberties and privileges they already enjoy; let them agree to sit down with us at the negotiating table and discuss peace and cooperation like equal sovereign sister-states, not like victors and defeated — and I assure you that together we shall devise an "open frontier" formula for peace which will give full satisfaction not only to the East Bank population but to the West Bank Arabs as well and, yes — I say this without hesitation — will open new vistas even to those Arabs who for the past twenty years have been citizens of Israel.

THE "OPEN FRONTIER" VISION

A thousand times more than the "open bridges" policy maintained during this time of hostilities, a wise and generous "open frontier" arrangement in time of peace would be wonderfully effective in bringing together the resources, skills, and capital of the two partners for the common good, and in facilitating the attainment of the national aspirations of both peoples. The effects of such a policy would amaze the world.

Such a bi-state arrangement (as distinct from the tri-denominational or even the bi-national) would serve as a natural starting-point for constructive projects aiming at ever broader regional cooperation in the economic, technological, scientific, and cultural spheres. In fact, it may blaze the trail for — why not dream? — a Middle Eastern Common Market and other frameworks of regional cooperation, from as far west as Greece to as far east as Iran. Without infringing on the sovereignty of the individual member-states, it could lead the peoples of the Middle East and the eastern Mediterranean basin toward the brighter future they deserve.

Sure, Dr. Abu-Lughod, the "Siamese twin" states that I propose here as my own vision will be progressive (and I truly mean that, without quotation marks). They will be democratic, of course (and here again I use the term in its old, conventional sense). Indeed, they may eventually become the nucleus of some future United States of the Middle East in which Christians, Muslims, Jews, and, for that matter, all their diverse sects and sub-denominations, will find that their respective religious divergences in no way conflict with their national identity or impair the privileges and liberties that citizenship in their state bestows upon them. For, unlike your "vision," Dr. Abu-Lughod, the progress and the democracy and the well-being of one will not be built on the "elimination" of the other.

And so, unlike a Greek tragedy, our situation bears hope. And if the Arab-Jewish past cannot supply us with a precedent, we can, I believe, gain some insight by way of analogy from the broader sense of our region.

Like the Turks and the Greeks, we may be in for a long period of no-war, no-peace, our two nations pitted against each other with clenched fists and anger in their eyes, biting their lips and burying their dead, grimly determined to stand fast, until — yes, until they realize that neighbors need not necessarily love each other in order to fight together against a common enemy and until each side discovers it can profit far more from the other side's experience than from its own pride.

Only then will a real solution emerge. And only then will there come also that which you, Dr. Abu-Lughod, pronounce *as-salaam* or *as-sulh* and which I call *shalom*, but which we all must understand and accept as PEACE.

INTRODUCTION

The Middle East conflict is not only marked by the ideological confrontation between Arab nationalism and Zionism, but also by the clash between diverse societies, each with deep, distinct religious, racial and social convictions. Thus, theological and ethnical factors, having joined the cause of nationalism, inevitably contribute to the widening abyss between the antagonists.

Arab society is not homogeneous either religiously or ethnically. It consists of both Moslems and Christians, Arabs and non-Arabs. Of the seventy million inhabitants of the Middle East, about ten percent are Christians of various denominations. And among both Christians and Moslems significant populations come from non-Arab stock.

Yet Islam, as a religion, plays a significant role in Arab nationalism, and the "Pan-Islam" idea of bringing under one flag all Moslems (from Indonesia to Morocco) is one of the pillars of Arab political ideology. In part, therefore, the Arab desire to restore control over Palestine is motivated by Islam's historical and traditional links to the area, and particularly to Jerusalem with its sites which are sacred to Moslems as well as to Jews and Christians.

While Islam lends a clerical coloring to Arab nationalism, the "Pan-Arab" notion is seeking the unity of all Arab people on the basis of their racial, cultural and linguistic heritage, rather than their religious heritage. This call for Arab unity does not stem from any special affinities between Islam and Christianity, but rather from demographic and political realities of the Middle East. Diverse religions and races have long been intertwined in the Levant. Moslem acceptance of large Christian populations is based not only on a history of relative religious tolerance, but also on present-day pragmatic considerations, while Christian adoption of Arab nationalism is partially motivated by fear of pressure and persecution by the majority.

Arab nationalists point with pride to their willingness to accommodate different religious and ethnic elements. This secularism, they claim, furnishes safeguards for Christian populations, sites and interests in the Holy Land. Relying on their Christian populations for support, the Arabs have thus sought to enlist the sympathies of world Christianity to their cause.

Zionism, on the other hand, is by definition the political ideology of a single

99

group collectively known as the "Jewish people." This ethnic assertiveness is intimately related to the theological context of Judaism and it is from these two that Zionism derives its spiritual nourishment and moral guidance. Jewish nationalism assumes that Jews can live fully Jewish lives only in the "land of their fathers" which houses shrines and traditions of incomparable sacredness. Since the possibility of assimilation or persecution, or both, is ever present in the Diaspora, the preservation of Jewish and ethnic life requires, according to the Zionist doctrine, that every Jew emigrate or at least foster emigration to Israel.

While the Arab-Israeli conflict exists mainly on the political plane, the antagonists, to further their opposing claims, have deliberately sought to Islamize, Christianize, and Judaize the confrontation by appeal to racial and religious symbols and interests world wide. The Arabs have accused Israel of "racial," "anti-Islamic," and "anti-Christian" activities, while the Israelis have accused the Arabs of "anti-semitism" and disregard for Jewish holy places.

The Arab position is expressed in two selections. The first contains excerpts from Khalid Kishtainy's VERDICT IN ABSTENTIA published as Palestine Essay No. 11 by the Palestine Liberation Organization Research Center (no date). The author deals with alleged "Anti-semitic Blackmail" which is being utilized by the Zionists aiming to promote the cause of the Jewish State. Translated from the French, the second selection was published in Beirut by the Fifth of June Society in February, 1969. The author, Jibran Majdalany, discusses the racial and religious aspects of Zionism and the Jewish State and the emergence of anti-Arabism as a new form of racialism. It also offers "a way out of the impasse."

The first Israeli selection is from Dafna Dan's ARAB RACIALISM published in Jerusalem by Keter in 1969. It describes the Arab efforts to indoctrinate students with racial and religious hatred against Jews, Zionists, and Israelis. The second selection, published by the Israeli Ministry for Foreign Affairs on September 30, 1969, contains excerpts of Arab writings on racial and religious issues. These statements are selected from Arab mass media in Egypt, Jordan, Syria, Lebanon, Libya, and Iraq.

THE
ANTI-SEMITISM
BLACKMAIL

Khalid Kishtainy

Israel was established after the savage bestiality meted out to the European Jews in a holocaust which stunned all men of good will. So great was the evil that its guilt seeped through to the soul of every civilised individual who inherited the heritage of the western world. Men of letters and thought became apprehensive of anything that might hurt the feelings of the victims. The Zionists, ever ready to exploit any opportunity, used this apprehension in the service of their own machinations. Anti-Semitism was reckoned by both Jew and gentile, Zionist and anti-Zionist as the best ally of Jewish nationalism. None of the Zionist leaders disputed this fact, although some of them paid lip service and condemned it. In fact, Theodor Herzl recommended the anti-Semites as prospective agents who would look after the interests and properties of the Jews following their departure to Palestine. "The anti-Semites will become our most dependable friends, the anti-Semitic countries our allies," he wrote to Count de Hirsch.(1)

Yet the Zionists have used anti-Semitism so effectively that the cry of anti-Semitic has become the ghost which haunts the mind of any judicious politician or writer who has dared to raise his voice or to doubt the words of the Jewish Agency. It is for this purpose that the WZO keeps the memories of the Nazi concentration camps aflame. Matzpen, the Israeli Socialist Organisation, observed:

"The relation between Zionism and anti-Semitism is surrounded by an emotional smoke-screen which deters many people, including Jews, from voicing their apprehensions concerning Zionism. This reluctance is well known to the Zionist public relations men who draw and harp on it incessantly. Often this harping becomes indistinguishable from emotional blackmail."(2)

This is why Eichman was hunted and his trial dragged on to the point of dreariness. This is also the justification for the excessive sums of money spent on tracking down the Nazi war criminals. Exhibitions of relics, letters, pictures and films of the concentration camps and gas ovens continue to tour the world to the revulsion of the younger generation of Jews.

There is no simpler way to win the sympathy of the public than to place any sign of opposition within the picture of this revolting anti-Semitism. True to the fashion of the commercial advertiser, the term has become a trade mark which is worth a lot and which should never be changed. Although the question may be simply one of anti-Israelism, anti-Zionism, anti-Judaism or anti-religion, it should be still called anti-Semitism in every case. The Arabs who are certainly nearer to being Semites than the American Jews, are accused by the Zionists of anti-Semitism. Edward Attiyah and other Arab publicists drew attention to the contradiction, an effort which is meaningless as the term denotes no more than the trade name of Coca-Cola or Nescafe. In fact, many anti-Zionist Jews who have defended the Arab case have been accused of anti-Semitism.

The Zionist publicity officer achieved a formula by which he made anti-Semitism, anti-Judaism and anti-Zionism one and the same thing. The result was simply breathtaking. In an atheistic state like the Soviet Union, religion is a customary target for Marxist ideologists, and the Orthodox Christian Church has been mercilessly subjected to attacks from countless impetuous young writers. Yet, Kychko's JUDAISM UNMASKED, which was published by the Ukrainian Academy of Sciences, was confiscated from the market by the authorities as soon as the formula of equating anti-religion with anti-Semitism was successfully applied. On the other hand, members of the American Council of Judaism, whose concern was basically over Jewish religious values, were accused of being anti-Semites(3) because of their criticism of Zionism and Israel.

The very obvious pragmatic use of anti-Semitism in blackmailing journalists and public figures can be shown by remembering that people who confessed to be anti-Semitic like R. Crossman, and others who revealed their anti-Semitism in various instances such as A. J. Balfour, Lloyd George and Sir Mark Sykes, received nothing but the highest praise from the Zionists, simply because they supported the Jewish National Home. Even the notorious butcher of the Jewish masses and instigator of the Kishinev Pogrom, the Tzarist Minister of Interior, Count Plehve, had the kindest words from Herzl — "un bien grand homme."(4) Count Plehve happened to write a letter to the Zionist Congress promising his help to the Zionist effort. On the other side of the scale, those who have never shown any trace of an anti-Semitic disposition, like the Labour leader, Mr. George Brown, have been accused of anti-Semitism as soon as they put a spoke in the Israeli wheel. Poland, which is more liberal than Rumania, was the target of the anti-Semitic charge. Far from being criticised at all, the policies of the Rumanian Government received refreshing words from the Zionist press. Rumania was the only socialist state which stood by Israel after the Six-Day War.

A brief study of a few victims of the Zionist outcry of anti-Semitism may throw some light on the obvious purpose of the procedure. The long list of such victims includes James Forrestal, Ernest Bevin, Count Bernadotte, General de Gaulle, George Brown, Christopher Mayhew and most of the leaders of the East European states (Rumania excluded).

James Forrestal, U. S. Secretary for Defence, was a man closely connected with the oil and imperialist interests of the United States. His views were also influenced by the Navy and the general staff who looked at the Arab World as a vital link which should not be lost. His position was simply that of any Secretary of Defence who has to resolve any problem in accordance with the interests and opinions of his country and not the aims or opinions of an exterior force or a minority pressure group. He accordingly endeavored to "lift the Palestine question out of American partisan life."(5) This brought him into clash with the

Zionist strategy of insuring support to the Jewish State by making it an election issue. He automatically became an open target for the charge of anti-Semitism. The Zionists seem to have been determined to make an example of him, and one of the most notorious campaigns of character assassination was launched against him. Two photographers employed by the Zionist Organisation, as revealed by the police after their arrest, shadowed him whenever he went out. His personal life was dragged into the smear campaign, accelerating his psychological break up.(6)

U. S. Ambassador James G. McDonald, one of the devoted Zionist gentiles, knew him personally and visited him during his ordeal. McDonald's remarks on him ran like this:

"He was in no sense anti-Semitic or anti-Israel . . . I am confident that he was then convinced that partition was not in the best interests of the United States. He certainly did not deserve the persistent and venomous attacks which helped to break his mind and body; on the contrary, these attacks stand out as among the ugliest examples of the willingness of politicians and publicists to use the vilest means in the name of patriotism — to destroy self-sacrificing and devoted public servants."(7)

Nevertheless, "He had been," according to his biographer, "marked as the victim of one of the biggest headhunts in the history of Washington politics."(8) He was forced to resign and finally disintegrate and take his own life.

Another of their victims was Mr. Ernest Bevin, the Foreign Secretary in the Attlee Government. Like Mr. Forrestal, he was driven to an anti-Zionist position not by any personal hostility to Jews or Judaism, but by the imperial interests of his country. His biographer(9) explains that Bevin looked at the Middle East as an area inhabited by the Arabs, upon whom a Jewish state could not be imposed. Britain's interests rested more in the millions of Arabs controlling the vital region with all its oil resources, than with a small Jewish community on a few thousand square miles. He, too, incurred the punishment of the charge of anti-Semitism as a result of this position, notwithstanding his long record in the Labour Party and the British Trade Union movement, as a friend of the Jewish community and former supporter of the same Zionist aspirations.

Even more absurd is the same charge against George Brown, who is married to a Jewish wife and who is on best terms with his numerous Israeli and Jewish friends. He caused a problem by insisting on an Egyptian diplomat shaking hands with an Israeli diplomat and friend of his, when both were his guests. The colourful ex-Foreign Secretary must have learnt the lesson of his Labourite predecessors and refrained from saying anything critical of Israel, Zionism or the Jewish community. His only sin was his assertion, during the difficult months in which Britain needed all the good will of the large Arab markets and oil resources, that the Arabs had a case which deserved a hearing. But this was enough for the Zionists to accuse him of treading in the anti-Semitic footsteps of Ernest Bevin. His fear and prudence over the issue deprived the Zionists of the helpful, unguarded statements which they could exploit against him. The press, however, found another weak point against him — his honest indiscretions and drinking habits. George Brown became a fixed figure for ridicule and scandal. He was unfit for office. Mr. Emanuel Shinwell advised that he would be better off in some job in industry.

General de Gaulle is the latest victim. The JEWISH CHRONICLE described his relationship with the Jews as a "love story," as "one of the utmost correctness, even of warm sympathy and understanding." Throughout his life, the General helped the Jews and the Jews rallied to his banner. He became the target of the anti-Semitic smear after his support to the Arabs following the Six-Day War. His speech of November 1967 in which he referred to the "domineering elite" is usually quoted in evidence. Yet, any student of French politics can see that the General was incurring the wrath of the Zionist much earlier than the cited speech. The same JEWISH CHRONICLE article, in fact, says that the disenchantment of the Jews with de Gaulle goes back to the days when he granted independence to Algeria.(10) Interesting to note also that the outcry against de Gaulle was not heard immediately after his press conference of the 27 November 1967 when he attacked the arrogance of Israel and the domination of the Israelites, but rather after the report that he was going to supply arms to the Arabs and maintain his embargo on the shipment of arms to Israel. It was then, on 12 December, that Senator Javits lamented de Gaulle's attack "on people of the Jewish faith in general" and called on the U. S. Government to supply Israel with the Phantoms in reply.

The Zionists dug up Count Bernadotte's past to prove his anti-Semitism and declared to the world that he was cooperating with the Nazis during the war on the final solution. Further independent enquiries revealed that, in fact, the Swedish aristocrat was working for the Red Cross during the war, and his work involved him with Germany in an effort to save, rather than liquidate, varying numbers of Jews. The general public, however, are not given to historical details, an unfortunate fact which enabled the journalists to ridicule men who have no racial prejudice.

The charge against the leadership of the socialist countries is another piece of pragmatism aimed at forcing their governments to grant the Jews (a dead loss for the Zionist cause now) what they have not granted the rest of their peoples, i.e., the right to emigrate and travel abroad at will. No communist can afford to be an anti-Semite with the bulk of his classic works written by Jews and a substantial number of his party workers coming from Jewish origin. In Poland, about a quarter of the Communist Party were Jews before the war, a fact which led a member of the Central Committee, Andrzej Werblan, to attribute the deviations which occurred after the war to the preponderance of the representatives of a minority in the Party. His article was condemned by Gomulka and the rest of the Central Committee.(11) Yet, it was the leadership of the Polish United Workers' Party which received the worst from the Zionist smear campaign. Werblan's article was quoted every time; Gomulka's condemnation of it was omitted every time. The fact is that Wladislaw Gomulka, himself married to a woman of Jewish origin, was the one leader in the People's democracies who made a devastating attack against Israel and its expansionist ambitions soon after the Six-Day War.

Authors and journalists have been accused of anti-Semitism by the dozen, for no genuine reason other than putting forward the Arab case. Professor Miller Burrow's book, PALESTINE IS OUR BUSINESS was libelled as anti-Semitic although its author was himself a Vice-President of the National Committee to combat anti-Semitism. Professor Toynbee, Sir John Glubb, Erskine Childers, Ethel Mannin and Michael Adams have all been accused of anti-Semitism.

Extensive research carried out under different headings in the United States and Britain on anti-Semitism has contributed to the efficiency of the anti-Semitism blackmail mechanism. It has reached such perfection and elaboration that there is practically no escape from its tentacles. George Kirk pointed out that the grasping of a detail or minor incident and then blowing it up into a full scale universal affair is the key to the Zionist propaganda technique.(12) It is, in essence, the basic successful advertising gimmick in which a broken trousers zip, filling the whole television screen, speaks for excellent pork pie, a film more erotic than "Silence," or simply for Hong Kong made buttons — according to the caption. The public are never bothered with the actual position of Gomulka, de Gaulle or Bevin. In fact, it is important that the Zionist publicist does not tell the public at all what it is all about. It sufficed to repeat that Bevin was speaking of the Arab rights because he was an anti-Semite, and that he was definitely anti-Semitic because he said that the Jews "should not jump the queue."

In the age of computers, figures and symbols are all that matter for a world which, thus, ends up with a colossal gap by starting with a minute numerical error. Over the decades of the Jewish question, a wide vocabulary of symbols and terms has emerged. The Zionists exploit this harvest by juggling with the symbols until the colossal gap in information is achieved, thanks to the ordinary writer or speaker who is not mindful of this computer system or its symbols. Thus was de Gaulle accused of anti-Semitism as soon as he used such terms as arrogance and domineering. "Arrogance" happened to be part of the title of a notorious German anti-Semitic society called the Society for Combating Jewish Arrogance, whilst "domineering" is a derivative of "domination," a key word in the "Protocols of the Elders of Zion."

The use of such evocative symbols is abundant in the Zionist propaganda attacks. British opposition to the Jewish Agency's illegal activities after World War II was described by Ben Gurion, not as imperialism or oppression but as "racial discrimination."(13) A similar abuse of terms is the resolution passed by a mass meeting in Israel in 1956 protesting against the demand of the world and the U. N. that Israel should refrain from the annexation of Gaza. The resolution said, "The citizens of Israel . . . strongly protest against the attempts being made in the Assembly and other U. N. institutions to strike at Israel's security and equality of rights by an act of discrimination which constitutes a violation of the charter."(14) The stilted insertion of "an act of discrimination" in this passage is a definite attempt at intimidation.

A similar situation reoccurred in 1968, when the United Nations opposed the military parade in Arab Jerusalem. There was nothing new in the position for the U. N. stood in opposition to all Israeli military parades in Jerusalem as they violated the U. N. decision on the internationalisation and demilitarisation of the Holy City. The 1968 parade made in the Old City and the occupied Arab part drew protests not only from the best friends of Israel but from important sections of the Israeli people themselves. However, Mr. Tekoah, the Israeli delegate to the United Nations, branded Jordan's submission of the issue to the Security Council with the spirit of the Damascus blood outrage. "Now they had chosen Jerusalem as the object of their blood libel."(15)

LE MONDE, which has become the latest target for attack, was described by Mr. Abba Eban as "the most horrible literature of incitement,"(16) incitement being the word normally used in dealing with racial and anti-Semitic holocausts, and incorporated in the British Race Relations Act.

The tacticians of Zionist propaganda have evolved a situation in which you are guilty whatever the answer to the charge may be. If you keep quiet and give no answer you are obviously guilty. If you reply you become even more guilty because you will be attacking Jews. It is a grand "Catch 22" brought from the realms of literature to life. The Zionists needle their victim and provoke him into saying more — and the more he says, the more they point out to the public, "Didn't we tell you?" Their best victims are usually found among the honest, the sensitive, the sincere, the plain-spoken, the innocent, the have-nothing-to-fear people. All the victims already mentioned are known for such qualities.

It is generally accepted that the unwillingness to admit to the U. S. A. the Jewish Displaced Persons was an essential factor in America's pro-Zionist policies after the war. Yet Bevin's blunt comment, "They don't want too many Jews in New York" was thrown at him over and over again as a definite sign of anti-Semitism. It is also admitted that the bitter hostility to Zionism was only revealed by Forrestal and Bevin in their later days after persistent provocation and humiliation.

Writers, politicians and journalists found that the best thing for them to do was to avoid any polemics with the Zionists and swallow their pride in peace if they were ever attacked. The OPINION NEWS reported in 1947 that 30 per cent of American editors supported the partition of Palestine and 50 per cent opposed it. It was also found that 57 per cent of the newspapers refrained, during the same period, from making any editorial comment on the Palestine question.(17) The result was the overwhelmingly pro-Zionist picture.

One man, however, decided to follow a different course and, by doing so, prove how easily the Zionists can be defeated once they are handled with intelligence, firmness and courage. Christopher Mayhew, M.P. ventured to defend the Arab case in the television programme, "Your Witness" on 15th June 1968. Reginald Freeson, M.P. protested to the Labour Chief Whip against Mayhew's views and called on the party to dissociate itself from them. Maurice Edelman, M.P. hastened to ascribe the charge of anti-Semitism to Mr. Mayhew in an article carried by the JEWISH CHRONICLE. The moral blackmail and conscious fabrication of the charge are shown by the fact that Mr. Edelman was quite aware that his Labour colleague had a long record of activities on behalf of the Jews in Britain and abroad.(18) A more timid politician would have followed the beaten track and avoided further trouble, but Mr. Mayhew took the JEWISH CHRONICLE and Mr. Edelman to court in a libel action and forced them to apologise publicly.

Although these accusations are made with the true object in full view, they are not without any emotional impact to the average Jewish reader. The persecution mania, inflicted on the majority of Jews over the centuries, finds its expression in ultra-sensitivity to any comment or gesture. Ben Azai's attack on the GUARDIAN drew a letter from a reader reminding him that it was not just the GUARDIAN but the entire British press which was anti-Semitic and "know not Joseph."(19) George Brown was also a mere figure head. The entire foreign office was anti-Semitic and deserved a complete book on this score.(20)

In dealing with the attitude of the British press, Mr. A. Sharf criticised the WORLD REVIEW for publishing a discussion on the Mandate of Palestine without referring to the Jewish war effort, although the declared purpose of the discussion was "to put the Arab case" in "a small effort to redress the balance." There were scores of Arab exhibitions held in London without even a mention by any paper. Yet the same author took exception that an exhibition on Jewish Palestine in the war was "certainly not ignored by the press. But some provincial newspapers of standing contented themselves with printing what was obviously no more than a condensed version of the exhibition's press release." Such treatment, according to him, cannot be given a simple "anti-Zionist explanation," i.e., it must be due to anti-Semitism.(21)

Readers' letters to the Jewish press everywhere are excellent samples of this mind. It is as good to tell them that no harm was intended in the New Oxford Dictionary definition of "Jew" as it is to tell a psychotic patient that she hasn't got a horse in her belly. In the analysis of the present work, it appears that not only does the patient believe that she has a horse in her belly, but also that everyone in the hospital also believes that this is actually so.

The fear of the anti-Semitism smear is a part of the post-war political climate which has tended to placate the minorities and eliminate all forms of discrimination. The fear of anti-Semitism is as real to a public figure as the fear of colour prejudice, and the reaction, in both cases, seems to be an over-reaction to the long centuries of racial and religious discrimination. It is for this reason that we find West Germany as one of the countries most sensitive to any anti-Israeli or anti-Zionist literature. Blanvalet of West Berlin published Ethel Mannin's Far East novels and Catholic novels, but none of her works on the Middle East. The publishers gave her a contract for her successful ROAD TO BEERSHEBA, which would have sold "like hot cakes," but soon retracted from it because of the fear of being accused of anti-Semitism.(22) Outside the ranks of the New Left, which have no fear of the charge — the more inclined to anti-Semitism, the more apprehensive you become of the charge — the Arabs have been even less able to find a voice among the German speaking peoples.

That the Zionists should exploit this advantage is something natural, but the extent to which they have gone has proved to be beyond all expectations or wisdom. Protests were even lodged against the issue of special Christmas stamps in the United States and the erection of a Christmas tree in the hall of the New York Post Office. The adventurous Jewish nationalists are not worried about the possible anti-Semitic reaction. If they succeed in cowing editors and politicians it will be a feather in their cap; if they fail and draw an anti-Semitic outburst they will prove their case, i.e., that anti-Semitism is a law of nature and that the Jews have no place outside Israel. This is the other "Catch 22."

NOTES

(1) Herzl, DIARIES, Vol. I, p. 84.
(2) THE OTHER ISRAEL, Matzpen, Tel Aviv, July 1968.
(3) NEW YORK TIMES, 16 July 1967.
(4) Herzl, DIARIES, Vol. IV, p. 1525.
(5) THE FORRESTAL DIARIES, London, 1952, p. 327.
(6) Rogow, A. A., VICTIM OF DUTY, London, 1966, p. 162.
(7) McDonald, MY MISSION TO ISRAEL, p. 12.
(8) Rogow, p. 276.
(9) Francis, W., ERNEST BEVIN, London, 1952.
(10) JEWISH CHRONICLE, 2 May 1969.
(11) MORNING STAR, 8 May 1959.
(12) Kirk, G., SURVEY OF INTERNATIONAL AFFAIRS, the Middle East 1945-50, Royal Institute of International Affairs, 1952, p. 203.
(13) ZIONIST REVIEW, 11 April 1947.
(14) Citation in Burns, BETWEEN ARAB AND ISRAELI, p. 249.
(15) U. N. MONTHLY CHRONICLE, June 1968. The Medieval blood libel in which the Jews were accused of killing Christian children and drinking their blood is a European invention unknown in Islam. With the imperialist penetration of France in Syria, Damascus was stirred in 1840 by the story of a blood libel inspired by the French missionaries. Leaders of the Jewish community were arrested and the Jews were mobbed in the streets. The matter was raised in Cairo and Muhammad Ali ordered the release of the Jews forthwith reminding his governor that such charges were foreign to the Islamic World.
(16) JEWISH CHRONICLE, 14 June 1968.
(17) Lilienthal, WHAT PRICE ISRAEL, p. 126.

(18) TIMES, 22 January 1969.

(19) JEWISH CHRONICLE, 22 September 1967.

(20) JEWISH CHRONICLE, 7 July 1967.

(21) Sharf, A., THE BRITISH PRESS AND THE JEWS UNDER NAZI RULE, Oxford University Press, 1964, pp. 126, 127.

(22) Mannin to the writer.

ON THE NECESSITY
FOR AN ANTI-RACIALIST SOLUTION
TO THE PALESTINE CONFLICT

Jibran Majdalany

Today we are witnessing a world revival of anti-Semitism and the crystallisation of a new form of racialism: anti-Arabism.

In Europe, pro-Zionism often hides the remains of an older well-established anti-Semitism. Support for the Zionist state represents on the one hand an "expiation" for the crimes committed by the Nazis (an expiation all the more hypocritical because achieved at the expense of the innocent) and, on the other, helps modern anti-Semites to get rid of an unwelcome, undesired presence in a way that does not weigh upon the conscience of a society that wishes to think of itself as humanist.

Simultaneously with the emergence of this hypocritical variant of anti-Semitism, the classical form of anti-Semitism has been intensified almost everywhere in the world and has even reached areas where it hardly existed before. The most striking example of this is the implantation of anti-Semitism in the Muslim world as a consequence of the creation of the state of Israel. This is a fact which is especially worth pointing out because, historically, Islam has always been more open toward the Jews than the Christian world and has never adopted the pogroms and inquisitions characteristic of both eastern and western Europe.

Moreover, for some time now, another branch of Semites has become the object of a wave of discrimination that often verges on distrust and hatred. These new victims are the Arabs. The war of June 1967 brought into the open the anti-Arabism which was latent in western Europe. It was as if the long tradition of anti-Semitism in the Western world was unleashed against the Arabs, and as if, by a process of unconscious transfer, the Arab has become the new Jew for Europeans. This discrimination and distrust towards Arabs has gone beyond the limits of traditional anti-Semitic circles and has attained the circles of yesterday's victims. In 1967 we saw that the most virulent anti-Arabs were Zionist Jews. Non-Jewish anti-Arabs expressed their dislike with that calm that marks a long-rooted prejudice, whereas Zionist Jews showed the agitation of recent converts.

Faced with these two apparently contradictory aspects which, far from neutralising, aggravate each other, an anti-racialist attitude only has real meaning if it is based on fundamental postulates; and if it seeks out the causes of the world growth of both forms of anti-Semitism: against Arabs and Jews. In this its aim should be to discover, by going further than a simple expression of pious wishes, the best way to eliminate this centuries-old scourge.

To begin with, anti-racialism must proceed from an absolute refusal of any form of discrimination between men, whatever reasoning or justification may veil it. There is no justification for discrimination: neither anxiety, nor suffering, and even less so torture and genocide. Those who have been victims of discrimination are all the more to be condemned when the roles are reversed: the greater the price that has been paid to discrimination, the more aberrant is racialism on the part of the former victims of persecution.

From this first generality follows a first conclusion which is equally commonplace but nevertheless of great importance: for an anti-racialist there does not exist a chosen people any more than there exists an inferior people. Races may have different collective characteristics but this variety has no implications of value. People placed in similar collective conditions tend to act and react, within certain limits, in the same way. There are no races which are more criminal or more humane than others. All peoples are capable of experiencing exaltation and degradation. Consequently attempts made to establish a scale of values in the classification of peoples are in reality only the left-overs of a shameful racialism which seeks to justify itself under the guise of science.

If we accept this second generality, we meet a new aberration which consists of preferring one people to another, one race to another, or one human group to another. It is possible for us to feel closer to one human group than to another but this subjective phenomenon should not be translated into value-judgments, or into an attitude which results in discrimination. This is to fall into a form of sentimental racialism. The attitude we adopt toward human groups can only be based on criteria independent of the preferences and intrinsic, or supposedly intrinsic, qualities of the groups. The rights of peoples and groups do not emanate from our feelings or from our guilt; they do not even emanate from a group's misfortunes. There is an international consensus which establishes the principles upon which the rights of human groups are based. These principles are the same for everyone and any attempt to adjust or to amputate them out of subjective motives is a form of racialism, and inevitably results in a situation of racial conflict.

Finally, anti-racialism is an absolute: that is to say, it is one and indivisible. A person who fights anti-Semitism only earns the right to the title of anti-racialist if he adopts the same militant attitude with regard to all forms of discrimination, and towards all human groups. Otherwise his "anti-racialim" is a form of Semitic racialism. The "leagues" which campaign against anti-Semitism and which remain silent when the victims of discrimination are non-Jews (and particularly when they are Arabs) are in reality hypocritical racialists, and instruments, whether conscious or unconscious, of Zionist propaganda. In the same way, those who protest against cases of anti-Arab racialism and ignore anti-Jewish aspects of anti-Semitism are also false anti-racialists and play into the hands of Arab racialists. By its very nature, anti-racialism is incompatible with compromise and half measures. It is the enemy of silence and of compromise. It does not measure out the force of its action in proportion to the degree of misfortune, real or supposed, suffered by human groups. It derives its absoluteness and its value from the fact that it is the expression of a total commitment of the person. It proceeds from our fundamental conception of the human being. And for these reasons it is impossible that it should take on an aspect of conformism or sentimentality.

If these general principles are not translated into concrete analysis and positions, there is a risk that they will remain a dead letter or degenerate into useless sermons. They are only a starting point, not an alternative to action and to the acceptance of responsibilities. Racialism in all its forms is the cause of too much devastation for it to be viewed calmly by observers or analysed as an academic exercise. Inaction in the face of racialism is no less criminal than racialism itself. And that is why I feel obliged to consider the practical aspects of these general principles, and the methods of action needed to put them into practice. It needs to be clearly stated that the taking of a stand is a sort of praxis in which the ideological option materialises into a political attitude; for the condemnation of particular ideologies must lead to a condemnation of the regimes and the political structures to which they give rise.

A lucid evaluation of the dangers involved in the different forms of racialism leads us to consider anti-Semitism in both its forms (anti-Jewish and anti-Arab) as the most serious threat at the present time to peace in the Middle East and, through its repercussions, to world peace. A radical solution to the problems raised by anti-Semitism on a political, economic, and social level may be the forerunner of a solution to all racialist anomalies.

ZIONISM AND ANTI-SEMITISM

It would be an oversimplification to claim that the current wave of anti-Semitism has resulted from the propagation of Zionist ideas. Historically the opposite is true, and it is indisputable that Nazism greatly helped to strengthen the Zionist movement and so enabled Herzl's dream to take a concrete form. But just as anti-Semitism played an important role in the crystallisation of the Zionist movement, so in its turn Zionism stokes the fires of anti-Semitic prejudice by a sort of fatal dialectic which admits no possibility of transcendence or synthesis. By opposing the assimilation of Jew and non-Jew it encourages the individualisation and isolation of the Jew in society. Starting from an acceptance of racialism, Zionism seeks to protect itself by operating a kind of selection. It does not fight against racialism as such, but only against certain racialists. And as it remains at the level of those against whom it is fighting, its option does not go beyond the limits of racialism. But this is racialism in reverse, expressing itself in a search for separation. It proclaims the impossibility of going beyond the racialist impasse and its ambition goes no further than a peaceful coexistence of racialisms.

This neo-racialist conception might have been less dangerous than the others if it had stayed in the realm of theory. The fact that it is a racialism of reaction, a racialism which had its beginnings in self-defence, might be taken as a mitigating circumstance. But the fact is that a political reality and its extension has had repercussions among both Jews and non-Jews. It has caused the uprooting of a people, the people of Palestine, and has exposed all the Jews of the "diaspora" to an ambiguous status which may be the cause of new racialist excesses.

By combatting anti-Semitism through its antithesis, which might be called "anti-non-semitism," the Zionist movement does not arrest the progress of anti-Semitism but, on the contrary, creates a new political problem. In other words, it constitutes an escalation of the racialist phenomenon: the anti-Semites find in Jewish segregation new pretexts and new recruits, and the political victims of the Zionist state are transformed into enemies who include in their denunciation all those whom the state seeks to mobilise. Thus, to the extent that the Jews of the world give the impression of backing Zionism, they are responsible for the development among non-Jews (and especially among the victims of Zionism and those in sympathy with them) of a counter-solidarity which reaches out beyond the framework of the State of Israel, to include all the allies of the State. This growing hostility is not unwelcome to the champions of an integral Zionism. It can only release a greater number of Jewish "exiles" from their countries of "exile" and result in a massive "return" to the "promised land." This in turn causes the anti-Semites and the political enemies of the Zionist state to harden their positions. And so on. Following the logic of the Zionist movement, we are witnessing the progressive deterioration of the relations between Jew and non-Jew by a succession of attacks and counter-attacks. And even if this inevitable deterioration, which is becoming more and more serious, does not fatally lead to collective massacres, it nevertheless plunges more and more people and states into a climate of continual tension and insecurity. Among individuals and among groups it will make more victims and cause more havoc.

If we try to estimate what the Zionist "solution" has cost in blood, time and money up to the present day, we would see that for that price we could have transformed, not the tiny Negev desert, but all the deserts of the East into fertile land and, instead of creating an islet destined exclusively for Jews amid a sea of hostility, we could have turned all the countries of the East into a refuge for all, at less expense, with less effort, and in a spirit of human solidarity.

ANTI-ZIONISM AND ANTI-SEMITISM

As, according to Zionist doctrine, all the Jews of the world are the children of Israel, any hostility shown towards this state or towards the ideology on which it is based is for them, at the same time, a manifestation of anti-Semitism. This schematisation is less absurd than some people think: it is both wilful and dangerous. It not only aims at paralysing anti-Zionists by making them out to be anti-Semites but, above all, it helps to foster this confusion in the mind of Jew and "gentile" alike. Anti-Semitism is necessary to the survival of Zionism and this confusion can only feed and encourage it.

In fact, in the Islamic countries, and especially in the Arab countries, it is becoming increasingly difficult to draw the line between Jew and Zionist. A succession of Arab defeats, accompanied by the growth of a feeling of frustration and humiliation among the mass of the people, have facilitated this process of confusion. This simplifying of the identity of the enemy and the crystallisation of his image served for some people as an outlet, and for others as an instrument of demagogy. It is in this context that the criminal and foolish slogan linked with Shukairy's name can best be understood: "Let us throw them into the sea." If a demagogue like Shukairy, who was not lacking in psychological understanding, was able to launch such a slogan it was because he knew that he could count on the receptivity of a great number of his listeners. This receptivity gives a fair indication of a state of mind which came into being after the creation of Israel. Far from being blunted as time goes on, the feeling of hostility toward the state of Israel is becoming more acute. Up to 1967 the Palestinian problem was treated like a commodity by most of the regimes of the region but, since the war of June 1967, it has really become an Arab problem — an Egyptian, Jordanian, Syrian problem, etc. But the Zionist crusade has prepared the conditions for a "counter-crusade" of the same nature. This tendency to "return to sources," which is symbolised by the Muslim Brotherhood, has found in the Zionist precedent one of its most telling arguments.

But just as the unleashing of Nazism on the European continent explains, without justifying, the Zionist impetus, so the Zionist defiance of the past twenty years has stoked the fires of a new form of racialism which also shelters behind the idea of eliminating the persecution of the Arabs (the "new Jews").

This kind of reaction to Zionism is an acceptance in practice of the ideology against which it is fighting: when religion is turned into a spring-board for political struggle, it is the enemy's religion that becomes the cause and aim of the hostility. Thus we see that Zionism and anti-Semitism run along parallel lines and that each success gained by one of the two antagonistic camps inexorably results in a counter-success in the opposite camp.

The attempt to mobilise the masses in order to drive the Jews out of Palestine is, in fact, a "neo-Zionist" response. It is the same process of selection but with the roles reversed. It is equally deserving of condemnation and forms the reactionary Arab counterpart to the Zionist aggression.

A WAY OUT OF THE IMPASSE

The interpenetration of Zionism and anti-Semitism is such that it is impossible now to eliminate the one without checking the other. This escalation in hostilities has reached a level where a compromise is no longer possible. We are obliged to make a radical choice. No other option has either meaning or weight. Either we condemn racialism — and this condemnation is equivalent to a categorical refusal of both Zionism and anti-Semitism with all that such a refusal implies on the political, economic and social levels. Or we refuse this total and unequivocal condemnation, and so are inevitably led by our silence or equivocation to support one or other of the racialist camps, Jews or Arabs.

In so much as anti-racialism is a refusal to discriminate between Jew and non-Jew, it cannot help being a contradiction to Zionism because, as we have seen, the call to non-assimilation is a call to discrimination, and in itself constitutes one aspect of the latter. Consequently there is no other course but to refuse and to combat the structure of a state which is based on this form of discrimination.

On the other hand, to confound the people living in this neo-racialist state with the structure of the state would itself be a reactive form of discrimination. Our refusal of Zionism can only be justly expressed by a refusal to confuse the Jewish people with the Zionist political structure. The only valid form of anti-racialism in this context is not counter-Zionism, but anti-Zionism. The anti-racialist struggle against the Zionist structure can only be manifested by the defence of the Jewish people against its Zionist and anti-Semitic enemies. To advocate the exodus of the Jews living in Israel in the course of the struggle against the Zionist state would be to accept discrimination between Jew and non-Jew.

That is why the true anti-racialist formula must be a simultaneous condemnation of the State of Israel in its Zionist structure, and of any formula which would consist of making the Israeli Jews suffer the same fate as that of the Palestinians. Its concern must be to give the Palestinians back their national rights, that is their right to their homeland, not to turn the Israelis into refugees. Beyond the quibbling on the subject of the name to be given to the state that would replace Israel — in spite of the symbolic importance of this choice — what needs to be established is the nature of the state. To say that Israel is the state of the Jewish people is just as misguided as to say that the United States is the country of the Protestants, or France that of the Catholics, or to claim that Lebanon is the country of the Christians and Syria that of the Muslims.

The fact of being an ethnic or a religious majority never gives a right to privileges or to the limitation of the rights of the minority. Even less does it give such a right when this majority has been acquired by a process of uprooting and colonisation. The beginnings of an anti-racialist solution are to be found in a clear formulation of the conception of the state. The only concept that goes beyond the dialectical impasse of Zionism and anti-Semitism is that which consists of transforming "the state of the Jewish people" into "the state of the Palestinian people." By this transformation Jew and non-Jew alike are integrated in a national melting pot which unites them in spite of their religious and ethnic differences. The conception of the state is only acceptable to the extent it brings into relief the common denominator of all the inhabitants.

There can be no compatibility between anti-racialism and the constitutionalisation of the privileges of a race or religion. Thus the formula "state of the Jewish people" is the consecration of a religious discrimination and only its abolition can open the way to true national solidarity, the way to the abolition of the gulf between Jew and non-Jew.

We have said that certain Arabs have advocated for Palestine the formula "the state of the Arab people of Palestine." This formula includes nearly all the Sephardic Jews but eliminates the Ashkenazim and dooms them to a new exodus. Although this Arab counter-formula is not discriminatory with regard to the Jews as such, nevertheless, it is discriminatory with regard to some of them (precisely those who dominate the present state of Israel), and, even though it is less racialist than the formula "state of the Jewish people," it is not the true anti-racialist solution to the present drama.

The only formula that can be defended from an anti-racialist stand-point is that which embraces all the original inhabitants of Palestine and their descendants, as well as all those who, for one reason or another, have become inhabitants of the present state of Israel. Any intention of subjecting the attitude to be taken towards this option to a calculation of percentages harbours an ulterior motive that is racialist. The refusal to discriminate is tantamount to a categorical refusal of this kind of reckoning.

In practice, this option can be realised by the adoption of two measures:

The first step that should be taken in this direction is the abolition of the "law of return." A Jew from the United States has no more political rights in the state of the Palestinian people than a Muslim from Pakistan for whom Jerusalem is a second holy city, or a Christian from Europe. As a spiritual centre, the non-racialist state to be established would be open to all followers of the monotheistic religions who find in it their geographical centre but, as a political entity, there would be place only for its own nationals, and not for the followers of these religions.

The second step would be to authorise all the Palestinian exiles and their descendants to return to their country of origin. In the press and elsewhere there has been a considerable amount of discussion as to the number of refugees who would agree to go back under the present circumstances. We are not concerned here with this kind of discussion. The importance lies in the authorisation itself, independent of the practical consequences, because this step, together with the first measure, constitutes the criterion of de-Zionisation of the state and its adoption of the anti-racialist formula.

114

Some people may think that such projects are rather utopian and that they fail to take into account the present state of affairs, the climate of distrust and even of hatred which reigns between the Israeli Jews and the Palestinian Arabs.

It is precisely through a thorough and conscious study of this hatred and its sources and evolution that we arrive at this option. The fact that it reflects a human postulate does not make it any less practical. I fail to see why the feeling of solidarity and fraternity should be any less realistic than that of hatred and discrimination. Both of them have always existed. In the case with which we are concerned there is no chance that a solution will be found in hatred. It will certainly lead to a total impasse from which every kind of excess and destruction will spring. But if we back solidarity, this opens up a serious possibility for a solution which has the merit of not keeping its followers (mainly the progressives) in a state of conflict. This possibility is all the more reasonable if we remember the long history of harmony which formerly reigned over the relations between today's antagonists. If there are Jews who can live today as minority citizens in Germany it is difficult to understand how people can reason that it would be impossible for Jew and non-Jew to live together on the soil of Palestine.

In Europe and in America, Jews have experienced persecution and discrimination which have never been equalled in the East, even in the darkest days. Circumstances fail to give a rational explanation of this and, even if they did, it would have no justificative value. Moreover we know that relations in this part of the world deteriorated after the creation of the state of Israel, and in consequence of it. If the causes of friction were eliminated a great step would have already been made to alleviate the present climate of tension. Arab antagonism, in general, and Palestinian antagonism in particular, are fed by the Zionist reality. This does not in any way imply that de-Zionisation would immediately eliminate the possibilities of antagonism. But it would set in motion a process of dialogue and eventual mutual understanding. The antagonisms that might still persist for a certain time would clearly be less aggressive and less harmful in character. Instead of war, guerilla warfare, and sabotage, ending in a real popular war, the struggle would take on a political aspect. This would extend beyond the present division and would put an end to the present dualism of Israeli parties which claim to be of the Left, but which, by their Zionism or their acceptance of Zionism, destroy any true links with the Left.

Meanwhile, the struggle to achieve anti-racialism is not to be satisfied with pious wishes or by an analysis of the future positive effects of de-Zionism. It is incontestable that one of the main reasons for the success of the Zionist movement among the mass of the Jewish people is the fear of a future outside a Jewish state: this fear is deliberately cultivated by competent organisations and is nurtured by any signs of anti-Semitism, which are immediately enlarged and exaggerated. The mass of the Jewish people can only be weaned from Zionist leadership by the elimination of this fear; it is not enough to note that 15% of Jews live in Israel (which fact alone contradicts the idea of the fundamental insecurity of the Jews of the "diaspora"). It is in fact the Zionist leaders who deliberately envenom relations between "diaspora" Jews and the citizens of the countries in which they have settled.

Thus the main effort should consist of doubling measures of de-Zionisation with consitutional and other guarantees which would rule out the hegemony of any one religion or ethnic group. De-Zionisation — which, in itself, is a negative measure — will only make sense if it leads the way to a formula which destroys, once and for all, the allegation of the psychological deracination of the Jew. But the climate which will result from de-Zionisation will not be enough to dispel fears aroused daily. Unless this fear has been overcome by a clear formulation of the anti-Zionist alternative, it is practically impossible to hope that there will be enough pressure in favour of de-Zionisation. What has to be done is to convince the mass of Jews that the real solution to the problem of anti-Semitism does not lie in the focus of "anti-non-Semitism" which Israel has become, but in a joint struggle against racialism together with the other victims of this racialism, the Arabs. It is the solution found on the soil of Palestine that will serve as a starting point for this long struggle, and upon its success will depend the chances of success of the struggle against racialism in general.

I think that the only worthwhile alternative to the Zionist state is a secular state whose constitution refuses to acknowledge ethnic or religious privileges, and precludes the hegemony of any ethnic group whatever its percentage of representativeness. The superficial and mystical infatuation with a "return to sources" barely dissimulates a step backwards of many centuries. It is not possible to look with impunity for a solution to the problems of the 20th century by going back to the era of Mahomet, Christ or Moses. In a world which is trying to find scientific ways of dealing with current problems, this Zionist and anti-Semitic backlash is an especially dangerous aberration.

I think that we are today forced to make a choice between capitulation in the face of an apparently intangible situation, which may bring about a final and dangerous division of the region (a division which can only lead to worse conflicts), and the search for a solution to the anti-Semitism/anti-non-Semitism dilemma by an unremitting struggle to achieve a secular state on Palestinian soil. In this state both Jew and non-Jew of Palestine will be nationals and equals, and no outsider, whether Jew or non-Jew, will enjoy any sort of political privilege.

When it is a question of basic principles it is still worse to try to be realistic than to have preconceived ideas. It consitutes a denial of human values, and it does not bring results. We know that anti-racialism is not simply the expression of a basic postulate, corresponding to the profound nature of the human being when stripped of its passions, but that it is also the only formula which is valuable for human integration and for the blossoming of societies. Facing us we have the Zionist reality and the Palestine Arab reality in its traditional conception. It seems to me that twenty years is a long enough time to prove that they cannot coexist peacefully. The Western world witnesses with surprise — some people, with anxiety — the "resurgence" of the Palestinian people, who have not been disintegrated by dispersion or humiliation. Instead they have gained a deeper awareness of themselves and have increased their determination to re-assert themselves as a people.

Two entities, both equally determined, lay claim to the same territory. Unless one of them wipes out the other, they have no alternative but to accept each other and join forces. And this acceptance rightly presupposes the abolition of racialist obstacles, both Zionist and counter-Zionist.

In his book "Israel en danger de paix," Marc Hillel speaks of the condition of oriental, and especially Yemeni, Jews and compares it to the Negroes. Zionism is so deeply embedded in racialism that even Jews, when they are Arabs ("Levantines" as some Zionist leaders call them), suffer the backlash of discrimination.

On the other hand, we have seen how the remains of classical anti-Semitism have been re-animated in some Arab milieux and, how the notion of a "diabolical and all-powerful race" has infiltrated into the minds of many. It is at this moment when the impasse seems complete that there is a chance of stemming the racialist flood. Just as the soil of Palestine is the place where the fervor of monotheists converges, so, on a human level, it can become the crucible in which all prejudices and discriminations are melted down. And this is a challenge to our own fidelity towards ourselves. It is also a matter of the salvation of the Jews and the Arabs, who are in great danger of being swept away in an infernal form of new-style racialism.

This solution has the advantage not only of reconciling Palestine with itself but also of reconciling it with the region. Instead of Israel continuing to be a foreign body artificially grafted into hostile surroundings, Palestine will be able to take part in the process of development and unification of this Arab complex. This integration will be brought about on the basis of the free choice of the peoples involved and the principles which govern all real progress: secularity and the abolition of economic exploitation and social antagonisms.

Like all the solutions proposed, this solution also involves a risk of failure. But it does have a serious chance of success, perhaps the only chance of solving the present tragic situation. This situation, which is the emanation and direct consequence of a refusal of anti-racialism, is not a hypothetical one; it is a living, searing reality, the expression of a carefully cultivated mesh of hate, and the source of all the ills that ravage the region. Even for the pseudo-realists — those who give the name "reality" to a situation which has been artificially immobilised and fixed — the risk is, in the circumstances, a better solution than the fatalistic acceptance of an increasingly dangerous impasse.

EDUCATION
IN
HATRED

Dafna Dan

If one were tempted to hope that with the disappearance of the present generation of Arab leaders, men more farsighted and enlightened might take their place, what is one to think when one sees the desolating campaign to indoctrinate the younger generation in the universities, colleges and schools, and give them an education in hatred and perverse prejudice.

How general in Egypt, one asks oneself, is the early morning 'hate'-ritual described in a Sarajevo magazine in February, 1969, by a Yugoslav journalist who has lived many years in Cairo? "The road to full and real recognition of Israel by the Arabs will necessarily be a long one," he writes. "Ways of thought and lessons drawn from the experience of many generations do not change overnight, and that goes for the entire existing politico-educational system. To give a concrete example: I am still woken up every morning by the drums of the school next door to me, where the children — before classes begin and after the national anthem is played and they have shouted their compulsory war-cries — have to listen to their daily lecture on the most important subject of all, the inevitable demise of Israel." And in order to drive home that he is not inventing the whole thing, the journalist gives the school's address: Madris el Sharq el Kasseh Muhmad Mizhar, Zamalek, Cairo.

In the press, radio and television, in text-books of all kinds, from simple readers for primary schools to grammars and works on history and sociology, in articles in supposedly learned periodicals, there are the same slogans, the same themes, the same monstrous misconceptions, propagated by misinformation and distortion shading into plain forgery and blatant lies.

There is no other way to substantiate these general charges than quotation and more quotation, because it is the very quantity and ubiquity of this material that is so frightening. The absence of anything to counter this dreadful stuff can only be shown by statistics.

Arabic text-books are woefully inadequate on subjects such as socialism, the nationalist movement in the Arab world, or the Egyptian "social revolution" under Nasser. But on "Palestine" and the "world Jewish conspiracy" they are effective, full-blooded and clear. If they can be faulted, it is only for prolixity, but as Hitler preached and Goebbels practised, the oftener you repeat your lie, the better. Of course, it is the work of the Nazis in Egypt that is behind the excellent organization and diffusion of anti-Semitic propaganda. Nor should it be forgotten that Egyptians (and former Palestinians) are today the majority of the schoolteachers in the countries of the Middle East and Libya (though not further west).

Let us take some examples of teaching material found after the capture of the Gaza Strip, Judea and Samaria and the Golan Heights. Text-books, maps, pictures, wall-newspapers, exercise-book covers — everything is made use of. Paradoxically, the atlas in common use in Arab schools is entirely oblivious of the existence of Israel; Israel is included in the "Hashemite Kingdom and Palestine," and no borders appear in the atlas at all. Yet, on the back of a standard exercise-book, there appears a map of Israel; encircling it are portrayed the Arab armies, and a missile is aimed at Tel Aviv; and above the lot is the caption: "We are returning!" Everything drips hatred and destruction, everything glorifies war on the Jews. The drawings are all Stuermer-type caricatures of Jews with scarcely human features — resembling vultures or bats or mice — puny, miserable scarecrows facing Arab "Superman"-type heroes.

There is the Syrian series, "Read and Write," one of which is called, "Salem in the Army." The picture on the cover shows Arab soldiers charging with drawn bayonets: in front of them, in the sea, are drowning Jews, and the Arabs are raising their bayonets to prevent any of the Jews from trying to struggle out onto dry land. This book is one of a series for adult education, considered suitable material for teaching Syrian soldiers to read and write. But in the reading primer for 1st Grade in Syrian schools, the child learns this sentence: "The Jews are the enemies of the Arabs. Soon we shall rescue Palestine from their hands." He should write it out in printed characters and in cursive script.

At a girls's school in Khan Yunis in the Gaza Strip — an UNRWA school — there was found a permanent exhibition of "art work" — posters, cartoons, drawings, covering three walls of a largish class-room — all devoted to the war against Israel, all in glorious technicolour. A little girl is seen brandishing a machine-gun and cheering on the tanks. There is a vivid scene of destruction and slaughter in a Jewish quarter — Stars of David on the walls — with soldiers shooting and corpses slumped on the ground: children too are shooting and cheering the killers, turning excited faces, as it were to the viewer.

In the 4th Grade (elementary) Arabic Grammer issued by the U.A.R. Ministry of Culture and Education, we find on p. 87: "Exercise 5: Decline the verb: 'The Arabs (plan) to destroy the Zionists.'" In the 5th Grade grammar, p. 73, we find: "Question: 'Why do we hate Israel? Why do we want to destroy her?' Answer: 'The fatherland must be victorious, Israel must be strangled.'" The same 5th grade, in Syria this time, gets the same sort of exercise: "Analyze: 'We shall expel all the Jews from the Arab countries.'" (Basic Syntax, 1963).

In the 6th Grade (elementary) "reading and entertainment" primer, issued by the U.A.R. Ministry of Culture and Education in 1960, we find an elevating moral tale about a little boy who blew up a Jewish strongpoint. The Jews let him through, because he said he was taking bread to his mother.

We now advance to "preparatory" (junior high) schools, which come between primary and high schools or colleges. First year (preparatory) grammer, published in '65, gives the following sentence for grammatical analysis (p. 244): "The Arabs do not cease acting for the extermination of Israel." The same first grade (preparatory) is given this literary text to study; a poem by Elia Abu Madi:

"You Jews shall never have a homeland —
You never had a homeland —
We will take over Palestine —
And bury you in its soil."

Now for history. The reader for the 3rd Grade (preparatory) teaches: (p. 34) "In Palestine lived King David, who turned his back on the evil Jews ... We can never forget how the Jews tormented Mohammed, the Prophet of Allah ... " (p. 90) "My Arab brethren ... Help me throw Israel into the depths of the ocean, to the remotest deserts." Here is some "History of the Arab Fatherland in Ancient Times," for 1st Grade (preparatory): (p. 52) "Pharaoh will always be honoured in our memory for destroying the Jews who endangered him." And some "History of the Arab Fatherland and its Culture," for 2nd Grade (preparatory): (p. 102) "The Hebrews were not true Semites, and their temporary occupation of the Holy Land disintegrated after the death of King Solomon." And not to beat about the bush, the 3rd Grade (preparatory) is told (The Arab Homeland, p. 79): "The Zionist claim that Palestine, which they call 'Zion' or 'The Promised Land', is the spiritual and national homeland of the Jewish people is utter nonsense." ... (p. 80) "The Jews have always claimed they were persecuted, in order to elicit sympathy. In actual fact, nobody every persecuted Jews anywhere." There is however less than perfect coordination. Children in the same grade (third "preparatory") in Jordan are told, "The Jews in Europe were persecuted and despised because of their corruption, meanness and treachery" (Modern World History, 1966, p. 150).

Third year junior high students in Syria are told, in "The Arab Homeland and its Foreign Relations" (1963/64, p. 64): "Carrying out the unity of the countries of the Arab homeland will provide them with the strongest possible weapon enabling them to restore the right they have been robbed of, to strangle Israel, to tear her ambitions to pieces and throw her into the sea."

There is really not much to choose between the different countries. The Israel Ministry of Education took out of use (for correction) no less than fifty text-books in common use in the schools in Jordan. We find in "Modern Arab History" for 6th Grade junior school: (p. 156) "In 1964, following the growing Zionist danger, the President of the U.A.R. called upon the leaders of the Arab countries to hold an Arab Summit Conference ... King Hussein was the first to respond. The conference ... formulated a comprehensive plan for the fulfilment of the greatest Arab aspiration, the extermination of Israel." The 7th Grade grammar, issued in 1966, gives: "The Arabs will never rest until they have reconquered the plundered Garden of Eden." The 8th Grade grammar, also issued in '66, gives as examples: "The enemy soldiers are led to the slaughter. The enemy is a trickster and a traitor."

"Glances at Arab Society" for first year high school in Jordan (1964) sets the pupil an essay exercise: " 'Israel was born to die!' Prove it."

In general, secondary school pupils can be given material that is less summary, and more literary and impressive. Here is a passage from "Zionist Imperialism," by Abbas Mahmud al-Akkad, 9th Grade, secondary schools (U.A.R.), p. 249:

Israel wishes to exist and does all that she can to further that aim ... The defence burden she bears is overwhelming, because of the enmity of her Arab neighbours. Should the Israel Army be defeated in battle, all the country will be destroyed ... Israel hopes to be the homeland of the Jews,

120

and they have the stubbornness of 4,000 years of history behind them. But Israel shall not live if the Arabs stand fast in their hatred. She shall wither and decline. Even if all the human race, and the devil in Hell, conspire to aid her, she shall not exist!

"The Rules of Grammar" for second year of secondary schooling in Jordan have these exercises: "It is arms that will free our stolen homeland," and, "The Arab soldiers will lead our enemies to the slaughter."

The book called "Arab Society," intended as a history book for second year high school students in Jordan, sums up: "Thus Israel was born and thus the malignant cancer came to infect the Arab homeland. The Emir Abdallah called it 'a cataract in the eye, a thorn in living flesh, and a bone in the throat.' Like the cry of Cato, the famous Roman orator, 'Carthage must be destroyed,' so you Arab boys and girls must cling to the slogan 'Israel must disappear forever'."

Logic itself is no longer pure either. "Advanced Logic" for 3rd Grade (secondary) in the U.A.R. offers this proposition: (p. 30) "If the Arabs unite — they will be able to destroy Israel. Therefore, the destruction of Israel depends on Arab unity."

Suitable material is also provided for teachers' training. An apparently serious work, "Arabic Islamic History," for third year teachers' training (in a 5-year programme) in Egypt tells students: "The Jews are always the same, every time and everywhere. They will not live anywhere save in darkness. They contrive their evil deeds clandestinely. They fight only when they are hidden, because they are cowards." (p. 47) Conclusions to be drawn? "The Prophet enlightened us about the right way to treat them, and succeeded finally in crushing the plots they had planned. We today must follow this way and purify Holy Palestine from their filth in order to bring back peace to the Arab homeland." (p. 48) Another Egyptian book, also for teachers' seminars, "History of the Arab Fatherland in Modern Times," writes: (p. 181) "While the U.A.R. strides gloriously forward, Israel screams with fear at her destiny and fate — her ultimate destruction by the Arabs." A Syrian book, intended for both Teachers' Training Colleges and secondary schools, called "National Culture," gives a large map (p. 190) showing Islam as covering a very large slice of the world, from West Africa to China and Indonesia. Below the map is the caption: "This is Palestine, in the heart of the Arab world. Every Moslem on earth has a duty regarding it, until it be purged of the robbers and aggressors."

Another book from Damascus, "The Culture of Islam," for 3rd year high school and teachers' seminaries, is liberally decorated with soldiers charging towards the map of Israel with drawn bayonets, tanks firing in all directions, and a child garbed in vaguely mediaeval dress, with turban, and a scimitar bigger than himself, chasing a Jewish boy wearing shirt and trousers and a peaked cloth cap (the exaggerated "Jewish nose" of the German Stuermer-type caricatures does not serve its purpose in the Arab countries, where it is not regarded as unusual, so the main stress has to be on distorted faces, puny bodies and Western clothing). The text says: "Palestine is Arab land dear to us. The Arabs are a strong nation that will not suffer degradation. The Jews are wicked criminals who came to Palestine and drove out its people. We Arab children will always remember Palestine. We will drive the wicked criminals out of the country. Long live Palestine, and long live the Arabs."

To a critical mind, the passages quoted above will seem very poor stuff, but it is unwise to underestimate the damage it has done and is still doing. And the accompanying illustrations — the noble Arab superman facing the vermin-like criminal of a Jew — are more important than the text, because they make their point immediately and unforgettably.

The hate-breeding material that has been cited includes no little misrepresentation. The attempt to mask or eliminate the Biblical record of the Jew in Palestine, the historical record of Judaism's ante-dating Islam and in fact fathering it, as Abraham fathered Ishmael, is no small matter. Or take this straightforward bit of fabrication about something more recent: "Modern Arab History," fourth year high school, (Jordan, 1966), p. 190: "Following the 1929 Zionist Congress in Zurich, which outraged Arab feelings, the Jews raised their flag over the Western Wall. Then the Arabs attacked and killed the Jews in the kibbutzim and the cities, principally in Galilee and Safad, until these places were cleansed of them . . . This was one of the major Arab revolutions in Palestine." Let it suffice here to say that there was no such "cleansing" and no "revolution."

From our still ample reserve of quotations, let us select a recurring element, which happens to have immediate and up-to-date implications. In "Basic Spelling" 6th Grade (elementary), Damascus, one lesson is devoted to Zionism, and the children are taught: (p. 55) "The Jewish Parliament, from the first day of its establishment, took as its motto: 'The boundaries of Israel are from the Euphrates to the Nile.' " This "Euphrates to the Nile" business turns up regularly in Arab polemics. Here, for example, is a statement allegedly made by Ben Gurion at the end of hostilities in 1949, "quoted" not in an Arab propaganda pamphlet but in the EGYPTIAN JOURNAL OF POLITICAL SCIENCE, an ostensibly scholarly journal: "We have returned our swords to their scabbards only as a temporary measure. We shall unsheathe them when liberty in this land is endangered and when the vision of the Prophets and the Torah will be fulfilled, for then the entire Jewish people will return to settle in the lands of our forefathers stretching out from the Euphrates in the east to the Nile in the west."

This peculiar mixture of pastiche and forgery is not only quite the wrong style for Ben Gurion, with its swords and scabbards and so on, but in content is not like anything he ever said. It is unsettling to realize, as Mr. Robert Alter points out in "Commentary," October, 1968, that "this statement, cited by a supposedly scholarly authority, is accepted by its readers and has precisely the same effect on them as though it really had been made by Ben Gurion." The commonest version of the "Euphrates to the Nile" story is that there is a large map in the Knesset building in Jerusalem, with "From the Euphrates . . . etc." printed under it. Another variation has it that the motto is engraved over the portico. When captured Egyptian officers were taken into the Knesset in 1956 to see that there was no such map, they decided that the Israelis had merely hidden it. In 1967, another batch of Egyptian prisoners was taken to Jerusalem and shown the new Knesset without the famous inscription on the facade — they doubtless concluded that there was nevertheless a map inside the building somewhere. In January '69, addressing an international pro-Arab congress in Cairo, Nasser asked rhetorically: "Can it be that stories from thousands of years ago should provide a pretext for the expulsion of an entire people from its land and make it possible to threaten other peoples dwelling between the Euphrates and the Nile?"

One could go on indefinitely. Here is a final exhibit, a show piece, a book entitled, "The Palestine Question," by Dhikan al Hindawi. Intended for Jordan secondary schools, 3rd Grade literature classes, it was published in 1964, printed by the Army press. All the text-books we have quoted from are official publications, bearing the State emblem of the country concerned. This one has the extra distinction of being written by someone who himself became Minister of Education two years later (from September '66 to October '67). In his book he affirms that the Jews are not satisfied with having stolen Palestine: they aim at ruling the entire world, because they consider themselves the chosen people. The Protocols of Zion are presented as the resumé of the deliberations of the First Zionist Congress of 1897. It is shown how these supposed directives are being carried out in practice: take-over of world finances, enslavement of governments, control of press and opinion. The Jews stir up strife, revolutions and wars. They use spies to pull the strings of governments, and most of the spies in the world are Jews. Spying is part of their religion with the Jews, the pupils are told, and as proof are given in detail (but not quite accurately) the story of Joshua and the spies he sent into Jericho. Another convincing example brought forward is that of the Russian Beriya (of all people!), who was shot when it was revealed that he was "an agent of Zionist intelligence," working not even for the Western Powers but for the Jews alone. And so it continues, the international network of brothels and all the rest, pages and pages of muddled, poisonous nonsense, fed to young people by "educators" and Ministers of Education who may even — appalling thought -- believe what they teach.

When the Israel Government made representations to the United Nations authorities over all this hate material in text-books used in UNWRA schools for the children of Palestinian refugees, the Director-General of UNESCO opened a correspondence with the Arab Governments on the subject. The Syrian Minister of Education, Suleyman Al-Khash, answered him, "The hatred which we indoctrinate into the minds of our children from their birth is sacred." (Reproduced in "A-Thaura" Ba'ath party organ, Damascus, 3 May 1968).

This is the hatred which broke out in uncontrollable frenzy in May, 1967, when the Arab masses were told by their leaders that the hour of Israel's destruction was at hand. The leaders have bred this hatred in their people's hearts, and both leaders and led are reaping the whirlwind. Hate has become their master.

Is there nothing to put in the other scale to counterbalance so much desperate harm? Would not even a gram of common sense and objectivity outweigh the cartloads of official rubbish? True, there have recently been some attempts to restrain the outpouring of venom, because of a belated realization that it "looks bad" and does the Arab cause harm. These attempts are beginning to bear fruit insofar as Arab spokesmen in the international arena have for the time being stopped calling aloud in foreign tongues for the annihilation of Israel. But what we are looking for is some trace of a capacity to recognize facts about the Jews in history and in the present. On 9 August '67, one Philip Glubb, son of the famous Glubb Pasha of Jordan, published an article in the paper, AKH'R SA'AH, in which he flatly condemned the use of the Protocols of Zion. Glubb referred to an article by Dr. Y. Harcabi, Israeli expert on Arab affairs, in NEW TIMES, which pointed to the Arab use of the Protocols as an index or barometer of Arab anti-Semitism. Glubb's attitude was presumably a matter of tactics only — that it is a mistaken tactic to use the Protocols, which can so easily be proved false, when to do so brings down these unpleasant accusations on the heads of the Arabs. Glubb brought down on himself a storm of abuse from the Egyptian press; he was called "a defender of the Jews in all their vileness and filth," etc. Glubb replied in an article in AL MATSUR (30.8.67) to the effect that he was concerned not to defend the Jews but to reduce the harm being done to the Arabs. But one would have to be blind indeed to take any comfort from this isolated (and non-Arab) instance. The voice of extremism and anti-Semitic hysteria has risen even higher and more shrill since 1967. Perhaps the only gleam of hope lies in the tendency of young people everywhere to disrespect the views of their elders. But it is to be feared that the stamp has been left, that the dye has "taken."

Without expatiating at length, and without too much self-congratulation on our own honesty, we must at least point to the fact that in Israel there is absolutely no incitement to hatred of the Arabs. After the Six Day War, there was a spate of articles about the Arabs, in the daily and weekly press and over the radio, some of them academic, some popular, on various levels of seriousness and competence. These talks and articles were concerned with description and explanation, history and politics. They may have contained mistakes of fact, here and there, or shown an emphasis open to question on one issue or another. But they all illustrated a lively, objective interest in the Arabs, a wish to know more about them and to understand them, to understand why they hate us with such deluded ferocity. It should be remembered that over half the population of Israel had immigrated into the country (or been born) after the establishment of the State and was not directly acquainted with the Arabs, unlike the old-timers. Contact with the small minority of Israeli Arabs, living mostly on the borders of the State, had been relatively slight. Now there was a sudeen demand for courses in Arabic, and the radio began to broadcast Arabic lessons, both beginners' and advanced.

Dr. Y. Harcabi, referred to above, in an article in the widely read evening paper, MA'ARIV, on 26.9.65, stated that many people in Israel had tried to dissuade him from writing about Arab anti-Semitism, because they feared it might lead to the Jews' beginning to hate the Arabs with the same irrational intensity.

There is no death penalty for murderers in Israel, not even for terrorists who are found guilty of having laid a mine or set a time-bomb that killed one person or many. Some Israelis are saying that the death penalty should be re-introduced for terrorists as a deterrent; some oppose it as likely to confer the halo of martyrdom, and others because it will lessen the inducement for them to surrender and cooperate with their captors once they have been taken prisoners. Some 1,700 Arab terrorists in Israel prisons lead lives of routine and discipline, hear lectures, work in the prison workshops. In Dec. 1968 they put on an exhibition of their handicrafts, liberally sprinkled with doves of peace.

An Israeli army doctor, who lost an arm from wounds received while attending to wounded soldiers on the battlefield, was interviewed on the air, so that his successful rehabilitation as a practising physician might encourage other war cripples in their struggle to fit into society again. In the course of the interview, the doctor described how his small sons, aged 8 and 5, visited him in hospital and saw his arm for the first time. The older one was speechless, but the younger one asked, "How did it happen? Who did it to you?" "I didn't know how to answer him," said the father, "but I had to. So I said, 'The Jordanians did it.' He had heard of Egyptians but not of Jordanians. 'Are the Jordanians Arabs?' he asked. So I had to tell him. But we are on good terms with the Beduin who camp near where we live, and I hope I shall succeed in bringing my sons up not to hate Arabs."

ON ARAB
ANTI-SEMITISM

Ministry of
Foreign
Affairs
(Jerusalem)

PRESS UNDER ZIONIST INFLUENCE
Nasser in his speech opening the 3rd session of the ASU National Congress,
said:

> Certain forces help in the psychological war: the imperialist forces, the
> imperialist agents, all the US and British propaganda media, and the press
> under Zionist influence. [Radio Cairo, 23.7.69, quoted from BBC
> Monitoring Service]

NOTORIOUS PROTOCOLS CITED
Said the Egyptian Minister of State, Amin Howeidi, in an interview on
Egyptian television:

> That the Jews are the 'chosen master people,' their leaders announce at
> every opportunity. This is also stated in the PROTOCOLS OF THE
> ELDERS OF ZION and in the Talmud (sic!).
> This is the secret of the conflict with Nazism which talks of the
> superman and the superiority of the Aryan race. It was inevitable that the
> 'chosen master people' and the racist theory of Nazism came into conflict.
> [Al-Gumhurya, Cairo, 9.7.69]

THE COMPARISON OF ISRAELIS
TO NAZIS 'UNFORTUNATE'
At a press conference in the Hague, on 19.6.69, Egyptian Foreign Minister
Riad said: "The Israeli occupation is worse than anything the Germans did in
Holland." Seeing that his listeners were outraged, and the Dutch Foreign
Minister suggested "to cross this remark from our minds," Raid withdrew and
asked that "the unfortunate comparison" be forgotten.

125

From a poem by Mustapha al Khoussi:

If I live, oh my beloved land,
I will destroy Tel Aviv over their heads
I will purify my stolen land,
and cleanse Jerusalem from the stench of Rachel (the Jewess).
[Al-Gumhurya, Cairo, 31.3.68]

ANTI-SEMITIC LITERATURE FROM CAIRO

"Jewish Aggressors from Moses' to Dayan's Days," a book by Muhamad Sabih was published by The Arab World publishing house in Cairo. The book discusses Jewish aggression against Egypt and the Arab countries and its foundation in historical and ideological Judaism. The author attempts to prove that today's Jewish presence in Palestine is not the result of 'Nazi — or any other — persecution' but rather the outcome of an ancient plan, quoted in the Torah, and of a fundamental hatred against the Arabs nurtured by the Jews for 3.500 years. [Al-Arabi, Kuwait, 1.4.69]

'CHOSEN PEOPLE' — A LEGEND
SNEAKED INTO THE FORGED AND UNJUST TORAH

Leave off the legend of the 'chosen people' which has been sneaked into the forged and unjust Torah! Had you been 'chosen' and not 'embarrassed' (in Arabic — this is a play on words), Allah would not have dispersed you in the world. [Al Massawar, Cairo, 9.5.69]

THE MISSION: UPROOT ZIONIST COLONIALISM
The editor-in-chief of the Egyptian ideological monthly, Lufti al-Houli wrote: "To fight Zionist colonialist occupation and uproot it, that is the mission of today's generation in the Arab homeland. The present Arab generation has no right to exist unless this mission is carried out." [At-Tali'a, Cairo, May 1969]

JEWS HAVE NO HISTORIC RIGHTS IN PALESTINE;
THEIR PRESENCE IS PART OF IMPERIALIST PLOT
The Egyptian weekly 'Akhir Sa'a' regularly devotes a special section to statements by important leaders. A study by Nasser's personal representative on the 'true trends of Israel and its secret plan' appeared in this space. Dr. Hassan Zabri al-H'uli wrote:

The present situation in the Middle East demands a study of historical writings and documents to reach the roots of a problem which has existed for some hundreds of years. As to the repeated claims of the Israelis regarding their historical rights to the country known as Palestine, these have no historical basis. All writings and documents show that the passage of Jews to Palestine was a temporary incident in history, one which neither left any trace nor grants any historical rights.

History further determines that no other people preceded the settling of Arabs in Palestine, but that, 5,000 years ago tribes of Arab Canaaites settled there, giving it the name 'The Land of Canaan.' Nobody objected to this right of theirs.

They were joined later by groups of Hebrews, together with the prophet Abraham, and they lived together with the Arabs. When the Hebrews became united and independent, they imposed their government on the country for seventy years, during the period of the kings David and Solomon. It is of interest that, at the time of their short regime, they used methods of violence and subjugation to which the Scriptures attest, when God said to His people in the Talmud: 'When you enter a town, do not neglect to kill its inhabitants with the sword and to annihilate everything in the town.' And that is what is said in the Book of Isaiah: 'They killed all inhabitants of the town, men, women, children and old people, even the cattle, sheep and the beasts were massacred with the sword, and they set fire to the town, sparing only the gold and the silver which they seized for their Temple treasures.'

Zionism, according to its political doctrine, aspires to sovereignty and is, therefore, one of the most prejudiced racial and imperialistic dogmas on earth. Palestine is its closest objective, serving as a starting point for the distant objective.

. . . Imperialism became the partner of Zionism for the purpose of its own plans, so as to continue to establish its influence and authority for the benefit of its interests in the Arab area. Its plans, as defined by the British Prime Minister at the time, were to concentrate on two issues: (a) to perpetuate the split in the Arab area, its backwardness and weakness; (b) to divide the African part of the area from the Asian by a strong and foreign human buffer in the Suez Canal neighbourhood, which would be friendly towards Europe and hostile towards the Arabs.

Thus Israel realizes the objectives of imperialism and Zionism:

— It serves as bridge-head for the imperialism and a base for neo-imperialism in Asia and Africa.

— It serves as an instrument for squeezing the resources of the neighbouring Arab States, leaving them weakened and torn.

— It serves as a starting point for establishing a Jewish State from the Nile to the Euphrates.

— It serves as base for the consolidation of Zionist ambitions, unlimited expansion and sovereignty over the world. [Akhir-Sa'a, Cairo, 14.5.69]

THE ARABS WILL SAVE THE WORLD
FROM A NEW TARTAR (ZIONIST) CONQUEST.
ISRAEL TO BE DESTROYED BY RETURNING REFUGEES

The nationalized daily, catering for the educated elite, used Nazi terminology in an article analyzing the situation of the Arabs vis-a-vis Israel:

Our struggle with Israel is a continuous one which started long before its creation in 1948, and did not end in June 1967. It will be continued in various forms until the Palestinians' rights will have been restored and the danger of racist Zionist aggression is eliminated.

Israel, as a State, is not like other States in the world, and it is not true that we fight only against a military and political establishment dominating the soil of Palestine.

Israel is part and parcel of a powerful international establishment — I do not mean the USA but world Zionism, the present ally of the USA. Not for nothing does the Zionist establishment turn Israel into an independent nuclear power. It matters not that Israel, for the time being, is not in possession of an atom bomb. What counts is that it is working to acquire it.

It would be naive to believe that this effort of world Zionism is directed exclusively against the Arab world. It is intended chiefly as a part of the Zionist strategy to achieve superiority, and to seek domination as a strong world power.

It would also be naive to believe that Israel really wants all Jews to immigrate to Palestine. It is planning immigration to a certain extent, but it wishes to leave a force of influential people in other countries, to act for it in the spheres of economics, politics, propaganda, arts and espionage.

There can be no doubt about the influence of the Zionist establishment in the USA, and the USA leaders are not ashamed to acknowledge this.

It has become clear that among the leadership of European Socialist States there are some elements who have links with Zionism, using their position and influence in the party and State to sway the general policy and create unrest.

A member of the Central Committee of the Soviet Communist Party, Ivanow, writes in his book 'Zionism — Beware' that Zionism has managed to appear in many different guises and that it has had a part in turmoils and troubles, like military adventures and economic crises, all over the world. It has incited angry youth to revolt. The author apparently refers to the economic turmoils in France and the rebellions of youth and students in both East and West.

Fate has laid upon us the burden to save humanity from a new tartar conquest . . . Thus, to restore the Palestinian people to its country means to negate all that Israel stands for. Returning the refugees is a fundamental part of the world struggle against Zionism and is likely to shake its foundations. [Al-Akhbar, Cairo, 4.7.69]

CLEANSE SOIL FROM ENEMIES OF RELIGION

Sheikh al-Ahzar addressed the Moslem Summit Meeting and called for unification to cleanse the soil from the enemies of humanity and religion. [MENA, Cairo, 22.9.69]

HATE-FILLED ARAB TEXT-BOOKS

A UNESCO Commission of experts examining the text-books used in UNRWA schools in the Arab countries and Judaea and Samaria has recommended to take out of circulation 18 text-books, correct and make changes in 65 and permit the use of 48 books, about which there were only some reservations. The recommendation to take 18 books out of circulation is based on hate-filled passages about Israel and the Jewish people. . . The Commission's report was submitted to the Director-General of UNESCO. [Ha'Aretz, Tel Aviv, 17.4.69]

ISRAEL TO DESTROY ARAB CULTURE
Hassan, King of Morocco, said:

The Israeli occupation aims at the destruction of Arab culture. The continued occupation of the territories is part of a plan to destroy Arab culture and its values. [Radio Amman, 29.5.69]

ALLOW US, ALLAH, TO BECOME MURDERERS
The following are samples from poetry of hatred, by prize-winning renowned Arab poets:

> Allow us, oh Allah, to become murderers!
> . . . Oh hatred! Grow extraordinarily!
> [Written by renowned poet, Nazar Qabani, published in Syrian army paper, Jeish ash-Shaab, 5.11.68]

This poem by Thamed Hasan was awarded first prize by Syrian Ministry of Culture:

> We have sworn by Jerusalem, that the city will be the grave of the conqueror. They have defiled the purity of its soil, . . filled our land with hatred and revenge. We are death, sowing fear and terror. Our flag is conquest and victory with God. [Jeish ash-Shaab, 29.10.68]

PRESIDENT AL-ATASSI AT A MASS RALLY IN DAMASCUS

> No doubt, the battle is inevitable. Long live the one Arab nation. Death to the colonialist Zionists! [Radio Damascus, 7.4.69]

EXPLOSIVES IN SYNAGOGUE

> The Lebanese Security Forces arrested Ali Shaaban and charged him with having carried out a campaign of incitement in the State. He admitted to having placed explosives in the synagogue in Aleyh and to being a member of the Syrian intelligence services. [Al-Jarida, Beirut, 28.4.69]

INCITING AGAINST JEWISH MERCHANTS;
NOTORIOUS PROTOCOLS POP UP AGAIN

> Lebanese leaders have to fulfil their national duty and protect Lebanese merchants and industrialists from their Jewish merchant 'colleagues,' the cheaters, who revealed their true face as mean Zionists and who will not be deterred from destroying the State which has sheltered, fed and enriched them, and who proved beyond any doubt that every Jew, wherever he is, is a Zionist, from beginning to end, is loyal to Israel . . .
>
> The Lebanese merchants do not want a recurrence of what has been done by six Jewish merchants to dozens of Lebanese. The last victim was Jamil Damasqieh, who lost more than 800 thousand Lebanese pounds through a Jewish merchant from Saida, who was Mukhtar of Saida's Jewish quarter.
>
> Is this story the first one? No, it is only one link in the chain of treacherous cheating which started after the June disaster and which was carried out by five Jewish merchants from Tripoli and Beirut. This was the sixth; there may be more robbers. The matter is not yet closed, and it is nothing unusual in Jewish mentality. On the contrary — it fits perfectly the teachings of the Torah (sic!), the Talmud (sic!) and the Protocols of the Elders of Zion. [Al-Ahad, Beirut, 8.6.69]

JEWISH DOMINATION OF INFORMATION SERVICES

Israel fully exploits international public opinion taking its side, so that it comes near to imposing Jewish domination on the world's information services. [An-Nahar, Beirut, 15.6.69]

The Lebanese authorities have taken steps to prohibit Jews of Lebanese citizenship from leaving their country, because the emigration of Jews after the Six-Day War damaged Lebanon's economy and because it had become known that many of the Jews had settled in Israel. [Saut al-Aruba, Voice of Arabism, Beirut, 6.8.69]

JEWS AN ACCURSED CANCER, STINKING BODY

Moscow, as well as Washington, fears a heavy Israeli defeat which may result from the Arab existence, in the course of which it will be eradicated from among the Arabs, and returned as a dead and stinking body to the place it came from, namely the slums of German towns, Poland and Russia, where the Zionists had been living as accursed cancer. [Al-Haqiqa, Libya, 22.5.69]

COMMUNICATIONS CONTROLLED BY ZIONIST CAPITAL
A listener's letter from Libya says:

In recent years there has been a great advance in the development of television and radio broadcast via satellites. This represents a serious danger to the Arab area since such communications systems are controlled by Western monopolies and Zionist capital. [Radio Cairo, 21.7.69, quoted from BBC Monitoring Service]

IRAQI BA'ATH 22 ANNIVERSARY STATEMENT

Mankind has not known a fiercer, harsher or more intense struggle than that against the imperialist-Zionist alliance. The Ba'ath's new experiment gives new hope by which the revolutionary Arab generations aspire to leave behind the traditional forms of the struggle which characterised the phase prior to 5th June. By raising the slogans of the armed popular struggle, united front action and freedom of popular action, this new experiment will determine the revolutionary criteria for every unitary, liberating and progressive or socialist action in this phase, as the Arab nation is witnessing a direct and fateful confrontation with and struggle against the imperialist-Zionist alliance. The history of mankind has not known a fiercer, harsher or more intense struggle. [Baghdad Radio, 7.4.69, quoted from BBC Monitoring Service]

INTRODUCTION

The collision between Arab nationalism and Zionism, drawing also upon religious and ethnic antagonism, has produced tragic consequences to the peoples involved. Over a half million Arab refugees left the territory that became Israeli. Among the others particularly affected by hostility and war are the Arabs residing in Israel, the Arabs in the territories occupied by Israel since 1967, and the Jews in the Arab countries.

Difficult questions relating to minority and human rights have resulted from the Arab-Israeli conflict. The Arab countries speak of the Arab community in Israel, which in 1949 included some 170,000 naturalized Israeli citizens and has since doubled its numbers, as a population that has lost its land and property, as well as the majority in its own home, to alien Jewish intruders. As inferior citizens of a Jewish state, these Arabs are subjected to racial and religious discrimination, and to brutal mental and physical persecution. Israel is accused of imposing and enforcing a policy of apartheid upon its minority; of restricting freedom of movement; of denying equal opportunities in all fields; of expropriating and consfiscating villages and towns; and of ruthlessly arresting and banishing masses of innocent inhabitants. This policy's aim, it is claimed, is not only to further reduce the Arab population in the formerly all-Arab state, but, more importantly, to discourage the Arab refugees in neighboring countries from pressing for their return to their rightful homes.

Israel vehemently denies these charges and proudly acclaims its record of accomplishments on behalf of the Arab minority. Specific measures are being pointed to: Arabic has become one of Israel's official languages; Arab cultural and local affairs have been promoted; Arabs are fully represented in the Knesset (Parliament); Arab advisors serve in government ministries; Arab communities have been furnished with water, electricity, medical care and education; and joint enterprises in commerce, labor, and the arts have been established. Finally, the military rule set up for security reasons in sensitive border areas with heavy Arab populations, was abolished in 1966. Since the June, 1967 War, moreover, Israeli Arabs have been granted freedom of movement in and out of Israel.

Sabri Jiryis's article, published in English by Beirut's Fifth of June Society in May, 1969, attempts to present the "truth" of Israel's treatment of its Arab minority. The author, an Israeli Christian Arab lawyer, deals also with questions connected with the military government and land expropriations laws. The

131

Israeli position is contained in "The Arabs of Israel," a document of the Israel Ministry for Foreign Affairs published in March, 1968.

A separate issue involves the rights of the Arabs in the West Bank of Palestine (previously held by Jordan) and in the Gaza Strip (previously under Egyptian control.) These territories have been under Israeli control since the June, 1967 War. Now consisting of one million people, their population was to have lived in a "Palestinian Arab State," envisaged by the 1948 U. N. Partition Resolution, but never established. A large segment of these Arabs are refugees of the 1948 war when Israel was created. Following the war, Jordan annexed the West Bank and granted Jerusalem citizenship to its Palestinian population. Egypt, occupying the Gaza Strip, confined the people to this narrow region, denying them Egyptian citizenship and opportunities for political, economic and social development.

The position of the Arab states concerning Israel's administration of the West Bank and the Gaza Strip has been expectedly critical. It is charged that the Arab populations in these areas have been intimidated and terrorized by collective punishment: the imposition of curfews, demolition of houses, confiscation of land and property, arrests and expulsions.

Israel, on the other hand, has argued that life in all fields go on normally with minimum intervention by the military government. It points to the fact that over 22,000 refugees who during the Six Day War had deserted the West Bank have been permitted to return to their homes under the "family reunion" program and other schemes; that Arab residents on either side of the Jordan River have an opportunity to travel, visit, or engage in work and business activities as a result of Israel's "open bridges" policy; and that Israeli preventive and punitive measures are intended to keep violations of military regulations and sabotage operations "under control."

An excerpt from monograph No. 55 published by the Palestine Research Center in Beirut (no date) presents an account of the alleged "reign of terror" in the occupied areas. Specific violations by Israel of the Fourth Geneva Convention for the protection of civilian populations in time of war are being cited.

A booklet published by the Ministry of Foreign Affairs in Jerusalem discusses "Israel in the Administered Areas" (no date). The account is based on addresses by Ambassador Netanel Lorch in the Special Political Committee of the General Assembly of the United Nations on September 10, 1970, and by Ambassador Mordecai Kidron at the 27th session of the United Nations Commission on Human Rights in Geneva on March 12, 1971. The Israelis assert that their administration goes beyond the requirements of the Geneva Convention. Despite the Arab states' insistence upon a continued state of war, Israel claims that its policy of open bridges permits the resumption of cultural, social, and economic links between the inhabitants of the occupied areas and the Arab states.

A third aspect of minority and human rights issues is the problem of the Jewish refugees from the Arab countries. Israel has focused attention on this problem because there has been a mass exodus of Jews from Arab countries in recent years. Moreover, those who have remained are, according to Israeli reports, subjected to severe discrimination and persecution, casting doubt on the Arab proposal for a "pluralistic state," where Jews will live in peace as a minority. The Israeli position is discussed in an excerpt from Dafna Dan's ARAB RACIALISM published in Jerusalem by Keter in 1969. Here the author surveys the difficult conditions under which Jews in each of the Arab states live and their exodus to Israel, concluding that this experience demonstrates the extent of Arab prejudice and hatred.

One Arab response to this specific accusation was reported in the CHRISTIAN SCIENCE MONITOR of December 2, 1971, attributing to Colonel Chazi Bby Akl, Syrian Army Information Officer, the statement: "they (the Israelis) are trying to use a smoking screen to hide the bad treatment of Arabs in the occupied territories, and (to hide) the discrimination against Arabs and Oriental Jews in Israel itself." In general, the Arabs have always insisted that their confrontation is with Zionism and Israel as its national state and not with Judaism or the Jewish people. The Arabs repeatedly point out that relations between Moslems and Jews in the Arab countries have throughout history been friendly and peaceful. They attribute the worsening of this cordial situation to the emergence of Zionism. The migration of their Jewish populations to Israel they view as a result of Zionist propaganda rather than as a product of Arab animosity. The Arabs assert also that they cannot be anti-semites because they, like the Jews, are ethnically of the semitic stock.

THE ARABS
IN
ISRAEL

Sabri Jiryis

Ever since the establishment of the State of Israel, large areas of that country (Galilee, the Triangle(1) and the Negev), have been ruled by a Military Government which has extensive powers and works through military courts.

These three areas each have a Military Governor appointed by the Ministry of Defence. In them 75 percent of the country's Arab inhabitants live. In the Northern Area, Galilee, there are about 130,000 Arabs living in 65 villages and small towns; the Central Area, the Triangle, has about 50,000 inhabitants living in 27 villages; and in the Southern Area, the Negev, there are about 20,000 Bedouin and nomads belonging to some 18 tribes.

The whole system owes its existence to the British Mandate Government's Defence Laws (State of Emergency) 1945, and the Israeli Defence Laws (Security Areas) 1949. Under the 1945 laws, the British carried out most of their operations against the terrorists of Irgun Zvai Leumi and the Stern Gang.

At that time the Jewish settlers violently opposed these laws. In February 1946, at a conference of Jewish lawyers in Tel Aviv, Dr. Dunkelbaum (later to become a Supreme Court Judge) said: "These laws contradict the most fundamental principles of law, justice and jurisprudence." Other leading Israeli figures who, then, opposed these laws include Dr. Bernard Joseph (as Dov Joseph he became Minister of Justice), and Mr. Ya'acov Shimshon Shapiro. A conference of Jewish lawyers passed a resolution which stated: "The community of Jewish lawyers in the land of Israel, assembled in Tel Aviv on 2 July 1946, hereby decide:

> 1. The powers granted to the authorities under the Emergency Laws deprive the Palestinian citizens in the land of Israel) of the fundamental rights of man.
>
> 2. These laws undermine law and justice, constitute a grave danger to the life and liberty of the individual and establish a rule of violence without any judicial control. The conference demands the repeal of these laws . . .

These lawyers seem to have forgotten their decisions; for it was they who became judges and legal advisors in the State of Israel. At its establishment that State did not repeal the laws but, with the exception of clauses concerning immigration and the acquisition of land, they left them on the Statute Books. Only one Jewish judge found himself unable in conscience to apply them — Judge Shalom Kassan.

These laws affect almost the whole range of a person's life. A person may be restricted in his movements and required to inform the police of them; he may have to appear at the nearest police station when required. Under these laws a person can be detained, for an unlimited period, without trial. He can be denied his possessions or refused access to them. A person's property can be destroyed if it is suspected that a bomb has been thrown or a shot fired from it. The government can banish a person permanently from the country. Curfews can be imposed and inhabitants can be required to provide food and lodgings for the military.

All cases under these laws are tried by Military Courts. There are two kinds of Military Court. The first, called plainly a Military Court, has a senior officer as president and two other officers. It can impose any penalty that the Central Court can impose, including life imprisonment and the death penalty. The other, a Summary Court, consists of one Israeli army officer. It is empowered to impose sentences of imprisonment for up to two years and fines of not more than I £ 3,000.

Until 1963 there could be no appeal to any other court against the sentences of the Military Courts. Now, when an appeal is made to the Supreme Court, that Court has made it a general rule not to interfere with the Military Government when its actions are based on "security reasons."

The Emergency Laws of 1949 impose the same restrictions as the Defence Laws of 1945, but they also give the Ministry of Defence very important powers of permanent eviction in "security areas" or "closed areas." The Military Government can declare an area closed, which means that one may not travel in it or visit it without a military permit.

In theory, the Defence Laws of 1945 are enforced throughout the country, but, in fact, they are only enforced in those areas under Military Government. In practice they are only enforced with their full rigour against the Arabs.

The restriction of movement is often used as a threat and invoked against Arabs who have linked themselves with political organisations not approved of by the Military Government. When it fails to subjugate Arab citizens by restricting their movements, it employs fiercer measures such as expulsion from their home areas and police supervision.

Expulsion requires that a person should reside in a remote area where he has no house of his own and no means of providing a living for himself or his family. He may also be required to report to a distant police station at least twice a day. Villagers in the Triangle have been banished to Upper Galilee and told to report twice a day to a police station, 20 kilometres from their place of exile. Others have been told to report to police stations, 15 kilometres away from their villages. Two villagers in the Triangle were ordered to remain in their homes all night (from one hour after sunset until sunrise), and report twice a day to a police station, eight kilometres from their homes. A particularly cruel and "amusing" case is that of Ahmad Hassan, a Bedouin of the Al-Wadi tribe. He was ordered to sit every day for six months, from sunrise to sunset, under a large carob tree. There are innumerable similar cases.

In addition to this, the Military Government has made much use of its power to enforce detentions. In 1956—1957, 315 detention orders were issued. The villages of the Triangle were put under curfew for 14 years. The curfew was not finally raised until February 1962.

What is the real purpose of the Military Government? All classes of the Arab population of Israel regard the Military Government as an institution which was established to achieve the following three fundamental objectives: 1. To facilitate the expropriation of Arab land by the authorities, 2. To interfere in elections to the Knesset and municipal councils, in the interests of the Mapai Party and a group of hypocritical Arabs who do what they are told by this party, and 3. To prevent the formation of any Arab political movement which is either independent, or linked with any political movement other the Mapai.

LAND EXPROPRIATION AND THE
ESTABLISHMENT OF JEWISH COLONIES

The acquisition of land in Israel has been one of the central aims of the Zionist movement ever since its foundation. The establishment of Israel eliminated many of the obstacles in the way of Jewish attempts to acquire land and the system of Military Government provided Israel with one of the means of doing this.

At first, in 1948, the Israeli forces simply drove the Arab inhabitants over the armistice lines or to another part of the country. This, however, was too flagrant a way of doing things with so much world attention on the refugees. Therefore Israel passed a series of amended articles and orders to justify the expropriation that had already been carried out, and give the authorities additional powers to seize further Arab lands. From that time two complementary methods have been used for the acquisition of land — forcible expropriation and the invocation of these laws to justify it.

Under Article 125 of the Defence Laws, the Military Government can declare certain areas closed areas. Inhabitants can be refused entry to their own villages, expelled from them, or, if they were expelled during hostilities, prevented from returning.

The inhabitants of Rama were evacuated from their village on November 5, 1948; then on November 15 the Arab population of Kafr Bar'am was evacuated. Three months later, the inhabitants of Anan were expelled from their village; half of them were forced to cross the armistice lines. Three years later the villagers applied to the Supreme Court to be allowed to return to their village. All the houses were blown up by the Israeli Defence Army.

On February 28, 1949, 700 refugees were expelled from the village of Kafr Yasif. Most of them were put in trucks and taken to the frontier, which they were forced to cross. In June 1949, the Israeli army and police surrounded the villages of Hisam, Qatiya and Jauneh and expelled the inhabitants.

The villagers of Ghabisiya were given two days notice to leave their homes on 24 January, 1950. Later they appealed to the Supreme Court, which ruled that the order was not valid until it was published in the Official Gazette. The authorities refused to allow the villagers to return, and the order declaring it a closed area was published.

At the beginning of 1950, the inhabitants of Batat were expelled from their village. On 17 August, the villagers of Mijdal received an expulsion order, and the first group of them was taken to the Gaza Strip. The expulsion was completed in three weeks. Thirteen villages in Wadi Ara were evacuated and the inhabitants taken across the Israeli frontier in February 1951.

In November 1951, a military detachment surrounded the village of Buwaishat, expelled the inhabitants and dynamited their houses.

In September 1953, the inhabitants of Umm al-Faraj were expelled from their village, which was blown up immediately afterwards. In October of the same year, seven families were expelled from Rihaniya, despite a Supreme Court judgement that the expulsion was illegal. The Baqqar tribe, which lived in the north of the country, was forced to cross the frontier into Syria on 30 October, 1953.

In 1948 the Israeli Defence Army occupied the village of Aqrat in Western Galilee. Six days later the villagers received an order to leave their village for two weeks until military operations in the area were concluded. Much more than two weeks passed. They appealed to the Supreme Court in 1951, which declared that there was no legal impediment to their returning to their village.

The villagers, then, asked the Military Governor to allow them to return. He referred them back to the Minister of Defence who referred them back to the Military Governor. They were ordered to leave again. They appealed to the Appeals Committee and from there to the Supreme Court. But on Christmas Day, a month and a half before the day the Supreme Court assigned to hear the case, all the houses of this Catholic Christian village were blown up.

A similar incident concerns the village of Hasas, in Upper Galilee, near the Israeli-Syrian border. The population was expelled from this village in 1949. They stayed away until 1952, when they appealed to the Supreme Court to be allowed to return. The Court ordered that they be allowed to return, but the authorities immediately served "removal orders" on them. The Court then decided that it had no power to interfere with the authorities who had given the "removal orders" as they "were absolute in so far as they were connected with security matters."

The above list of villages by no means includes all the Arab villages whose inhabitants have been expelled. Nearly all these areas have been given to Jewish colonies to cultivate.

The links between the Military Government and the Israeli Lands Directorate can be seen from the fact that Military Governors and their representatives are readily employed by the Lands Directorate when their services are terminated. Although they are not specialists in land affairs, their experience during their years as Military Governors is extremely useful to the Israeli Lands Directorate.

Alongside the methods of expropriation and expulsion, Israel uses other means of acquiring land. One of the most notorious is the Law on the Acquisition of Absentees' Property of 1950. It first appeared in the form of emergency articles for absentee property until this law replaced it.

The function of this law was to define the legal status of property of absentees who had left the country. Their property was transferred to the Custodian of Absentee Property, who was appointed by virtue of the law. However, it defines "absentee" to mean any person who was a citizen of the Land of Israel and left his residence in the country after 29 November 1948 to: (a) a place outside Israel before 1 September 1948 or (b) a place inside Israel that was then occupied by forces hostile to Israel.

By this law people who had left their villages or had been driven out of them by the Israelis — even if they remained in areas that were Israeli-controlled — were prevented from returning to their villages, and their lands were confiscated from them. An Arab who visited a neighboring land at any time before 1 September 1948 would have his land expropriated, even if he returned to his village before Israel occupied it. If he changed his residence during this period, his land could also be confiscated.

Aharon Cohen, in his book 'Israel and the Arab World' says: "Inasmuch as the Law for Absentees' Property has been enforced in the mixed towns where the majority of the population were forced to change their place of residence, this means, in practice, that all Arab property is regarded as "absentees" property, unless the contrary can be proved. It is by no means unusual for an Arab who has moved from one quarter in the same town to another to be forced to pay the Custodian of Absentees' Property rent for the house he has moved to, while, at the same time, he receives no rent for his former house, in which others are living, and paying rent to the Custodian."

The law empowers the Custodian to decide what persons are absentees on no further evidence than the testimony of a Mukhtar (head of a village) or a collaborator. He may not be questioned about the information sources which led him to a decision, so that he is protected from future attacks in the courts. No deal made by the Custodian in connection with property he believed to be absentee property may be invalidated, even if it is later proved that such property was not absentee property.

This law is enforced against villages that were annexed under the armistice agreement between Israel and Jordan on 3 April 1949, despite the fact that its enforcement is in direct contradiction to that agreement, which says: "Whenever villages are affected as a result of the armistice demarcation line the inhabitants of such villages shall be entitled to keep their rights — these rights being protected by the law — as regards their places of residence, their property and their freedom . . . " When some villagers appealed against the Custodian to the Supreme Court, it informed them that the armistice agreement was not in the competence of the Court and that it was up to the states concerned to enforce it.

This law is also enforced against Islamic Waqf property. According to the religious laws of Islam, Waqf property is considered as belonging to God, income from such property being devoted to the members of the Islamic community to charitable projects or to the purpose for which the property was mortmained in Waqf. This property has been transferred to the Custodian of Absentees' Property, on the assumption, perhaps, that God also is an absentee by virtue of this law.

The value of Islamic Waqf property was enormous. Today it is impossible to find out how much it contributes to the State of Israel, the matter being left to the discretion of the Custodian.

Despite frequent attempts by the Islamic community to secure its release and restoration to the control of the community, the reverse has happened; for a proposal was submitted in 1964 and approved in 1965, which transfers this property to the government once and for all.

The income from Waqf property is estimated in tens of millions of pounds, yet in the financial year 1963—1964 only I £ 700,000 were allocated to Islamic education, social affairs, holy places, mosques, etc.

Another law the Israelis use to expropriate land is the Emergency Articles for the Exploitation of Uncultivated Lands. They claim that the object of this is to encourage people to cultivate their land, by giving the Ministry of Agriculture power to take it from them if they don't.

Its real object, however, is to help in the expropriation of land. The Military Government declares a certain area closed and allows nobody to enter it without permits. For "security reasons" it is unable to give the owners of the land in the closed areas permits. Soon their land becomes "uncultivated" and the Ministry of Agriculture can step in to ensure its cultivation by "handing it over to another party to cultivate it." The "other party" is always the neighboring Jewish colonies.

138

Despite all these laws, the Arabs still managed to hold on to some of their land. So the Israeli Government promulgated the Law for the Requisitioning of Land in Times of Emergency. This law gives the government the right to take over land "for the defence of the State and the security of the people, to safeguard essential provisions or essential public services or to absorb immigrants, or retired soldiers, or men disabled while on active service." At first the land could only be retained for three years. But then it was extended to six and again further until 1 August 1958. Lands retained after this date are regarded as having been expropriated by the State!

Most of these laws spoke of 'transfer', 'requisitioning' or 'usufruct'; they did not mention 'ownership'. From a legal point of view the ownership of the land still remained with the original owners. Moreover most of the laws were subject to the existence of a state of emergency in the country. [A state of emergency was declared four days after the establishment of the State and is still in existence today.(2)] These temporary measures had to be made permanent. To do this the Law for the Acquisition of Land (Operations and Compensations) was passed in 1953.

This law enables the Minister of Finance to transfer lands expropriated under previous laws into the possession of the State of Israel. The Ministry issues certificates for property subject to three conditions: (1). That such property was not at the disposal of its owner on 1 April 1952. (2). That between 14 May 1948 and 1 April 1952 such property was employed for essential purposes of development, or (Jewish) settlement or security. (All previous laws for expropriation had been passed before 1 April 1952, and the object of most of them was the expropriation of land for purposes of development, settlement or security.) (3). That the property is still needed for the purposes mentioned. All this property the law transferred to the ownership of the Development Authority which had the right to take immediate possession of it.

Seven months after this law, the Minister of Finance issued certificates providing for the expropriation of 250 Arab villages. Most of these villages belonged to absentees — those who had left their homes and property and crossed the frontier during the war. But the certificates also covered large portions of land belonging to Arab citizens who are still living in Israel.

The land of absentees was transferred without any payment on the grounds that there was no one to pay. For the Arabs who remained the compensation was so trifling as to be a cover for expropriation of Arab lands without payment.

The law makes 1 January 1950 as the date of expropriation for the purposes of assessing compensation. The law was passed in 1953 — why make the date 1950? In 1950 there were very few land sales so that the price of land was low. Moreover then the Israeli pound was equivalent to the pound sterling, while in 1953 it was only worth 20 percent of the pound sterling. I £ 12 million was paid for 104,000 dunums (1 acre = 2.5 dunums) of land — that is about I £ 140 per dunum. In 1961, similar compensation was paid for 20,000 dunums, although the price of land in the free market had risen to hundreds, and sometimes thousands of pounds per dunum.

The next in the series of laws concerning the confiscation of Arab property is the Law of Prescription. Besides civil matters this law also contains provisions which help in the acquisition of much land in Galilee.

The Ottoman Land Law of 1858 and the Mandate Land Law of 1928 stipulate that anyone who controls and exploits land for ten consecutive years is entitled, at the end of these ten years, to ask for the land to be registered in his name.

The draft of the Israeli law changed this period to fifty years. This immediately brought a storm of Arab protest and the period was then fixed for land at 15 years and for other property at seven. However, if a man started to cultivate land after 1 March 1943, the first five years from that date were not to be taken into account, so that for such people the period was, in effect, twenty years. But before 1 March 1963 all lands became subject to survey so that these people had no chance of occupying the land for the twenty years required.

In one dispute over the period of occupation of land, the government representative produced an aerial photograph with the number 45 written at the bottom of it. He said that it was an aerial photograph of the land taken in 1945 and showed that the land was not being cultivated. The Supreme Court accepted this and the Arab lost this land although no proof was given that this photograph had, in fact, been taken in 1945.

Owing to the conflicting figures from various government departments, no exact figures can be given for the total area of land of the Arabs living in Israel that has been expropriated, but the estimate of one million dunums seems reasonably accurate.

In 1960 the Israeli Government made another attempt, unsuccessful this time to dispossess the Arabs of further land. In order to concentrate government land in one area, the government intended to exchange land in one area for land in another or, if there was no land for exchange, to offer "compensation."

This time the Arabs resisted. 13 Arab municipal councils adopted resolutions demanding the withdrawal of the draft. Meetings and conferences were held. Strikes and demonstrations were organised in several Arab villages.

As a result of such opposition, it was decided not to submit the draft law to the Knesset. This was the first time that a government conspiracy against the Arab population was defeated by organised mass action.

There are two further expropriation laws which the authorities have used after they had exploited, to the full, most of the powers granted to them by laws already mentioned.

The first of these is the Forest Law. According to this law the government can declare forest lands which were previously registered for the use of villages as Government forests. The villagers are forbidden to enter these areas. This is merely the prelude to reclassification of the land to change it from common land to government owned land. Many villages have lost thousands of dunums of land by the operation of this law.

The second of these two laws is the Law for the Acquisition of Land in the Public Interest. By this law the government, the municipal authorities or public institutions may expropriate any land they require. So far this law's use has been rare; the most important occasion being when it was used to acquire 1,200 dunums of the best land in Nazareth. The Supreme Court rejected an appeal against this because it was satisfied that the land was needed for the building of government offices. However, when the land was acquired, it was used for building houses for newly arrived Jewish immigrants, and for spinning and weaving and chocolate factories. The aim of the authorities seems to be to establish a new Jewish Colony, called Upper Nazareth, in the heart of Nazareth, in order to strangle the Arab City.

The expropriation of Arab lands is the most painful chapter of the Arabs of Israel. One of the first results of the expropriation of land was the removal of some 20,000 Arabs from their villages. They have become refugees, living only a few kilometres from their villages, which are now used as Jewish settlements. They can only enter lands that were their own as paid labourers for the new "owners" of their lands. Israel Hertz, in an article in 'Al-Hamishar', writes: "mostly (they) live in humble houses of tin, sacking or wood, that have been erected on the outskirts of their villages, the authorities regarding them as temporary residents. Very few of them are rich enough to have succeeded in buying a plot of land on which to build a house in the villages they live in, or in renting a house in one of these villages. In some, but not all, of the villages of these refugees new immigrants have settled, while most, though not all, of the cultivable land has been annexed to already existing Jewish colonies to meet their land requirements or granted to new colonies.

"The great majority of these refugees — nearly all of them — ask to be allowed to return to their villages, refusing to sell their rights to their land, inspite of their unfavorable material conditions. They do not become absorbed by other villages, firmly maintaining their positions."

Until 1952 they received aid from the U. N., but then the U. N. decided that they were "property owners" in Israel and stopped the aid. After ignoring them for so long, in 1958 the Israeli Government announced a plan to settle them and provide loans for them. But when the majority of these refugees discovered that this plan was conditional on their giving up their rights, they refused.

Every Arab village has had some of its land expropriated. This has done great harm to Arab agriculture and brought into existence a new generation of unemployed, men who were formerly agricultural workers, and have not been able to learn another trade since they have been dispossessed of their lands.

The vast majority of Arab landowners refuse to accept compensation — which is extremely small. Nor will they take compensation in the form of land belonging to "absentees," either still living in Israel or living abroad as refugees. To encourage the Arabs to accept compensation, it was raised by 15 percent. But even this "generous" proposal was not accepted by the Arabs.

The Arabs continually demand the return of their land and will accept nothing in its place. The efforts made by the authorities to expropriate Arab lands constitute a danger to the very existence of the Arabs in Israel.

Israel is determined to smash Arab control of two areas in Israel, Galilee and the Triangle, in both of which the Arabs are in the majority. To do this it expropriates Arab lands and builds Jewish settlements.

Most of the confiscated land is situated in areas which, by virtue of the resolutions of the United Nations of 1947, belong to the Arab State of Palestine. The Israelis are afraid that there might come a time, should there ever be peace talks between Israel and the Arab countries, when the Arabs, who are a majority in these areas, might ask to be attached to such Arab or Palestinian state as might be established, on the grounds that there is an Arab majority in these areas.

That is why the Israeli Government is hastening to settle Jews in these areas, thus transforming the Arab population everywhere into a minority, and confronting the Arabs, both inside and outside Israel, with a fait accompli.

THE STRONG—ARM POLICY

The names of Deir Yassin and Kafr Qasim are landmarks in the history of the Arabs in Israel. Deir Yassin's frightful massacre, when 250 of the Arab inhabitants, men, women and children, were butchered by armed members of Irgun Zvai Leumi and the Stern Gang, has become notorious throughout the world.

It achieved its object, which was to terrorize the Arabs out of the country. However, for those Arabs who remained behind, despite the fact that they had become citizens of Israel, there was still some danger.

On 29 October 1956, 49 innocent Arab citizens in the Israeli village of Kafr Qasim were killed. It was the eve of the British-French-Israeli aggression against Egypt. A curfew was put on the village — but the villagers out in their fields had not been informed. As they returned to their homes in little groups, they were stopped and shot down by Israeli Frontier Guards. Those killed included women and children.

At first Ben Gurion, in the Knesset, described the incident vaguely, referring to some people being injured. But eventually the public outcry became so great that there was an investigation and the men responsible were brought to trial. They received sentences of imprisonment. However, these sentences were drastically reduced and the last of these guilty men, the two officers, came out of prison in 1960 after serving only 3½ years.

Moreover in 1960, Joubrael Dahan, the Lieutenant in charge, who was convicted of killing 43 Arabs in an hour, was engaged by the municipality of Rama as the "Officer responsible for Arab affairs in the city."

POLITICS AND SOCIETY

The second aim of the Miliary Government is the strengthening of the Mapai rule among the Arab population. In this way it does harm to all other political circles in the State, both left and right, both Jewish and Arab. All other circles, whatever their political aims and opinions, are unacceptable to the Military Government and cooperation with them is liable to a violent clash with it.

For this it has the support of the Special Operations Department of the Israeli police and the Internal Security Organisation, and its agents in all classes of Arab society. Through enormous efforts of pressure, threats, bribery and exploitation of every point of weakness in Arab society, it has succeeded in creating a large number of collaborators, especially among the older generation.

In addition to these forms of collaboration, it uses the regular weekly reports of the Arab Mukhtars (the heads of villages). Originally Turkish, then adopted by the British, the Mukhtar system includes the most reactionary elements of the Arab population. Apart from the 18 Mukhtars of the Bedouin tribes, there are only three other officially recognized Mukhtars, but the Military Government recognizes 100 Mukhtars in about 80 villages in Galilee and the Triangle.

Thanks to the Military Government, most of the municipal authorities in Arab villages are instruments in its service. When the time comes for elections to these councils, it prepares careful lists of candidates, forcibly opposing any list it does not approve.

However, when the Minister of the Interior has been a member of Achdut Haavoda or the General Zionist Party, there have been clashes between the ministry and the Military Governor. In 1958 the Supreme Court was convinced that a number of the actions of the Military Governor in the Triangle proceeded from a desire to induce people to change their minds over the election of a president for the Tira Village Council, and that expulsion orders were issued in order to diminish the influence of the people expelled.

During elections to the Knesset, interference by the Military Government is more extensive and forceful. The Mapai Party wins all elections to the Knesset. Four or five Arab members of Mapai are elected. Their sole function is to support Mapai and draw their monthly stipends. These Arab members voted against the abolition of the Military Government.

A typical example of Military Government interference in parliamentary elections took place in a village in Galilee three days before elections to the Fifth Knesset. At a meeting called by all the heads of clans of the village, the representative of the Military Governor told the villagers whom the government had decided they should vote for. He went on to say that, in order to enforce this, the villagers were to be divided into small groups of 15-20, a supervisor for each group being appointed by the Military Governor. They were not to use the printed ballot papers but special sheets of white paper, on which they were to write the letter to indicate the list of candidates they chose in a special way; one group was to write in Arabic at the head of the paper, another in Hebrew at the head of the paper, another in Arabic at the bottom, another in Hebrew on the right and so on. This would ensure that the government knew the names of those who refused to cooperate and their infringement of these instructions would not be viewed favourably.

As a result of such pressure a higher percentage of Arabs than Jews go to the polling stations and they duly elect the Mapai representatives.

Other Israeli political parties have tried to combat this hold the Mapai has on the Arab electorate. The General Zionist Party and Achdut Haavoda have both attempted to put up Arab candidates, but have failed at the elections. The Mapam Party (United Labour Party) has also tried. Although unsuccessful at the polls, this party has won some support from some of the younger Arabs. Its position is somewhat contradictory; for while it supports movements of national liberation and self-determination outside Israel, it does not apply them to the Arabs of Palestine. Nevertheless the Mapam has done much for the Arabs in many fields. Many young Arabs have found work for long periods in its kibbutzim and other projects, when they could find no other work. The ministries that have been entrusted to Mapam members, particularly the Ministry of Health, have made considerable efforts to improve the conditions of the Arabs.

The Israeli Communist Party is the only party with a high proportion of Arab members. It has played a unique role in the history of the Arabs in Israel. By going into opposition shortly after the establishment of the state, it became the principal defender of the rights of the Arabs. The party has been supported by Arab circles who have cooperated with it, because it was only through it that they could oppose the conspiracies of the authorities.

The party's influence on Arab society increased to the point that in the year 1956—1957 it became the virtual spokesman of the Arabs in Israel. At that time any Arab who refused to submit to the government was dubbed a "Communist."

Between 1954—1958 the Communists, both in Israel and the Arab world, supported the Arab struggle without reserve. In 1958 the Israeli Communist Party, along with various Arab leaders, formed the Arab Front, called the Popular Front.

Cooperation with the Communist Party continued for six months. Then an open split occurred between Arab nationalism and the communist parties in the Arab world. Within a few months the Popular Front had split into two groups. The first group, only three or four members, continued to cooperate with the Communist Party. The second group decided to continue its activities separately.

It immediately founded the organisation known as Al-Ard and issued its own programme. It submitted an application for a license to publish a weekly newspaper in Arabic called 'Al-Ard.' Publication started at once, pending the granting of a licence. After 13 issues the paper was closed and six of its editorial staff prosecuted. A short time later Al-Ard applied for the registration of a printing and publishing company. At first this was refused, but later this decision was rescinded.

However, when it applied for permission to publish an Arabic weekly, its application was refused. In this situation there was no alternative to comparatively silent action.

Early in 1964 the group decided to register its association with the Journalists' League, under the name of the Al-Ard Movement, and sent a statement to this effect, containing the movement's constitution, to the authorities. The authorities replied that the Al-Ard Movement was illegal because it had been established with the aim of prejudicing the security of the very existence of the State of Israel. The group appealed to the Supreme Court.

They stated that their aims were: to raise the educational, health, economic and political standards of all its members; to achieve complete equality and social justice for all classes of people in Israel; to find a just solution of the Palestine problem as a whole, as an indivisible unit — a solution that would restore their political entity to the Palestine people, who were an indivisible part of the Arab nation; to support liberation, unionist and socialist movements in the Arab world by all legitimate means; to work for peace in the Middle East in particular, and the world in general; to support all progressive movements in all parts of the world, to oppose imperialism and to support people who wish to liberate themselves from it.

The Supreme Court rejected Al-Ard's application on the grounds that its objectives were utterly destructive to the State of Israel; that it was against recognition of the State of Israel and that any state had the right to protect itself from the establishment of a fifth column within itself.

The Communist newspaper, 'Al-Ittihad,' pointed out that Al-Ard had recognized the State of Israel by making one of its objectives the achievement of the complete equality and social justice of all classes of people within Israel. It regarded the Court's decision as political, rather than legal, and said that it was aimed at depriving a group of citizens in the State of the right to engage in political activity and to work in a clear and legitimate manner for entirely constitutional objectives.

A few days after this judgement, certain of Al-Ard's leaders were arrested and a search was carried out of most of its centres. A week later, invoking the Defence Laws (State of Emergency) 1945, the Minister of Defence declared that the Al-Ard movement was an illegal association. The result of this statement was that every member of this group, who allowed himself to engage in any activity whatsoever, became liable to ten years imprisonment.

The Government of Israel has not hesitated to interfere in religious matters. It has succeeded because it has "bought" the greater part of the religious leaders, whether Moslem, Christian or Druse.

As far as the Christians are concerned, Israel's interference has not been so great because the spiritual centres of these communities are in countries whose aid Israel still requires. However, certain fanatically religious Jewish elements do engage in hostile activities against Christian missions in Israel.

The Moslem community has suffered more than any other in Israel; the majority of Islamic Waqf possessions have been confiscated so that financial resources available for religious purposes are extremely meagre. Under the British Mandate, the Moslem religious community used to enjoy almost complete liberty, and the Higher Moslem Council supervised religious affairs. The Israel Government has abolished this council and formed a committee (three, at least, of whom must be non-Moslems) to appoint Qadis (judges in the religious courts) in Israel. However, Islam does not recognize judges appointed by non-Moslems so that chaos reigns in Moslem circles. Islamic funds have been squandered by committees appointed by the government, often with government help and encouragement.

The sanctity of a number of Moslem holy places, such as mosques and tombs, has been violated in a most regrettable manner. One of the reasons for this hostile attitude is the widely held Israeli idea that Islam is linked with Arab nationalism.

The Israeli treatment of the Druses is quite different. This is a result of an Israeli attempt to weaken the position of the Druses in Arab countries and to separate them from the Arab community. The Israelis put forward the idea that the Druses are not Arabs. In Israel today, Jews often differentiate between Arabs and Druses. They even tried to show a marriage relationship between the prophet Shu'aib, whom the Druses hold in particular veneration, and the prophet Moses. They claimed that he married Shu'aib's daughter and before that Shu'aib had married an Israelite woman. This claim does not conform with the religious tenets of the Druses, according to which Shu'aib never married.

In fact the Druses are an Arab religious sect — founded at the end of the tenth century A. D. Ethnically this community is an indivisable part of the Arab nation. It should be emphasized that the great majority of educated and younger Druses are strongly opposed to the creation of this new nationalism, and are proud of belonging to the Arab nation. In any case the myth of "Druse nationalism" has not protected the Druses from the expropriation of their land in just the same way as the other Palestinian Arabs.

EDUCATION

The number of Arab pupils studying in Arab elementary schools has increased, but in comparison with the figures in Jewish schools this increase is inconsiderable; more than a third of Arab children of school age are still not in schools. Even then there is an extensive network of confessional and missionary schools providing elementary education, which receive little help from the Ministry of Education.

The educational standards in the Arab schools are extremely low in comparison not only with Jewish schools in Israel, but also with present standards all over the Middle East and with the standards prevailing in Palestine under the Mandate. There are many reasons for these low standards: Arab schools in Israel suffer from a grave shortage of buildings, equipment, furniture, books and professional teachers, and the teaching curricula are liable to be changed at any time.

There has been a shortage of teachers ever since the establishment of the state when most of the best teachers left the country and their places were taken by untrained teachers. As the numbers of Arab schools have increased, the teaching staff has been increased by teachers who have completed their secondary education. These teachers are chosen, not for their qualifications but because the Military Government or the Ministry of Defence approve of their appointment, or because of nepotism.

In 1962 the Israeli Government was "gracious" enough to open an Arab Teachers' Training College in Jaffa, for both men and women teachers. But this college can only train fifty teachers a year. Half of these are unable to find employment after they graduate. All Arab teachers in Israel are constantly intimidated by threat of dismissal.

The Government has been responsible for the deplorable situation in Arab education because it has appointed dozens of untrained teachers to Arab schools and kept them at their posts for years without giving them a chance to obtain teaching diplomas. It has been responsible for the dismissal of dozens of trained teachers for political reasons and has ignored the urgent requests of Arab schools for trained teachers.

Another reason for the low educational standard in Arab schools is the absence of clear and permanent curricula, as these are being constantly changed by the Ministry of Education, sometimes just before the Secondary Certificate Examination.

There is a serious shortage of books in secondary schools. This shortage applies also to books in general. Up until April 1964 only 270 books in the Arabic language had been published, 45 of them written by authors resident in the country, the remainder reprints of books first published in Arab countries. Even the Educational and Cultural Committee of the Histadrut (the General Federation of Jewish Labour) has called upon the Ministry of Education to overcome this shortage of Arabic books, to which it attributes the low standard of education among the Arabs in Israel.

The shortage of maps and laboratory equipment is also acute.

Most of the school buildings are not fit to be used as schools. They are old constructions with small, dark rooms and few sanitary amenities. In the course of five financial years the state allocated I £ 3 million for the improvemnt of Arab schools. This is an extremely small proportion of the Ministry of Education's budget, which totals tens of milions of pounds.

Needless to say the failure rates of Arab pupils who sit for the secondary certificate examination is higher than 85 percent. These results have disastrous effects on Arab society and they have caused widespread unemployment and despair among younger educated Arabs. Only 171 Arab students out of a total population of a quarter of a million are receiving university education, as against 14,000 Jews. So it is hardly surprising that the Arab population of Israel are now nearly all labourers or small tradesmen.

The neglect by the Israeli Government of Arab education is a studied plan to keep the Arabs in ignorance and diminish national consciousness among them. A large percentage of those who leave Arab elementary schools can only read and write Arabic with difficulty, although they come from Arab stock. Many passages from famous Arabic poems and prose are omitted from the curricula, being replaced by weak and banal passages drawn from obscure authors. In Arab secondary schools, the study of the Old Testament is compulsory, while the Islamic and Christian religions are not studied at all.

The whole attitude of the Ministry of Education is to distort and misrepresent Arab history and glorify Jewish history. Much more time, too, must be spent on the study of Jewish history. In the secondary examination there are never questions about the Prophet Muhammad, the Caliph Harun al-Rashid, the Omayyad Caliph Muawiya, or Saladin, who were some of the greatest men in Arab history.

The whole aim is to judaize the rising generation of Arabs.

AGRICULTURE

Under the British Mandate, and since the establishment of Israel, Arab society in Israel has been essentially agricultural. There have been many obstacles put in the way of Arab agricultural development and tens of thousands of the best Arab agricultural land has been expropriated.

The prices of Arab agricultural produce are fixed at a much lower level than the prices of Jewish produce. This is particularly so with their principal crops, tobacco and olive oil. Arab farmers are obliged to sell their tobacco crop at a very low price to Jewish monopoly companies, whereas other private companies purchase equivalent quantities of Jewish-grown crops at higher prices. The Jewish monopoly company withholds one third of the Arab tobacco crop for any one year until the farmer undertakes to sell it in his following year's crop and so on.

The prices of olive oil produced by Arabs were subject to direct government control until 1955. This injustice applies in the case of all other crops. For example in 1961–1962 a ton of Arab-grown barley was sold for I £ 215, while Jewish-grown barley was sold for I £ 225 per ton.

Arab farmers who want to buy modern machinery frequently have their requests for loans ignored and delayed for long periods. Jewish agriculture, however, is very highly mechanised.

The combination of these factors — lack of machinery, lower prices, less irrigation (43.9 percent of Jewish land is irrigated compared with 3.6 percent of Arab land) have resulted in a very great difference in the yield per dunum between Arab and Jewish land. Added to this is the fact that most of the best Arab land is now in Jewish hands and two-thirds of all presently-held Arab land lies in mountainous and rocky areas that are difficult to cultivate. It is not surprising, therefore, that the yield from Jewish land is nearly 400 percent greater than from Arab land.

Behind this treatment of the Arabs is the desire that more and more of them should leave the land so that Jews can take it over.

LABOUR

Arab labour was not fully organised under the British Mandate. Whenever any organisations that there were became general and comprehensive, they were dissolved. However, the Jewish labour organisations, especially the Histadrut (the General Federation of Jewish Labour), grew yearly stronger. The only Arab Labour organisation left in 1948 ceased to exist shortly after the establishment of the State.

Thus Arab workers had been easily exploited by Arab capitalists and feudalists. Now the Zionist Movement, in the form of the Labour organisations attached to it, joined this attack on Arab workers under the racialist slogan "Jewish Labour." After the establishment of the State hundreds of Arab workers were driven from their jobs, and special penalties were inflicted on any Jews who gave them jobs.

There was no organisation to defend Arab rights and they were opposed by the Histadrut. They were forced to sell their labour on the black market, where they had to accept much lower wages than those paid to Jewish workers for the same work, and they were liable to dismissal on the grounds that they were "not organised." At certain periods when there was a high level of Jewish unemployment, dismissal of Arab workers became a daily event.

Sometimes Arab workers received less than half the wages paid to Jews for the same work. For example, in 1952, the unskilled Arab workers used to be paid one Israeli pound for a day's work for the Public Works Department, whereas a Jewish worker doing the same work, in the same grade, used to receive I £ 2.63. Similarly a skilled Arab labourer received I £ 2.50 per day, his Jewish counterpart was paid I £ 3.14. It was the government that enforced this discrimination against Arab workers. The same was true in education. In 1952 an unmarried Jewish teacher, holding a Secondary Teachers' Training College Certificate, was paid I £ 69 per month, while an Arab with the same qualifications was paid I £ 41.

The Jewish writer Ahron Cohen, in his book 'Israel and the Arab World', has described the lot of Arab workers and employees as follows: "The Arab worker who managed to find a job in the first ten years after the establishment of Israel was restricted to unpleasant jobs that Jewish workers would not accept, like in sewage or building. The wages paid to Arab workers never equalled those paid to Jews, even if the Arab was doing the same work. In practice many jobs were closed to Arab workers and employees. The Arab worker who found a temporary job in a remote Jewish colony could be dismissed on the grounds that he was 'not organised.' "

Although now Arabs have been admitted into the Histadrut on an equal basis (by the end of 1962 there were 36,000 Arab members), the general situation of Arab workers has not improved. Many still do not belong to any labour organisation and are obliged to find work by their own efforts, having no protection from dismissal and unemployment.

Arab workers have to travel great distances to their places of work; many of them are only able to return home once a week, or once a month. Out of 54,000 workers, 27,000 are itinerant.

The number of non-agricultural workers is increasing. The reasons for this include the lack of Arab agricultural land, the increase in Arab population and the small income they derive from Arab agriculture. But behind all this is the fundamental Israeli plan to sever relations between the basically agricultural society of the Arabs of Israel and mechanised agriculture, in order to facilitate the acquisition of Arab land. So all sorts of obstacles are placed in the way of Arab agricultural development and the Arab village in general, and the drift to the towns has been encouraged in such a way as to ensure the complete success of the policy.

DEVELOPMENT AND SERVICES

At first the Ministry of the Interior did not permit elections to Arab municipalities. Eventually, with the utmost reluctance, it started to permit some activity in this field. Between 1950—1953 it allowed the formation of eleven local councils, between 1953—1959 another nine, and a further ten between 1959—1963. In 1961 in nearly 57 percent of the areas inhabited by Arabs, where 38 percent of the total Arab population live, there was no municipal representation at all.

Such a situation is bound to impede the progress of the Arab village and paralyse its development. Many local councils are appointed by the Ministry of the Interior, without prior consultation with the local inhabitants.

The absence of any local authorities in many villages stands in the way of building and construction operations in these villages, for it is impossible to demarcate boundaries or survey building sites. It is quite normal for the villages to wait a whole year before receiving replies to their requests for building permits. As a result nearly 4,000 houses have been built in Arab villages without permits and the authorities are now threatening to demolish them.

Electricity has so far been installed in only a few Arab villages. The Arab village of Tayyiba in the Triangle was the first to have electricity in 1955. By 1961 lines had been laid to five more villages and during the last few years a few more have received electricity supplies.

The standards of the postal services are on a par with the electricity service. There is only one post office, one branch office and fifteen sub-divisions amongst all the Arab villages. There are telephone services in 26 Arab villages — one quarter of all the Arab villages in the country.

Although the Health Service in the Arab villages has somewhat improved, the standard of the health service provided to Arabs is by no means as high as is the case with the Jews. Many Arab villages have no dispensaries, and sometimes there is no doctor, nurse or pharmacist within easy reach. No medical services are provided for mothers in 46 Arab villages. In 5 villages in the Acre area the villagers have not been vaccinated and in the year 1963—1964 no doctor or nurse visited 17 villages in the Acre area, although the medical services are supposed to cover these villages.

Despite the fact that the government has ordered the Ministry of Health to provide medical services for 82 of the Arab villages, this has not been done. This helps to explain the high infant mortality rate — for example, in 1964, 15 infants died of measles in the Arab village of Kisra in Galilee.

Arab standards only approach those of the Jews in the prison services. There are many more Arab prisoners than Jewish prisoners; this is particularly so with offenders against the Defence and Emergency Laws.

CONCLUSION

It has become clear that the policy of Israel towards the Arabs in Israel is nothing less than a policy of racial discrimination and repression. David Ben Gurion is one of the men who devised the nervous system of the State of Israel, basing it on a concept that has long been dear to him and which is dear to many of today's Israeli leaders — hatred of the Arabs and all things Arab.

On April 30, 1958, the newspaper, 'Haritz', published a report which revealed Ben Gurion's real attitude to the Arabs. "Ben Gurion," it stated, "refused the identity card issued to him because it was written in Arabic as well as Hebrew." Commenting on this report in the periodical, 'Haolam Hazeh', Uri Avneri wrote: "Ben Gurion has always been utterly reactionary in his opposition to anything Arab. The Prime Minister has never visited an Arab town or village since the establishment of the State. (In July 1959 he visited the Druse village of Julis in a helicopter.) When he visited the Jewish town of Upper Nazareth, he refused to visit Arab Nazareth, only a few hundred metres away from the Jewish town. In the first ten years after the establishment of the State, Ben Gurion did not receive a single delegation of Arab citizens, though under party pressure he did condescend to receive the Arab members of the Knesset, who were subservient to the Mapai; though this was his only meeting with Arabs, and during it he made them insincere promises."

When he visited Negev, he insisted on the immediate removal of a signpost bearing the Arabic name, Ain Ghadban, saying that he found this Arabic name disagreeable.

It cannot be said that Ben Gurion bears the responsibility for Israel's anti-Arab policy alone; he has advisors, assistants and directors who are even more extremist in their views, which they hold to this day, and it is they who have been directing Israel's policy since Ben Gurion retired. But it was he who switched on the green light and no one has turned it off.

Further evidence of Israel's racial discrimination can be found in the Nationality Law passed in 1952. Jews are granted Israeli citizenship automatically, by virtue of the Return Law of 1950, but an Arab is considered to be an Israeli citizen only if (a) he was registered as a resident in Israel on 1 March 1952, (b) he was resident in Israel on 1 April 1952, and (c) he was from the date of the establishment of the State and until 1 April 1952 in Israel or in an area that was attached to Israel after the establishment of the State and until 1952 or had entered Israel legally during that period. On the basis of these provisions the

Ministry of the Interior has refused to recognize the nationality of thousands of Arabs, who, on the eve of the establishment of Israel, happened to be in areas which were at the time outside its frontiers, but were later occupied by Israeli forces or annexed. In 1961 an inhabitant of the village of Ana attacked these provisions in the Supreme Court and received judgement in his favour. This was the first and only occasion in which Arabs prevailed over a repressive law that had been enacted to persecute them.

In the Knesset debate on the Citizenship Law of 1950, Moshe Sahpira, then Minister of the Interior, referred to the important rights granted to the Arabs when "the State granted automatic Israeli citizenship to '63,000 foreigners' who were registered on November 30, 1948." These "foreigners" had been born in a country where they and their ancestors had lived for hundreds of years before the establishment of the State of Israel.

NOTES

(1) During the Mandate, the Triangle was the district enclosing Nablus, Tulkarm and Jenin. In the Rhodes agreement of 1949, half of the Triangle was incorporated by Israel. This Israeli Triangle, or the little Triangle as the Israelis call it, is about 25 miles to the east of Tel Aviv.

(2) The State of Emergency was repealed in December 1966, but after the June 1967 war the treatment of Arabs by the Israeli authorities again hardened.

(3) A full description of this incident as well as its legal sequences can be found in the complete edition of THE ARABS IN ISRAEL (Institute for Palestine Studies) pp. 91-118.

THE ARABS
OF
ISRAEL

Ministry
of Foreign Affairs
(Jerusalem)

Not the least of Israel's achievements since 1948 has been the record of progress of its Arab and Druze citizens. Then a not very forward-looking community of about 108,000, it had by 1967 grown in number to 313,000, or 11.8% of the total census (not counting the approximately one million Arabs living in the areas under Israel administration since the Six-Day War of June 1967). More striking, however, than the numerical data is the extraordinary metamorphosis in the life and ways of this ethnic group, and its various religious sub-groups, within the periphery of Israel's democratic and independent society.

There are two reliable yardsticks by which this can be precisely measured. One is comparison between the situation of the community in 1948 and in 1967; the other is to place side by side, year by year, the manifestations of its development and those of any other Arab group in the Middle East.

Material advancement by itself, of course, is no guarantee of friendship and loyalty either between or within societies. The relations between the Jews of Israel and its Arabs may, therefore, be a notable exception. They were put to the test during the Six-Day War of June 1967. The overwhelming majority of Israel's Arabs expressed and displayed a personal identification with the country's defence and security. Moslem and Christian Arab alike volunteered to help in the war effort. They came forward as blood-donors. They took over the field-work of Jewish villagers called to the colours. Druze soldiers fought bravely alongside their Jewish comrades-in-arms. Not a single incident of dissension or disloyalty disturbed the internal harmony and peace of embattled Israel.

These unchallengeable facts are heartening to all who believe in a positive and peaceful settlement of the Israel-Arab conflict. They show that Jews and Arabs can live constructively and harmoniously together in a communion of friendship and progress. By now, Israel's Arabs may well have a key part to play in bringing about a just, pacific and lasting conclusion to the unhappy clash between two Semitic peoples.

The prospects of their succeeding are, indeed, bright and boundless. The war of June 1967 has torn down barriers between Israel's Arab community and a

151

million of their brethren living on the West Bank of the Jordan and in the Gaza Strip. Instead of the cleavage which a twenty-year-long siege of Israel by the Arab States had wrought, there is daily contact between Arab and Arab and between Arab and Jew. The evolutionary impact that Israel's democracy exerted upon its Arab citizens ever since 1948 has begun to make itself felt. Whatever the ultimate political destiny of the liberated areas, that impact may prove to have been a cardinal contribution to an enduring Middle East peace.

THE BEGINNING

The Arab community that emerged as citizens of Israel from the War of Independence of 1948-49 was a residual part of the Palestine Arab community of Mandatory days. Occupation of the Gaza Strip and the West Bank of the Jordan by the Arab States had put most of the Palestinian Arabs outside the State of Israel. They were joined by something less than 500,000 other Arabs, who, before the War of Independence, had lived in the territory which became Israel, but during the fighting, in obedience to the behests of Arab military commanders, had left their homes: they had been promised a speedy Arab victory and, on safe return, a share in the loot to be taken from the vanquished Jews. But it was the Arab invaders that were vanquished, not the Jews, and these Arabs became refugees: they found themselves in Palestinian areas seized by the Arab armies, and in Syria, Lebanon, Saudi Arabia and oil sheikhdoms of the Persian Gulf.

The 108,000 Arabs who stayed on Israel soil were, then, one remnant of a fragmented community. Their leaders had been the first to decamp when fighting began. Their economy was in chaos. Communications between many of their villages and with much of the rest of Israel had been severed. Not a few villages had been destroyed in whole or in part.

The unremitting beleaguerment of Israel by the Arab States thereafter placed its Arabs in a quandary. The Arab States castigated cooperation with Jewish authority as 'collaboration'. The Jews did not know in those early days where the real sympathies of Israel's Arabs lay and how far they could be trusted.

Things were aggravagated by the organized despatch of saboteurs and desperadoes into Israel territory from the neighbouring Arab States. Most of Israel's Arabs live in areas contiguous to the borders. Security precautions had to be taken there to ensure general safety. Hence, movement by Arabs and Jews in particularly sensitive areas was controlled, but controls were soon relaxed and began to be lifted progressively as it became clear that, by and large, Arab citizens of Israel were not willing to work with trouble-makers and Israel's security forces showed that they could tackle infiltration and terrorism.

In 1949, apart from the urgency of integrating and rehabilitating Arabs, Israel had other tremendous human and social problems. Survivors of Hitler's Europe, and war refugees from the Arab States of North Africa and the Middle East, streamed into its ports and airfields. Penniless and without skills in all too many cases, the newcomers arrived by the hundreds of thousands in those first years. It was against that background that Israel began to embark on programmes through which its Arab community, first and foremost, could help itself. This, indeed, has been the governing principle of Israel's policy from the very start. The guiding lines were set in the Declaration of Independence of 14 May 1949, in these words:

> The State of Israel will rest upon foundations of liberty, justice and peace as envisioned by the Prophets of Israel. It will maintain complete equality

of social and political rights for all its citizens, without distinction of creed, race or sex. It will guarantee freedom of religion and conscience, of language, education, and culture. It will safeguard the Holy Places of all religions. It will be loyal to the principles of the United Nations Charter.

Even amidst the violent attacks launched against us for months past, we call upon the sons of the Arab people dwelling in Israel to keep the peace and to play their part in building the State on the basis of full and equal citizenship and due representation in all its institutions, provisional and permanent.

We extend the hand of peace and good-neighbourliness to all the States around us and to their peoples, and we call upon them to cooperate in mutual helpfulness with the independent Jewish nation in its Land. The State of Israel is prepared to make its contribution in a concerted effort for the advancement of the entire Middle East.

A POLICY OF PROGRESS

Subjectively, Israel's Jewish citizens were determined to translate the spirit and the letter of the Declaration into practical every-day terms. They realized that the gap in standards of living, in social and educational levels, between the Arab community and themselves could not be bridged overnight. In an ambience of freedom, it was evolution, geared to the needs and the will of that community, that would have to determine the formative — and reformative — policy. Coercion, in any shape or form, was utterly incompatible with the spirit and the ethics of this new democratic State. And evolution meant years of 'gradualness'. The Jews were conscious that its point had been mainly of European origin, heir to a European level of civilization and to Europe's technical norms. The Arab element was a product of centuries of a Middle Eastern lag. Government policy, therefore, was founded on two axioms: to bridge, as swiftly as possible, the gap between the standards of living and to respect, encourage and help to develop Arab ethnic and religious distinctiveness.

It was natural that there should be setbacks and imperfections. Israel's simultaneous problems — mass intake and integration of Jewish immigrants, defense and security — and a lack of raw materials and economic resources set their own tempo of development. The national loaf had to be sliced very thin, too thin to satisfy all appetites. At times, the importance that Israel attached to speeding up progress among its Arab citizens meant that the opportunities offered were beyond what they felt willing or able to use. At other times, by reason of limited budgets, opportunities fell short of their capacity. All in all, however, the rate and extent of advance have been more than impressive.

If we have dwelt on these objective circumstances, it is because visitors have occasionally been tempted to apply the wrong criteria of analysis. They did not compare how the Arab community was circumstanced at any subsequent moment with how it stood in 1949, but sought contrasts with the standards of the Jewish community, forgetting that the Jewish starting-point had, in great part, been European. Critics unfriendly to Isreal, particularly propagandists of the Arab States, have consistently exploited the disparity in a demagogic manoeuvre to show that Israel discriminated against its Arabs. Such fabrications have paid poorer and poorer dividends as the gap narrowed demonstrably year by year. In short, the testament of history has been re-written.

Since 14 May 1948, every Isreali, without distinction of origin, sex or creed, has had parity of rights, civic social and political. Every man and woman from the age of eighteen may vote in parliamentary and municipal elections, every man and woman from the age of twenty-one may be a candidate for election. In every successive polling since 1948, at least four out of every five of all the eligible Arabs and Druzes cast their ballots; there have been times when the percentage was nearer ninety. Arab and Druze Members of the Knesset, Israel's Parliament, take vigorous part in debates, not confining themselves to championing sectional interests but evincing a high sense of responsibility for national needs.

Arabs, like Jews, have free entry to all health and educational services, to the benefits of social welfare and to the advantages of the conprehensive development undertaken by central and local government. Arabic, like Hebrew, is an official language, in Parliament and over the radio and on television, and is, of course, the medium of instruction in Arab schools. The Arab community exercises uninhibited cultural and religious autonomy.

RELIGION AND COMMUNITY

For centuries, religion in the Middle East, unlike much of Europe and the Western world, has been not merely a matter of private or individual conscience, but an integral part of the fight by minorities to be emancipated from oppression. This was particularly true in the Ottoman empire. Israel's policy, therefore, has been, and is, to extend freedom of faith to every citizen and to recognize, as on a par, the authority of the ecclesiastical institutions of Jews and Arabs. It is an authority that embraces issues of personal status — marriage, divorce and alimony, guardianship, wills and legacies, and the affairs of minors. Moslem and Christian religious courts, in point of fact, exercise a wider jurisdiction than the Jewish; the Shari'a (Moslem) tribunals possess exclusive competence in any and every question of personal status. For the individual, the virtue of this freedom of faith, of the statutory and constitutional recognition of clerical authority, is all the greater, seeing that Israel's Arabs are subdivided into several denominational and communal groupings: most of them are Moslems, but Christians, who belong to several Churches, are a sizable percentage, and there are, besides, some thirty thousand Druzes professing an eclectic religion of their own.

At the same time, Israel's civil law governs all creeds without exception: the marriage of a girl younger than seventeen years is forbidden, and so is polygamy; no wife may be divorced against her will; a woman's rights of inheritance are fully secured. Once and for all, the legal status of women in Israel has been equated to that of men.

Through the Ministry of Religious Affairs, the Government looks to the welfare, and supports the authority, of the religious organs and establishments of Moslems, Christians and Druzes, as it does for the corresponding institutions of the Jewish community. Public funds are as readily voted to protect and improve the sacred and historical sites of those three communities as they are for Jewish shrines and monuments. The Ministry scrupulously refrains from interfering in their domestic concerns; there is not the slightest trespass on Arab prerogatives to develop and conduct religious ceremony and worship, to determine suits of personal status, to maintain ecclesiastical and charitable agencies, and to manage the widest gamut of internal affairs.

The Jewish Sabbath is only one among the official weekly days of rest. The Moslem Friday and the Christian Sunday are co-equally recognized. For all faiths, there is an absolute and statutory privilege to stop working on their weekly restdays and on the holy days of their religious calendars.

Until the Six-Day War was fought, the number of Moslem Arabs to be vouchsafed this communal and religious liberty exceeded two hundred thousand.

154

Since then, with the extension of Israel administration to Judaea, Samaria and the Gaza Strip, hundreds of thousands more have been granted it. The re-unification of Jerusalem has given back to the Arabs of Israel the unimpeded and unconditioned access to the shrines of Islam and Christendom in the Old City — an access that had been denied by the Jordanian Government all through its presence in East Jerusalem, except at Christmas and Easter, when a limited quota of Israeli Christians was accorded dispensation by it to cross the artificial border for a few hours. Of all the — in sum total, over the years — thousands of Israeli Christians who would thus make the crossing into Jordan for their seasonal devotions, not a single one ever failed to return punctually; this surely attests a genuine attachment to Israel.

Israel has striven unremittingly to gain permission for its Moslem citizens to perform the pilgrimage to Mecca and Medina, and, at long last, in the light of the new conjunctures brought about by its administrative responsibility for the West Bank and the Gaza Strip, it has succeeded in negotiating the desired right of transit from the Jordanian authorities, and the Government of Saudi Arabia will not withhold the consequent right of entry. For its own part, Israel offers free access to Nebi Shueib, near the Horns of Hittin, to Druzes from Syria and Lebanon who wish to join their fellow-sectaries in the annual celebration at the legendary tomb of Jethro.

By 1967, there were a hundred and twenty mosques in Israel, and new houses of Moslem worship were under construction in Nazareth, Kfar Yassif and Jedida. Two hundred Moslems officiants were being paid their salary from Israel's exchequer. The Knesset had passed a law permitting the delivery of Moslem religious endowments (awqaf) to committees of Moslem trustees in towns and villages, so that the income might be devoted to communal, educational and charitable purposes; under the same law, family foundations of that kind can be handed over to the legitimate beneficiaries.

By June 1967, there were in Israel fifty-eight thousand Arabs professing Christianity. The heads of their Churches attended ecclesiastical conferences abroad with no let or hindrance; Christian clergy from other countries visited Israel freely, including clergy resident in the Kingdom of Jordan.

Most of the almost thirty thousand Druze citizens of Israel live in large villages in the north. Till 1948, the group had not been recognized in the Holy Land as a distinct religious entity. Four years ago, a Supreme Religious Council of the community was established and Israel law brought Druze religious courts into being, with standard communal jurisdiction in all Druze matters of personal status and religious endowments. Administratively directed by a young Druze gradutate of the Faculty of Law in the Hebrew University of Jerusalem, the courts apply Lebanon's Druze Personal Status Law of 1948, as adopted also by the Druzes of Syria. Testimony of the successful integration of the Druze community is that, since 1957, young Druzes have been conscripted into the Israel Defence Forces at the express wish of the community.

The Six-Day War has widened the vistas and the orbit of religious freedom in the Middle East. The Holy Places of Judaism, Islam and Christianity in the Old City of Jerusalem, in Bethlehem and Hebron, are now totally and unreservedly accessible to the faithful, as have always been the Holy Places within sovereign Israel. Israeli Moslems can fraternize in prayer with co-religionists in the historic mosques of the Old City. Chrismas in Bethlehem in 1967 drew greater significance than ever it did in the last twenty years from its newly-won accessibility and as a hopeful augury of the tranquil harmony that must one day illumine all peoples and all faiths in this region which saw civilization born.

LOCAL GOVERNMENT

Twenty years ago, elected local government existed in only three Arab centeres. Today there are forty Arab local and municipal councils, with seventy per cent of Israel's Arab population as their constituency. They have engaged in extensive development works of their own planning, with grants from the State of approximately one half of the costs involved. The works range from public parks to street lighting, from modern markets to factory zones, from classrooms to clinics. To design and carry out these projects has incidentally been excellent training in local government.

Israel's five-year plan for improving Arab and Druze village life entered its final phase in 1966-67. It included the provision of such essential services as village approach-roads, electricity, piped water, health and educational amenities and new housing, and the setting up of municipalities wherever population and modernization had outpaced the capacity of local councils. An important part of the plan was to guarantee the new investments which would create and multiply openings for work and raise the level of income in farming and artisanry, in industry and commerce. The Arab-Israel Bank, in partnership with the Government, makes rewarding loans available to industry: for example, in Nazareth, for constructing ready-to-use workshop centres. This five-year plan had been estimated to cost I £ 55,000,000, of which I £ 25,000,000 was to come from the State Department Budgets, but, in the course of performance, it was considerably enlarged and the eventual outlay was I £ 85,000,000, of which I £ 44,000,000 came from the Treasury.

Thousands of homes have been built to settle nomadic Bedouin permanently, to house Druze ex-servicemen, young couples and workers. The extensive network of modern buildings in the Arab areas of Israel today is one outcome of the plan, not to speak of noteworthy advances in municipal services, in the realms of health and schooling and in the ramification of farming, handicrafts and industry.

And once the initial scheme had been carried through, a more advanced, finalizing stage was blueprinted. The aims now are: completion of the infrastructure of rural services — education, electricity and other 'municipalized' requirements; further capital investment to assure the fullest employment, to raise living standards higher yet and to step up productivity in farm and factory and in workshop; a closer alignment of the employment complex to the needs of a modern economy; easement of the livelihood and the conditions of Arab labour by housing it nearer the job, directing village manpower to conveniently-placed economic centres, and developing rural-urban communications; expansion of vocational *pari passu* with general education; strengthening of the social and cultural fabric of Arabs in mixed towns by providing better homes and the essential periphery of schools, colleges and institutions of health and welfare; and, by no means least, the stabilization of Bedouin tribesmen throughout Galilee and the Negev in planned villages that, from the start, incorporate all the imperative adjuncts of even the simplest gainful life — drinking-water, ways of access, schools and clinics.

This larger plan is likely to cost about I £ 130,000,000.

BEDOUIN SETTLEMENT

Of all the changes impinging upon the lives of Israel's Arab community, perhaps the most remarkable have to do with its thirty thousand Bedouin. Many of them are already domiciled for good in up-to-date villages with the most modern of municipal arrangements. Each new point of settlement was carefully chosen and patterned, with an eye, in each instance, to the specific values and needs of the tribes. Construction, entirely at the State's charge, includes public buildings and services. One village was built near Ramla, in the centre of Israel, whither Bedouin had moved to find work, and over five hundred already live in it. The tribesmen are profiting greatly from Israel's free and compulsory elementary education, and, beyond that, Bedouin pupils are now to be found in high schools and Universities. Near Beersheba, where a large Bedouin village has been in existence for some years, a new trade school is being built to help its inhabitants to adjust themselves to a twentieth-century economy.

LIVING STANDARDS

Most dramatic has been the rise of Arab living standards: they have altered out of recognition since the days of the British Mandate. This reflects not only the tremendous strides made by Israel's economy as a whole in that brief interval, but also the self-effort and changing values of the Arabs of Israel themselves. A traditionally closed Arab husbandry has been transformed by mechanization, irrigation and the variegation of crops into an ever-expanding and sophisticated agricultural economy. This substitution, in its turn, has led to a movement of part of the village labour-force to mushrooming urban areas and its absorption there in industry, so that income levels and living standards have climbed rapidly.

According to a survey recently made in Nazareth, the average annual income of an urban Arab family is practically identical with that of an urban Jewish family. It is higher today, for example, than the income of Jewish newcomers from Asia and Africa. The real worth of Arab farm-produce is sixfold what it was twenty years ago. The Israeli Arab today earns, on an average, four times as much as his fellow-Arab in any neighbouring country.

Once the mainstay of the Arab population, agriculture today need occupy only forty per cent of its workers. Crop rotation, scientific farming, land reclamation and planned marketing have brought about this agrarian revolution. The land is vastly bountiful, and much higher earnings from it furnish the means for its further development. This development has been sedulously fostered by the Government: training by demonstration techniques on a large scale; credit on easy terms; the same minimum prices guaranteed for Arab produce as for Jewish; a fourfold rise in the area under irrigation, and the process is continuing; spectacular development of orchards; a four hundred per cent increment of livestock. Certain traditional crops are being circumspectly replaced by sugar-beet, groundnuts, cotton and tobacco, which, apart from yielding ampler returns, are neutralizing the Arab farmer's stereotyped, and, in the past, often ruinous, dependence on a single crop. Twenty years ago, only five combine-harvesters were to be found in Arab hands; today, there are hundreds. Young Arabs by the score are studying scientific farming in Israel's widespread vocational schools and, on graduation, ought to make a valuable contribution to the further diversification and prosperity of the rural scene.

The Bedouin economy, too, has been revamped fundamentally: until a few years ago, it was almost exclusively grazing of flocks and primitive cultivation of wheat and barley in virtually rainless areas; today, irrigation and mixed farming assure handsome proceeds and a stable husbandry for the tribes.

As we saw, farming, intensified by irrigation and mechanization, requires fewer hands to tend it, and, correspondingly, more Arabs seek, and readily find, employment in workshops and factories, in building and services. This occupational re-direction has led to far-reaching shifts of habit and convention.

157

Industry signifies more than an urban way of life; it brings out such qualities as punctuality and diligence, alacrity and technical skill, all of them attributes that are strangers to much of the Middle East. Moreover, enrolment in industry makes for direct and continuous contact between Arab and Jewish workers. Industrialization accelerates the pace of Arab integration into the society of Israel.

During the Mandate, there were marked differences in wage levels between Jewish and Arab factory operatives. In the State of Israel, practically the whole labour-force belongs to one or other trade union and its conditions are protected by statute; Arabs and Jews are members of the same unions and get equal pay for equal work. The law regulates how long the working-day shall be and guarantees days of rest and vacations on full wages. It obliges employers to ensure their workers against accidents; it provides for social benefits in line with the most forward precedents. The Employment Service Law grants all citizens the elementary right to work, regardless of faith, race or sex. Labour conditions in Israel for Arab and Jew alike can, therefore, be claimed to be far in advance of any in the Arab States, and even ahead of many parts of Europe.

Already, more than half of the Arab workers of Israel have joined the largest labour federation, known as the Histadrut. The Histadrut is especially active in improving the lot of Arab women; it arranges vocational courses, educational and cultural interests and other means of elevating their status to equality with their menfolk. It helps Arab workers to organize themselves in producers' and consumers' cooperatives, a trend which has transfigured Arab life not a little; under the Mandate, the cooperative movement was largely a Jewish concern, and the Arabs kept to traditional marketing and purchasing methods on an individual or family basis, but, since 1948, Arab societies have achieved excellent progress and have begun to embark upon enterprises and investments of sizable dimension.

It was not easy to make Arab industry and handicrafts self-sufficient. In Mandatory days, it had been rudimentary and microscopic. Lack of resource, and reluctance to risk capital, retarded development. Technical know-how and the right substratum were not to be had in the villages. But, since 1948, thanks to copious expenditure, mainly by the State, on communications, waterworks and electricity, and to the adoption of a new way of life, an industrialization of modern form and magnitude has been characterized by constant progress. The Government encourages joint Arab-Jewish manufactures. It has opened vocational training centres for Arabs, and one such centre at Tamra, for example, offers instruction for young people and refresher courses for grown-ups.

There has been marked extension in the Arab sector in recruitment, and training, for service vocations, and, though there is still room for a good deal of improvement here, more and more qualified Arabs and Druzes are entering the Civil Service as teachers, administrators, doctors, Police officers, nurses and social workers, for instance. A few 'pockets' of the casual unskilled linger on, usually in restaurants and garages: as a rule, they do not belong to any trade union, and their terms of employment leave much to be desired.

HEALTH AND EDUCATION

Apart from campaigns to counter epidemics, the Mandatory Administration did not do much to install medical services in Arab and Druze villages. The villagers' neglect or ignorance of the rules of hygiene was complicated by the unavailability of an independent health agency. Preventive medical services and

158

treatment in Israel, today, are of very high standard, and Arab citizens profit accordingly, getting the necessary care in modern clinics, with the fees covered by insurance. About eighty per cent of the Arab population already have their local medical services, which comprise, *inter alia*, 79 village clinics and 64 mother-and-child stations. Soon, almost every village will have its own clinic or health establishment. These continuing improvements speak for themselves with statistical eloquence. The death-rate among Israel's Arabs dropped from 20 per thousand in 1948 to 6.1 per thousand in 1965 and is today one of the lowest in the world. Infant mortality fell from 68 per thousand in 1948 to 40 per thousand in 1965 (the figure in Egypt, in 1962, was reported to be 134), and should be lower from year to year, as already eighty per cent of Arab children are born in hospital; in Israel, all expectant mothers who enter hospital to have their babies get a grant from the National Insurance Institute. Natural increase among Israel's Arabs went up from 34 per thousand in 1952 to 44.5 per thousand in 1965, among the highest figures in the world and nearly three times that of Israel's Jews.

Education, key to the future of any modern community, has undergone spectacular change. Israel took over from the Mandatory a narrow, rudimentary, network of sixty Government primary schools and a solitary high school, serving a total of hundred and eleven Arab towns and villages. Within eighteen years, the Israel Ministry of Education and Culture was responsible for 360 schools in Arab areas: 160 kindergartens attended by 8,200 children, 183 State primary schools with over 53,000 pupils, a 'special care' and two 'working youth' schools with a total of 1,685 pupils. Moreover, there were 11,500 pupils in Christian confessional and Mission establishments.

Some 23,000 Arab girls are at school today, in kindergarten and primary classes in the main, but the first 200 have by now reached secondary level; the figure represents no less than seventy-five per cent of all Arab girls of school age. The percentage of Arab boys of school age attending classes had, at the time of writing, risen above ninety-five per cent. Compared to pre-State times (when school attendance was less than fifty per cent, nearly all boys), the educational map of Israel's Arab community has been re-scaled and re-drawn.

The expansion was launched at the end of the 1948-49 fighting under tremendous handicaps. One serious difficulty was an acute shortage of teachers, due to the flight of so many of the Arab intelligentsia. The Government, therefore, gave priority to teacher-training. A teacher-training college for Arabs was established in Haifa, and today it has 135 men and women students; the money for its construction came from the budget of the Ministry of Education and Culture, which regularly provides loans to the students to defray the expenses of the entire course. At the moment, there are 2,000 Arab teachers, but, though eight times what it was in 1949, this cadre is far from enough to answer current demands.

Over 350 Arabs are now studying either at the Hebrew University of Jerusalem in the Faculties of Humanities and Natural Sciences, of Medicine, Law and Agriculture, or at the Israel Institute of Technology in Haifa in all engineering subjects. The Histadrut has started classes in journalism for Arab women and runs a course in office management for fifty Arab students at a time; graduates of this course are to be given appointments in the Ministry of Finance and as managers in the Histadrut's own banks and factories.

Of especial interest are the thirty-four schools opened for Bedouin children exclusively, fourteen in the Negev and twenty in Galilee. Nineteen years ago, not one such school was in existence. It is of hardly less significance that almost half of the Arab students now being trained as teachers are women. Progress may also be reckoned by the statistic that, while, in 1958, the proportion of Arab elementary pupils who passed the examination for admission to secondary level was twelve per cent, the figure today is thirty-two percent. In 1962, only from ten to fourteen per cent of Arab secondary pupils passed their matriculation; about three times as many now succeed. In 1952, only ten Arab students were enrolled in institutions of higher learning in Israel; the present enrolment is almost thirty times as large, as we have noted.

To assist University students in adjusting themselves to new surroundings, generous aid is granted in housing, in loans, in special coaching and professional guidance; it is most rewarding aid, for the Arab community is in pressing need of doctors, social workers and agronomists.

All this is adding steadily to the number and competence of Arab civil servants, which means that the Arab population can begin to take a proper part in the management of public affairs.

This, however, is not to say that the training of young Arabs in the vocational skills that are indispensable in any balanced communal economy in a technological world is neglected.

The Government does all that it can, as well, to foster Arab cultural development, but it feels that it may fairly expect the main inspiration and action to come from within the community itself. Until the Six-Day War, the frontiers between the Arabs of Israel and of the surrounding Arab countries were almost impassable in the cultural as well as in the physical sense. Now, although permanent frontiers, mirroring permanent peace, are yet to be negotiated, there is already good ground for believing that contact and communication between Israel's Arabs and the Arabs of Samaria and Judaea in particular should develop with mutually advantageous cultural stimulation. Israel's Arabs have always enjoyed full cultural and intellectual freedom of expression in their own language, history and religion — whether Moslem or Christian. Arabic newspapers have wide circulations, as have periodicals and books in Arabic, including the translated works of foreign authors. The Hebrew University of Jerusalem has a regular programme for translating Arabic classics into Hebrew and Hebrew classics into Arabic. Jewish and Arab writers conduct a joint literary forum. An Arabic theatre is being established in Jerusalem. With the re-unification of East and West Jerusalem, the Arabs of the Old City can take a larger interest and share in the cultural life of Israel's Arabs.

NEW HORIZONS

For Israel and its Arab community, the June war opens up the newest and brightest of horizons. For almost twenty years, it had been beset, its security constantly imperilled, its frontiers undefined. The armistice lines marked out in 1949 were regarded as provisional until a permanent and directly negotiated peace would replace them by agreed frontiers. The lines encompassed a territory of less than 8,000 square miles or 20,700 square kilometres. But, by reason of topography, they were disproportionately long — 1,025 kilometres. A land-length of as many as 951 kilometres was the transient demarcation between Israel and the Arab States. The midriff of Israel from the Jordan armistice line to the Mediterranean was no wider than 14.6 kilometres. Such elongated boundaries, within easy striking distance of areas vital to Israel's existence, rendered maintenance of security exceedingly difficult and were an ever-present temptation to the aggressor.

The Arab States, in those twenty years, agreed neither to discuss peace and, with it, permanent frontiers, nor to recognize the validity of the armistice lines. Terrorists and spies were smuggled across the lines to harass Israel's civilians. Because many of the Arab villages of Israel were contiguous to Jordanian, Syrian, Egyptian or Lebanese territory, Israel was constrained to apply the Mandatory's Defence Regulations, and set up a military control in the highly sensitive areas. The reasons for it were geographical, and the only task of the military administration was to counter hostile action, whether from across the lines or by a handful of local intransigents.

At the beginning, travel in the controlled areas required identity documents and permits, for Jews and Arabs alike. By the early 'fifties, however, restrictions were being progressively relaxed. Soon, they had become a formality, and movement to the centre of Israel was uncomplicated and unhindered. By 1 December 1966, the control apparatus and all its ramifications could be abolished. At no time, however, while this especial vigilance was necessary, had there been interference with the normal life of Israel's Arabs: they were no whit less free than the rest of the inhabitants.

The fighting of June 1967 has re-designed the security patterns of Israel in every detail. The armistice lines of 1949, eroded into empty fiction by unending Arab violations, lost any historical importance that they might have had. They have been replaced by cease-fire lines, marking, geographically, the contours where the fighting stopped, namely, the Jordan River, the Suez Canal, the Gaulan Ridge and the Mediterranean. Twenty years of bitter taste of Arab aggression are Israel's warrant for insisting upon directly negotiated, permanent and secure frontiers, within the context of a durable and guaranteed peace, as the only acceptable alternative to cease-fire lines. True, the cease-fire line along the Jordan River tends to circumscribe Israel's security problem, because it is far shorter than the one that had to be defended before June 1967, and is much further withdrawn from critical points in Israel. At the same time, controlling the Gaulan Ridge, the West Bank of the Jordan River (Judaea and Samaria), the Gaza Strip and the Sinai peninsula, Israel is now answerable for a new Arab population which a recent census puts at one million and whose economic level is nothing like as high as that which the Arabs of Israel have reached. The June war, though it was swift, left its legacy of suffering and havoc. Not less swift has been Israel's reinstatement of normality in the administered areas. Services have been restored everywhere. In extent and scope, economic activity already shows promise of outreaching its pre-June bounds. If the Arab States persist in their recalcitrance toward Israel, if they will not negotiate a permanent peace, it is not unlikely that Israel influence on the life of the Arabs in the administered areas will begin to produce effects no different from those which, ever since 1948, the Arab community of Israel has been experiencing to its manifest well-being.

But whatever the measurable future has in store — a protracted status quo or a genuine peace — the Arabs of Israel, by their very precept and example, are bound to be a decisive factor in shaping the relations between Israel and the Arabs of Judaea, Samaria and the Gaza Strip, if not beyond, too. What has been demonstrated above all doubt and challenge is that Jews and Arabs can dwell together peacefully and constructively, that the Arab citizens of Israel are loyal in peace and war, and that, given democracy and an environment of cooperative friendship, an Arab community, by its own efforts, will find itself garnering the harvest of every boon and benefit that this century can bring.

REIGN
OF
TERROR

Palestine
Research
Center

The Fourth Geneva Convention was conceived for the protection of civilian populations in time of conflict. This Convention was signed in 1949 by most countries of the world. Israel signed it in 1951. According to this Convention, the civilian population in a territory occupied by a foreign power falls under the category of "protected persons" defined as follows: "Persons protected by the Convention are those who, at a given moment and in any manner whatsoever, find themselves, in case of a conflict or occupation in the hands of a party to the conflict or Occupying Power of which they are not nationals."

Yet, if anything, there could hardly be two more ironical words, for the Arabs under Israeli occupation, than "protected persons." Both during the June War of 1967 and its aftermath, Israel, which likes to pose as the pillar of civilization in the Middle East, committed grave violations of the ruling of the Geneva Convention. Both prisoners of war and civilian population, as well as members of resistance movements, are protected by these rulings, and all the military and civilian personnel of an occupying power are bound by them, whatever orders they might have received from their superiors or government. Furthermore, they are liable to prosecution for transgressing them.

In the week of November 10, 1967, a member of the PEACE NEWS staff interviewed an Israeli journalist who was stationed with the occupation forces after the June war of 1967 on the West Bank near the Jordan. He recounted what he himself had seen of the shooting of refugees and the so-called "infiltrators" crossing the Jordan from the East Bank, and described, in detail, interviews with soldiers who had themselves taken part in the operations. He also spoke of destruction of Arab villages. Following are some of the accounts(1) of the Israeli soldiers who took part in the operations.

> Every night Arabs crossed the Jordan from East to West. We sealed off the passages and were ordered to shoot to kill without warning. In fact we fired every night on men, women, children, even on moonlit nights when we could distinguish between men, women, and children.

In the mornings we searched the area and, acting under explicit orders from the officers on the spot, shot the living, including those who had hidden and those who were wounded. Again, these included men, women and children. After killing them, we covered them with earth, or left them lying until a bulldozer came to bury them.

Some of the people were intelligence agents, some were armed infiltrators, some were smugglers. But mostly they were former inhabitants of the West Bank who had not received an Israeli permit to return.

There were cases I will never forget. Once we found two men wounded, and the officer ordered us to kill them. We shot them on the spot. Another time, we found two men wounded in the leg. We talked with them and took their papers, and then the officer ordered us to kill them. They understood what was happening from our gestures, and desperately pleaded for their lives. We all left the place except one man who had volunteered to kill them. He had to fire six times before they were dead.

The stories are many, but I am telling only of events that I saw with my own eyes. Accounts by other soldiers are abundant. I heard of stories setting fire to heaps of bodies. One morning I myself saw bodies in a heap, among them the body of a young girl. On another occasion an El Fatah man pleaded for his life. When he saw that it was useless, he cursed and took the bullets. Another night a group of about twenty crossed. We shot them. In the morning we found eleven bodies . . .

I am disclosing this information in the hope that it will become known to as many Israeli citizens as possible. Perhaps some will be able to use their influence to put a stop to these events.

THE BLOW-UP-AND-EXPEL POLICY

On August 31, 1967, the Israeli authorities mercilessly eradicated the three Arab villages of Emaus, Beit Nuba, and Yalu, driving the poor Arab inhabitants out, after torturing women, children and men alike. The description of the brutality of the Israeli soldiers was actually given by a soldier who took part in the eradication operations. Amos Kenan, a freelance Israeli writer, sent a description of the events to the Israeli newspaper, HAOLAM HAZEH, but of course, the statement was never published, but it was duplicated and circulated in Israel.(2) The only acknowledgement of the Israeli Government to these events was a brief report in the press saying that the Cabinet had discussed "the purity of Israeli arms." This esoteric term has definite meaning in Israel. It is used whenever suspect activities of the army come to public attention.

Amos Kenan, in his statement, spoke how the decision to destroy Emaus, Beit Nuba, and Yalu was justified by the Israeli authorities who ordered the soldiers to destroy the houses and expel the villagers.

The Unit Commander told us that three villages in our sector were to be destroyed . . . The decision was justified by strategic, tactical, and security considerations: to straighten out the border at Latrun; to 'punish the nests of murderers;' to eliminate future bases of infiltration . . .

. . . the orders were to shoot over their heads and to warn them not to enter the village. We did not shoot in the air, but took cover and some soldiers who spoke Arabic went over to explain our instructions. There were old people who could hardly walk, old women murmuring, women carrying babies, and small children. The children wept and asked for water. We told them to go to Beit Sura. They said they had been walking on the roads from everywhere and forbidden to enter any village. For four days they had been walking on the roads without food and water. Some of the children cried and some of our soldiers were crying too.

Our unit was outraged. At night we were ordered to guard the bulldozers, but the soldiers were so angry that no one would carry out the duty. In the morning we were moved from the area. None of us understood how Jews could behave in such a way. No one understood why the farmers should not be allowed to take their stoves, blankets and some food.

After the eradication of the three villages, a foreign correspondent asked an official military spokesman for an explanation to the action. The answer offered was that "fewer than 67 houses had been destroyed and it had taken place during the war." The same correspondent, trying to push the question further, never received an answer and was told there was nothing to add to the earlier reply.(3)

But the latter example is one of hundreds of others which proved the disregard with which the Israeli occupation authorities treated the Geneva Convention or, more specifically, Article 53, which stated that "any destruction by the Occupying Power of movable or immovable property belonging individually or collectively to private persons, or the State, or to other public authorities, or to social or cooperative organizations, is prohibited except where such destruction is rendered absolutely necessary by military operations." It is difficult to explain how the destruction of Beit Nuba, Emaus, and Yalu could be justified by "except where such destruction is rendered absolutely necessary by military operations."

A report presented by the United Nations to the General Assembly based on the report of Mr. Nils Göran Gussing, Personal Representative of the Secretary General, after his visit to the Gaza Strip, said on September 15, 1967, "The Israeli authorities have killed citizens and destroyed houses even after the end of military operations." The policy of blowing up houses by the Israeli occupation was even condemned by the U. S. During a press conference on March 8, 1968, an official U. S. State Department spokesman urged Israel to abide by international laws in the Arab territories seized in the June war and insisted that the destruction of the houses of "suspected" terrorists contravened international agreements.

The blow-up-and-expel policy followed by the Israelis is not new and is evidently aimed to achieve the following:

1. Blowing up a house or houses which have been allegedly used to hide or protect Arab freedom fighters was in fact aimed at setting an example to the Arab inhabitants for future actions.

2. By spreading a reign of terror, the Israelis hoped that the greatest number of Arabs would leave the occupied territories for other Arab countries thus, on the one hand, decreasing the number of Arabs, and on the other, making more room for Jews to settle in their places.(4)

3. By acting as such, the Israeli authorities wanted to soothe the fears of the Israeli populace that there is a government which is doing something to protect them no matter if the action of blowing up houses was justified, humane, legal or not.

The destruction of houses by the occupation authorities since the June war has numbered in the hundreds and every time a house was blown up, a new wave of refugees crossed the Jordan River to the East Bank. One could only cite a few examples:

— On November 28, 1868, Israeli security forces blew up a number of Arab houses in Deir Al Balah village in the Gaza Strip in retaliation for the murder of a farmer.

— In order to intimidate the population, the military authorities dynamited houses where freedom fighters might have found shelter or help.(5)

— On January 11, 1968, the JERUSALEM POST reported that "a number of shacks in the Shati refugee camp were demolished by the security forces on January 9."

— The London TIMES said on March 7, 1968, "The order to destroy houses of anyone to be connected with saboteurs or to have sheltered them is still enforced. At least 100 houses have been destroyed."

— Just before that, the OBSERVER, on January 28, 1967, said, "Non-Arab residents of the (Gaza) Strip share the Arab view that punishment is meted out to tens of thousands of people who could not possibly be implicated in the incidents: the destruction of houses, whose inhabitants' only crime is to be living at or near the spot where a bomb explodes, is out of all proportion to the acts committed."

Thus the destruction of property was actually carried out on entire villages, whole quarters, and individual homes in addition to the blowing up of shops, offices, and in, some cases, hospitals.(6)

The absence of any plausible justification in most cases is made obvious by the trivial reason adduced for such drastic measures. On some occasions, the excuse has been that an electricity wire has been cut, or a grenade thrown in the neighborhood. On others, that a relative of the owner is suspected of being a member of the resistance. Sometimes no excuse whatsoever is given. In an almost insignificant number of cases the reasons alleged were the harbouring of Arab commandos, the possession of arms or membership to a resistance movement. Whatever the motive, the destruction of movable or immovable property is a direct infringement of human rights and is explicitly prohibited by Article 53 of the Fourth Geneva Convention and Article 17, paragraph 2 of the U. N. Declaration of Human Rights.

In most cases of destruction of property, it should be emphasized, the owners would not be allowed to take away their belongings or would at best be given a few minutes to save what they could. The intention was obviously not only to deprive the victims of their dwellings, but also of all means of subsistence or, in other words, to leave them altogether destitute.

Such lack of restraint prompted the Chairman of the U. N. Commission of Human Rights to call upon the Israeli government on March 13, 1968, to "desist forthwith from indulging in such practices and to respect human rights and fundamental freedoms."(7)

The Israeli version of demolitoin actions was explained by the head of the Israel Military Government for the Occupied Territories, Brigadier Shlomo Gazit. In an interview with Kol Israel, he said, "The act of blowing up houses is essentially . . . a deterrent action, a punishment which is supposed to deter others. I am not sure that expropriation would achieve the same deterrent effect; first of all, because of the consideration that expropriation may be reversed. Although I repeat that the subject needs further fundamental study, expropriation does not seem to be a practical method."(8)

The intentional destruction of houses without justification even evoked the anger of Israelis themselves. Dr. Israel Liff, of the Hebrew University in Jerusalem, described the situation as follows:

Now, with the bombing of houses in the heart of East Jerusalem and Beit Hanina, public opinion in Israel and abroad against such atrocities has been aroused. Demolishing houses (like the expulsion of leaders) causes only harm to our case . . . The suspects whose houses were demolished were not brought before the court martial and have not yet been convicted. Even if they were convicted in the future, there is neither justice nor advantage in avenging their wives and children and robbing them of their shelters . . . "(9)

SUMMARY ARRESTS AND INTIMIDATION

According to the Fourth Geneva Convention, Article 33, "collective penalties are prohibited" while Article 32 states the following:

The high Contracting Parties specifically agree that each of them is prohibited from taking any measure of such a character as to cause the physical suffering or extermination of protected persons in their lands. This prohibition applies not only to murder, torture, corporal punishment, mutilation and medical or scientific experiments not necessitated by the medical treatment of a protected person, but also to any other measures of brutality . . .

The arbitrary arrest of peaceful civilians often on whimsical charges has, perhaps, been the commonest feature of Israeli conduct. While it is not possible to give an exact figure of all those who have been so arrested, it is estimated that at least 10,000 Arab civilians have seen the inside of Israeli prisons since June 5, 1967. At any one point of time since this date, there have been at least 2,000 civilians in prison held either indefinitely or serving terms longer than one year.

On August 11, 1967, the Red Cross submitted a report to the International Red Cross office in Geneva to the effect that "the Israeli army has often arrested citizens in downtown Gaza in the daytime, for the sole reason of spreading terror."

Examples that could be cited are inumerable and one could only mention a few:

— In the period of only two days, on January 11 and 12, 40 persons suspected of sabotage were arrested in the Gaza Strip.(10)

— The intimidatory measures imposed by the Israeli authorities on the village of Al Arish in the Sinai Desert during the week of December 11, 1967, were so strengthend that it was difficult to find a single boy in the town who had not been imprisoned for some days without any reason. It was also reported that during that week, and between midnight and 3 a.m. each night, every family lived in a state of anxiety and expected to be arrested by the security forces at any minute; the men have been taken off for several days or weeks and during this period of detention would be subjected to the ugliest possible forms of torture.(11)

— The Red Cross, in Report Number 4 on August 23, 1967, reported that "adult Egyptian males, who had lived in Gaza and are presently imprisoned in Al Arish, are undergoing extreme hardships. They are held in concentration camps, which do not come up to the necessary sanitary conditions required."

A frequent practice is that of detaining individuals without any apparent reason, submitting them to interrogation accompanied by torture to obtain information, and releasing them after a certain period of time. One such case was that involving the student Youssef Attiyah Abu Youssef of Al Nusseirat Camp in Gaza, who was detained on August 21, 1967, for interrogation and freed one week later after having been beaten with iron bars on all parts of his body to the extent that — according to his own testimony, he could not stand on his own feet for some time after his release.(12)

Thus, to the obvious injustice of arbitrary and unwarranted detention is added the crime of physical coercion despite the fact that Article 31 of the Fourth Geneva Convention explicitly states that "no physical or moral coercion shall be exercised against protected persons, in particular to obtain information from them or from third parties."

The apparent object of this Israeli policy is to engulf the population in an atmosphere of continuous fear and insecurity in which no one feels himself beyond the reach of physical harm of degradation at the hands of the occupying authorities.

EVICTION AND DEPORTATIONS

In its Reprt Number 3, issued on August 11, 1967, the Red Cross reported the following, "Public cars leave Gaza regularly every morning to the West Bank of Jordan. The number of travellers vary from 400 to 500 daily, only 10 percent of which return to Gaza in the evening." This eviction of Arabs from their own lands by the occupation authorities was bluntly admitted by an Israeli newspaper, which reported that the "Israeli authorities force the Arab citizens of Gaza to seek refuge in Jordan."(13)

In fact, following the June war, the Israeli Government had promptly followed the mass eviction of the Arabs and individual deportations of Arab leaders in each of the Gaza Strip, the West Bank of Jordan, and the Golan Heights. Between June 5, 1967, and May 30, 1968, a total of 399, 248 Arabs from the West Bank and the Gaza Strip were evicted to the East Bank.(14)

In the immediate aftermath of the war, and particularly in the Gaza Strip, large numbers of young men were rounded in most towns and villages and marched off to the Suez Canal and the River Jordan and obliged to cross over. These initial collective measures resulted in the eviction of some 5,000 men from the Gaza Strip in one batch, of whom 2,000 came from Khan Younes, over 800 from the Coastal Camp and 600 from the Jabalia Camp.

An Israeli newspaper reported on June 13, 1967, that Israeli Major General Yosef Said had said that the "Israeli forces are endeavoring to persuade the Arab inhabitants . . . or to oblige them to cross the Suez Canal . . . and that many of them are afraid to leave their homes."(15)

One particular measure that has been interminably implemented by the occupation authorities in this respect is the deportation of prominent personalities from the West Bank, thus gradually depriving the Arab population of its leadership in the civic, religious and intellectual domains. This is an obvious attempt to break the morale of the Arabs and undermine their collective will to resist the step-by-step incorporation of the occupied territories into the State of Israel.

In fact, between August 23, 1967, and November 25, 1968, 34 Arab leaders, men and women, were actually deported by orders of the Ministry of Defense or the Military Governor.(16) Among these was the President of the Supreme Moslem Council Abdul Hamid Al Sayyed, Mayor of Jerusalem Rohi Al Khatib, former Jordanian Minister Kamal Dajani, and many other lawyers, teachers, school principals, doctors and school inspectors.

The blow dealt to the fabric of the community as a whole by this continuous erosion of its elite is naturally in addition to the moral and physical damage inflicted on the deported themselves, who are never given the chance to challenge the allegations made against them.

TREATMENT OF PRISONERS

Blowing up of houses, evictions, and deportations all contravene the stipulations of the Geneva Convention. Yet these measures have proved bearable when compared to the treatment of Arabs in prisons by the occupation authorities — treatment which has defied all human values, rights and principles. Nazi treatment has already been matched by the Israeli occupation authorities and long bypassed. What one could mention is only a little. The rest remains to be experienced in Israeli torture houses if it is to be comprehended.

In this regard, one cannot but quote the Declaration of Human Rights, which was primarily designed for treatment of people under occupation, for human beings imprisoned while fighting for their rights and their country. For the Declaration, among other things, dictates the following:

— that a human person should be treated in a spirit of brotherhood (Article 1).

— that he should have the right of life and security of person (Article 3).

— that no one shall arbitrarily deprive him of his property (Article 17/2).

— that he has the right to a fair trial by an independent and impartial tribunal. That he has the right to be presumed innocent until proved guilty according to the law in a public trial at which he has had all the guarantees necessary for his defence (Articles 8-11).

But the Declaration concerns itself merely with values, while the question of rights was best stipulated by the Geneva Convention of 1949, which Israel signed in 1951. More specifically, the Fourth Convention pertains to the protection of civilian persons in time of war. Only some of these articles could be mentioned here and the description which follows will reveal to what extent the Israelis have abided by them:

— use of physical or mental coercion against protected persons to obtain information by force from them or from third parties is prohibited (Article 31).

— it is also prohibited to take any measures resulting in the physical torture (Article 32).

— internees should also be accommodated and administered separately from prisoners of war and from persons deprived of their liberty for any other reason.

— accused persons shall have the right to be assisted by a qualified advocate or council of their own choice, who must enjoy the necessary facilities for preparing the defense (Article 72).

Very few Westerners have been able to have access to Israeli prisons and to report to the outside world the exact treatment of Arab prisoners. In fact, the International Red Cross has often been refused admittance to prisons under one pretext or the other. Israel has also refused to allow a United Nations delegation to investigate into the lives and treatments of Arabs, despite a U. N. General Assembly resolution urging this, on the pretext that another delegation should also probe into the Arab treatment of Jews living in the Arab countries.

As a result, the best sources for detailed accounts of Israeli treatment of Arabs has been from prisoners themselves who had either served their sentences and were deported to the East Bank of Jordan or prisoners who had been able to appeal to the outside world through their lawyers and through international organizations.(17) In many cases, the information proved embarrassing to the occupation authorities. In one such case, a Jewish journalist from Stockholm, Bo Kuritzen, produced evidence incriminating Israel for torturing any one suspected of being a member of the resistance organizations.(18) Kuritzen cited the example of a student from Nablus, Moayed Osman Al Bohesh, 21, who was detained for months in Israeli prisons, tortured, deprived of the right to contact a lawyer for six months and was prevented from getting medical help which resulted in his arm becoming partially paralyzed as a result of the torture methods used with him.

After writing the article about Bohesh, the Jewish journalist was summoned by Moshe Dayan, after the publication of his article had been banned by the censorship, only to be told the following: "No doubt there are some cases of mistreatment which actually happened . . . I am a military man and declare that individuals are sometimes cruel, but we are no angels. We must think of our nation . . . If some Arabs in the occupied territory spoke of the battle against the occupation, we regard this as a serious matter."

This is the official reply to mistreatment and torture to death of Arab prisoners. It needs no further comment.

According to the accounts of those who had served their sentences in Israeli prisons, Arabs are distributed in the following prisons: Hebron Prison (700); Jerusalem Moscovite Prison (100); Ramallah Prison (80-200); Nablus Prison (450-500); Tulkarem Prison (75-100); Central Ramleh Prison (150); Atleet Prison (150-250); Shata Prison (150-200); Beit Lidd Prison (200); Ghaza Prison (550); Damoun Prison (100); Sarafand Concentration Camp (100-200).(19)

It should be pointed out that in almost all these cases, the prisons were jammed with much more than they can take. For example, the prison of Nablus can take no more than 250 prisoners while in some cases it held more than 500. The administration of the prison had to detain in badly ventilated cells double what the cells could hold of prisoners. In some cases, 20-25 persons were crammed in a room 10 x 4 meters with no lavatory facilities, not enough ventilation or light. In other cases, the cell was 80 cms. long and 60 cms. wide. This was home for the prisoners. No blankets, no beds, mattresses or places to relieve nature except a bucket usually full to the brim.

In fact, if one were to sum up Israel's violations of the requirements for the treatment of prisoners as spelled out by the Geneva Convention, the following could only be pointed out in brief:

— In many of the prisons, the cells are cold and damp as the sun never enters them, a matter which often resulted in the spread of many diseases among internees.

— Water taps are left open in some prisons, on purpose; the result is leakage of water that flows inside the cells in which prisoners are made to sleep on the floor.

— Israel did not provide Arab prisoners with medical care.(20) In some prisons, an internee who happened to be a doctor was assigned to take care of his colleagues without being assigned with sufficient tools or drugs. The prisoners of the Aroha Prison confirm the fact that at one time they were not visited by a doctor for a period of four months, despite the fact that some of their conditions were considered serious by the internees.

— Internees are assigned, in some cases, to work of a military nature for the benefit of the Israeli army such as knitting nets for camouflage used by Israeli forces during military operations, a matter strictly prohibited by law.

— There are no recreation facilities in any of the prisons. Internees are also forbidden to read. Israel claims that Arab prisoners do not have sufficient knowledge of reading. The fact that these prisoners had requested the administration of the prison and the representatives of the Red Cross who happened to visit them, more than once, was finally met with the provision of one Koran to each dormitory.

— The responsible administration of these prisons does not permit religious ministers to visit the prisons or to minister to members of their community, contrary to the provisions of Article 93 of the Geneva Conventions.

— Several provisions of the Fourth Geneva Convention provide that trial of accused persons who are to be examined by Courts of the occupying power should take place as soon as possible. These provisions also prohibit detention without due cause and detention on the grounds of an act which does not constitute a crime of the Penal Law.

Israel does not act according to these basic principles. Ordinances applied in the occupied areas permit detention for unlimited periods of time. Some of the prisoners are not even informed of their charges in spite of the fact that they have been imprisoned for more than one year.

— Article 84 of the convention provides that "internees shall be accommodated and administred separately from prisoners of war and from persons deprived of liberty for any other reason." Yet in spite of this, the prison of Nablus includes a mixture of Jordanian prisoners and Israelis convicted of crimes of the public law in addition to a group of Egyptian prisoners of war, who Israel claims have been arrested in civilian clothes as they tried to reach Eastern Jordan. At the Gaza Prison, at one time, there were 292 political prisoners and 87 prisoners convicted in crimes of the penal law. The same was repeated in the Ramleh and Ramallah prisons.

— Israel does not apply any of the provisions of Article 90 of the Convention pertaining to clothing of prisoners. Many have to live without any under-wears.

— Lavatories are filthy — in all prisons — that no one can use them unless reluctantly. Asaad Abdul Rahman, who served a one-year sentence in occupied territories, described the situation at one time as follows, "The cell was divided into two by iron bars across the middle. On the other side of the bars there was a tin full of faeces. In my cell, this side of the bars, there was no one place to relieve oneself. One urinated through the bars into the tin. But for other purpose, one looked around for scraps of newspapers on which one relieved oneself and then depostied them through the bars into the tin."(21)

— Arab prisoners complained of the insufficiency of the quantities of food allowed for them. Prisoners in Gaza complained that fish was their only meal every day and that they could not eat it. Meat was not served until after the intervention of the Red Cross, and after numerous hunger strikes staged by the prisoners.

— Article 106 to 115 of the Geneva Conventions refer to the right of internees to send letters, telegrams and receive parcels. Even Article 107 notes that "if the detaining power deems it necessary to limit the number of letters and cards sent by each internee, the said number shall not be less than two letters and four cards monthly." This is never respected by the Israeli authorities. At the Ramallah prison, for instance, parcels sent for prisoners are not delivered to them. Instead they are consfiscated.

But perhaps the psychological torture and the war of nerves are the most draconian for the prisoners. The moment they are arrested, prisoners are subjected to two influences simultaneously: inducements and threats. The latter assumes many forms, but the most common include: threatening with beating or torture, with the arrest of those dearest to them like their father, mothers, sisters, brothers; with the blowing up of their homes, rape of nearest women relatives, with imprisonment in cells containing Israeli thieves and murderers and, if the prisoner is a woman, with imprisonment in cells containing Israeli prostitutes.

Following this psychological war of nerves, the prisoners are then thrown into cells — blindfolded, handcuffed, or shackled. The cells are often powerfully lit day and night without interruption. They are sometimes fitted with loudspeakers which continuously broadcast sounds and words aimed at wrecking the prisoners' nerves. At other times, the cells are fitted with blowers which direct strong waves of cold and hot air alternately. Not rarely, dogs are set loose into the cell. They tear the prisoners' clothes and body and expertly snatch at the cloth blindfolding the prisoners' eyes.(22)

Sometimes, the prisoners are led to an open grave and told that the grave was specially dug for them. Sometimes the leg of a corpse, probably artificial, is sticking out of the grave covered with dirt and prisoners are told that it is the body of this or that friend. At other times they are led into the torture chamber to watch some of their friends or strangers undergoing torture. According to Asaad Abdul Rahman, at least 60 percent of those arrested on charges of helping the resistance receive some variations of this type of psychological torture.

Physical torture, however, is not applied to all the prisoners. The proportion varies. On the West Bank of Jordan, about 15 percent receive this physical treatment. In the Gaza Strip the proportion is higher, reaching up to 25 percent of those arrested.

A number of those who had served prison sentences in Israeli prisons have agreed upon about 16 different methods of torture used by the Israelis. They are not all practiced on the same person nor are they all used with the same frequency.(23)

These different methods of torture can be described as follows:

— The prisoner is made to strip completely of all clothes. The body is whipped or beaten with sticks. No part of the body is spared. The beating and whipping continues until blood spurts out. Salt is thrown on the lacerations and the beating resumed.

— Lit cigarette ends are applied to varoius parts of the body.

— The prisoner is forced to sit naked on cactus leaves fixed on platforms.

— Enormous dogs are let loose on the prisoner, who is usually handcuffed with hands behind the back. The dogs are trained to throw the prisoner on the ground. The prisoner is ordered by an interrogator, whip in hand, to get up on his feet as soon as he falls down.

— The fingers of the hand are placed on the edge of an open door and the door is slammed on the fingers.

— Finger nails are pulled out with ordinary pincers.

— The prisoner is injected with pepper solutions.

— The prisoner is suspended from the ceiling from his wrists or ankles. The interrogator throws his weight on the prisoner or pulls him in a downward motion.

— Electric shocks are passed through the ear lobes, the chest, and the privy parts.

— The prisoner is injected with solutions which he is told induce instant insanity. He is shown what he is told is an antidote which he would be given if only he would confess in time.

— A large metal container is fitted over the head and neck and held firm to the body by extensions that are held in place by a waist-band. The container is then hit with sticks and rods on the outside, at first slowly and in routine fashion, and then with increasing tempo. The more battered the container is the more difficult it is to pull out.

— A certain chemical substance, possibly a nerve irritant, is put in the hand of the prisoner who is ordered to clench it. The substance gives the effect of an electric shock.

— Water hoses are applied to the mouth or anus and the water turned on.

— The motions of sodomy are enacted apparently by a negro kept for the purpose.

— One of the prisoners' arms is firmly tied to the fixed bars of a window, the other to the handle of a door. The door is slowly opened in the other direction.

— Match sticks are inserted into the urinary-genital tract. Sometimes they are lit. Or, alternately, the fillings of dry ink pens are inserted in the tract.

These methods of physical torture, it should be pointed out, are practiced with great skill and artistry in order to avoid permanent damage. But the interrogators sometimes lose control of the situation, and certain, perhaps unwanted results, follow, such as partial paralysis, injury of the stomach, the loss of an eye, or total nervous breakdown.

Numerous examples could be cited to prove that these tortures were actually applied and in many cases led to the death of the Arab prisoners(24) Among these, one could mention the death of Mohammed Shalul, with four others, in the Nablus Prison on September 6, 1967, as a result of tortures practiced on them; the Mukhtar of Khan Younes, who was tortured and died in prison on January 5, 1968. In Jericho, a policeman, Mohammed Dhib Rashid, was tortured to death in February, 1968.

The prisoners are not all men and there were many women who were tortured in equally cruel methods. Abla Shafiq Taha is a case in question, for she was arrested on her way back from Amman to Jerusalem and put in a cell usually reserved for prostitutes.(25) These Israeli harlots attacked her, giving her a violent and painful beating in the presence of an Israeli policeman, although Abla was in her third month of pregnancy. She asked the prison authorities to help her and to bring a doctor to see her, but they replied, "If you confess we will do what you want; if not, we shall kill the child inside you." She was interviewed by an Israeli woman lawyer, Felicia Langer, who, having heard what the prisoner had to say, complained to the police of the way in which Abla had been attacked and maltreated. The complaint was submitted first orally, and then in writing. The reply came that she had been attacked by prostitutes of bad character and that nothing could be done about them.

It is truly regrettable to be speaking of "cases" and not of humans at a time when the Declaration of Human Rights continues to be ignored. Human rights are still being violated daily in Palestine by the ruling Israeli authorities. More than one million Palestinian Arabs have been subjected to the injustice of the authorities of Zionist occupation since June, 1967. Such authorities have discarded all moral values, and have violated elementary principles of right and justice through blowing of houses, evictions, pressure, and torture. Israeli Defense Minister Moshe Dayan said, "We are not angels." One only hopes that the Israelis would become human.

NOTES

(1) For full details of accounts, see PEACE NEWS, November 10, 1967.

(2) Ibid. See THE ARABS UNDER ISRAEL OCCUPATION, Palestine Research Center.

(3) For further description of destruction of three villages, see Michel Adams

in the SUNDAY TIMES, June 16, 1967.

(4) This fact has been emphasized a number of times. Two British MP's, in a letter to the TIMES on February 10, 1968, said, "There was a well-attested intimidation of Arabs in the Gaza Strip and elsewhere to encourage them to leave."

Furthermore, a Red Cross Report No. 3 on August 11, 1967, spoke of the "Israeli policy which aims at spreading fear amongst the citizens so that they leave Gaza."

(5) LE MONDE, January 2, 1967.

(6) On February 7, 1967, Reuters news agency reported that the Israeli forces attacked the Al Shifa hospital and imprisoned a number of doctors. Some patients were killed as well as the head nurse, Samiha Fehmi.

(7) Telegram to the Israeli Government, U. N. Economic and Social Council Document, E/CN. W/L-1040.

(8) NEW OUTLOOK, Vol. II, No. 6, July—August, 1968, p. 50.

(9) In letter sent to the Israeli newspaper, HAARETZ, March 19, 1968.

(10) LE MONDE, January 18, 1968.

(11) This was reported by all press agencies on December 18, 1967.

(12) The testimony of Youssef Abu Youssef was made in a survey carried out by the Institute for Palestine Studies on April 12, 1968.

(13) KOL HA'AM, January 17, 1968.

(14) Report of the Higher Ministerial Committee for Refugee Affairs, Amman, May 1968, p. 3.

(15) Israeli newspaper DAVAR, June 13, 1967.

(16) A list of these leaders, reported in Israeli and Arab newspapers, has been compiled by the Institute for Palestine Studies, Beirut.

(17) Asaad Abdul Rahman, an M.A. graduate student of the American University of Beirut and a research assistant at the P.L.O. Research Center, Beirut, served a one-year prison sentence between December 21, 1967, and September 29, 1968. During his stay in various prisons, he was able to gather specific and well-documented facts about the treatment of prisoners. Much of the information described in this chapter is based on his first-hand account and research, part of which were depicted during a press conference held in Beirut on November 21, 1968. His memoirs were compiled in a book published by the Palestine Research Center.

(18) He wrote an article depicting one such case in AFTONBLANDOX, August 15, 1968.

(19) These figures were collected by the above-mentioned Asaad Abdul Rahman, who carried out the research while in prison. The figures in parenthesis are the number of prisoners found in each prison.

(20) This was verified in numerous cases, including that of Bohesh.

(21) Described during press conference in Beirut on November 21, 1968.

(22) In describing all this, Asaad Abdul Rahman pointed out that not all these methods were used with all the prisoners.

(23) Commenting on these methods, Asaad Abdul Rahman says, "All have actually been practiced. This conclusion is based on continuous research I carried out with my prison inmates. It is based upon a close examination of evidence given by these inmates, on a long rigorous process of checking and counter checking and on objective appraisal of the informants."

(24) Investigations into these cases were led by survey teams of the Institute for Palesinte Studies, Beirut.

(25) A report on her treatment and those of others was published by the Arab Women Lawyers' Bureau in Jordan on August 1, 1968.

Minority and Human Rights
arabs in the 1967 occupied territories

ISRAEL
IN THE ADMINISTERED AREAS

Ministry of Foreign
Affairs (Jerusalem)

It was not the Government of Israel which concentrated its troops on the borders of the neighbouring countries in May 1967; it was not the Government of Israel which publicly proclaimed that it would choose the time and place for the final battle against a neighbouring country; it was not the Government of Israel which asked the Secretary General of the United Nations to withdraw the UN Emergency Forces stationed along the Armistice Lines; it was not the Government of Israel which blocked the Straits of Tiran and sought to strangle the economy of one of its neighbours. If, in 1967, Israel used force, it was legitimately used in exercise of its right of self-defence under the Charter of the United Nations.

The Arab States which did not then go to war against Israel did not become involved in the fighting. Indeed, King Hussein of Jordan admitted some time after the war that his country was not attacked by Israel, but that he went to war voluntarily, to help Egypt. Thus the occupation is a result of legitimate use of force, and will continue as long as there is no peace in the area, as has been the case in every comparable situation on this planet. The speciously self-righteous critics of the occupation are the same authoritarian regimes that are inherently antagonistic to the very notion of human rights in any ordinary sense of the term, and would suffer no scruples in such a contingency. As nobody expects anything from them in the first place, any slight move in the direction of a more humane and liberal policy — such as the cessation of hangings in public squares, or the reprieve of persons sentenced to death for offences unknown to the law of civilised nations, or the release from prisons and concentration camps of innocent detainees — is regarded as the herald of a new dawn. But Israel is poles removed from authoritarianism.

For what is Israel's corroborative policy in these Areas? It has been summed up many times and its basic principle is this: even though the inhabitants do not regard the Government of Israel as their government — and naturally so, having had no part in its election — the Government of Israel is bound by law, by humanitarian considerations and by enlightened self-interest to treat them in a manner that is, it is convinced, incontrovertibly civilised and liberal, and provide them with all the services, and safeguard all the rights, to which they are entitled. This is not only duty — it is, we say it outrightly, plain self-interest. Whatever solution may be found for the conflict in the Middle East, whatever boundaries are drawn, secure and recognised as Security Council Resolution 242 ordains, we shall go on being the neighbours of the Arabs of Judaea and Samaria, of the Gaza Strip and Sinai.

For over twenty years the minds of these people have been systematically saturated with hatred for Israel, for all Israelis, sometimes for all Jews. They have been taught that this hatred is sacred, that the Israelis are assassins and rapists and must disappear from the face of the earth. But today we are in daily contact with them, with no barriers, no hermetically dividing Armistice Lines. Now, for the first time in over twenty years, we have the chance to show them who and what we are — not in the distorting mirror of Arab propaganda, but in sober truth. From the outset, the Government of Israel determined to make the fullest use of this opportunity.

The principal guide-line of its policy in the Areas has been achievement of normalisation: to permit the population to carry on its life and works as nearly as possible as it had done before June 1967. The policy takes form in three ways — non-presence, non-interference and open bridges.

The Israeli presence is as discreet as it can be. There is a minimum of Israeli symbols, of Israeli armed forces and patrols, of anything that might lead to friction between the authorities and the population. In principle, the objective of the military government vis-a-vis an Arab resident of the Areas is that he may be born in a hospital, grow up and be schooled, marry and bring up his children — all without the help or intervention of an Israeli civil servant or even setting eyes on one. Economic and administrative responsibility has been left in Arab hands. The military government stands aside and limits itself to fixing budgets for the various operations. The money comes chiefly from the Israeli tax-payer — a hundred million Israeli pounds were voted for the Areas by the Government of Israel from its own budget in the last fiscal year.

The population takes care of itself with its own personnel and in the way that it deems best.

Except for a handful of cases in which the military government had to end the services of personnel who were endangering the security of Israel and of the Areas no less, all the officials responsible for the administration of the Areas are the ones appointed by previous Governments; we say 'appointed,' because free elections were not then customary, even to the normally elective posts of mayor or chairman of local council.

Apart from matters that may jeopardize life inside Israel for ill — for example, sanitation, or economic acts that might bear adversely on conditions in Israel, the military government does not meddle or try to constrain the population to do anything against its will.

Ongoing contacts with Israel have understandably given rise to an impulse to make changes, to develop and advance. Whenever the prompting comes from the people of the Areas — and only then — the military government exerts every effort to help and to improve their standards of living.

The policy of open bridges vividly reflects the principle of normalisation. It was decided by the military government that little risk was involved in sanctioning continuing touch between the Arabs of the Areas and the Arabs of the surrounding States. The overall profit transcends the losses. After all, for twenty years and more, Israel had been willing to keep open land borders with those States. The Israelis, therefore, would not be the ones to close them.

The first step was the renewal of trade activities. Within weeks after the war, the agricultural produce of Judaea and Samaria was once again flowing eastwards, to its usual markets. Then the importation of goods was allowed: at first, only those that had already been paid for or had already arrived in the warehouses of the East bank; later, all that were needed in the Areas and whose natural sources were to be found in the East Bank.

The next step was to allow people to cross the lines. Since the beginning of 1968, except for individual cases barred on security grounds, anyone who wishes may apply for an exit permit to cross the cease-fire lines. This is required only for leaving the Areas — once it is granted, movement to all the Arab States is free and uncontrolled. When necessary, it is granted for a long-term absence, for purposes whether of study or work.

The latitude of the open-bridges policy was strikingly exemplified when the funeral of President Nasser took place: a delegation of dignitaries from Gaza and the West Bank travelled to Cairo to attend the obsequies of the man who had regarded — and comported — himself as Israel's arch-enemy, and returned to their homes in peace. Can it be conceived, for example, that a delegation of Jews from the UAR, or Iraq, or the Lebanon, or Syria would have been allowed to cross the Jordan to come to the funeral of Prime Minister Eshkol?

The next step follows of itself. Once visits from the Areas to the East Bank were allowed, so were visits from the East to the Areas. If there are no security grounds for disallowance, visiting permits from the East are granted for the Administered Areas and also for Israel.

The highlight of the open-bridges policy is the summer visits, which were made for the third time in 1970. Within the compass of this indulgence, the inhabitants of the Areas may ask the military government to allow kinsfolk from beyond the cease-fire lines to stay with them for from one to three months. In 1968, there were 16,000 such summer visitors; in 1969 — 26,000, and in 1970 — 54,000, thousands among them students from the West Bank and the Gaza Strip studying in Universities and colleges in Arab lands and elsewhere, and once again everything went smoothly without hitch or incident.

To ease the economic situation in the Areas, labourers may cross into Israel and take up gainful employment there. Well over 30,000 of them do so every day and never in nearly four years have there been any untoward incidents involving them, working side by side, as they do, with Jewish labourers in field and factory and on building sites. The Jews and Arabs toil together as good neighbours, which Jews and Arabs must be and which it has been shown that they can be. Again for reasons of enlightened self-interest, the Arab labourers are paid the same wages as their Jewish fellow-workers, which often means that they earn three or four times their previous pay — if, indeed, they had been lucky enough, then, to be employed at all. They have not been slow, either, to avail themselves of Israel methods or of the institutions of labour unions. All this will, no doubt, have a profound and far-reaching impact on the structure and outlook of Arab society.

At the same time, a great deal has been done to better and modernise the agriculture of the West Bank, by diversifying crops, introducing export varieties, extending the use of fertilisers, and by long-term planning and extension services. Total farm production went from 135 million Israeli pounds to 180 million Israeli pounds in one year, and exports multiplied tenfold — from a hundred to a thousand tons. In three years, 3.5 million trees were planted in the West Bank — as many as in all the past fifty years. In 1968, the tobacco crop there was tripled. In that year, too, industrial productivity went up by 54% thanks, largely, to loans and other aid from Israel. The budget for education has gone up by 20 per cent. The scholastic year 1969/70 opened and ended without interruption. The number of children attending school has risen by 11 per cent. Pupils may sit for the examination of their choice, including those of the Jordanian and Egyptian educational systems, the papers being brought in through the good offices of UNESCO. Of those who passed the examination, about 10,000 for the two years, some 3,000 have been accepted by Universities in the UAR; half are already there, the rest will follow at the beginning of the new academic year. About 1,200 of the other 7,000 are already enrolled in trade and vocational schools run by the Israeli Ministry of Labour in the Gaza Strip.

These details are a background for the discussion of Israel's policy in the Administered Areas. It must be remembered that the work there is carried out in the face of the violent and incessant hostility of the Arab States, and under the constant threat of terrorism in the Areas and within Israel. The terrorists are a deadly menace to the lives of civilians — Jews and Arabs alike. It is their declared aim to thwart cooperation between Jew and Arab, to disrupt normal life within the Areas and in Israel. In the last three years or so, more than two thousand men, women and children have been killed or wounded in terrorist outrages, over half of them Arabs: 117 killed, 933 wounded.

International Law grants Isreal the right, indeed it imposes on Israel the duty, to preserve public order in the Administered Areas. This is sometimes a difficult task, in Gaza frequently an unpleasant one. Morally and physically, young policemen and soldiers are under tremendous strain. Their assignments are long and arduous. They are subject to considerable provocation. Their lives are often in danger.

When things are done that are harmful to the security of the State and its citizens, Israel is bound to act. Not only bound, but entitled to, under the legislation in force in the Areas and equally under the provisions of International Law. This is the only sphere of administration in the Areas which is in Israeli hands.

The Jordanian or Egyptian legislation in force fully empowers the Government of Israel to inflict the death penalty on terrorists and instigators to terrorism. But Israel has refrained from applying the death penalty in the Areas. Subject to that limit alone, any person acting to imperil the security of the State or of the population of the Areas will, to be sure, be punished with the full vigour of the law.

But this Israel is portrayed by representatives of Iraq, Lebanon, the UAR, the Soviet Union, in terms of atrocity propaganda, its Government described as if it were a pack of ravening wolves, its treatment of the population in the Areas likened to the massacres of the Crusades, the Mongol invasions or the horrors of Nazidom. The purveying of this arrant nonsense is not only debasement of the truth, it degrades the United Nations.

Not that Israel professes that the Areas under military government are an earthly paradise — they cannot be. Military government is, at best, an unwelcome necessity. Israel lays no claim to a happy occupation. It hopes that the occupation will come to a speedy end, that peace will reign at last, that secure and recognised boundaries will be established, and the need for a military government vanish. But, for the moment, the need exists, and Israel believes that it has honestly done as well as is humanly feasible in its determination to deal fairly and decently with the people who, in the outcome of events beyond their control, have come under its jurisdiction and care.

The record of the military government is one that it need not be ashamed of. If one strips the noxious verbiage away, one finds that the nub of the complaint against Israel is that we allegedly try, by fair means or foul, usually foul, to compel the Arab population of the Areas to collaborate with us. Since World War II collaboration has become a very emotive word, which can be distorted to mean almost anything. But the delegation that took part in Nasser's funeral was not a delegation of collaborators; the schoolboys of Gaza who sat for the UAR matriculation are not collaborators; the 54,000 people who spent their summer holidays with their families in the West Bank are not collaborators. They are people who are trying to live, as far as possible, normal lives. They are people who have resolved to free themselves from the intolerable pressure of terrorist gangs which, in the name of nationalist liberation, murder and rob fellow-Arabs. We do not say that they love us. We know that many of them would gladly see us go. But we also know that our administration has earned their respect, grudging though it may be. More than anything else, this is proved by the rejection, in the West Bank Area, of the self-styled liberators of Palestine. They find no support among the people for whose cause they claim to be fighting. They have been cast out, with anger and contempt.

Our administration is there for all the world to see and judge. There is no restriction on travel into the Administered Areas — diplomats, journalists, tourists visiting Isreal, all are free without any let or hinderance whatsoever to move in and out, to speak to whom they wish, to form, and register and publish, their own opinions.

These opinions have been overwhelmingly favourable. The correspondent of the Daily Telegraph, for instance, writes on 30 April 1969:

> Israel's occupation of the conquered territories has been the most humane and generous in modern history . . . On its record so far Israel can have a clear conscience before the UN or any other international bar on its handling of the occupied Arab territories. Economic conditions for Arabs in the occupied territories are improving. Many of them, even the professional refugees, are better off than they have ever been before.

Mr. J. D. F. Jones, Foreign Editor of the Financial Times, writes on 20 May 1969:

> The Military Administration on the West Bank, for example, still strikes me as being one of Israel's most impressive achievements. By and large the essential discretion of the occupation has been maintained, despite Al-Fatah's attempts to sabotage the security operations and intimidate 'collaborators.' There are still scarcely 300 Israelis all told in the Military Administration and they work with the 7,000 or so Palestinian civil servants who are inevitably responsible for most of the administration of the area.

Raymond Gunter, a former British Minister of Labour, declared, in October 1969, that Israel's occupation in the Areas was "unique in the history of humanity," that he had seen no signs of pressure, of suffering "of the kind one expects to find in areas under occupation," and was particularly impressed by "the lack of troops there." The French Socialist Senator Pierre Giraud said, in October 1970: "In Jerusalem's Old City you see fewer policemen than on the Boulevard St. Michel in Paris. Israel, a country at war, does not put people in jail for crimes of opinion." The Gambian newspaper, The Nation, writes in June 1970: "What exactly has Israel been doing? — The activity can be summed up in the astounding total of nearly $30 million budgeted annually for civil administration in the Territories."

And the editor of the East Jerusalem paper El kuds, Muhammed Abu Zuluf, in November 1968: "We are for the withdrawal of the Israel occupation from the West Bank, Jerusalem and Gaza. But the question to be asked: is this paper really able to express its opinions freely?" And he answered: "There is no doubt and I must speak the truth: we now have freedom of the press, which, to my great regret, the Arab reader has never before enjoyed." The issue was illustrated with a photograph of King Hussein.

The November/December issue of the World Federalists prints an article by Dr. Frank H. Epp entitled "The Palestinians — A hi-jacked people." As its title indicates, the article is far from being pro-Israeli; indeed, it is redolent of undisguised hostility to Israel and all its works. Yet, after describing the situation in Gaza and the West Bank, Dr. Epp writes:

> To be sure, the Israeli military occupation is one of the most liberal and enlightened military occupations in history, but the fact remains that in the latter half of the twentieth century an enlightened military occupation is a contradiction in terms. The awareness of occupied peoples, the conscience of humanity, and international law do not allow for any unilateral military occupation, however generous.

How, then, is it possible that the conclusions of the Three-Man Special Committee (Doc. A/8089. Special Committee to investigate Israeli practices affecting Human Rights of the population of the Occupied Territories.) could diverge so widely from those of all objective observers? How did it happen that its Report was so unilaterally inimical to Israel? Why this glaring contrast between the Report and reality?

The Committee came into being as an upshot of General Assembly Resolution 2443 [XXIII] of 19 December 1968, which was adopted by the votes of a minority of member-States, almost all of them Arab, the rest pro-Arab. In the light of the one-sided character of the Resolution, and the manner in which it prejudged the issue which the Committee was supposed to examine, none of the uncommitted States that were approached would agree to serve upon it. The only ones willing were Somalia, Yugoslavia and Ceylon. That willingness was not to be sought in any sense of duty to the UN; they have no monopoly of that sense. It is to be sought elsewhere. These three States have certain things in common: none has diplomatic relations with Israel, and all have identified themselves with Arab hostility towards Israel. All three belonged to the minority of member-States which voted for Resolution 2443 [XXIII].

On the attitude of the Government of Somalia towards Israel, it is enough to quote its Foreign Minister, who not long ago pronounced that his country considered itself "in a state of war with Israel." Somalia's membership on the Committee is to be read as an act of war, of the war of propaganda which is so important an element in overall confrontation. Its representative was there not to establish the truth, but to provide wordy weapons for that campaign.

Yugoslavia broke off relations with Israel in 1967, identifying itself with the policies of the Arab Governments, and particularly with those of President Nasser, long-time friend and ally of President Tito.

The Ceylonese Ambassador Amerasinghe has on many occasions shown where he stands on the issues of the Middle East. It is his view that the action which led to the establishment of Israel was wrong, that it was, in his phrase, "the most painful irony of all." All the same, or perhaps on that account, he eagerly accepted the nomination, and plunged into the task of finding facts to support his preconceived convictions. Is not this itself the most "painful irony"?

Such are the credentials of the three members of the Committee which purported to investigate Israel's administration of the occupied territories. Would they not be enough, and more than enough, to disqualify any judge or jury?

Ceylon's delegate in the last Third Committee, speaking on human rights in armed conflict, flatly contradicts his country's Ambassador:

> With regard to international assistance in and supervision of the application of humanitarian rules to armed conflict, although his delegation endorsed the need for some evaluating machinery, it wished to point out that the creation or expansion of international agencies with a possible judicial or quasi-judicial status was open to major abuse. The principles to be considered in establishing such machinery were impartiality, complete absence of political motivation, specialised intellectual capacity and internationally approved procedures, but his delegation believed that no steps should be taken in that respect until the relevant instruments had been brought up to date.

Impartiality, complete absence of political motivation, specialised intellectual capacity and internationally approved procedures are the key words. The Committee headed by the Ambassador of Ceylon stands condemned by the criteria of Ceylon itself.

As the Committee declined to enquire into the plight of Jews in the Arab States, and as its mandate and composition were hopelessly compromised from the start, the Government of Israel decided not to cooperate with it. This, however, did not prevent impartial individuals and organisations from probing conditions in the Administered Areas, as is attested by the statement of M. Claude Pilloud, of the International Red Cross in Geneva, who told the Committee that "there was constant cooperation and collaboration between our delegates and the authorities in Israel."

The conduct of the Committee was in line with its membership. Skirting the fact that objective Governments and organisations were, in general, unwilling to work together with it, the Committee proceeded to organise a show of gathering "evidence" from witnesses who were, for the most part, supplied by Arab Governments and organisations. The result was a collection of dated and easily-refuted Arab allegations and distortions. It goes without saying that the long list of pre-selected, indoctrinated and rehearsed witnesses thus made available to the Committee produced lurid and often pathological tales of ill-treatment and atrocity. The procedures were, of course televised by Arab stations. It was soon evident that the interpreter, in many cases, doubled as director and prompter — from time to time, when witnesses forgot their lines, he helped them out and told them what to say . . . This was in sharp divergence from the meticulous examination to which the Red Cross interpreters were subjected; one wonders what criteria were set by the Committee for its own interpreters.

It is hardly necessary to embark upon an itemised analysis of the Committee's Report and rebut each and every one of its often absurd allegations but a few instances might serve to underscore its overall value — or, rather, dearth of value. There is the evidence of Mohammed Debras, who appeared before the Committee in Cairo on 23 April 1970, and described graphically how, following the 1967 war, he was forced into an Israeli hospital and castrated by an Israeli surgeon, with an Israeli nurse assisting. The truth is that, for medical reasons, Debras had undergone two operations for the removal of his testicles. These were performed by Arab surgeons in the Gaza Strip in 1965 and 1966 respectively — that is to say, long before the 1967 war. Already in June 1966, Debras had gone to Egypt from the Strip in the vain hope of cure by transplantation, as is recorded by an Egyptian professor in a medical report of 28 July 1966. This report was placed before the Committee by the Israeli delegation. The episode tells how human misfortune can be cynically exploited for propaganda ends.

In fairness to the Egyptian doctors who examined Debras, it should be added that their report contained nothing about either the date or the circumstances of the operations performed on him which would gainsay the facts. If the Committee was misled by this "witness", it was because of its propensity to credit anything that might be damaging to the Government of Israel; as loyal servants, they were swayed by the policies of their own Governments.

In Amman, on 15 April 1970 (UN Press Release HR/503), Nadim Zarou, a former mayor of Ramallah, testified that two young Arabs had been taken from that town and shot by two Israeli soldiers, that one of the soldiers had gone free because the Military Governor said that he had simply obeyed orders, and the second been adjudged insane; in any event, there had been no judicial proceedings.

The facts are these: on 8 October 1968, two employees of the Public Works Department were shot dead on the highway between Ramallah and Latrun, and on 8 November the District Court of Jerusalem sentenced two members of the Frontier Guard, Sergeant Albert Alus and Constable Eliyahu Elias, to the maximum penalty — life imprisonment — for premeditated murder.

The quondam mayor's allegation was omitted from the Committee's Report, presumably because someone had drawn its attention to the public proceedings of the District Court of Jerusalem. But we do find the following in the Report:

> The evidence of Mr. Nadim Zarou, who was mayor of Ramallah at the time of the occupation, deserves special attention ... He is a responsible citizen ... In the Special Committee's opinion, Nadim Zarou satisfied these tests (norms of credibility) and deserves credence.

In other words, while the Committee knew that at least one part of Zarou's evidence was false, and had to be stricken from the record, it yet asserts that he "deserves credence," a deliberately misleading assertion if ever there was one.

The tendentious suppression of evidence also took another form. As we have said, the Government of Israel withheld its cooperation from the Committee, for reasons which are fully vindicated by the Committee's procedures. But Israel is a free country, and individual Israelis were at liberty to offer evidence to the Committee if they chose, and some of them did. The Committee quoted extensively, even reproduced in toto, the damaging evidence of such Israeli witnesses as Mr. Joseph Abileah, who appeared on behalf of the Israeli League for Human and Civil Rights. Mr. Abileah, in the course of his oral testimony, made no secret of the fact that his "evidence" was based on newspaper reports, and afterwards declared that he did not himself believe what newspapers printed.

Nevertheless, the Committee chose to print, verbatim, the written evidence put in by him, although he had patently discredited himself in his oral testimony. The written evidence put in by Alexander A. Aviram, who was Civil Administration Officer in the Gaza Strip was designedly burked. Here is a part of it:

When I was appointed Deputy Governor of the Gaza Strip, acting as officer in charge of civil administration, the instructions that I was given clearly stipulated that my task was to restore civilian life in the zone to its accustomed course. It was, moreover, explained to me that the assistance that I would have to extend to local residents must serve to raise their standard of living above the level prevailing at the time of the Egyptian occupation.

1. In Gaza schools, studies used to be carried out in shifts, the Gaza-born children attending the first, while refugee children studied in the second. This practice of separating one category of pupils from the other was carried out with the full knowledge of UNRWA. Quite evidently, I could not agree to pursue such a policy of discrimination between Arab and Arab.

2. During the entire period of Egyptian rule, the inhabitants were subjected to a night curfew. Although I am not an Arab, I felt outraged by this measure, and a few weeks later rescinded the curfew altogether.

3. Refugee camps lacked all sanitary facilities. Upon assuming my duties, I gave instructions to start the installation of a proper water supply. Today arrangements are being made for bringing in electricity, too.

4. During the period of Egyptian occupation (I use the term 'occupation' because the area was governed by an Egyptian Military Governor, and all the senior positions were entrusted to Egyptian officials, appointed by the Governor), residents desiring to leave Gaza for Egypt or any other Arab country met with great difficulties. Two weeks after our arrival, the inhabitants were permitted to travel and visit their relatives — whom they had not seen for twenty years — in Jordan, the West Bank or Israel.

5. All personnel, from policemen, street-sweepers and clerks to the mayor, remained at their posts. No officials were appointed by the Israeli military government, so as to leave the entire local administration in the hands of the residents.

6. Courts of law were enabled to function, and are trying offenders in accordance with local laws in force prior to the entry of Israeli forces. The death penalty, however, has been abolished, and sentences of forced labour are not implemented. The tribunals set up to try offences relating to Army jurisdiction deal in this regard with Arabs and Israelis alike. Every accused is defended by a lawyer, either called in by the defendant, or appointed for this purpose and paid for by the Army.

7. Apart from the international relief organisations UNRWA and CARE, Israeli rule provides relief to the destitute, while the Ministry of Religious Affairs pays the salaries of the imams and other religious officials, and the Ministry of the interior pays those of the mukhtars.

8. A revolutionary change has taken place in the prisons. At the time of the Egyptian occupation, prisons were run only as penal institutions. Today, they operate under a scheme of rehabilitation, wherein all inmates are taught a trade, traffic offenders as well as terrorists. Food rations have

improved both in quality and quantity, and the fare in Gaza prisons is the same as in prisons inside Israel. Corporal punishment has been forbidden. International Red Cross representatives have repeatedly visited Gaza prisons, and have approved all the conditions therein.

9. Although Israeli rule could levy taxes and duties to cover the occupation costs, it has refrained from doing so, and Israel is shouldering the expenses of maintaining the Army and running the civil administration.

10. In cases of damage done to private property by the Israeli Army, compensation is granted after due inquiry, and losses are made good.

11. Almost no complaints of looting or rape — which are not uncommon occurrences in occupied territories — have been lodged. Whenever, in rare instances, there was a suspicion that an act of this kind had been perpetrated, the suspects were brought to justice and, if found guilty, were severely punished with the full rigour of the law. I am willing to give evidence before the Committee if called upon to provide additional explanations . . . "

Mr. Aviram volunteered to go wherever necessary, to submit himself to cross-examination and to furnish orally whatever additional information the Committee might be interested in. Here the Committee had an opportunity to hear from a witness who, unlike Mr. Abileah, had first-hand knowledge of the situation. But, again unlike him, Mr. Aviram was not invited by the Committee to testify.

In Cairo, on 23 April 1970 (Press Release HR/509), Tewfik Hassan Wasfi, who had been in charge of the Arab League's office in the Old City of Jerusalem when the Six-Day War broke out, testified that, on the second day of the fighting, he was arrested by the Israeli authorities and jailed in Ramla for eight months. This was true — Wasfi was an Egyptian citizen and, as such, during the war between Israel and Egypt, had to be regarded and treated as an enemy alien.

The evidence given in Beirut on 7 April (Press Release HR/490), by Mr. Ahmed Khalifa, is described by the Committee as "particularly impressive, because he did not give the impression that he was moved by rancour towards his former captors. . . . Despite his experiences, he seemed to have retained his objectivity and sense of proportion." The Committee omits to inform us that the witness, long before his detention, was, by his own admission, a political officer in George Habash's Liberation Front, one of the most extreme terrorist organisations. The Committee, though well aware of this fact, failed to mention it in its Report. And we are asked to believe that such a witness is "objective"!

The Committee says that Professor Sayegh informed it of the serious effect of the occupation on the economic life of the Areas. Professor Sayegh — a well-known Arab propagandist and Director of the Planning Centre of the Palestine Liberation Organisation — here contradicts what any casual reading of the press makes obvious. The Report says that the citrus fruit trade in Gaza has been virtually ruined. Statistics available to anyone will show that the diametrically opposite is true. Here is the demonstration: in 1968, the value of the local citrus crop was IL. 21.6 million, in the following year it was IL. 27.0 million — which is hardly ruination, any more than is the rise in shipments of citrus from Gaza from 97,000 tons in the 68/69 season, to 120,000 tons in the next.

The Report affirms that there is a distinct lack of respect for the religious susceptibilities of the inhabitants of the Areas. A cursory glance at Israeli legislation and at the testimonies of religious leaders who live in, or have visited, the Areas discloses that this is the reverse of the truth.

I found all these Holy Places in fine condition. I have been told that the Government even contributes to the expenses for the upkeep and safeguarding of the Holy Places . . . I would be failing in my duty as a true Moslem if I did not tell the Moslems in my country the real truth and the facts about their Moslem brothers here in Israel. [Mr. Salih Ututalum, Moslem member of Philippines Cabinet, 5 June 1969]

How good it would be if those who have heard unfounded rumours of desecration and interference in the regular work of the Mosque could come to witness the peace and tranquillity which prevail in this holy place . . . [Tawfiq Mahmoud Asaliyah, Qadi of Jaffa and Jerusalem, 1 January 1970]

Thank God, I could visit them [Holy Places in Israel] and find religious communities, Moslems among them, with whose members I spoke for a long time. I found that they enjoyed absolute freedom in the religious field. In addition, they are receiving much help from the Government for the improvement and safeguarding of the Holy Places. [Mahamat Rahama Saleh, Minister for Public Service in Tchad, 8 September 1969]

Rest assured that the Moslem and non-Moslem holy places are in good hands, and that freedom of religion is assured to all the members of the various faiths. [Hajj Abdul Karim el Gazali, Chairman of All Islamic Congress in Sierra Leone, 20 June 1967]

Contrary to the propaganda disseminated by certain elements in Africa, the Moslems in Israel enjoy complete freedom in observing their religious precepts. [Al-Sheikh Abdo Kamulageya, Deputy Chairman of the National Association for the Advancement of Moslems in Uganda, 9 July 1967]

One must come to Israel to see for oneself to what great extent peace and tranquillity reign here, how false is the picture disseminated by Arab propaganda. It is difficult for us to understand why these two peoples —the Jews and their Arab cousins —cannot live together in peace. [Sheikh Salim Ibn Issa, Adviser on Moslem Affairs to the President of the Malagasy Republic, June 1968]

The Report expresses concern that legal assistance is not forthcoming for persons in detention. "It appears," says the Committee, "that the only legal assistance that is available . . . is rendered by one office, which has three or four lawyers working in it." The truth is that every detainee has the right to avail himself of the services of a local or an Israeli lawyer. If the charge is serious, the court appoints a lawyer for the defense at the expense of the Military Governor. The number of lawyers available is, for all practical purposes, unlimited. In the Gaza Strip, the defence is undertaken by ten local lawyers, but in Judaea and Samaria the local lawyers, except five, decided to strike, and thus deprived the inhabitants of legal defence. Thus most of the accused are represented by Israeli lawyers chosen by them. Their choice has to be, and is, respected by law.

Of particular objectivity, in this regard, is this passage from a judgement delivered by the wholly Arab Court of Appeal of Ramallah on 17 June 1968, reversing the verdict of the District Court of Hebron to disallow an Order by the Israeli Army commander as to the appearance of Israeli advocates before Arab courts in the West Bank:

> .... the present situation necessitated the issue of the Order because, of the dozens of advocates in the West Bank, a very small minority have agreed to practice, while the majority prefer to stay at home and leave the inhabitants confused, with no one to turn to to represent them in the civil and military courts and with no one to defend them, or assert their rights.

The proceedings of the courts in the areas are public, and eminent jurists from many countries, who have witnessed them, have voiced admiration for their complete fairness. The Government of Israel offers safe conduct to any person residing outside Israel who wishes to make a complaint to the competent authorities. The 54,000 visitors who came to Israel last summer from the surrounding Arab States are all silent witness to the truth — if any one of them had believed what is written in the Committee's Report, would he have wittingly exposed himself to arbitrary jailing, to Dantesque torture?

The London Times of 30 October 1970 reports the case of Mrs. Leila Bakr, wife of Ibrahim el-Bakr, a member of the Executive Committee of the Palestine Liberation Organisation. At the height of the civil war in Amman, she and her two children came to the Damya Bridge and were admitted to the West Bank. She knew that the Israeli authorities were cognizant of her husband's activities, but she had no least fear. She knew that they would deal with her in absolute equity, that nothing would happen to her and her children. She knew that the Committee's conclusions were baseless and she proved their baselessness by what is a thousand times more eloquent than speech, by entrusting herself and her children to the military authorities of Israel.

The series of testimonies reproduced by the Committee were manufactured directly or indirectly by those who conduct hostilities against Israel and who will seize any and every opportunity to wage a propaganda campaign as well. Some came into court with their hands stained with the blood of Arabs and Jews alike. Those who are responsible for the fratricidal battles that recently raged in Jordan and in which more Arab lives were lost than in twenty years of conflict with Israel, as many as 20,000 according to some Arab sources, those who have made it so shockingly plain how they would treat a Jewish population if it should ever fall into their hands — they are the ones who produced and directed the evidence. And the Committee served as their willing tool.

If any doubt lingers as to the basic orientation of the Committee and its Report, it is dispelled by the following passage in the document:

> The weight of international opinion should be brought to bear on the Government of Israel to apply forthwith the principles declared in Security Resolution 242 (1967), and in conformity with that Resolution to withdraw Israel armed forces from the occupied territories and to bring the occupation to an end.

This deliberate misquotation from the Resolution, this wilful distortion of its intent and purpose, is the trademark of the Committee. Not a word of a just and permanent peace, not a word of agreement, not a word of secure and recognised boundaries. Just unconditional withdrawal from the Areas — that is the interpretation which the Committee gives to the Resolution. Even Arab delegations, speaking in the debate on the Middle East in the General Assembly, did not have the effrontery to read such a twisted meaning into the Resolution.

And the same jaundiced political slant is evident in the rest of the recommendations of the Committee.

The Chairman of the Committee took issue with a statement made by the Israeli delegation in another place, concerning the Committee's wish to prolong its existence and its travels to the Middle East. He protested that the Committee had said nothing of the sort. Part of the relevant paragraph (156) reads:

> The Special Committee feels that, until such an arrangement is made, it should continue its work. For this purpose the Committee would require certain facilities to enable it to keep abreast of developments in the occupied territories which have a bearing on the protection of human rights of the population of those territories, to receive allegations and evidence of violations of those rights, to conduct studies of relevant developments as they occur, and, if necessary, to return to the Middle East for further work in the execution of its mandate.

No doubt the member-States serving upon the Committee believe that its prolongation will be useful for Arab propaganda. But would it be useful for the United Nations and the cause of human rights? Fact-finding on disputed matters requires the highest standards of objectivity, and those have been conspicuously absent in this case. The United Nations has been misused as a propaganda instrument for one side, which, admittedly, has many votes at its bidding. But the more the United Nations becomes identified with one side in a conflict, the less are its opportunities for acting impartially to bring about a solution. In his message to the Commemorative Assembly, the Secretary General referred to those who scoff at the United Nations, and many speakers at the Assembly gave expression to the fear that the Organisation is losing prestige. To countenance, in the sacred name of human rights and under the auspices of the United Nations, propaganda exercises such as those in which the Committee has indulged will only serve to discredit the Organisation and diminish its authority.

As for Israel, not because of this Report, but in spite of it, it will persevere in doing everything possible to safeguard the human rights of the people in the Administered Areas, to keep the Areas open for all visitors, and to strive for a peace based on secure and recognised boundaries and mutual respect for the sovereignty and territorial integrity of all the States in the Middle East. With the coming of that peace the need for a military government will have passed.

JEWS
IN
ARAB COUNTRIES

Dafna Dan

In view of the state of mind of the Arab world today, one would rather not go into the treatment of the Jewish minorities in the different Arab countries, helpless victims of so much venom. To postpone entering on this dark chapter, let us glance at the past in order to recall that there were periods — if not a Golden Age, at least golden intervals — in Spain and elsewhere in the Moslem world, mainly in the 10th and 11th centuries, when Moslem princes and chieftains on the one hand and Jewish viziers, physicians, scholars and merchants on the other, lived together in tolerance, peace and prosperity, periods like brief candles of humane civilisation in the long night of man's inhumanity to man. It was in these golden islands of enlightenment in the Dark Ages that Arab and Jewish philosophers, linguists, mathematicians, cartographers and astronomers salvaged the thought, learning and science of the ancient world for re-discovery in the bright dawn of the Renaissance and prepared the way for the exploration of the globe.

When pressure increased from the Christian north, the Moslem rulers in Spain called in the desert — the later-comers in North Africa — to their aid. In the result, the historian Cecil Roth tells us, "All who were not Moslems must be forced to don the turban; the only alternatives were extermination or expulsion ... When the Almohades had entered Fez, many of its Jewish inhabitants suffered martyrdom rather than change their faith. An identical policy was pursued by the invaders in Spain. In every city which they captured, the Jewish and Christian inhabitants were put to the sword ... "

To come nearer to the present, the Arab country with perhaps the oldest Jewish diaspora of any of them, the Yemen, has already been described. Jews started leaving the Yemen for Palestine at the beginning of this century, but the majority stayed there, living as they always had done, as small traders, artisans and fine craftsmen. After the establishment of the State of Israel, the pressure of Arab hostility surrounding the community was such that in effect it was liquidated, removing itself piecemeal to Aden, where those few who had some means found room and a livelihood in the small Jewish merchant community long established there. The poor, stripped of the little they had, crossed the desert in pitiful caravans and encamped on Aden territory, whence emissaries from Israel, with some British assistance, flew them all to embattled Israel. There, too, only tent encampments awaited them. But that is a different story.

In June 1967, the last hundred and fifty Jews in Aden were evacuated by the British, after an unknown number had been murdered, three synagogues burnt down and all Jewish property looted or destroyed.

Even in less peripheral lands than the Yemen, the Jewish position of "protected," second-class citizens was always a highly vulnerable one, and the "protection" afforded by the forces of law and order often more theoretical than real. In supposedly liberal or at least constitutional regimes, where Jews had the right to organize as communities, to establish schools and so on, political leaders used to make a distinction between Jews and Zionists (or Israelis) and declare that a minority which had lived where it was for a thousand years or more had nothing to fear. But these good international manners wore thin in the late 1930's and during the war, and after 1948 vanished entirely.

The anti-Jewish riots in Bagdad in 1941, instigated by the Mufti of Jerusalem and company, were the turning point in the modern history of the Jews in Iraq, then a community of some 150,000, whose history in Iraq went back 2500 years, "protected" under the Turks, given theoretical equality before the law and practical advancement under the British Mandate, and then discriminated against in increasing measure after the Mandate gave way to independence. After World War II, opportunities of advancement and the possibilities of earning a living narrowed steadily, and the Jews of Iraq, who had numbered in their ranks many a savant and many an eminent servant of his country, began to emigrate. Early in 1949, Iraqi Jews began to be attacked in the streets, their places of business were broken into, many were murdered in cold blood. Jews were dismissed from all branches of public and civil service. Their movements were restricted, their children were barred from public schools. Hospitals were closed to them. They were barred from public institutions, and refused import and export licenses. In December '49, an official reign of terror began, with thousands of Jews being imprisoned on charges of "Zionism." The head of the Jewish community of Basra was hanged in his own backyard and a public holiday was declared to celebrate the event.

At this stage, registration for emigration was encouraged. Then in March 1950 legislation was put through retroactively depriving of their citizenship those who had registered for emigration, freezing Jewish bank accounts and forbidding the sale of Jewish property without a special licence. The property of those who had already left was sold by public auction. Emigration became mass flight. The better-off left behind professions they could no longer exercise and property they could not realize; the poorer — many of them humble people from the distant Kurdish north — left behind homes, market stalls and artisans' cubby-holes. By mid-July 1950, 110,000 Iraqi Jews had fled to Israel, arriving in utter destitution, to live in barracks and transit camps and try to strike root anew.

Successive Iraqi governments tightened the screws on the remnant that remained. A ban was put on all Jewish cultural, social and communal organization apart from strictly religious observances. The community status accorded the Jews by the law of 1931 was cancelled in 1958 (Iraqi Government Gazette, 25 February, '58), and control of communal property (schools, hospitals, etc.) was transferred from a 'Jewish Lay Council' to a Government body created for the purpose.

In 1963, new regulations were passed decreeing that all Jews who had left the country between January 1960 and March 1963 and did not return within six months of the date of the decree would lose their citizenship and have their property and funds — shareholdings in public companies, etc. — "frozen." This meant that such property and funds as had still remained, legally at least, in the names of these particular Jews was finally lost to them. And Jews who had not managed to leave were prohibited from dealing in their own real estate or shares, or collecting their company profits (Law No. 122 of 1964). The citizenship law of '63 laid down that all Jews had to apply to the Directorate of the Passport Police for new citizenship documents, which would only be granted on their renewed declaration that they were retaining their Iraqi citizenship and had not acquired any other citizenship during any time spent abroad. It seems odd that the Government should still try to stop Jews from getting out. Jews must get permits to travel, and bring proof that the journey is for medical treatment or for study; otherwise it is limited to four months.

Today there are perhaps 3,000 Jews left in Iraq; a tiny handful of the very rich; a thin layer of professional men and executives, mostly employed by foreign corporations, who are increasingly molested and harassed; and the poor, who live cheek by jowl with their Moslem neighbours and daily fear the worst. The atmosphere of hatred and threats has of course darkened still more since the Six Day War, when Jews were arrested by the score, and only released on the payment of heavy ransom. (Some thirty of them were still in prison at the end of '67). The Chief Rabbi of Bagdad was constrained to condemn Israeli aggression and to thank the Government for its treatment of the Jews, who were told that they would not be hurt "at the present time":

> The Jewish cancer in Iraq constitutes a serious danger for our struggle to exist and for the future of our country. If interest, circumstances and the law require that we do not hurt them at the present time, at least it is incumbent on us to place them under strict surveillance and freeze their activity. [SHAWT AL ARAB, 17.6.67.]

In October 1967, a representative of the Red Cross visited Iraq. He was told that the Jews there lived in fear and trembling, but he did not meet any representative of the Jewish community, which feared the results of making contact with a foreigner.

On 3 March 1968, the Iraqi Government Gazette published yet another amendment to the law about 'Supervision and Management of the Property of the Denationalized Jews,' on top of the amendments in Law No. 64 of 1967. These Laws speeded up and tightened up the process of seizing Jewish property. Furthermore, Government and private offices and businesses were forbidden to pay out any sums due to Jews, but had to notify the Minister instead. Excepted were only salaries up to 100 dinars a month — approximately the starting salary of a junior clerk, certainly not enough to support a family. The Government was thus given complete control over all Jewish income except that of the lowest-paid employees.

Apparently the Jews were still needed as objects of hatred and derision, as scapegoats for the Arab failure to dislodge the Jews of Israel and as proof of the existence of the great conspiracy:

> If we demand of the Government that it put an end to the activities of the destructive forces operating within our homeland, we do so only to defend

ourselves against the enemy's plots. The first thing that we must do to purge our ranks is to establish that the Jews living within Iraq shall be second-class citizens . . .

This 'taking it out' on the miserable remnant of an ancient once-flourishing community, this witch-hunt for some-one to blame for Iraq's descent into an economic and political bog as vast as the country's own marshlands, reached the limits of absurdity when former Prime Minister al Bazzaz, the nearest thing Iraq had to a statesman in recent years, was arrested in December '68 on the charge that he too was spying for Israel. But there was nothing laughable about the spy trials of January '69, when nine Jews were condemned to death with all due process of television, and then hanged in the main square of Bagdad for the delectation of the populace, local and provincial, the latter brought up for the occasion by excursion train. There have certainly been Israeli agents in Arab countries. These Jews were not. They were hanged — and they were not the last — because they were Jews.

Since Syria became independent of France, Syrian Jews have been subject to numerous disabilities. From the start Jews were practically excluded from government service. Jewish schools functioned only with difficulty: they were forbidden to use Palestinian text-books for the study of Hebrew; teachers suspected of harbouring Zionist ideas were dismissed; the text of every lecture delivered to a Jewish club or society had to be cleared first with the political police. A Jew with a valid Syrian passport and who succeeded in obtaining one of the few, much-sought-after British entry visas to Palestine would find himself denied a Syrian exit visa.

On VE Day in May 1945, demonstrators in Damascus were prevented by the police from breaking into the Jewish quarter; a month later a Jewish schoolteacher was murdered in the street in broad daylight. In the autumn of the same year, a meeting of Moslem religious leaders in Damascus sent a telegram to the Allied Governments, warning them that a holy war would be declared against the Jews if immigration into Palestine were to continue. The leader of the Young Moslems declared from the pulpit of the famous and beautiful Umayyad Mosque in Damascus after the Friday prayers — the chosen hour for riot incitement — "If the Palestine problem is not solved in favour of the Arabs, the Arabs will know how to deal with the Jews living in their countries." On 18 November, a mob broke into the Great Synagogue of Aleppo, smashed candlesticks, beat up two old Jews reading there and burnt prayerbooks in the street.

Small wonder that illegal Jewish emigration increased apace, though Syrian Jewry was so far from being Zionist that the majority did not go to Palestine or later to Israel, but to Beirut and further afield; of those who did not go to Israel many migrated further.

The Jewish Community Council of Damascus was dissolved in December 1949. Of about 40,000 Jews in Syria at the end of World War II, something between 2,500 and 3,000 are still left there, most of them Syrian nationals, though a few are Persian, Iraqi or stateless. They are not only legally discriminated against but systematically persecuted under successively more arbitrary and tyrannical governments. The word "Jew" is stamped on their identity cards in red. They are not allowed to move out of a radius of five kilometres from their place of residence without a movement permit. While no Jews are allowed to enter Syria, none are legally allowed to leave it either, unless they formally abandon all their property and declare that they are leaving for good. The Jews must purchase exemption from army service for a sum equivalent to U.S.$600, a very large sum for them. They are forbidden to deal in land. They have been so browbeaten, terrorised and broken in spirit that in 1953 when an Israeli escaped from a Syrian prison and in utter exhaustion and despair took refuge in a synagogue, the congregation turned him over to the police.(1)

Year after year, the screws are tightened. Jewish property — banking accounts, working equipment, harvested crops —is all "expropriated," that is, stolen purely and simply. Shopkeeping — the main occupation and source of livelihood left — is strangled by an official boycott.(2)

Every so often a synagogue is set on fire or just closed down; some Jew is beaten up or simply killed. During the 1967 war, in the only other centre besides Damascus where there are any number of Jews, Qamishli, some 200 Jews were arrested and 57 others were killed by the mob. Next to no news gets out about the position of Jews in Damascus, who are kept going by aid from U.S. sources. American visitors to Damascus in 1968 were shown a Jewish school, with a dozen or so small, silent children at their desks. The two teachers, with tears in their eyes, begged the visitors to go away: "You cannot help us, you can only do us harm." The Jews pay for the police who "guard" their quarter, and they pay bribes to the Palestinian Arabs who are purposely housed alongside them. They are afraid even to apply to foreign consulates for exit visas. Stoning and insults are their daily ration. There are midnight arrests. People are tortured.

Israelis who by one means or another fell into Syrian hands over the years were tortured with patient ingenuity for long periods past the brink of madness. Some committed suicide. Some died under torture. Of the handful that were at long last returned to Israel, one committed suicide in his parents' home, and the rest have had to be taken care of in institutions. Only one man remained sane enough to recount what had happened to them.(3)

Before we pass to another torture chamber for Jews, Egypt, let us have a brief respite by completing the round-up of Arab North Africa, in countries where Jews may be murdered but it is not with Government sanction.

Under the Italians, Libyan Jews were granted equal rights and communal autonomy. The Fascist racial laws were not very enthusiastically applied. During the war, however, the Jews were either conscripted as labourers or put in a concentration camp, and the Allied advance was hailed as liberation. Relations between Jews and Arabs had been peaceable, but real friction started with incitement by Egyptians who came to Tripoli as minor officials of the British occupation authorities, as teachers and as businessmen. Two days after pogroms in Egypt in November '45, false rumours were spread in Tripoli that the Jews had murdered the Mufti and the Kadi and burned down the Moslem Law Courts. Organised crowds attacked the Jewish quarters, and within three days over a hundred Jews were murdered in Tripoli and Benghazi.

Soon the Jews of Tripoli, too, were on the move — some to Tunisia, some to France or Italy (most Libyan Jews were Italian nationals), the majority to Israel. There may have been some 30,000 Jews in Libya in 1945. By June 1967 there were at most 4,500. In that month, 18 Jews were killed in street rioting. The mob entered Jewish houses, threw people from balconies into the street, sacked Jewish shops, burnt down synagogues. The greater part of the property that remained to these Jews was destroyed. Some 3,500 Jews were taken to a military camp to protect them from the mob, and those who wished to were then allowed to leave the country with a suitcase-full of clothes and the equivalent of fifty pounds sterling a head.

In 1948, Moroccan Jewry had scarcely broken out of the confines of the 'mellah' (oriental ghetto). They lived — except for a very few of them — in abject poverty, earning their livelihood as artisans, shopkeepers and hawkers. They were not eligible for employment in the French civil service, because they were *indigènes*, subjects of the Sultan, ruled on in matters of personal status by their own religious courts. Nor did they enjoy any special favour at the hands of the Sultan's administration. Local Jewish communities functioned as such, with a very limited measure of autonomy, and there was no single official Jewish representative body.

When Morocco became independent, some Jews of the first 'emancipated' generation helped set the new State on its feet both as technicians and administrators, and the Sultan proclaimed admirable principles of toleration and equality. These principles, however, were not admired by his non-Jewish subjects. The Jews came under all kinds of pressure in matters of education, religious and personal freedom. Young Jewish women were being more or less forcibly carried off, converted to Islam and married. Outbursts of popular hatred finally drove this numerous community, too, to emigrate. Jews whose forbears had been expelled from Spain in 1492, Jews from Casablanca, from Fez, from Marrakesh, from Meknes, humble people from the Atlas Mountains —rich and poor, merchant, shoemaker, peasant and peddler — they left by the scores of thousands. Those who could went to France, to the United States, even to Spain. Those who had little or no means managed to get to Israel.

At least 350,000 in 1948, they numbered at most 60,000 by 1967. At the news of the Arab defeat there were street demonstrations. Jews were attacked, and in Meknes two were killed. Anti-Semitic leaflets were circulated by the opposition Istiklal party, and Jewish shops and businesses were boycotted. King Hasan condemned the disturbances and the boycott and took police measures to protect the Jews. But hatred and jealousy have been kept warm by propaganda and incitement from within the country and without, and the Jews that are left in Morocco have despaired of ever renewing tolerable relations with their Arab neighbours. Those who can will leave.

It is a relief to turn to Tunisia, though even here it is sad to see ancient communities liquidated after existing peacefully side by side with Berber and Arab in Djerba, Sfax and other places for nearly 2,000 years. When the French left, perhaps something over half the Jews of Tunisia left too, and not unnaturally they went to France — Tunisian Jews had been French citizens for nearly a century. About 20,000 stayed on. The Government of Tunisia has maintained law and order and firmly repressed all demonstrations of the kind that elsewhere inevitably led to rioting, pillage and murder. The Government has held aloof from the wilder policies of the Arab League, arguing that the State of Israel could be liquidated or at least pruned down by international diplomacy, negotiation and rational policies short of war.

Nevertheless on the 5th June 1967, the mob succeeded in burning down the central synagogue in Tunis, sacking Jewish shops and attacking Jews in the streets. One Jew was killed. Many of the rioters were arrested, and their ringleader was sentenced to 20 years' hard labour. Pres. Bourguiba publicly condemned the outbreak and personally went to see the damage done. He sent an apology to the Chief Rabbi and promised that compensation would be paid. The main synagogue has since been rebuilt.

Of the 20,000 or so Jews that were still in Tunisia in 1967, there are now probably less than 15,000 left. The Government of Tunis has asked the Jews not to leave, but does not attempt to prevent their doing so.

The Jews of Algeria were more numerous than those of Tunisia (or of Egypt, for that matter) — probably over 120,000. They were French citizens and they left when the rest of the French left. There are still a few thousand there, but the Algerians do not seem to make much of it. In their propaganda, they still distinguish between Jews and Zionists or Israelis.

Perhaps this is the place to mention the Lebanon, where the uneasy truce between Moslem and Christian Arabs permits some 8,000 Jews to live in Beirut discreetly and more or less unmolested. During the Six Day War the authorities, fearing that anti-Jewish riots could set the mob off against Christians too, took steps to prevent trouble. But Jews are beginning to leave, when they can get themselves exit permits. These are valid for a year, but for one journey only.

Traditionally, the connection of Jews with Egypt goes back to Joseph, and historically there was a centre of Jewish dispersion in Egypt in the 6th century B.C. But the modern history of the Jews in Egypt begins in Turkish times.

Over the last hundred and fifty to two hundred years, the Jews of Egypt were on the surface a prosperous and progressive community, while beneath the surface their position was utterly insecure. Under the Capitulations, the Jews preferred the nationality or protection of a European Power to the dubious benefits of Turkish citizenship under distant and arbitrary authority. The Jews acquired French, British, Italian or some other nationality; they educated their children in foreign schools in Egypt and then in universities in Europe, sometimes even distributing them as evenly as might be among universities in different countries. They constituted a truly cosmopolitan layer in the very variegated cake of Egyptian society. They were attached though not fanatically to their religion and its customs. They were an elite, educated, efficient and exceptionally honest.

When the regime of the Capitulations came to an end, Jewish applications for Egyptian citizenship were not easily granted. Jews who were not foreign nationals, and who were in many instances second and third generation native-born Egyptians, remained legally without nationality, stateless.

With the attainment of Egyptian independence, the overwhelming Egyptian and particularly Moslem majority began to claim its place in all walks of life and to replace the leading Jewish families, which had played so big a part in trade and industry, banking and public works, agricultural development and Government service. After World War II, the Arabic language replaced French and English in all official and public correspondence, and the growing number of educated Arabs began crowding out the Jews from "white-collar" jobs.

The founding of the Arab League with headquarters in Cairo was the beginning of the end for Egyptian Jewry, then numbering about 76,000. Fanatical organisations such as the 'Moslem Brotherhood,' and Fascist organisations such as 'Young Egypt' began open incitement against the Jews. The latter were called upon to dissociate themselves from Zionism, and Jewish leaders did produce disclaimers. On the 2nd of November, 1945, a protest strike against the Balfour Declaration was proclaimed in Egypt for the first time. The demonstrators forced Jews — and non-Jewish foreigners as well — to close their shops, many of which were looted. Synagogues were wrecked, and Scrolls of the Law were burnt in the streets.

The pressure of 'Arabization' mounted steadily. By a law of 1947, 75% of the clerical staff of companies and 90% of the workers employed by them had to be of Egyptian nationality. (As already explained, most Egyptian-born Jews were not Egyptian nationals.) Egyptian nationals who stayed abroad for more than six months lost their nationality. On the day the State of Israel was proclaimed, the 14th of May 1948, 2,000 Jews were arrested in Egypt; hundreds more were placed under police surveillance and many others were thrown out of their homes. A fortnight later a law was passed "freezing" the property of anyone arrested or placed under police surveillance on suspicion of "activity directed against national security."

The next few years saw profound political and social changes in Egypt. Gamal Abdel Nasser emerged as unquestioned leader, with both Communists and 'Moslem Brothers' in jails and concentration camps. In these years the ranks of the secret police, army, intelligence and propaganda networks slowly filled up with ex-Nazis of considerable expertise and determination. Instead of the traditionally easy-going, erratic and corrupt Egyptian way — arresting people, then beating them up just for fun, sometimes more severely, sometimes less, and then letting them go if a satisfactory amount of baksheesh were forthcoming — a steadier, more consistent, more deeply murderous design became apparent. The Jewish community was being systematically squeezed out, systematically plundered, suffocated, eliminated. On the eve of the Sinai clash of '56, "foreign" Jews who had till then been unable or unwilling to pick up and leave were forcibly expelled. Some 4,000 were ordered to get out, with a suitcase and LE20 each. Later, the amount of cash was cut, and only a small brown paper parcel could be taken out. The property they had to abandon represented a not inconsiderable slice of Egypt's wealth: those who left signed documents renouncing all title to property in Egypt and all financial claims whatsoever. Some British and French nationals did recoup something later from their respective governments, but that was not the fault of the Egyptians.

Early in 1957, new rulings were promulgated, one after the other, making more and more Jews liable to arrest and expulsion. Citizenship was taken away from any Jew who had acquired it later than 1933, then from any Jew whom someone decided was a Zionist, then from any Jew who had acquired citizenship since 1900, then from any Jew who had ever been convicted of a crime, then from those who, though they had acquired citizenship before 1900, had not been in continuous residence since then.

Some Jews got out of the country and reached Israel, if not by the thousands by the hundreds. The rest still stayed on, helpless or fatalistic, or refusing to abandon home and property, relying on the old distinction between Jews and Zionists. At bottom they stayed because they were Egyptians. But the Jewish community as such was already in a state of collapse. By 1960, synagogues were being closed down; some of them were converted into mosques and the rest were completely neglected. When the Jewish hospital was confiscated, the sick were put out into the street and the doctors and staff arrested. All the other community institutions — old aged homes, orphanages, schools — were taken over, confiscated or closed down. Even the cemeteries were confiscated, sealed off, closed.

By June '67, there were probably no more than 2,500 Jews left in Egypt, 1,500 of them in Cairo and the rest in Alexandria. During May, Jews connected with or employed by public institutions had received letters sending them on vacation *sine die* and then follow-up letters dismissing them. Jewish bank accounts were frozen. When Nasser announced the blockade of the Straits of Akaba, and told the world's press, "We say to the Jews" — to the *Jews*, not to 'Israelis' or 'Zionists' — "We say to the Jews, 'We are waiting for you,' " the Jews of Egypt knew that there would be war, and they knew that they would be arrested. As one who got out reported afterwards, "In 1948 and '56, anti-Semitism was still courteous. This time the Jews knew they would not simply be given as fodder to the special services. It would not be enough to leave everything — homes, cars, carpets to the officers of Section. 94. The auction room in Nimr Street, whose owner was a member of the Jewish community and whose shadow-partner, Col. Sharawi, was Director of the Department for Jewish Problems, would no longer be the shortest route from prison to Paris. There would be something else, but what? . . ." The writer recounted how he was summoned by telephone to see a special service officer. "He offered me coffee and asked me if I could prove that I was Egyptian. I could. 'And of course you have a certificate of nationality?' That had been my act of triumph. A certificate of nationality proved that one had not always been Egyptian. I was Egyptian well before the birth of Egypt, when everyone was still Turkish. I had never had anything to prove it . . . He said I was certainly a son of my country . . ." But this time it was precisely the Egyptian Jews who were "it," and the writer found himself in an old rattle-trap of a car with three policemen and three other prisoners headed for Abu Zaabal just outside Cairo, where there were soon some 600 Jews, aged 20 to 50. Some 200 more were in the Al-Barga prison in Alexandria, among them the vice-president of the community, aged about 70, and the Rabbi of Alexandria. The prisoners in Alexandria were brought to Cairo to join those in Abu Zaabal; on arrival the Rabbi was strung up to the prison gate in the form of one crucified and beaten unconscious. The Chief Rabbi and the Ashkenazi Rabbi of Cairo, the latter a very old man, were both put under house arrest. (All the rabbis were released by the end of '67.)

What followed these arrests — a prolonged orgy of torture, part simply spiteful and part murderously sadistic, which continued for many months thereafter — has been described by one of those arrested, in an account published in December '67 in the French weekly L' EXPRESS. This account, which in its ironic and painful detachment bears the imprint of truth, makes extremely unpleasant reading. But most of those arrested — in effect, every adult male Jew in Egypt — are still there, in prison, subject to renewed torture whenever the bribes run dry or the itch takes their tormentors. Meanwhile their families starve.

The Egyptian authorities divided the Jews into three categories: Jews of foreign nationalities, Stateless Jews, and Egyptian Jews. The foreign embassies in Cairo, horrified by the reports seeping through, made every effort to rescue these unfortunates. The Egyptian Government was prepared to let them have "their" Jews and even Stateless ones; many of the latter were thrown out of the country straight from prison, without even being allowed to inform their families. The Spanish Government repeated a gesture it made during World War II to save Jews from the extermination camps. It granted Spanish nationality to Sephardic Jews, that is to say, to every Jew whose family name or place of birth lent him some colour of Spanish descent. The Jewish community, practically paralysed as it is, still tries to help and advise Stateless and foreign Jews who are trying to leave the country. It helps them to get papers, and provides the completely penniless with sea passage and LE50 a head. Those who leave are warned by Egyptian officials not to spread reports about the treatment of Jews in Egypt, lest those remaining there be made to suffer still more. As regards Egyptian Jews, the Egyptian Government has turned a deaf ear to all pleas to let them go. However, the Red Cross was finally allowed to visit them, including those under arrest; it concentrates its efforts on trying to get exit permits for the old and sick, but it can do little for them and nothing for the rest, who live in complete destitution and bodily fear.

The U. N. General Assembly passed a resolution in the autumn of '68 requesting the Secretary General to send a commission to inquire into Israeli treatment of the Arab inhabitants of Israeli-occupied areas. Israel agreed to give official aid to such an inquiry, on condition that a similar inquiry be undertaken into the treatment of Jews in Arab countries. This was turned down.

JORDAN AND JERUSALEM

For twenty years Jordan refused to honour her undertaking in terms of the 1948 Armistice Agreement to allow Jews from Israel access to the Western (Wailing) Wall in Jerusalem. Guards at the Wall forcibly prevented anyone, including Christian pilgrims, priests and pastors, from standing and facing the Wall, lest some one vicarious prayer might find its way from the voiceless stones to the unheeding heavens. Similiarly Christians were not permitted even to move their lips in silent prayer or to kneel even for a moment in the Coenaculum, the place of the Last Supper, on Mount Zion, when this was under Jordan control.

The Arab Legion avenged itself for its 1948 defeat by destroying, defacing and defiling the Jewish Quarter of the Old City of Jerusalem. Synagogues and religious schools that were not razed to the ground were ransacked and stripped bare, turned into store-rooms, rubbish dumps, stables or goat-pens. The spite vented on stones in default of human victims found its finest exercise in the desecration of the ancient Jewish cemetery on the Mount of Olives. The Jordan Government, the Legion and a chief contractor shared between them the quarry of thousands of gravestones from the graves of Jews who came to the Land of Israel over the centuries to be buried in holy soil so that their bones might be present at the end of days, gravestones from the graves of fathers and grandfathers of Jews alive in Israel today. Not that there is any shortage of building stone in Judea and Samaria. But stone-masons have to be paid, and ready-hewn stones by the thousand are a windfall for a building contractor, a godsend as one might say. The stones are to be seen everywhere in former Jordan-held territory, in a wall, in a bunker, as stepping-stones in a muddy field, as anchor for a tent-rope, as the sill of a latrine-hole.

There are no Jews in Jordan, but this country outdoes all the other Arab States in the virulence of its anti-Jewish propaganda and official systematic indoctrination of school-children.

NOTES

(1) PRISONERS OF HATE. Yehezkel Hameiri. Keter Books. Jerusalem. 1969. pp. 61-62.

(2) The following is a translation of an Army Circular dated 8 February 1967: "The Syrian Arab Republic . . . Ministry of Defence . . . Armed Forces General Headquarters . . . Administration Branch . . . Department of Military Administration — Military Police Section — No. 26/27/2 — Circular No. 4 — 8 February 1967. The following is a partial list of names of Jewish merchants and their businesses in Damascus. For security reasons, all Army personnel are forbidden to deal with them. Anyone who violates these instructions is liable to the severest penalties." The list attached gives 47 Jewish shops with their addresses and description — e.g., second-hand clothing, textiles, copper-work, etc.

(3) Hameiri. Op. Cit.

INTRODUCTION

It is on the issue of the Arab refugees that the positions of both the Arabs and Israel are probably more entrenched and uncompromising than on any other outstanding difference. The antagonists violently disagree not only as to who must assume the burden of responsibility for the refugee tragedy, but also as to what measures would be adopted towards its solution. Even the number of refugees involved has become a matter of contention.

The Arab states have asserted that the wholesale displacement of "millions" of Palestinian refugees is the cause rather than the product of their conflict with the Jewish state, for the Zionists have intentionally and ruthlessly uprooted the indigenous Arab population from its land in order to create a purely racist Zionist state. This displacement was carried out in accordance with a premeditated plan, beginning with the first Zionist immigration to Palestine some ninety years ago. Seeking the "ingathering" of its own "exiles," Israel, according to the Arabs, launched upon a land purchasing program, calculated terror tactics, and aggressive wars, thereby precipitating the flight of the defenseless Arabs from their ancestral homeland. Once displaced, the refugees' properties had been seized, appropriated, and confiscated. Moreover, all successive U. N. resolutions calling upon Israel to repatriate the homeless to their rightful country, and pending their return, to cooperate with the U. N. custodian for refugee property, had been defiantly ignored.

The Arab states insist, therefore, that the refugees, who have been living in deplorable and pathetic conditions, must be permitted to return and that their rights as a people and as individual human beings must be restored in a new Palestine. Any other attempt to treat the problem merely in economic or humanitarian terms — through resettlement or emigration — is evasive and superficial; it will not curb the aggressive mentality and behavior of Israel and, consequently, cannot guarantee peace.

Israel has been equally adamant on the refugee problem. It has stressed that the refugee problem was born out of the Arab states design to destroy the new fledgling state, and is, therefore, a by-product of the wars unleashed by the Arabs in disregard of the U. N. Partition Plan. Israel claims that the Arab states are not only guilty of creating the problem, but have sought to preserve it as a prime political weapon by steadfastly obstructing the resettlement of the refugees in Arab territories with suitable room and opportunities. The refugees, furthermore, have been cast in the role of a military spearhead against the Jewish state, and are constantly incited to undertake sabotage and terror activities inside and outside Israel.

Israel, furthermore, insists that it has already permitted the return of thousands of refugees under "family reunion" schemes, that it has released refugee bank accounts and safe deposits in its banks, and is ready to compensate the refugees for abandoned property. Beyond this the Arab refugee problem must be viewed in the context of the unplanned exchange of ethnic minorities (Jewish and Arab) that has taken place as a result of the Arab-Israeli conflict. Israel, for its part, and without the aid of any international body, has integrated some 600,000 destitute Jewish refugees who were brutally expelled from the Arab countries. It expects a reciprocal move on the part of the Arab states to resettle their refugees. But the ultimate solution of this problem, Israel concludes, can come only within the framework of a peace settlement, on the basis of regional cooperation and international financing.

An excerpt from Sami Hadowi's PALESTINE IN FOCUS, published by Beirut's Palestine Research Center (no date) presents the Arab view of the refugee question, particularly in relation to the pre-1967 period. The document places the responsibility for the Arab refugees on Israel and calls for implementation of U. N. resolutions affirming the legitimate rights of the refugees.

The Israeli's position is stated by Ambassador Michael Comay in an address delivered before the 23rd Special Political Committee of the U. N. General Assembly on November 26, 1968. Ambassador Comay stresses that the question of the Arab refugees must be viewed in the perspective of other refugee problems and concludes that it can be solved humanely by the Arab states themselves.

THE
ARAB
REFUGEES

Sami Hadawi

The number of Arabs who had left their homes by 14 May 1948, was in the neighbourhood of 400,000. By the time the last Armistice Agreement had been signed, another 350,000 had been forced to leave the country, bringing the total number of refugees who had been expelled from their homes inside Israel to some 750,000.

According to the 1966—1967 report of the United Nations Relief and Works Agency (UNRWA), the number of refugees registered with the Agency as on 31 May 1967, had risen, through natural population increase, to 1,344,576, of whom 860,951 were in receipt of rations.(1)

These figures do not include, however, Palestinians who have lost their means of livelihood but not their homes, and as such, do not qualify for relief according to UNRWA regulations. Also they do not include persons who have been able to re-establish themselves in neighbouring Arab countries without outside help and therefore are not in need of relief; or Palestinians who are now scattered throughout the world. The total number of Palestinian Arabs on the eve of the War of June 1967, was some 2,350,000. The approximate breakdown of this total: refugees, whether or not on relief: 1,345,000; non-refugee population of the West Bank: 475,000; non-refugee population of Gaza Strip: 130,000; persons never listed as refugees, living outside Jordan and Gaza: 100,000; and Arabs staying in Israel since May 1948: 300,000.

THE U. N. RESOLUTION ON THE RIGHT OF RETURN

On 11 December 1948, the United Nations General Assembly met to consider the report of the late U. N. Mediator Count Bernadotte, and, among other things, resolved "that the refugees wishing to return to their homes and live at peace with their neighbours should be permitted to do so at the earliest possible date, and that compensation should be paid for the property of those choosing not to return and for loss of or damage to property which, under principles of international law or in equity, should be made good by the Governments or authorities responsible."(2)

On 14 December 1950, the General Assembly met once again, and this time adopted a resolution "noting with concern that agreement has not been reached . . . repatriation, resettlement, economic and social rehabilitation of the refugees and the payment of compensation have not been effected, recognizing that . . . the refugee question should be dealt with as a matter of urgency . . . directs the United Nations Conciliation Commission for Palestine to . . . continue consultations with the parties concerned regarding measures for the protection of the rights, property and interests of the refugees."(3)

Between 1950 and 1967, eighteen resolutions were adopted by the General Assembly affirming and reaffirming annually the right of the refugees to repatriation or compensation under the provisions of paragraph 11 of the resolution of 11 December 1948.(4) The Israelis continue to refuse implementation and to demand resettlement of the refugees in Arab countries.

The Israeli position is contrary both to the desire of the refugees, who in their overwhelming majority want to return to their homes and homeland, and to specific U. N. resolutions affirming the refugees' right to return. The attitude of the refugees, on the one hand, and of Israel, on the other hand, need defining and exploring here.

ATTITUDE OF THE REFUGEES

There is a myth current outside the Arab world that the refugees would accept to be resettled where they are, outside Palestine, and that it is the Arab governments that block resettlement for political reasons. This is the reverse of the truth. The Arab governments refuse resettlement because the refugees refuse it, not the other way round.

The attitude of the refugees has been made clear and has remained unaltered since 1948 — namely, insistence on implementation of their right to return. It is true that the Arabs in the host countries are "brother Arabs" and that they and their governments have been hospitable to the refugees. It is true that land and work — all the material needs of life — could be found for them outside Palestine. What they insist on as a right, is to live in their own country, with a sense of collective identity as Palestinians.

Successive directors of UNRWA (the U. N. agency which looks after the refugees) have acknowledged the desire of the vast majority of refugees to return. This desire was no less strong and compelling in 1967 than it had been in 1948, and it is even stronger today after the expulsion by Israel of a few hundred thousand more since the June 1967 war.

Ten years ago one UNRWA Director in reporting to the General Assembly said: " . . . the great mass of the refugees continues to believe that a grave injustice has been done to them and to express a desire to return to their homeland."(5)

Another report stated: "All that he [the new Commissioner-General of UNRWA Mr. Laurence Michelmore,] has so far seen and heard since assuming his present responsibilities confirms the view recorded in previous reports that the refugees in general strongly maintain their insistence on the idea and aspiration of returning to their homes . . . The refugees have also expressed the wish that they should be enabled to receive redress for the loss they have suffered without prejudicing their claims to repatriation or any other political rights mentioned in resolution 194 (III). The modalities of implementing that paragraph of the General Assembly resolution may be differently conceived by the refugees, but what is not in doubt is that their longing to return home is intense and widespread . . ." The refugees "express their feeling of embitterment at their long exile and at the failure of the international community, year after year, to implement the resolution so often reaffirmed. They feel that they have been betrayed and their resentment is directed not only against those whom they regard as the chief authors of their exile, but also against the international community at large whom they hold responsible, for the partition and loss of their homeland, which they regard as an offence against natural justice."(6)

In 1966, the Commissioner-General, Mr. Michelmore, emphasized: "As year succeeds year, there is no sign that the refugees are becoming any less embittered by their conviction that a grave injustice has been done to them through the loss of their homes and country and the continued deprivation of any benefit from the property they left behind. The implications for peace and stability in the Middle East of the continued existence of the Palestine refugee problem thus remains as grave as ever."(7)

ISRAEL REFUSES RESPONSIBILITY

To justify their rejection of United Nations directives to repatriate and compensate the refugees, the Israelis invented the myth that the Arabs left of their own accord under the orders of their leaders, and that they were not driven out. This being so, the Israelis claim, the refugees have forfeited their right to return to their property.

Whether the Arabs left voluntarily or otherwise, their rights to freedom of movement and property ownership are governed by the Universal Declaration of Human Rights to which Israel is a signatory. Article 13[2] provides that "Everyone has the right to leave any country, including his own, and to return to his country"; and Article 17[2] prescribes that "No one shall be arbitrarily deprived of his property."

However, the following testimonies from neutral and Jewish sources prove that the Palestine Arabs did not leave of their own free will, nor at the orders of their own leaders.

Erskine B. Childers, British writer, reported in 1961: "Examining every official Israeli statement about the Arab exodus, I was struck by the fact that no primary evidence of evacuation orders (by Arabs) was ever produced. The charge, Israel claimed, was 'documented'; but where were the documents? There had allegedly been Arab radio broadcasts ordering the evacuation, but no dates, names of stations, or texts of messages were ever cited. In Israel in 1958, as a guest of the Foreign Office and therefore doubly hopeful of serious assistance, I asked to be shown the proofs. I was assured they existed, and was promised them. None had been offered when I left, but I was assured again. I asked to have the material sent to me. I am still waiting."

Childers went on: "I next decided to test the undocumented charge that the Arab evacuation orders were broadcast by Arab radio — which could be done thoroughly because the B.B.C. monitored all Middle Eastern broadcasts throughout 1948. The records, and companion ones by a U. S. monitoring unit, can be seen at the British Museum. There was not a single order or appeal, or suggestion about evacuation from Palestine from any Arab radio station, inside or outside Palestine, in 1948. There is repeated monitored record of Arab appeals, even flat orders to the civilians of Palestine to stay put. To select only two examples: On April 4, as the first great wave of flight began, Damascus Radio broadcast an appeal to everyone to stay at their homes and jobs. On April 24, with the exodus now a flood, Palestine Arab Leaders warned that 'Certain elements and Jewish agents are spreading defeatist news to create chaos and panic among the peaceful population. Some cowards are deserting their houses, villages and cities... Zionist agents and corrupt cowards will be severely punished.' Even Jewish broadcasts (in Hebrew) mentioned such Arab appeals to stay put. Zionist newspapers in Palestine reported the same; none so much as hinted at any Arab evacuation order."(8)

Sir John Bagot Glubb, former Officer Commanding the Arab Legion, said: "The story which Jewish publicity at first persuaded the world to accept, that the Arab refugees left voluntarily, is not true. Voluntary emigrants do not leave their homes with only the clothes they stand in. People who have decided to move house do not do so in such a hurry that they lose other members of their family — husband losing sight of his wife, or parents of their children. The fact is that the majority left in panic flight, to escape massacre. They were in fact helped on their way by the occasional massacres — not of very many at a time, but just enough to keep them running."(9)

Professor Arnold Toynbee, British historian, wrote: "If the heinousness of sin is to be measured by the degree to which the sinner is sinning against the light that God has vouchsafed to him, the Jews had even less excuse in A.D. 1948 for evicting Palestinian Arabs from their homes than Nebuchadnezzar and Titus and Hadrian and the Spanish and Portuguese Inquisitions had had for uprooting, persecuting and exterminating Jews in Palestine and elsewhere at diverse times in the past. In A.D. 1948 the Jews knew, from personal experience, what they were doing; and it was their supreme tragedy that the lesson learned by them from their encounter with the Nazi Gentiles should have been not to eschew but to imitate some of the evil deeds that the Nazis had committed against the Jews."(10)

Professor Erich Fromm, a noted Jewish writer and thinker, had this to say: "It is often said that the Arabs fled, that they left the country voluntarily, and that they therefore bear the responsibility for losing their property and their land ... But in general international law, the principle holds true that no citizen loses his property or his rights of citizenship; and the citizenship right is *de facto*, a right to which the Arabs in Israel have much more legitimacy than the Jews. Just because the Arabs fled? Since when is that punishable by confiscation of property and by being barred from returning to the land on which a people's forefathers have lived for generations?"(11)

M. Stein and A. Zichrony, of the Third Force Movement in Israel, wrote in 1961 in connection with the trial of Adolf Eichmann: " ... with deep sorrow and shame we ask: Does Israel, which for 13 years has been imposing exile and misery on hundreds of thousands of men, women and children, whose only guilt is that they are Arabs; which has deprived her Arab inhabitants of elementary human rights, confiscated most of their lands and forces them to beg for a permit for every move in the country — does the Israel of Libya, Gaza, Kafr Kassem and the wanton attacks on Egypt have the moral right to sit in judgement? Israeli leaders and newspapermen vehemently denounce those Germans who were silent during the beastly Nazi reign. Even the 'good Germans' profitted from the plunder of Jews. Even German liberals and leftists became Nazis, it is said. But how do the Jews in Israel behave? Do they not approve — not tacitly, but quite loudly — the inhuman actions of their Government? Are there many Jewish houses in Israel that do not harbour Arab property? Do not the Kibbutzim build 'socialism' on robbed Arab land? What a spectacle: In the City of the Prophets and under the eyes of Humanity, they are sitting in judgement!"(12)

JUNE 1967

During the Six-Day War the impetus of the Israeli attack took them right through the West Bank of Jordan as far as the River Jordan (now the cease-fire line). Surprised by the suddenness of the attack and terrified by modern war weapons, such as napalm, of which they had had no previous experience, the Arab villagers again fled in panic, along with some refugees from the 1948 war, many of whom had been settled in camps in Western Jordan. Altogether about 200,000 people fled during the brief war. Another 210,000 have since followed them, impelled by fear, the dynamiting of their houses or loss of their menfolk, to leave their homes and land.(13)

Pressure at the United Nations(14) after the cease-fire squeezed out of the Israelis a reluctant promise to readmit the refugees, who were now mostly assembled in makeshift camps along the east bank of the Jordan River. Out of the original 200,000, over 176,000 filled the appropriate return forms under the supervision of the International Red Cross. The return was set for July 1967. In fact, only 14,000 have since been allowed back.

Until February 1968 most of the refugees clustered in 6 large camps along the Jordan Valley. But after two air and artillery attacks in which over 100 refugees were killed and wounded, the refugees moved again to higher, safer ground farther to the east. To their number is now added a fourth category of refugee: Jordanians from the Ghor Valley, forced to leave their farms by Israeli shelling and strafing. The ratio of refugees to non-refugees in Jordan is now (June 1968) 2:1.(15)

Ever since their attack on June 5th, the Israelis have been trying to prove to the world that, because they are safer, the Palestinian problem is solved. Far from it. The whole Palestinian people is now either under occupation or uprooted. It would be most unrealistic to expect them to accept this.

NOTES

(1) U. N. Document A/6713—UNRWA Report 1966—1967.

(2) U. N. Resolution 194(III) of the December 1948, Para. 11.

(3) U. N. Resolution 394(V) of 14 December 1950, Para. 2(C).

(4) For numbers and dates of resolutions, see UNITED NATIONS RESOLUTIONS ON PALESTINE 1947—1966, ed. Sami Hadawi, (Beirut: Institute for Palestine Studies), pp. 73-111.

(5) U. N. Document A/3686—UNRWA Report 1956—1957.

(6) U. N. Document A/5813—UNRWA Report 1963—1964.

(7) U. N. Document A/6313—UNRWA Report 1965—1966.

(8) From an article entitled 'The Other Exodus,' published in the LONDON SPECTATOR, 12 May 1961. The same finding was made independently by Mr. Walid Khalidy after research undertaken at the British Museum. See Walid Khalidy in THE MIDDLE EAST FORUM, Beirut, December 1959; and in ARAB REVIEW, London, January 1960.

(9) Glubb, A SOLDIER WITH THE ARABS, p. 251.

(10) Toynbee, A STUDY OF HISTORY, Vol. VIII, p. 280.

(11) JEWISH NEWSLETTER (New York), 19 May 1958.

(12) Ibid., 3 October 1960.

(13) See Halim Barakat and Peter Dodd, REFUGEES: UPROOTEDNESS AND EXILE (Institute for Palestine Studies, Beirut, 1968) — A sociological field study on the June refugees.

(14) U. N. Resolution 2252 (ES-V) of 4 July 1967.
(15) See ORIENT (Beirut daily), 1 June 1968, p. 7.

THE
ARAB
REFUGEES

Michael Comay

Mr. Chairman,

After twenty years of debating the Arab refugee problem, my delegation will not spend much time on its historical background, in spite of the weird lectures to which the Committee has been treated on this theme. The Israel Government is today concerned with a peace settlement that will finally end the Israel-Arab conflict, and with a constructive approach to the problems of human displacement caused by that conflict. It is in this spirit that we shall address ourselves to the item before the Committee.

The bitter fruit of wars everywhere in the world has been death, destruction and displacement for both sides. That grim axiom applies as well as to the three wars spawned by Arab hostility to Israel in the two decades of our statehood.

The 1948 war did not wipe Israel out at birth, as it was meant to do. What it did do was to launch a two-way migration. More than half a million Arabs moved from the areas under Israel control to adjacent Arab areas. They did not move far afield, and 85 per cent of them approximately remained and still remain in the area that had been Palestine under the British Mandate. This fact was to have a strong bearing on their subsequent absorption, since they were Arabs remaining in a familiar Arab environment.

The displaced Jews from the Old City of Jerusalem and a number of Jewish villages occupied by Arab forces in the 1948 fighting were taken into Israel. After the war a movement took place into Israel of about 500,000 Jews uprooted in the Arab countries. With natural increase, the families that came into Israel as refugees from the Arab countries number today about 900,000 souls. A vast amount of their property was confiscated in the countries which they left behind; no offer was ever made to pay compensation for it. Only small remnants of the ancient Jewish communities remain in the Arab countries of the Middle East; they are repressed, and not allowed to leave.

POPULATION EXCHANGE

What took place at that time, therefore, was an unplanned and spontaneous

205

population exchange, corresponding to what has happened in other regions. In times of war and stress, groups which feel insecure tend to move into areas where they have an affinity with the local population, based on race, religion, language or culture. Historically these migrations have not been put into reverse — least of all, as in the present case, where the movement took place in both directions, and the war was not followed by peace. For twenty years Israel and its Arab neighbours have faced each other across military frontiers — first armistice lines, and now cease-fire lines. On both sides of these lines the displaced groups have put down fresh roots among their own kin.

There was, however, a sharp contrast in the handling of the two refugee groups. The United Nations never became seized of the problem of Jews displaced from the Arab countries. Most of them were resettled in Israel and absorbed into the life and economy of the country. That required a staggering national effort and financial burden, willingly borne by the people of Israel, with material help from their Jewish brethren elsewhere in the free world. No comparable effort was made by the Arab world to absorb their own displaced kinsmen.

On the contrary, the official Arab position towards them hardened. The refugees were cast in the role of a political and military spearhead in a continuing struggle against the existence of Israel. They were preyed upon by professional agitators; the children were brainwashed in the schools; and thousands of young men were armed and trained while remaining wards of UNRWA. Even before the June 1967 war, the Secretary-General had reported to the Assembly on the danger to peace of the so-called Liberation Army deployed in the Gaza Strip and along the Sinai border, under Egyptian command. Several thousand of these trainees are now in Egypt receiving UNRWA rations, and we must again question the propriety of this aid. Responsibility for them should devolve on the United Arab Republic Government which recruited them. In brief, the refugees were taught that the only solution to their problem lay in the dissolution of the State of Israel. The concept was scornfully rejected that this was a humanitarian problem, to be settled on economic lines.

More and more of the Arab refugees did become spontaneously absorbed in the host countries or elsewhere in the Arab world. But this vital fact was not reflected in the statistics. After being inflated from the beginning, the official total swelled each year, and with it the gap between myth and reality.

REGIONAL ECONOMIC INTEGRATION RESISTED . . . ABANDONED

UNRWA itself became a political prisoner of the unresolved conflict, and lost its original purpose. It is almost forgotten that UNRWA was created nearly twenty years ago to carry out a crash programme for the regional economic integration of the Arab refugees.

In 1948, before the hositilities were over, the United Nations Mediator had put forward his views on an over-all settlement of the conflict. He recommended, *inter alia*, that those refugees who wished to go back to their homes and live at peace with their neighbours should be allowed to do so, while the others should be paid compensation for their property. He was referring to people who at that time had left their homes only months or even weeks before. He also assumed that there would be a quick peace settlement.

Paragraph 11 of resolution 194(III), adopted by the General Assembly on 11 December 1948, echoed the recommendations of the Mediator regarding the refugees, though it already held out resettlement as an alternative to repatriation. That paragraph was contained in a resolution calling for a final negotiated settlement of all Israel-Arab issues, and setting up a Palestine Conciliation Commission to assist the parties in their negotiations. It soon became apparent that these peace expectations were unduly optimistic.

It became unreal to suggest that anything could be done just by invoking paragraph 11. Assembly resolutions continued to pay lipservice to it — as they still do — and it became the focus of a sterile textual exercise in the annual debates in this Committee. But United Nations policy on the refugee problem turned in a new and more long-term direction as early as 1949.

In that year, the Palestine Conciliation Commission sent an Economic Survey Mission to the Middle East — the Clapp Mission. The General Assembly approved its programme of public works and projects for "the re-integration of the refugees into the economic life of the Near East." A $ 200 million Rehabilitation Fund was voted by the Assembly to finance this programme. UNRWA was created as an instrument for carrying it out. Relief was to be temporary, and incidental to the main constructive approach.

Because of Arab political resistance, all integration and rehabilitation projects were abandoned many years ago, and the word "works" in UNRWA's title ceased to have any meaning. UNRWA became that anomaly, a permanent relief agency for a self-perpetuating refugee problem.

ONCE A REFUGEE, ALWAYS A REFUGEE?

UNRWA's working rule has in effect been "once a refugee, always a refugee." Even those persons who became self-supporting and no longer needed or received the Agency's help remained registered with it, and could come back on relief at a future time. Meanwhile they were included in its refugee totals. (In Annex I of the Report presently under discussion, the figure for such "N" category refugees is given at 121,939.) Furthermore, UNRWA has come to assume in practice that the status of refugee is handed down from the original displaced persons to their children and their children's children and all subsequent generations.

My delegation has recalled the history of UNRWA's mandate because it has some relevance for the future. The question is not whether the international community should help needy or uprooted people, on humanitarian grounds. On that we all agree. The question is whether the help over a long period should concentrate on their rehabilitation or keep them on relief. After twenty years, the time has come to take a fresh look at the problem and prepare the way for a constructive settlement, in the framework of peace and regional and international co-operation.

Security Council resolution 242 (1967) of 22 November 1967 has placed the refugee problem once more in the broad context of peace-making, and wisely refrained from tying its settlement to previous United Nations resolutions on the subject. My Government is anxious to participate actively in a renewed attack upon the substance of the problem, and my delegation will make some further observations on this matter later in this statement.

In asking what has happened to the rehabilitation side of UNRWA's task which was originally its main function, my delegation would not wish to underrate the work the Agency is doing in the field of education and vocational training for youth. The value of these activities is generally and rightly recognized, though at some stage they will need to be merged with the education systems in the host countries. My Government intends making a special contribution of IL 200,000 for the expansion of UNRWA's vocational training center in Gaza. I would mention here that our authorities are developing their own vocational training services in Israel-held areas, with an emphasis on imparting skills to adult workers, including many refugees.

ISRAEL CO-OPERATES WITH UNRWA

Pending an overall solution of the problem, it is self-evident that UNRWA should continue to operate. Any sudden and drastic change in its present activities, unaccompanied by a broad programme for permanent integration, would only cause fresh hardship and instability. My Government will, therefore, support a reasonable extension of the Agency's mandate, and will continue to extend full co-operation to the Agency in all Israel-held areas.

On the basis of our own day-to-day contacts with the Agency in the area, my Government is glad to associate itself with the tributes already paid in this Committee to the dedication and zeal with which Mr. Michelmore and his colleagues have carried out their task in difficult circumstances.

If we have expressed certain criticisms about the way UNRWA's role has evolved since the Agency was founded, it will be appreciated that these are objective comments, not levelled personally against the men who have directed the Agency's affairs. They have often been caught between the political attitudes of the host Governments and the lack of firm and precise directives from the Assembly.

Our working relations with the Agency have been harmonious, and specific questions have been discussed and dealt with in a spirit of goodwill and pragmatism. My delegation can confirm the statement in paragraph 14 of the Report that the co-operation between UNRWA and the Israel authorities has continued to be effective.

The financial cost of the UNRWA operation to the Israel taxpayer is considerable. As is reflected in Table 22 of the Report, the direct contribution of the Israel Government to the refugees for the year ended 30 June 1968, was over $ 2.5 million. That figure covers education, social welfare, medical, housing, security and other services. To this must be added a direct cash contribution for the period under review of IL 1 million and almost IL 2 million for port services transportation, storage and other expenses. The total cost to my Government of services and contributions to UNRWA and the refugees during the year under review was, therefore, nearly IL 11 million, the equivalent of over $ 3.5 million at the then rate of exchange.

HOW MANY REFUGEES?

I would comment briefly on a few other points in the Report that concern the UNRWA operation in Israel-held areas.

We would make a general reservation about the figures given in the Report for the number of refugees remaining in the areas, after allowing for movement out of them. The Agency has adjusted its figures downwards, but they are still above the levels of the Israel figures. As the Report states in paragraph 14 —

> Consultations have also been held with the technical staff of the Government of Israel on the reconciliation of the UNRWA statistics with those produced in the census conducted by that Government in September 1967. More recently, emphasis has shifted to the statistics produced from the issue of identification cards. (A/7213, para. 14)

This effort at reconciling the figures is still in progress and my delegation will refrain from drawing any conclusions in the present debate. We are not aware of any such scrutiny of the rolls through a joint technical study in any of the Arab host countries, and in our opinion the statistics for those countries remain inflated and unreliable.

SCHOOL-BOOKS AND HATE

There is also no need to comment in detail on the question of school textbooks, to which the Report refers in paragraphs 17 to 19. In Israel-held areas textbooks containing offensive passages or incitement to hatred are no longer in use, whether in refugee or non-refugee schools and I would add here that there has been no interference with anybody's religious or cultural education. The question of the replacement of books in refugee schools will no doubt be considered by the Committee of Experts set up by the Director-General of UNESCO with Israel approval. To the best of our knowledge, no steps have yet been taken in any Arab host country to remedy this serious problem. As the Report indicates, those Governments have raised objection on the grounds of sovereignty, cultural heritage, and so forth. These arguments beg the real question, which is, whether United Nations agencies should be responsible for teaching children hatred and incitement against another State or people. The issue is at last being faced, and UNESCO rightly though belatedly sees it as a challenge to its own fundamental principles.

ECONOMIC IMPROVEMENT V. CONTINUOUS TERROR

The Report makes a point of the economic dislocation and hardship caused by the war and its impact on the refugees. Without going into details, it can be stated that, in general, economic activity in Israel-held areas is at least back to the pre-war level. There is no longer any serious unemployment. Wage levels have risen. On the West Bank, private building activity is reviving, after being at a standstill for a long time after the war, and measures are being initiated to promote investment.

The 1968/69 budget — that is for one year — for the maintenance of public services and for economic development in Israel-held territories is IL 140 million. Of that amount, only one-fifth is covered by local revenues, and the rest is provided by the Israel taxpayer.

The refugee communities in the Israel-held areas also benefit from this general improvement in economic conditions and the constructive efforts of the authorities.

In his report, the Commissioner-General lays stress on the problem of persons displaced as a result of the June 1967 hostilities, and he urges that their return be facilitated to their former homes and camps. This point was stressed by the Secretary-General and by certain of our colleagues.

I would assure those representatives that my Government is acutely conscious of the human aspect of this question. My delegation will inform the Committee of what we have done and what we propose to do about it, under present circumstances. I say "under present circumstances" because it is not helpful to discuss the matter as if it existed in a vacuum and not in a complicated local context. The extent and rapidity with which a return can be facilitated is inevitably affected by the political and security conditions on the spot. We still live in a situation that officially rests on a cease-fire but that is in practice marked by continuous border warfare and by efforts to promote violence and disrupt orderly administration within the Israel-held areas The Jordan Government, which foments and supports all these activities, is itself making any large-scale repatriation as difficult and as sensitive as possible.

Bombs and mines are laid under cover of darkness to blow up farmers' sleeping families, or a busload of schoolchildren on an outing, or ordinary Jews and Arabs in marketplaces — these squalid murders are being glorified to the Arab world as heroic exploits. They are at war against innocent civilians and at war against peace itself. They will not deflect us from our humane and positive policies towards the local population, nor from our search for dialogue and reconciliation with our neighbours. We accept the sincerity of the moral advice we hear from our friends; they should also accept the sincerity of our own wish to reduce human hardship as much as we can.

FAMILY REUNION

Pending a peace settlement, Israel is doing its best to reconcile the return of displaced persons with responsibility for the safety, welfare and security of the local population and the security of the State itself. A programme for an influx of returnees obviously needs to be carefully regulated, though it can be reviewed and expanded as the situation permits.

Last year, as we have been told, 14,000 persons were repatriated in our project, and another 7,000 were given permits but did not appear. After that, the Government initiated a family reunion scheme under which the local inhabitants could apply for the return of relatives. By the end of June 1968, as Mr. Michelmore reports, 3,000 persons had been returned under this heading. Since that date, another 3,000 have been admitted and several thousand more approved.

In his statement to the General Assembly on 8 October last, the Foreign Minister, Mr. Eban, declared :

> As an interim measure, my Government has decided, in view of the forthcoming winter to intensify and accelerate action to widen the 'uniting of families' scheme, and to process 'hardship cases' amongst refugees who had crossed to the East Bank during the June 1967 fighting. Moreover, permits for return which had been granted and not used can be made available to other refugees who meet the same requirements and criteria as the original recipients. (1686th meeting, page 47)

Administrative arrangements have already been made to carry out this undertaking.

The processing of family reunion and hardship applications is being intensified and accelerated, and this will result in a substantially higher rate of return in these categories, without placing on them specific limitations of time or numbers. In addition to this continuous flow, a further 7,000 persons will be readmitted on the basis of permits issued but not used last year. The Ministry of the Interior, which is the responsible Ministry, published an announcement last week, on 19 November, that all permit-holders would be given a fresh opportunity to come back by the end of January, after which unused permits would be made available to other applicants.

It should be mentioned here — and I think this point is important—that migration eastward across the river has virtually ceased. Except for a few scattered individuals the flow is now entirely westward, back to Israel-held areas. It is this flow which the most recent arrangements will augment.

JORDAN'S BORDER ATTACKS CREATE NEW REFUGEES

Some further comment is required on the nature and dimensions of this problem. An estimated 400,000 persons are alleged to have crossed from the West Bank into Jordan and become registered there. If this is meant to be a figure of West Bank residents who were displaced by the fighting and moved into Jordan, it is grossly exaggerated.

In addition to those who actually fled as a result of the hostilities — that lasted for seventy-two hours on the Jordan front — the registration in Jordan may be presumed to include various other groups. For instance: there is no doubt that a number of those listed are local residents who are in need or who have suffered economic hardship because of the war. By way of analogy, it may be recalled that in a 1949 report on the Arab refugees the then Secretary-General pointed out that a great number of needy non-refugees had got onto the rolls; the Clapp mission estimated the number at 160,000.

Since then, between 60,000 and 70,000 inhabitants from the Jordan Valley east of the river have moved further inland, and a number of them have presumably swelled the relief ranks in and around Amman. They have been displaced by the terrorist organizations that have established their bases in that zone and operate from it with the support of the Jordan Legion, thus turning it into a battlefield. The answer to their problem is for the Jordan Government to halt the operations of regular and irregular armed forces from Jordan territory and to ensure a scrupulous observance of the cease-fire.

In this connection, it might be pointed out that Jordan's failure to halt border attacks also accounts directly for the fact that the temporary camps are in the uplands and not down in the Jordan Valley where the winter climate is mild. As appears from the foot-note on page 6 of the Commissioner-General's report, he had reported last March that the refugees had fled from the previous camps in the Jordan Valley because of the security situation created there. The gunfire and the terrorist raids from Jordan have taken their toll in death, injury and destruction on our side of the line. They have also brought about the evacuation of both inhabitants and refugees from the areas of Jordan adjacent to the line on that side. The reports of a recent accommodation between the Government in Amman and the terrorist groups do not hold out much prospect of an early pacification of the border. Maintaining the cease-fire is the concern of the Security Council, not of this Committee. But it is pertinent in this debate to refer to the human price paid for the policy of limited warfare across the cease-fire line.

It must also not be assumed that people from the West Bank area now in Jordan necessarily crossed over during or since the hostilities of last year. That area has always been a source of migration. In the Mandatory period there was a population movement from this hill region into other parts of Palestine, and even overseas. In the nineteen years of Jordanian rule, the movement was into East Jordan — where investment and development was deliberately concentrated — and from there a number travelled onwards into the oil-producing Arab countries. In the decade before 1967, an estimated 200,000 persons from the West Bank settled across the river. Relief is now claimed from the Jordan authorities or UNRWA for a number of persons who were already in East Jordan before the hostilities last year, but are now described as having been displaced by those hostilities.

AFTER THE CEASE-FIRE

After the cease-fire last year, migration eastward was resumed for a variety of reasons connected with family ties, means of livelihood and sources of income. A sense of insecurity or reluctance to remain under Israel control may also have stimulated this movement. But it was a free, orderly and voluntary one, and the migrants were not wartime refugees. My Government has never felt entitled to hold any of the inhabitants in Israel-held territory against their will. But, as I have already stated, this eastward movement has also dried up by now.

From the beginning of July 1967, our authorities have kept a record of the persons migrating eastward across the river. Together with our best estimate of the number that crossed during and soon after the hostilities, we believe the total to be less than 250,000, up to the present.

It is not for my Government to suggest how many persons should be assisted in Jordan. The above comments are made simply to keep the record straight about the number of persons who were displaced in the West Bank by the June war and moved into Jordan. The human fact remains that, wherever they came from, a large number of families face a hard winter in the camps in Jordan, and that UNRWA needs to raise additional funds so that the camps can be made more habitable. Bearing this in mind, my Government intends to make another special contribution to UNRWA of IL 1 million, to be utilized in cash or building materials at the Agency's option.

The Commissioner-General states, in paragraph 11 of the report, that:

> Some easing of the difficulties faced by the refugees and other displaced persons in East Jordan has resulted from the greater freedom of movement across the river Jordan in both directions, which has been permitted in recent months.(A/7213, para. 11)

This freedom of movement is one expression of the general policy of the Israel Government. Our authorities have gone to great lengths in order to encourage the passage of people, goods and mail.

AN OPEN FRONTIER

A stream of Arab visitors come and go across the Jordan bridges, thus maintaining family, social and business ties. Since the beginning of this year 180,000 persons have crossed from the West Bank into Jordan and beyond on temporary passes, and returned; and 23,000 Arab visitors have come across from Jordan and Arab countries further away. This latter figure includes 6,000 students in Arab countries who came to spend their summer vacations with their families in the area in Israel control. Over 1,000 of them sought and obtained permission to remain permanently, thus forming yet another category of returnees.

During this year also, many thousands of truckloads of farm produce from the West Bank have crossed the river to Jordan and beyond, returning with imports of produce and merchandise. The volume of this traffic is about what it was before June 1967. At peak periods, over 300 trucks a day have crossed over. The truck drivers automatically change the license plates each time they cross.

The exchange of mail between Israel-held areas and the Arab States is also functioning smoothly, with the co-operation of the International Red Cross.

This policy of an "open frontier" not only lessens present difficulties, as the Commissioner-General says, but it widens the areas of contact and intercourse between all the populations concerned, and has a bearing on the prospect of peaceful co-existence.

A NEGOTIATED SOLUTION

I shall now revert to the question of a permanent, over-all solution to the main Arab refugee problem.

In his statement in the general debate at the present session on 8 October, the Israel Foreign Minister referred to the refugee problem, in the course of outlining nine principles for peace. Mr. Eban proposed that:

> 1. A conference of Middle Eastern States should be convened, together with the Governments contributing to refugee relief and the specialized agencies of the United Nations, in order to chart a five-year plan for the solution of the refugee problem in the framework of a lasting peace and the integration of refugees into production life. This conference can be called in advance of peace negotiations.
> 2. Under the peace settlement, joint refugee integration and rehabilitation commissions should be established by the signatories in order to approve agreed projects for refugee integration in the Middle East, with regional and international aid. (1686th meeting, page 47)

We are waiting for a positive response to that proposal which would turn the discussion of the problem away from useless polemics and into practical channels.

The Israel Government contemplates that a refugee programme would include a reintegration and compensation Fund, which would provide the financial means for land settlement, economic self-support, training, migration and compensation for abandoned property. I would reaffirm the willingness of my Government to give prompt and substantial financial support to such a fund.

I would also recall what my delegation said in the Committee last year, in proposing consultations on a five year plan:

> At the disposal of such a constructive and comprehensive plan, we shall place whatever resources we can make available, and all the extensive skills and experience in settlement and development we have gained in our own nation-building, and in the programmes of economic and technical co-operation between Israel and over sixty other developing lands.

In our opinion the practical aspects of a solution should not be unduly formidable, once the political roadblocks have been removed. It is a fictitious impression that there are 1,333,000 Arab refugees eking out a precarious existence on international charity. The real picture is less bleak, and attention should be drawn to some of the encouraging facts about it.

For one thing, the total number of needy refugees actually existing in the area is considerably lower than the registered total. This fact is not contested in any serious quarter, and I do not need to dwell on it.

ECONOMIC ABSORPTION

Moreover, there has been substantial economic absorption. In most areas, refugee levels of employment and family income are at or close to those of the non-refugee population. In addition, many tens of thousands of refugees have good jobs in Kuwait and the other oil countries, and send remittances home to their families.

Four years ago, the Commissioner-General reported to the Assembly that destitute and nearly-destitute refugees might constitute some 40 to 50 per cent of the registered total, and that the rest were either economically independent or partially self-supporting. Two years ago Mr. Michelmore stated that:

> With the passage of time and changes in the economic circumstances, the rations have become for many of the recipients a modest economic subvention from the international community to assist them in their struggle to support themselves and improve their economic conditions. The Commissioner-General believes that it would be misleading to attach undue importance to the number of ration recipients as an index of the dependence or independence of the refugees on international aid. (A/6313,Supplement 13, pp. 8-9)

In last year's report, the Commissioner-General developed the theme that for some years prior to the June war there had been a steady rise in the economic and social conditions of the refugees. He attributed the progress in rehabilitation to economic development in the Arab countries, the capacities of the refugees themselves, and the education and training which young refugees had received. He described the economic aid supplied by UNRWA as subsidiary to the principal factors at work, though not unimportant in itself.

Mr. Michelmore stated that the hostilities had had a disruptive effect on this steady absorption, but at any rate the Israel-held territories have shown an economic recovery since then, as I have already said.

Our own observations in Israel-held areas tend to bear out Mr. Michelmore's description. I would mention here a study in depth of one of the large camps in the West Bank area, carried out by a research team from the Hebrew University of Jerusalem. In the group studied, the average family income and level of employment was nearly equal to local standards, and even a little higher, when adding the cash value of the UNRWA rations. What is more, very few of the original refugees were left in the camp, and a number of local inhabitants had gradually moved in.

Not only economically but also as far as their places of habitation are concerned, the refugees have to a large extent merged with the indigenous population. Even including the special case of the Gaza Strip, only a third of the refugees live in camps at all. The camps themselves have in the course of time evolved into villages, small townships and urban quarters. The original homes have been expanded into family dwellings by the refugees from their own resources.

It is also of interest to note that the majority of names on UNRWA lists today are those of children and young people who were born after the events of 1948 that created the refugee problem. The proportion will be even larger when the lists catch up with the undeclared deaths.

"INTEGRATION DE FACTO"

It appears, therefore, that behind the dust and smoke of political rhetoric, the natural absorption into the local life and economy is quite far advanced. In most areas the distinction between refugee and non-refugee has become very blurred. A practical solution would not, therefore, start from scratch. It would consist largely in speeding up and consolidating the existing process of integration; ensuring a productive life for all those able to work; and merging refugee and non-refugee education, health, social welfare and relief services. The need for re-location would apply in particular to the refugees in the Gaza

214

Strip, where the numbers certainly exceed the absorption potential on the spot. One recalls what was said in the remarkable report drawn up in 1959 by Secretary-General Dag Hammarskjold, in which he developed the thesis of what he called, "integration de facto." Mr. Hammarskjold wrote:

> The unemployed population represented by the Palestine refugees should be regarded not as a liability but, more justly, as an asset for the future; it is a reservoir of manpower which in the desirable general economic development will assist in the creation of higher standards for the whole population of the area. (A/4121 of 15 June 1959, Part I, para. 11)

As I have indicated, that reservoir is already being substantially tapped. In last year's Report, in dealing with this matter, the Commissioner-General admitted that UNRWA's published statistics do not adequately reflect the extent of refugee rehabilitation. We commend this candour but find the explanation unsatisfactory. There have doubtless been other reasons for this credibiltity gap — for instance, the fact of political inhibitions in the host countries; the fact that UNRWA's staff consists of a hundred-odd "international" employees and 11,000 local Arab refugee employees; and the fact that a refugee card has become a political, emotional and even commercial vested interest. Whatever the reasons, the result has been that an exaggerated and unduly gloomy picture of the refugee problem has been projected outwards and has been exploited for propaganda purposes. The first stage in any final settlement of the problem will have to be a thorough factual survey that will reveal how many bona fide refugees there actually are and what the real extent is of their absorption. Only then can any serious and practical planning be done to rehabilitate those that still need it and to start winding up a twenty-year relief operation.

HIGH COMMISSIONER FOR REFUGEES
I would like to glance now at the record of the parallel United Nations institution, that of the High Commissioner for Refugees. The experience of the United Nations High Commissioner for Refugees in different regions of the world confirms that as a general rule refugees who have left their original country get resettled elsewhere. In the Secretary-General's annual Report to this Assembly Session, the section on the UNHCR stated that local integration in the countries of asylum has been the main solution. It continues:

> Of a total of 222,000 refugees benefitting under UNHCR current operations and the Emergency Fund, 214,000 were assisted in their local integration, some 206,000 of whom were in Africa. (A/7201, p. 139)

At page 138 it is stated that the High Commissioner's programmes were mainly devoted to helping refugees to become self-supporting.

My delegation has tried to present these facts and views in a sober and realistic spirit. It is our hope that the present debate will be free from rancour and that no contentious proposals will be pressed. With all the differences and hazards that remain, there are also grounds for renewed hope. Over a large area today, one can witness movement and mingling such as has not existed for twenty years. The peoples on both sides of the line are weary of bloodshed and strife and long for the chance to lead their daily lives and bring up their children in peace. The United Nations is once more engaged in a serious peace-making effort many years after the last such effort faded. The realities of the refugee problem are emerging more clearly, and it appears less grim and intractable than the propaganda picture.

What is essential is to leave the past behind and move toward a better future in which Israeli and Arab will live and work together in amity for the good of our shared region.

INTRODUCTION

There have never been stable boundaries between Israel and her Arab neighbors. After the demise of the Ottoman Empire, Britain obtained a League of Nations trusteeship over Palestine, including Trans-Jordan. In this territory a national home was to be established for the Jews. In 1922, by British decision, the lands east of the Jordan were turned into an independent Arab state. Later, when Arab-Jewish hostilities peaked, various programs for the partition of Palestine were advanced. In 1947, the U.N. finally approved such partition under which both an independent Arab and independent Jewish state were to be created. The objecting Arab states then invaded Palestine, but the new state of Israel resisted. The resultant armistice agreement left within Israeli control more than the U. N. had originally decreed. But Jordan annexed one part of the Arab Palestine to be and Egypt occupied another. No Arab Palestine was created and subsequent warfare between the Arabs and Israelis further increased the Israeli territorial holdings.

While the Israelis had originally accepted the 1948 U.N. partition proposal the Arabs have continued to challenge the very creation of Israel in what was at the time a predominantly Arab populated country. Responding to the challenge, the Israelis point to the Arabs as mere latecomers to a land which was previously promised to the Jews.

The Jews lived in Palestine from about 1200 BC until the Roman destruction of the Jerusalem Temple in 70 AD. Palestine then became a Roman province until it was conquered by the invading Arabs in 637 AD. In the next thirteen centuries the area changed hands from one domination to another. Since 1071 Palestine was ruled by the Seljuk Turks, the Crusaders, the Kurds, the Mamelukes, and from 1516 by the Ottoman Turks who, after the First World War, renounced their rights to the land. The British Mandate in Palestine, which followed, lasted until May 14, 1948.

The U. N. partition plan granted Israel 5893 square miles. The 1949 Armistice Agreements signed between Egypt, Jordan, Lebanon, and Syria, on the one hand, and Israel, on the other, concluding the first round of Arab-Israeli hostility, left within Israeli occupation 7992 square miles. Although these agreements were intended to assist the antagonists to move towards a peace settlement and thus resolve the outstanding territorial issues, no such progress has been made. Responding to alleged Egytian provocations, Israel in October, 1956, after a lightning victory, occupied the Gaza Strip and Sinai from Egypt. The 1949 Armistice Agreement was, however, reinstated when arrangements were made early in 1957 to evacuate Israeli troops and to introduce an United

Nations Emergency Force (UNEF) into the area in order to secure tranquility on the Egypt-Israeli border and freedom of navigation in the Suez Canal and the Gulf of Aqaba. The withdrawal of UNEF ten years later, in connection with increased military and political tensions, led to the 1967 Six Days War and the suspension of the 1949 Armistice Agreements between the Arab states and Israel. Cease fire arrangements were set up by the U. N. and the antagonists after Israel captured the Gaza Strip and Sinai from Egypt, the West Bank, and East Jerusalem from Jordan, and the Golan Heights from Syria.

Five years after that event it becomes clear that the 1967 ceasefire has not produced a peaceful settlement. What once appeared as a temporary Israeli occupation seems to be acquiring permanent characteristics. The Arabs view these developments as a classical illustration of Zionism's "expansionism" and "imperialism." Israel, on the other hand, insists that it is entitled to determine what are her vital security interests, and therefore, it intends to never return to the pre- "Six Days War" frontiers.

In this chapter, an excerpt from Sami Hadawi's PALESTINE IN FOCUS (Beirut: Palestine Research Center, no date) discusses Israel's designs of expansion from the early days of Zionism through the June, 1967, war and its aftermath. Israel's Ministry of Foreign Affairs states its views on the subject in "The Provisional Nature of the 1949 Armistice Lines," published in March, 1971. The article analyzes the nature of the 1949 demarcation frontiers, the rights of the Arab states in the West Bank and Gaza, and the question of Israeli administration of these territories.

ISRAELI
EXPANSIONISM

Sami Hadawi

Each time the Arabs point out the dangers to them of Israeli expansionism, they are met with emphatic denials. It is just not possible to reconcile such denials with Israeli planning and action. It has already been pointed out that the limits of "Eretz Israel," as loosely defined by the Zionist movement in the late nineteenth and early twentieth century, coincide with the so-called "biblical" and "historical" boundaries of the "Promised Land," namely from "the Nile to the Euphrates."

The concrete political steps leading to the realization of this objective began with the Balfour Declaration which gave the Zionists a foothold in Palestine in the form of a "national home," followed by the establishment of a "Jewish state" in 1948. Since the June 1967 war, there has been great pressure inside Israel to establish "Greater Israel," including the territories occupied in June 1967.(1)

The extension of Israel's geographical horizons, to which we have just referred, is neither a recent nor an isolated phenomenon. Apart from the adoption of an expansionist, centrifugal policy by Zionism before the establishment of the State, there is no shortage of evidence of the same tendency since 1948, although one would expect a state to be more aware of international obligations than an ideological movement that is not tied by diplomatic constraints. The declarations of Israeli leaders make their expansionist intentions much clearer than Israel's Western sympathizers would like to admit.

Dr. Chaim Weizmann, President of the World Zionist Organization for more than three decades, and first President of Israel, during a visit to Jerusalem on 1 December 1948, told his audience: "Do not worry because part of Jerusalem is not now within the state. All will come to pass in peace. Again I counsel patience." He added: "Fear not, my friends, the old synagogues will be rebuilt anew and the way to the Wailing Wall will be opened again. With your blood and sacrifices you have renewed the Covenant of Old. Jerusalem is ours by virtue of the blood which your sons shed defending it."(2) Nineteen years later, the Israeli army followed the counsel of Weizmann and opened the way to the Wailing

Wall: not peacefully or through patience, but by bombshell and napalm. The reader is reminded that Jerusalem means spiritually at least as much to the Arab — Moslem and Christian alike — as to the Jew. This is apart from Arab attachment to and identification with a city in which the Arabs have lived and which they have controlled for many centuries without interruption.

David Ben Gurion said in an official publication that the state "has been resurrected in the western part of the land" of Israel and that independence has been reached "in a part of our small country." He added: "Every state consists of a land and a people. Israel is no exception, but it is a state identical neither with its land nor with its people . . . It must now be said that it has been established in only a portion of the land of Israel. Even those who are dubious as to the restoration of the historical frontiers, as fixed and crystallized from the beginning of time, will hardly deny the anomaly of the boundaries of the new State."(3)

David Ben Gurion, speaking at a meeting of the Mapai Party in 1952 said: "I accept to form the Cabinet on one condition, and that is, to utilize all possible means to expand towards the south." Could the Sinai campaign in 1956, but have been a fulfilment of this undertaking?

On 12 February 1952, Moshe Dayan, as Chief-of-Staff of the Israeli army, said on the Israeli radio: "It lies upon the people's shoulder to prepare for the war, but it lies upon the Israeli army to carry out the fight with the ultimate object of erecting the Israeli empire."(4) This is probably one of the clearest and most unhypocritical of statements by responsible Israelis. In using the term "empire," Dayan called things by their right name.

On 12 October 1955, Menachem Beigin, leader of the Herut Party and member of Parliament and Government, said in the Knesset: "I deeply believe in launching preventive war against the Arab States without further hesitation. By doing so, we will achieve two targets: firstly, the annihilation of Arab power; and secondly, the expansion of our territory." Again an unhypocritical statement.

Another spokesman of the Herut Party, declared in New York in 1956, months before the Suez campaign: "Peace with the Arab countries is impossible with the present boundaries of Israel which leave Israel open to attack." He advised that "Israel should take the offensive immediately and capture strategic points along its border, including the Gaza Strip and then should take over the British-backed Kingdom of Jordan."(5)

With these declarations as a recent background, and with earlier declarations before the establishment of the State, the Arabs cannot but view with apprehension the dangers which the creation of Israel represents to Arab territory and peace. And there has been no lack of concrete acts of agression to substantiate Arab fears.

THE INVASION OF EGYPT IN 1956

The reasons the Israelis gave for their action varied. In a communiqué issued on the eve of the invasion, the Israeli Ministry of Foreign Affairs described the campaign in terms of both a "preventive war" and a "retaliatory raid."(6) General Moshe Dayan's order to his troops read: "Today the Southern forces will fight across the border and will enclose the Nile army in its own country."(7) When asked to explain the Israeli action, the Liasion Officer for Armistice Affairs at the Ministry of Foreign Affairs qualified the terms of the official communiqué and confirmed that "this was not just a retaliatory raid, but that the Israel forces were going to stay in Sinai."(8)

In announcing the invasion of Egypt to the Knesset, David Ben Gurion was even more explicit. He said: "The army did not make an effort to occupy enemy territory in Egypt proper and limited its operations to free the area from northern Sinai to the tip of the Red Sea." Referring to the occupation of the Island of Tiran, south of the Gulf of Aqaba, he described it as "the Island of Yotvat, south of the Gulf of Elath, which was liberated by the Israeli army."(9) The reader will remember that Elath itself (originally Um Rashrash) had been occupied merely half a month after Israel signed the Armistice Agreement with Egypt in which she undertook to respect the demarcation lines defined in the Agreement; these lines excluded Elath.

The repeated references to "liberation" and to old biblical names of places, like the indication of the intention to stay in Sinai, are reflections of the expansionism motivating the campaign. In any case, when Israel had to withdraw under pressure from the United Nations and more specifically from the United States, it still insisted on changing the status quo ante by making its withdrawal conditional on the Gulf of Aqaba being opened up for Israeli shipping. The Arab contention that the Gulf was without doubt territorial water was refused by Israel, as was the Arab suggestion to take the issue to the International Court at the Hague for a ruling. Few people recall that the International Law Commission in 1956 found no grounds for considering the Straits an international waterway subject to the rules appropriate to such waterways.(10)

THE JUNE WAR 1967

Because it is more sensitive to threats to Israel than threats to the Arabs, public opinion in the West believed that the June 1967 war began with the U.A.R.'s closing of the Straits of Tiran to Israeli shipping in May and with the entry of U.A.R. troops into the Sinai Peninsula; and that the Israelis had to attack to prevent the destruction of their state. Because of this, the Israelis got political, moral and financial support from many nations and were able to brand the Arab states as the aggressors. In fact, President Nasser's actions in May were in answer to Israeli threats and attacks against Syria in April, though, because these went almost unnoticed in the Western press, very few people realised their occurrence.(11)

A sampling of Israeli statements made before the June War and after it shows a wide gap: the statements preceding the war invariably containing assurances and pledges regarding Israel's innocence of expansionist aims; the ones after explicitly stating Israel's intention to hold on to certain occupied territories, no matter what outcome the negotiations demanded by Israel might have. The Israelis have adopted as the main plank in their Arab policy the idea of direct negotiations. Few Westerners have seen clearly the dishonesty of calling for negotiations, while declaring certain issues (e.g. Jerusalem) "non-negotiable."

STATEMENTS BEFORE THE WAR

On 8 November 1966, Michael Comay, then Israeli representative at the United Nations, told the Special Political Committee — in rebuttal of Arab accusations of Israeli expansionist designs on Arab territories: "I would like to inform the Committee quite categorically that the Government of Israel covets no territory of any of its neighbours, nor does it feel obliged to hand over its territory to any of its neighbours. We are all members of the United Nations. We have signed the Charter obliging us to respect each other's political independence and territorial integrity. My government fully and reservedly accepts this obligation towards the other 120 Member States of the United Nations."(12)

Levi Eshkol, Prime Minister, in an address to the Israeli Parliament "told Arab countries that Israel has no aggressive designs."(13)

Moshe Dayan, Minister of Defence, said, "We have no invasion aims. Our only target is to foil the Arab armies' aim of invading our country."(14) On another occasion he was quoted as saying: "Soldiers of Israel, we have no aims of territorial conquest."(15)

Gideon Rafael, Israeli delegate to the United Nations, read the following statement by the Israeli Defence Minister to the Security Council on 5 June 1967 — the day of the attack: "We have no aim of conquest. Our sole objectives are to put an end to the Arab attempt to plunder our land, and to suppress the blockade."(16)

On the day of the attack Levi Eshkol declared: "We do not demand anything except to live in tranquility in our present territory."(17)

STATEMENTS AFTER THE WAR

Levi Eshkol: "A new political reality in the Mideast" has been created;(18) "Israel intends to keep the former Jordan part of Jerusalem and the Gaza Strip. Israel without Jerusalem is Israel without a head . . . "(19)

Abba Eban, Foreign Minister: "Israel will, under no circumstances, return to the 1949 Armistice Agreements."(20) "Sometimes you cannot gain peace and security without territorial gains."(21) "If the General Assembly were to vote by 121 votes to 1 in favour of Israel returning to the armistice lines . . . Israel would refuse to comply with that decision."(22) "Israel has no intention of 'squandering' the position won by its Middle East war victory and will hold lands captured from the Arabs until a satisfactory peace settlement is reached."(23) "The military victory is neither stable nor successful unless it is ratified by peace. What happened in 1967 happened because in 1957 Israel had been persuaded to give up the fruits of victory. This time there will be a different map of Israel . . . Israel does not have to be recognized. Israel exists."(24)

Yisrael Galilee, Minister of Information: "Israel cannot agree to return to the status quo before this [conflict] happened."(25)

Yigal Allon, Minister of Labour: "We must have depth, especially in the central part of the country and the vicinity of Galilee and Jerusalem."(26)

David Ben Gurion, former Prime Minister: There are "no grounds for Israeli negotiations on Old Jerusalem."(27)

Moshe Dayan, Minister of Defence: "The Gaza Strip is Israel's, and steps will be taken to make it part of this country."(28) "Israel must not return to its 1948 borders. We need to consider the reality of 1967 and the map of 1967. We need, not only permanent borders, but borders that will ensure peace."(29) "There are about a million Arabs whom we don't want, I should say as citizens of Israel, in the Jordanian part. We certainly don't want Egypt to go back to the Gaza Strip. This is the same story like Sinai . . . I don't think that we should in any way give back the Gaza Strip to Egypt or the western part of Jordan to King Hussein." Asked whether there was any way whereby Israel could absorb the huge number of Arabs whose territory Israel now occupies, he said: "Economically, we can; but I think that it is not in accord with our aims in the future. It would turn Israel into either a bi-national or poly-Arab-Jewish State instead of the Jewish state, and we want to have a Jewish State . . . We want a Jewish State like the French want a French State."(30) "On no account will we force ourselves to leave, for example, Hebron. This is a political programme but more important, it is a fulfilment of a people's ancestral dream."(31)

It was reported from Jerusalem that all maps issued by the Israeli Survey

Department with markings of the 1949 armistice lines have now been classified as 'antiquated and historical.'(32)

The Israeli Government has now declared that the areas occupied as a result of the June 1967 war are no longer recognized as 'enemy territory'. This action has the double purpose, on the one hand, of overcoming criticism that the Israelis, in their treatment of the civilian Arab inhabitants, are contravening the 1949 Geneva Conventions; and, on the other hand, of acquiring freedom to expropriate property.(33)

EXPANSIONISM: THE RECENT EVIDENCE

Merely for the sake of the argument, one could say that the foregoing quotations only suggest a growing appetite for territory on the part of the Israelis, not premeditated expansionism. This might be so. However, the record of events indicates that, once given the slightest chance, Israel does not take long before actually expanding. Admittedly, one is on firmer ground in condemning Israel on the basis of actions taken and adhered to, than on the grounds of intentions — no matter how strongly circumstantial evidence supports the accusation of expansionist intentions. It ought to be remembered that the circumstantial evidence is not limited to the immediate past of a year ago; nor are the expansionist acts limited to the aftermath of the June 1967 war.

Israel's expansionism can be said to be based on her occupation of Egyptian, Jordanian, and Syrian territory and her refusal to withdraw, in spite of the Security Council Resolution to this effect of 22 November 1967 (No. 242, 1967), and in spite of blanket condemnation in the U. N. Charter of occupation of the territory of other states by member states.

But we will not use the evidence of occupation in broad terms. We will assume, again for the sake of the argument, that Israel is willing to negotiate partial withdrawal, against certain Arab concessions.

Therefore, the expansionist acts will, by elimination, involve those areas occupied by Israel and declared "non-negotiable" by Israeli leaders, that is, areas that Israel will unequivocally refuse to include in any "negotiation agenda," under any circumstances. The non-negotiable areas are those occupied in excess of the territory set for the Jewish state in the Palestine Plan of 1947 and held until 5 June 1968, plus parts of the territory occupied in the June war. These last include Jerusalem, Gaza, the Golan Heights, and "certain parts" of the West Bank of Jordan "needed for strategic purposes," according to the Israelis.

The Israelis are most emphatic about Jerusalem. Its occupation is irrevocable, according to Israeli official sources at all levels, from Prime Minister Eshkol and General Moshe Dayan down. Indeed, Israel's Foreign Minister Abba Eban declared at the United Nations on 16 June 1947, that even if the whole membership voted against the annexation measures taken by Israel (regarding the Arab parts of the City and a few villages surrounding it), Israel would still not budge or remove these measures.(34) Gaza, the Golan Heights, and "certain parts of the West Bank" are likewise considered non-negotiable in Israeli statements, some of which have been quoted above.

Whether premeditated or not, the determination to continue the occupation of Arab territory has no other name but expansionism. Yet so far emphasis has been placed solely on territorial expansion. There is another aspect of expansion that also deserves examination. This is Israel's policy of emptying the occupied territories of as many of their inhabitants as possible.(35) This was done in the 1948-49 war. Some 200,000 Arabs were expelled from the West Bank during, but mostly right after, the brief fighting in June 1967. Another 200,000 have since been expelled, many from the Gaza Strip. These figures do not include Syrians expelled from the Golan Heights, Egyptians from Sinai towns, or East Jordanians forced to move out of the Jordan Valley further east, beyond the range of Israeli artillery.

The United Nations took action regarding the "new refugees." Thus, the Security Council called upon the Government of Israel "to ensure the safety, welfare and security of the inhabitants of the areas where military operations had taken place and to facilitate the return of those inhabitants who had fled the areas since the outbreak of hostilities."(36)

Only 14,027 refugees have been allowed to return, plus a total of 1,847 admitted under a "family reunion plan." It is worth noting that against the odd 16,000 permitted to return out of the 200,000 expelled in June 1967, some 200,000 additional Arabs have since been expelled from the West Bank and the Gaza Strip. And the flow continues.(37)

In addition to actual expulsion, whether or not accompanied by large-scale destruction of dwellings, there is another form of pressure used by the Israeli authorities in order to empty the occupied territories of their inhabitants. This is economic pressure. It takes many forms, hidden and overt, coarse and subtle. It is only the high morale of the Arabs living under occupation, plus the financial aid which the Jordanian Government sends that enables the West Bankers to hold on. This, and the fear of the fate of becoming refugees living on relief.

There is hardly any more need to establish the case that Israel, like Zionism, the ideology underlying it, is expansionist. To the Arab, and to the impartial observer, the establishment of the state in 1948 against the will of the Arab majority and its land, was an act of aggression, of colonialism in the classical sense. To have further occupied more than the Partition Plan allowed it, made of Israel an expansionist state. To have occupied yet more territory in June 1967, and to announce blatantly the determination not to give up several parts of this territory, confirms the expansionist label, if confirmation is still needed.

The reader will no doubt ask why the Arabs have allowed themselves to be bettered, in diplomatic manoeuvring and on the battlefield. He will ask why, this being the clear course of events, the Arabs do not negotiate to retrieve, and protect what they can in the face of Israeli expansionism.

The questions are legitimate. But the story carries the answer. World Zionism, in alliance first with Britain and then with the United States, has been far too strong for the Arabs to confront successfully. The Arabs have relied too heavily on the inherent justice of their case and on world conscience. But the new Arab does not believe that his fate permits any more self-pity or passivity. He refuses to negotiate with Israel because Israel's precondition for negotiation is advance acceptance of further loss of territory and long-term humiliation. He does not trust Israel's word in view of its record of broken promises and of expansion. He does not negotiate because no United Nations injunction in existence asks him to do so, while the United Nations Charter and its many resolutions on Palestine all provide for the use of the intermediary of the United Nations and its agencies. He is yet to see one sign of Israeli compliance with United Nations orders, calls, requests, whether with regard to territory or the return of refugees. He refuses to take Israeli declarations of peaceful intentions seriously, because to him deeds are much more eloquent than words. And he has not yet seen one act that concretizes Israeli admission of guilt, or Israeli redress of the many injustices done to the Arabs.

This is a sad story. But the sadness is more in the bitterness, frustration, and violence it is going to engender than in what it has so far engendered. A whole people, the Arabs of Palestine are today either under occupation or uprooted. They number 2,350,000 — exactly equal to the number of Jews in Israel. The Arab rightly asks: What has the creation of Israel solved? It has put into the land as many Jews as the Arabs uprooted or subjugated. But the Jewish inhabitants have not essentially solved even their own problem. Today they are harassed. Tomorrow they might be besieged. Can the Arabs be justly expected to do less than fight, dispossessed and continuously threatened as they are?

NOTES

(1) The evidence is voluminous, so we will select a few references:

a. On 18 July 1967, in Paris, Mr. Walter Etyan, Israeli Ambassador to France, declared that Israel had not taken anything that belonged to anybody else. See THE TIMES (London), 27 July 1967.

b. On 29 October, Levi Eshkol, Prime Minister, spoke of Greater Israel as defined in the text above. See INTERNATIONAL HERALD TRIBUNE, October 30, 1967.

c. "A Movement for Greater Israel" has been formed in Israel. According to LE MONDE (20 December and 28 December, 1967) this Movement insists on the annexation of the areas now under occupation. It includes in its membership many leading professors, journalists, Knesset members, and is supported by such members of the Israeli Cabinet as Menachem Beigin, Yosef Sapir, and Moshe Dayan.

d. Mr. Yigal Allon, Minister of Labour, announced that official maps of Greater Israel had been issued, and that the old maps (with the 5 June borders) had become merely historical. See LE MONDE, 23 February 1968.

(2) Joseph, Dov, THE FAITHFUL CITY: THE SIEGE OF JERUSALEM 1948, p. 332.

(3) ISRAELI GOVERMENT YEARBOOK   1951-1952, p. 64; and YEAR-BOOK 1952, pp. 63 and 65.

(4) From a statement broadcast on the Arabic Programme, Israel radio, 12 February 1952.

(5) NEW YORK TIMES, 25 January 1956.

(6) For text of communiqué, see U. S. POLICY IN THE MIDDLE EAST DOCUMENTS, (Washington: Department of State, 1957), pp. 135-6.

(7) JEWISH OBSERVER, 9 November 1956.

(8) Burns, E.L.M., BETWEEN ARAB AND ISRAELI   (New York: Ivan Obolensky, 1963), p. 180.

(9) NEW YORK TIMES, 8 November 1956.

(10) See reference to the report of the International Law Commission in a letter by Harvard Professor Roger Fisher to the Editor of the NEW YORK TIMES, 10 June 1967.

(11) E. Rouleau, J. F. Held, and S. Lacouture, ISRAEL ET LES ARABES (Paris, Editions du Seuil, 1967), pp. 73, 176. Also, John S. Badeau, "The Arabs, 1967," in THE ATLANTIC (U. S. Monthly), December 1967, p. 108.

(12) U. N. Document A/SPC/PV.505 of 8 November 1966.

(13) THE WASHINGTON POST, 23 May 1967.

(14) From an Israel radio broadcast on 5 June 1967. However, compare this statement with that of General Hod, Commander of the Israeli Air Force, who indicated that the attack plan had been in preparation for 16 years in these words: "Sixteen years' planning had gone into those initial 80 minutes [the air strike on 5 June 1968]. We lived with the plan, we slept on the plan, we ate

the plan. Constantly we perfected it." Article by Randolph and Winston Churchill, in THE SUNDAY TIMES (London), 16 July 1967, p. 7.

(15) THE NEW YORK TIMES, 5 June 1967.

(16) Statement made before the Security Council on 5 June 1967.

(17) From an Israel radio broadcast from Jerusalem on 5 June 1967.

(18) UPI Despatch, 9 June 1967.

(19) From an interview with DER SPIEGEL. Reported in JERUSALEM POST, 10 July 1967.

(20) UPI Despatch, 17 June 1967.

(21) From an interview on West German television, 5 July 1967.

(22) NEW YORK TIMES, 19 June 1967.

(23) Reuter Despatch, 14 August 1967.

(24) THE DAILY STAR (Beirut), 19 September 1967.

(25) UPI Despatch, 10 June 1967.

(26) From a statement made on 12 June 1967.

(27) UPI Despatch, 19 June 1967.

(28) THE CHRISTIAN SCIENCE MONITOR, 7 July 1967.

(29) THE GUARDIAN, 11 August 1967.

(30) From statements on C.B.S. "Face the Nation" programme, televised from New York.

(31) UPI Despatch, 9 August 1967.

(32) Quoted in THE DAILY STAR, 22 February 1968.

(33) For contraventions against the 1949 Geneva Convention, see ISRAEL AND THE GENEVA CONVENTIONS, The Institute for Palestine Studies, Beirut, 1968.

(34) Three resolutions have been taken calling on Israel to cancel her measures to change the status of the city:

a. General Assembly Resolution 2253 (ES-V) of 4 July 1967;

b. General Assembly Resolution 2254 (ES-V) of 14 July 1967, which was taken when the Secretary-General was unable to report compliance by Israel with the first resolution; and

c. Security Council Resolution S/RES/252 (1968) on 21 May 1968. All these resolutions have been defiantly and totally ignored. More recently, reacting to the last quoted resolution, Israel had again stated its categorical refusal to comply with U. N. resolutions involving the cancellation of annexation measures.

(35) We will not stop long here to talk of the harsh treatment of the Arabs living in the occupied territories, including mass shootings, mass graves, large-scale dynamiting of houses, destruction of whole villages, plundering of shops and offices, depriving Arabs of their means of livelihood. Many cases like these have been reported on the Western press, particularly the destruction after the war of about two-thirds of the town of Qalqilya. See for instance: a. David Holden, in the SUNDAY TIMES, 19 November 1967; b. ISRAELI IMPERIAL NEWS (London), March 1968, pp. 9 and 10; c. World Peace Council, Report on a visit to the Middle East, 27 September to October 1967, in THE TRUTH ABOUT THE MIDDLE EAST, (London, undated), p. 4; d. Jordan Government Letter of Protest to U Thant, 10 August 1967; e. Letter from the Jordan Government to the United Nations regarding violations listed above, particularly the destruction of Qalqilya after the cease-fire dated 21 June 1967; f. United Press International despatch on 11 June 1967, regarding strafing by Israel planes of large masses of refugees running for safety; and g. The same information was reiterated in a UPI despatch of 23 June 1967.

(36) Security Council Resolution 237 (1967) of 14 June 1967, and General Assembly Resolution 2252 (ES-V) of 4 July 1967.

(37) A great deal of propaganda accompanied the return of the 14,027 refugees — the Israelis providing photographers and journalists to cover the event. Commenting on this propaganda, Ian Gilmour and Dennis Walters, British Members of Parliament, in a joint statement commented: "The Israeli attitude to the refugees becomes clearer when their return rather than their expulsion is considered. Most people in Britain probably believe that Israel has agreed to their return and that repatriation is now satisfactorily proceeding. Nothing could be farther from the truth. Certainly on one day, in front of television cameras, 144 were allowed to return over the Allenby Bridge. Unfortunately, there was no television to record that over the other bridges on that same day, more than three times that figure were still going in the other direction. And since July 10, so far as we could establish, not one single refugee has been allowed to return and the sad traffic of exodus has continued at a rate of about 1,000 a day." THE TIMES (London), 27 July 1967.

THE PROVISIONAL NATURE
OF
THE 1949 ARMISTICE LINES

Ministry of Foreign Affairs
(Jerusalem)

In 1949, Israel and the neighbouring Arab States negotiated and signed General Armistice Agreements. The Agreements established demarcation lines, based on military considerations. They specifically stated that the lines should not prejudice the future political settlement. In other words, they did not determine legally settled and recognized boundaries between Israel and its neighbours.

These fragile and frequently violated lines lasted for eighteen years, until the Six-Day War of 1967. The Israeli administration of territories occupied in that War accords with international law. Israeli withdrawal is necessarily linked with secure and recognized boundaries and not with Armistice lines.

THE NATURE OF THE ARMISTICE LINES

The texts of the Agreements between Israel and Lebanon, Syria, Jordan and Egypt clearly point to the fact that the lines dividing them were of a provisional and non-political nature: they were not intended to, and did not constitute international boundaries. Article V (2) of the Agreement with Egypt states, for example:

> The Armistice Demarcation Line is not to be construed in any sense as a political or territorial boundary, and is delineated without prejudice to rights, claims and positions of either Party to the Armistice as regards ultimate settlement of the Palestine question.
>
> It is also recognized that no provision of this Agreement shall in any way prejudice the rights, claims and positions of either Party hereto in the ultimate peaceful settlement of the Palestine question, the provisions of this Agreement being dictated exclusively by military considerations.
> (Article II (2) of the Israel-Jordan Agreement)

Statements from Arab and other sources between 1949 and 1967, while the Armistice was in force, also imply acceptance of the provisional nature of the lines. During the debate in the Security Council before the Six-Day War, the Jordanian ambassador to the United Nations stated:

> There is an Armistice Agreement. The Agreement did not fix boundaries; it fixed a demarcation line. The Agreement did not pass judgment on rights political, military or otherwise. Thus I know of no territory; I know of no boundary; I know of a situation frozen by an Armistice Agreement. (1345th Meeting of the Security Council, 31 May 1967)

In the BEIRUT DAILY STAR, Professor Mughraby wrote:

> Israel is the only State in the world which has no legal boundaries except the natural one the Mediterranean provides. The rest are nothing more than armistice lines, can never be considered political or territorial boundaries. (28 May 1967)

President Lyndon Johnson, in outlining his five points for peace in the Middle East declared:

> The nations of the region have only had fragile and violated truce lines for 20 years. What they now need are recognized boundaries and other arrangements that will give them security against terror, destruction and war. (Address on 19 June 1967, 57 DEPT. OF STATE BULLETIN 33)

In an interview broadcast on the National Broadcasting Company's 'Meet the Press' programme, Joseph Sisco, Assistant Secretary of State for Near Eastern and South Asian Affairs, said:

> We feel that this time what we need is a peace agreement, not a de facto armistice agreement which existed for 20 years and gave rise to several wars during the period. (12 July 1970)

Jurists, too, have noted the limited effect of the Armistice Agreements.

> Quite understandably, each of these Agreements concluded between Israel and her neighbours contains a provision that the armistice lines therein laid down shall not prejudice the future political settlement. It would not, therefore, be accurate to contend that questions of title, as opposed to temporary rights of occupation, depend on the Armistice Agreements. Questions of sovereignty are quite independent of the Armistice Agreements. (Elihu Lauterpacht, JERUSALEM AND THE HOLY PLACES, London, 1968, p. 45)

Stephen M. Schwebel, writing in 64 AMERICAN JOURNAL OF INTERNATIONAL LAW:

> Israel has better title in the territory of what was Palestine, including the whole of Jerusalem, than do Jordan and Egypt ... modifications of the 1949 armistice lines among those states within former Palestinian territory are lawful. (pp. 346-347)

In a footnote, Schwebel adds that the Armistice Agreements of 1949

229

expressly preserved the territorial claims of all parties and did not purport to establish definitive boundaries between them.

RIGHTS OF THE ARAB STATES IN THE ADMINISTERED AREAS

Four areas were occupied by Israel in the Six-Day War: the Gaza Strip; the West Bank of the Jordan; the Golan Heights; and the Sinai Peninsula. The Gaza Strip and the West Bank fell within the borders of Palestine during the British Mandate.

> The facts of the 1948 hostilities between the Arab invaders of Palestine and the nascent state of Israel further demonstrate that Egypt's seizure of the Gaza strip, and Jordan's seizure and subsequent annexation of the West Bank and the old city of Jerusalem were unlawful. Israel was proclaimed to be an independent state within the boundaries allotted to her by the General Assembly's partition resolution. The Arabs of Palestine and of the neighbouring Arab states rejected that resolution. But that rejection was no warrant for the invasion by those Arab states of Palestine, whether of territory allotted to Israel, to the projected, stillborn Arab state or to the projected, internationalized city of Jerusalem. It was no warrant for attack by the armed forces of neighbouring Arab states upon the Jews of Palestine, whether they resided within or without Israel. But the attack did justify Israeli defensive measures, both within and, as necessary, without the boundaries allotted her by the partition plan (as in the new city of Jerusalem). It follows that the Egyptian occupation of Gaza, and the Jordanian annexation of the West Bank and Jerusalem, could not vest in Egypt and Jordan lawful, indefinite control, whether as occupying Power or sovereign: *ex injuria ius non oritur.* (Schwebel, 64 AMERICAN JOURNAL OF INTERNATIONAL LAW, p. 346)

The West Bank and East Jerusalem were under Jordanian rule for almost twenty years. One year after signing the Armistice, Jordan purported to annex the territories west of the Jordan River, including the Old City of Jerusalem, which had been occupied by the Arab Legion during the hostilities in Palestine.

> [T]he position of the State of Jordan on the West Bank and in East Jerusalem itself, insofar as it had a legal basis in May 1967, rested on the fact that the State of Transjordan had overrun this territory during the 1948 hostilities against Israel. It was a belligerent occupant there. (Julius Stone, THE MIDDLE EAST UNDER CEASEFIRE, 1967, p. 12)

The fact that these territories were within the Armistice lines separating the Jordanian and Israeli troops did not confer on Jordan legal title to them. On the contrary, the Hashemite Kingdom of Jordan could legally exercise only the rights of a belligerent occupant whose occupation rested solely on aggression.

The position of Israel, the State most affected, was made plain by its Foreign Minister, Mr. Moshe Sharett, on 3 May 1950 in the Knesset (Parliament):

> This is a unilateral step, which in no way binds Israel. We are tied, with the Hashemite Jordan Government, to the Armistice Agreement, and are unreservedly decided that it must be strictly applied. But this Agreement contains no final political settlement, and no final settlement is possible without negotiations and the establishment of peace between the two

Parties. It is, therefore, necessary that it be clear that the question of the status of the Arab areas west of the Jordan remains open as far as we are concerned.

The Jordanian action brought about a clash with the other Arab States, since it violated the Arab League resolution of 13 April 1950, barring any Arab country from annexing part of Palestine. The Egyptian Government called for a meeting of the Political Committee of the League to study the consequences and Premier Mustafa Nahas Pasha asserted that Egypt would stand firm in its opposition to the annexation. The Cairo newspaper, AL BALAGH, called the act 'aggression by one Arab State against others.' The 'League seriously considered applying sanctions to Jordan or even seeking to expel it.

Elihu Lauterpacht puts things in their correct perspective:

> Thus Jordan's occupation of the Old City — and indeed of the whole of the area west of the Jordan river — entirely lacked legal justification; and being defective in this way would not form any basis for Jordan validly to fill the sovereignty vacuum in the Old City. Jordan's prolonged *de facto* occupation of the Old City was protected exclusively by the Armistice Agreement which prohibited Israel from initiating action to displace Jordan; and Jordan's occupation could last no longer than the protection thus afforded. This bulwark was abandoned when Jordan destroyed the Armistice Agreement by its attack on Israel Jerusalem on 5th June 1967. [JERUSALEM AND THE HOLY PLACES, 1968, p. 47]

Only two countries, the United Kingdom and Pakistan, recognized the annexation as valid. The British Government was careful to qualify its recognition:

> This action is subject to explanation on two points. The first of these points relates to the frontier between this territory and Israel. This frontier has not yet been finally determined. The existing boundary is the line laid down by the Armistice Agreement signed between Israel and Jordan on April 3, 1949, and is subject to any modification which may be agreed upon by the two States under the terms of that Agreement or of any final settlement which may replace it. Until the actual frontier between Israel and Jordan is determined by a final settlement between them, HMG regard the territory to which the Anglo-Jordan treaty is applicable as being bounded by the Armistice line or any modification of it which may be agreed upon by the two parties. (Mr. Kenneth Younger, Minister of State, in the House of Commons, 27 April 1950, see Keesing, p. 10678)

Julius Stone compares Israel's position in this context to the status of Egypt and Jordan:

> The legal titles by which the above Arab States formerly held the more important territories which they lost in the recent war with Israel may be said therefore, ironically enough, to have been no better than the title acquired by Israel in that war. (THE MIDDLE EAST UNDER CEASE-FIRE, 1967, p. 12)

231

THE ADMINISTERED AREAS AND WITHDRAWAL

Israel's presence in Sinai, the Golan Heights, the West Bank and the Gaza Strip is the result of defensive action. This fact has far-reaching legal implications. Two subsequent developments also have direct bearing on the situation: the Security Council Resolution 242 of 22 November 1967 and the position taken by the United States under Presidents Johnson and Nixon. Key political elements are covered in both the Security Council Resolution and the American attitude: the establishment of peace and Israeli withdrawal.

International law requires a clear distinction between aggressive and defensive conquest. A further distinction can be drawn between the taking of territory legally held and the taking of territory illegally held.

The effect of these distinctions and their application to the Six-Day War are summarized by Schwebel, in 64 AMERICAN JOURNAL OF INTERNATIONAL LAW:

> (a) A state acting in lawful exercise of its right of self-defense may seize and occupy foreign territory as long as such seizure and occupation are necessary to its self-defense. (b) As a condition of its withdrawal from such territory, that state may require the institution of security measures reasonably designed to ensure that that territory shall not again be used to mount a threat or use of force against it of such a nature as to justify exercise of self-defense. (c) Where the prior holder of territory had seized that territory unlawfully, the state which subsequently takes that territory in the lawful exercise of self-defense has, against that prior holder, better title.
>
> The facts of the June, 1967, 'Six-Day War' demonstrate that Israel reacted defensively against the threat and use of force against her by her Arab neighbors. This is indicated by the fact that Israel responded to Egypt's prior closure of the Straits of Tiran, its proclamation of a blockade of the Israeli port of Elath, and the manifest threat of the U.A.R.'s use of force inherent in its massing of troops in Sinai, coupled with its ejection of UNEF. It is indicated by the fact that, upon Israeli responsive action against the U.A.R., Jordan initiated hostilities against Israel. It is suggested as well by the fact that, despite the most intense efforts by the Arab states and their supporters, led by the Premier of the Soviet Union, to gain condemnation of Israel as an aggressor by the hospitable organs of the United Nations, those efforts were decisively defeated. The conclusion to which these facts lead is that the Israeli conquest of Arab and Arab-held territory was defensive rather than aggressive conquest. (pp. 345-346)

The Security Council Resolution of November 1967 laid down two general principles for the establishment of a 'just and lasting peace.' The Resolution,

> Emphasizing the inadmissibility of the acquisition of territory by war and the need for work for a just and lasting peace in which every State in the area can live in security,
> Emphasizing further that all Member States in their acceptance of the Charter of the United Nations have undertaken a commitment to act in accordance with Article 2 of the Charter,
> 1. Affirms that the fulfilment of the Charter principles requires the establishment of a just and lasting peace in the Middle East which should include the application of both the following principles:

(i) Withdrawal of Israeli armed forces from territories occupied in the recent conflict;

(ii) Termination of all claims or states of belligerency and respect for and acknowledgement of the sovereignty, territorial integrity and political independence of every State in the area and their right to live in peace within secure and recognized boundaries free from threats or acts of force . . .

The meaning of the Resolution is clear insofar as the Armistice lines are concerned. There was nothing sacred about them; they were not internationally recognized boundaries. If Israel is to withdraw from the present cease-fire lines, it must be to 'secure and recognized boundaries free from threats or acts of force.' Since there have never been any such boundaries, secure or otherwise, lines must be determined before any withdrawal. This is, after all, only pure logic: one cannot withdraw (or advance) to a boundary that has never existed and which is not known. In this context, the Resolution means change, new lines which will be international boundaries, and a new state of peace, where none has existed so far. In an address to the American Society of International Law on 24 April 1970, Eugene V. Rostow said:

The agreement required by paragraph 3 of the resolution, the Security Council said, should establish 'secure and recognized boundaries' between Israel and its neighbours 'free from threats or acts of force,' to replace the Armistice demarcation lines established in 1949, and the cease-fire lines of June 1967. The Israeli armed forces should withdraw to such lines, as part of a comprehensive agreement, settling all the issues mentioned in the resolution, and in condition of peace. (64 AMERICAN JOURNAL OF INTERNATIONAL LAW, p. 68)

Continued Israeli occupation is justified pending a peace settlement, on the ground that the danger to which Israel responded by defensive action remains.

The 'no acquisition' phrase in the preamble to the Security Council Resolution does not indicate that territorial changes cannot be negotiated and agreed upon by the States concerned. In an address to the American Foreign Law Association in New York on 27 October 1970, a former State Department official, Robert H. Neuman, said:

It is important to seek a meaning from the phrase 'inadmissibility of the acquisition of territory by war' in the preamble. This is a major premise of the Resolution and the foundation of the Arabs' case. It would seem that the phrase cannot possibly mean that territory cannot be acquired as the result of negotiation — certainly neither the practice of States nor the judgments of tribunals would support that conclusion. Thus, the phrase could only mean that territory cannot be acquired as a (proximate) result of armed conflict. Yet, if all such acquisitions were reversed, even in this century, the map of the world would be drastically altered. (p. 5)

The necessity for territorial change can be found in the comments of statesmen. On 10 September 1968, President Johnson said:

We are not the ones to say where other nations should draw lines between them that will assure each the greatest security. It is clear, however, that a return to the situation of June 4, 1967, will not bring peace. There must be secure and there must be recognized borders. (59 DEPT. OF STATE BULLETIN, p. 348)

Article 1 (i) of the Resolution does not call for Israel to withdraw from 'all territories' or from 'the territories' taken in the Six-Day War; it speaks only of 'territories.' The British Government, author of the Resolution, has explicitly announced that it provides for territorial change and not for return to the Armistice lines. Thus the Foreign Secretary, Michael Stewart, in the House of Commons on 9 December 1968 stated:

> As I have explained before, there is reference, in the vital United Nations Security Council Resolution, both to withdrawal from territories and to secure and recognized boundaries. As I have told the House previously, we believe that these two things should be read concurrently and that the omission of the word 'all' before the word 'territories' is deliberate.

That President Nixon was of the same mind can be seen in his comment that 'Israel must withdraw to borders, borders that are defensible . . .' (Television interview, 1 July 1970). The Armistice lines were neither borders, nor defensible. The President meant new lines.

Schwebel writes:

> If the foregoing conclusions that (a) Israeli action in 1967 was defensive and (b) Arab action in 1948, being aggressive, was inadequate to legalize Egyptian and Jordanian taking of Palestinian territory, are correct, what follows?
>
> It follows that the application of the doctrine of according no weight to conquest requires modification in double measure. In the first place, . . . Israel has better title in the territory of what was Palestine, including the whole of Jerusalem, than do Jordan and Egypt . . . In the second place, as regards territory bordering Palestine, and under unquestioned Arab sovereignty in 1949 and thereafter, such as Sinai and the Golan Heights, it follows not that no weight shall be given conquest, but that such weight shall be given to defensive action as is reasonably required to ensure that such Arab territory will not again be used for aggressive purposes against Israel . . .
>
> The foregoing analysis accords not only with the terms of the United Nations Charter, notably Article 2, paragraph 4, and Article 51, but law and practice as they have developed since the Charter's conclusion. In point of practice, it is instructive to recall that the Republic of Korea and indeed the United Nations itself have given considerable weight to conquest in Korea.

The preamble to the Resolution also emphasises 'the need to work for a just and lasting peace.' Territory would not, in any event, be acquired by war, but, if at all, by the force of peace treaties. The law on the question of territorial change has been summarized by Elihu Lauterpacht:

> . . . territorial change cannot properly take place as the result of the *unlawful* use of force. But to omit the word 'unlawful' is to change the substantive content of the rule and to turn an important safeguard of legal

principle into an aggressor's charter. For if force can never be used to effect lawful territorial change, then, if territory has once changed hands as a result of unlawful use of force, the illegitimacy of the position thus established is sterilized by the prohibition upon the use of force to restore the lawful sovereign. This cannot be regarded as reasonable or correct. (JERUSALEM AND THE HOLY PLACES, London, 1968, p. 52)

Posing Israel's choice as 'peace or territories' is a grave and misleading oversimplification. Israel's position has consistently been that peace and secure and recognized boundaries are a prerequisite of withdrawal, a position sound and solid in both international law and practice.

VI. The Status of Jerusalem

INTRODUCTION

Who is to have political control over Jerusalem? Can the question of the legal status of the "City of Peace" be separated from the international concern for appropriate guarantees of freedom of access, worship, and administration in the numerous religious sites of Islam, Christianity, and Judaism located in Jerusalem as well as in all of the Holy Land?

The great common denominator among Christians, Moslems, and Jews in their attitude towards Jerusalem has been their common concern for the city's Holy Places. In principle, all agree that these sites must be inviolate, and those who wish to visit them and worship there should be given full opportunity to do so without hindrance. Yet to both Moslems and Jews the city is more than a historical and sacred memory. A large Arab population has continuously dwelled in the city since the first Moslem occupation, and for most of the present century the Jews have constituted a majority in Jerusalem, the capital of their ancient kingdom. The Moslem and Jewish ties with the Holy City are physical as well as spiritual.

Due to the unique history and sanctity of the City, it is not surprising that when the United Nations considered the problem of Palestine in 1947, one of its major concerns was the future of Jerusalem. The General Assembly's "Partition Resolution" of November 29 proposed that Jerusalem be established as an international *corpus separation* to be administered by the United Nations through the Trusteeship Council. As a result of Arab opposition to international-ization, the United Nations Palestine Conciliation Commission, during its 1949 work, suggested that as a minimum a United Nations Commissioner be made responsible for the protection of the Holy Places, the observance of human rights, and the demilitarization of the city. When this plan failed, the Trusteeship Council prepared a Statute for the internationalization of Jerusalem. Once more, this scheme was rejected by Jordan and Israel, the parties most directly involved in Jerusalem, and was finally shelved by the United Nations.

The status of Jerusalem had thus been determined not by the United Nations, but rather by the de facto Jordanian and Israeli division of the city. Separated by armed forces, minefields, barbed wire in 1948 the city was not again reunited until the Israelis gained total control in 1967. Several weeks after the June War, the reunification of Jerusalem was legally formalized by Israel's Knesset (Parliament). The adopted legislation extended the laws, administrative institutions and public services of Jewish West Jerusalem to East Jerusalem, the former Jordanian sector, and fixed the new boundaries of the reunified city. The Knesset also passed the "Protection of Holy Places Law 5727-1967" which provides for freedom of access and worship to all.

It is obvious from the selections that follow that Arab-Jewish coexistence in post-1967 Jerusalem is facing many difficulties. The first article deals with the "Judaization of Jerusalem" as seen by Rouhi Al-Khatib, a former mayor of the Arab section of the city. Published by the Palestine Liberation Organization Research Center in Beirut in July, 1970, this study surveys the steps leading to the annexation of Jerusalem, Israel's "occupation" policies, and the imposition of a Jewish character upon the city. The second selection is Yosef Tekoah's "Barbed Wire Shall Not Return to Jerusalem," published in Washington, D.C. by the Embassy of Israel. Generally it constitutes a plea to permit Jerusalem to continue its present status as a unified city.

THE JUDAIZATION
OF
JERUSALEM

Rouhi Al-Khatib

The Judaization of Jerusalem, which the Israeli occupying authorities have been carrying out since June 7, 1967, is part of a series of well-prepared plans. They constitute a violation of all human, civil and international conventions. They aim at usurping Arab land, dispersing and liquidating its owners, and, gradually, seizing the Muslim Holy Places. The Israeli policy-makers are intent on changing the face of the city in as short a time as possible so that the Judaization of Jerusalem and the liquidation of Arab presence (Muslim presence in particular) from the city, be achieved before the Arabs succeed in closing their ranks, before Muslims and Christians respond to the Arab appeal to save the city and before the conscience of the world awakens. The Israeli authorities have been working, at the same time, towards cutting the Holy City off from neighboring Arab towns and villages, in the hope of confronting the world with a *fait accompli.*

The preliminary steps in this scheme were sketched out during the First Zionist Congress at Basle, Switzerland, in 1897. The Zionist design has been executed in stages, of which the most important are the following:

a) The Balfour Declaration in 2/11/1917 by the British Government granting Jews a National Home in Palestine.

b) The appointment of Sir Herbert Samuel, a British Zionist, in 1/7/1920 to be the first British High Commissioner in Palestine to prepare the ground for the implementation of the Balfour Promise.

c) The facilitation of Jewish immigration and settlement from 1920 to 1948, at first at the point of British bayonets, later with American and German assistance. The number of Jews in Palestine, thus, rose from 56,000 in 1918 to approximately 650,000 in 15/5/1948; in Jerusalem it rose from a few thousand in 1918 to approximately 90,000 in 1948.

d) The United Nations Palestine Partition Resolution of 29/11/1947 and the occupation of the greater part of the city by the Zionist terrorist organization before the evacuation of the British Army in 14/5/1948.

e) The proclamation of the State of Israel, 15/5/1948, and its recognition by the United Nations, the dispersion of the majority of the Arab inhabitants of the city and the usurpation of their property in accordance with what the Israelis term the Absentees' Property Law.

f) The proclamation of Jerusalem as the capital of the State of Israel, 23/1/1950, and the transfer of the Knesset to it, as well as the increase of Jewish immigration and settlement in the city. The number of Jewish residents, thus, rose from 90,000 in 1948 to 190,000 in 1967.

g) Finally, the Israeli military occupation of what remained of the city, 7/6/1967, followed by the realization of the final stages of its Judaization through a number of military, legal and administrative measures, as well as through terrorism. Following is a list of these measures in the order in which they have occurred. I have relied on my own observations during the nine months I remained in the occupied city, and on information I have collected since, from travelling Jerusalemites and from newspapers, periodicals and books, both Hebrew and Arabic, which have appeared in the occupied territories. I have relied also on documents and maps.

MURDER, ARREST AND PILLAGE

Upon occupying the city, the first step towards changing its status taken by the military authorities was identical to the methods the Zionist terrorist organizations had practised in the massacres of Deir Yassin, Kafr Kassem and elsewhere in the previously occupied territories. During the first day of fighting and for the following two days, although the Jordanian Forces had withdrawn, there was continuous Israeli ground and air bombardment of the city. The Israeli Forces used incendiary bombs and machine guns. Three hundred civilians were killed. Whole families were wiped out, some inside their homes, others in the streets and lanes, during their flight from raging fires.

Bombs tore down hundreds of residential and business buildings, both inside and outside the city walls. They caused fires in dozens of stores outside the city walls, and heavy damage to a number of churches, mosques and hospitals. Of these we cite St. Anne's Church (also known as al-Salahiya, which at the time happened to be sheltering over three hundred refugees from outside the city walls), the chapel in the Schmidt's College for Girls outside Bab Al-Amoud, Al-Aqsa Mosque, the minaret of Bab Al-Asbat and the Augusta Victoria Hospital on the Mount of Olives. (This place was overflowing with the sick and wounded at the time.)

The Israeli Army then occupied most of the large buildings in the city, mostly schools and hotels, and looted much of their contents and those of numerous stores and dwellings. They pillaged cars as well. All this took place after the 'fighting' had ceased.

The occupying authorities imposed successive curfews, lasting for many hours at a time, during which they rounded up residents of whole quarters and detained them for long hours both in the night and under the scorching sun. These authorities took away hundreds of citizens to undisclosed concentration camps where they subjected them to various kinds of physical and mental torture, regardless of age. The fate of many of these people is still unknown.

These waves of brutal acts and crimes of terrorism have caused about 5,000 people, mostly 1948 refugees, to flee the City.

DESTRUCTION OF PROPERTY

The second measure taken during the process of Judaizing Jerusalem was a succession of acts of demolition of Arab property inside and outside the city walls. These began as early as 11/6/1967, four days after the Israeli occupation was effected. Within less than a week the following edifices ceased to be part of Arab life: a) 135 houses in Al-Maghariba (Moroccan) Quarter in which 650 people lived, b) Two mosques in Al-Maghariba Quarter, c) A plastics factory near the Armenian Quarter inside the city walls which used to employ 200 workers, and d) Nearly 200 houses and stores in No Man's Land.

Further acts of destruction of property were carried out during the first months of occupation. Various dwellings (24 separate ones) were blown up by the Israeli Army in answer to alleged Resistance activities. The Israeli civil authorities also blew up 14 historical and religious sites on 14/6/1969, on pretext of extending the exposed part of the Western Wall of Al-Haram Al-Sharif called the Wall of the Holy Buraq, also known as the Wailing Wall. This set of buildings included a mosque and Al-Zawiya Al-Fakhriya, the seat of the Mufti of Al-Shafi'i sect. As a result of these acts of destruction, nearly 1,000 Jerusalemites became homeless.

ANNEXATION OF JERUSALEM

On 27/6/1967 and the two following days, the Knesset, the Israeli Cabinet and the Armed Forces passed three decrees aimed at altering the sovereignty, the administration and the Municipality of the Arab City.

On 27/6/1967 the Knesset passed a resolution to insert a paragraph in an Israeli law called the Administrative and Legal Rules Ordinance, 1948. The new paragraph empowers the Israeli Government to apply this law to any new area which the Government decides to annex to the Israeli territories.

On 28/6/1967 the Secretary to the Government issued an order called the Law and Administration Ordinance No. 1, 1967, declaring the areas included in the chart appended to the order to be areas under the jurisdiction and the administration of the State of Israel. They include the municipal area of Jerusalem which had been under Jordanian jurisdiction. They are bounded in the north by the village of Qalandiya and the Qalandiya Airport, in the west by the Armistice Line, in the south by the villages of Sur Bahir and Beit Safafa and in the east by the villages of Al-Tur, Al-Isawiya, Anata and Al-Ram. At the time, 100,000 Arabs inhabited this area.

On 29/6/1967, the Israeli Defense Army issued an order dissolving the Municipal Council elected by the residents of Arab Jerusalem, dismissing its Mayor and transferring the employees of the Arab Municipality to the Israeli one.

The Israeli military authorities enforced these orders with a high degree of severity. They seized all property, furniture, equipment and records belonging to the Jordanian Government and to the Municipality of Jerusalem. They brought all Government Departments and Courts under their Israeli counterparts. They abolished Jordanian laws and regulations replacing them with Israeli ones. They imposed an Israeli Military Government to which Arab residents became subject.

The Arabs of Jerusalem and of the rest of the West Bank objected to these measures, as did the Jordanian Government. They complained to the U.N. The U.N. passed two resolutions, on 4/7/1967 and on 14/7/1967, considering these Israeli measures as invalid; they called upon Israel to rescind them and to desist immediately from taking any action which might lead to a change in the status of Jerusalem.

SEALING OFF JERUSALEM

To secure the annexation of the Holy City, the occupying authorities set up a number of Army, Police and Customs posts across all the roads linking the city to the neighboring Arab towns and villages. Jerusalem was considered a foreign area accessible only to the carriers of military permits. These permits are very difficult to come by, and, even then, are granted only after lengthy and repeated petitioning, lasting sometimes for days. As many Jerusalemites who live in the suburbs, and many inhabitants of other neighboring areas who work in Jerusalem, have had to move between the city and the areas surrounding it, large numbers of people have found their lives greatly affected by these restrictive measures, sometimes tragically so.

JUDAIZATION OF ARAB ECONOMY

No sooner did the occupying authorities finish sealing off Jerusalem politically and administratively from the neighboring areas, than they confronted Jerusalemites with another set of measures this time aimed at liquidating Arab economy and incorporating it gradually into the Israeli economy. The authorities closed down Arab banks (The Arab Bank, The Cairo-Amman Bank, The Bank of Real-Estate, The Jordanian Bank, Al-Ahli, and Intra) and took possession of their funds. The Ottoman and British Banks, too, were closed down for a time. The authorities exchanged Jordanian currency for Israeli currency. Finally they prevented any West Bank agricultural or manufactured product, or any other Arab commodity from reaching the Jerusalem market; instead, only Israeli products and merchandise were imported.

This restriction prevented the Arab of Jerusalem from consuming Arab products even though these might be of his own production. He was forced to buy Israeli goods. Some Arab merchants were forced to deal with their Israeli counterparts. The nearby Arab producer who depended on the Jerusalem market was now deprived of the main outlet for his products and was forced to cut down on his production. Workers who were laid off, either joined the ranks of the unemployed, or, under the pressures of earning a living, had to seek employment with the Israeli occupying authorities or with Israeli institutions.

In the face of this restriction, a number of West Bank agricultural and industrial producers approached the occupying power for permission to export their products to the markets of the East Bank of Jordan. The Israeli authorities found this arrangement agreed with their wider plans since it alleviated the problem of distribution. It would, thus, consecrate the restrictions imposed on Jerusalem for the purpose of separating it from the rest of the West Bank. At the same time, this arrangement could make the citizens on the one hand, and the Jordanian Government on the other, accustomed to these measures and lead them to accept a *fait accompli.*

CENSUS OF ARAB RESIDENTS

On 25/7/1967 the Israeli authorities carried out a general census of the inhabitants of Jerusalem during which they registered the names of all citizens present requiring them to obtain Israeli identity cards within three months (these cards do not entitle their carriers to Israeli nationality). The authorities, furthermore, considered those absent at the time of the census to be absentees and denied them the right to reside in the city.

Because of this measure, all Jerusalemites who were absent in jobs held in neighboring areas or countries, or elsewhere in the world, prior to or since 1948, as well as those who had temporarily left during the 1967 fighting, were considered to be absentees and were denied the right to return to their country.

These people and their families total no less than 100,000 Arabs. They are compelled, as a result of the Israeli occupation, the change in the status of the city, and the census, to forfeit their international right to belong to Jerusalem. This same right is bestowed upon Jews everywhere.

ABSENTEES' PROPERTY LAW

On 31/3/1950 the Israeli Government passed a law called the Absentees' Property Law, 1950, empowering the authorities to seize all the movable and immovable property of Arab or Palestinian residents of the areas occupied who had left these areas (now under Israeli jurisdiction) after 29/11/1947, in the case of any non-Palestinian Arab citizen, or, after 1/9/1948, in the case of any Palestinian.

By means of this unfair law, the Israeli authorities confiscated all the movable and immovable property of all the Palestinian refugees and their brethren who had shared with them the right to reside in the areas occupied in 1948.

As soon as the annexation of Jerusalem by Israel was proclaimed in 27/6/1967, and after the above-mentioned census was carried out, the Israeli authorities hastened to apply the Absentees' Property Law on all Arabs absent from the newly occupied areas. Israeli Government Offices were set up in Jerusalem. Registration of all movable and immovable property belonging to these people was started. Thus, in this new operation, the Israeli authorities seized vast tracts of land that had remained in Arab hands. They seized also a considerable amount of real-estate and are still sequestering whatever movable property and stocks and bonds come to their attention. All this property is placed at the disposal of an Israeli administrator to be gradually Judaized as was the Arab property expropriated in 1948.

JUDAIZATION OF THE ARAB EDUCATIONAL SYSTEM

Arab education was not excluded from the Israeli authorities' plans. Very soon after the occupation, they hastened to take over all government schools and the Department of Education in the city. They abolished the programs taught in these schools and forbade the use of the assigned text books, replacing them by those taught in Arab schools in the areas occupied in 1948. The Israeli authorities also requested the Director of Education and his staff, as well as all principals and teachers, to join the school system under the Israeli Ministry of Education and the Municipality of the Israeli sector of Jerusalem.

The Director of Education, his staff and all the teaching body refused to cooperate as a matter of principle. They persistently refused to join the Israeli educational system, in spite of the material enticements offered to them, until the order for the annexation of Jerusalem was rescinded. They argued that their cooperation in the application of the Israeli educational programs would mean an acceptance of this annexation.

The occupying authorities retaliated by arresting the Director of Education and the Assistant Director for three months. They ordered schools to go back to their normal schedule. The authorities, next, began to put various pressures on the Arab teaching body and on parents to induce them to cooperate for the sake of starting the scholastic year.

At the time there were in Jerusalem 30 Arab government schools, 18 for boys and 12 for girls, in addition to 14 private and confessional schools.

The government schools were forcibly started and some teachers resumed their work; but a large number still refuse to do so. As to the private and confessional schools, they resumed their classes after a short close-down, when they saw that it

242

was feasible to continue their private programs.

Jerusalemites used this opportunity to send their children to private schools. A large number of students transferred to them after their parents requested the different school administrations to enlarge these schools to accommodate as large a number of students as possible. This arrangement led to a sharp drop in student attendance at government schools, high schools in particular.

This turn of events worried the occupying authorities. They passed a new law called the Supervision of Schools Law, 1969, which appeared in the Israeli Law Digest, No. 564, July 17, 1969. The law will be effective as from January 17, 1970.

In general, the law in question is yet another link in the chain of measures aimed at furthering the Israeli Judaization of Jerusalem. It stipulates that all private and confessional schools and their staff acquire Israeli licences in order to continue operating. The law stipulates also that their curricula and their sources of income be subject to complete Israeli control.

The Israeli curricula, as Arab educators have observed, suppress all materials which help develop the spirit of Arab nationalism, and they draw the new generation of Arabs away from their Arab culture and values, so that, in the end, having lost their authentic identity, they fade into the Jewish identity and melt into the Israeli State.

JUDAIZATION OF ARAB PROPERTY

As part of the Israeli plan towards the Judaization of the city of Jerusalem, the occupying authorities started another series of acts, this time with the intention of expropriating large sections of Arab property inside and outside the city walls. Through the expropriation of Arab lands and through the encirclement of the Arabs of the Holy City, the Israelis intend to liquidate Arab collective identity and destroy Arab shrines.

Israel expressed its readiness to compensate the owners of these lands. But Arab landowners refused such offers and gave the authorities to understand that they regarded their properties as part of the Palestinian fatherland, not subject to any bargaining or sale. In spite of persistent Arab refusal, the Israeli authorities went on implementing their plans. They confiscated these properties by force and began construction.

As soon as the Israelis occupied the Old City, they started to implement their plans. They removed all the Arab buildings in the vicinity of the Wailing Wall.

On 8/8/1967 the Israeli authorities paved the way for their action by allowing THE JERUSALEM POST to publish an item about the necessity of clearing up 82 meters of the Wailing Wall.

No sooner did the news spread than the Muslim Committee in Jerusalem proceeded to investigate the meaning of the information released in the paper. The committee discovered that the realization of such a scheme required the demolition of the remaining buildings between Bab Al-Maghariba, one of the gates leading to the Haram, and the south-western corner of the Haram close to Al-Aqsa Mosque, in addition to the building housing the old Shari'a court and Bab Al-Silsila in the north. Upon ascertaining the existence of these new plans, the Muslim Committee presented to the occupying authorities a memorandum on 9/8/1967 requesting the discontinuation of any new expansionist measures.

The Israeli occupying authorities did not respond to the demands of the Muslim Committee. Instead they allowed a number of their agencies to begin vast excavations for archaeological purposes. In effect, these excavations weakened or destroyed the foundations of the buildings in the area. While these excavations were going on, the Israeli authorities dismayed Jerusalemites by ordering the area to be sequestered. The quarters affected are, in addition to the Moroccan Quarter already destroyed, Bab Al-Silsila Quarter, Al-Sharaf Quarter and part of the Assyrian Quarter. This wide circle of neighborhoods inside the walls constitutes about 20 per cent of all property in the Old City.

On 14/6/1969 the preliminary works towards uncovering the southern section of the Wall of Al-Buraq (Wailing Wall) were intensified. The excavations were deepened and this caused cracks to appear in the walls of the 14 buildings still standing against the wall of Al-Haram. Among these was Al-Fakhriya Zawiya, the seat of the Mufti of the Shafi'i sect. At this point the Israeli authorities issued orders for the evacuation of these buildings, by force if necessary. Next they ordered these buildings to be bulldozed. A week later, bombs were discovered in the streets leading to the Wall of Al-Buraq. Arabs were accused; but I suspect the Israeli authorities planted them there to give themselves an excuse to confiscate more buildings in order to further the Israeli expansionist designs on the Old City. (See also the Haifa newspaper AL-ITTI-HAD, June 27, 1969.) Thus, on 20/6/1969 the Israeli Military Governor proclaimed the confiscation of 17 Arab buildings. Some stand against the Wall in an area which constitutes a continuation of the area of the Wall referred to in THE JERUSALEM POST on 8/8/1967. The others lie on both sides of certain streets in the Old City.

This time, the confiscated buildings include an historical building of great antiquity known as Al-Tankiziya school. It used to house the Shari'a Court. When it was confiscated, it housed the Muslim Institute of Preachers and Teachers. Situated as it is at the main entrance to Al-Haram Al-Sharif, its confiscation means another step in the direction of encircling Al-Haram Al-Sharif, and making access to it easier.

These buildings include several historical Waqf properties. The confiscation of these buildings has brought all the properties along the southern side of Bab Al-Silsila Street into Israeli hands. The authorities have decalred that they will bring no less than 10,000 Jews to live in them.

The fifth stage in the Israeli plans to Judaize the Old City were revealed on 15/7/1969. An Israeli Government official declared that his government was considering exposing a further 200 yards or more of the southern wall of Al-Haram. Reuter was the source of this news and THE HERALD TRIBUNE reported it on 16/7/1969.

The method of releasing this information was identical to that used when THE JERUSALEM POST (8/8/1967) published the information which preceded the Israeli expansion discussed above. (Stages 2, 3, 4.)

Exposing the 82 meters of wall as mentioned above led to the appropriation of nearly 595 Arab buildings, to the demolition of 150 buildings and to the sequestration of 17 buildings. We expect, therefore, that the information released this time will lead to further Israeli expropriation of 300 Arab buildings, 4 gates of Al-Haram Al-Sharif (Bab Al-Mathara, Bab Al-Qattanin, Bab Al-Hadid and Bab Al-Habs known also as Bab Ala'iddin Al-Busairy). The area includes also two mosques and the most ancient of the Arab suqs in Jerusalem, Suq Al-Qattanin. In the area live 3,000 Arabs. Their fate is going to be like the fate of their other brethren—displacement and dispersion—followed by further liquidation of Arab presence in the city.

The two schemes discussed above indicate clearly the Israeli intentions of continuing to usurp Arab property in Jerusalem, encircling Al-Haram Al-Sharif inside the City and the City itself from the outside with fortress-like buildings and Jewish inhabitants. The authorities aim by this to convert Jerusalem into a Jewish city when they have got rid of its Arab inhabitants.

The Jordanian Government complained to the U.N. Security Council about the acts of pillage and the acts of changing the status of Jerusalem. A heated debate took place on the Jordanian complaint, during the April/May sessions, 1969. The resolution passed considered all the above-mentioned measures as null and void being contrary to previous U.N. resolutions. It called upon the Israeli Government to rescind its measures and to desist from taking further action on the matter.

JUDAIZATION OF THE ARAB CITIZEN

On 23/8/1968, the Israeli authorities passed yet another law to be applied to the Arabs of Jerusalem, called the Law and Administration Ordinance Law, 1968.

As I have already explained, the measures taken by the occupying Israeli power change the political, administrative, geographic, economic and cultural status of Jerusalem's Arab inhabitants. The new law closes the loopholes. It aims at Judaizing Arab professionals and craftsmen, as well as the various other aspects of Arab life in the city by giving legal justification to the measures already taken.

The Law and Administration Ordinance Law, 1968, stipulates the following:

a) Every Arab resident who practised his profession, labor or any other occupation under a Jordanian licence must obtain a new licence under Israeli legislation within six months, ending 22/2/1969. This category includes 5,000 professionals, businessmen and craftsmen.

b) Every Arab company, be it private, limited or ordinary, which is situated in Jerusalem and was registered under Jordanian Law must apply to the Israeli courts for a licence under Israeli law within a period ending 22/2/1969. This law affects 180 companies (with a total capital of approximately 5 million Jordanian Dinars). Thus, 4,000 shareholders and a further 4,000 employees are also affected.

c) Every Arab Cooperative Society which is situated in Jerusalem and was registered under Jordanian legislation must obtain a new licence according to Israeli legislation no later than 22/2/1969. 23 societies with a total membership of 1,518 persons are, thus, affected.

d) Every Arab physician, engineer or public accountant who practised his profession in Jerusalem under Jordanian legislation must obtain a new licence under Israeli legislation, no later than 22/2/1969. 80 such people are affected by this law.

e) Every Arab lawyer who practised his profession in Jerusalem under Jordanian legislation and was still a resident of the city shall become a member of the Israeli Bar Association. The Minister of Justice shall, no later than 22/2/1969, publish in the OFFICIAL GAZETTE the names of the persons to whom the law applies, without their application for such membership. 30 lawyers are affected by this law.

f) Every person who had registered ownership rights in a patent, pattern or trade-mark under Jordanian legislation in Jerusalem was entitled to such rights under Israeli law within a period which ended on 22/2/1969.

g) Any persons, to whom paragraphs (a) to (f) apply, who do not obtain licences under Israeli laws and regulations are guilty of violating these laws and are subject to punishment and to the payment of a fine as decreed by Israeli legislation. In cases when such persons continue in their violation, they shall be prevented from practising their professions further. Persons to whom this law applies have found themselves faced with one of two painful choices. They either lose their means of livelihood and are obliged to leave their homes to become refugees, or, they are obliged to collaborate with the enemy.

h) The said law stipulates also that immovable properties owned by Jews which the Jordanian Government administered shall be released to the original owners or their heirs. On the other hand, the law does not release Arab property confiscated under the Absentees' Property Law, 1950. This exclusion of Arabs from the benefits of this law takes place, even though the owner is present in the area of jurisdiction, and has been a resident thereof, on the day the law comes into force.

i) The Arabs of Jerusalem objected to this law and refused to comply with its provisions. The Israeli authorities were obliged to amend it and to authorize the different ministers in charge of the regularization of businesses and professions to renew automatically all licences granted under Jordanian legislation, as if they had been applied for under Israeli legislation.

j) The Jordanian Government complained to the U.N. Security Council (June/July session, 1969) about these measures which are contrary to the U.N. resolutions concerning the change of status of the city and its residents. The U.N. passed a resolution considering these measures as null and void and requesting Israel to rescind them and to desist from taking any further action in that direction. The resolution, also, called on the U.N. Secretary General to pursue the matter and to report his findings to the Security Council.

JUDAIZATION OF MUSEUMS AND ANTIQUITIES

The Israeli authorities have taken measures towards changing the status of the Museum and Arab antiquities. A memorandum was presented by the previous director of the American School of Oriental Research in Jerusalem, Professor Lapp, to his government's representative in Jerusalem on 7/4/1968. Professor Lapp was residing in Jerusalem at the time the Israeli occupation occurred. Due to the nature of his work he had ample occasion to observe the Israeli activities.

He wrote that the 9th Archaeological Convention of New Delhi, December 5, 1956, and the Hague Convention, 1954, deal with the protection of antiquities and other cultural possessions in the case of an armed conflict. He mentioned Article 32 of the New Delhi Convention which states that in the case of war, a power occupying the territories of another power shall refrain from carrying out any archaeological excavations. In the case when antiquities are discovered during the construction of military installations, the occupying power shall take all the measures necessary for the protection of these antiquities, and upon the termination of the said occupation it shall deliver them, along with all pertinent documents, to the authorities with powers over the areas previously held.

The second convention contains a number of provisions applicable to the conditions prevailing in the occupied territories. On the whole the provisions of the Hague Convention, 1954, prohibit the removal of antiquities from the areas occupied without the supervision of a representative from UNESCO. The provisions, also, call for the extension of assistance to the curators of antiquities for the purpose of safeguarding these antiquities during the period of occupation.

While the first document may be considered as a collection of recommendations, the second is a body of rules mandatory upon the signatories.

The occupying power has taken a number of decisions and measures in blatant contradiction to the resolution of 1956. A large number of robberies have been committed and permits have been granted for incidental excavations. The robberies have persisted notwithstanding the Israeli claims of having stopped them. Archaeological findings have been sold secretly by antique dealers in the Israeli sector of Jerusalem. The Israeli Government has, thus, failed to discharge its commitments regarding the convention of 1954 which makes it mandatory upon the signatories to prohibit the removal of antiquities from occupied areas for the duration of the occupation.

The UNESCO Acting Director-General has assured me that archaeological excavations are forbidden without prior authorization by the Jordanian Government, or, at least, its explicit consent. Accordingly, every American who conducts any excavations is violating all existing conventions. The excavations which were carried out under the southern and western sections of Al-Haram Al-Sharif's wall are particularly noteworthy. The traditions of Judaism, Christianity and Islam hold the area in which the excavations were carried out as one of the most sacred in the whole world. The Anglo-French excavations that were conducted in the vicinity of Al-Haram Al-Sharif between 1961 and 1967 could not be brought close to the said wall on account of the refusal of the Department of Islamic Waqf. I have been informed by the UNESCO Acting Director-General that the objections of the Department of Islamic Waqf to the excavations, carried out by Professor Mazar and sponsored by the Hebrew University, were much stronger than the objections to the Anglo-French proposals. The recent Muslim objections, however, did not get to the point of open confrontation in order to avoid Israeli retaliations.

THE JERUSALEM POST referred to the Arab objections against the said excavation works. But the Israeli Director of Antiquities considered the Arab and Israeli sectors of Jerusalem as being merged, to form one archaeological unit subject to the Israeli laws on antiquities.

It should be emphasized here that the archaeological community raised strong objections to these excavations. The Director of Antiquities in the Hebrew University confessed that the person responsible for the said excavations was not qualified to conduct earthworks underneath the wall and that his work may result in the destruction of existing antiquities of great value to the three religions. The archaeological community is greatly angered at the highly irregular excavations carried out without prior consultations with the archaeological mission who conducted the previous works, particularly since some of the recent excavations have included the trenches opened by the Anglo-French mission. The Israelis went even further and invited Father Pierre Douveau to participate in their excavations. There is no precedent in the history of scientific archaeological excavations for an archaeological dig to take place in a spot already dug up, without explicit authorization. Let it be emphasized here that the excavations in question were carried out by 20-25 paid laborers and a number of student volunteers from the Hebrew University working under utterly unqualified government employees.

It is clear, then, that the excavations in question have been conducted on Waqf property contrary to the proposals of the afore-mentioned convention, contrary to the interests of Muslims and Christians and contrary even to the interests of a segment of the Jewish community. Finally they are contrary to all the scientific practices and archaeological conventions approved by scientific organizations.

The Israeli occupying authorities, generally, consider the Palestine Archaeological Museum to be part of the Israeli Museum and, as such, a property of the Government of Israel. The Director of the Israeli Department of Antiquities has declared this to Father Douveau and to myself. Following are some details pertaining to the Israeli policies and violations.

Upon entering the museum on June 6, 1967, the Israeli soldiers led its Arab curators up a tower at gunpoint where they fired their guns over the heads of these employees. Three hours later, the Israelis drove them into a narrow room next to the lavatories. Since the Jordanian Army had not used the museum for military purposes, the Israeli action is a glaring violation of Articles 4 and 5 of the Hague Convention. The Israeli action, also, is incompatible with the provisions of the said convention because it exposed cultural possessions to the dangers of war and prevented the Jordanian curators from continuing in their jobs and protecting the cultural possessions of their country. Over a month passed after the end of the war, before the Israeli authorities allowed these men to return to their work and then only as employees of the Israeli Government. These persons are now working under a large number of Israeli employees from the Department of Museums and Antiquities. The Israeli Government has taken no steps towards enabling them to carry on their duties properly. The gate to the Palestine Museum now carries a sign indicating that it is one of the Israeli museums. The entrance hall assigned for the sale of brochures contains an enormous number of political pamphlets of a blatantly propagandist nature, as well as medallions commemorating the Six Day War.

As for the plates which used to carry explanations in Arabic and English, they have been replaced by signs in Hebrew only, an act which is incompatible with the respect due to cultural possessions.

The museum has been used as a center for collecting items discovered during surface earthworks and for exhibiting some antique objects discovered in Israel. On April 2, 1968, a special exhibition of ancient settlers in the Jordan Valley 8,000-5,000 B.C., was opened. The invitations to the exhibition were issued by the Israeli museum in Jerusalem. They mention the place of the exhibition as the "Rockefeller Museum." Most of the items shown were pictures and tools discovered in Jericho. Miss Kenyon, who had discovered them, had not been consulted. The other items came from Israel.

At the same time the Israeli authorities were organizing an exhibition of scrolls. For that occasion, they removed from the Palestine Museum the unique Lachish scrolls. This action is nothing but a scandalous violation of the Hague Convention which states that the signatories shall refrain from removing cultural possessions from areas occupied after an armed dispute (Article 1). Leading archaeologists in the various schools of archaeology in occupied Jerusalem have declared that the exhibition which was held in the Palestine Archaeological Museum is but a precedent and a prelude to the removal of the contents of the Palestine Museum to Israel, including the Dead Sea scrolls.

The Israeli stand *vis a vis* the Dead Sea scrolls does not differ from their stand *vis a vis* the Palestine Archaeological Museum, for both are complementary. The Director of Antiquities, Biran, told Father Douveau that the Israeli authorities considered the Dead Sea scrolls in the Palestine Museum to be the property of the Israeli Government and that keeping them in that museum is but a temporary arrangement. Father Douveau, it should be noted, is studying these scrolls which the Israelis claim form part of their collection in "The Shrine of the Books." Similar statements have been made to all archeologists by Dr. Biran, the Israeli Director of Antiquities, and by Yadin.

Important Dead Sea scrolls were removed from the Palestine Museum on June 6, 1967, under the pretext of protecting them. They form a section of the Smithsonian exhibition, particularly the part pertaining to the psalms. These scrolls have not been returned to the Palestine Museum. Had the scrolls been removed for safekeeping as the Israelis claim they would have been immediately returned. However, the Israeli authorities have not returned them. The Israelis are, thus, violating Articles 17 and 18 of the Hague Convention. Nor have the Israeli authorities apprised the UNESCO Acting Director-General of the event, either before or after removing them as stipulated in Article 19. I firmly believe that the act of removing the scrolls on June 6, 1967, during the course of the war was definitely not for the sake of protecting them. The scrolls were being kept in a safe and inaccessible place. However, removing them in cars which ran the risk of being attacked constitutes a most serious offence. Removing the scrolls from their place during military operations by the enemy and before any cease-fire came into effect was not only exposing them to unnecessary dangers but also committing a glaring violation of the Hague Convention (Article 4) dealing with the safety of cultural possessions. The Israeli action is in fact an act of theft.

There is yet another consideration. Supposing, for the sake of the argument, that Israel is really the legitimate heir to the museum, its competence entails certain responsibilities towards the museum's standing commitments. For example the International Advisory Board signed a contract with Mrs. Elizabeth Hay Bachtel whereby she provided a sum of money towards publishing the scroll of psalms on condition the scroll remained on permanent display in the Palestine Archaeological Museum and was removed from its place only occasionally to be shown at foreign exhibitions. The clauses of the contract grant Mrs. Bachtel and her partner Mr. Essor the right to demand that the said scroll be returned to the Palestine Museum. The museum contains also most of the fragments of the scrolls discovered in Cave 4. These were being studied by an international group at that museum. Father Douveau has seen the fragments recently but he says that a number of these have been removed to be restored. The fact has been recorded in the register kept by the museum. Although Father Douveau did not object to this action, it is, nevertheless, a violation of the Hague Convention concerning the transportation of cultural possessions from an occupied territory to a foreign one without due international supervision, as stipulated in Section 3 of the regulations appended to the Hague Convention.

There is further the case of the famous Temple scrolls, which were removed from the Kando residence in Bethlehem before the cease-fire came into effect. According to Jordanian legislation this act constitutes theft. Additional scrolls discovered in the occupied West Bank have been seized and fragments of them have been transported outside the occupied area and then sold.

Finally it should be noted that all the afore-mentioned materials in the Palestine Archaeological Museum which were removed during the war, as well as the objects discovered during the excavations in Jerusalem and elsewhere in the West Bank before and since the occupation, and all the Dead Sea scrolls discovered in Jordan should remain in, or, be returned to, the occupied areas. All the above-mentioned items should be returned upon request within six months after the state of belligerency comes to an end—as stipulated in Article 18 of the regulations appended to the Hague Convention.

The Jordanian Government has filed a complaint against these violations with UNESCO. UNESCO conducted a full-scale investigation and the matter was discussed during several sessions of the UNESCO Executive Board. The Board passed a number of resolutions on several occasions. On 10/10/1969 a final comprehensive resolution was taken which expressed great concern at the repeated violations by Israel in its treatment of the Holy City. The resolution called on Israel to preserve the city's heritage and to desist from any further attempts to change its status.

THE JUDAIZATION OF CIVIL AND RELIGIOUS COURTS

In the wake of the Israeli occupation of Jerusalem 7/6/1967, the occupying authorities closed down all the civil courts in the city and took the following measures towards changing their status: a) The High Court of Appeal was transferred from Jerusalem to Ramallah, b) The District Courts of Justice were merged with their Israeli counterparts. All their furniture and registers were removed to the Israeli sector of the city, c) Arab judges and other court officials were requested to apply for transfer to the Israeli Ministry of Justice, and d) The judiciary in Jerusalem was separated from West Bank affairs and attached to the Israeli judiciary.

The members of the Arab judiciary considered these measures to be confirmation of the Judaization of Jerusalem. They rejected them and refused to cooperate with the Israeli occupying authorities. The vast majority still refuse to cooperate up to the moment of preparing this memorandum. Only four have cooperated.

The Arab lawyers in Jerusalem and the rest of the West Bank have refused to cooperate with or appear before Israeli military and civil courts, to show their support for the judiciary body and their rejection of Israeli plans. They have expressed their rejection in several memoranda and documents presented to international bodies and to the occupying authorities themselves.

In the case of the Muslim religious courts, the occupying authorities at first made no move towards closing them down. Instead they tried to convince the judges and the other employees by means of incentives, then through pressure and threats, to join the Israeli system. When they failed, the authorities expelled the head of the Shari'a Court, Sheikh Abdul-Hamid Al-Sayeh from Jerusalem in the hope of intimidating the others.

The Shari'a judges in Jerusalem continued their refusal to cooperate with the occupying authorities. They were supported in this by the vast majority of Shari'a judges and court personnel as well as the Waqf Departments in the West Bank. They are still persisting in their refusal to cooperate up to this moment.

In answer to this Arab stand, the occupying authorities directed their agencies to disregard any judgement or decision rendered by Muslim courts, and to ignore any complaint filed by the Waqf agencies or by the Muslim Committee formed, since the occupation, to look after the affairs of the Muslims in the West Bank, Jerusalem included.

The Israeli authorities, thus, do not recognize the certificates pertaining to marriage, divorce, inheritance, guardianship. Waqf and other matters connected with the personal status of the Muslim inhabitants, including all births resulting from new marriages. This situation has created innumerable problems for the Shari'a judges, the Waqf authorities and the Muslim population. In spite of these inconveniences all have borne their fate with patience and calm to an extent which worried the Israeli authorities. In an effort to create chaos and division among the Muslims, the Israeli authorities have appointed the Jaffa Shari'a judge to take charge of religious affairs in Jerusalem and directed the Muslim community in Jerusalem to refer to him in matters relating to their religious practices.

Jerusalemites have not recognized this appointment and have refused to cooperate with the new judge. They consider him unfit to make judgements in Shari'a matters as long as he does this via the Israeli Government and as long as he accepts the Judaization of Jerusalem as evidenced by his acceptance of the new post.

GREATER JERUSALEM

On 26/3/1969 the Israeli newspaper MA'ARIV (Tel Aviv) published an article under the title "Greater Jerusalem as the Capital of Israel." In this article the newspaper uncovered, for the first time, the details of a project which was being planned as far back as June 1967 (possibly much earlier) for widening the limits of the city of Jerusalem The new limits are to extend to Ramallah in the north and Bethlehem in the south. The paper said nothing about the eastern limits. It added that the project as planned covered fifty years and presupposed an increase in the population up to 900,000 persons, predominantly Jewish.

The project has been called "Al Ab Project." Four Israeli agencies are taking part in it: the Municipality, the Ministry of Housing, the Ministry of Communications and the Ministry of the Interior.

The expenses necessary for constructing the roads leading to Greater Jerusalem and the internal roads are estimated at 500 million Israeli pounds.

Among the aims of the project is the removal of a large number of the Arab houses and buildings inside the city walls under the pretext that they are overcrowded and insanitary.

The demolition of these dwellings will result in the dispersion of even greater numbers of Arab Jerusalemites and the removal of still more historical, cultural and religious Arab buildings which link the Arabs to their past in the Holy City.

The British Mandatory Administration had preserved these edifices and had promulgated laws for their maintenance and the preservation of their architectural styles. The mandatory government had absolutely prohibited the demolition of any of their parts or the introduction of changes in their charactersitic traits. So did the Arab Administration. It held faithfully to all these principles and applied all the rules and regulations pertaining to city planning for the purpose of preserving these buildings for posterity.

On 10/7/1969 UNESCO censured the Israeli occupying government for carrying out the demolition of the Arab buildings in Al-Maghariba Quarter. The United Nations General Assembly and Security Council had, earlier, censured Israel for these acts and for others, on the grounds that such measures change the features of the city, disperse its inhabitants and convert it slowly into a Jewish city.

On 7/4/1969 the newspapers, MA'ARIV and HA'ARETZ, mentioned that an agreement had been signed between a Canadian Jewish company and the Israeli Housing Ministry for the building of 600 housing units on an area of 900 dunums. This area forms part of the Arab lands confiscated in northern Jerusalem. According to the two newspapers, the housing units will be earmarked for wealthy Jews in the West.

The newspaper, YEDIOT, (8/5/1969) reported a statement by the Israeli Minister of Justice in which he declared that the building to house the Israeli Supreme Court will be built on the Mount of Olives near the August Victoria Hospital.

HA'ARETZ (11/5/1969) uncovered further details about the Israeli project of Greater Jerusalem. These are connected with yet another part of the expropriated area in the vicinity of the Hebrew University and Hadassa Hospital (in the northern section of the Mount of Olives). The newspaper mentioned that the Administration of the Hebrew University had decided to transfer a number of its Schools from Western Jerusalem (previously Ein Karem) to Mount Scopus near the Mount of Olives. The schools in question are the School of Social Sciences, the Law School, the School of Education, and the Buber and Truman Centers. The administration had decided, also, to erect dormitories to house 10,000 students. 200 million Israeli pounds were assigned for the project. Work on the site has been going on at great speed, the intention being to achieve quickly the encirclement of Arab Jerusalem, to change the features of the city and to increase its Jewish population.

The project of Greater Jerusalem aims, also, at erecting large buildings to house the various Israeli ministries. Heading the list are the buildings for the Ministry of the Police, the Housing Ministry, the Ministry of Justice and the Ministry of Religious Affairs. The Arab Government Hospital in Sheikh Jarrah has already been converted into offices for the Israeli Ministry of the Police which were officially opened early in September, 1969.

THE BURNING OF AL-AQSA MOSQUE

The circumstances surrounding the burning of Al-Aqsa Mosque on 21/8/1969 lead one to believe that the event is but another link in the chain of Israeli-Zionist plots to destroy this holy Muslim Shrine and the nearby Dome of the Rock, and rebuild on their site the Temple of Solomon, presenting the world with a *fait accompli.*

In the background to the act of arson against Al-Aqsa one notes the following declarations and measures:

a) The various statements made by the Jewish religious leaders urging the government to confiscate Al-Haram Al-Sharif and all it contains.

b) The expropriation, sequestration, and demolition of Arab property in the vicinity of Al-Aqsa.

c) The occupation of Bab Al-Maghariba, one of the gates of Al-Haram Al-Sharif leading to Al-Aqsa Mosque; the admission through the gate of all Jewish visitors without Muslim supervision. The denial to Waqf employees of the right to check those who pass through the gates; the continued occupation of the gate since 31/8/1967, despite strong opposition by the Muslim Committee and its repeated demands to check the visitors.

d) The holding of prayers in the courtyards of Al-Aqsa by members of the Israeli Army, by rabbis and later by some Jewish organizations.

e) The excavations around Al-Aqsa.

Among the statements made by religious leaders are the following:

a) On 12/8/1967 the Israeli Minister of Religious Affairs declared at an international Jewish religious convention held in Jerusalem: "The liberation of Jerusalem has placed all the Christian holy places and a part of the Muslim holy places under Israeli jurisdiction. It has returned to the Jews all their synagogues. But Israel has other holy places in Transjordan and Al-Haram Al-Sharif. To Jews this last is the holy of holies."

b) On 22/7/1969 MA'ARIV published an appeal by the Chief Rabbi of Israel to all Jews in Israel and elsewhere to observe as usual the Jewish traditions of mourning in remembrance of the destroyed Temple of Solomon. The Chief Rabbi drew the attention of World Jewry to the fact that the Israeli occupation of the Old City of Jerusalem did not return to the Jews their Temple. They had no alternative but to continue spending that sorrowful day in fasting and prayer until the Temple was reconstructed in the courtyard of Al-Haram Al-Sharif.

c) Three days before the arson at Al-Aqsa, YEDIOT reported the following:

At 4:30 p.m., 18/8/1969 a group of 25 Zionist youths from Europe on tour in Israel, paid a visit to the Wailing Wall, then to the Holy Place. They went in spite of the prohibition against visiting it. They organized themselves quickly and paraded on the steps leading to the courtyard between the two Mosques (Al-Aqsa and the Dome of the Rock). After a moment of silence as a mark of respect for the holiness of the place, the group began to circle the Dome of the Rock chanting psalms, hymns and verses from the Old Testament. Next they sang the Zionist Bitar. The group-leader then addressed the youths in French. He explained to them that their feet were touching the most sacred spot for the Jewish people, a spot which the foreigners had tried to seize. In the future, this place would become for the second time the center of Jewry when the Holy House would be built anew. The group-leader added that the purpose of their visit was to demonstrate Jewish presence in the sanctuary. After repeating 'Hatikva' the group left the place.

Concerning the appropriation, and sequestration of Arab property and the acts of demolition in the vicinity of Al-Haram Al-Sharif, I refer the reader to sections 9 (pp. 16-21) and 2 (pp. 9-10) of this memorandum.

The occupation of Bab Al-Maghariba demonstrates Israeli malevolence. It is enough to mention in this connection the mere act of occupying the gate, keeping it under the supervision of the military authorities without permitting joint Muslim participation, allowing Jewish crowds to enter Al-Haram Al-Sharif during the daytime and possibly during the night. Muslims look with foreboding at the continued occupation of the gate despite their strong opposition to it. They would not be surprised if something comparable to the arson in Al-Aqsa occurred and in the near future.

As to conducting Jewish prayers inside the sanctuary, the first to do so was the Chief Rabbi of the Israeli Army, Shlomo Gorin. He led the first group through Bab Al-Maghariba on 15/8/1967. On four other occasions, groups belonging to the military and the religious, as well as to Jewish organizations, have held prayers there. The last occasion was on 18/8/1969 as I have mentioned earlier.

The excavations around Al-Aqsa have been extended along the western and southern walls. In some places, the excavations run as deep as 10 meters.

I still maintain that there can be no doubt that the fire which broke out in Al-Aqsa was not the deed of a single person. Basing my judgement on past experience, I have reason to believe that the arson was planned and executed, possibly with the blessings of the Israeli authorities, by the same agencies responsible for the following events: 1. The assassination of Lord Moyne, the British Minister-Resident in Egypt during the Second World War, 2. The blowing up of the King David Hotel in Jerusalem, 1946, 3. The massacre of Deir Yasin, near Jerusalem, on 10/4/1948, and 4. The assassination of Count Folke Bernadotte in the occupied sector of Jerusalem, 1948.

In each of these cases the Jewish Agency, the Israeli leaders and later the Israeli authorities hastened to wash their hands of the deed and to declare their disapproval of it. Every time they expressed their deepest concern and hastened to pay the victims the last honors. Time and again, it came to light, eventually, that the leaders of Israel and its ministers (some of whom are now at the head of the state) were the ones to plan and execute these incidents.

So it was in the past. We have reason to believe that so it is now. As the news of the fire spread in the world, the Israeli Government and leaders declared their deep sorrow over the incident, and the Israeli Government formed an investigating committee.

But in Jerusalem, the Chairman of the Muslim Committee, Sheikh Hilmi Al-Muhtasib, held a press conference in which he declared the following: (JERUSALEM POST, 22/8/1969)

1. The fire was a deliberate act of arson, not one caused by a fault in the electric system of the mosque.

2. The municipal water main controlled by the occupying authorities was turned off from the area as soon as the fire started.

3. The Israeli municipal fire engines were late in reaching the place of the fire.

4. It was the arrival of the Ramallah and Hebron firemen which helped to extinguish the fire.

The reports of the Arab engineers commissioned to examine the place indicate that the flames started in two different spots, one near the mimbar (pulpit), the other in the south eastern section of the roof. The mimbar was totally burnt. The roof over three aisles in the southeastern section and a large part of that section were destroyed.

The pictures taken of the above-mentioned spots immediately after the conflagration show that the first fire did not reach the ceiling above the mimbar. It remained intact. The flames in the second fire did not touch the columns nor the walls supporting the roof. The carpets covering the floors in that section were not affected by the flames. Finally, the two fires did not meet. Since the distance between the floors of the mosque and the ceiling is 15 meters and there is no short-cut between the area where the mimbar is situated and the south-eastern roof, and in the absence of any indication that the fires extended from one to the other, it becomes evident that two separate fires occurred simultaneously.

At first the Israeli authorities tried to put the blame on the Jerusalem Electrical Company. But the company had hastened to send its engineers to the scene of the fire and to switch off the electric current feeding the mosque as soon as the fire was discovered. The technical examinations made on the mosque's electric wiring showed no connection whatsoever between electricity and the fire. Deprived of one excuse the Israeli authorities searched for another. A young man from Australia was made the villain in what I believe to be an Israeli concocted drama. Although the scenes of the play were meant to revolve around the insanity of the accused young man, they also exposed Jewish covetousness of Al-Haram Al-Sharif, the eagerness of Jews to see Al-Aqsa destroyed and their hopes of erecting a new temple on the site of Al-Aqsa and the Dome of the Rock. In all this, the Israelis have been careful not to disclose their intentions concerning the future of this Muslim holy place.

Had they harbored any really good intentions, the Israeli authorities would have appointed a neutral committee to investigate the causes of the fire. It would have become immediately apparent to the investigating committee that, under no circumstances, could one person have set fire, a whole hour after sunrise, to two distant spots — the floor and the roof. Moreover, the two spots are at least two hundred meters apart and the stairway leading to the roof winds up for more than 15 meters. In such a case how can one person carry the heavy incendiaries and explosives and run upstairs, then downstairs and away before being discovered?

Anyone who stands in front of the place of the fire and examines the area inside the mosque and on the roof will, no doubt, see the impossibility of one person setting the two different places on fire concurrently. The observer must come to the conclusion that the act of arson in Al-Aqsa was the work of more than one person. But the occupying authorities dismissed this possibility. They limited themselves to bringing an accusation against the man whom, we strongly suspect, they dressed up to be the victim in a drama directed by various Israeli agencies.

MUNICIPAL ELECTIONS

On 1/1/1969, LAMERHAV reported that the Knesset passed the draft of a law entering the Arab inhabitants of Jerusalem in the Israeli electoral register to enable them to vote in the municipal elections.

On 6/5/1969, HA'RETZ reported that the Ministry of the Interior was completing the list of Arab voters living in the areas annexed after 7/6/1967 i.e., in the Old City, Wadi Al-Joze, Al-Thori, Silwan, Al-Tur, Al-Isawiya, in addition to the villages of Beit Safa (east), Sharafat, Sur Bahir and Mount Scopus.

On 19/9/1969 HA'RETZ casually pointed out an order by the Minister of the Interior enlarging the Jewish Municipal Council in Jerusalem from 21 members to 31. The order came as a result of the unification of the city and the resulting increase in its population.

These measures aim at changing the status of the Arab citizen in Jerusalem and dressing him up as an Israeli citizen. They emphasize his separation from the Arab citizen of the West Bank and consecrate the annexation of Jerusalem by Israel. These measures are, also, a continuance of the Israeli disregard for the U.N. General Assembly and the Security Council, which have not recognized the annexation of Jerusalem and have requested Israel to desist from introducing any changes in the status of the city.

The Israeli agencies in the various ministries, and particularly those of the Municipality of Israeli Jerusalem started campaigning among Arabs to induce the latter to nominate their representatives. They urged them, men as well as women, to participate in the municipal elections set for 28/10/1969.

The Arabs of Jerusalem received these calls with either indifference or coolness. They refused to nominate anyone and were determined to boycott these elections.

Such attitudes greatly disappointed the Israeli authorities. They had built castles in the air. They had hoped for a minimum of collaboration in order to use that as material for propaganda. They had hoped to lead world public opinion to believe that the Arabs of Jerusalem approved of the annexation of their city by Israel.

Since the Israeli schemes necessitated holding such elections with Arab participation, even by means of threats and falsifications, the various Israeli agencies, particularly those belonging to the Israeli Municipality of Jerusalem became very active. They initiated wide campaigns among the various social classes and communities in Jerusalem and in the nearby Arab villages annexed administratively to the city. They offered attractive rewards to those who participated in the elections and threatened all those who boycotted them.

HA'RETZ (29/10/1969) reported an interview with Mr. Maron Benvenesti, the Director of Arab Affairs in Israeli Jerusalem. He boasted: "I have worked long and hard during the past months. I spoke at length with one hundred and twenty Mukhtars and heads of families (hamulah) until I succeeded in winning over a number of them to participate in the elections."

On the other hand, YEDIOT (31/10/1969) reported some of the threats and the intimidation to which the employees of the Israeli Municipality and their aides had resorted. The newspaper's Israeli correspondent wrote:

'This is democracy ... This is a farce ...' I was told in a coffee house by an Arab resident of the Old City, after the elections. This Arab citizen expressed, in a few words, the impressions of nearly 20 persons of various ages with whom I had spoken on the same day. Israeli democracy has been imposed on them.

The correspondent went on to write:

In the morning (on the day of the elections) rumors began to spread that anyone who did not have his identity card stamped indicating his having gone to the polls would be dismissed from his work, refused permission to visit relatives in Jordan and not allowed to run his own business.

Up to mid-day, no Arab Jerusalemite had taken part in those elections.

Losing all self-control, members of the Israeli police and the Administration started to collect people from the streets, houses and coffee-shops. They drove them in trucks to the polls. Next day the Israeli information agencies surprised the world by announcing that nearly 4,000 Arabs cast their votes out of a total of 37,000 potential voters.

On 30/10/1969 AL-QUDS reported two contradictory news items. In the first the paper mentioned that the two parties, the National Religious Party and the extreme right-wing Gahal, who had taken part in the Jerusalem municipal elections, were investigating the possibility of presenting the Israeli Supreme Court with a request to nullify the Arab ballot. The two parties had received information indicating that Arab voters had been taken to the polls in a manner that was, to say the least, contrary to the accepted electoral practices.

The second item reported by the paper was a statement by Teddy Kollek, the Mayor of the Israeli Sector of Jerusalem, in which he denied the rumors and accusations that had begun to spread in the city accusing him and the Israeli police of having conducted a campaign aimed at intimidating the Arabs of Jerusalem. He denied their having threatened anyone who abstained from voting with dismissal from work, or withholding travel permits or creating difficulties for him.

While Teddy Kollek denied the allegations against him and the Israeli police, we see Mr. Maron Benvenisti (Kollek's right-hand man) declare to YEDIOT (31/10/1969): "The Arab electors did not come to the polls willingly. We have worked hard and firmly towards that for months."

AL-MIRSAD (the Israeli Arabic periodical) commented on 6/11/1969: "The vote of 10 per cent of the Arab residents, downtrodden and intimidated as they have been, cannot be interpreted as acquiescence to the policy of Mr. Teddy Kollek or that of his government by the Arabs of Jerusalem."

The news coming out of Jerusalem has emphasized that in spite of inducements and threats, the Israeli authorities have failed to persuade any Arab in the city to stand for candidacy for the Municipal Council. The Arab boycott of this event, in particular, is proof of the failure of the Israeli policy towards the Arabs of Jerusalem.

EXPULSION OF CITIZENS

As part of its plan to empty the homeland of its owners and weaken the Arab spirit of resistance and steadfastness, the enemy has resorted to expulsion. A large number of political leaders and representatives of the various sectors of society have been expelled to the East Bank for alleged activities against the security of the occupying power. The methods followed have been arbitrary and terroristic, clearly indicative of the mentality of conquest and oppression. The act of expulsion would take place without forewarning, the expelled person being told at the bridge. He would have no opportunity to communicate with his family or carry with him any of his personal belongings. This condition means that the person expelled is cut off from his family and loses his livelihood. Israel has so abandoned itself to this course of action that it has expelled workers, teachers and students. So far 94 people have been expelled, of whom 13 are Jerusalemites. Among them are the Head of the Muslim High Committee, the Mayor of Jerusalem, ex-ministers, an ex-member of parliament, a surgeon (head of a charitable hospital), a lawyer, a merchant, teachers, students and workers.

Through the act of expulsion, Israel aims to realize the following:

1. Getting rid of a number of political and popular leaders.

2. Weakening the spirit of resistance among the citizens through fear of becoming subject to expulsion.

3. Avoiding the embarrassment of keeping people in person without any specific charges being brought against them.

4. Obliging the families of the expelled persons to leave after them due to the extreme difficulties, both material and psychological, resulting from the expulsion.

The Israeli authorities resort to expulsion on the basis of the Defense Laws applied during the British Mandate over Palestine. These laws are incompatible with:

1. The Fourth Geneva Convention (to which Israel is a signatory), Article 49, which prohibits the removal of protected persons by force from an occupied area to the territories of the occupying power or to another occupied or unoccupied area, irrespective of reasons.

2. The U.N. Security Council Resolution 237 of July 14 which emphasizes the necessity of avoiding the infliction of harm on civilians and prisoners of war as well as the necessity of observing the principles of human rights and the Geneva Convention.

The Arab citizens of the West Bank have presented several memoranda to the United Nations. In these they have objected to the practice of expulsion and requested that it be stopped and that those expelled be allowed to return. Other memoranda were presented through the Red Cross. Israel's answer to the Red Cross inquiries (Letter of Red Cross Representative in Amman, 14/3/1969) was that it did not intend to reverse its position for reasons of security. Israel, however, expressed its willingness to review each case separately upon receiving such a request from the person expelled, if such a person declared that he would refrain from undertaking any action that might threaten the security of the occupying forces and from engaging in any political activities.

The occupying authorities have recently resorted to a new method. They pursue certain detained persons and others serving prison terms with offers to sign statements indicating their willingness to depart to the East Bank if they are released from prison. It has happened, also, that the occupying power has threatened a number of citizens with prosecution and detention for alleged resistance activities. But these citizens, the occupying power has gone on to suggest, can avoid imprisonment by agreeing to sign a statement to the effect that they choose to depart to the East Bank.

Expulsion of citizens is another act in the Israeli drama of the Judaization of Jerusalem. It is neither the last nor the least of the acts related here. This memorandum is but a brief survey of what awaits Jerusalem, the Arabs of Jerusalem and the religious and historical places in the Holy City.

Perhaps greater determination and further counter-planning may still save the city.

BARBED WIRE
SHALL NOT RETURN
TO JERUSALEM

Yosef Tekoah

Within the span of Jerusalem's long chronicles, only once, for a brief 19 years, did the city know division. Those were the years between 1948 and 1967, when its eastern sector, site of many Holy Places sacred to Judaism, Christianity and Islam, was occupied in war by the Kingdom of Jordan. During that time of truncation, Jerusalem became a front-line city, an arena of barbed wire and gun emplacements. Freedom of access to the Holy Places was inhibited; for the Jews it was barred altogether.

In June 1967, the Kingdom of Jordan, for the second time in two decades, launched an offensive assault against Jerusalem in an attempt to occupy the whole of the city, Israel's capital. The Israeli forces hit back, ousted the attackers, and reunited the city. The 19 years division was brought to an end; the barbed wire was removed; the city's inhabitants (200,000 Jews, 60,000 Arabs) intermingled again in free association and dialogue; a start was made to repair the vandalism perpetrated against the Jewish religious institutions and to rehabilitate the squalor of long neglected border slums; Jews returned to their holiest of shrines, the Western Wall; laws were passed guaranteeing the integrity and welfare of the Holy Places of all denominations; and on May 2, 1968, Israel celebrated its 20 years of independence in united Jerusalem by a ceremonial parade of its defense forces.

THE AGONY OF JERUSALEM IS NO LONGER

The world has not forgotten how Jordan, together with other Arab States, trampled the United Nations Charter and its resolutions, invaded Israel in 1948, and proclaimed: "This will be a war of extermination and a momentous massacre which will be spoken of like the Mongolian massacres."

That is what actually took place wherever the Arab forces succeeded in retaining territory invaded by them. On the West Bank, the Jordanian armies did not leave a single Jewish community intact. All Jewish villages in the areas occupied by Jordan were completely wiped out. Not a single Jew was left alive in the territories under Jordanian control. When, for instance, the village of Kfar

Etzion surrendered to the Jordanian Army, after having defended itself to the last round of ammunition, all the 220 inhabitants, except for four, were mercilessly butchered before the eyes of Jordanian officers. However, the worst fate was reserved for Jerusalem.

The Arab Legion besieged the city and launched an indiscriminate artillery bombardment sparing no residential quarter, disregarding completely the Holy Places. Jerusalem was cut off on all sides. Starvation, pestilence and thirst stalked the streets, and death dug daily ever new graves. The siege continued for weeks. The toll of death increased. Convoys with food supplies to the unfortunate inhabitants were ambushed. The Arabs did not take prisoners. All men and women were being massacred. Not even medical assistance was respected. On 13 April 1948, for instance, a convoy of doctors and nurses and medical supplies to the Hadassah Medical Center was ambushed and set afire. Seventy-seven eminent doctors and nurses were killed.

The Jews of Jerusalem looked in desperation towards the United Nations to stop the killing, to put an end to aggression. The Jews of Jerusalem looked expectantly towards the great powers to relieve the city's agony. In vain. The aggression continued. The aggressor stayed on in the city. He stayed on for nineteen years.

This is how Abdullah el-Tal, the commander of the Jordanian invasion forces, describes the battle in his memoirs:

> ... The operations of calculated destruction were set in motion ... I knew that the Jewish Quarter was densely populated with Jews who caused their fighters a good deal of interference and difficulty ... I embarked, therefore, on the shelling of the Quarter with mortars, creating harrassment and destruction ... Only four days after our entry into Jerusalem the Jewish Quarter had become their graveyard. Death and destruction reigned over it ...
>
> As the dawn of Friday, 28 May 1948, was about to break, the Jewish Quarter emerged convulsed in a black cloud, a cloud of death and agony.

When the din of battled died down the invader was able to apply himself more thoroughly to the rape and ravage of the city.

In the Jewish Quarter all but one of the thirty-five Jewish houses of worship that graced the Old City of Jerusalem were wantonly destroyed. The synagogues were razed or pillaged and stripped and their interiors used as hen-houses and stables. In the ancient historic Jewish graveyard on the Mount of Olives, tens of thousands of tombstones were torn up, broken into pieces or used as flagstones, steps and building materials in Jordanian military installations and civilian constructions, including latrines. Large areas of the cemetery were levelled and converted into parking places and petrol filling stations.

Again the world stood by in silence. Nobody raised his voice. Where are the Security Council resolutions about the destruction of Jewry's Holy Places and religious sites in Jerusalem? Where are the Security Council resolutions condemning the desecration of the cemetary on the Mount of Olives? Where are the Security Council interventions about Jordan's refusal to allow free access to Holy Places and to the humanitarian institutions on Mount Scopus, in accordance with the General Armistice Agreement? When has the Security Council called on the Jordanian invaders stationed on the Old City walls to desist from keeping Jerusalem's population under constant menace, from firing indiscriminately, from satisfying the lust for blood in the murder of children, innocent archaeologists, unsuspecting tourists? What action did the Security Council take last May when Jordan joined the conspiracy of the Arab States that closed the Straits of Tiran, amassed huge armies on Israel's borders and proclaimed that the time for Israel's annihilation has come?

Last June, when Jordan faced the choice between peace and war, it wilfully rejected peace and chose war. King Hussein described it as follows:

> On 5 June, after the fighting had already started, the Norwegian General of the United Nations, Odd Bull, handed me a communication from the Israel side to the effect . . . that if we would refrain from attacking we would escape the consequences that otherwise would be inevitable. By that time, however, we had no choice.

When the Jordanian Army opened its frontal attack against Israel, it was again Jerusalem that became the target of the principal onslaught. Jerusalem was again under Jordanian shell fire. Jordanian guns placed within the confines of the Holy Places, Jordanian machine-guns firing from the roof of the Omar Mosque opened up with a deathly barrage against the city, aiming to kill as many inhabitants as possible and destroy as much of the city's housing as could be attained.

The June hostilities were the most televised, the most fully reported war in recent history; nothing could be concealed from the lens of the camera or the eye of the Press. THE SUNDAY TIMES of London, for instance, published on 11 June 1967, the following eyewitness account by its correspondent, Colin Simpson:

> The infantry platoons swung left through the cloisters of the Fort of Antonia and into the vast courtyard of the great Mosque of Omar. From the small gate-houses beside the Mosque, machine-guns opened up and the Arabs used their mortars horizontally, the bombs sliding crazily across the paving stones before exploding.
>
> I called on the Little Fathers of Saint Nicholas who attended the wounded and marvelled at the nuns from the Monastry of the Sisters of Zion who were incredibly calm. Both told me that their buildings had suffered no damage. One of the really impressive things was the tremendous care taken by the Israelis not to damage private or religious property. Every soldier I saw seemed to venerate the City, and several times held his fire when sniped on from a church roof.

The Jordanians did not confine themselves to the destruction of the thirty-four synagogues and innumerable houses of learning in the Jewish quarter. They did not stop at the profanation of the ancient Jewish cemetary on the Mount of Olives. They were not satisfied with their indiscriminate shelling of Jerusalem, causing numerous casualties and damage to such buildings as the world-renowned Dormition Abbey. They, as THE SUNDAY TIMES reported, turned Holy Places into military bases and army positions. The eastern ramparts of the Haram Al-Sharif area where the Mosque of Omar is situated served as a gun emplacement; artillery and mortar fire was directed from the wall towards western Jerusalem; caves and cisterns in this holy compound were used as ammunition dumps; an ammunition store guarded by Jordanian soldiers was found even in the Holy Cave underneath the Rock of the Mosque of Omar; military tents, lorries, motor-cycles and army offices were located inside the

Haram area adjacent to the Gate of the Tribes — Bab-es-sbat. The minarets of the Mosque of Omar and the El-Aksa Mosque were used as sniper positions; so was the minaret of the Mosque of Sheikh Jarra; a military lorry full of explosives and ammunition was exploded by the Jordanian Army next to the El-Aksa Mosque at the approach of the Israel forces.

It is instructive, indeed, to compare this utter disdain shown by the Jordanians for the holiness of Moslem mosques with the protestations of concern for religious values voiced in Jordanian statements. How this alleged regard for religion appeared in the eyes of the local inhabitants is illustrated in a report entitled "Into Jerusalem, on to Bethlehem" by Mr. Royce Jones, printed in THE SUNDAY TELEGRAPH of 11 June 1967. The report states, inter alia: " 'After Saturday comes Sunday, an Arab tells me' — the proverb meaning that after the Jews are massacred it will be the turn of the Christians. Several of them crossed themselves to prove their religion." Referring to this very victory, the report continues: "This is the best thing that could have happened to Bethlehem, said a Franciscan in the church."

A letter published in the JERUSALEM POST on 30 April 1968, on behalf of American Christians resident in Bethlehem states:

> We have been in the Arab world for the past twenty years and know what would have happened if the victory had been reversed. There would have been no thought of sensitivity towards feelings of confiscated lands; all would have been destroyed just so the Arabs could sit in bombarded buildings and brag as to what happened to the Jews and their fine buildings, letting the country and corpses deteriorate as they allowed their land to deteriorate in the past few centuries.
>
> We Americans, Christians, were here before, during and after the six-day war. Local residents were in our house during the shooting, first to protect us from the mobs who had threatened. After the victorious army had occupied our city for one month, residents felt they had been liberated but their propaganda-instilled minds still feared reprisals from a united Arab army, which still promises them a total victory from one lost battle. The Jews have desecrated nothing that is holy to another religion, either Christian or Moslem. They have cleared away rubble and filth which have accumulated for years and are in the process of restoring their own holy places that had been desecrated, ignored or allowed to decay by all other religions for centuries.

The Jordanian Government is apparently not satisfied with the destruction it has brought upon the City. According to Jordan the destruction, the desecration, the humiliation must not be touched by anyone, it must remain Amman's forever.

The Book of Kings in the Bible states: "Thus saith the Lord; Hast Thou Killed, and also taken possession?" This is what we ask of Jordan today. Is it not enough that you have shattered, killed, and destroyed? Do you want to take possession? Should our synagogues remain ruined and defiled? Should the tombstones of our forefathers continue to serve as stepping stones and pavements? Must the Hebrew University and Hadassah hospital on Mount Scopus remain paralysed in squalor? Should construction stop in the City? Should slums remain uncleared and gardens not planted? All this only because the lust of war and bloodshed and annihilation still hovers over the region?

Is there any juridical technicality, any private claims that would be allowed anywhere in the world to stand in the way of urban reconstruction and improvement? Why should we allow this to be the case in efforts to heal the wounds inflicted on Jerusalem?

Israel's aim remains peace with its neighbors. Israel shall continue to pursue it steadfastly. It is convinced that this aim can be attained. It is certain that it will bring vital benefits to all nations of the Middle East.

If there is to be progress toward understanding and agreement, active warfare must cease. If the nations of the Middle East are to move toward a peaceful settlement, warfare by terror, warfare by threat and warfare in the international organs must stop.

We have faced acrimony in the Security Council, in the General Assembly and in other organs of the United Nations for twenty years. For the good of our peoples we must not continue on this course. Their interest lies on the road to peaceful agreement.

FROM ROMAN DESTRUCTION TO ISRAEL REBUILDING

For three thousand years Jerusalem has been the focal point of Jewish history, Jewish civilization and religion. Even when the cohorts of Imperial Rome conquered Jerusalem and destroyed the Temple, Jerusalem remained Israel's eternal capital. It is the Bible that says: "If I forget thee, O Jerusalem, let my right hand forget her cunning. If I do not remember thee, let my tongue cleave to the roof of my mouth; if I prefer not Jerusalem above my chief joy." For two thousand years, every day, three times a day, Jews all over the world have prayed: "And to Jerusalem, thy city, return in mercy, and dwell therein as thou hast spoken; rebuild it soon in our days as an everlasting building, and speedily set up therein the throne of David. Blessed art thou, O Lord, who rebuildest Jerusalem." Every day, three times a day, they have thus prayed in all the corners of the world.

In Rome, where eternal civilisations were born, and the ancient world started, there stands an arch of triumph, an arch to mark one of the most significant contests of the Roman Empire. It is a monument to a victory that Rome considered a particularly significant expression of its grandeur, a victory over a people that in its struggle against foreign domination challenged Rome's hegemony in the East. Few of the innumerable wars and conquests by Rome were considered as decisive for the future. This was the war against the people of Israel, the Judean State, its freedom and civilization. The arch depicts the defeated Hebrews being led into captivity bearing the symbols of the destruction of their sovereignty and their civilization, the symbols and paraphernalia of the demolished Temple. In Jerusalem there stands the Western Wall, the last remaining relic of this Jewish Temple.

Ever since the Roman conquest in the first century of this era, history seems to have reserved a distinct destiny for the Hebrew people: oppression, denial of rights, martyrdom. The Prophet Jeremiah said: ". . . the children of Israel shall come, they and the children of Judah together . . . All that found them devoured them all their adversaries said, We are not guilty . . ." (Jeremiah, Chapter 50:4 and 7).

Israel has survived through defeat and enslavement by Imperial Rome, through the rebellions against the foreign conquerors, through the centuries of dispersion of the people and occupation of the land by a succession of invaders, through the massacres of the Crusaders, through the *autos-da-fe* of the Inquisition, the pogroms, the blood-libels, the holocausts. We have survived and regained our national freedom and reestablished our sovereignty in our land. Yet, Jeremiah's prophecy is not of the past; some still try to devour us and then say, "We are not guilty."

In the Arab States the spirit of the Damascus blood-libel is still alive. This is the spirit that shapes and guides the Arab policy toward Israel. This is the spirit that dominates the Arab attitude in the United Nations. Today they have chosen Jerusalem as the object of their blood-libel — Jerusalem, sanctified and revered as Rome and Mecca are.

There is an old Jerusalem saying: "Ten measures of beauty came into the world; Jerusalem received nine measures, and the rest of the world one. Ten measures of suffering came into the world, Jerusalem received nine, and the rest of the world one." However, whether in bliss and beauty or in suffering, Jerusalem has always remained Israel's eternal capital.

By the time it was conquered in the year 70 of the present era by the legions of Rome, Jerusalem had served as Israel's capital for more than a thousand years. Though defeated, the people of Israel refused to be subdued, and in the year 132 rose in revolt against the Roman invader. Jerusalem was freed and the nation's leader, Bar-Kochba, set his government up in the capital. He struck coins inscribed "Jerusalem" and "Year One of the Liberty of Israel." He succeeded in holding out for three years until the weight of the Roman cohorts overcame the Jewish people again.

Then followed a long period of Roman and Byzantine rule. In 614, the Jewish population helped Persia to dislodge Byzantium, and for a while Jews governed Jerusalem again. Then, in the year 638, Jerusalem was captured by the Arabs who had come from Arabia. Jerusalem was under Arab domination till the year 1077, but the Arab conquerors never made it a seat of government, not even of provincial administration. They ruled the area from Damascus, from Baghdad from Ramle. In 1077, the Seljuk Turks conquered the land and the city of Jerusalem. It never returned to Arab rule again except for the nineteen years of grim Jordanian reign in part of the city.

In 1099, the Crusaders succeeded in wresting Jerusalem from the Turks. They put the entire Jewish and Moslem population to the sword. They maintained their power, except for a brief interval during the time of Salah ed-Din, until 1244, when they lost out to the Tartars. These were followed by the Mamelukes, who, in turn, were conquered by the Ottoman Turks in 1516.

Like the Arabs, neither the Mamelukes nor the Turks ruled from Jerusalem. Under the Mamelukes the seat of provincial government was Gaza: under the Turks — Acre. In 1917 the Turks were ousted from the land of Israel and from Jerusalem by the allied forces which included a Jewish legion fighting under Israel's colours.

Jerusalem has never ceased to be part of the Jewish saga. It was no more Arab by virtue of the Arab conquest than Turkish when the Turks occupied it or British when the British ruled in it. Arab annals record the Arab conquest of Jerusalem. Jewish history is permeated with the memories of Jerusalem's defense, the desperate attempts to preserve its Jewishness, the destruction of the Temple, the fast and mourning that the Jewish people have observed ever since the ninth day of the month of Ab.

Jerusalem's name is Hebrew. "Yerushalem", the city of Peace. One cannot separate Jerusalem from Hebrew history, martyrdom and redemption. However, it is with profound respect that Israel recognizes the universal interests in Jerusalem. Jerusalem is venerated by three great religions and all three share in the city's glory. The people are the city, and the Jews have never left Jerusalem.

Even after the most sanguinary of massacres they came back to it — the heart of Judaism — again and again, to heal the city's wounds and rebuild its ruins.

Jerusalem repaid the love and loyalty of its people. It remained for ever faithful to it. It served as the capital of one nation, and one nation alone —the capital of the Jewish people.

JEWISH MAJORITY

Since statistics of Jerusalem's population have become available, it has been evident that Jews have for generations constituted a majority in the city. In 1844, of a total population of 15,510, there were in Jerusalem 7,120 Jews, 5,000 Moslems and 3,390 Christians. In 1876, there were 12,000 Jews, 7,560 Moslems, and 5,470 Christians. In 1896, the Jewish population rose to 28,112, the Moslems numbered 8,560, the Christians 8,748. The number of Jews in Jerusalem reached 40,000 by 1905, in a total population of 60,000; the number of Moslems declined to 7,000. In 1910, there were 47,400 Jews, 9,800 Moslems, 16,400 Christians. By 1931, the Jewish inhabitants of Jerusalem numbered 51,222; there were 19,894 Moslems, and 19,335 Christians. In 1948, Jerusalem was a city of 100,000 Jews, 40,000 Moslems and 25,000 Christians. On the eve of last June's hostilities, 200,000 Jews, 54,903 Moslems, 12,646 Christians resided in Jerusalem. Today Jerusalem, a living city again in its freedom and unity, is the hearth of more than 200,000 Jews, about 60,000 Arabs, and 6,000 of other nationalities.

What precept of law, what tenet of justice, what principle of morality would deprive Jerusalem's citizens — Jews and Arabs alike — of their rights to the happiness and beauty and inspiration of their city as a whole? Why should those who have treasured Jerusalem for 3,000 years as their chiefest joy be shorn of the fullness of it? Why should Jerusalem's Jewish and Arab inhabitants be despoiled of their heritage in the City's unity? Does a conquest in defiance of the United Nations, a nineteen year occupation unrecognized by the nations of the world, including the Arab States themselves, give Jordan the right to oppose Jerusalem's revival in integrity and radiance? Does the presence of 54,000 Moslems and 12,000 Christians, in addition to the more than 200,000 Jews necessitate a bisection of the City's body?

King Solomon's biblical judgement between the two contesting women cries out to us through the ages. Could a real mother ever agree to have her baby cut in two? Could a people ever accept that its eternal capital be divided? There are many cities in the world with large national or religious minorities. Have such communities ever claimed that their cities should be artifically divided and separate public services set up for them?

Jerusalem has existed for thousands of years, and it was only during the brief nightmare of Jordanian occupation that part of it was carved out and wrested away from the city and its people. A crime that the world witnessed in silence, a transgression that brought death and destruction, terror and desecration to Jerusalem — how can Jordan now come and demand approval of it? History, justice and faith will never pardon the nineteen years of darkness, profanation and ruin in eastern Jerusalem.

Jerusalem is too precious to all of us to wrong it. Jerusalem is too central and too significant a part of the entire Jewish saga, Jerusalem is too highly venerated by the world's three great religions, for the Amman Government to play with it as if it were just another weapon in the campaign of hate and hostility against Israel on which Jordan subsists.

THE TESTIMONY OF CHURCHMEN
WHO KNOW THE TRUTH, SPEAK THE TRUTH
On April 30, 1968, in a letter to the United Nations Secretary General, the Foreign Minister of Israel, Mr. Abba Eban, elaborated Israel's policy towards the Holy Places as follows:

> ... While I have spoken of Jerusalem's special and unique place in Israel's history, we are deeply aware of the universal interests which are concentrated in the City: the equal protection of the Holy Places and houses of worship; the assurance of free access to them; the daily intermingling of Jerusalem's population in peaceful contact; the removal of the old military barriers; the care of ancient sites; the reverent desire to replace the old squalor and turmoil by a harmonious beauty — all these changes enable Jerusalem to awaken from the nightmare of the past two decades and to move towards a destiny worthy of its lineage. I reaffirm Israel's willingness, in addition to the steps already taken for the immunity of the Holy Places, to work for formal settlements which will give satisfaction to Christian, Moslem and Jewish spiritual concerns. Israel, unlike previous governments in the City, does not wish to exercise exclusive and unilateral control over the Holy Places of other faiths. Accordingly, we are willing, as I stated to you on 10 July, 1967, (A/6753, S/8052), to work out arrangements with those traditionally concerned, which will ensure the universal character of the Christian and Moslem Holy Places and thus enable this ancient and historic metropolis to thrive in peace, unity and spiritual elevation.

On the eve of the six-day war the slogan in Jordan was: "Sunday comes after Saturday. On Saturday we murder the Jews; the next day the Christians." That was plainly understood to mean what it said. However relieved the Christian communities may have felt at the liberation of Jerusalem by the Israel Defense Forces, weeks passed before the story about this slogan was repeated, and then only reluctantly by laymen and clergy to Christian visitors from overseas. Discrimination against Christian communities actually found its way into Jordanian legislation. The Parliament of Jordan enacted a law in 1958 prescribing that all members of the Brotherhood of the Holy Sepulchre should become Jordan nationals. Since its foundation in the fifth century, the members of the Brotherhood have always been Greek; and, if applied, the law would have deprived the bishops and the Patriarch of the Orthodox faith of their Greek citizenship.

Another ordinance, concerning the use of immovable property by moral bodies, was adopted in 1965; it curtailed the development of Christian institutions in Jerusalem by an embargo on their acquisition of further land or property within the bounds of the municipality and its surroundings, whether by purchase, testament, gift or otherwise. The sponsors of that ordinance were apparently Moslems opposed to the building of a church in the neighborhood of El Aksa Mosque. Yet in recent years, wherever possible, the Jordanian Government has built mosques cheek-by-jowl with churches, or, wherever that was not possible, sequestered a room in the premises of a church for Moslem worship and installed a loudspeaker in it.

In October of 1964, the Jordanian Government decreed a stoppage of the work of the Jehovah's Witnesses. That work had been officially permitted by an order of 21 February 1960. The Jehovah's Witnesses were accused of maintaining contacts with Jews, and were consequently persecuted.

In October 1966, the Jordanian Government took other steps, discriminating against Christian ecclesiastical institutions and clergy; for instance, the exemption from customs duty, including that on food-stuffs, formerly granted to churches was withdrawn. Education in Christian schools and institutions was narrowly supervised by the Jordanian authorities, who required that the curricula be sanctioned by them. Christian schools were bidden to close on Fridays, Christian civil servants and army officers suffered, in comparison with their Moslem colleagues, in advancement and often were pensioned off before the age-limit in order to make way for the promotion of Moslems. Christian prisoners of war taken by Israel during the six-day war were beaten up by their Moslem superiors and comrades, who charged them with disloyalty as citizens and soldiers.

It is without the slightest hesitation that I invite comparison between the Jordanian attitude and Israeli policy, not only towards Christians and Christian Holy Places but towards Moslem Holy Places and Moslem institutions. The Haram Al-Sharif, where the mosques of Omar and El-Aksa are situated, remains entirely under Moslem jurisdiction. The entrance to it is guarded by Moslem Arab policemen. Special instructions are posted to prevent entry in attire unbefitting the holiness of the site. The Moslem Waqf (religious, charitable funds), continues to charge entrance fees to the various shrines. During prayers entrance is forbidden to non-Moslems. When, last August, Mr. Thalmann, Personal Representative of the Secretary-General, tried to visit the Haram Al-Sharif area on a Friday morning when prayers were being conducted in the mosques of Omar and El-Aksa, he was barred by guards employed by The Supreme Waqf. Moslem Council meets regularly, the Moslem Sharia Court continues its work in accordance with traditional sharia law; the Waqf Council functions normally; all Waqf officials continue in their posts; revenues from Waqf properties are collected as in the past; the first Moslem hospital in Jerusalem, situated on the Mount of Olives, has completed construction of its premises and the outfitting of its wards and will begin operation shortly.

The Red Crescent Society, the Moslem orphanages, Moslem cemeteries, Moslem private schools function normally under unchanged Moslem supervision; private prayers, sermons in mosques, celebration of holidays continue in accordance with all traditions; on Moslem festivals streets are decorated and illuminated and cannon salvoes announce the beginning of the holiday. For the first time since 1948, Israeli Moslems are free to worship in the shrines of eastern Jerusalem; Moslem visitors from Arab States and other continents have again begun to visit the city: the Moslem inhabitants have resumed their pilgrimages to Mecca.

The Moslem Kadi of Jaffa, Sheikh Toufiq Assliya, summarized his impressions of united Jerusalem as follows:

> We prayed today with our Moslem brethren of Jerusalem in the blessed El Aksa Mosque. This is a great day for us to be able to pray at the site for which we were yearning for many years. I pray to the Almighty that He may bestow peace upon our region. We are convinced that these Holy Places continue to be closely guarded, as they were before. From here we send our blessings to all our Moslem brethren and request of them that they be reassured in the knowledge that the Holy Places are in faithful hands. Let it be known to every Moslem in the world that religious freedom, which we have enjoyed since the establishment of the State of Israel, will continue forever.

Thus, it was that, on 14 July, 1967, the Foreign Minister of Israel was able to state in the General Assembly:

We have a deep and respectful understanding of the concern of Moslems for their Holy Places. It goes without saying that the custody of the Moslem Holy Places in Jerusalem should be in the hands of authoritative representatives of Islam, with free access to all Moslems fully ensured. Accordingly, we shall welcome consultations with Moslem representatives in the vicinity of our country and throughout the world.

Let not the Jordanians come now and speak of Israeli behaviour in terms of the sanguinary bloodbath they were preparing for us. The facts are there for all to see. Let others bear witness. This is what the representative of the Secretary-General, Mr. Thalmann, had to say about the situation in Jerusalem in his report:

Prime Minister Levi Eshkol, meeting on 7 June with the spiritual leaders of all communities, declared: "Since our forces have been in control in the entire city and surroundings quiet has been restored. You may rest assured that no harm of any kind will be allowed to befall the religious Holy Places. I have asked the Minister of Religious Affairs to contact the religious leaders in the Old City in order to ensure orderly contact between them and our forces and enable them to pursue their religious activities unhindered."

On 27 June, the Knesset (Israel Parliament) adopted a special law for the protection of the Holy Places, and I continue to quote from the report by Mr. Thalmann:

These statements and statutory measures were very favourably received. Various religious representatives in fact told the Personal Representative spontaneously that so far the Israel authorities had conformed to the principles which had been laid down and that there was, therefore, no ground for complaints. They hoped that whatever difficulties still existed or were feared — mostly of a practical and physical nature — would be resolved in a spirit of co-operation.

Although the attitude of representatives of other Christian denominations was, rather, one of 'wait and see', they also described the present situation as satisfactory.

At the beginning of July 1967, the following letter addressed by His Beatitude Theophilos, Patriarch of the Church of Ethiopia, to the Israeli Ambassador in Addis Ababa, was received in Jerusalem:

The Patriarchate of the Ethiopian Orthodox Church would like to express its appreciation to the Israeli Government for the proper care with which it handled the sanctuaries in the Holy Land in general and the Ethiopian convent in particular. We also extend our thanks to the Israeli authorities for having granted unhindered and free movement to our clergy in Jerusalem during the war and after. We hope that such good care of the Holy Places will continue to enable our people in Jerusalem to perform their religious duties without any difficulty. Please convey this message to your Government.

On 14 July 1967, a group of Dutch Catholic and Protestant theologians issued the following statement in Amsterdam:

Catholic and Protestant theologians connected with Het Leerhuis (the Inter-confessional Center of Bible Studies) feel themselves called to issue the following statement on Jerusalem, which they hope may offer for Jewish and Islamic theologians an acceptable point of departure for common thinking on the future of Jerusalem.

The Jewish people, the Promised Land and the City of Jerusalem are, through Bible and history, linked with one another in a unique way. To separate by thought or deed the Jewish people from the land or from Jerusalem is tantamount to challenging Jewish identity.

The autonomous existence of the Jewish people in its own country, with Jerusalem as its capital, is felt by the overwhelming majority of the Jewish people throughout the world as a vital condition for its existence. Recognition of the international character of the Holy Places cannot imply any denial of the above-mentioned biblical and historical links binding the Jewish people with undivided Jerusalem. Neither can such recognition imply distrust with regard to the Jewish people, as if it could not be trusted to have sufficient understanding and respect for the links connecting Christians and Moslems with Jerusalem.

A manifesto on a united Jerusalem by America's leading Christian theologians, published in the NEW YORK TIMES on 12 July, 1967, stated inter alia:

During the past twenty years the City of David has experienced an artificial division. This has resulted in a denial of access to their Holy Places for all Jews and for Israeli Arabs of the Muslim faith. It has also severely limited accessibility to Christian shrines for Israeli Christians. This injustice, we must confess, did not elicit significant protest on the part of the religious leaders of the world.

We see no justification in proposals which seek once again to destroy the unity which has been restored to Jerusalem. This unity is the natural condition of the Holy City, and now once again assures the world's religious peoples the freedom of worship at the shrines which remain the spiritual centers of their faith.

This manifesto was signed by theologians representing the entire spectrum of American churches.

On 6 October, the CATHOLIC HERALD of London published a letter from Les Filles de la Charité de l'Hospice Saint Vincent de Paul of Jerusalem in which a campaign of lies against the Israelis since their victory in the Six-Day War is deplored — and I quote from that letter:

We do not know the source from which those who are hawking such rumours are drawing their inspiration, but they fill us with profound grief. There is no question for us of 'taking sides'. Our service is at the disposal of all who stand in need of it. This is confirmed by the fact that of the 400 inmates of this Hospice approximately 360 are Arabs of all ages, from babes in arms to the senile.

Some are in good health, others suffering from every conceivable kind of ailment. This, of course, in no way means that we deny a brotherly hand to the Jewish population. Within the charity of Christ we love both Jew and Arab. But we owe it to truth to put on record that our work here has been made especially happy and its path smoothed by the goodwill of the Israeli authorities — in peace and in war alike — smoothed, that is, not only for ourselves but (more important) for the Arabs in our care. . . .

The Jews, like the Christians and Moslem communities, number among themselves a spiritual elite whose moral quality none can mistake and which we, at least, cannot but admire.

Like us, too, they also have their black sheep. But all in all, after an experience extended now over a number of years, we have found amongst them much to appreciate and indeed to applaud. The recent war, moreover, has revealed them to us — both the soldiers and the civilians — as deserving of our deepest admiration.

War is war, and the Jews prosecuted theirs with the sole object of preserving their existence, while saving every single human life that they possibly could.

On April 12, the Greek Orthodox Patriarch of Jerusalem, Benedictos, made the following declaration:

It is true, and we would like to stress it again, that the Holy Places in general, monasteries and churches were given full respect and protection by the Israelis before the war, during the war and afterwards, and we hope that in the future they will be respected as well and the status quo which existed will be safeguarded.

On 8 April the Armenian Patriarch of Jerusalem wrote as follows:

I have the honor to refer to Your Excellency's kind visit of today to our Patriarchate and to thank you sincerely for the genuine regard shown by the Israeli authorities for the Holy Places.

In this connection I also present my deep thanks to Your Excellency for your willingness to render us every help in order to restore our Monastery of the Holy Saviour and cemetery, situated on the front line for twenty years.

I am confident that the Israeli authorities have always been animated by a spirit of justice and equity and that the great consideration and respect they have shown for the Holy Places will continue with the same spirit and feeling.

This is how Bishop Don Jose Goncalves da Costa of Brazil paints the situation in Jerusalem in the JORNAL DE BRASIL of 30 September, 1967:

For many hours I walked through the streets of Old Jerusalem and watched the faces of the merchants and peddlers. I went into bars and into shops. They all looked lively and very much satisfied with the excellent business they were doing. I felt no signs of anxiety or hate on the part of the Arabs in Jerusalem, Jericho and Bethlehem.

The Government of Israel immediately put the municipal services of the great City of Jerusalem on a joint basis. There is no doubt that the ridiculous situation of before the war must not recur, where a street dividing two countries passes through a single city, and soldiers armed to their teeth faced each other from the rooftops, looking at each other with hate. The Mandelbaum Gate, of which little is left now, was a serious obstacle for Christian pilgrims.

The atmosphere of the city was best reflected when the Christian communities, joined by thousands of tourists from abroad, including visitors from the Arab States, celebrated recently the Easter festival. The Moslem community celebrated the holidays of Id el-Fitr and Id el-Adkha in accordance with its own traditions.

On 27 April 1968, the Latin Custos of the Holy Land wrote:

Thanks be to God, pilgrimages to the Christian Shrines are increasing in number from day to day, and pilgrims make their visits as they did a year ago. Only occasionally they are advised, though not prevented by force, to omit the visit to the River Jordan, on account of some danger of shooting in that zone.

All services are going on as usual in the Christian Churches. It would be enough to mention how orderly was everything during the recent celebrations of Holy Week and Easter.

As I had occasion to state on previous occasions, practically none of our Holy Places and churches were damaged or destroyed during the Six Day War. In one or two places minor damage was caused, because the fight went on in the immediate vicinity of the Church or monastery. One place which suffered quite a bit was our monastery on Mount Zion.

What I have stated so far are facts that everybody can check. Of course a war is a war; yet in general we must be grateful to Almighty God that the Holy Places were preserved from destruction, and almost in all cases from damage, even small. I suppose that all can see for themselves in what conditions are our churches. And again I should say 'Thanks be to God' that Christians and pilgrims have been able to continue their divine worship in our churches, practically without any break since last June.

These are significant testimonies of non-Jewish leaders. They leave little doubt as to the true situation in Jerusalem.

THE REJUVENATED CITY —
VENTURE IN COEXISTENCE

Jerusalem is a living city, a city made up of people, a city of Holy Places, a center of universal interest, veneration and pilgrimage. The problems facing us are not of abstruse and contestable interpretations, but of pressing practical needs. Should measures adopted for the protection of Holy Places be considered regrettable? Must Jewish Holy Places remain desecrated? Should the local authorities stop issuing licenses for the construction of houses by Arabs or by Jews? Must we tear up the pavements and roads and restore the ruins and barbed wire? Must we refuse the Moslem and Christian population of Eastern Jerusalem increased quantities of that most precious of commodities in the Middle East, water, supplied now from West Jerusalem — and all this merely to satisfy the belligerent whims of an aggressor State?

The development of the situation in Jerusalem since last June constitutes a long awaited revival, a return of the city to its normal state, casting away nineteen years of tragic, artificial division. This is not an Israeli view. This is the opinion shared by all who hold dear Jerusalem's welfare and happiness. No objective and unbiased observer could suggest today that the nightmare of Jordanian occupation deserves to be preserved. The United Nations itself has not been able to ignore the grim implications of the Jordanian conquest of part of this city. As early as 1951, the report of the Director of UNRWA states: "The separation of the Old City of Jerusalem from the more modern and prosperous part has deprived many persons of their livelihood, depressed the tourist trade and created great congestion and severe competition for the few jobs that remain."

Even an organization commissioned by the Jordanian authorities found it unavoidable to emphasize this city's unhappy state. The Brown Engineering International report submitted to Jordan in 1963 says: "Modern Jerusalem is largely a product of unnatural circumstances. That which was once a complete organism was cut in two."

It is this basic fact, this overriding circumstance, that explains why Jerusalem today is a rejuvenated city and why all its inhabitants — Jews, Arabs and others — are gradually joining together to rebuild it, beautify it, and to make it worthy again of its name.

The situation soon after the cease-fire was described in the report submitted by the Secretary-General on 12 September, 1967. The findings of the Secretary-General's Special Representative, Mr. Ernesto Thalmann, based on a visit to the area as far back as last August, includes the following:

> ... the Personal Representative was struck by the great activity in the streets of the city ... The uniforms were few and weapons fewer ... The picture of the crowd in the Old City was dominated by the tourists. Arabs and Jews were mingling ... Most of the hotels had reopened. Before dawn and during the day the muezzin could be heard, as well as the church bells ... (5/8146, paras. 19, 20 and 21) The Arab personnel of the Old City was absorbed in the equivalent departments in the Israel municipality ... (Ibid., para. 29) It was reported that from the time that access from Israel to East Jerusalem had become free, the shopkeepers there had been unusually active, selling at the rate of two million Israel pounds a day in the first day in the first month and at a steady rate of one million pounds a day at present ... Service establishments were reported to have greatly increased their activities. The workshops, after an initial period of dislocation, were said to have all reverted to routine and normality and to be going through a process of adjustment to new marketing conditions ... (Ibid., para. 67)

Israel does not suggest that Jerusalem's problems have been resolved. We discuss these problems openly and freely, We realise that after nineteen years of division and Jordanian education and hostility, propaganda and hate, difficulties of a technical and psychological nature do arise at times. We are fully aware of the challenges that remain to be met. We cannot expect all of the 60,000 Arab inhabitants of East Jerusalem to show friendship to the 200,000 Jews of this city. We do, however, hope that the animosity of the few would not be used to harass and injure the many.

We do also affirm without any hesitation that whatever measures have been taken in the last ten months are aimed at ensuring the welfare of the city and the happiness of its people. We do say that the situation today for Jew and Arab alike is better than in the years of division and Jordanian occupation in Eastern

Jerusalem. We do agree with Pere Riquet, the former Predicateur de Notre-Dame, who, upon return from a recent visit to Israel stated, according to FRANCE SOIR of 25 April 1968: "The Israel authorities are practising true coexistence in peace between the religions. In Palestine, public security is greater today than ever before."

This is Jerusalem today — a venture in coexistence, a trial of faith. After all these years of hostility and suffering, Jerusalem is still groping on its way; but Jews and Arabs in it are already living together, working together, building together and dreaming together the dream of peace. For the first time in nineteen years, Israelis and Arabs talk one to another, shake hands and sometimes even smile at each other. If, at long last, agreement and peace will come to the area, it will have drawn much of its inspiration from united Jerusalem. If the beginnings of understanding and community sprouting today in Jerusalem were impaired, peace would be dealt a grievous blow. They must be nurtured with the utmost care for in them are the real interests of the peoples of the Middle East.

One of the pretexts for the Jordanian complaint is a concoction of unfounded allegations about housing development in Jerusalem. Most of the land involved in the reconstruction projects is not Arab-owned, but Jewish-owned and public domain. No attempts by Jordan to distort this basic fact could succeed. The land records happen to be in Jerusalem, not in Amman. No mosque or church, no Holy Place would be affected. It is sufficient to look at the map to realize this. All of the land in question situated outside the Jewish Quarter is empty. In the Jewish Quarter itself no home of any Arab inhabitant who has settled there in the last two decades is involved. The undertaking is one of normal urban development, of cleaning ruins, restoring houses of worship and reconstructing slum areas. Many of these projects had been worked out not by us, but by the Mandatory Administration before the Jordanian occupation in 1948. Had the attitude of the occupying Jordanian authorities towards the City of Jerusalem been different, they would have carried out those projects themselves a long time ago.

With regard to the urban development, slum removal, clearance of ruins and new construction, it should be noted that three particular projects are involved. The first one is the plan to develop the area of the Jewish Quarter from its western edge to the Western Wall. This is the area destroyed by the Jordanians during their 1948 onslaught on Jerusalem and immediately thereafter, and includes the Moghrabi houses adjacent to the Wall, a district which the Jordan authorities allowed to deteriorate into a slum.

A UNESCO delegation visited this area in 1960. The annual report of the Director-General of UNESCO for that year emphasized the danger of leaving the area in such a condition. The report stated inter alia: "There should be no deception about the necessity of large-scale future improvements to prevent parts of the Old City becoming ever-increasing slums."

In 1963, the Brown Engineering International submitted a report to the Jordanian authorities stressing the need for urban development. For example, recommendation No. 5 of the report reads: "Construction of shell public housing units to facilitate the clearance and reconstruction of deteriorated houses in the Old City." Recommendation No. 6 reads: "Reconstruction of destroyed areas along lines similar to the original."

Recommendation No. 2 reads: "Removal of temporary structures in the courtyards of the Old City, after a rehousing programme has provided living space for the inhabitants of these structures in shell public housing units." All the inhabitants affected by this project have, as already stated, been provided with alternate housing by the Israel authorities.

A second area is a complex of about 3,345 dunams — or about 800 acres —in and around the Hadassah Medical Center and the Hebrew University compound on Mount Scopus stretching from there through vacant land westward. Here, in addition to the rehabilitation of the humanitarian institutions on Mount Scopus and the construction of the Truman Center for the Advancement of Peace, new housing construction is planned on empty land for Jews and Arabs.

The development of this area is based on a master plan prepared by a British engineer, Mr. Kendall, in 1946, who was engaged for that purpose by the Mandatory authorities well before the Jordanian occupation. Moreover, the Brown Engineering International recommended specifically housing developments in this very area.

The third urban development project concerns the area of the Jewish village of Neveh Yaacov in the northern part of East Jerusalem. This village was razed to the ground by the Jordanian Army in 1948.

I reiterate; most of the land in question is Jewish property and public domain. No photo-montage charts, no allegations irrelated to the records can change this fact. All private claimants would receive compensation. Indeed, this is the fact that necessitated the announcement concerning acquisition of the land and the intent to compensate private owners.

There is one way, and one way only, to judge the present condition of Eastern Jerusalem; not by the bellicose pronouncements of hostile Governments; not by statements of disgruntled agents of Jordanian rule; but by the reaction of the people themselves. The Arab residents of Jerusalem have rejected all attempts made by outside elements to prevent Israel-Arab co-operation in the administration of the City. Arab inhabitants of East Jerusalem now voice their views, their complaints and demands through a committee of thirty-nine Mukhtars, neighborhood leaders who represent all sections and clans of the population of East Jerusalem. The Mukhtars constitute an advisory committee to the Mayor and are the same persons that had functioned in this capacity prior to 5 June 1967.

Moreover, frequent question-and-answer meetings are held between the Mayor and municipal department heads and the local public. Hundreds of Arab citizens, and in particular persons prominent in public life and professions, attend. At the meetings of the Mukhtar advisory committee and at the public assemblies, the needs of the City are aired, the interests of the inhabitants voiced.

It is through such meetings between the Mayor and the public and their representatives that the municipality is able to act upon suggestions and advice offered to it freely and democratically. Many of the measures taken in East Jerusalem in the last several months are in response to such suggestions and advice: 110,000 square metres of roads have been paved; free medical services organized; public libraries opened.

It is of significance that the Arab citizens of Jerusalem adopt this attitude of joint effort for the benefit of the City as a whole, as well as in respect of the very measurses and projects around which the Jordanian complaint attempts to create a controversy. Jordan takes exception to housing construction plans. Not so did 200 Arab families, who, together with 250 Jewish families, will be settled in these new homes; nor the Arab workers who will be employed in their construction. The Jordanian representative finds only words of criticism for the clearing of slums around the Western Wall, in accordance with international recommendations. Not so the inhabitants of these slums, who have been provided with new housing. The following is the text of a letter dated 8 January 1968, addressed by forty-one heads of families to the Mayor of Jerusalem, Mr. Kollek:

> We, the undersigned, who constitute part of the residents of the Jewish Quarter and of the Moghrabi Quarter in the Old City, who were evacuated from our homes there as a result of the six-day-war, wish to thank His Honor, as well as Mr. Meron Benvenisti, in charge of East Jerusalem, and Mr. Faris Ayub, head of the public relations bureau in the eastern part of the city, for the financial aid and human care which was extended and is still being extended to us, which impressed us profoundly and which afforded us and our families more decent alternative accommodations. We pray God will grant you long life and a continuance of your good deeds.

Jordan tries to paint a bleak picture of the situation in Eastern Jerusalem and the prospects of joint Israel-Arab endeavours for the good of the City. The well-known Nusseibeh family, which the representative of Jordan enthusiastically extolled at a meeting of the Security Council seems to disagree with him. The Nusseibeh family is now constructing a six-story, 140-room hotel in Jerusalem. Verily, it must be emphasized that the building activity is not confined to the Jewish sector. The district planning board is approving an average of ten applications a week, submitted by Arab residents for construction permits. In general, an unprecedented economic boom prevails today in Jerusalem. Thousands of Arab workers make a living in factories and construction firms in that part of the City which until a year ago they were told to consider as enemy territory.

There is a shortage of manpower in the building industry. Mixed Jewish-Arab enterprises, such as construction firms, restaurants, souvenir stores, are mushrooming. The Arab Chamber of Commerce, under the old leadership, is pursuing its activities and expanding them. A special advisory committee was formed by the Chamber to work with the municipality on the assessment of income tax. Workers, government and municipal employees in Eastern Jerusalem have joined the Israel Federation of Labor.

The most striking feature of present-day Jerusalem is probably the freedom of movement enjoyed by the City. Not only are the walls, minefields and barbed wire fences separating the two parts no longer there; not only are all Israeli citizens — Jews and Arabs alike — free to come to Jerusalem and bask in the fullness of its glory; not only are all Gaza inhabitants free to do so; not only can the Arab inhabitants of Jerusalem move freely through all Israel, but they are also free to visit the East Bank, including Amman and other Arab countries, and then to come back. There are regular daily bus and taxi services between Jerusalem and Amman. In the last few months 6,000 Arab citizens of Jerusalem have availed themselves of these services to visit the East Bank and return, thereafter, to their City.

The credibility of the claims made in Jordanian statements and the material distributed on their behalf is probably best illustrated by the following. An allegation was voiced in the Security Council that 3,000 persons have been evacuated from the Jewish Quarter. The true figure is 160 families, or about 700 souls, who were moved only out of the ruins of the synagogues in which they had settled after the Jordanian capture of the Old City in 1948. All have received alternative housing and full compensation, totalling 120,000 Israeli pounds. 3,500 Arab citizens continue to reside in the Jewish Quarter and, as I have already stated, the restoration project would not affect them.

Nor is it necessary to expatiate on the myths of the alleged Israeli pressure on Arab inhabitants to leave the City and the resultant question of absentee property. Again, let the testimony of third parties serve as an answer to slander. Mr. Byford-Jones, a well-known writer on the Middle East question states in his book, "The Lightning War," that the Israeli Government did all it could to prevent the Arabs from leaving their homes in Old Jerusalem. There are numerous other eye-witness reports, including reports by representatives of the International Red Cross.

In respect of the size of this problem and the question of absentee property that remained behind, it has to be poined out that relatives have been allowed to take over the homes of members of their families who had left, and that out of 8,000 houses in Eastern Jerusalem, only 160 are considered as absentee property.

I have analyzed the situation prevailing in Jerusalem at present and the reaction to the situation by church heads, leaders of local communities and foreign observers, as well as the attitude of the people themselves.

I have emphasized in particular that the people are the city. The welfare of Jerusalem and its future cannot depend on questionable claims and allegations born in the passion of debating contests. Jerusalem is the life of its people — 200,000 Jews, 60,000 Arabs and 5,000 of other nationalities. These people have been innocent victims of international conflict for nineteen years. Their hope lies in never returning again to the grim past.

The past — the nightmare of barbed wire and minefields, of bombardment, of sniping from the Old City walls, of desecration of Holy Places and prevention of free access to them, the past of hate and hostility is best illustrated in the caricature circulated in Jerusalem under Jordanian rule and published in the Jordanian daily Al-Manar on 28 January 1965. It shows a Jew, the Star of David on his clothes and fear in his eyes, kneeling under the guillotine's axe ready for the slaughter. The Arabic caption under the caricature reads: "No words needed."

The past is symbolized by the text book, one of many similar ones, used in the second year of high school in Jerusalem's sector occupied by Jordan. In the text book entitled "Arab Society" we read: "You Arab boys and girls must cling to the slogan 'Israel must disappear forever'." That was the past — dark and sanguinary.

The present is characterized by the following description by Sister Stephanie Stueber, which appeared in the Jesuit publication AMERICA of 3 February 1968:

> Throngs of Jewish pilgrims, old and young, of Muslim pilgrims, of Christian pilgrims, were going to their own Holy Places, and to each other's Holy Places — places that some had been barred from for twenty years and some had never seen. Jews were seeking out their fathers and grandfathers' tombs in the desecrated cemetery lying beyond the Golden Gate in the eastern part of Jerusalem.
>
> Arab and Jew intermingled in the Old City. Colorful in their oriental dress, Arab families strolled through modern Jerusalem, bought squash from Israeli shopkeepers, peered into shop windows, enjoyed the parks and wide streets, smiled back at the joy of happy, carefree children.

The present is a venture in coexistence. In today's Jerusalem, Jews and Arabs live together, build together and dream together the dream of peace. Not only do all Arab institutions continue to function normally, but there is also a beginning of united endeavours, of undertakings in which Jews and Arabs join hands together for the common good.

The present is not characterized by the atmosphere of malevolence and alienation that hostile spokesmen try to create. The present is characterized by the meetings between Jewish and Arab school children, by the participation of forty Arab students in the "Municipal Youth Orchestra," by tours of Israel organized for hundreds of Arab school pupils and adults. The present is Jewish-Arab symposia taking place regularly with the participation of Arab leaders, including former ministers in the Jordanian cabinet, high government officials, journalists and scholars. These symposia are attended by hundreds of citizens, Arabs and Jews alike. Hundreds of Arabs and Jews are studying each other's language in specially conducted courses. Joint Jewish-Arab sport events are held regularly.

For the first time, Eastern Jerusalem has Arab theatrical activities. Arab theatre ensembles from Israel have begun their performances in the City, while a local Arab theatre group has been organized and is preparing to appear shortly on stage. The municipality is constructing a special theatre hall in east Jerusalem. The world-renowned Khaledia Library, one of the best in the Arab world, closed during the last decade because there was no Jordanian incentive or interest in opening it, is about to be reactivated. The Moslem Museum adjacent to the Al Aksa Mosque, bolted and neglected for years, has already been reopened. Negotiations are on the way to reopen the Palestine Ethnological Museum, abandoned and closed during the Jordanian occupation.

Old friends, long-time Jewish and Arab residents of Jerusalem, have found each other again after nineteen years of separation. There are again reunions of Arabs and Jews in Israeli homes in Jerusalem and elsewhere in Israel. Jews visit again with Arab families in the eastern part of the City.

That is the situation which Jordan, in the name of belligerency and destruction and desecration, wishes to undermine. Jordan does not speak for Jerusalem's happiness. Jordan does not speak on behalf of the City's population, not even on behalf of the 20 percent which are not yet ready for peace and understanding with Israel. It is, however, peace and understanding that our peoples desire. It is peace and understanding that we must be helped to find.

The Arab Mayor of Nazareth addressed himself to the Arab governments on April 5, 1968, and said: "The Arab States have tried war and brought upon themselves ruin and destruction. Let them now try peace. Let them put aside the deceptive dreams of destroying Israel and come to the peace table."

It is in the spirit of that brotherly appeal by Mr. Mussa Khatili, Mayor of Nazareth, that we too appeal to the Government of Jordan and to other Arab Governments; for the good of the Arab and Israeli nations let us join together in a concerted, dedicated effort to attain peace, at last, so that our peoples shall know war no more.

VII. The Jordan River

INTRODUCTION

The disagreements between the Arabs and Israelis regarding the exploitation of the Jordan River waters is particularly characteristic of the state of relations between the antagonists. Both camps realize that a regional development of the waters of this international river, whose sources are in Lebanon, Syria, and Israel, and which flows through the territory of Jordan and Israel, could benefit all the peoples of the area. More specifically, the riparian states have recognized that a regional approach could contribute to extensive economic improvements, through the development of irrigation and hydro-electric power, which might also create an economic base for a substantial number of Arab refugees. Nevertheless, none of the various water schemes proposed over the years, some dating back to the British Mandatory period, have been implemented because of the hostile political climate which has militated against any step-by-step effort to build a de facto peace in the region.

The Arabs have maintained their objection to enter into any joint venture with Israel, whose existence they do not recognize. Denying Israel's standing as a riparian state, with rights that legally accrue to riparian states under international law, the Arab league decided in 1964, with Syria taking the lead, to divert the two sources of the Jordan River from flowing into Israel. Some beginnings were made by the Syrians on the digging of diversion canals, but the work stopped as a result of Israeli bombings. Moreover, Lebanon was reluctant to actively engage in these works for fear of provoking Israeli retaliation. Jordan, on the other hand, proceeded with its own plans to divert the waters of the Yarmuk River, one of the tributaries of the Jordan River after Israel, without waiting for Arab consent, implemented various projects based on plans originally advanced by international engineering and water experts. Moreover, as a result of the June, 1967 War, Israel gained a significant strategic advantage by occupying the Golan Heights, including the Syrian source of the Jordan River. Thus, most of the Arab diversion scheme has come to a standstill. And yet, more comprehensive development of the Jordan region remains impossible as long as the parties continue to insist on their opposing positions.

The first selection in this chapter is from Omar Z. Ghobashy, THE DEVELOPMENT OF THE JORDAN RIVER published in New York by the Arab Information Center in November, 1961. The author describes Arab, Israeli, and American plans for the utilization of the Jordan River waters, the Arab efforts to halt Israel's unilateral actions, and the legal issues involved. The Israeli view on the subject comes from a publication of the Ministry for Foreign Affairs, dated April, 1965. It deals with "The Arab Plan to Divert the Headwaters of the River Jordan" and Israel's reaction.

278

THE DEVELOPMENT
OF
THE JORDAN RIVER

Omar Z. Ghobashy

In the Middle East, and particularly in the Arab World, there are two important resources, water and oil. There are some states which are blessed by the possession of both. There are some which have one resource and lack the other. Finally, there are the less fortunate countries having neither oil nor a water supply sufficient for normal and gradual economic and agricultural progress.

The Arab States bordering the Jordan River have one thing in common. They are not among the oil producing countries of the Middle East, and they depend heavily upon water resources. In the case of Jordan, which is a major beneficiary of Jordan River waters, the case is most acute, for its existence depends upon its maximum use of water resources through the development of the Jordan River. It is evident, therefore, that the Jordan, an international river, is of primary concern to the three Arab states of Lebanon, Jordan and Syria, through which it passes, and the utilization of its waters by any or all riparians raises matters of an economic, political and legal nature.

The Jordan is 156 miles long, 73 miles in Israeli controlled territory, and the rest in Syria, Lebanon and Jordan. The total flow of water which passes down the River annually is 1880MCM (Million Cubic Meters), of which 77% or 1488MCM originates in the three Arab states, and 23% or 432MCM, in Israel.

The River is composed of two important sections, the al-Sharea and the Jordan. The al-Sharea River, which is the name of the Jordan before it enters Lake Tiberias, descends from a height of 230 feet above sea level to Tiberias, 650 feet below sea level. The al-Sharea has three branches: the Banyas, extending from the city of Banyas in the northwest of Syria to Gabal El-Sheikh, the Hasbani, extending from southern Lebanon near Hasbia in the southwest of Gabal El-Sheikh, and the Dan, extending from Tel Kadi in Israel. These three sources of the Jordan River meet 9 miles north of the Huleh area, forming one river, the al-Sharea.

The name 'Jordan' is given to the River from Lake Tiberias to the Dead Sea, a distance of 120 miles. During its course it drops nearly 600 feet until it empties into the Dead Sea, 1300 feet below sea level. At Gisr Al-Magameh, at the intersection of Syria, Jordan and Israel, the Jordan River meets in a small area known as the Triangle of Yarmuk. Here the River becomes the line separating Jordan and Israel until south of the city of Besan, at the end of Truce line. From there, the River becomes Arab on both banks.

The main tributaries of the Jordan River are: the Yarmuk, which flows down from the Syrian hills westward and extends 47 miles from Huran in Syria until it meets the Jordan four miles south of Lake Tiberias, the Zarka, which extends from the town of Zarka north of Amman in Jordan until it meets the main river near the Jordanian town of Al-Salat, and the Galant, which runs from Besan in Israel to the Jordan River near Bisen.

Because of the great drops in the Jordan River it has long been recognized that the River could readily be used for generation of hydroelectric power, as well as for gravity irrigation of lands in the river valley. These measures would revolutionize the economic conditions of the region. For this reason successive plans have been set forth for the use of Jordan waters. The plans center particularly around the Dan, Banyas, Hasbani and Yarmuk tributaries and the al-Sharea and Jordan sections of the River itself.

It is clear that any regional plan for the use of the Jordan and its tributaries must provide equitable benefits for all riparians. The situation has arisen, however, in which Israel has attempted to unilaterally divert the waters for its own use, without consideration for the rights of the Arab states. Thus, in the light of the great potential of the River for the development of the region, and in view of the threat to peace posed by Israel's action, it is pertinent to examine the technical, political and legal aspects of the various plans that have been proposed.

ZIONIST PLANS TO UTILIZE THE WATERS OF THE JORDAN

Zionist plans for utilizing Jordan waters for their exclusive benefit which threaten peace today, have been continuous and deliberate efforts which began during the Mandate period, continued after the creation of Israel, when successive plans were seriously considered and actively set forth, and are now being implemented by the present Israeli diversion plan. The purpose of all Zionist plans has been the cultivation of more land in order to make room for more Jewish immigrants.

As early as 1916, British Zionists asked the British Government to claim all the Jordan River for mandated Palestine. The King-Crane Commission sent by President Wilson to the Middle East in 1918 reported the Zionist argument that: There is no need to displace the present population, for with afforestation, modern methods of agriculture, utilization of water power, reclamation of waste lands, scientific irrigation, and the like, the land can contain several times its present number of inhabitants.(1)

At this time, however, the British Government was not very susceptible to Zionist pressure and was unwilling to commit itself to actions having an adverse effect on Syria and Lebanon, which were under French mandate.

The British Mandate Government examined different projects for the development of the Jordan River, and in 1937 sent the Peel Commission to Palestine. The Commission reported that the Jordan was the only potential source of river irrigation, that there were possibilities of irrigating northern Palestine by draining the Huleh marshes and that the Jordan Valley could be watered by running canals from the river. As a result of this commission's work, the first hydrographic survey of the Jordan Valley was made from 1937 to 1939 by M. C. Ionides, Director of Development in Trans-Jordan at the time.

The investigations of the Mandate Government were motivated by a desire to find a solution to the increasing tension between Arabs and Jews. However, Zionist pressure was constantly exerted, in an attempt to change any water projects to fit their program. The Joint Palestine Survey Commission had been employed by the Jewish Agency for Palestine since the beginning of the Mandate to study land utilization with a view to absorbing an increased number of new immigrants. As a result, water became the main preoccupation of Zionist leaders and definite plans were soon set forth for the seizure of Jordan waters.

THE LOWDERMILK-HAYS PLAN

In 1939, the Jewish Agency in Palestine invited Mr. Walter Clay Lowdermilk to study irrigation problems in Palestine. He prepared an elaborate report on irrigating the Negeb, and published a book in 1944 in which he presented his plan, which was designed to permit four million Jewish immigrants to settle in Palestine. He proposed the transfer of water by canals and pipes to irrigate the Negeb and the construction of dams and reservoirs in south Palestine to conserve rain and well water. Because this would cut off the important water flow to the Dead Sea which is rich with mineral resources, he proposed the digging of a canal near Haifa from the Mediterranean to the Dead Sea as a substitute for the loss of the Jordan waters. This new canal would be utilized to produce electric power for Palestine. The Lowdermilk plan called for the irrigation of Palestine land in the north and center, irrigation of large areas in the Negeb, the industrialization of the Negeb and the conservation of the Dead Sea resources.

Among the technical features of the Lowdermilk plan were the following:

1. The full utilization of the Jordan waters and its sources in Tel-al-Kadi, the Hasbani River and the Banyas River.

2. The drainage of Huleh Lake and the opening of wide canals for irrigation in the Besan area, and the transfer of Jordan waters to the south for irrigation of lands in the Negeb.

3. The full utilization of the waters of the Litani in Lebanon by diverting its waters in northern Palestine to an artificial lake in the village of Nabit al-Battauf, north of the city of Nasra, and from there to the Negeb.

This plan of Lowdermilk was soon followed by a series of engineering studies by two other U.S. consultants to the Jewish Agency, James B. Hays, and J. V. Savage. Lowdermilk's ideas were incorporated into Hays' study, T.V.A. ON THE JORDAN, which was published in 1948.

The basic concept of the Lowdermilk-Hays plan, as promulgated even before the existence of Israel, was "to take as much as possible of the Jordan's waters right out of the Jordan's own valley, away from the people of it, and run it over the watershed of the basin to irrigate lands far away."(2) This became the guide to all future Zionist plans.

It is to be noted that the Zionists had this project in mind when expressing their views on the Partition Plan, since they insisted that the Jews be allocated lands situated in the areas envisaged in the project. Dr. Emanuel Neumann in the introduction to T.V.A. ON THE JORDAN wrote that by the Partition Resolution, "The Jewish state was awarded an area embracing the upper reaches of the Jordan in the north . . . thereby the opportunity was given for carrying out the basic conception of the Lowdermilk Hays project . . ."(3)

In promoting Lowdermilk and Hays' vision of large scale immigration and use of Jordan waters outside the river valley, the Zionists carried on a propaganda campaign, parallel to their Jewish National Home policy, that land could be found for unlimited irrigation.(4)

The fact of the matter is, that there are limited water resources in the Jordan Valley to satisfy the needs of the people of the area, and since this fact is known to Israel, its policy is based on increasing its water supplies by taking it away from the Arabs, depriving them of their minimum water needs, for the benefit of new Jewish settlers. This is presented to the outside world as a great project for economic development, a major contribution to peace in the area, a classic case of economic cooperation and a work of engineering genius to develop an area which the Arabs could not cultivate due to their backwardness and lack of technical know-how. It is never mentioned, and the general public is not aware, that their unilateral national project is based wholly on the unlawful encorachment on Arab waters, the illegal diversion of Arab rivers, and the exclusive use of an international river for selfish ends, ignoring the rights of the legitimate riparians.

ISRAEL'S SEVEN YEAR AND TEN YEAR PLANS

The Israeli Seven Year Plan, largely based on the Lowdermilk-Hays proposals, was set forth in 1953 and subsequently incorporated into a Ten Year Plan in 1956. The principal difference between the two plans was the allocation in the Ten Year Plan of an additional 160MCM of Jordan River waters to Israel. The broad outline of the schemes remained substantially the same.

The Seven Year Plan envisaged the receipt of 540MCM of Jordan River water by Israel through the drawing of the following amounts from Jordan River resources:

A. Drainage of Lake Huleh	120MCM
B. Diversion of the Jordan at Gisr Banat Yacub	340MCM
C. Diversion of Lake Tiberias via Kinneret-Besan canal	80MCM

The first of these projects involved draining the rich marshes north of Lake Huleh and utilizing the waters of the Dan and upper Jordan tributaries to irrigate northern Israel to the southern end of the Lake. This project remained substantially unchanged in the Ten Year Plan.

The Kinneret-Besan canal project was also included in both plans. It was to draw water from the southwest corner of Lake Tiberias to irrigate southern Israel to the Besan district. Such a canal would seriously deplete the waters of the Jordan below Tiberias. A feeder canal from the Yarmuk to Tiberias was included in the maps of the proposed Seven and Ten Year Plans. Furthermore, since the Ten Year Plan envisages Israeli use of 700MCM of Jordan and Tiberias waters, and the flow at and above Tiberias is only 600 MCM, exeuction of the Ten Year Plan would appear to imply some use of Yarmuk waters for the project.

The key feature of the Seven and Ten Year Plans was the proposed diversion of the Jordan at Gisr Banat Yacub to the Negeb. It was in this project that the major changes were made in the plans regarding construction and volume of water.

Under the Seven Year Plan the Jordan was to be diverted at Gisr Banat Yacub and conveyed by a canal through the demilitarized zone between Syria and Israel to a proposed power plant at Tabgha, where part of the flow would be diverted over a 250 meter fall into Lake Tiberias to generate power. Most of the flow, however, would be channelled westward to the al-Battauf reservoir. The Tabgha plant, with a capacity of 25,000 kilowatts and an expected output of 50 million kilowatts annually, would supply power to pump water from the canal into al-Battauf reservoir. From the reservoir, the main conduct, a cement pipe of 108'' diameter would lead southward to Faluja, and thence through smaller pipelines to the Negeb, linking with local projects along the way.

The Ten Year Plan envisaged the same diversion of the Jordan at Gisr Banat Yacub as in the Seven Year Plan, but differed in that 500 MCM of water was to be taken at this diversion point, an increase of 160MCM, and major storage of the water was to be in Lake Tiberias rather than in al-Battauf reservoir, which had been found to leak. Also, because of the additional pumping of fresh water at Gisr Banat Yacub, it proposed the diversion of 30MCM of the saline spring water downstream, to avoid undue salinity in the Lake.

Thus, Israel's Ten Year Plan, which amounted to an extension and slight modification of the original Seven Year Plan, envisaged the receipt of 700MCM of Jordan waters by Israel through the diversion of the following amounts from Jordan River resources:(5)

A. Drainage of Lake Huleh 100MCM
B. Diversion of the Jordan at Gisr Banat Yacub 500MCM
C. Diversion of Lake Tiberias via Kinneret-Besan canal 70MCM
D. Diversion of saline spring water from Lake Tiberias downstream 30MCM

These diversions would result in only 540MCM of Jordan River water remaining for Arab use. Therefore, Israel's share would be 56% although the quantity of water which flows in the Jordan from Israeli sources is only 23%, the rest originating in Lebanon, Syria and Jordan.

THE COTTON PLAN

In May 1954 the Israeli Government proposed a modification of its Seven Year Plan as an answer to the proposals made by the Johnston Mission. The Israeli Minister of Agriculture termed it a "genuine regional plan" embracing all available water resources in the Jordan watershed and part of the Litani River waters which flow entirely in Lebanon.

The plan involved the diversion of all upper Jordan River waters, including the Dan, Banyas and Hasbani tributaries, for use in Israel. They were to be utilized either in upper Israel or conveyed to the al-Battauf canal and ultimately through the main conduct to the Negeb. In addition to this, 400MCM of Litani River waters were to be diverted by tunnel to the Hasbani and thence through al-Battauf to the Negeb, leaving but 301MCM of Litani water for Lebanese use. Such a diversion had been envisaged in neither the Seven Year Plan nor the Johnston Plan.

Unlike the Seven Year Plan, which did not specifically include the utilization of Yarmuk water, the Cotton Plan clearly stipulated that 100MCM of Yarmuk water would be for Israeli use, the rest for Syria and Jordan via a canal system. The Cotton Plan followed the Johnston Plan in advocating main storage of Yarmuk waters in Lake Tiberias, with but a small storage dam and reservoir at Maqarin.(6)

PRESENT ISRAELI PROJECTS

Since the promulgation of its Seven and Ten Year Plans Israel has proceeded with the diversion of Jordan waters for its own use. The first portion of the project was completed in 1956 with the draingae of the Huleh Lake and the channeling of this water into a canal with a capacity of 80 cubic meters of water per second, thereby conserving 100MCM of water for Israel. Israel built a pipe factory in Magdel to supply the needed pipes for tne project. Subsequently, work was begun on a pumping station at the southwest tip of Lake Tiberias, to pump water into a canal extending to the Besan district, for the irrigation of the Jordan valley in southern Israel.

The key section of Israeli development plans is the diversion of the waters of the upper Jordan and Lake Tiberias to the mid-Negeb. Just as this could be seen to dominate all past Israeli plans, so it is the center of the present efforts. Since the Security Council in 1953 blocked Israel's effort to divert the river through a canal from Gisr Banat Yacub, which would have passed through the demilitarized zone, Israel is planning a new diversion to by-pass this area. This diversion, it is hoped, would be carried out by pumping water from a point on the northwest corner of Lake Tiberias, and conveying it by canal to al-Battauf reservoir, and from there to the Negeb by pipelines.

Israel has thus far completed construction of the canal from Lake Tiberias to al-Battauf reservoir, the reservoir itself, and many sections of the 108 inch pipelines to the Negeb. It has laid much of the pipeline and built two tunnels to carry the water through mountainous regions. The entire project is estimated to carry a total of 320MCM of water from the Jordan River to the Negeb, a distance of 110 to 155 miles.(7)

The first stage of the project involves the laying of pipelines to a point where they would meet the Yarkon-Negeb pipelines of the local scheme and convey additional water through them into the Negeb. This stage would bring 180MCM of Jordan River waters to the Negeb by 1963. Initially intended for completion in 1964, it was shortened as a result of an Israeli cabinet meeting on May 1, 1960, in which funds were allocated for completion in three years.

The whole project is to be completed by 1968. It would involve extension of the main 108 inch pipeline further into the Negeb, the addition of two long 70 inch distribution lines, and the construction of reservoirs and boosters.

Israeli sources have estimated that the most costly item of this Jordan-Negeb project is the pipeline.(8) Consequently, in late 1959, Israel persuaded United States officials to agree to U.S. financing of the pipelines. After the failure of the Johnston Mission, the United States Government had offered to finance local projects that did not conflict with regional plans, and it was in such context that Israel presented its scheme. Such financing, which would have amounted to a sanctioning of Israel's right to unilateral diversion of Jordan waters, brought a sharp reaction from the Government of the United Arab Republic, with the complete support of the other Arab States. The U.A.R. established two committees to study the matter on December 1, 1959, and requested an urgent meeting of the Arab League Council. Subsequently, the United States Government decided not to finance Israel's project. Israel has continued with the project by insisting, in official declarations throughout 1959 and 1960, that it has the right to divert the Jordan without Arab consent and will do so regardless of consequences.

CONCLUSION

The unilateral diversion of the Jordan River by Israel for its own benefit, without the consent of the Arab riparian states and without consideration of Arab economic interests or prior vested rights in water appropriation, is an act that is contrary to international law, is a serious enfringement on Arab legal rights and constitutes a threat to the peace and security of the Middle East.

Unless the United Nations and the international community take concrete and positive actions to prevent Israel's diversion of the Jordan River, the peace of the area will soon be disturbed, for no Arab state will remain aloof to an action by Israel which would deprive the Arab people of their right to continue the utilization of water resources in their territories. It is unlikely that civilized nations will permit the Zionists, who are in illegal possession of the territory of another nation, to proceed by illegal means to seize Arab waters through the diversion of an international river in territories under its de facto control.

The Arabs, in a spirit of conciliation, have carefully considered many regional schemes to develop the Jordan River. These schemes have taken into account water needs in Israeli controlled territory. This is in contrast to Israel's actions of ignoring Arab rights and thereby depriving them of their vital and essential needs. Water is a resource on which depends the survival of most Arab countries, and any Israeli plan to infringe on these rights will entitle the Arabs to exercise the rights of collective defence and self-preservation.

It is to be emphasized that, unlike Israel's diversion plans, present Arab projects are to utilize waters of rivers that flow almost entirely in Arab territories. The effect of these projects will not cause a substantial decrease of waters available in areas under Israeli control. Therefore, Israel is under two limitations which make it insufficient in law to submit any counter complaint against the Arabs for carrying out their small local projects. First, to constitute a valid case for diversion, the effect must be a substantial diversion of waters with resulting substantial injury to other riparians. The second and most important is the fact that Israel cannot maintain any legal action to a court applying international law unless and until it can prove legal title to territories under its actual control. Since Israel's title in its territories is based on the now defunct right of conquest, and is derived from the debatable power and competence of the General Assembly of the United Nations to partition a state contrary to the will of its population, an international tribunal would of necessity reject any Israeli judicial complaint, which must allege legal title.

It is unequivocal, therefore, that the development of Jordan waters is as important as any other aspect of the Palestine question. It is, therefore, a serious error to attempt to ignore it when coping with the deep-rooted controversy. The Palestine question and the disputes that arose from it are one unit and cannot be separated. It cannot be solved piecemeal, but only by squarely facing the entire matter objectively, and bearing in mind always the principles of law and justice.

NOTES
(1) FOREIGN RELATIONS OF THE UNITED STATES: The Paris Peace Conference, 1918, Washington, D.C., 1947, Vol. XII, p. 851.
(2) M. C. Ionides, "The Disputed Waters of the Jordan," MIDDLE EAST JOURNAL, Vol. 7, 1953, p. 157.
(3) James B. Hays, T.V.A. ON THE JORDAN, Washington, D.C., Public Affairs Press, 1948.
(4) Ionides, op. cit. pp. 154-155.
(5) United Nations Relief and Works Agency for Palestine Refugees, SPECIAL REPORT ON JORDAN, Bulletin of Economic Development No. 14, Beirut, 1956, pp. 95-100.
(6) UNRWA, SPECIAL REPORT ON JORDAN, p. 98.
(7) Yehoshua Prushansky, WATER DEVELOPMENT, Israel Today, No. 11, Jerusalem, January, 1960, pp. 24-25.
(8) Ibid., p. 24.

THE ARAB PLAN
TO DIVERT THE HEADWATERS
OF THE RIVER JORDAN

Ministry of Foreign Affairs
(Jerusalem)

The Arab Governments have announced the intention to divert the natural flow of the headwaters of the River Jordan. This intention conflicts with, and undermines, the Unified Water Plan for the utilization of the waters of the Jordan-Yarmuk River System by the four riparian States—Lebanon, Syria, the Kingdom of Jordan, and Israel. The primary aim is to wreck Israel's national water carrier, which has been constructed, and is being operated, on the basis of the Unified plan.

THE UNIFIED WATER PLAN

The Unified Plan was drawn up in 1955 by the late Ambassador Eric Johnston, after lengthy and exhaustive negotiations with the four riparian States. It gave full satisfaction to the specific demands of each of the three Arab States for enough water to meet agricultural and other requirements, and was designed to forestall any conceivable claims, objections or reservations on their part at a later stage. It accepted, without qualification, the highest figures that were put forward in the 'Arab Plan for Development of Water Resources in the Jordan Valley' formulated in 1954 by the Arab League's Technical Committee, namely, up to an annual maximum of 35 million cubic metres for Lebanon from the Hasbani tributary which rises in that territory and of 20 million cubic metres for Syria from the Banias tributary which rises there (THE EGYPTIAN ECONOMIC AND POLITICAL REVIEW, October 1955, pp. 42-44). To the Kingdom of Jordan it allocated from the Jordan-Yarmuk River System the quantity needed to irrigate all of its irrigable area. It left the remainder for Israel.

Although it believed that the three Arab States had each been allocated to an excessive quantity of water, the Government of Israel announced its readiness to accept the Unified Plan. The Arab Governments had accepted it on the technical level, but the Arab League, meeting in Cairo in October 1955, deferred consideration and thus withheld formal approval, on the ground that the Plan would also benefit Israel.

The course of events has been described by President Eisenhower and Ambassador Johnston. President Eisenhower's report to the United States Congress for 1955 says:

> From the middle of August to the middle of October, Ambassador Johnston was again in the Near East for further negotiations. By their end, all the major technical problems of an over-all plan appeared to have been resolved satisfactorily. Under the plan that evolved, approximately sixty percent of the water of the Jordan River system (which includes the Yarmuk that empties into it) was to be allocated to Lebanon, Syria and Jordan and the remaining forty percent to Israel... At the end of Ambassador Johnston's second visit to the area in 1955, only formal political concurrence on the plan remained to be obtained.

Ambassador Johnston wrote:

> A comprehensive plan for the Jordan Valley is already in being. Its technical aspects have been approved by the Arab States and Israel. All that it lacks is the political go-ahead signal. (NEW YORK TIMES MAGAZINE, 10 August 1958)

The sequence, then, was this: a Unified Water Plan, worked out on the basis of proposals from the Arabs and from Israel, was accepted by the technical experts of the Arab League and, individually, by the Governments of Lebanon, Syria, Jordan and Egypt. It was an acceptance in detail, and specifically in respect of the quantity to go to each riparian State.

The Government of Israel also agreed. But the Political Committee of the Arab League deferred its formal approval. This deferment, based as it was on purely political grounds, in no way affects the international validity of the Plan as the equitable division of the waters of the Jordan-Yarmuk River System between the riparian States. Since then, ten years have passed.

Development in the riparian States which depends on irrigation from the Jordan-Yarmuk River System could not be held up indefinitely simply because political agreement was lacking. Syria and Lebanon are taking supplies from the headwaters. The Kingdom of Jordan has diverted the River Yarmuk through the East Ghor canal. Israel is operating the Lake Kinneret-Negev project. Thus, in effect, the Unified Plan is being carried out by a series of unilateral actions. Israel, all along, has affirmed that it is ready to cooperate with the three other riparian States to ensure the fullest efficacy of the Plan. This offer remains unanswered and now the three States proclaim that they mean to circumvent the Unified Plan, and wreck Israel's national water project, by diverting the Jordan headwaters.

At two Arab Summit meetings, one in Cairo in January 1964, the other in Alexandria in the following September, Israel's right to its share of the waters of the Jordan-Yarmuk River System was challenged. Different Arab States sent Foreign Ministers and other emissaries to canvass support in many capitals. The envoys met with little or no success.

Disappointed in this global diplomatic manoeuvring to knock the props from under the Unified Water Plan and now left to their own devices, the Arab Governments set to the planning and execution of a diversion which would radically contract the flow of River Jordan water to Israel.

WHAT IS THE ARAB DIVERSION?

The River Jordan proper is formed by the confluence of three main headwaters, the River Dan which rises in Israel, and the Rivers Hasbani and Banias which rise in Lebanon and Syria respectively, the Banias at a point only a few hundred yards from the Israel frontier. Their flows unite in the north of Israel. The River Jordan then continues southward through Lake Kinneret (Sea of Galilee, Lake Tiberias), situated entirely within Israel territory, and passes from Israel into the Kingdom of Jordan. The Arab diversion is meant to stop the headwaters from flowing in their natural channels to Israel. The main features, reported in the Cairo daily, EL-GUMHOURIA, of 24 October 1964, are as follows.

Lebanon is to take up some 90 million cubic metres of water from the Upper Hasbani, of which 40-60 million cubic metres are to be diverted to the River Litani and 20-30 million cubic metres to Wadi S'rid, thence to the Banias in Syria and on to the River Yarmuk in the Kingdom of Jordan. Sixteen million cubic metres from the Wazzani Springs, on the Lower Hasbani, are to be allocated for local use, and the remainder, 30-35 million cubic metres, will be diverted to the projected Banias-Yarmuk canal. Of the waters of the Banias itself, 110 million cubic metres are to be diverted to the Yarmuk, in that way associating the Kingdom of Jordan with the diversion.

In place of the 35 million cubic metres which Lebanon was allotted under the Unified Water Plan and 20 million cubic metres similarly assigned to Syria, the threat is now to withdraw 220-250 million cubic metres from the headwaters in Lebanon and Syria.

It is a 'spite' diversion. It has aggressive intent. It is a deliberate violation of the Unified Water Plan. Under the Unified Plan, all the waters of the Hasbani and the Banias as they flow southward are available to Israel except to the extent required to irrigate lands adjacent to those two rivers and up to the maximum specified quantities (Hasbani—35 million cubic metres for adjacent irrigation in Lebanon; Banias—20 million cubic metres for adjacent irrigation in Syria). Equitable apportionment is a general principle for the allocation of the waters of river systems that are of concern to more than one State. The equitable apportionment of the Jordan-Yarmuk River System upon which the Unified Plan rests is, then, as is usual in such cases, based upon the established needs of each of the four riparian States, Syria, Lebanon, the Kingdom of Jordan, and Israel. The needs were established in the light of data which each Government had furnished as to the availability of its water resources and the requirements of its irrigable areas. It was after those data had been checked independently, and the negotiations described had been conducted, that the equitable apportionment materialized in the Unified Plan. No riparian State may take more than its share without the consent of all the riparian States. No riparian State may, without the consent of all the riparian States, transfer to any other State water which had been allocated to it for a specific requirement or locality of its own, and, by so doing, unilaterally alter the type, or place, of use of any water thus equitably apportioned to it. But that is precisely what the Arabs now intend to do—each State exceeding its share and each transferring water to another State—by means of joint works of diversion from the Hasbani in Lebanon to the Banias in Syria and from there to the Yarmuk in the Kingdom of Jordan.

The diversion would rob the villages in the northern Hula district of the waters of the Hasbani and the Banias which they have been using for centuries. As ancient canals and their ancient names still testify, those waters have been their principal source of irrigation for hundreds of years.

But what is even more serious: the effect of the diversion on Israel would be to diminish, by at least a third, the supply of water to its Lake Kinneret-Negev water project, to cut off the sweet waters of the River Jordan's tributaries, and to add heavily to the salinity of the Lake, which is the intake point of the project, thereby rendering its waters largely unfit for irrigation.

ISRAEL ALREADY USING ALMOST ALL OF ITS WATER RESOURCES

Israel has no margins of water, and, with the national water carrier in full operation, will be using about ninety percent of its total resources. Seventy percent had been in use before the Lake Kinneret-Negev water project began to operate in June 1964. The project has turned to account most of the remainder, but, even so, the annual average of all of Israel's resources is only enough to irrigate forty percent of its arable area.

Israel, as a voluntary measure of good administration, has instituted a strict internal water regime as one means of securing the fullest effective application of its water potential and to prevent waste.

In an endeavour to supplement its limited resources, Israel is also undertaking long-term and diversified research into non-conventional methods of producing sweet waters and, in particular, into the possibilities of desalting sea-water. But the undertaking is circumscribed both by cost and by the quantity of sweet water it will yield: it may help to alleviate shortages, it may add to the natural flow guaranteed to Israel under the Unified Plan, but it will never be a substitute for the flow.

DIVERSION PLAN IS UNRELATED
TO INTRINSIC ARAB WATER NEEDS

Neither Lebanon nor Syria had practical plans for any extensive use of the Hasbani and Banias tributaries beyond the allocations of the Unified Plan until the Arab Governments resolved to exploit their waters as a weapon against Israel. This is proof that the diversion has no genuine relation to established or traditional Arab needs for water. All irrigation plans for southern Lebanon have turned, in the first instance, on utilizing the River Litani with its annual flow of 850 million cubic metres, of which, to this day, most runs to waste into the Mediterranean. Now, a good deal of the flow of the Upper Hasbani is to be wasted as well.

Lebanon has ample water for irrigation; arable land, not water, has always been the factor limiting the development of Lebanese agriculture. So much so, indeed, that a survey made in 1949 for the United Nations (Gordon Clapp Mission) mentions the possibility of transferring surplus water from the Litani to Israel.

'The Arab Plan for Development of Water Resources in the Jordan Valley', as stated, put the highest quantities that could be effectively taken from the two tributaries for local purposes at 35 million cubic metres from the Hasbani in Lebanon and at 20 million cubic metres from the Banias in Syria. Both figures were accepted in the Unified Plan.

AGGRESSION AGAINST ISRAEL IS THE ULTIMATE TARGET

The concern of the Arab Governments is not more water for Lebanon, Syria and the Kingdom of Jordan, but less water for Israel. This was frankly admitted by President Nasser in an interview with the editor of an Indian magazine which was broadcast by Radio Cairo on 7 February 1964, after the first Summit meeting: "We are now preparing, with all the means at our disposal, to take steps to foil Israel's project . . . What we are concerned with is not to allow them to strengthen themselves."

On 9 January 1965, Nur-ed-Din Atassi, Deputy Chairman of the Syrian Presidential Council, was reported by the Italian News Agency, ANSA, as saying: "Syria is pursuing, without respite, the implementation of the plans conceived to prevent Israel's domination over the Arab waters of the Jordan. Syria will not neglect any measure designed to give effect to the Arab plan which has as its purpose the elimination of the Number One enemy of the Arabs — Israel."

In a press conference in Beirut on 13 November 1964, Salim Lachud, of the Lebanese Parliament, stated: "The problem of the diversion of the River Jordan can brook no further delay — Israel will exist until it is eliminated by the Arabs, and every means should be employed towards this end, including the water problem which is decisive to Israel . . . Israel is actively engaged in exploiting the water and in so doing assures its survival." (ES-SAFA, Lebanon, 14 November 1964)

Dr. Muhammed Ahmed Selim, Chairman of the River Jordan Arab Technical Committee, said: "The Arab plan to divert the River Jordan's headwaters constitutes the guarantee that the basic purpose of the Jewish scheme to irrigate the Negev will be foiled." (EL-MANAR, Jordan, 3 January 1964)

The underlying aim of the diversion was broadcast by Radio Damascus on 19 January 1964: 'The diversion of the Jordan constitutes, basically, one stage of the decisive deeds for the liberation of Palestine.'

One military instrument of this design is the Unified Arab Command which was created, simultaneously with the design, in the Summit conferences. Its primary objective was declared to be 'to provide definite protection to the diversion project against attacks, sabotage and obstacles' (AL-AHRAM, Cairo, 8 September 1964). The ultimate objective was proclaimed by President Nasser in his address to the second conference:

> The target is to liquidate Israel and uproot it completely and decisively. With this target in mind, the UAR has been seeking to achieve superiority over Israel in respect of land, sea and air force. There are two aims along the course towards this target, namely, to strengthen Arab defence and to place the coordinated Arab force in the right position to embark on achieving the ultimate target. (Radio Cairo, 8 September 1964)

Lebanon has not concealed its misgivings at being chosen to be the first to start the diversion. Nevertheless, at a meeting of Arab Prime Ministers in Cairo in January 1965, the Lebanese delegation acquiesced under pressure, but subject to parliamentary approval. In secret session on 21 January, the Lebanese Parliament confirmed the acquiescence, on condition the foreign troops of the Unified Arab Command would only be allowed to enter Lebanon if specifically authorized by the Council of Ministers.

In Syria, levelling operations have already begun to the north and south of the Banias tributary, which would seem to be a preliminary to the digging of diversionary canals. The Syrian daily, EL-BAATH, wrote on 21 December 1964:

> Fauzi el-Habbaz, Director of Public Works and head of the Syrian delegation on the River Jordan Exploitation Authority, reported on the diversion works being implemented in Syria. He stated that work is continuing on the canal which will join the Banias with the Hasbani. The

canal's length will be eight kilometres and it is being constructed to divert the Hasbani to the Banias.

The diversion of the Jordan headwaters is not only an act of political hostility towards Israel. It is an act of physical aggression. In this connection there is relevance in a statement by Charles Ammoun of Lebanon in the Sixth (Legal) Committee of the General Assembly of the United Nations on 14 January 1952. The question of defining aggression was then under debate. Criticizing a draft Soviet definition, Ammoun said that it failed to mention such concrete cases as 'the possibility that a State . . . might alter (a stream's) course so that the neighbouring country suffered hunger and thirst.' (Official Records of the General Assembly, 6th session, Sixth Committee, p. 202, Paragraph 27.)

The Arabs themselves make no secret of this: 'Denying Israel the waters of the Jordan means that the Arabs have gone over from defence to attack. The diversion of the Jordan is basically the start of serious action for the liberation of Palestine.' (Radio Damascus, 19 January 1964).

Prime Minister Levi Eshkol made Israel's position clear in the Knesset on 16 January 1965: 'Any attempt to deprive Israel of its just share of the Jordan River system under the Unified Water Plan will be considered an encroachment on our borders.'

ISRAEL'S POSITION

Israel has, from the outset, sought the cooperation of the other riparian States to ensure the most effective application of the Unified Plan to the benefit of all concerned. Israel's project is, in any case, so designed that it can, at any time, be incorporated into a regional project, whenever the Arabs are prepared to cooperate in one.

In constructiong its own national carrier, Israel has publicly undertaken to remain within the limits of the allocations of the Plan. Prime Minister Levi Eshkol told the Knesset on 20 January 1964: 'We have undertaken to remain within the framework of the quantities specified in the Unified Plan — and we shall honour this undertaking.'

Israel has, however, made it plain that it will oppose unilateral and illegal measures by the Arab Governments and will take all appropriate action to protect its vital water rights and interests.

The diversion is illegal and violates the Unified Water Plan which constitutes an accepted and equitable division of the waters of the Jordan-Yarmuk River System among the four riparian States — Lebanon, Syria, the Kingdom of Jordan, and Israel.

The diversion has no relevance to the established and intrinsic water needs of the Arab riparian States. The scheme has been conceived in unreasoning hostility and not in sober economics.

The sole purpose of the diversion is to harm Israel by curtailing the flow of the River Jordan to Israel and so wreck Israel's national water carrier.

Precisely because of its manifestly belligerent and destructive character, the Arab plan of diversion has been rejected by enlightened public opinion throughout the world. More and more, Governments and public opinion are realizing that what the Arab States are planning has no connection with water but only has meaning in the context of their denial of Israel's right to exist and of their aggressive designs.

Israel hopes that water will once again become a source not of strife and misery but of peace and blessing in the Middle East.

VIII. Freedom of Navigation

INTRODUCTION

In addition to the utilization of the Jordan River, another outstanding Arab-Israeli issue concerning water involves the freedom of navigation through the Gulf of Aqaba and the Suez Canal. Freedom of navigation was clearly one of the major contributing causes for two out of the three wars that have been fought between the Arabs and Israelis.

Involved in the Gulf of Aqaba are the four littoral states — Egypt, Jordan, Saudi Arabia and Israel. Since each of these states claims only a strip of the 98 miles along the Gulf as territorial waters, the remaining part of the Gulf is considered high seas. At the entrance to the waterway, on the other hand, where it narrows to a width of about six miles, the uninhabited islands of Tiran and Sanafir are entirely included within the territorial waters of Egypt and Saudi Arabia, respectively.

Egypt erected military installations on these islands, as well as on Sharm-el-Sheik on the Egyptian owned Sinai coast opposite them. Using these military posts at the mouth of the Gulf, Egypt excluded Israeli naval traffic and Israel-bound shipping of other nations between 1951 and 1956. Egypt justified these activities on the ground that the Gulf constituted "Arab historic waters" and that there was no international agreement to which Egypt was a party declaring it otherwise. Furthermore, Egypt was technically at war with Israel and therefore obliged to take all measures to defend its security, including a blockade in the Gulf.

Israel, on the other hand, asserts that the Gulf of Aqaba represents its sole outlet to certain parts of the world with which it maintains commercial relations. One of Israel's major objectives in the 1956 Sinai War was therefore to break the maritime blockade of the Gulf and gain control of the Straits of Tiran and the western coast of the Gulf so that navigation to and from Eilat, Israel's most southern port, could resume.

Early in 1957, Israel withdrew her forces from the captured territory after receiving assurances from the U. N. and several maritime powers that they would uphold the international status of the waterway and the freedom of navigation in the Gulf. With the posting of the U. N. Emergency Force (UNEF) at Sharm-el-Sheikh, maritime traffic in the waterway resumed without interference. After a ten year lapse, Egypt, in May 1967, demanded and secured the removal of UNEF and once again announced the closure of the Gulf to Israel-bound shipping. This act was one of the principal factors in precipitating Israel's military action the following month. As a result, Israeli troops are once again in control of the entrance to the waterway, and international maritime traffic has resumed.

The legal and political roots of the Gulf of Aqaba conflict are analyzed in two selections. The Arab position is stated in an excerpt from THE PALESTINE QUESTION published in Beirut by the Institute for Palestine Studies in 1968. The Israeli view is presented in an excerpt from a Ministry for Foreign Affairs document on "Egypt's Unlawful Blockade of the Gulf of Aqaba" published in Jerusalem and not dated.

The second navigational problem relates to the Suez Canal. Although all the Arab States are directly or indirectly involved in the Middle East conflict, it is only Egypt as the abutting state which plays a unique role vis-a-vis maritime traffic in the Suez. In instituting a blockade upon navigation through the Canal in 1950, Egypt justified its restrictions by the state of war with Israel and her right of self-preservation under international law.

Although the U. N., at the requrest of Israel in 1951, rejected Egypt's claim and urged it not to interfere with international navigation through the Canal, Egypt ignored the Security Council's resolution by stopping and confiscating Israeli-bound cargo. In the summer of 1956, Egypt nationalized the Canal, formerly controlled by an international corporation authorized by the Constantinople Convention of 1888. In October of 1956, Israeli forces occupied Sinai, while British and French units invaded the western bank of the Suez Canal Zone. Egypt countered by sinking a number of ships to block the Canal.

In March, 1957, Israel withdrew from Sinai and the Canal after obtaining international pledges that navigation through the Suez would not be restricted. Subsequently, Egypt cleared up the Canal, but continued to keep it closed to Israeli ships, although for almost two years it refrained from interfering with maritime navigation of other nations carrying Israeli goods. As a consequence of the 1967 War, the Canal is once more clogged, and the question of free passage for all nationas, including Israel, is deadlocked.

An Arab perspective on Suez is contained in Cherif Bassiouni's "Some Legal Aspects of the Arab-Israeli Conflict," published in Beirut by the Palestinian Liberation Organization Research Center in August, 1969. The Israeli viewpoint is given in "Egypt and the Suez Canal" published in Jerusalem by the Ministry for Foreign Affairs in June, 1959.

THE GULF OF AQABA
AND
THE STRAITS OF TIRAN

Institute for Palestine Studies

Israel has regarded the ban imposed on the passage of her ships(1) through the Straits of Tiran and the Gulf of Aqaba as a "casus belli."

In fact, Israel's right of passage does not exist and has never existed; for international law could only be invoked by the Zionists if they were riparians of the Gulf of Aqaba or if these waters (those of the Gulf and of the Straits) were waterways for international navigation.

In the case in question neither of these two conditions is met.

The Partition resolution which gave the Negev to the "Jewish State" cannot constitute a legal title in favour of Israel. This resolution is in fact null and void; what is more, it has neither been accepted nor applied by the Zionists themselves, who have only observed the part that suited them, i.e., the principle of the creation of a State. The remainder they have disregarded, resorting to force in breach of the U. N. resolutions regarding the truce and of the Armistice Agreements concluded with the Arab States.

The Security Council has sought, by various resolutions, to check the invasion by Israeli forces of "territories which were respectively under Egyptian and Jordanian sovereignty."(2) The resolution of 4 November 1948 obliges Israel to withdraw those of its "forces which have advanced beyond the positions held on 14 October, 1948."(3) The United Nations mediator was authorised "to establish provisional lines beyond which no movement of troops shall take place."(4) Despite this clear obligation Israel resumed its advance in the same region of the Negev, and the Security Council was forced to intervene once more to reaffirm its previous resolution which the Zionists had not obeyed. According to this fourth resolution,(5) the Governments concerned were to implement, without further delay, the instructions issued by the Acting Mediator, "these instructions making it imperative upon Israel to withdraw its troops from the positions which they had occupied after 14 October."

However, Israel did not see fit to submit either to this or to other resolutions; her military action did not come to a halt, and then only temporarily, until March 1949, when her forces had reached the shores of the

Gulf of Aqaba.

But before this date, another event had occurred which aggravated the illegality of the Israeli action: the Israeli-Egyptian Armistice Agreement signed in Rhodes on 24 February 1949.(6)

That the occupation of the coast, and particularly of the village of Umm Rashrash, where the port of Elath was later established, came after the conclusion of the Armistice, is beyond a shadow of doubt.(7) Besides, the Israelis themselves do not deny this fact: one of their commanders in Aqaba stated that Israel had violated the Armistice in order to secure an outlet on the Red Sea through the Gulf of Aqaba.

It is hardly worth pointing out that the Armistice Agreement expressly prohibited the resumption of hostilities;(8) this, indeed, was its sole raison d'être.

It is true that, unlike that with Egypt, the Armistice with Jordan was signed after the occupation of the coast by Israel. But there is nothing in the text of this agreement, or in the appended map, which indicates or implies that Jordan accepted the situation which had been created by violations of the truce.

Nor does the conduct of Jordan and of Egypt after the signature of the Armistice Agreements give any indication that they accepted the situation. As we have already seen, not only did recognition of Israel by the Arabs never come about, but, what is more, their relations contunue to be characterized by a state of war.

If, therefore, hostilities are, in principle, suspended between the parties — but history has proved that the opposite is the case — Israel's acquisitions remain without any foundation in law.

It is, of course, clear that the succession of events leaves no doubt as to the illegality of this sudden invasion by Israel of the Gulf of Aqaba, and it is hardly necessary to emphasise the elementary point that an illegality, far from creating a right, actually pledges the responsibility of the party committing the illegality. For, on the one hand, the Security Council, which cannot possibly be regarded as suspect by the Zionists, explicitly stated, in its resolution of 19 August 1948, that "no party is entitled to gain military or political advantage through violation of the truce."(9)

On the other hand, the Armistice Agreements, which were imposed on the Arab States by the Security Council,(10) to the advantage of Israel, and which were signed by the latter, clearly show that not only do the parties "recognize the principle that no military or political advantage should be gained under the truce ordered by the Security Council . . .,"(11) but that their very existence cannot be invoked as a basis for any right whatsoever at the time of the final settlement of the Palestine question.

"As a de facto occupation occurring during the period of the cease-fire, and notwithstanding the formal provisions of the Armistice Agreement, it cannot be converted, in law, into territorial sovereignty in favour of the belligerent State, and, still less, result in an annexation pure and simple, such as the annexation of the Negev to the State of Israel."(12)

This "State" cannot, therefore, avail itself of any alleged right of riparianship on any part of the Gulf of Aqaba. Juridically, it is a third party whose very existence is a constant threat to the security of neighbouring States.

The principle of freedom is the dominant feature of international law concerning the high seas. But from the first, with a view to safeguarding this freedom, a right of sovereignty was recognised for States over certain waters, or parts thereof, which wash their territories.

The Gulf of Aqaba, which is a sort of closed sea 95 miles long and from 7 to 14 miles wide, washing the territories of three Arab States, is "blocked" at the end by the islands of Tiran and Sanafir, Egyptian and Saudi Arabian territory respectively. There can be no doubt that it is not subject to this principle of freedom, because it does not in any way form part of the high seas. Its waters are internal and, therefore, national waters, whether we take into consideration the rules of international law relating to historic bays, or those relating to the determination of the base line of the territorial sea.

The problem of the width of territorial waters gives rise to another problem — that of the base line, i.e., of the starting point for the measurement of the territorial sea. On the occasion of the conflict between Great Britain and Norway, the International Court of Justice enunciated the rules applicable in that case.(13) The 1958 Convention on the Territorial Sea and Adjacent Zone sanctioned the solution worked out by the Court.

According to the terms of Article 3 of this Convention "the base line follows the line of the lowest ebb-tide along the coast." However, it is not always easy to put this rule into application and often "geographical realities dictate the solution" that must be adopted in each case.(14) In fact, the method applied "consists in choosing points along the lowest ebb-tide line and joining them by straight lines; this method is especially applicable in the case of well-defined bays."(15) The Geneva Convention has adopted this rule.

However, as regards bays, the problem has been to determine the length of the opening which permitted a State to draw a straight line serving as a base line for its territorial sea. Early arbitral sentences considered that this opening should not exceed ten nautical miles;(16) but the Court has held that "the ten-mile rule has not acquired the authority of a rule of international law."(17) The Geneva Convention has definitely settled this question by stipulating in its Article 7, that "if the distance between the lowest ebb-tide lines of the natural points of entry to a bay does not exceed 24 miles, a demarcation line can be drawn between these two lowest ebb-tide lines, and the waters thus enclosed are considered as internal waters."

This provision of the Convention applies very precisely to the Gulf of Aqaba, for to penetrate therein from the Red Sea the only opening is that of the Straits of Tiran, barely four miles in width, between Ras an-Nasrani, a promontory on the Sinai peninsula to the east, and the Island of Tiran on the west, both belonging to Egypt.

The fact that there are three States on the Gulf of Aqaba does not in any way alter this situation, particularly as the three States are taking joint action to claim the same right.(18)

To show the historic nature of the Gulf of Aqaba, it is not necessary to repudiate the international law drawn up by the West to suit its own interests. The Arab states could, quite legitimately, refer to Moslem Law to determine the rules applicable to their relations with other nations. For, even if modern international law often has its roots in "the prescriptions and practices of Islam,"(19) it differs from Islamic law in particular as regards the concept of the State in Islamic countries.

According to this law, "the Moslem State cannot, in theory be anything but a unitary State."(20) If one takes one's stand on this law, the following will be the conclusion: the Gulf of Aqaba, located as it is entirely within one State, incontestably forms part of the territory of that State.(21) In other words, one can say that the Gulf has a national character, and this conclusion exactly corresponds to reality.

But modern international law which, with certain adaptations, tends to become universal, provides the Arab countries with sufficient juridical means to arrive at the same final result. The fact that there are three States on the shores of the Gulf of Aqaba does not constitute an obstacle to the recognition of its historic nature.(22) All this is quite obvious and it will, therefore, not be necessary to dwell on it any further.

As for the conditions which must be met in order to create historic title, it is generally admitted that three factors must be taken into consideration: 1. The authority exercised over this area by the State claiming historic title; 2. Continuity in the exercise of this title; and 3. Attitude of other States.(23)

However, in the opinion of certain writers, it is only necessary to establish whether the claim is justified by economic necessity, national security, vital interest or other considerations.

In the case under consideration all these conditions are amply fulfilled.

The riparian Arab States exercise rights of sovereignty over the whole stretch of the waters of the Gulf. While publicists are of the opinion that "as regards the nature of appropriation acts, it is difficult to be very specific about their characteristics," they are certain that the "exclusion of foreign ships or their subjection to the laws of the riparian State . . . would clearly be acts fully indicative of the will of the State."(24) Such acts have taken place in the Gulf of Aqaba: in 1951, a British ship carrying goods for Israel was intercepted in the Gulf by Egyptian forces.

The States concerned maintain military forces for the purpose of keeping watch over the coast; Egyptian and Saudi troops are permanently stationed on the islands of Tiran and Sanafir to ensure control over the entrance to the Gulf.

Finally, the Arab States exercise legislative and police powers over this part of their territory. An example is provided by Egyptian Circular No. 39/1950, of 21 December 1950, which stipulates that the part of the waters lying to the west of the line between Ras Muhammad and Ras an-Nasrani is closed to navigation.(25) For these are acts which provide undoubted evidence of the effective sovereignty of these States over these waters.(26)

This sovereignty has been exercised continuously; as far back in history as one wishes to go, one always finds authority being effectively exercised over the area. As early as the first days of Islam, a treaty concluded with the Christians with regard to the port of Aqaba imposed upon them "the payment of the *jizya* and expressly put their ships under the protection of Islam."(27) It can thus safely be said that "the Gulf of Ayla (now Aqaba) and the Red Sea were, already at that time, an Arab sea held by one party, hermetically closed, through which plied Moslem ships exclusively.(28)

History has not changed this situation. When the Ottoman Empire established itself in the region, it became, with the Pasha of Egypt, co-successor to Arab sovereignty. At the end of the First World War, which led to the final disappearance of this Empire, Great Britain extended her occupation to the shores of the Gulf.

Since their independence, the present Arab States have succeeded to the authority which had always been exercised either by the Moslem State itself or on its behalf.

The third condition raises the problem of the acquiescence of foreign States in the exercise of sovereignty by the riparian State or States over waters which are claimed to be historic. Publicists are unanimous in regarding this condition fulfilled when other States refrain from expressing their opposition.(29) Thus, the absence of any reaction by foreign States is sufficient to confer historic character on a bay.(30) In fact, proof of international acquiescence is established by long use.(31)

This opinion has been sanctioned by court decisions, according to which "public knowledge of the facts, general acquiescence by the international community . . . would in any case enable Norway to oppose its system to the United Kingdom."(32)

The mere fact that "acquiescence" by foreign States is not absolutely general, does not constitute sufficient reason to deny historic title to the State claiming it.(33) For, generally, the problem of such a claim only arises in cases of dispute, i.e., when a foreign State, with good reason, declares its opposition.

In the case of the Gulf of Aqaba, the only opposition has come from Israel and the United States.(34) Israel's opposition is inoperative because it emanates from an entity which the Arab States have never recognised as a State, and which has been imposed upon them by force. Opposition by the United States has been of a purely political nature and cannot be taken into consideration by the jurist; it is rather a manifestation of hostility towards Egypt than concern by the United States for the safeguarding of a legitimate interest.

Publicists have adopted different views about these oppositions. Gidel, the great master on the law of the sea, writes: "Oppositions cannot all be put on the same level without making a distinction as to their nature, to the geographic or other situation of the State from which they emanate.(35) And this opinion is rightly considered as "wise and realistic."

On the other hand, but following the same line of reasoning, acquiescence on the part of a State having real navigational interests in the waters under consideration, can have decisive importance. Thus, acquiescence by Great Britain in a letter recognising Egypt's right to visit foreign ships in the Gulf,(36) offset American opposition considerably.

There can be no doubt that the three conditions generally required for the establishment of historic title are fully met in the case of the gulf of Aqaba. But there is another view which holds that historic character can exist, not only on the basis of the factors discussed above, but "on the basis of other particular circumstances, such as geographical configuration, requirements of national defense, or other vital interests of the riparian State."(37) This is not an isolated doctrine; on the contrary, it has been advanced or supported by governments in attempts to codify international law; it is clearly and unequivocally enunciated; Article 7 of the draft International Convention submitted to the Conference held in Buenos Aires in 1922 by the International Law Association defined it as follows:

> The State can include within the limits of its territorial sea estuaries, gulfs, bays or parts of the contiguous sea over which its jurisdiction has been confirmed by continuous and age-old use, or, in default of these precedents, in case such jurisdiction is absolutely necessary according to the concept of Article 2, to guarantee defence and neutrality and to ensure navigational and coastal maritime police services in all their forms.(38)

This criterion of the vital interest of the riparian State, on which historic title is based, was also reaffirmed by the declarations of certain governments at the 1930 Hague Conference.(39)

But in the case of the Gulf of Aqaba, no one has yet been able to deny the interest of the Arab States without committing a serious offence against history and reality. The need to safeguard territorial security is all too evident, as has been shown on several occasions by the behaviour of Israel. Moreover, the riparian States can quite legitimately claim exclusive rights over the riches of the sea in this region.

In view of the above it is clear that the Gulf of Aqaba very definitely has the characteristics of a historic gulf. Hence, all its waters are internal water, the use of which the adjacent State may withhold from the other members of the international community, and this includes the sub-soil, the soil, the body and surface of the water and the air above."(40)

Straits are natural passageways between two seas. To be considered as a strait, such passageway must not be wider than double the width of the territorial sea. If the strait does not connect two parts of the high seas, no obligation is imposed by international law to open it to international navigation.(41) But if the strait links two parts of the high seas, international custom imposes the obligation to open it to international navigation, even if it is located in the territory of one State only.

This principle was expressly confirmed by the decision of the International Court of Justice in the Corfou Strait Case. The court stated that, by general admission, and in accordance with international custom, States have the right, in time of peace, to sail their warships through straits which are used for international navigation for communication between two parts of the high seas, without securing prior authorisation from the riparian State, on condition that such passage be innocent.(42) Article 16, paragraph 4, of the Geneva Convention, does not restrict the right of passage to straits connecting two parts of the high seas and assigned to international navigation; it extends it to cover straits connecting the high seas with the territorial waters of a third party state.(43)

But even thus modified, the text of the law is not applicable to the Straits of Tiran, for the latter do not connect the Red Sea with allegedly Israeli territorial waters.(44) Indeed, a ship proceeding towards Elath must travel over 95 miles of Arab internal waters, after passing through the Straits, before reaching its destination.

On the other hand, it is an established fact in international custom that States have the right, in time of war, to exercise control over ships transiting such straits if they are located in their territory.(45) Similarly, they can refuse passage through such straits to enemy ships, and to those transporting contraband goods to the enemy, even after the conclusion of an armistice.(46)

Thus the Montreux Convention of 1936, relating to the regulation of navigation in the Bosphorus and the Dardanelles, explicitly recognised the right of Turkey, should she find herself in a state of war or under the threat of war, to make passage through the straits subject to her own free will. She was also to have the right to build fortifications there.

Moreover, during both World Wars, England constantly insisted on exercising control not only over the Straits of Gibraltar, but also over the Straits of Magellan in South America.

Again, very recently, the Soviet Union objected to the passage of two American ice-breakers through the Straits of Kara and Vilkitsky in the Arctic Ocean, each of which is 40 kilometres wide. The Soviet Union made it known that these Straits formed part of Soviet territorial waters, and that the passage of the two ice-breakers would constitute a frontier violation.(47)

Thus, the Straits of Tiran cannot be considered as a waterway for international navigation, because they connect the Egyptian territorial sea with the internal waters of Arab states acting jointly. Due to this fact, and quite apart from a state of war, Israel cannot claim right of passage through the Straits.

NOTES

(1) To Israeli ships we should add ships owned by third parties carrying goods for Israel.

(2) Ed. Rabbath, MER ROUGE ET GOLFE D' AKABA DANS L'EVOLUTION DU DROIT INTERNATIONAL, Beirut, p. 57.

(3) This resolution reaffirms those of 15 July and 19 August 1948, imposing the truce and denying all legal effect to violations thereof.

(4) Quoted by Ed. Rabbath, op. cit., p. 57.

(5) Resolution of 29 December 1948.

(6) Israel's violation of the Armistice came after other indisputable violations of Security Council resolutions.

(7) Cf. The telegram sent on 22 March 1949 by the President of the Security Council to the United Nations Mediator.

(8) Article 1, paragraph 2, of the Egyptian-Israeli Armistice Agreement stipulates that: "No aggressive action by the armed forces — land, sea, or air — of either Party shall be undertaken, planned or threatened against the people or the armed forces of the other."

(9) Quoted by Ed. Rabbath, op. cit., p. 57.

(10) A. Gervais: LES ARMISTICES PALESTINIENS, A.F.D.I., 1956, p. 17 sqq.

(11) Article 4, paragraph 1, of the Egyptian-Israeli Armistice Agreement. This provision alone is sufficient to deprive the occupation of the coast of all semblance of legality, even if such occupation had occurred before the signature of the armistice agreements.

(12) Ed. Rabbath, op. cit., p. 58.

(13) International Court of Justice: AFFAIRES DE PECHERIES, 18 December 1951, Recueil, p. 116 sqq.

(14) I.C.J., op. cit., p. 128.

(15) I.C.J., op. cit., p. 129-130.

(16) Mme Bastid, COURS DE DROIT INTERNATIONAL PUBLIC, 1964-65, p. 602.

(17) I.C.J., op. cit., p. 131.

(18) ANNUAIRE DE LA COMMISSION DU DROIT INTERNATIONAL DE L'ONU, 1962, Vol. II, p. 24.

(19) Baron de Toube, RECUEIL DES COURS DE L'ACADEMIE DE DROIT INTERNATIONAL, 1926, vol. I, p. 380 sqq.

(20) "The unity of the Moslem *Umma* is a basic postulate of the theory of the Moslem State." (Ed. Rabbath, op. cit., p. 43.)

(21) This solution applies to gulfs whose opening on the high seas does not exceed a width which, though not precisely determined, can certainly be up to 24 miles (Geneva Convention on the Territorial Sea and Adjacent Zone, art. 7) V. Bouchez: THE REGIME OF BAYS IN INTERNATIONAL LAW, Leyden, 1964, p. 16 sqq.

(22) YEARBOOK OF THE U. N. INTERNATIONAL LAW COMMISSION, 1962, vol. II, p. 24 (Fr. edit.) "It does not appear that the existence of several riparian States to any considerable extent modifies the conditions required for the formation of a historic title." Cf. also Madame Bastid, COURS DE DROIT INTERNATIONAL PUBLIC, 1964-65, p. 602, who asserts that "when there are several riparians on the bay the waters will be shared; there is, therefore, a delimitation in the internal waters and Article 12 of the Convention (on the territorial sea) contains fairly precise provisions on this point." Court decisions have also sanctioned this point. See Central American Court of Justice, decision

of 9 March 1917 rendered in the case of the Gulf of Fonseca, reported in MEMORANDUM OF HISTORIC BAYS, prepared by the U. N. Secretariat (Doc. A/Conf. 12/1), OFFICIAL DOCUMENTS OF THE U. N. CONFERENCE ON THE LAW OF THE SEA, Vol. I, p. 8 sqq.

(23) Yearbook of the I.L.C., op. cit., p. 15 (French edit.)

(24) Gidel: LE DROIT INTERNATIONAL DE LA MER, Vol. III, p. 633, quoted in the Yearbook of the I.L.C., 1962, II. p. 17 (French edition), similar view by Bourquin: BAIES HISTORIQUES IN MELANGES GEORGES SAU-SER-HALL, 1952, p. 43.

(25) This circular was sent to all navigation companies and consulates which were at that time in Egypt.

(26) Draft convention prepared for the Hague Conference of 1930, for the codification of international law, in Bustamante: LA MER TERRITORIALE, 1930, p. 257. See also United Nations Memorandum on HISTORIC BAYS (A/Con./13-1), p. 14, for an identical provision embodied in the draft submitted in 1933 to the Seventh International Conference of American States.

(27) E. Rabbath, op. cit., p. 35.

(28) Ibid., p. 36.

(29) See references listed in the YEARBOOK OF I.L.C., op. cit., p. 19 sqq.

(30) Bourquin: op. cit., p. 46.

(31) Gidel: op. cit., Vol. III, p. 651; Ed. Rabbath, op. cit., p. 50.

(32) International Court of Justice, FISHERIES CASE, decision of 18 December, 1951, RECUEIL, 1951, p. 138.

(33) Bourquin: op. cit., p. 47-48. Gidel: op. cit., p. 634, who expressly states that "opposition by one State cannot invalidate a custom."

(34) Aide-Mémoire presented by the Government of Israel on 11 February, 1957, op. cit., p. 634; similar view in Bourquin, op. cit., pp. 47-48; Fitzmaurice in BRITISH YEARBOOK OF INTERNATIONAL LAW, 1953, pp. 31-32.

(35) Yearbook of I.L.C., 1962, Vol. II, p. 21 (French edition;) Gidel, op. cit., p. 634.

(36) Letter addressed by the British Embassy to the Egyptian Government on 29 July 1951 ... Egypt had, on several occasions, exercised her right of control over ships of different nationalities transiting through the Gulf of Aqaba. But the fact which rendered international recognition of this control even more decisive was the precedent of the British ship Empire Roach which, on 21 December 1950, having disobeyed the instructions relating to passage through the Straits of Tiran, was seized by the Egyptian authorities. In the exchange of notes between Egypt and Great Britain which followed, the British Government accepted that its ships proceeding to the Gulf of Aqaba could be visited (Cf. Gamal El-Oteifi: LE GOLFE D'AQABA ET ISRAEL, REVUE DE LA POL-ITIQUE INTERNATIONALE, Belgrade, No. 414-415, 5-20 July, 1967, pp. 6-8.)

It must be observed that, in 1955, England went back on the contents of this letter by stating that she considered the Gulf of Aqaba to be an international maritime waterway. In 1957, during the discussion in the United Nations of the problem of the withdrawal of Israel from Egyptian territory, almost all the other Western States followed the British and American positions on the character of the Gulf of Aqaba. It is incontestable that, for these countries, recognition of the international character of the Gulf constitutes one of their means of supporting Israel against the Arab States. Their opposition, therefore, is of very limited value.

(37) YEARBOOK OF THE I.L.C., op. cit., p. 23, references found in Document A/Conf. 13/1.

(38) Mentioned in Yearbook of I.L.C., op. cit., p. 23. (French edit.)

(39) In the view of publicists as well as of governments, this criterion is alternative and not cumulative.

(40) Gidel: op. cit., Vol. III, p. 625; Ch. Rousseau: DROIT INTERNATION-AL PUBLIC, Paris, 1953, p. 445; Mme Bastid: COURS DE DROIT INTERNA-TIONAL PUBLIC, 1964-65, p. 610.

(41) Rousseau: op. cit., p. 445; Colombos: LE DROIT INTERNATIONAL DE LA MER, p. 125; Baxter: THE LAW OF INTERNATIONAL WATERWAYS, 1964, p. 163-164.

(42) Corfou Strait Case Decision of 9 April 1949, RECUEIL, p. 28.

(43) At the United Nations Conference on the Law of the Sea, the Arab States opposed this article, but without success. So they have, in general, refrained from ratifying the Convention adopted by the Conference. Some of these States expressed reservation on this subject at the time of signing.

(44) See above our discussion of the internal nature of the waters of the Gulf of Aqaba.

(45) Baxter, op. cit., p. 215.

(46) It will be recalled that the port of Elath, occupied after the armistice, cannot be legally considered as Israeli, even by those who recognize the validity of the acts creating Israel (Cf. supra, p. 242-243).

(47) LE MONDE, 3-4 September 1967. Yet, the U.S.S.R. and the United States are not at war.

EGYPT'S UNLAWFUL BLOCKADE
OF THE GULF OF AQABA

Ministry of Foreign Affairs
(Jerusalem)

The Red Sea, at its northern end, splits up into two sections — the Gulf of Suez, which, together with the Suez Canal, forms one link with the Mediterranean Sea; and the Gulf of Aqaba, which forms a similar link in conjunction with the land route across southern Israel. Between these two bodies of water lies the peninsula of Sinai.

The 230-mile coastline of the Aqaba Gulf is shared by four countries — Saudi Arabia, Jordan, Israel and Egypt. Its two main ports are Eilat (Israel) and Aqaba (Jordan).

Two uninhabited islands — Tiran and Sanafir — are situated at the southern end of the Gulf, restricting the navigable area between the Gulf and the main body of the Red Sea to a 3-mile channel, between Tiran and the Sinai coast, known as the Straits of Tiran.

The actual sea-lane that can be used by vessels is even narrower, as coral reefs and rocks confine shipping to a 500-yards channel, about 1,000 yards from the shore and running parallel to it.

Towards the end of 1949, the Egyptian Government erected military installations on Tiran and Sanafir, as well as at Ras Nasrani on the coastal strip facing those islands. The United States Embassy in Cairo, concerned over the possible significance of this move, addressed an inquiry to the Egyptian Government and, on 28 January 1950, received in reply an aide-memoire stating, in part:

> This occupation being in no way conceived in a spirit of obstructing in any way innocent passage through the stretch of water separating these two islands from the Egyptian coast of Sinai, it follows that this passage, the only practicable one, will remain free as in the past, in conformity with international practice and recognized principles of the law of nations.

INCIDENTS

Contrary, however, to the promise and assurance contained in this state-

303

ment, the Egyptian Government began using its gun batteries at the entrance to the Gulf of Aqaba to block this waterway to all shipping bound for the Israel port of Eilat — this in open violation of internatonal law and of the United Nations Charter.

On 1 July 1951, the ss "Empire Roach," a British vessel carrying a cargo of arms for Jordan, was fired upon by the Tiran batteries and denied entrance to the Gulf. On 3 December 1953, Egyptian shore batteries fired at the United States vessel "Albion" at the entrance of the Gulf, in the belief (as the Egyptian authorities later explained) that the ship's destination was Eilat. (Actually, the "Albion" was carrying a cargo of wheat to the Jordanian port of Aqaba.) On 1 January 1954, Egyptian gunfire was directed, at the entrance of the Gulf, against the Italian ship "Maria Antonia" on her way from Massawa to Eilat. The ship was compelled to return to her port of origin. On 10 April 1955, the British ss "Anshun" was fired upon and hit by the Egyptian batteries because she failed to stop and identify herself.

On two occasions, the matter was raised in the Security Council. In the autumn of 1951, there was a lengthy debate in the Council on the subject of the Egyptian blockade of Israel, and, in the course of it, the Egyptian interference with navigation to Israel and the maintenance of the blockade were strongly denounced as being inconsistent with the establishment of permanent peace in the region. The matter was discussed again by the Council in February and March 1954, with special reference to the Egyptian interference with shipping proceeding to Eilat, when the representatives of several member-States reiterated their condemnation of the Egyptian practice. On this occasion, Mr. (now Sir Leslie) Munro, the representative of New Zealand, stated:

> Any impartial survey of events since the Resolution of 1 September 1951 must record that the Egyptian Government has with every appearance of deliberation ignored the injunctions of this Council. This course of conduct, persisted in for over two years, has resulted in many ships, which would otherwise have gone on their lawful occasions through the Suez Canal or the Gulf of Aqaba, being deterred from trading with Israel or diverted at great cost over other routes to their destination. No Government interested in the preservation of the rule of law in international affairs, and least of all any Government depending for the livelihood of its people on maritime trade, can contemplate this unhappy state of affairs without an earnest desire to bring it to an end . . .

The same view was expressed by other members of the Council.

ISRAEL MEASURES TO REOPEN GULF

During the Sinai campaign of 1956, the Israel Army took over the Egyptian positions. On 3 November of that year, the guns of Ras Nasrani were spiked, and, for the first time in seven years, navigation through the Straits of Tiran and in the Gulf of Aqaba was free to the ships and cargoes of all nations, as is every other international waterway.

Thus freed from an illegal stranglehold, Eilat fast grew to become today an expanding township of already over ten thousand inhabitants, and a vital interest to Israel. It has been developed as a main port of Israel, and a centre of communications of crucial importance. It is the maritime outlet of the Negev, which is its rapidly developing hinterland, and it increasingly serves international trade between Israel and East Africa, South-East and Eastern Asia, and the

Antipodes. It is joined to the Mediterranean by a major system of highways. An oil pipeline has been laid from Eilat to Haifa, with a branch to the new harbor of Ashdod: through this passes the bulk of Israel's oil imports. Plans are settled to extend the Haifa-Beersheba railroad to Eilat, and a proposal had been formulated for transforming the port into the southern terminal of a Mediterranean-Red Sea canal.

On 1 March 1957, in the General Assembly, the Foreign Minister of Israel, Mrs. Golda Meir, responding to a call from the United Nations that it withdraw from the occupied area, declared the readiness of her Government to quit Sharm-el-Sheikh — the point on the mainland opposite Tiran Island, in the confidence that there would be continued freedom of navigation for international and Israeli shipping in the Gulf and through the Straits.

Here is the full text of what Mrs. Meir said in the General Assembly on 1 March 1957:

We have repeatedly stated that Israel has no interest in the strip of land overlooking the western coast of the Gulf of Aqaba. Our sole purpose has been to ensure that, on the withdrawal of Israel forces, continued freedom of navigation will exist for Israel and international shipping in the Gulf of Aqaba and the Straits of Tiran. Such freedom of navigation is a vital national interest for Israel, but it is also of importance and legitimate concern to the maritime Powers and to many States whose economies depend upon trade and navigation between the Red Sea and the Mediterranean Sea.

There has recently been an increasingly wide recognition that the Gulf of Aqaba comprehends international waters in which the right of free and innocent passage exists.

On 11 February 1957, the Secretary of State of the United States of America handed to the Ambassador of Israel in Washington a Memorandum on the subject of the Gulf of Aqaba and the Straits of Tiran.

This statement discusses the right of nations in the Gulf of Aqaba, and declares the readiness of the United States to exercise those rights on its own behalf and to join with others in securing general recognition of those rights.

My Government has subsequently learnt with gratification that other leading maritime Powers are prepared to subscribe to the doctrine set out in the United States Memorandum of 11 February, and have a similar intention to exercise their rights of free and innocent passage in the Gulf and the Straits.

The General Assembly's Resolution (II) of 2 February 1957 contemplates that units of the United Nations Emergency Force will move into the Straits of Tiran area on Israel's withdrawal. It is generally recognized that the function of the United Nations Emergency Force in the Straits of Tiran area includes the prevention of belligerent acts. In this connection, my Government recalls the statements by the representative of the United States in the General Assembly on 28 January and 2 February 1957 with reference to the function of the United Nations Emergency Force units which are to move into the Straits of Tiran area on Israel's withdrawal. The statement of 28 January, repeated on 2 February, said: "It is essential that units of the United Nations Emergency Force be stationed at the Straits of Tiran in order to achieve there the separation of Egyptian and Israeli land and sea forces. This separation is essential until it is clear that the non-existence of any claimed belligerent rights has established in practice the peaceful conditions which must govern navigation in waters having such an international interest."

... My Government has noted the assurance embodied in the Secretary-General's report of 26 February 1957, that any proposal for the withdrawal of the United Nations Emergency Force from the Gulf of Aqaba area would first come to the Advisory Committee, which represents the General Assembly in the implementation of its Resolution of 2 November 1956. This procedure will give the General Assembly an opportunity to ensure that no precipitate changes are made which would have the effect of increasing the possibility of belligerent acts . . .

In the light of these doctrines, policies and arrangements by the United Nations and the maritime Powers, my Government is confident that free and innocent passage for international and Israel shipping will continue to be fully maintained after Israel's withdrawal.

It remains for me now to formulate the policy of Israel both as a littoral State and as a country which intends to exercise its full rights of free passage in the Gulf of Aqaba and through the Straits of Tiran.

The Government of Israel believes that the Gulf of Aqaba comprehends international waters and that no nation has the right to prevent free and innocent passage in the Gulf or through the Straits giving access thereto, in accordance with the generally accepted definition of those terms in the law of the sea.

In its capacity as a littoral State, Israel will gladly offer port facilities to the ships of all nations and all flags exercising free passage in the Gulf of Aqaba. We have received with gratification the assurances of leading maritime Powers that they foresee a normal and regular flow of traffic of all cargoes in the Gulf of Aqaba.

Israel will do nothing to impede free and innocent passage by ships of Arab countries bound to Arab ports or to any other destination.

Israel is resolved on behalf of vessels of Israel registry to exercise the right of free and innocent passage and is prepared to join with others to secure universal respect of this right.

Israel will protect ships of its own flag exercising the right of free and innocent passage on the high seas and in international waters.

Interference, by armed force, with ships of Israel flag exercising free and innocent passage in the Gulf of Aqaba and through the Straits of Tiran will be regarded by Israel as an attack entitling it to exercise its inherent right of self-defence under Article 51 of the Charter and to take all such measures as are necessary to ensure the free and innocent passage of its ships in the Gulf and in the Straits.

We make this announcement in accordance with the accepted principles of international law under which all States have an inherent right to use their forces to protect their ships and their rights against interference by armed force. My Government naturally hopes that this contingency will not occur.

In a public address on 20 February, President Eisenhower stated: "We should not assume that, if Israel withdraws, Egypt will prevent Israeli shipping from using the Suez Canal, or the Gulf of Aqaba."

This declaration has weighed heavily with my Government in determining its action today.

Israel is now prepared to withdraw its forces from the Gulf of Aqaba and the Straits of Tiran in the confidence that there will be continued freedom of navigation for international and Israeli shipping in the Gulf of Aqaba and through the Straits of Tiran.

UNEF PRESENCE

The presence of the United Nations Emergency Force at Sharm-el-Sheikh was a visible expression of international determination that any attempt to renew hostile acts in that area would be denied. The effectiveness of the Force in such a contingency was never put to the actual test, but it did carry out its prophylactic purpose as a keeper of the peace in the Straits.

Israel had sought clarification of the procedures that would be adopted if Egypt were, unilaterally, to demand evacuation of the Force before its presence had established an abiding guarantee of freedom of navigation for all shipping in the international waterway. In his reply to a pertinent Israel memorandum, which had also asked for assurances that the Force would oppose belligerent acts, the Secretary-General of the United Nations, Mr. Dag Hammarskjold, wrote on 25 February 1957: "With regard to the function of UNEF in the prevention of belligerency, the answer is affirmative, subject to the qualification that UNEF is never to be used in such a way as to force a solution of any controversial, political or legal problem."

On the question of notification to the General Assembly, it was added, an indicated procedure would be for the Secretary-General to inform the Advisory Committee on the United Nations Emergency Force, which would determine whether the matter should be brought to the attention of the Assembly.

AMERICAN STAND

John Foster Dulles, in his memorandum of 11 February 1957, answering the same question put to him by Israel, wrote that the United States would certainly anticipate that any proposals to withdraw the Force would be considered by the General Assembly before such withdrawal was carried out. In such consideration by the General Assembly of any proposals to withdraw the Force from the Gulf of Aqaba area, the United States would be guided by the concept of the functions of the Forces as defined by Ambassador Lodge on 28 January and on 2 February.

In a Press conference on 26 March 1957, the Secretary of State was asked what the United States position was, in view of the fact that it seemed to be the position of some Powers that the Force was in the area on Egyptian sufferance, and must vacate it whenever Egypt decided that it must go. This was Mr. Dulles' answer:

> The generally accepted view in the United Nations is that the General Assembly has no right to impose upon any nation the presence of any observers or representatives or forces of the United Nations, and that for them to enter upon the territory of another State they have to have the consent of that State. Now once the consent has been given, then I think a good argument can be made that the consent cannot be arbitrarily withdrawn, frustrating the original project, because other people change their positions in reliance on the original consent, forces are set in motion, a chain of events has occurred. And we would question, certainly, whether Egypt has the right arbitrarily to alter and change a consent once given until the purpose of that consent has been accomplished.

Regrettably, the procedure thus authoritatively expounded was not followed by Secretary-General U Thant in the month of May, 1967: he at once conceded an Egyptian demand that the Force be withdrawn.

ISRAEL'S STAND ON GULF AND STRAITS — 1967

Following this incontinent and ill-timed withdrawal of the Force at the insistence of Egypt, President Nasser, on 23 May, announced that Egypt had sealed off, to ships flying the Israeli flag and to ships under other flags with cargoes of a strategic character meant for Israel, their free and innocent passage through the international waterway of the Straits of Tiran into and from the Gulf of Aqaba.

On that same day, Mr. Levi Eshkol, Prime Minister of Israel, made the following statement in the Knesset, Israel's Parliament:

> Any interference with freedom of passage in the Gulf and the Straits constitutes a gross violation of international law, a blow at the sovereign rights of other nations and an act of aggression against Israel. As the Knesset is aware, a number of Governments, including the major maritime Powers, have publicly stated, since 1957, their intention of exercising their rights to free passage through the Straits of Tiran and the Gulf of Eilat.
>
> During the past few days, the Government of Israel has been in close touch with the Governments that have proclaimed and exercised the principle of free passage in these waters since 1957. After these exchanges, I can say that international support for these rights is determined and widespread.
>
> And indeed, what is at stake here is a clear and formal international undertaking on compliance with which the maintenance of international law and order depends. We are confronted with a fateful hour not only for Israel, but for the whole world.
>
> In view of this situation, I call upon the Powers once again to act without delay for the maintenance of the right to free passage to our southernmost port, a right which applies to every State without distinction. The Government of Israel will adhere to the policy which it announced in the United Nations Assembly on 1 March, 1957. Since this statement was made, free passage in the Straits and the Gulf has taken shape as an established international reality, expressed in the form of hundreds of sailings under dozens of flags and the creation of a variegated and developing network of commerce and communications.
>
> The statement of the Egyptian President is another link in the chain of infractions of law that Egypt has been perpetrating for many years by its blockade in the Suez Canal, in violation of its undertaking to permit free passage through the Canal to all ships of all nations . . .
>
> If a criminal attempt is made to impose a blockade on the shipping of a member of the United Nations, that will be a dangerous precedent, with grave consequences for international relations and the freedom of the seas. The latest development clearly demonstrates the serious significance of Egypt's moves. I call upon the world community to demonstrate practical and effective responsibility for the preservation of peace.

NAVIGATION RIGHTS
IN THE SUEZ CANAL

C. Bassiouni

Israel's most insistent demand in its quarrel with the U.A.R. has been for the use of the Suez Canal. This demand, supported by the United States and some other governments, has been based on the theory that the Canal is an international waterway open on equal terms to all states.

The Maritime Suez Canal links the Red and Mediterranean Seas across the Isthmus of Suez. It has been and is still governed by the terms of the Constantinople Convention of October 29, 1888.(1) The parties to this convention were France, Germany, the Empire of Austria-Hungary, Spain, Great Britain, Italy, Holland, Russia, and Turkey. When Egypt achieved independence she succeeded to the rights and obligations of Turkey, across whose territory the waterway was constructed, in accordance with international law governing successor states. Article 8 of the Anglo-Egyptian Treaty of 1954 reasserted that "The Maritime Suez Canal . . . is an integral part of Egypt." In addition, Egypt enjoyed certain rights and bore certain obligations specifically set forth in the 1888 Convention.

The Convention delegated to Egypt execution of the principles and obligations established by the agreement, with these words in Article 9: "The Egyptian Government is to take . . . the necessary measures to enforce the execution of said treaty . . ."

The language is specific, and Egypt remains the sole judge as to the measures required to be taken for implementation of the treaty. This cannot be considered a discretionary power to take measures that do not conform to the terms of the Convention.(2) Article 14 of the Convention stipulated also that obligations imposed by that treaty were not to be limited in time to "the duration of the concessions granted the Universal Company of the Suez Canal," and this article assumes special significance because it clearly distinguishes between the Canal itself and the Universal Maritime Suez Canal as the operating agency for the waterway.(3)

Article 14 of the 1888 Convention amounted to a clear acknowledgement that Egyptian sovereignty over the Canal and the rights and obligations of the

309

company were two separate matters, in fact and in law.

The Universal Maritime Suez Canal Company was an Egyptian corporation, established under Egyptian law and, like any other private corporation, subject to that law.(4) It was set up to perform a specific, needed public service: construction and operation of a waterway between two seas. It had no independent existence outside the terms of its establishment and no rights or authority beyond those specifically granted to it by the Government of Egypt. Its character was no different from that of a public utility corporation, say, in the United States, authorized to distribute electric power to communities and individuals within the area prescribed by the terms of its charter and subject to regulation under the laws of the chartering government. That the shares of the company were all owned outside Egypt had no bearing whatever on the character or status of the company. A corporation is in itself a legal entity, whoever may own or control its stock.

The Egyptian decree of July 26, 1956, nationalized the assets of the Canal Company. It did not nationalize the Suez Canal because there was neither need nor reason to assert Egyptian control over what had always been Egypt's own. The right to transmit through the Suez Canal had been spelled out in the Convention of 1888, the terms of which Egypt was obliged to carry out. In law the decree of July 26, 1956, altered none of the rights and obligations arising under international law, but merely substituted one operating agency for another. It did, however, have a powerful political impact, and this — a dramatic shift of political power in the whole Middle East region — created the situation that faced the world in the year 1956.

Great Britain and France, strongly supported by the United States and less eagerly by some other governments, attempted not only to compel Egypt to permit operation of the Canal on their terms but even to undermine Egypt's territorial sovereignty in the Canal Zone.(5) Britain, France, and Israel resorted to war to achieve these aims but abandoned their aggression in the face of overwhelming pressure from the United Nations and world opinion. This conclusion of the 1956 Suez affair settled for all time the question of Egyptian sovereignty over the Canal and the juridical status of the Suez Canal Authority. Unrestricted use of the Suez Canal, however, remains a prime political and economic goal of the State of Israel.

The Treaty of Constantinople guarantees the right of free navigation in the Canal, and it still stands today as the basic document guaranteeing that freedom.(6)

Of prime importance in the Treaty are Articles 1 and 4 which establish the principle of freedom of passage.(7) Article 1 provides:

> The Suez Maritime Canal shall always be free and open, in time of war as in time of peace, to every vessel of commerce or of war, without distinction of flag.
>
> Consequently, the High Contracting Parties agree not in any way to interfere with the free use of the Canal, in time of war as in time of peace.
>
> The Canal shall never be subjected to the exercise of the right of blockade.

The first paragraph of Article 4 declares:

> The Maritime Canal remaining open in time of war as a free passage, even to ships of war of belligerents, according to the terms of Article 1 of the

present Treaty, the High Contracting Parties agree that no right of war, no act of hostility, nor any act having for its object to obstruct the free navigation of the Canal, shall be committed in the Canal and its ports of access, as well as within a radius of three marine miles from these ports, even though the Ottoman Empire should be one of the belligerent Powers.

Israel was not, of course, in existence when the 1888 Convention pledged the right of passage to ships of all nations in peace and war. It has been argued that this right accrued to it as a continuing right available to all states. Authorities have pointed out, however, that this dedication — a stipulation in favor of third parties — is a concept of domestic private law and has no place in international law because it is alien to the techniques and incompatible with the characteristics of this discipline. In 1929 the International Court of Justice ruled specifically that stipulation in favor of third states is not a rule of international law.(8)

It thus appears that Israel acquired no right to the beneficial use of the Suez Canal under the Convention of 1888 and that, having never acquired such a right subsequently through the implied unanimous consent of all contracting parties by unobstructed habitual transit of the Canal,(9) there is no avenue open to Israel under international law now to assert such a right.

On May 4, 1948, Israel declared its independence, and on the same day Egypt, as a member of the Arab bloc, established a general blockade against Israel in the Suez Maritime Canal.

On February 6, 1950, King Farouk I of Egypt issued a decree on the procedure of ship and airplane searches and seizure of contraband goods in connection with the Palestine War. This decree, known as the Embargo Act of February 6, 1950, provided for the continuance of "visit and search" practices. Article 2 of the Act provided for customs officials to inspect the suspected ship's manifest and cargo for such contraband as arms, munitions, war material, or other war contraband. In Article 3 it was stated that "force may be used at all times against any ship attempting to avoid search, where necessary, by firing so as to force the ship to stop and submit to search." An amendment to the decree added to the list of contraband, "foodstuffs and all other commodities which are likely to strengthen the war potential of the Zionists in Palestine in any way whatever." The Egyptian authorities drew up a "black list" of ships known to be carrying certain materials to Israel and also established a Prize Court at Alexandria to dispose of confiscated goods.

The most frequent argument raised against Egypt's actions of visit, search, and confiscation pursuant to the Embargo Act of 1950, states that such blockade actions are a direct breach of the Treaty of Constantinople which guaranteed free passage and prohibited blockades in Articles 1 and 4. This argument can be resolved by an examination of Article 10 of that Treaty which provides:

> Similarly, the provisions of Articles 4, 5, 7, and 8 shall not interfere with the measures which His Majesty the Sultan and His Highness the Khedive, in the name of His Imperial Majesty, and within the limits of the Firmans granted, might find it necessary to take for securing by their own forces the defense of Egypt and the maintenance of public order.

It is in reliance on this provision of the Treaty that Egypt exercised her sovereignty right of search for reasons of her own defense. One writer comments:

> For though there is an explicit freedom of use, even in wartime, laid down
> in the Convention of Constantinople, there is also a provision in Article 10
> that neither that liberty nor the other stipulations of the agreements shall
> hinder measures necessary for the defense of Egypt and the maintenance
> of public order. In any event, it would be less than realistic to expect a
> state at war to allow free passage through any portion of its territory to
> the ships, supplies, or nationals of an enemy.(10)

It should also be noted that in Article 9 of the Treaty of Constantinople it is
declared that, "the Egyptian Government is to take the necessary measures to
enforce the execution of the Treaty," and Article 12 provides ". . . that all rights
of Turkey [to which Egypt is the successor state] as the territorial power are
still reserved."

Taking a historical approach, Egypt's actions are certainly not without
precedent. During both World Wars Great Britain blockaded the Canal against
use by Germany and her allies. The procedure used by Great Britain was first to
stop and search the enemy vessel at the entrance to the Canal, and if contraband
was found, the vessel was directed to proceed through the Canal. Having passed
safely through, the enemy halted the vessel and seized the contraband, the effect
being a de facto blockade.

Another argument advanced against the blockade practices of Egypt in the
Suez Maritime Canal, and the Gulf of Aqaba as well, contends that the Armistice
signed at Rhodes by Egypt and Israel on February 24, 1949, prohibited any
further hostilities by the opposing parties and that Egypt's actions pursuant to
the Embargo Act of February, 1950, after the Armistice had been signed,
constitute acts of aggression in violation of the Armistice. But paragraph 2 of
Article 2 of that Armistice declares: "No element of the land, sea or military or
para-military forces of either party, including non-regular forces, shall commit
any warlike or hostile act against the military or para-military forces of the other
party . . ."

As was noted above, under the provisions of the Embargo Act of 1950, it is
provided that visit and search of Israeli and suspect neutral ships be conducted
by regular Egyptian customs officials. Strictly interpreting the above article of
the Armistice, customs officials are neither military nor para-miltitary forces.

A further interpretation of the crucial Article 2 of the Armistice is contained
in a statement by the Chief of Staff of the United Nations Truce Supervision
Organization: ". . . interference with the passage of goods destined for Israel
through the Suez Canal is a hostile act, but not necesarily against the General
Armistice Agreement, because of the limitations imposed on the term 'hostile
act' in the text of Article 2, paragraph 2 of the General Armistice Agreement."(11)

The crux of the argument, and the point which was never resolved, centered
about the interpretation to be given the effect of the Armistice by the parties.

The Egyptian Representative told the United Nations Special Committee of
the Mixed Armistice Commission on June 12, 1951, that, "We are exercising a
right of war. . . . We are still legally at war with Israel. An Armistice does not put
an end to a state of war. It does not prohibit a country from exercising certain
rights of war."(12)

Oppenheim has stated the effect of Armistices as they are traditionally
considered:

312

Armistice or truces, in the wider sense of the term, are all agreements between belligerent forces for a temporary cessation of hostilities. They are in no wise to be compared to peace . . . because the condition of war remains between the belligerents themselves, and between belligerents and neutrals, on all points beyond the mere cessation of hostilities. In spite of such cessation the right of visit and search over neutral merchantment therefore remains intact.(13)

In July, 1951, the Representative of Israel complained to the Security Council of the United Nations that the Armistice signed at Rhodes had terminated the Egypt-Israeli war, yet Egypt continued to blockade Israeli vessels and neutral vessels destined for Israeli ports. As a result, the Security Council passed a resolution on September 1, 1951, calling upon Egypt to lift its blockade.

Commenting on this action of the Security Council, Colonel Howard S. Levie wrote: "It is considered more likely that the Security Council's action was based on a desire to bring an end to a situation fraught with potential danger to peace than it was attempting to change a long established rule of international law. By now it has surely become fairly obvious that the Israeli-Arab General Armistice Agreement did not create even a de facto termination of the war between those states."(14)

Before the Security Council, the Representative of Egypt stated the position of his Government on the General Armistice Agreement:

The fact that the Armistice Agreement is silent on this point [i.e., the right of visit and search] although it is fairly common practice to include a provision on this subject in armistice agreements, shows, as indeed the Mixed Armistice Commission has confirmed, that the Armistice Agreement of the classical type concluded between Egypt and Israel expressed the joint will of the signatories and left them free to exercise their legitimate right of visit and search.(15)

On October 29, 1956, Israeli forces invaded the Sinai peninsula, and within a few days occupied Sharm al-Shaikh, thereby gaining control of the Gulf of Aqaba. This invasion by Israel brought an end to the General Armistice Agreement, and in the words of Premier Ben Gurion of Israel to the Israeli Knesset in November, 1956, ". . . the Armistice with Egypt is dead and so are the Armistice lines. No magician can bring back life to those lines."(16)

After Israeli forces withdrew from the Sinai peninsula and were replaced by the United Nations Expeditionary Force, the Egyptian Government, which had nationalized the Universal Company of the Suez Maritime Canal, availed itself of the rights of a belligerent and continued to adhere to its interpretation of the Constantinople Convention. On July 18, 1957, however, Egypt accepted the "compulsory" jurisdiction of the International Court of Justice in all matters relating to the interpretation of the Constantinople Convention or freedom of navigation in the Suez Canal. While Egypt is willing to permit the entire question to be settled through the International Court of Justice, Israel has not communicated a corresponding intent.

NOTES

(1) M. Cherif Bassiouni, "The Nationalization of the Suez Canal, and the Illicit Act in International Law," DE PAUL LAW REVIEW, 14, 1965, p. 258.

(2) Ibid., p. 265.

(3) Ibid., p. 266 et. seq.

(4) Mustapha El-Hefnawy, LES PROBLEMES CONTEMPORAINS DU CANAL DE SUEZ (Paris, 1953).

(5) Anthony Nutting, NO END OF A LESSON (New York: Potter, 1967), pp. 52-71.

(6) Simcha Dinitz, "The Legal Aspects of the Egyptian Blockade of the Suez Canal," GEORGETOWN LAW JOURNAL, 45, 1956-1957, p. 175.

(7) See also U.S. Department of State, THE SUEZ CANAL PROBLEM (Washington: U.S. Government Printing Office, 1956), pp. 16-19.

(8) International Court of Justice, Case of The Free Zones of Upper Savoy and District of Cos, 19 August, 1929. See also REPORT OF COMMITTEE ON USES OF INTERNATIONAL RIVERS AND CANALS, International Law Association Conference, Hamburg, 1960, p. 58.

(9) Oppenheim, op. cit., pp. 926-927.

(10) P.E. Corbett, LAW AND SOCIETY IN THE RELATIONS OF STATES, 1951.

(11) Treaty No. 654, between Israel and Egypt, signed at Rhodes, February 24, 1949.

(12) Bloomfield, EGYPT, ISRAEL, AND THE GULF OF AQABA IN INTERNATIONAL LAW, 1957, p. 50.

(13) L. Oppenheim, INTERNATIONAL LAW: DISPUTES, WAR AND NEUTRALITY, Lauterpacht, ed., 1952, pp. 546-551.

(14) Howard S. Levie, "The Nature and Scope of the Armistice Agreement," AMERICAN JOURNAL OF INTERNATIONAL LAW, 50, 1956, pp. 880-906.

(15) United Nations, Security Council, OFFICIAL RECORDS, 661st Meeting, March 12, 1954, pp. 9-13.

(16) United Arab Republic, Information Department, NAVIGATION IN THE SUEZ CANAL (Cairo, 1962), p. 33.

ISRAEL
AND
THE SUEZ CANAL

Ministry of Foreign Affairs
(Jerusalem)

Ever since the establishment of the State of Israel, and to this day, Egypt has blocked the Suez Canal to Israel shipping, in contravention of United Nations decisions and recognized international conventions, and has denied the use of this international waterway to all vessels coming from or bound for Israel.

Israel has never consented to these arbitrary Egyptian acts, whose primary aim has been to thwart Israel's economic development, to prevent it from establishing and expanding relations with the countries of Africa and Asia and, in general, to carry out economic warfare against it.

As far back as 12 July 1951 the head of the United Nations Truce Supervision Organization, General Riley, reported to the United Nations Security Council: "It is quite clear to me that action taken by the Egyptian authorities in interfering with passage of goods destined for Israel through the Suez canal must be considered as aggressive action."

Nevertheless, Egypt persisted in its blockade, and Israel raised the matter for discussion at the Security Council in August 1951. Egypt's legal and international claims were rejected by the Council, which on 1 September 1951 decided that complete freedom of navigation must be maintained in the Suez Canal and that Egypt had no right to impose a blockade or exercise any kind of belligerent rights there. The Council explicitly and unequivocally called "upon Egypt to terminate the restrictions on the passage of international commercial shipping and goods through the Suez Canal wherever bound and to cease all interference with such shipping beyond that essential to the safety of shipping in the Canal itself and to the observance of the international conventions in force."

In flagrant violation of this decision of the United Nations Security Council, Egypt persisted in its maritime blockade of Israel in the Suez Canal and even expanded its scope. Egypt prevented the passage of all Israel vessels through the Canal, confiscated all cargoes of Israel origin or bound for Israel and withheld all services and facilities from foreign vessels that appeared on the blacklist of the Arab Boycott Office — a list running into many hundreds of names. A large number of ships (such as the Norwegian, Rimfrost, the Greek, Konitza, the

315

Italian, Franca Mari and many others) were stopped at the entrance to the Canal and their cargoes confiscated.

Early in 1957, Israel again raised the question at the Security Council. A resolution was put forward referring to the decision of 1 September 1951, noting with regret that Egypt had not complied with it, and calling upon Egypt to comply with that decision, in accordance with the United Nations Charter. The resolution won overwhelming support in the Council but failed of passage because of the Soviet veto.

A new development came in September 1954, when an attempt was made to secure the passage of an Israel flagship, the Bat Galim. The vessel was detained and its crew imprisoned. The episode came under discussion at the Security Council, which passed no resolution, but the Chairman summarized the debate with the declaration that the decision of September 1951 was still in force.

Following Egypt's nationalization of the Suez Canal in the summer of 1956, the Security Council once again took up the anti-Israel blockade (13 October 1956), adopting six principles for the safeguarding of freedom of navigation in the Canal for all nations and removing the matter "from the politics of any country." The Egyptian Government's acceptance of these principles was announced at the Council's meeting.

At the start of the Sinai Campaign (October, 1956) Egypt blocked the Suez Canal to all shipping, as a means of exerting pressure on the United Nations and the nations of the world. In the course of the political moves that followed, in the effort to solve the crisis, Israel reiterated its demand for the lifting of the blockade against it. The demand was given international recognition. On 20 February 1957, President Eisenhower said: "We should not assume that, if Israel withdraws (from Sinai), Egypt will prevent Israeli shipping from using the Suez Canal or the Gulf of Aqaba. If, unhappily, Egypt does hereafter violate the Armistice Agreement or other international obligations, then this should be dealt with firmly by the society of nations."

It follows from this that freedom of navigation for Israel in the Suez Canal constituted one of the conditions for the withdrawal of Israel forces from Sinai and the Gaza Strip in 1957.

Yet Egypt continued to carry out its belligerent policy in this respect. On several occasions Israel tried to exercise its right of innocent passage through the Canal; in every case, the ships were detained by the Egyptians. The Danish freighter, Inge Toft, was seized on May 1959 and held for nine months. In the case of the Greek ship, Astypalea, Egypt had previously given United Nations Secretary-General Dag Hammarskjold its agreement in principle for the vessel's passage. However, when the Astypalea entered the Canal on 17 December 1959, it was refused permission to use the Canal and its cargo was seized. Commenting on the incident on 8 April 1960, Mr. Hammarskjold declared that the detention of the Astypalea and the confiscation of its cargo were "against the principle upheld by the United Nations."

Egypt persisted in its policy of denying freedom of passage to Israel vessels and cargoes in the Suez Canal right up until the Egyptian attack on Israel in June 1967. Egypt even threatened that the Canal would be closed to all foreign vessels that would attempt to run the renewed blockade of the Tiran Straits, at the entrance to the Gulf of Aqaba. Similar threats had been voiced on previous occasions against countries whose policies irked the Egyptians. Matters came to a head when, on 6 June 1967, Egypt blocked the Canal by sinking a number of its own ships in it, in the hope of being thus able to extort concessions in its favour from the Powers — while claiming, at the same time, that it was Israel that had blocked the Canal.

Twice, then, Egypt has closed the Suez Canal to all navigation, utilizing this international waterway as an instrument of political blackmail. So far, it would appear that in terms of actual damage, Egypt herself is the loser; but this fact does not in any way detract from the gravity of the act.

Egypt continues its opposition to Israel navigation in the Suez Canal, terming any attempts at such navigation a violation of the cease-fire agreement.

Israel continues to maintain its right to free navigation in the Canal under the Constantinople Convention and in accordance with the express decisions of the United Nations on this question. Prime Minister Levi Eshkol on 18 July 1967 reiterated that Israel will insist on the exercise of its right of free navigation in the Suez Canal, an international waterway. On the following day, U.S. Secretary of State, Dean Rusk, declared that the United States supported freedom of navigation in all international waterways, including the Suez Canal.

Israel will insist on this right in any arrangement that may be reached on the problems of the region.

IX. Aggression and Self-Defense

INTRODUCTION

The concepts of "aggression" and "self defense" may imply that there are in international law and custom common standards of behavior within which relationships between states and peoples are to be conducted. In reality, however, the recent efforts of the international community (pursuant to U.N. urging) to develop general agreement on a comprehensive definition of "aggression" have been unsuccessful. It is not surprising, therefore, that there is a great deal of confusion as to what constitutes "aggression" on the one hand, and legitimate acts of national or collective self defense, on the other.

Expectedly, these concepts have also been a source of controversy in the context of the Arab-Israeli conflict. What one party calls "aggression," its antagonist regards as "self-defense," and vice versa.

The Arabs assert that the Zionists had prepared plans for attacks against the Arab majority in Palestine even before the establishment of Israel. They cite the activites of the Zionist underground forces, some of which were involved in atrocities such as the massacre at Deir Yasin in April 1948. The Arabs claim that before the entry of the Arab armies into Palestine in order to "defend" the Arab inhabitants and avert a direct threat to the "security" of the neighboring countries, Jewish units occupied Arab areas outside the territory reserved for the Jewish State. Similarly, Israel, in collusion with Britain and France, attacked Egypt and occupied Sinai and the Gaza Strip in 1956. Finally, the Arabs observe, Israel initiated the June 1967 war and conquered substantial territories from Egypt, Jordan, and Syria. These activities, coupled with Israeli sporadic "retaliatory operations," against guerilla activities constitute "aggression."

The Israelis view history and their legal rights differently. They cite the Arab "disturbances" against peaceful Jewish settlers during the 1920's and 1930's as hostile acts. This was followed by the operations of irregular Arab armies, in the six months period before Israel's birth, with the declared aim of liquidating the Jewish community in Palestine. The failure of this "aggression" resulted in the invasion of the emerging Jewish State by the regular armies of the neighboring countries in May, 1948. Defeated in this war, the Arabs nevertheless did not refrain from the threat or use of force against the integrity and sovereignty of Israel. Facing Egypt's war preparations in Sinai, Israel took "security measures" in October 1956, including the temporary occupation of the Peninsula. Since the Arab goal of destroying the Jewish state had not been given up and the military buildup had continued for the next decade, culminating in the dramatic events of May and June 1967, Israel was once again "compelled" to successfully "defend" its very existence. As a result of the war Israel has secured "defensive"

318

borders which, according to Israeli officials, can be modified only if the other side shows a sincere readiness for a lasting peace.

Some aspects of these polarized approaches are discussed in the following three selections. The first is excerpted from Ibrahim Al-Abid, A HANDBOOK TO THE PALESTINE QUESTION published in Beirut by the Palestine Liberation Organization Research Center, in October 1969. The author deals specifically with the questions of Israeli retaliatory acts as well as its military responses to the closing of the Gulf of Aqaba.

Two excerpts from Abba Eban's speeches represent the Israeli view. In an address delivered before the first emergency special session of the General Assembly on November 1, 1956, Eban described Israel's action in Sinai as an "inherent right of self defense." In another address by Eban, this time delivered in the U.N. Security Council on November 13, 1967, he surveys Arab "aggression" leading to the Six Days War.

PALESTINE: QUESTIONS
AND
ANSWERS

Ibrahim Al-Abid

Question: Are the Israeli acts of aggression "retaliatory acts" against military operations mounted or abetted by the Arab countries?

Israel uses border incidents as a pretext to expand its territories. Moshe Brilliant, the Israeli military commentator, concedes that they are part of Israel's cold and calculated policy to force the Arabs to accept peace with Israel. The U.N. files between 1948 and 1967 include 92 testimonies by various delegations and U.N. observers in the Middle East that the Israeli military campaigns into Arab territory have been the source of conflict not vice versa.

Let us take the attack on Egypt in 1956 as an example. On October 1954, five months before the attack on Gaza, the Israeli authorities and press began a publicity campaign against saboteurs infiltrating from Gaza. On November 4, 1954 the JERUSALEM POST said that conditions were deteriorating due to the British evacuation from the Suez zone. On November 11, 1954 General Burns, Chief of Staff of the U.N. Truce Supervision Organization at the time, proposed that the armistice lines be sealed with barbed wire; but, strange to say, Israel turned the proposal down. In January 1955 a spokesman for the Israeli Army made public an order calling upon every Israeli army officer to train for guerrilla warfare and parachute landing. It came to light later that the two contingents deployed against Gaza were the first group to graduate from that program.

When the attack came (February 28-29, 1955) Israel explained that it was in retaliation for the detention of the S.S. Bat Galeem preventing it from crossing the Suez Canal. It should be noted that the Israeli Prime Minister had declared in the Knesset (January 27, 1955) that he left it to the good judgement of the members not to connect the safety of the Israeli borders with any such incidents as the detention of the Bat Galeem or the Cairo trials. (JERUSALEM POST, Jan. 27, 1955).

He had also declared on that same day that the borders had witnessed a period of relative quiet during the past months. The Chief of Staff of the Israeli Army had made a similar declaration on January 26, 1955.(1)

Question: Are retaliatory raids justifiable under the U.N. Charter?

U.N. Mediator Count Folke Bernadotte realized that Israel had expansionist designs which she planned to execute under one pretext or another. Moshe Sharett, then Minister of Foreign Affairs, had mentioned to the Mediator that Israel would reserve for herself the right to retaliate militarily if the Arab countries broke the Armistice agreements. Sharett had told him also that the area of Israel must expand, now, after the establishment of the State. Count Bernadotte said:

> Shertok even hinted that any partitioning of the Arab part of Palestine might result in the Jews resuming military operations — a statement that seemed inconsistent with the Jews' own criticism of certain Arab countries for trying to interfere in the domestic affairs of the Jewish State. Clearly Shertok was laying himself open to much the same charge now.
> Shertok continued: the decision of the Jewish Government to call a peace conference was dictated by a sincere and honest desire to put an end to the war. But he realised that the Arabs would probably refuse. As to the shape the Jewish State was to assume, he shared my view that the frontiers laid down in the United Nations resolution of 29th November 1947 could not be maintained. They were impossible to defend militarily; in view of the tension that existed between the two parties some modification must be sought. The Israeli territory would have to be expanded. The great Arab promontories thrusting into Jewish territory would have to be abolished. That, Shertok asserted, would be the best way of preventing future Jewish expansion. If Jewish territory were made too small from the start, a tremendous outward pressure among the population was bound to arise that would lead to serious complications. I interpreted this as meaning that the Jews would after a time make use of the argument that the number of immigrants at a given moment had become so great — and would become still greater later on — that Jewish territory was inadequate. This was a line of argument completely in accordance with what the Arabs believed Jewish plans for the future to be.(2)

Count Bernadotte reported his fears to the Security Council which took a decision on August 19, 1948 forbidding any of the parties from violating the truce either by way of retaliation or deterrence. (S/982, sec. d).

The Security Council reaffirmed this same decision four times in the same year: On October 19, November 4, November 16 and December 29, 1948.

Furthermore, the philosophy of so-called "retaliation" has been examined by the Security Council with great thoroughness, and has been condemned in the statements made by the majority of the Council members during the debates on Israel's invasions, as well as in the Council resolutions. Thus, in its resolution of 19 January 1950 the Council proclaimed that the alleged "provocation" which Israel claimed had prompted its invasion "in no way justifies the Israeli action," and proceeded to "remind" Israel that it (the Council) had "already condemned military action in breach of the General Armistice Agreements, whether or not taken by way of retaliation." (Paragraphs 1 and 2). The Council, moreover, "condemned" that attack as a three-fold "flagrant violation" — "of the cease-fire provisions of its resolution of 15 July 1948, of the terms of the General Armistice Agreement . . . and of Israel's obligations under the Charter." (Paragraph 3).

Finally, the Secretary-General, in his reports on the visit he made to the Middle East in pursuance of the Security Council's request of 4 April 1956, had examined thoroughly the question of "retaliation" and of the right of a state party to the Armistice Agreements to undertake military action if another party violates some other provision of these Agreements. The findings of the Secretary-General, submitted to the Council on 12 September 1956, merit quoting at length:

In my report to the Security Council of 9 May 1956 I pointed out the complications which had arisen because of confusion concerning the extent to which compliance with the Armistice Agreements could be conditioned by reciprocity. I said in this context:

"As a matter of course, each party considers its compliance with the stipulations of an Armistice Agreement as conditioned by compliance of the other party to the Agreement. Should such a stand be given the interpretation that any one infringement of the provisions of the Agreement by one party justifies reactions by the other party which, in their turn, are breaches of the Armistice Agreement, without any limitation as to the field within which reciprocity is considered to prevail, it would in fact mean that the armistice regime could be nullified by a single infringement by one of the parties. Although such an interpretation has never been given from responsible quarters, it appears to me that a lack of clarity has prevailed. From no side has it been said that a breach of an Armistice Agreement, to whatever clause it may refer, gives the other party a free hand concerning the Agreement as a whole, but a tendency to regard the Agreements, including the cease-fire clauses, as entities may explain a feeling that in fact, due to infringements of this or that clause, the obligations are no longer in a strict sense fully binding, and specifically that a breach of one of the clauses, other than the cease-fire clause, may justify action in contravention of that clause."

In view of this lack of clarity I considered it essential to lift the cease-fire clauses out of the Armistice Agreements so as to give them an independent legal status as obligations, compliance with which was conditioned only by reciprocity in respect of the implementation of the same obligations by the other parties to the Armistice Agreements. As a result of the negotiations last spring such an independent status was established for the cease-fire obligations to be found in Article II:2 of the Egypt-Israel Armistice Agreement, and in Article III:2 of the Jordan-Israel, Lebanon-Israel, and Syria-Israel Armistice Agreements. Thus, no party could any longer justify a violation of the cease-fire by reference to an alleged non-compliance by other parties with other clauses of the General Armistice Agreements than the cease-fire clause itself, and then only if and when such non-compliance were found to be a reason for the exertion of the right of self-defense as recognized (and subject to the conditions) in Article 51 of the Charter. Any such measure must be immediately reported to the Security Council and is subject to decision by the Council. In this connection, circumstances make it necessary to emphasize again that acts of retaliation have repeatedly been condemned by the Security Council.

The assurances given to the United Nations of unconditional observance of the cease-fire clauses, further, made the United Nations itself a party to the cease-fire obligations. Its right to take steps for securing the implementation of these obligations was thereby again clearly established in line with the decision of the Security Council on 11 August 1949.(3)

Question: Has Israel observed the general armistice agreements?

Up to 1962, Israel had violated the General Armistice Agreements (AGG) 63,161 times.

Israel has been strongly condemned by the U.N. Security Council and the General Assembly on numerous occasions: Qibya, on 11-15 October 1953, in which 75 people were killed and the village demolished; Nahhalin, on 28-29 March 1954, in which 14 people were killed and the village demolished; the Gaza Strip, on 8 February 1955, in which 38 people were killed and 31 wounded; Khan Yunis, on 31 August 1955, in which 46 people were killed and 50 wounded; El-Buteiha, on 11-12 December 1955, in which 50 people were killed and 28 were taken prisoners; Qalqilya, on 10-11 October 1956, in which 48 people were killed and 31 wounded; El-Tawafiq, on 1 February 1962, in which the village was razed to the ground; and Sammu', on 13 November 1966, in which 18 people were killed, 130 wounded and 125 houses (including the school, clinic, and mosque) demolished. (PALESTINE IN FOCUS, pp. 91-92).

No Arab State has been condemned by any U.N. organ for violating the GAA or the cease-fire.(4)

NOTES

(1) Quoted from I. Al-Abid, VIOLENCE AND PEACE: A STUDY IN ZIONIST STRATEGY, (Beirut: P.L.O. Research Center, 1967).

(2) Bernadotte, TO JERUSALEM, Joan Bulman, trans. (London: Hodder and Stroughton, 1951), p. 211-212.

(3) E.L.M. Burns, BETWEEN ARAB AND ISRAELI (London: George Harrap and Co., 1962), p. 139 and pp. 144-145. Also U.N. Document S/3659 (September 27, 1956), Section II, pp. 2-4.

(4) For details see I. El-Abid, VIOLENCE AND PEACE, Lists 1-7.

ISRAEL'S ACTION IN SINAI
AND
FROM A STATE OF WAR TO A STATE OF PEACE

Abba Eban

Surrounded by hostile armies on all its land frontiers, subjected to savage and relentless hostility, exposed to penetrations, raids and assaults by day and by night, suffering constant toll of life amongst its citizenry, bombarded with threats of neighboring Governments to accomplish its extinction by armed force, overshadowed by a new menace of irresponsible rearmament, embattled, blockaded, besieged, Israel alone amongst the nations faces a battle for its security anew with every rising dawn and with every approaching nightfall. In a country of small area and intricate configuration, the proximity of enemy guns is a constant and haunting theme.

These are the fears and provocations which hover over us everywhere, but they fall upon us with special intensity in the frontier areas, where development projects vital to the nation's destiny could be paralyzed or interrupted by our adversaries from a position of dominating geographical advantage. In short, it is a small country where every activity by farmers or citizens becomes a test of physical and moral courage. These are the unique circumstances in which Israel pursues its quest for security and peace.

On many occasions the active defense of Israel life and territory has been compromised in deference to international opinion. We know that Israel is most popular when it does not hit back, and world opinion is profoundly important to us. So, on one occasion after another, we have buried our dead, tended our wounded, clenched our teeth in suppressed resentment and hoped that our very moderation will deter a repetition of these offenses. But sometimes the right and duty of self-preservation, the need to avoid expanding encroachment, the sentiment that if the claim to peaceful existence is not defended it will be forever lost prevails in the final and reluctant decision.

ISRAEL'S DEFENSIVE ACTION

. . . Egyptian belligerency . . . is a new device for making war and for making it with safety. The doctrine is one of unilateral belligerency. The Egyptian-Israel frontier is to be a one-way street. It is to be wide open for these armed Egyptian

324

units to penetrate deeply into Israel to accomplish their mission and to return. It is to be closed in their favor against any defensive response.

It was in these circumstances that the Government of Israel has faced the tormenting problems of its duties and obligations under the Charter of the United Nations. We are not satisfied with a justification of our actions in terms of national expediency. There is no Member of this Organization more sensitive to the currents of international opinion, more vulnerable to the dissent of friendly world opinion, broader in the scope and extent of its universal associations, less able to maintain its existence on any principle of self-sufficiency and autarky.

It was with a full knowledge of this fact that we have been forced to interpret Article 51 of the Charter as furnishing both a legal and a moral basis for our defensive action. Under Article 51 of the Charter the right of self-defense is described as "inherent"; in the French translation it is *naturel* — something which emerges from the very nature of states and humanity. This "inherent right of self-defense" is conditioned in the Charter by the existence of "an armed attack," against a Member State.

Can anyone say that this long series of murderous encroachments upon us did not constitute in its totality the essence and the reality of an armed attack? Can it seriously be suggested that we made no attempt to exhaust peaceful remedy? Time after time at the table of the Security Council and in meetings of the Mixed Armistice Commission efforts were made to bring about tranquility on the frontier. Yet all of this well intentioned, enlightened, and, at certain times, hopeful effort ended without making the life or security of a single citizen of Israel greater than it was before.

ISRAEL'S PERIL RECALLED

There has never been an aggressive war for which responsibility is more explicit and unmistakable than the UAR's responsibility for this war.

The representative of the United Arab Republic has told the Security Council nothing of all this. His Government now comes here saturated with war guilt, heavy with responsibility for nineteen years of purposeful aggression, to lay complaint and accusation against Israel.

What is the Egyptian Foreign Minister's complaint against Israel? His complaint is that Israel energetically refused to be destroyed. What is his proposal? His proposal is that Israel put itself in the position most congenial for the next attempt to destroy it. What is his purpose? His purpose is to refuse negotiation and agreement. To the offense of making war, Cairo adds the offense of refusing peace. For this refusal, the United Arab Republic seeks the Security Council's sanction.

But the dramatic facts which the UAR representative has wantonly suppressed are not forgotten in Israel. They will never be forgotten there. A new dimension has been added to the national memory, and the exploration of it will long continue. Our nation still lives intimately with the peril and solitude which afflicted it in those agonizing weeks. We still remember the cold horror which that peril evoked in world opinion. We still recall how the imminent extinction of Israel's statehood and the massacre of its population were seriously discussed across the world, in wild intoxication of spirit in every Arab capital — and with tormented but impotent sorrow in other lands. We take unbounded pride in the six days of resistance by which the danger was gloriously overcome. And we remember the heavy price exacted in death and bereavement in mutilation and anguish and suffering.

These are our memories. I evoke them here in vehement rejection of the attempt by the Egyptian representative to wash his hands clean of his government's sustained aggression against the security of Israel and the peace of the Middle East. I recall them also because these memories lie at the heart and center of Israel's policy today. If you ignore our memories, you cannot understand our policy. That policy can be expressed in a single sentence: It is our firm resolve never, never to return to the danger and vulnerability from which we have emerged. This resolve must prevail over every other consideration. To avoid a return to any of the conditions which prevailed on June 4 is a supreme national purpose, worthy of every effort and any consequence.

In their speeches to the Security Council on November 9, the Soviet and the United Arab Republic representatives sought to persuade the Security Council of two things: First, that Israel's refusal to be strangled and bludgeoned to death was an act of "aggression"; Second, that the way to get peace in the Middle East is to reproduce the precise conditions which brought about the war.

These are the only two ideas which the Soviet and Arab delegates have expressed during the long discussions of the summer and autumn months. I submit that there is not a single grain of truth or value in either of them.

CONSPIRACY OF VIOLENCE

It is especially important that the problem of aggression be faced and probed. It is the starting point for any rational understanding of past events and of future necessities. The Egyptian Foreign Minister spoke of Israeli "aggression" 61 times. The Soviet representative only 24. Frequency of reiteration is a typical symptom of weak argument. Never has this been more true than in this case. To the charge of aggression I reply that Israel's resistance to the assault concerted against it last summer will resound across the generations as a triumphant assertion of human freedom. From the dawn of its history, the people now rebuilding the State of Israel has struggled, often in desperate conditions, against tyranny and aggression. Our defense last June falls nobly within that tradition. As Israel freed itself from the aggressive stranglehold, we could hear the cry of ardent relief that resounded across the peace-loving world from end to end. Alone, embattled, neither requesting nor receiving aid, Israel by independent effort and sacrifice had withstood a conspiracy of violence. In the life of our generation, it is hard to think of any other hour in which progressive opinion has rallied in such tension and agony of spirit to any cause. Never have justice, honor, peace, national freedom and international morality been more righteously defended.

Something of this world opinion found expression even in the international organizations where Arab and Soviet positions have a great numerical advantage. Proposals seeking to define Israel's action as "aggression" were rejected in the Security Council on June 14, and in four separate votes in the General Assembly on July 4. In each case, the rejection of the charge was so emphatic as to imply a rebuke to those who had invented it. Of special significance was the defeat of what the spokesman of the Latin American group called "the ridiculous Soviet resolution" on Israel "aggression" for the discussion of which the General Assembly had been convened in emergency session.

I am aware that Israel's decision to survive has caused some difficulty for Arab representatives and those who support them. But in the light of international judgments and of massive world opinion, everyone who speaks of Israel "aggression" is uttering a violent untruth. Israel's defensive action was taken when the choice was to live or perish, to protect the national existence or to

326

forfeit it for all time. We even have Arab acknowledgement that this was our choice. The official Cairo Radio on May 23 defined the situation with unusual veracity. It said:

> Israel is faced with two alternatives, either of which will destroy it. It will either be strangled to death by the Arab territorial and economic blockade, or it will perish by fire of the Arab forces encompassing it from the South, from the North and from the East.

I repeat: "It will either be strangled to death by the Arab territorial and economic blockade, or it will perish by fire from the Arab forces encompassing it from the South, from the North, and from the East."

The most important action which the U. N. has taken, beyond the cease-fire, has been to determine the non-aggressive character of Israel's operations in early June. Everything in our policy flows from this premise. Our thinking on the political, juridical, territorial, and security aspects of the Middle Eastern problem is based on the secure premise that we have repelled aggression, are still being threatened with its renewal, and must now so act as to insure that it shall not succeed in any new assault.

X. Economic Warfare

INTRODUCTION

Battlefield warfare and guerrilla activities, as demonstrated in the 1948 Palestine War, the 1956 Suez episode, the 1967 Six Days War, and a host of dramatic aircraft hijackings, have remained the major forms of conflict in the Middle East. Yet other confrontations between the antagonists have persisted in the past twenty-five years.

The economic boycott against Israel, instituted by the Arab states, as well as the Palestinian Arab groups, is a case in point. The primary purpose of these economic sanctions, according to the Arabs, is to prevent imports to Israel of Arab products and exports from Israel to the neighboring states. Another major aim of these sanctions is to block capital from flowing into Israel.

To implement their plans the Arab League established a boycott office which has sought, for instance, to prevent foreign companies having regional offices or direct investments in Israel from operating in the Arab countries and from selling their products in the Arab markets. Justifying these activities, the Arabs assert that since a state of war exists with Isreal they have a right to exercise the boycott even against third parties. In short, the economic boycott is designed to extend the consequences of the Arab-Israeli conflict into the international world of trade.

Isreal views the Arab boycott as an extension of Arab military "aggression" against her and claims these sanctions to be in violation of international legal principles and practices. For example, the Arabs' belligerent practices are alleged to be incompatible with common membership in the U.N., an organization to which all the antagonist states belong. The Arab action is furthermore viewed as an unjustified measure against third parties not directly involved in the conflict. Israel views economic boycotts as part of a total program of Arab economic warfare, of which the maritime blockades are a portion. These modes of conflict have, in the Israeli view, made a negative impact on the economic situation of all countries and peoples involved, and have adversely affected their socio-economic development.

The first selection in this chapter is an excerpt from Marwan Iskandar's THE ARAB BOYCOTT OF ISRAEL, published in Beirut by the Research Center of the Palestine Liberation Organization in November, 1966. The author deals with the legality of the Arab boycott in terms of international legal principles and practices and with reference to the basic Armistice Agreements which regulated the relations between the Arab states and Israel.

The second Arab view is by N. I. Dajani, "Economic Impact of the Israel Aggression" published in Amman by the Ministry of Culture and Information in

July, 1969. Dajani deals specifically with the impact of the June, 1967, war on Jordan's economy. The Israeli position is reflected in an excerpt from Abba Eban's statement before the U.N. Security Council on November 12, 1953. A more recent response to the Arab boycott is presented in an excerpt from a document by the research division of the Ministry for Foreign Affairs in Jerusalem published on August 10, 1969.

THE ARAB BOYCOTT
IN INTERNATIONAL LAW

Marwan Iskandar

Appreciation of the Boycott's legality requires that it should be described in its historical origins. Early in the 20th century, the Arab population in Palestine began to suspect the motives of Zionist settlers. These were demonstrating a negative attitude toward the indigenous population. Zionist settlers did their best to achieve as high a degree of self sufficiency as was possible for an incoming minority. In agricultural settlements, the drive towards self sufficiency and non-cooperation with the indigenous population manifested itself in a partial boycott by the Zionists against the Arabs. This boycott which developed around 1907-1908, subsequent to the Basel Convention of 1897, took the form of prohibition of Arab employment in Zionist settlements and the purchase of agricultural products from the Arabs by Zionist settlers. But these acts produced localised reactions only, especially as the total number of Zionist settlers and Palestinian Jews represented by 1918 some 10 percent only of the total population in Palestine and owned around 2.5% of the land. Nevertheless, the use of an economic boycott as a tool for political ends was introduced into Palestine by the planned acts of Zionist settlers.

Arab suspicion turned after World War I into acute awareness of the drive by Zionist Jews to control Palestine. In 1917, Lord Balfour's promise that Britain would help World Jewry to establish a national home, coupled with the disclosure of the Sykes-Picot agreement by the new Russian regime, helped to increase the apprehensions of the Palestine Arabs, then 90 percent of the total population.

Zionist practices and increasing numbers of immigrants could not but cause the indigenous Arab population to view its own future with fear. Consequently, in 1936, the Arabs rose in violent opposition to the policy of open immigrantion for the Jews sanctioned by the mandatory authorities in Palestine. In the four preceding years, the rate of inflow of immigrants had increased from 9,500 in 1932 to 62,000 in 1935. This development was most significant to the Arabs in that the increase in Jewish population from immigration and natural birth in 1935 amounted to practically three times the increase in the Arab population. In absolute figures, whereas the Arab population then numbering some 960,000 increased by approximately 25,000, the Jewish population then numbering 290,000 increased by approximately 70,000.

It is no wonder that the Arabs around this time, having witnessed the proportionate increase of the Jewish population from 10% of the total population in 1918, to 28 percent in 1936, and the latest triple rate of increase in the numbers of the Jews as opposed to their own, began to adopt measures which they hoped would prevent Zionist ambitions from being realized.

During World War II, immigration could not take place at the rate it had reached before the War. Moreover, as the Germans advanced in North Africa towards Egypt and Palestine, the Jewish population became restless and immigration practically came to a stand still during the first four years of the war. In consequence of these developments, Arab-Jewish conflicts subsided during this period. But by 1945, the Arabs, fearing a resumption of Zionist activities intended to secure control over Palestine, took an important step toward frustrating them. The Arab League, which had been formed in 1944, decided to begin an economic boycott of Jewish products in Palestine, with the object of retarding their industry and thereby weakening their power to establish a Zionist state in Palestine. This move is important in that the Arab League states which decided on this boycott were independent states taking an action intended to preserve the rights of the Arab indigenous population in Palestine which was still subject to the mandate system.

The Arab League states were acting in support of the Palestine Arabs who were prohibited from organizing para-military groups by the mandatory power, in contrast to the freedom granted in this respect to the Jewish population. The only open alternative that was left for the Palestine Arabs to oppose Zionist designs was that of continuing their economic boycott of Jewish products which had started in 1936. They were supported in their renewed effort by the decision of the Arab League. Technically speaking, however, the Arab boycott of 1945 was not implemented efficiently.

In the wake of the Palestine War, the Arab League took a unanimous decision in May 1949 to establish boycott offices in all Arab countries under the supervision of a head office to be located in Damascus. By this time, the Arabs were trying to use the boycott to deny Israel the economic power to make further progress towards achieving its territorial ambitions. This is the background to the boycott which is alleged to be in contravention of international law. The allegation is based on the notion that the Arab Boycott represents the use of a right only granted to belligerent states during wartime. But, the argument continues, as the Armistice Agreements between Israel on the one hand, and Egypt, Jordan, Syria and Lebanon on the other were intended to lead to a peaceful settlement, continuity of the economic boycott contradicts the spirit of the Agreements and international law, in so far as these Agreements regulate outstanding matters between parties to the Palestine war.

At the 381st meeting of the Security Council held on November 16, 1948, it was resolved that: Council " ... calls upon the parties directly involved in the conflict in Palestine, as a further provisional measure under Article 40 of the Charter, to seek agreement forthwith, by negotiations conducted either directly or through the Acting Mediator on Palestine, with a view to the immediate establishment of the armistice including: (a) the delineation of permanent armistice demarcation lines beyond which the armed forces of the respective parties shall not move: (b) such withdrawal and reduction of their armed forces as will ensure the maintenance of the armistice during the transition to permanent peace in Palestine."(1)

Between February 1949 and July 1949, Armistice Agreements were concluded successively between Israel and Egypt, Lebanon, Syria and Jordan. These agreements were novel in one respect. "It was implicit in the Security Council's approach to the problem that there was nothing even remotely approaching a victor and vanquished relationship between the parties, who were negotiating upon the basis of absolute political and military equality."(2) By contrast, in all modern precedents, armistices were dictated by the victor and not negotiated.

Due to the negotiated character of the Armistice Agreements between parties exercising equal rights, it was an essential pre-requisite to restrict the military operations of all parties. The Armistice Agreements were to stand or fall on adherence by the parties involved to the terms restricting military operations. If violations were to be serious and numerous, then one could not expect the Armistice Agreements to be provisional measures leading to permanent peace.

The importance attached to the aim of preventing military aggression is manifestly clear in the Armistice Agreements. "The Egyptian, Lebanese and Jordan Agreements contain an identical Article I laying down four principles to be fully observed by both parties during the armistice. This was done with a view to promoting the return of permanent peace in Palestine and in recognition of the importance in this regard of mutual assurances concerning the future military operations of the parties."(3) In the Syrian agreement, the text was slightly modified without any substantive changes. In their respective order, the four principles referred to were:

1. The injunction of the Security Council against resort to military force in the settlement of the Palestine question shall henceforth be scrupulously respected by both parties.

2. No aggressive action by the armed forces — land, sea or air, of either Party shall be undertaken, planned or threatened against the people or the armed forces of the other; it being understood that use of the term "planned" in this context has no bearing on normal staff planning as generally practised in military organizations.

3. The right of each Party to its security and freedom from fear of attack by the armed force of the other shall be fully respected.

4. The establishment of an armistice between the armed forces of the two Parties is accepted as an indispensable step toward the liquidation of armed conflict and the restoration of peace in Palestine. (4)

It is clear that the first three principles constitute the corner stone in each of the four Armistice Agreements that were concluded. The fourth principle is no more than a logical legal conclusion that obtains in case the first three principles are meticulously observed. Moreover, it is an accepted principle in international law that "Armistice" does not signify termination of the state of war between belligerent parties. To any state involved in war, the state of war does not end in respect of its international legal ramifications until that state agrees to such termination of its own free or forced will.

Already we have noted that the Palestine war produced nothing like a victor-vanquished relationship. Consequently, termination of the state of war between the signatories of the Armistice Agreements had to depend on decisions taken by their own free will. The Arab countries were given no opportunity by constant Israeli aggression in violation of the Armistice Agreements to decide on termination of the state of war.

To substantiate this interpretation of events subsequent to signature of the Armistice Agreements it is sufficient to stress few salient features of Israel's military violations by contrast to military actions by the Arab states. It is important to recollect at this point that military action in violation of the Armistice Agreements constitutes an outright abrogation of international legal commitments. For the purpose of lessening strain between the parties to the Armistice Agrements three areas were delimited and declared as non-military or de-militarized zones. No military actions or movements or personnel were to be allowed in any of the demilitarized zones.

Against this background made absolutely clear to Israel and the Arab states, Israel:

1. Undertook the planning and execution of organized military action in violation of all the principles of the Armistice Agreements.

2. Transgressed over parts of all the demilitarized zones, and despite censure by the Security Council and General Assembly still violated, on what seems to be a continuing basis, areas of two of the three demilitarized zones.

3. Achieved the highest rate of international criminal delinquency as between all states, members and non-members of the United Nations, since it became obliged by international agreements to strive towards maintaining peace.

By contrast, not one Arab state has been censured for military action in violation of the Armistice Agreements. Had it not been for Arab adherence to the spirit of the Agreements, and effective, though in many instances, belated interference by the organs of the United Nations, widespread war would have erupted in the Middle East.

The status of tension perpetrated by Israeli aggression and intended oblivion to international obligations cannot be interpreted in any way as progress towards a peaceful settlement over Palestine. Consequently, the Arab view that a status of war still exists and warrants the exercise of an economic boycott against Israel is perfectly in line with the principles of international law.

This view is supported by the implicit admission at the time of negotiation of the Armistice Agreement between Syria and Israel that the former had the right to exercise an economic boycott against Israel without this action leading to any violation of the Armistice terms. At no point in the Armistice Agrement do we find explicit reference to the Boycott. Yet, the Armistice Agreement between Syria and Israel was finally signed on July 20, 1949, long after the establishment of the Head office for the Arab Boycott in the capital of Syria in May, 1949. Had the boycott been in violation of the Armistice Agreement, surely explicit reference ought to have been made to that particular.

In view of the above arguments, it is clear that the Arab Boycott of Israel is an act that conforms to international legal principles. As a matter of fact, the Arab states in view of Israel's actions would have been entitled to military reprisals and neglect of the Armistice Agreements' terms. That the Arab states have chosen to exercise the least belligerent of their international legal rights to curb Israeli aggression is a clear testimony of their collective good will and adherence to international law.

NOTES

(1) Rosenne, Shabtai, ISRAEL'S ARMISTICE AGREEMENTS WITH THE ARAB STATES –A JURIDICIAL INTERPRETATION (Blumstein's Bookstores Ltd., Tel Aviv, 1951), p. 22.

(2) Ibid., p. 31.

(3) Ibid., p. 42.

(4) Ibid.

ECONOMIC IMPACT
OF THE ISRAELI AGGRESSION

N. I. Dajani

The question that comes to one's mind is "In what way have the events of last June affected Jordan's economy"?

These effects can be classified in the following categories though it is very difficult to quantify, at this stage, the amounts involved:

1. Direct war damages which would require reconstruction. Under this category we could include damaged bridges, hospitals, farms, dwellings, etc.

2. A substantial reduction in anticipated internal revenue for the balance of the current fiscal year. The main area affected under this category will be receipts from customs since imports have more or less come to a stop and if the occupation of the West Bank continues for a few months this will certainly have a significant effect on the volume of output and the level of economic activity and hence on taxes in general.

3. There is no doubt that there will be some delay involved in the completion date of several projects which are already under construction, coupled with an increase in their original cost estimates. This will affect such activities as the current expansion of the port of Aqaba, which involves the construction of a deep berth for the accommodation of bulk carriers, the construction of storage facilities at Aqaba, the extension and expansion of Jerusalem Airport, the improvement and relocation of the Jerusalem-Bethlehem highway, and many other projects which were originally scheduled for completion either at the end of this calendar year or some time within the next 12 months.

4. Delay in the initiation of several projects which were scheduled for execution during the second half of this year. The major project affected under this category is the start of the execution of the Potash Project for which loan agreements were supposed to be signed by the middle of June this year and construction work on certain phases of the scheme was originally planned for the balance of this year. The delay in this project under these circumstances is estimated at about one year at least.

5. Substantial reduction in the flow of foreign investment and private

334

investment. Jordan has tried during the last decade and succeeded in establishing a climate for the encouragement of foreign investment and the promotion of private enterprise and investment. This was achieved by developing a proper institutional legislative structure within the framework of free enterprise and monetary and price stability.

The last events will certainly have an influence on the confidence of potential investors which will reflect itself in a lower rate of both foreign and private investment and possibly the need for either more public funds or other incentives and guarantees than was normally expected from the government. The sectors which are affected most under this category include housing, manufacturing, mining and hotel construction.

6. Political instability in the area will no doubt have some bearing on Jordan's prospects for marketing its products and particularly the conclusion of long-term marketing contracts of its mineral products.

7. A possible shift from development to military budget. The aggressive acts carried out recently point to the necessity of maintaining a larger budget for military preparedness which was maintained at somewhat constant level during the last few years and which as judged by recent events has proved to be inadequate. This will of course depend on the outcome of the political discussions and the role played by the major powers and the United Nations.

PRESENT STRATEGY

Jordan at present is no doubt facing a major economic problem. There has been a substantial increase in its population coupled with a major reduction in its natural resources, thereby constituting a serious threat to its economic unity and structure. What is also significant is that most of the refugees who moved across the River belong to the least productive part of the population including a good number of UNRWA in-camp refugees, while the people who stayed behind are mostly the people who can be classified as the entrepreneurial class of the West Bank. They include such people as the industrialists, the hoteliers, the shop owners, dwellings and the real estate owners and so on. What this means is that the East Bank has received a large number of people who have to be sheltered, fed, schooled, etc., without any additional means which would make this added burden endurable. So far the contributions made were on strictly emergency basis and are not adequate to cope with the problem.

The Jordan Development Board is now developing a certain number of projects which are labour intensive and could employ as many of the evacuees as possible and at the same time have a short construction period so that the output from these prolong. The list of these projects include road construction particularly village roads, farm-to-market roads, relocation of some primary and secondary roads which have been subject to certain slides, irrigation schemes, low cost housing, clearance and improvement of certain touristic sites, etc. The list also includes the acceleration of some agricultural and irrigation schemes which were originally scheduled for completion by next year so as to shorten the construction period to the shortest extent possible. The government is also planning to give certain soft term loans to industrialists to enable them to maintain employment of their workers during the present economic crisis.

The occupation of the West Bank is considered by the Jordan Government to be of temporary nature, and plans are being prepared for the reconstruction and rehabilitation of the area after withdrawal of the occupying forces. The plans are per force of short term nature in view of the various elements of uncertainty, since the whole bases and assumptions for planning will have to be

335

reviewed in the light of the military and political framework which it is hoped will be resolved within the course of months, otherwise the whole economic structure and the role of foreign aid will have to be re-examined to determine the direction in which the economy will move.

After the withdrawal of the occupying forces from the West Bank, the implementation of the Seven Year Program would be resumed. We are firmly convinced that the objectives of this Program can be achieved and that Jordan has a unique opportunity to demonstrate, under the leadership and guidance of His Majesty King Hussein, how a determined and conscientious people are able to shoulder the grave challenges of our time, without foregoing their cherished values or their faith in a free and responsible society.

ECONOMIC EFFECTS

Abba Eban

Political hatred is reinforced by a violent economic war. The Council of the Arab League maintains a special section for centralising economic warfare against Israel. Boycott committees exist everywhere under the auspices of the Arab League. At every meeting of the Arab League Council steps are taken to insure that no intercourse of trade should inadvertently take place across Israel's frontiers and thus create links of common economic interest. In the absence of mutual economic interchange, both Israel and the Arab States, deprived of markets and sources of supply within their own region, are forced into wasteful commercial practices with the result that both sides become artificially dependent on external financial aid. Third parties, especially countries which generously finance economic aid abroad, are thus called upon to endorse and pay the bill presented by the Arab League for the emotional luxury of its boycott policy. There is a purposeful attempt to impose the anti-Israel economic siege upon other countries. The outstanding example was the intrusion of Arab States, fortunately rebuffed, into the economic agreement between Israel and Western Germany. Efforts are made to force other countries and industrial concerns to adapt themselves to the Arab policy of regional economic hostility, in other words to join the siege on Israel's frontiers.

At the peak of this economic warfare, which threatens the sovereignty of all states exposed to its pressure, stand the Egyptian blockade regulations ruled by this Security Council on 1 September 1951 to be a violation of the Egyptian-Israel Armistice Agreement. These regulations continue in full force, exercising all the deterrent effects of a blockade with respect to shipments through the Suez Canal, and imposing such risks of illicit intervention as to make the transportation of cargoes to or from Israel through the Canal precarious and, therefore, rare.

The economic siege goes beyond defiance of international law or blockade and pervades every manifestation of Arab policy. Water sources essential for Israel's economy have twice within four years been the subject of obstructive Syrian complaints, although these waters are historically, politically and geographically unavailable to Syria except on the assumption of aggressive Syrian expansion beyond its recognized frontiers. The superficiality of these complaints assures their ultimate collapse, but in the meantime vital economic development is delayed. Together with this attempt to deny Israel the ability to carry out its national development schemes, there goes a comprehensive Arab opposition to every project of regional economic development. Thus any inter-state progress involving irrigation and power is subjected to a double veto. The Arab states will neither agree to regional cooperation with Israel nor will they leave Israel alone to utilize its available resources within national limits. In brief, we have the only instance in contemporary international relations of a group of states making the economic strangulation of their neighbor an active objective of their policy and seeking international support for that objective.

ARAB
BOYCOTT

Ministry of Foreign Affairs
(Jerusalem)

Addressing the meeting of Arab boycott officers, the Secretary-General of the Arab League said: "The boycott of Israel is one of our rights and is authorized in the UN Charter." [MENA, Cairo, 2.8.69]

BOYCOTT A MOST EFFECTIVE WEAPON
Speaking to the Arab boycott officers, the Egyptian Minister for War, Fawzi said:

> The principal motivation for war in our times is actually the economic factor ... You know that one of the ways to wreck the (enemy's) economic potential is by boycott and blockade ... The Arab boycott is, no doubt, one of the strategic elements against an enemy, who has stolen precious parts of our Arab land ... Israel's economy is an artificial one and not natural ... The boycott is considered one of our most effective weapons in our historic struggle against the base of Western imperialistic expansion in the region, namely Israel ...

Fawzi stressed that Egypt, under Nasser's leadership, would not hesitate to sacrifice all it holds dear to support the Arab right, to return every inch of Arab land and to restore their legal rights to the Palestinians.

> (We must) ... check again how the Arab boycott is directed, the measures and methods to be adopted to turn it into a more effective instrument of our confrontation with Zionist imperialistic activity, whose severity and vileness get ever stronger.'[MENA, Cairo, 2.8.69]

BOYCOTT IS INTEGRAL PART OF ARAB STRATEGY

> It is a known fact that closing the Arab markets to Israel, in addition to the boycott, has left a deep mark on the enemy's economy, causing him

339

many difficulties. To strengthen this boycott must, therefore, be one of the goals of a strategy of escalation. [Al-Ahram, Cairo, 27.7.69]

CUTTING FILMS, INHIBITING SALES OF VEHICLES AND BLACK LISTS

The 28th meeting of boycott officers took place on 5.8.69. It was decided to work out special regulations concerning the transit between Arab States of vehicles made by blacklisted manufacturers, so as to ensure the full application of the boycott and prevent the smuggling and sale of these vehicles in any of the Arab States. The Chief Boycott Officer, Ahmed Mahjoub, said that the meeting discussed how to cut parts out of films, in which boycotted film-stars appear in minor roles, so that the film itself should not be mutilated. [MENA, Cairo, 5.8.69]

Libya has decided to blacklist nineteen companies in several States for having infringed the rules of the Arab boycott. [Libyan News Agency, 4.8.69]

INTRODUCTION

The conflict between the Arab states and Israel is a confrontation between internationally recognized legal and political entities. In recent years, particularly in the post-1967 period, Palestinian Arab organizations have emerged on the scene claiming a status of national revolutionary movements. The assert their legitimacy under international law and claim a parallel to the Chinese revolution, the revolutions of Vietnam, Algeria, and Cuba. They conclude that their struggle is, like that of some African peoples, for liberation from the rule of a white minority.

The Arab organizations, to be sure, have been active de facto for more than fifty years. During the mandatory period Arab Palestinian groups initiated terror operations against the Jewish community in an attempt to control the country. As the birth of Israel drew near, guerrilla groups inside Palestine and from the neighboring countries had been engaged in systematic sabotage activities hoping to prevent the establishment of the State. After the Jewish entity came into being in 1948 another wave of guerrilla activities was commenced by Arab Palestinian groups, particularly by the "Fedayeen" who raided Israel from across the armistice lines. In 1956 it was the "Fedayeen" units, organized, trained, and armed by Egypt, against which Israel moved in the Sinai campaign.

For the next ten years, guerrilla activities continued and, in fact, intensified with the establishment of the Palestinian Liberation Organization (P.L.O.) and its Palestinian Liberation Army (P.L.A.) at a Summit Conference of the Arab League in Casablanca in 1964. The P.L.O. is a political umbrella organization for numerous guerrilla groups. Of these "El-Fatah" is the largest and most influential and its leader, Yasir Arafat, is chairman of the P.L.O.

While guerrilla movements have been able to win a limited right to exist within several Arab states, Israel does not accept them as legitimate revolutionary organizations. On the contrary, Israel regards them as "terrorists" whose sole aim is the destruction of a recognized member of the family of nations. Resorting to deliberate terror, often against civilian and foreign populations, with the political, financial, and military support of the Arab states, they fail in the Israeli view to resemble any genuine revolutionary movement. In addition, their activities are not a "people's war" because major segments of the Arab Palestinians, including those residing within Israel's territory, have failed to identify with the forces of the revolution. Israel concludes that it is the Arab terror groups which block the path to peace and seek to drag the Arab people into another Middle East war.

The Arab view of this problem is contained in an article by Ezzeldin Foda.

341

This selection was published in ZIONISM AND ARAB RESISTANCE by Beirut's Palestine Research Center in February, 1969. The Israeli position is given by the Ministry of Foreign Affairs in a document entitled "War by Terror," published in Jerusalem in September 1970.

THE LEGITIMACY OF RESISTANCE
AND
HUMAN RIGHTS IN THE OCCUPIED TERRITORY

Ezzeldin Foda

The nature of wars has become different and the concept of war has underwent a change in modern times. War is no longer a legal state (situation de droit) irrespective of its actual existence as a material state of affairs (situation de fait), as the case used to be in the age of the rise of international law following the Peace of Westphalia in 1648. International circumstances then — in the age that witnessed the rise of the nation-state, the appearance and triumph of capitalism, the splendor of state sovereignty and the organization of international relations on the basis of a traditional balance of power between states — have called for a justification of war as a characteristic feature of modern state sovereignty and as an indispensable means for the execution of national policy at the expense of other states and groups. Hence, the idea of the "just war" that justifies the existence of any state of material warfare as long as its causes and aims agree with the teachings of the Church, was no longer accepted by Royal thrones and men of colonialist ambitions. The creation of a state of war has become subject to the sovereign will of States and in accordance with the rights to sovereignty. A state of war has to imply certain legal provisions and conditions that qualify it for a legal war, i.e. a war that commences or ends under International Law, not a mere state of armed hostilities.(1)

When the sovereign states embarked upon the task of writing down some of the principles of the Law of War they did not aim, under any circumstances whatsoever, at a denunciation and condemnation of war, or at a prohibition of war as such. What they did instead was to collect and commit to writing some principles already established in international usage as customary, and dictated by considerations of international ethics, religious teachings and public human conscience, the purpose being to organize hostilities and war operations, and to diminish the sufferings of humanity from the evils of wars.

On this basis, conventional international Law regulated the State of War and the conditions for applying the law of war to such a state in the light of the following considerations:

— That it be a war between states, whereby open armed hostilities and fighting occur between the regular armies of two or more states.

This does not mean that traditional jurisprudence (Grotins, Zouche, Pufendorf, Vattel) did not know other kinds of armed hostilities falling outside the scope of legal war. Side by side with legal wars, there always arose other kinds of fighting and belligerence called "Rebellion," "Insurrection," "Revolution" and "Civil War." All of these taken together are of one nature in so far as they denote a struggle between the state as a person and parts of its subjects. But such kinds of hostility do not bear, under International Law, the attribute of Public War between Sovereign States. In spite of that, traditional International Law has recognized the phenomenon of civil war, as a result of the recognition willfully accorded by States to the rights of belligerents in those revolutions bound by rules and customs of war.(2)

— That there be a declaration of a state of war and an issuing of an explicit warning to that effect (Ultimatum) on the part of the State that wishes to absolve itself from the condition of peace existing between it and the other State or States. These latter "entities" have no choice in such a case but to respond to this hostile desire and take the stand of self-defense.(3) On this basis, constitutional Jurisprudence in the Anglo-Saxon countries (the U. S. in particular) has refused to consider any state of hostilities not preceeded by a declaration of war as a legally existing state of war. It is for such a purpose that the Third Hague Convention of 1907 stipulated for the High Contracting Parties the necessity of issuing a warning of war in the form of an ultimatum containing a "conditional but definite threat."

However, international jurisprudence has achieved much development in this respect, in taking into consideration the fact that a mere recognition on the part of one belligerent side of an existing state of war with the other side, is in itself an expression of this existing state of war. Failure to meet the obligation stipulated in the Convention of 1907, i.e. failure to issue the necessary Ultimatum, constitutes only a violation of this international obligation on the part of the High contracting parties.(4)

— Lastly, war under traditional international law is not a state of actual or material armed hostility calling for the application of Laws and Regulations of War irrespective of conditions for commencing open hostilities, or persons of the belligerent parties. It is rather a legal state arising out of certain existant conditions that qualify an actual state of affairs, for a "State of war under International Law," and hence require the implementation of international customs and regulations in the conduct of war and for diminishing the evils of war.(5)

It goes without saying that this traditional theory of the concept of war and the protection of mankind in war has impaired, by its nature, the appropriation of modern developments in international relations and the occurrent wars of national liberation, without taking into consideration these constitutional developments resulting from the rights of peoples to self-determination and rights of individuals to protect their basic liberties.

In its definition of "legal wars" and the distinctions drawn between these wars and various other kinds of armed hostility and belligerence, the traditional theory has fallen short of according protection to wars possessing no international character, and to armed hostilities that break out within the domain of the one State or between militant Revolutionaries and the regular armies of the Strife-torn State (such as the case is in Vietnam, the Congo and North of Iraq). More important still, that same theory stood as an obstacle against the resort to

344

armed force through means other than international war for the sake of self-defence (self-help) on the part of small peoples and states.(6)

Furthermore, the content of such a theory can no longer give legitimacy to an international war as a means for executing national policies of States, since the Pact of Paris (the Kellog-Briand Pact of 1928) and the Charter of the United Nations Organization (1945). This latter Charter stipulated clearly and explicitly the prohibition of "the threat or use of force against the territorial integrity or political independence of any state, or in any other manner inconsistent with the Purposes of the United Nations" (Article 2, paragraph 4). Chapter VI of the Charter has provided for pacific settlements of disputes through such means as "negotiation, enquiry, mediation, conciliation, arbitration, judicial settlement, resort to regional agencies or arrangements, or other peaceful means of their own choice." (Art. 33).

If the U.N. Charter was clear and explicit in prohibiting international wars and the non-recognition of any territorial gains resulting from such wars and claimed in the name of a legitimate war, or the right of conquest under traditional international law, it has also provided for other kinds of wars or warlike actions arising to deter aggression and denounce it by means of a collective system for the maintenance or restoration of international peace and security (Chapter VII of the Charter). According to Article 51 of the U.N. Charter, "Nothing in the present Charter shall impair the inherent right of individual or collective self-defense if an armed attack occurs against a Member of the United Nations, until the Security Council has taken the measures necessary to maintain international peace and security."

Clearly then, when modern international law prohibits the use of armed forces or the threat of force in international wars and disputes, and when it permits the resort to armed force for the sake of self-defense, i.e. the "just war of self-defense," this law purports to recognize the existence of a new situation created by the practical necessity of international life and channeled towards a new position that combines the two traditional states of war and peace. The phenomenon of revolutionary wars, such as wars of liberation and movements of national resistance conducted on the part of the occupied people for the sake of self-determination, or for detering an act of aggression committed by forces of occupation in wars of a criminal character, can thus occupy the same legal status enjoyed by wars of self-defense.(7)

This attitude has had the support of small states since the time of those first attempts to write down the regulation concerning the Laws and Customs of War in the Brussels Conference on War-Law (1874), and in the first Hague Conference of 1899. In the face of Big States' insistence upon retaining freedom of political action and imperialist expansion, and upon legalizing the purely armed conflict by means of regular armies only, there arose resistance on the part of the small states participating in those Conferences and refusal to limit the concept of a legal war to this single form or kind of armed hostilities. Hence, small member-states were determined to have national resistance included within the scope of legal wars and protected under the law of war. Disagreement between the participants reached such a degree of tension that it threatened the Conference with failure and collapse. A declaration was then issued to the effect that, the rules and usages of war as appearing in the conventions drafted by this Conference, do not cover all the circumstances which arise in practice, nor do they intend that "unforeseen cases should be left to the arbitrary judgment of military commandes." In other words, self-defense was tacitly recognized as a just means.(8)

It is a known fact that the Rules respecting the Law of war and its Regulations, as they have been written down in the Hague Conventions of 1899 and 1907, the Geneva Protocol of 1924, and the Geneva Conventions of 1949, constitute a set of principles that reveals some of the rules established in international practice and usage. But they do not constitute a universal or comprehensive limitation on the inhuman means of using wars and arms.(9) The Hague Conferences were especially convened to deal with limiting the kinds of arms used in wars and to appropriate the peaceful means for settling disputes, but not to write down every kind of principle or usage established by humanity as far as prohibiting the inhuman use of arms or the resort to various kinds of armed hostilities. Both Conventions, that of 1899 and 1907, did provide for this. The Preamble of the 4th Hague Convention (1907), for instance, stated the following:

> Until a more complete code of the laws of war has been issued, the high contracting Parties deem it expedient to declare that, in cases not included in the Regulations adopted by them, the inhabitants and the belligerents remain under the protection and the rule of the principles of the law of nations, as they result from the usages established among civilized peoples, from the laws of humanity, and the dictates of the public conscience.(10)

The Geneva Protocol of 1924 indicates that acts contrary to the public conscience of the civilized world are no doubt committed against international law. Furthermore, what is prohibited by provisions of the Protocol, should become the accepted and established principle of international law on a world-scale, as long as such principles are sanctioned by the public conscience and international practice.

Should there be any more need, in view of what has already been said, for further discussion on the essence and nature of war, in that it is a war calling for compliance with the laws intended to diminish its human evils? Does a Declaration of War on the part of one State against another constitute a basic condition for abiding by those conventions? Or, does the mere existence of armed hostilities, actual or material between two organized and regular belligerent forces, lead automatically to an implementation of the above mentioned rules commensurate with the degree and extent attained by hostile operations?(11)

In the light of these considerations revealing the humane character and objective of the legal rules mentioned in the special conventions on the law of war, and in the light of the prescriptive (normative), not constructive (descriptive) nature of these rules, and in view of the necessity of going back to what has been established by international usage and accepted by the public conscience — in any case not provided for in the aforementioned conventions, it could be said that the distinction between an international and a limited (localized) war is no longer relevant to the scope of applying these conventions whatsoever.(12) Perhaps this distinction has become so thin, that it only pertains at present to an extension of the scope or "locale" of war in both cases, and to be extent of applying the rules of international public law to them. Should these rules be complied with from the commencement of open hostilities, such as the case is in international wars where no change occurs in the person of the two belligerent states? Or, does the application of these rules change, following the stages in the process of rise and development of the international character and pending upon the extension of war operations necessary for its recognition as such?(13)

But is it logically possible to maintain that in all these stages and conditions a state of actual, material war ought not come under a regulation provided by the law of war which intends to diminish the human evils of warfare? Or, do all inhumane acts, immoral and contrary to civilized custom, become legalized and permissible in this case? Is it allowed under modern international law for a state to seek refuge in the law of war in order to exercise the right to international war in the traditional concept of war, whereas the U.N. Charter prohibits the threat or use of force? In such a case, the United Nations cannot stand still, by virtue of its Charter. Rather it has an obligation to apply such measures as "complete or partial interruption of economic relations and of rail, sea, air, postal, telegraphic, radio, and other means of communication, and the severance of diplomatic relations," up to military intervention by armed forces of Members of the U.N. against that state or party failing to comply with measures decided upon by the Security Council. Does not this in itself mean that, when the World Organization embarks upon intervention in order to prevent an aggravation of a situation likely to endanger the maintenance of international peace and security, it would be only exercising the right of the international community to prevent or denounce any open armed hostilities of whatever degree, scope and duration (See Articles 34, 41 and 42 of the U.N. Charter).(14)

What is the rule of a war conducted by the United Nations in this case, either as a police action or as an act of suppression required by collective security? Or what is the rule of a war permitted and regulated under the Charter of the World Organization for the sake of self-defense? Do not the Law and principles of humane war as stipulated in the Hague and Geneva Conventions apply to this war, too? Modern international law has prohibited the resort to an international war in order to score territorial gains against the territorial integrity or political independence of any state, whereas it has permitted other kinds of wars such as wars of a non-international character (local wars), of such a nature and objectives that place them outside the scope of wars legalized by traditional law. It follows then, that modern International law provides for applying the Law and Regulations of War as a means of defense against the inhuman use of war devices and tools in the latter kind of non-international (local) wars. To maintain the contrary means that we still subscribe to the position of traditional jurisprudence where a link is posited between international war as a "legal state," but not legalized yet, and the application of the law of war. Or else, we take an opposing and radical stand with respect to developing the law of war and extending the efforts to diminish the evils of war on the basis of prohibiting the right to wage war and negating its aforementioned objectives, bearing in mind at the same time that there do exist other kinds of non-international wars and of armed hostilities in general.

International public Law in its modern development does not condemn those other kinds of war regulated by the U.N. Charter, and those armed hostilities that develop within the social body of the one State into a civil war, where rights of belligerents are recognized and also their right to apply the laws and customs of humane war to themselves.

Furthermore, where traditional law has embarked upon reorganizing the rules of war and committing some of its usages and customs to writing, the intention was not to justify or prohibit war as such, but rather to prohibit certain acts contrary to humane practice. It should be absurd to maintain that such rules apply only to those acts considered in the past as having been committed under law, whereas the same rules should not apply to those acts committed in the Post World War II period, in view of that movement on a world-scale towards liberation in the colonies, and deemed legal and legitimate under the U.N. Charter.

The Law and Regulations of war for the sake of diminishing its human evils still stand, and are in constant need of development and modification, as long as acts of social and collective violence do exist in international relations. Also as long as there do exist western schools and opinions of jurisprudence that still consider those provisions of the U.N. Charter prohibiting the threat or use of force to mean war in its old traditional concept, and not any act of violence or force that falls short of international, open, armed force, such as reprisals or acts in retaliation, naval blockade, acts of sabotage and preventive wars.

All this is extremely important in limiting the scope of our discussion with respect to the necessary application of international written conventions on the laws regulating wars and aiming at diminishing the evils of war, and the inherent basic rights of peoples and individuals (These rights are much more older and deep-rooted in the history of mankind than those laid-down human rights in the legal grab that is called for at present in constitutions and international agreements) to those armed hostilities of a non-conventional international character, especially with respect to the law governing acts of occupying territories and acts of national resistance. It goes without saying that a great number of these rights and freedoms mentioned in the Universal Declaration of Human Rights (1948), and in the two political, social and economic conventions open for signature during this present year of human rights, have been included in the Four Geneva Conventions of 1949 relative to the Protection of war victims and considered as complementing the two Hague Conventions of 1899 and 1907 with respect to war on land and at sea.

International Conventions and Agreements concerning the protection of human rights make it a point to stipulate the right of States party to them to take those measures that run contrary to their obligations in safeguarding the rights of the individual within those limits required by war circumstances or other considerations of internal conflict threatening the nation (Article 15 of the European convention for the Protection of Human Rights and Fundamental Freedoms, Article 4 of the Draft International Convention on Civil and Political Rights). Such stipulations must then include within their jurisdiction, in order to guarantee such rights for peoples and individuals, those conventions regulating the law of war relevant to the protection of war victims and belligerent parties. This inclusion applies particularly to the Geneva Conventions of 1949.(15)

It is worth mentioning in this context that the Geneva Conventions have discarded the concept of war in traditional jurisprudence as a legal state subject to conditions, and adopted instead the concept of Actual War as defined by the outbreak of armed hostilities in a battlefield ("locale"), not necessarily conducted by belligerent parties that have to be States aiming at executing Their policy to the detriment of one another.(16)

Article 2 of the Geneva Convention on the Protection of Civilian Persons in Time of War (12 August, 1949) stipulated the following:

> In addition to the provisions which shall be implemented in peace time, the present Convention shall apply to all cases of declared war or of any other armed conflict which may arise between two or more of the High Contracting Parties, even if the state of war is not recognized by one of them.
> The Convention shall also apply to all cases of partial or total occupation of the territory of a High Contracting Party, even if the said

occupation meets with no armed resistance.

Although one of the Powers in conflict may not be a party to the present Convention, the Powers who are parties thereto shall remain bound by it in their mutual relations. They shall furthermore be bound by the Convention in relation to the said Power, if the latter accepts and applies the provisions thereof.

Article 3 provided for the following:

In the case of armed conflict not of an international character occurring in the territory of one of the High Contracting Parties, each Party to the conflict shall be bound to apply, as a minimum, the following provisions:

1. Persons taking no active part in the hostilities, including members of armed forces who have laid down their arms and those placed *hors de combat* by sickness, wounds, detention, or any other cause, shall in all circumstances be treated humanely, without any adverse distinction founded on race, colour, religion or faith, sex, birth or wealth, or any similar criteria.

To this end the following acts are and shall remain prohibited at any time and in any place whatsoever with respect to the above-mentioned persons: a) Violence to life and person, in particular murder of all kinds, mutilation, cruel treatment and torture; b) taking of hostages; c) outrages upon personal dignity, in particular, humiliating and degrading treatment; and d) the passing of sentences and the carrying out of executions without previous judgment pronounced by a regularly constituted court, affording all the judicial guarantees which are recognized as indispensable by civilized peoples.

2. The wounded and sick shall be collected and cared for. An impartial humanitarian body, such as the International Committee of the Red Cross, may offer its services to the Parties to the conflict.

The Parties to the conflict should further endeavour to bring into force, by means of special agreements, all or part of the other provisions of the present Convention.

The application of the preceding provisions shall not affect the legal status of the Parties to the conflict.

As a matter of fact, some writers on the subject have interpreted the phrase: "armed conflict not an international character" (as stated by the Geneva Convention relating to implementation of the Law of War on the belligerents) as being a state of civil war following the recognition of belligerents' rights accorded to revolutionaries. This opinion is no longer part of any respected trend of thought in modern international law. Hence, it is no longer maintained that the law to be implemented in the case of revolutionaries or rebels during the phase of pre-recognition of belligerents' rights, is no other than the internal penal code of the existing authority inside the State that is divided against itself and torn by dissension and insurrection. But modern interpreters on the whole, and especially in Anglo-Saxon jurisprudence, tend to favor the opinion that as soon as a revolution breaks out and revolutionaries declare themselves hostile to the existing authority and in rebellion against it, it becomes necessary to apply the international rules of the Law of War *Jus in bello*, even to a limited degree. The more a revolution extends in scope and the more the hostilities spread, the scope of applying the Law of War should be extended accordingly. In one way, the issue depends upon the material or concrete quantitative development of events. The international character of revolutionaries follows the trail of such development. The scope of applying international public law is extended respectively, so as to include all aspects of the conflict: in its transition from a conflict or hostility of no international character to one between two entities possessed by an internationally recognized belligerent status. Or, until such a time comes for the "extinction" of one belligerent party politically and legally — either the revolution triumphs and replaces the old government, or it is crushed and thereby the legal character and status of the revolutionaries disappear.(17)

In view of this, it appears that there is no room for the distinction between succeeding or different stages of the course taken by a revolution, i.e., its transition from the stage of rebellion or insurgence, to that of revolution followed by a civil war. These are stages of quantitative, not qualitative nature. During these stages, the international character develops concurrently with the developing hostile operations, their extended scope and duration. Such different names are mere variations expressing one single character of an actual and concrete state, where revolutionary activity develops under criteria that differ in political but not legal thought.

Since traditional international law has not really provided us with any definite criteria for distinguishing between stages of conflict prior to civil war with no international character, and between civil war as one kind of conflict, it becomes extremely difficult to distinguish between them on the basis of protection or non-protection under the law of war which in turn, is a law aiming at one goal in all of these cases.

If such is the case of an internal armed conflict raging between a government and its subjects, then the armed conflict that rages between men of the resistance and force of occupation primarily calls for applying the law of war to regulate resistance operations and protect its men from dangers. In cases of territories coming wholly or partially under occupation, sovereignty still belongs to the legitimate State. A provisional status of occupation does not entail any change in the relation between the legitimate state and its sovereign rights over the said territory. Furthermore, the occupant has no legitimation of authority, from the legal point of view, to alter the international status of the occupied territory, through annexation, partition, alteration of judicial laws in force of the country, or intervention in the daily life of inhabitants of the territory occupied, unless he intervenes within the narrowest limits that guarantee security for his forces and accord protection to his military operations. The occupied State continues legally to exercise "territorial concern" over the occupied territory, no matter how long the occupation endures, inspite of the fact that its exercise of authority or "concern" has been actually obstructed or suspended by the emergence of another actual status when the territory was occupied by military forces of the hostile army.

What this amounts to, is that the emergence of a certain situation whereby the territory has fallen to a hostile army or passed under its control and authority, does not mean a negation of the national character of the said territory. Nor does it entail an absence of loyalty and allegiance on the part of its inhabitants to their country and legitimate State. A territory actually placed under the occupation of a hostile army is not supposed to turn into a hostile territory, or that its inhabitants become hostile to their fellow countrymen, families, kinship and State. In this respect the judgment pronounced by the prizes Court in the Gerasimo Case on April 2, 1857 stated the following:

It is inconceivable, no matter how long this occupation has to endure, that Moldavia should become part of Russia, or that its inhabitants should become enemies of those who are fighting Russia. The most that could be reached is the temporary interruption of the High Porte's Sovereignty and a temporary assumption of Russian authority. But the national character of this territory remains unaltered and unchanged, as it used to be. Any attempt to the contrary of this principle, on the part of Russia, will be met with refusal.(18)

Since the authority exercised by forces of occupation is based on a "de facto" situation and an actual state of affairs, and not on grounds of exercising powers of legal sovereignty, occupation authorities usually resort to exemplary punishment (maltreatment and torture) of occupied inhabitants, compelling them to obedience and swearing allegiance. The occupant forces them to disclose secrets and furnish information about their fellow-citizens or military forces. Then, those inhabitants have no choice but to resist occupants and carry arms against them. An authority established on force rather than law, as is the case of occupation authorities in general, can only be resisted by force. The inhabitants have, under these conditions, to organize themselves into movements of armed national resistance, as the only unavoidable legitimate means under international public law for self-defense, protection of property and maintenance of the status of affairs where the transfer of authority does not lead to insurance of any legislative measures on the part of occupation forces in the form of orders-in-council. These orders do not assume the character of laws pertaining to the original State whose territory has passed under occupation, but only aggravate the provocative nature of occupation and call the occupied people to arms. For the purpose of illustration, not exhaustion, one could cite the measures resorted to by Israeli authorities in the occupied territories, such as the annexation of the Holy City of Jerusalem, changing school curriculae and educational programs, altering judicial procedures, demolishing houses and buildings, evacuating the population and expelling inhabitants, and acquiring lands, etc. All said measures which run contrary to the general rules to be duly applied under temporary cases of complete or partial occupation, and as stipulated in the articles of the Geneva Convention for the protection of civilian inhabitants.(19)

An important domain of international jurisprudence has concerned itself with the question of justifying people's resistance to occupation authorities and determining its legitimacy, to the same extent that it has called for applying laws of war and humanitarian rules respecting the attempts to diminish the evils of war suffered by members of resistance forces apart from the treatment accorded to members of regular armed forces. Resistance to occupation authorities means resisting the occupation as an illegal presence resulting from an invasion of the occupied territory contrary to International law that prohibits such a kind of territorial war conducted for the sake of scoring political or territorial gains. Whereas civilian inhabitants become free to defend themselves and their country against the invaders by resorting to all possible means, forces of occupation remain bound to follow war rules and customs with respect to the treatment of the civilian population and prisoner members of the Resistance.(20) Of relevance to this, is the decision made by the Polish Supreme Court in the "Greiser Case," to the effect that: a) Acts considered legitimate under international law make it impossible for Polish Court, to pronounce penal judgments against those committing them; b) A war of aggression cannot be justified under International Law; and c) Acts committed by occupation authorities are considered illegal acts, as long as the occupation resulting from a war launched contrary to international law is an illegitimate occupation.

Finally, the legitimation of resistance acts on the part of inhabitants of occupied territories is based upon the temporary nature of occupation and the allegiance of the inhabitants to their former state. As long as forces of occupation exercise more "de facto" authority, and not "de jure", the inhabitants' obligation to obey belongs to the original state as bearer of legal sovereignty. This original State has the right to punish individuals who squander their allegiance to it, as soon as it resumes the actual exercise of its authority upon the termination of occupation, and as long as no agreement to the contrary has been reached in a peace treaty whereby the State of origin renounces the territory to the occupant State. Hence, "there is no obligation, moral or legal, on the part of inhabitants of occupied territory towards the occupant State and forces of occupation; so much so that secret resistance against the enemy in the occupied territory becomes a legitimate and permitted kind of war." (21)

There is nothing under international public law to impair the inhabitants of occupied territories from resorting to acts of national resistance against the occupant. There is also nothing to prevent, but rather everything calls for implementation of rules of the Law of war and for diminishing the human evils of war on the inhabitants of occupied territories, whether occupation is met by resistance or not. (Article 2 of the Geneva Convention on the Protection of Civilian persons).

Finally, there is nothing to prevent, but rather everything calls for treating members of the national resistance forces as prisoners of war. Article 4 of the Geneva Convention, relative to the Treatment of Prisoners of War (August 12, 1949), stipulates that

> prisoners of war, in the sense of the present Convention, who have fallen into the power of the enemy, belong to one of the following categories:
>
> Members of other militias and members of other volunteer corps, including those of organized resistance movements, belonging to a Party to the conflict and operating in or outside their own territory, even if this territory is occupied, provided that such militias or volunteer corps, including such organized resistance movements, fulfil the following conditions: a) that of being commanded by a person responsible for his subordinates; b) that of having a fixed distinctive sign recognizable at a distance; c) that of carrying arms openly; and d) that of conducting their operations in accordance with the laws and customs of war.(22)

NOTES

(1) What this amounts to, in other words, is the existence of a legal state of war without military activity on either side, or the existence of actual hostilities. It also means that a state may resort to the use of armed force against another without a legal state of war maintaining. See Lord McNair — THE LEGAL EFFECTS OF WAR, 1966, pp. 2-6.

(2) Grotins has named such kinds of hostilities as "mixed wars" (Guerres mixtes) arising between the state and its subjects. Dufendorf called them wars that exist within the one society. De Martens has described them as wars conducted between members of the one State. Calvo gave such wars the name of "struggle" between citizens inside the one state. Lastly, E. de Vattel said: "When a nation is split against itself, divided into 2 opposing parts, with each one of them resorting to arms, this is civil war".

(3) Julius Stone — LEGAL CONTROLS OF INTERNATIONAL CONFLICTS, (London, Stevens, 1954), p. 305. Such was the case witnessed in the Spanish Civil War and the Korean War, inspite of the United Nations' non-recognition for the government of North Korea. That also applies to the Algerian war of liberation.

(4) Ibid. See also Mc Nair, op. cit., p. 7.

(5) Mc Nair, op. cit., pp. 7-8.

(6) Note in this respect the attitude of small states at the Hague Conference of 1899, and their insistence upon permitting all kinds and means of self-defense other than resorting to regular armies. See: W.J. Ford — "Resistance Movements in Occupied Territory", — NETHERLANDS INTERNATIONAL LAW REVIEW (Oct. 1956), p. 355.

(7) Metin Tomboc — INTERNATIONAL CIVIL WAR (Ankara, 1967), pp. 67-87.

(8) Ford — op. cit., p. 35.

(9) These early conventions (The two Hague Conventions of 1829 and 1907) are especially noted with respect to protection of belligerents in a war that breaks out in a legal State under customary international law. Both conventions have provided for the following:

— "The right of belligerents to adopt means of injuring the enemy is not unlimited" (Article 22 of the 2nd Hague Convention, 1899 and of the Hague Convention 1907).

— Prohibition "to employ poison or poisoned arms", and "to kill or wound treacherously individuals belonging to the hostile nation or army" (Article 23).

— "The attack or bombardment, by whatever means, of towns, villages, dwellings, or buildings which are undefended is prohibited". (Article 25, 4th Hague Convention of 1907).

— "The bombardment by naval forces of undefended ports, towns, villages, dwellings, or buildings, is forbidden" (Article 1 of the 9th Hague Convention, 1907).

— Pillage, plunder and hostages are formally forbidden even when a town or place are taken by assault. (Article 28 of the 2nd Hague Convention, 1899 and Article 47 in the 4th Hague Convention, 1907, and Article 7 of the 9th Hague Convention, 1907).

— "A Belligerent is forbidden to force the inhabitants of territory occupied by it to furnish information about the army of the other belligerent, or about its means of defense". (Article 44 of the 4th Hague Convention of 1907).

— "No general penalty, pecuniary or otherwise, shall be inflicted upon the population on account of the acts of individuals for which they can not be regarded as jointly and severally responsible". (Articles 50 of the 2nd Hague Convention, 1899 and 4th Hague Convention of 1907).

— The statement issued by the Hague Conference of 1899 has prohibited the use of poisonous gases.

— The Geneva Protocol of June 17, 1925, "prohibiting the use in war of Asphyxiating, Poisonous or other Gases, and of Bacteriological Methods of Warfare".

(10) The General Assembly of the United Nations called on all States, in its recommendation N& 2161 (521) of 5 December 1966, to observe the principles and aims stipulated in the Geneva Protocol of 1925, to condemn any violation of these principles, as well as to the necessity of becoming signatories to this Protocol. See: BULLETIN DE LA COMMISSION INTERNATIONALE DE JURISTES (Sept. 1968), pp. 5-6.

(11) This provision is known as "de Martens Provisions"

(12) BULLETIN, op. cit., p. 7.

(13) See on this subject: Jean Siotis — LE DROIT DE LA GUERRE ET LES CONFLITS ARMES DE CARACTERE NON INTERNATIONAL, (Paris 1968), pp. 21-22. Siotis writes: "Le seul élement qui les différencie est d'une nature quatitative, le degré d'application du droit de la guerre".

(14) Customary International Law refuses to recognize rebels as "an organized political entity" (Stage of Civil War) before acknowledging their rights of belligerents. These are the rebels belonging to militia groups, resistance movements or volunter corps. They have to fulfil the following requirements:
— that of being commanded by a person responsible for his subordinates,
— that of having a fixed distinctive sign recognizable at a distance,
— that of carrying arms openly,
— that of conducting their operations in accordance with the laws and customs of war,
— continuance of armed hostilities for a sufficiently reasonable period of time.
See: A. Rolin — LE DROIT MODERNE DE LA GUERRE, 1920; W. L. Walker — RECOGNITION OF BELLIGERENCY AND GRANT OF BELLIGER-ENT RIGHTS; Lothar Kotssch — THE CONCEPT OF WAR IN CONTEMPO-RARY HISTORY AND INTERNATIONAL LAW, (Genève, 1956).

(15) Siotis, op. cit., p. 20.

(16) Dietrich Sschindler — "DAS HUMANITARE IN RAHMEN DER INTERNATIONALEM GARANTIE DER MENSCHEM". (INTERNATIONAL ROUND TABLE DISCUSSION OF HUMAN RIGHTS) (Berlin 1966) pp. 40-50.

(17) Kotssch defines actual war as "Material War implies a continuous dash of arms conducted by organized armies which engage the responsibility of Government. It does not presume the conditions that the belligerents must be States. The existence of war in the Material sense is something to be judged by evidence not of intentions, but of activities of military forces in the field". Op. cit., p. 56.

(18) Siotis, op. cit., pp. 21-23.

(19) See, for instance, the following articles in the agreement dated 12 August 1949: 2, 27, 32, 47 and 49.

(20) E. S. Poscoe — REPORTS OF PRIZE CASES: 1745 — 1859, Vol. II (London, 1905), pp. 584-590.

(21) An opinion voiced by the Prosecution in the Hostages Case before the American Military Tribunal V. See Folk. Op. cit., pp. 357.
The Dutch Jurist G. Sawicki is of the same opinion and trend. See his article "Châtiment ou encouragement?" REVUE DU DROIT INTERNATIONAL, (Sottele) 1948, No 3, pp. 240 ss. See also the article of the Soviet Jurist, I.P. Trainin — "Questions of Guerilla Warfare in the Law of War". AMERICAN JOURNAL OF INTERNATIONAL LAW, 1946, pp. 534 ss.

(22) Ruling of the Hague Special Tribunal on May 4, 1948 on the case of "Höhere SS — und Polizeifuhrer", See Folk — Op. cit., p. 366.

WAR
BY
TERROR

Ministry of Foreign Affairs
(Jerusalem)

> Mr. Baroudy, representative of Saudi Arabia, in the United Nations
> Security Council: "Thirteen Arab Leaders were shot like birds on the
> rumour that they were going to talk with Israel during the last two
> decades." [UN document S/PV 1358, page 82, 13 June 1967]

For half a century, violence, terrorism and the endless indoctrination of
hate — through radio and press, in schools and mosques — have been cardinal
principles of policy with the Arabs, not only in their dealings with the Jews of
Palestine and, since 1948, with the State of Israel, but also — indeed, to a much
larger extent — in their dealings with each other.

In 1920, an extremist minority faction of Palestinian Arabs, headed by Haj
Amin el-Husseini, the former Mufti of Jerusalem, terrorized their way to
power — and the prospects of Jewish—Arab cooperation in the economic
development of the Middle East and in the advancement of the national
aspirations of both groups signalized by the 1919 Feisal—Weizmann Agreement
were shattered. The decades that followed were marked by constant incitement
to violence against the Jewish community of Palestine and by repeated acts of
extortion and "personal terror" directed against Palestinian Arabs who refused
to toe the Mufti's line in these as well as other matters.

In the summer of 1929, Arab extremist circles unleashed a terror campaign
through Palestine which culminated in the savage attack on the old-established
Jewish community in Hebron. Of the 600 Hebron Jews, 66 were massacred, 58
wounded and the rest forced to flee the town, leaving all their property behind
them.

The 1936-39 disturbances cost many more lives of Jews and of Arabs. The
Jerusalem correspondent of the NEW YORK TIMES reported on 15 October
1938:

> Extremist Arab followers of the Mufti . . . are rapidly achieving their aims

by eliminating political opponents in Palestine who are inclined toward moderation. More than 90 per cent of the total casualties in the past few days have been inflicted by Arab terrorists on Arabs.

In 1947-48, following the UN partition decision of November 1947, Arab irregulars from Transjordan, Syria and Iraq penetrated into Palestine and launched a war of ambush and terror that was to pave the way for the full-scale Arab invasion of Israel on 15 May 1948.

The Sinai Campaign (October-November 1956) was preceded by a concerted campaign of terror conducted by the notorious Egyptian-trained fedayun during 1955 and 1956.

The civil war in Lebanon (April-June 1958) was preceded by an Egyptian and Syrian-inspired campaign of terror and assassination in that and in other Arab countries. (At various times, the Egyptian Military Attaches in Jordan, Iraq, Lebanon, Sudan, Libya and Tunisia have been expelled from those countries for organizing subversion, intrigue and political murder in the Arab capitals to which they were accredited.)

In April 1957, the Jordanian authorities uncovered a terrorist conspiracy against the regime, organized with Egyptian and Syrian inspiration. Later that year, another plot came to light, this one headed by the Jordanian Chief of Staff, Ali Abu-Nawar.

The Moslem Brotherhood, active in several Arab countries and particularly in Egypt in the mid-fifties, also used murder and sabotage as instruments to achieve its political aims.

At the Arab League Council meeting at Shturah, Lebanon, in August 1962, the Syrian Delegation submitted a complaint against Egypt which included the following passage:

> ... The Cairo rulers were not content with calling for and instigating sedition and revolution. They exceeded this and plotted against the Syrian entity. They instigated terror and sabotage and supported mercenary elements in order to create an atmosphere of anxiety and disturbances which would prevent Syria from following its chosen course ... [Syrian Memorandum to Arab League Council, quoted by Radio Damascus, 22 August 1962]

In 1963, the governing Ba'ath Party in Iraq organized terrorist bands to "liquidate" members of the Iraqi Communist Party. Hundreds of persons lost their lives in this terrorist operation. Again, in 1964, subversion, intrigue and murder escalated into open combat as civil war exploded in Yemen, with active Egyptian intervention. Throughout 1966, the world press was filled with reports from Aden of terrorist acts committed by rival Arab groups.

The closing of the Tiran Straits by Egypt in May 1967, and the concerted Arab drive against Israel that immediately preceded and followed it, came as the climax to the two-year terrorist campaign of the El-Fatah organization, operating chiefly out of Syria.

Saudi Arabia's representative, in his statement before the UN Security Council quoted above, did not spell out the names of the thirteen Arab leaders who "were shot like birds on the rumour that they were going to talk with Israel." Facts are that the number of Arab leaders murdered in the period referred to by Mr. Baroudy is much higher, and that the great majority of them were done away with for reasons which have little or nothing to do with Israel.

One could, however, draw up a list of thirteen Arab heads of government, disregarding other prominent personalities, who have been victims of political murder in the past two decades.

Placed thus in its historical perspective, the current terrorist activity of El-Fatah and other infiltration-and-sabotage groups may be seen for what it really is: not a reaction to the events of June 1967 — but simply yet another phase of the continuing war against Israel waged by the Arab States. They may modify their tactics according to the exigencies of the moment, but their basic assumption remains the "non-existence" of Israel — and their ultimate aim: the translation of that assumption into reality.

> I have the honour to express to you the very strong disapproval of the International Union of the Resistance and Deportation, which ... comprises more than 500,000 former members of the Resistance Movement and victims of Nazism, with respect to the reckless terrorism which in Israel, and lately in Athens, Zurich and Baghdad, has caused the death of defenceless and innocent men, women and children.
>
> On behalf of its unanimous members, the Union fundamentally challenges any comparison of the struggle carried on by the Resistance against Nazism to these criminal acts inspired by fanaticism and racialism whose sole purpose is to arouse insecurity, fear and violence ... [Letter sent on 12 March 1969 by the President of the International Union of the Resistance and Deportation, Major-General Albert Guerisse, to the United Nations Secretary-General]

ARAB TERRORISM 1970: NATURE AND PURPOSE

Perhaps it will be easier to explain, first of all, what Arab terrorism is decidedly not: Arab claims in that context notwithstanding, it is not a "protest" or "resistance" or "liberation" movement by local Palestinians against "Israel military rule in the occupied areas". The Arab Governments would very much like the world to believe that it is. There is, however, not the least difficulty in demonstrating that what we are dealing with is not a local resistance movement but simply the continuation of Arab warfare against Israel, in another form, conducted by the Arab States from without, with the avowed aim of "keeping their irons in the fire" while making ready, again, as speedily as they can for a genocidal onslaught on the State of Israel. The following are the facts:

The initiative for Arab terrorist activity comes from the Arab capitals — particularly Damascus, Cairo and Baghdad — with Beirut, Amman, Algiers and Tripoli (Libya) in supporting roles of various kinds. "Initiative" means inspiration, organization, counsel and guidance. Support is given in the form both of material aid and of incendiary propaganda. Headquarters, bases, recruiting offices, fund-raising agencies, training camps, arsenals, broadcasting stations and newspapers of the terrorist organizations operate in the Arab countries in the full glare of publicity.

The activity invariably involves shooting and shelling across the cease-fire line and, to a much lesser extent, infiltration across that line into its immediate vicinity for acts of ambush and sabotage under the cover of night. Frequently, the crossings are accompanied by covering fire from regular army positions on the Arab side of the line. These activities thus constitute an incontestable violation of the cease-fire of June 1967.

The earlier attempts of terrorist groups to establish themselves in bases inside the Israel-administered areas, or to instigate a "popular uprising" in these areas, have met with unique failure and were given up. The infiltrator units have quickly been rounded up by Israel's security forces, while the mass of the Arab population refuses to harbour terrorists or cooperate with them. Aside from shooting and shelling from Arab territory on Israeli villages and towns situated near the border, the much-vaunted Palestinian "resistance movement" has come to consist almost exclusively of terror acts against "collaborators" (mostly Arabs from the Gaza Strip going to work in Israeli enterprises), on the one hand, and of dastardly attacks on passenger planes, offices and diplomatic precincts in Europe and America, on the other. Sabotage acts in localities inside Israel still occur, but their extent has greatly diminished.

The extreme inhumanity of Arab terrorism bears eloquent testimony to the true nature of the so-called "resistance movement". In nearly all cases, the terrorists' attacks are aimed not — as might have been expected of a "resistance movement" — at Israeli military personnel, but at the civilian population, both Jewish and Arab, and, at times, at citizens of other countries having no connection whatever with the Middle East conflict. What are the terrorists' targets? A public market place, a super-market or a bus station, an apartment house, a bus transporting children to a village school or on a spring outing, a university cafeteria, a passenger plane at a European airport going to or coming from Israel, a pick-up truck carrying Arabs to work, a crowded cinema, a barn or a childrens' house in a kibbutz, and the like. The Arab terrorists reached a new low in callous inhumanity when, in February 1970, they blew up a Swissair jet in mid-air through the use of an altimeter attached to a detonating device. This act of murder-by-remote-control resulted in the death of all the passengers and crew in the aircraft.   The leader of one of the terrorist organizations was quoted in the 10 June 1968 issue of U.S. NEWS AND WORLD REPORT as saying:

> Time is on our side. We're getting more and better recruits. With practice, we'll learn. And then we have to go after more Israeli civilians. We would prefer to restrict our attacks to Israeli soldiers and police, but killing civilians is the only way this kind of war can be won.

Most of the terrorist organizations, however, have found killing civilians increasingly difficult inside the borders of Israel, so they shifted their area of operations to Athens, Zurich or Asuncion, Paraguay. This can also be "rationalized". Witness the following statement of Georges Habash, head of the Popular Front of the Liberation of Palestine, in an interview with the correspondent of LIFE magazine (8 June 1970): "To kill a Jew far from the battleground has more of an effect than killing a hundred of them in battle; it attracts more attention".

The immediate purpose of the Arab terrorist organizations and their backers in the Arab capitals is — now as before the Six-Day War — to weaken Israel and undermine Israel morale, keeping tensions and para-warfare alive in the Middle East, while the Arab States and their military establishments prepare to renew their total attack. By their own admission, the ultimate purpose of the terrorist organizations, as it is of the Arab States, is not the restoration of the 1949 Armistice lines but the total destruction of Israel.

In defiance of the facts, the Arab terrorist organizations and their supporters persist in the propaganda effort to present to world public opinion the image of a "resistance movement" similar to the European partisans of World War II, or the Algerian rebels against France, or the Vietcong guerrillas. Apart from all the cardinal differences in aims and issues, the Arab terrorists are neither "partisans" nor "guerrillas" because 1. they hardly act at all inside the "occupied territory" but keep shooting from sanctuaries across the border in States which direct and support them openly; 2. their perpetually photographed men in camouflage uniforms are paraded before newsmen not on the battleground, but in bases in Jordan, Lebanon or Kuwait; they maintain a propaganda machine (on a scale unequalled in the history of resistance movements) whose methods of false reporting about imaginary "victories" have become proverbial; and, 3. most important difference of all, the Arab terrorists shun encounters with Israel's armed forces and instead indulge in unscrupulous practices of murder, involving hardly any risk, directed against civilians — men, women and children — and against offices or passenger airplanes in far-away neutral countries.

No resistance movement in history has ever had recourse to such monstrous acts. The remaining portions of this pamphlet are devoted to the documentation of this recital of facts.

THE HATCHETMEN

Who are the terrorists — or, as the official Arab spokesmen spuriously call them, the "resistance fighters", the "soldiers in the popular war of liberation"? The "Fatah Corner" of Radio Cairo on 19 May 1968 was given up to a discussion of the "mistaken notions" that guide "some" of the members of the El-Fatah organization in their decision to join its ranks. Among these "mistaken notions", the following were mentioned: a. personal problems that drive the individual into those ranks; b. financial pressure (namely, the lure of the wages paid to the terrorists by the Arab Governments); c. the personal satisfaction derived from becoming known as a "revolutionary" or a "fedayi"; d. emotional impressionability (that is, being carried away by the extensive and intensive Arab Government propaganda to which the would-be terrorist is exposed).

Who are the terrorists? They are people who, for various reasons (most of which have little or nothing to do with the Six-Day War), gang up together, or are pressed into one of the gangs, allow themselves to be trained as infiltrators and saboteurs and, in the dark of the night, cross into Israel to dynamite farmhouses or water-pipes, or to plant mines in dirt-tracks so that the first vehicle that comes along will be blown up — whether it be a lorry taking people, Jews or Arabs, to work, or a tractor or a school bus.

Money, that is, the relatively high salaries paid to the members of the terrorist groups, certainly is one of the chief attractions. Not a few of the terrorists rounded up by Israel's security forces turn out to be people with a criminal record who had been released from jails in Arab countries against an undertaking to join the terrorists' ranks. The London DAILY TELEGRAPH reported on 4 September 1970 that several terrorist organizations in Jordan and Lebanon purchase Soviet and Chinese arms with funds secured by the smuggling of large quantities of hashish to the United States, via Canada.

Children, too, have often been used by the terrorist organizations where adult "volunteers" seemed to be lacking for such exploits as throwing grenades at Israeli lorries passing in the streets of Gaza — usually hitting Arab passers-by — or throwing bombs at Israeli offices in European cities. The attackers of the Israeli Embassies in the Hague and Bonn and of the El Al Airlines office in Brussels in September 1969 were boys aged between 13 and 16 who had been brought over from the Arab countries and led to their targets by adults who disappeared from the scene before the bombs were thrown.

These "deeds of heroism" are organized and financed by the neighbouring Arab Governments, but the terrorists occasionally make house-to-house collections, to help make ends meet. The following item is from the JERUSALEM POST of 10 March 1968:

> A 50-year-old man from Bani Naim, near Hebron, died in Hussein Hospital in Bethlehem on Friday of wounds incurred when two Fatah terrorists assaulted him on Wednesday. In a statement at the hospital, Halil Mahmoud Mansara said that two men called at his house and, at gunpoint, demanded that he contribute money to the Fatah. When he said he had none, the extortionists took him outside the village, beat him and threw a hand-grenade at him. He was found unconscious by the police the following morning.

In the Gaza Strip alone, the terrorists' victims among the local Arab population number more than 800 (52 dead and 762 wounded) in the period between the end of the Six-Day War and July 1970. Many of them have been hit by bombs thrown at passing Israeli vehicles — usually missing their targets — without regard to passers-by. But many others were wilfully shot by criminals who have found the "resistance movement" a convenient cover for settling private accounts.

From time to time, as the opportunity arises, the terrorist organizations make use of the services of foreign agents, in the hope that these will avoid detection.

On 23 June 1970, Brono Bregue, a Swiss citizen, arrived in Israel by ship and was detained by the Customs authorities at Haifa port when his behaviour aroused suspicion. In the ensuing search of his person, Bregue was found to be wearing a belt which held ten bricks containing 200 grams of explosives each. Additional sabotage material was discovered in his baggage, as well as emblems of the Palestine Liberation Organization.

Bregue's contacts with that organizaton had been made in Beirut, where he had received equipment, training and detailed instructions, after agreeing to carry out sabotage activities in Israel. From Beirut, he had been flown back to Europe and from there had set out for Haifa by ship.

THOSE WHO SEND THEM —
OR AID AND ABET THEM

Different Arab Governments differ somewhat in their tactical appraisal of the role of terrorism in the overall Arab strategy against Israel, but they fully agree on the need to stimulate, encourage and support that form of operations against Israel — conducted, preferably, from Jordanian or Lebanese territory.

In his speech before the Arab Lawyers' Conference on 10 April 1968, President Nasser declared:

> We must support the Palestinian resistance movement for the sake of the rights of the Palestinian people and for the sake of victory. Egypt is ready to give such support and to arm the resistance movement, because this movement is part of the fateful battle of the entire nation.

More than a year later, Nasser's support of the terrorists was even more pronounced and comprehensive. Speaking before the Arab Socialist Union (Radio Cairo, 23 July 1969), he said:

> Brothers! The renaissance of the Palestine people is an incredible phenom-

enon. It is clear that the Arab people support their resistance. On our part, we give all we have, in the military, political and technical spheres. We are ready to do so without accounting, unreservedly.

Or the following, by the spokesman of the Iraq Government:

Iraq, which has repeatedly announced its full and absolute support for the fedayi (terrorist) action, reaffirms its desire to strengthen this action, to protect and broaden it, and to enable it to achieve its high aims of complete liberation.

The valiant Iraqi forces stationed in Jordan will find no substitute for fulfilling their obligations to protect the aspirations of our masses, to continue and strengthen the fedayi action in every way and by every means, and to enable it to perform its basic tasks as the vanguard of liberation. [Radio Baghdad, 11 February 1970 — BBC Monitoring Service]

Similar expressions of support have become standard in statements and resolutions of Arab leaders and Governments.

Even after the inception of the Middle East cease-fire, arranged on America's initiative in August 1970, the Egyptians — in addition to moving SAM-2 and SAM-3 missiles into the standstill Canal Zone — continued to give their unstinted support to the terrorist organizations. Thus we read in the Government-operated Cairo daily, AL-AHRAM, on 22 August 1970:

The Palestinian nation is not a party to the current efforts to reach a peace settlement. The results of these efforts, therefore, do not bind them in any way, and they retain complete freedom of action.

Another Government-inspired journal, the Cairo weekly AL-MUSSAWAR, wrote on 7 August 1970:

Neither the US initiative nor any response to it affects their (the extremist Palestinians') position; the contrary, in fact, is true: Egypt's answer reserves for them the freedom to continue in their struggle and to achieve their goals ... The eradication of the results of the aggression and the liberation of Palestine may be regarded as complementary goals. The Palestine resistance movement will remain one of the most important phenomena of modern Arab life.

Addressing a session of the Palestinian Council in Cairo on 28 August 1970, Abdel Latif Balatiya, Secretary-General of the Egyptian National Council, made the following statement:

The Palestinian Arab nation has the right to fight an armed revolutionary battle for the liberation of its stolen country, and it is the duty of all armed Arab forces to provide effective assistance until such time as this victory is achieved.

The struggle for the liberation of the land conquered both before and after June (1967) is part of the struggle for liberation, progress and unity in the Arab homeland.

A period of real war against the enemy still lies ahead of us, and it is our dearest wish that our guns will be ready on that day.

SKYJACKINGS: ACCESSORIES BEFORE
AND AFTER THE FACT

The terrorist organization responsible for most of the hijackings of civilian aircraft — or "skyjackings," as they have come to be known — is the Popular Front for the Liberation of Palestine, headed by Georges Habash. The recent hijacking, within a few days, of four airliners (TWA, Swissair, PAN-AM and BOAC) carrying more than 400 passengers, and the unsuccessful attempt to hijack a fifth (El Al), drew angry protests from many countries — and even Egypt and some of the other Arab States expressed reservations concerning the crimes. The utter meaninglessness of these "reservations" is demonstrated by two facts:

1. Egypt, Lebanon and other Arab countries have consistently and actively supported the extremist terror group headed by Habash, have received the perpetrators of past hijackings as heroes and have, time and again, goaded them on to further acts of indiscriminate international lawlessness. Indeed, if it were not for the facilities granted to the Popular Front in Cairo and Beirut, Damascus and Baghdad — in the form of offices, training camps, financial and propaganda backing — the group would have collapsed long ago.

2. The most recent spate of hijackings evoked official Arab lip-service to the general feeling of outrage; at the same time, however, the actions of these Governments, even as the acts were being committed, and after their commission, point in the diametrically opposite direction. Thus, members of Habash's gang were permitted to land the hijacked PAN-AM at Cairo international airport (after refuelling in Beirut) and there to blow it to smithereens; and another band belonging to the Popular Front was allowed to bring down the BOAC plane which it had earlier seized in mid-air at Beirut international airport and to re-fuel, while other members of the Front boarded the plane freely and placed aboard explosive charges used later to blow up the TWA, Swissair and BOAC planes forcibly brought down in the Jordan desert. Not only were these terrorists able freely to carry out their activities at the Beirut and Cairo international airports, but several of them remained in these Arab capitals — where training and organizational activities continue, with the full knowledge and permission of the Governments — and have not been brought to justice.

Even more significant is the fact that the Arab rulers make no secret of the active, material aid which they extend to the terrorist groups, whether in supplying them with money and arms, or training their recruits, or guiding their actions. Thus, following the Arab summit conference in Rabat in December 1969, Cairo Radio reported that —

> the Arab Kings and Presidents have decided to allocate £26 million to meet the financial commitments of the Palestine Liberation Organization in the coming year, including £12 million for the support of the Palestine revolution and £11 million for the support of citizens' resistance in the occupied territory. It has been learned that Libya has decided to contribute 25 per cent to the Palestine revolution budget. [Cairo Radio, 25 December 1969 — BBC Monitoring Service]

At the same time, beyond the facade of the general "support for the Palestine revolution", there are obvious differences in the degree to which each of the terrorist groups benefits from the support of the different Arab Governments — depending on the degree to which this or that group proves useful or amenable to the string-pullers in the Arab capitals. Thus, the Ba'ath regime in Damascus created the Saiqa ("Thunder") terrorist organization which, to all intents and purposes, acts as an arm of the Syrian army and indeed is composed in good part of Syrian servicemen. Egypt, on the other hand, openly favours Yasser Arafat's Fatah organization, and the "Voice of Fatah" is broadcast from Cairo. Iraq, again, has established and nurses its own Arab Liberation Front, but at the same time maintains a close link with George Habash's "Popular Front for the Liberation of Palestine" which specializes in acts of unbridled terror, like the attacks on civil planes in Europe. Iraq maintains the 421st Palestine Commando Battalion as part of the regular Iraqi army. Officers and men of this unit participated in terrorist infiltrations into Israel, and many of them were killed or captured in the Israel army raid on the Karameh terrorist base in Jordan in March 1968.

The extent to which the terrorists actually serve as a tool in the hands of certain Arab Governments is further illustrated by the pattern of their geographical deployment. Whereas their principal supporters are the so-called "revolutionary" Arab regimes — chiefly Egypt, Syria and Iraq, these three Governments, for their own good reasons, maintain close control of the terrorists' activities both inside their countries and on the front-lines; it is their weaker neighbours — Jordan and Lebanon — which are made to bear the brunt of the terrorists' pressures and to suffer the consequences of their actions. If these Governments demur, as has occurred time and again particularly since mid-1969, they are quickly bullied into line through the pressure of the "revolutionary" capitals.

Thus, the clash in the fall of 1969 between Lebanese forces and terrorist bands which had infiltrated from Syria was (temporarily) resolved by the "Cairo agreement" of 3 November 1969, signed by the commander of the Lebanese army and the leader of Fatah with the blessing of President Nasser, and granting the terrorists a large measure of "freedom of action" in southern Lebanon. For the terrorists and their Egyptian and Syrian mentors, however, this agreement merely served as a springlever for the further subversion of the authority of the Lebanese Government.

> The Arab masses in general (said the Voice of Fatah broadcast from Cairo on 18 January 1970), and especially the Lebanese, must unmask the new activity of the counter-revolutionary forces till they are overthrown. We do not say this to protect the Cairo agreement. We say this because the revolution considers this agreement as the minimum of support that the Lebanese authorities owe the revolution.

In fact, the tensions resulting from the terrorists' take-over in parts of Lebanon have persisted and led from time to time to renewed fighting between them and the Government forces, with Syria extending unabashed support in men, arms and propaganda to a drive designed to destroy the authority of the Lebanese Government. Sometimes this drive assumes very unusual forms indeed. Here, for example, is a report of the Beirut daily L'ORIENT of 11 June 1970:

> The most recent exploit of Saiqa (the Syrian-supported terrorist organization) took place in Tyre and is certainly unique in the annals of guerrilla. The day before yesterday, ten armed men of 'Saiqa' broke into a hall in Tyre where examinations for the Lebanese secondary school certificate were being held. They handed out to the students the answers

to the examination questions, ignoring the protests of the startled supervisors. Result: the examination has been declared void, to the great chagrin of the students. This is the decision that has been taken yesterday by the Ministry of Education.

Jordan's experience is no less instructive. Ever since the beginning of 1968, the rulers of Jordan adopted an "open door" policy towards the terrorist groups, underlined by King Hussein's "We are all fedayun" declaration on 23 March 1968. Not only have they maintained bases like that at Karameh (attacked by Israel forces in March 1968), complete with their own supply and arms depots, police force and jail, but many of their actions against Israel were carried out in collaboration with the Jordanian army, the latter usually providing covering fire to terrorist attempts to penetrate or escape across the cease-fire line. Check-points on key roads in Jordan had been manned jointly by Fatah men and Jordanian gendarmes. Notwithstanding all that, the terrorists' continued drive to arrogate more and more power to themselves and their complete disregard for the Government's authority have led, from time to time, to confrontation with the Jordanian army — but, until the civil war that erupted in the wake of the Popular Front's spate of hijackings in September 1970, King Hussein always shied away from a final, decisive showdown with the terrorists.

Typically, it was Egypt again that served as the nerve-centre from where the terrorists' moves in Jordan were directed. Radio Cairo allowed the "Voice of Fatah" extra broadcasting time to maintain contact with the disorganized Fatah men in Jordan. Other "revolutionary" Governments, farther away from the frontline, also stepped in to help the terrorists have their way. It was only when the terrorists began to attack Nasser for having accepted the American peace initiative in July 1970 that Nasser took a step against them by closing down their radio station in Cairo. Still, when civil strife broke out in Jordan two months later, he threw his weight behind the terrorists, who had sworn to fight on until the Jordanian Government was overthrown.

On 1 July 1970, the International League for the Rights of Man issued a statement from which it clearly emerged that it held certain Arab Governments responsible for the activities of the terrorist groups. The following is an excerpt from that statement:

> ... In the Middle East, we point to the recent succession of Palestinian terrorist assaults against non-military targets which have resulted in the deaths of innocent non-combatants, including women and children. Admitted incidents inside and outside the area of conflict have included the shooting at close range of rockets against a children's school bus; shooting at tourist buses; hijacking and blowing up civilian airliners; placing bombs in air terminals, a university cafeteria and public markets; setting fire to an old people's home; destroying the oxygen supply of a hospital and launching rockets against residential areas ...
>
> We call upon States which engage in terror and from which terrorist groups operate to put a stop to them.
>
> We call upon all Governments and leaders of world moral opinion to condemn terrorism directed against civilians as tending to engender counter-brutality and to erode human and moral standards. We call upon proponents of these tactics to disavow and to cease them ...

METHOD OF ACTION: MURDER UNLIMITED

In an article entitled "Whither the Armed Palestinian Struggle?," The Government-controlled Cairo daily, AL-GOMHOURIYA, on 17 November 1967 explicitly gave the lie to the Arab claim that Arab terrorism is an outgrowth of the 1967 war:

> These events are not a result of the aggression of 5 June and of Israel's conqest of part of the Arab lands. Already three years ago and more, several Palestinian organizations began armed operations within occupied Palestine; their activity was merely stepped up after the aggression.

Here is a sampling of terrorist exploits in Israel in the course of the years — just to give the reader a notion of the types of targets that these so-called "resistance fighters" have pinpointed for themselves.

On 12 March 1954, a gang of twelve Jordanian infiltrators ambushed a bus returning from Eilat Day celebrations and murdered eleven of its passengers — men, women and children. In April 1956, six children taking part in a prayer service in the school synagogue at the village of Shafir were murdered in an attack by a band of terrorists. On 19 August 1963, two young farmers at Almagor, a village north of Lake Kinneret, were killed by armed Syrian infiltrators.

On the night of 23-24 September 1967, a gang of Fatah infiltrators laid an explosive charge next to the last house in the small-holders' village of Ometz, in northern Israel. When the charge went off, the house was wrecked and the three-year-old child who had been sleeping inside was killed. On 8 October 1967, a time-bomb was discovered under a seat in the Zion Cinema in Jerusalem. Only the alertness and courage of a number of persons on the spot averted a tragedy.

On 2 March 1968, a 70-year-old Druze watchman at a tractor station near Abu Ghosh was murdered by saboteurs, who then proceeded to set off three explosive charges, damaging two tractors and a truck, as well as a small fuel-oil tank. On 18 March, a bus-load of children on a spring outing struck a mine near the children's village of Be'er Ora in southern Israel. A doctor and a youth leader were killed, and 29 boys and girls were wounded. On 8 June 1968, a child was wounded by a "pencil" equipped with a timing device that had been planted near the Zion Cinema in Jerusalem. On 17 June 1968, two button-shaped mines were found near the entrance of the Arlosoroff Elementary School in Jerusalem. The alertness of the finders (a pupil at the school and the school secretary) averted disaster.

On the night of 18 August 1968, three explosive charges went off in various parts of Jerusalem, injuring nine persons, two of them seriously. Most of the injuries were incurred when a grenade exploded that had been placed in a drainage outlet in the street opposite Bikur Holim Hospital, near the centre of town. Two additional charges were discovered before they could explode.

Shortly before noon on 4 September 1968, three bombs exploded near Tel Aviv's Central Bus Station, killing one pedestrian and wounding 51 others, five of them seriously. The explosions were caused by sticks of dynamite equipped with timing devices or delayed action fuses. (Within 24 hours, police rounded up the terrorist gang responsible for the outrage as well as for the bombing incidents of 18 August in Jerusalem and three earlier bombings in the Capital.)

On the night of 23 July 1968, the pilot of an El Al passenger plane en route from Rome to Tel Aviv was compelled at gunpoint to land the plane at Algiers airport. The hi-jackers were two Palestinian Arabs and a Syrian, bearing Iranian and Indian passports issued in Kuwait and Baghdad. The plane and its male passengers and crew were held in Algiers for 39 days before being released as a result of international efforts.

On Friday, 22 November 1968, a bomb concealed in a car exploded in the Mahane Yehuda market in Jerusalem while the place was crowded with people doing their Sabbath-eve shopping; 12 people were killed on the spot and 52 were injured. Both Fatah and the Popular Front for the Liberation of Palestine claimed credit for this outrage, and Baghdad Radio called the perpetrators "heroes." The "hero" himself later presented himself to the press in Amman and gave an account of how he smuggled the explosives-laden car from Jordan to Israel and escaped by taking advantage of Israel's "open bridges" policy, that is, the free traffic of goods and people between the Israel-administered areas and Jordan. Security measures on the Jordan bridges were subsequently tightened by the Israel authorities, but the "open bridges" policy has remained in force.

On 26 December 1968, two Arab terrorists opened fire on an El Al plane at Athens airport, killing one of the passengers. On 18 February 1969, an El Al plane was attacked at Zurich airport. Two of the plane's crew were wounded and one of them died later of his wounds. One of the three Arab attackers was killed by the plane's security officer.

On 21 February 1969, a dynamite charge concealed in a tin exploded in the "Supersol" supermarket in Jerusalem, killing 2 shoppers and injuring 8 more. Another charge was discovered in time and dismantled. On 7 March 1969, 29 students and staff members of the Hebrew University in Jerusalem were wounded when an explosive charge concealed in a briefcase went off in the University cafeteria.

On 29 August 1969, a TWA airplane on its way from Rome to Lydda was hijacked by three terrorists and forced to land at Damascus airport, where its flight deck was blown up. Two Israeli men who were on board, including Professor Samueloff, a physiologist of international repute, were held prisoner by the Syrians for more than three months, until 5 December 1969. The Syrian postal authorities (as reported by the German weekly STERN on 16 November 1969) issued a special stamp to mark this act of air piracy, portraying the heavily armed terrorists in front of the damaged airplane.

On 9 September 1969, Israel's Embassies in the Hague and Bonn, and the Brussels office of El Al airlines were attacked with bombs. Four persons were wounded in Brussels, but there were no casualties in the other two attacks. Three of the assailants — two Arab boys, aged 13 and 15, in Brussels, and a 16-year-old-boy in the Hague — were caught, but some others managed to get back to the Arab countries and receive a hero's welcome from Arab leaders. Thus, the 13-year-old Ali Ahmad al-Jaburi told the press that after attacking the Brussels office of El Al he fled from Belgium to France, where he was given a passport by the Iraq Embassy in Paris; on arrival in Baghdad, he was welcomed by Iraq's President, General al-Bakr (AL-ANWAR, Beirut daily, 18 September 1969).

On 27 November 1969, two Arab terrorists threw a bomb into the El Al office in Athens. A Greek baby was killed and five persons were injured, including the dead boy's brother, who lost his sight. On 10 February 1970, an airport bus in Munich, carrying passengers and crew about to board an El Al plane, was attacked by Arab terrorists. A grenade thrown into the bus killed one person and injured ten others. Two of the three attackers were wounded.

On 21 February 1970, a Swissair plane en route to Israel blew up in mid-air shortly after departure from Zurich. All 38 passengers and 9 crew members perished. The same day, an Austrian Airlines airplane narrowly escaped disaster when it managed to land at Frankfurt airport after an explosion during flight. The altimeter found among the debris of the Swissair plane was similar to the one that caused the explosion on the Austrian plane. Both were traced by German investigators to a dealer in Frankfurt who said that two Arabs had bought them from him a short time earlier.

On 4 May 1970, two Arab terrorists opened fire in the Israel Embassy in Asuncion, Paraguay. One woman of the Embassy staff was killed and another wounded. The two killers, originating from Gaza, were seized by the local police. On 6 May 1970, shelling with Katyusha rockets from Lebanon on the small town of Kiryat Shmona, in northern Galilee, resulted in the death of two persons, father and daughter. Three days later, three persons — all brothers — were seriously wounded in a similar attack.

On 22 May 1970, a school bus on its daily run from Avivim village, close to the Lebanese border, to a nearby regional school was attacked from ambush with bazooka shells. Eight children aged from 6 to 9, and four adults accompanying them were killed, and 20 others, mostly children too, were wounded. The Popular Front for the Liberation of Palestine (General Command) claimed credit for the attack.

On 1 June 1970, a 10-year-old schoolgirl was killed and three others were wounded outside their schoolhouse in Beisan by Katyusha rockets fired from across the Jordan. On 7 June 1970, two girls of Kibbutz Hanitha, near the Lebanese border were seriously wounded when they stepped on a shoe-mine buried in a dirt road near the kibbutz. On 4 June 1970, two explosive charges, wrapped in banknotes, were discovered in the courtyard of a school in Jerusalem. The banknotes were obviously put there to lure the schoolchildren. In the morning of 11 July 1970, two explosive charges attached to delayed action fuses went off on the beach of Achziv, in the north of Israel. Two bathers, women, were lightly wounded.

On 6 September 1970, three international airliners (TWA, Swissair, and PAN-AM) were hijacked by members of the Popular Front for the Liberation of Palestine. An attempt to hijack a fifth plane (El Al) was foiled by the quick action of the plane's crew and security guards. The PAN-AM was brought down in Cairo (after being allowed to re-fuel in Beirut) and there blown up by the terrorists, moments after the passengers had hurriedly emerged, nearly all of them sustaining minor injuries in the process. The other two aircraft were brought down in the desert of northern Jordan, joined later by a BOAC jetliner that had been seized in mid-air, on 9 September, on a Bombay-to-London flight. After several days of enforced detention in the hot desert, most of the passengers were released, but 54 of them were held by the terrorists as hostages for an undisclosed number of Arab terrorists convicted of similar crimes in the past and held in prison in Switzerland, Germany, Britain and Israel. The three aircraft were later blown up, with explosives put on board the BOAC liner on its re-fuelling stop, after having been hijacked, at Beirut airport. The civil war that erupted in Jordan, triggered by the mass hijacking, served to expedite the release of the remaining hostages, and by month's end all of them had been freed.

These then, are the targets. The driving force behind these crimes are the Arab States. What do they hope to achieve?

The cardinal objective of the terrorist organizations is by now well known far and wide: it is the "elimination of Zionist existence," or, more simply, the "destruction of the State of Israel." Here is one example of what is persistently preached, day in day out, in terrorist statements and broadcasts:

Our great masses! From the Voice of Palestine in Cairo we greet you and promise to continue our armed struggle and fulfil our blood-drenched duty — the duty to Jerusalem. We shall put an end to Zionist existence on the land of Palestine; we shall liberate all of Palestine by popular armed revolution. [Voice of Palestine, Cairo, 23 February 1970]

Needless to say, this has nothing to do with "elimination of the traces of the June 1967 aggression" — a formula often used by Arab spokesmen for consumption abroad to camouflage the continuing war against Israel as if it were merely the result of the Six-Day War. The tactical considerations which induce the Egyptian and Jordanian Governments to declare from time to time that they might accept "a political solution" or "the implementation of the UN resolution of November 1967" — do not apply to the terrorists' line: in their statements they take care to make it abundantly clear that they would not be content with anything but the total destruction of Israel by war. The attempt to deceive world opinion that underlies the apparently discordant notes struck by terrorist statements, on the one hand, and certain Arab official pronouncements, on the other, is illuminated by the following comment of the foreign editor of the Cairo AL-AHRAM in a talk with a Norwegian correspondent:

With regard to the resistance movements, the fedayun, they rely on the Egyptians. Therefore, we and the fedayun groups can work hand-in-hand, we think the same way and understand each other. There is no division between us. I cannot remember a single case where one can say that there was any basic disagreement. What one can say in this connection is that Egypt's official policy should not necessarily follow that of the fedayun groups. These resistance movements can say that they are absolutely determined to destroy Israel. Such a goal is understandable from the Palestinians' point of view. They are trying to regain their lost country. But as a Government, Egypt cannot have such a policy as its declared objective. What we say is that we understand the viewpoints and feelings of the fedayun groups. [AFTENPOSTEN, Oslo, 10 May 1969]

In fact, however, Arab rulers tend to have less scruples about their declared "objectives" than might appear from the comments of AL-AHRAM's foreign editor, and their support of the terrorists extends to the terrorist "war aims" as well. For example, a joint communiqué of Syria and South Yemen declares:

Both sides . . . decided to devote all their efforts and energies to support fedayun (terrorist) action — the first step towards a popular liberation war — and confront the Zionist and imperialist challenges with all means at their disposal until the Zionist existence was eliminated and the Palestinian Arabs succeeded in completely liberating their homeland. [Radio Damascus, 11 June 1969]

Iraq's President, Al-Bakr, had the following to say in an interview for the West German television:

There will be no peace until Zionist existence is completely removed. Then a natural atmosphere of co-existence of all Semitic faiths can be prepared and the return to the situation that prevailed before the establishment of the State of Israel. [AL-THAWRA, Baghdad, 2 June 1969]

Last but not least, President Nasser in a speech at a mass gathering in Benghati, Libya, openly expressed the view that — Arab unity means . . . elimination of Israeli aggression and of Zionist existence." [Radio Cairo, 25 June 1970]

What do the terrorist leaders and their members really mean by the standard slogans of "elimination of Zionist existence," "liberation of Palestine," etc.?

In the past, hardly any effort was made by the leaders of the "Palestine Liberation Organization" to disguise their genocidal aim of "throwing the Jews into the sea." The greatest notoriety in this respect has attached to the name of Ahmad Shukeiry, the former leader of that organization, but it has often been overlooked that Shukeiry's headquarters were in Cairo, his base of operations was the Egyptian-ruled Gaza Strip, and his political mentor was President Nasser.

After the débacle of June 1967, Shukeiry's successors have tended to use a somewhat more refined terminology: "throwing the Jews into the sea" has given place to formulations like "elimination of Zionist existence." In the terrorists' propaganda material peddled in foreign countries in particular, much stress has been laid on the objective of a "Palestinian democratic, secular State" to be established on the ruins of the "racist, religious Zionist State."

It does not need much effort to realize that this change of tone, rather than representing a change of heart, is a mere propaganda trick designed to pander to the tastes of "progressive opinion" abroad: the real aim of genocide has not changed a bit. As against the propaganda efforts to give the terrorist movement a more "humane" look, there stand out these facts:

The terrorist practice, far from becoming more humane, has tended to become more unscrupulous and barbaric. It needs a lot of imagination to envisage a "Democratic State" set up by those who perpetrate or encourage acts like killing small children, planting bombs in market places and cinemas, blowing up passenger planes, or making a spectacle of ripping up live animals.

The protagonists of the "secular State" do not seem to experience the least difficulty in switching to the theme of "iahad" (Moslem Holy War) when talking to other audiences. Here is one example in a UPI report from Kuala Lumpur, Malaysia, published in the NEW YORK TIMES of 25 April 1969: "Three Fatah commandos said today they will try to gate-crash the International Islamic Conference here on Saturday to get the 23 nations attending to declare a holy war against Israel."

The attempt to mislead world opinion by contrasting "the Zionist religious State" with some future "secular Palestinian State" is further underlined by the fact that, while Israel does not recognize any exclusive "state religion," all Arab countries except Lebanon have constitutionally declared Islam as the "State religion" and the main source of legislation. This is true not only of countries like Saudi Arabia, but also of the "revolutionary regimes" which the terrorist organizations consider as their spiritual kin: Syria, Egypt and Algeria, for example.

If these general considerations are not convincing enough, let us now see what the terrorist groups themsleves say about the character of the desired Palestinian State — when talking among themselves, not in "progressive circles" abroad.

In May 1964, a "Palestinian National Covenant" was promulgated by a Palestinian Congress held in Jerusalem when part of it was under Jordanian rule. The first article of the "Covenant" declares that "Palestine is an Arab homeland" — period. The prospect for the Jewish population was embodied in an Article 7 which stated that "Jews of Palestinian origin are considered

369

Palestinians if they are willing to live peacefully and loyally in Palestine."

This document has been reaffirmed by the representatives of the terrorist groups in a conference held in Cairo in June 1968 — one year after the Six-Day War — with a significant amendment. An article 6 has been added and it provides that "Jews who were living permanently in Palestine until the beginning of the Zionist invasion will be considered Palestinians."

Lest there should be any doubt about the exact date of "the beginning of the Zionist invasion," an explanatory chapter under the title "The International Palestinian Struggle" states as follows:

> Likewise, the Council affirms that the aggression against the Arab nations and its land began with the Zionist invasion of Palestine in 1917. Therefore, the meaning of the "removal of the traces of the aggression" must be the removal of all the traces of the aggression which was launched with the beginning of the Zionist invasion, and not just with the war of June 1967.

What then are the plans of the "Palestinian revolutionaries" for the Israeli Jews who were not "living permanently in Palestine" before 1917? This had not been spelled out. Dark plans are best left in obscurity.

However, the most striking exposure of the falsehood of the "democratic" slogans hawked by terrorist propagandists abroad is to be found not in Covenants and other formal documents, but in "informal chats" of terrorist leaders which occasionally filter into the Arab press. Thus, the Lebanese weekly AL-ANWAR, in its issues of 8 and 15 March 1970, has reproduced the record of a discussion held on the initiative of its editorial board by the representatives of six terrorist organizations on the theme of the "democratic Palestinian State." The following are excerpts from what the spokesmen of the major organizations stated in the discussion:

> It it useless to enter into detals on the subject of the Democratic State since the goal in proposing the slogan at this stage is to allow the Israeli enemy a small opening, so that if his military, economic and political powers are exhausted and Israel is in dire need — then it will have no choice but to turn to that small opening in order to find a way out. Then the Palestinian revolution will be able to dispel the obscurity so that the enemy may see things in their true light. Therefore, it is useless to dispel the obscurity at present. In the end, when the Israeli enemy or the Zionist State comes out of this opening — it will only happen according to the wishes of the Palestinian victory ... [Farid Al-Kahtib of the Palestine Liberation Movement]

> There is no merit in talking at length about the slogan of a "democratic State." It is not possible for such a State, devoid of affiliation, to come into being. If the slogan of a Democratic State is only intended as an answer to the charge that we aim at throwing the Jews into the sea, then it is a successful slogan and an effective political and propaganda act. But if we regard it as a matter of ultimate strategy of the national Palestinian and Arab liberation movements, then I think that it calls for thorough examination. [Shafiq Al-Hut, Beirut representative of Fatah]

Nobody who has read through this pamphlet need be taken aback by the degree of cynicism and falsehood displayed in these statements. They are a fitting complement to the bankruptcy, military and moral, that marks the Arab terrorist movement in the year 1970 as its loudly announced pretensions of representing the "guerrilla army of the Palestine people" have degenerated more and more to the practice of murder unlimited. And after all, those who daily feed the outside world with easily demonstrable lies about battles and victories which have never taken place — why should they feel any compunction about lying to the world on more intangible things, such as the nature of the "war aims" they are pursuing?

XII. The U.N. and The Big Powers

INTRODUCTION

While the Middle East conflict is primarily a confrontation between the Arab states and the Palestinian Arabs, on the one hand, and the Jewish State, on the other, other parties have become inevitably involved. The strategic importance of the region, its economic resources, religious affinities and cultural ties have turned the Middle East into an international problem. But, in particular, the U. N., the U. S., the U.S.S.R., Great Britain, and France have had a major role — mostly through the supply of armaments and political pressure — in either advancing hostilities or promoting the cause of peace in the area.

The U. N. sanctified Israel's right to exist on November 29, 1947, and has since been involved in various aspects of the Middle East conflict. The U. N. presence in the area is illustrated by the activities of the U. N. Truce Supervision Organization during 1949—1967, the U. N. Emergency Force in 1956—1967, and the U. N. Cease-Fire Observers since the Six Days War. Moreover, Dr. Gunnar Jarring, serving as the Special Representative of the U. N. Secretary General in the area, has been seeking to mediate between the antagonists specifically in connection with the implementation of Resolution 242 adopted by the Security Council on November 22, 1967. The aim to be attained, under the terms of that Resolution, was "a just and lasting peace," including freedom of navigation through international waterways, a just settlement of the refugee problem, territorial inviolability and political independence of every state in the area, withdrawal from occupied territories, and an end to all claims or states of belligerency.

Expected differences of interpretation of this Resolution have arisen, however, between the antagonists. Egypt, supported by the Soviet Union, insists that Israel must withdraw her forces to the pre-June 1967 borders before there could be negotiations. Israel insists that all the provisions of the Resolution have equal applicability and ought, therefore, to be implemented simultaneously.

Sharp differences of views also exist regarding the direct role of the Big Powers in the settlement of the conflict. The Arab states have been seeking the Soviet's involvement because of the massive political, military, and economic support they have received from it. The Western powers, similarly, have sought to mediate between the parties and to bring pressure upon them for a settlement compromise. Israel, on the other hand, rejects Big Power interference and insists on direct negotiations with the Arabs. After the failure of the 1950 guarantees by the three Western powers (the United States, France and Great Britain) for Israel's integrity, the ineffective assurances of 1957 regarding shipping in the Gulf of Aqaba, and the 1967 crisis, Israel has rejected Big Power intervention and assurances as alternatives for direct agreements with the Arabs.

The U. N. and Big Power roles are presented here in two selections. An undated booklet published in London by the Arab League Office outlines the work of the Jarring Mission in regard to implementing the Security Council Resolution of November 27, 1967. It includes extracts from British newspapers and texts of documents and statements relating to the problem. The Israeli view is discussed in "International Guarantees and International Police Forces" prepared by Jerusalem's Ministry of Foreign Affairs in April, 1971.

THE
JARRING
MISSION

The Arab League

The United Nations Security Council unanimously adopted resolution 242 (1967) on 22 November 1967. All 15 members of the Council — Argentina, Brazil, Bulgaria, Canada, China, Denmark, Ethiopia, France, India, Japan, Mali, Nigeria, USSR, United Kingdom, United States — cast positive votes for the resolution. The resolution read as follows:

The Security Council,

Expressing its continuing concern with the grave situation in the Middle East,

Emphasizing the inadmissibility of the acquisition of territory by war and the need to work for a just and lasting peace in which every State in the area can live in security,

Emphasizing further that all Member States in their acceptance of the Charter of the United Nations have undertaken a commitment to act in accordance with Article 2 of the Charter,

1. Affirms that the fulfilment of Charter principles requires the establishment of a just and lasting peace in the Middle East which should include the application of both the following principles;

(i) Withdrawal of Israeli armed forces from territories occupied in the recent conflict;

(ii) Termination of all claims or states of belligerency and respect for and acknowledgement of the sovereignty, territorial integrity and political independence of every State in the area and their right to live in peace within secure and recognized boundaries free from threats or acts of force;

2. Affirms further the necessity
   (a) For guaranteeing freedom of naviagtion through international water-ways in the area;
   (b) For achieving a just settlement of the refugee problem;
   (c) For guaranteeing the territorial inviolability and political indepen-dence of every State in the area, through measures including the establishment of demilitarized zones;

3. Requests the Secretary-General to designate a Special Representative to proceed to the Middle East to establish and maintain contacts with the States concerned in order to promote agreement and assist efforts to achieve a peaceful and accepted settlement in accordance with the provisions and principles in this resolution;

4. Requests the Secretary-General to report to the Security Council on the progress of the efforts of the Special Representative as soon as possible.

The Secretary-General promptly appointed Dr. Gunnar Jarring, Swedish Ambassador in Moscow, an experienced diplomatist and a talented linguist, as his Special Representative. After consultations in New York, Dr. Jarring established his headquarters in Nicosia, Cyprus on 10 December. Almost immediately, he went on his first round of visits — Beirut, Jerusalem, Amman, Cairo. On 22 December U Thant reported to the Security Council —

... During each of these visits he met the Head of State and other high officials. Ambassador Jarring reports that in all the countries he visited he was received with the utmost courtesy and with expressions of willingness to co-operate with his mission. He further reports that all the Governments visited welcomed the prospect of his early return to continue the conversations. Ambassador Jarring also reports that each of the Govern-ments visited agreed that the details of the conversations with him should be kept confidential ...

In the next three weeks or so Dr. Jarring visited Jerusalem four times, Cairo twice, Amman and Beirut once each. On 17 January 1968 U Thant reported —

... It would be premature at this time for me to report to the Council on the substance of Ambassador Jarring's talks thus far with the Governments concerned, since these talks are continuing at the wish of the parties and have not reached the stage at which any conclusions can be drawn. It may, however, be stated in general that the talks have covered two types of question. The first of these is concerned with the large and fundamental problems, which are of course, the most difficult ones and which are referred to in Security Council resolution 242 of 22 November 1967. The second type of questions are the kind of secondary problems, the solution of which would contribute to an improvement of the general atmosphere by relieving certain unnecessary hardships which have essentially resulted from the hostilities in June 1967. Such questions include the release of the ships stranded in the Suez Canal, the exchange of prisoners of war and certain measures of a humanitarian character . . .

... The Governments visited have also expressed the wish that the round of talks with Ambassador Jarring should continue, and he and I both take the same position. At the same time we are mindful of the time factor.

U Thant's third report, dated 29 March, covered rather more than two months and mentioned seven visits to Cairo, six to Amman and nine to Jerusalem. Dr. Jarring also went to U. N. Headquarters for four days for consultations with the Secretary-General —

... In his efforts to promote agreement between the Governments concerned, Ambassador Jarring has found a basic difference of outlook between the Governments of the United Arab Republic and Jordan on the one hand and the Government of Israel on the other, which have been described in some detail by the parties themselves in Security Council documents and at recent meetings of the Council.

The efforts of Ambassador Jarring have been directed towards obtaining an agreed statement of position concerning the implementation of the resolution, which could then be followed by meetings between the parties under his auspices. So far these efforts have not resulted in agreement. Moreover, they have been interrupted by recent events. However, Ambassador Jarring is now renewing his contacts with the parties and a further report may be submitted when the results of these contacts are known.

The "recent events" mentioned by U Thant included the Israeli military action on the Jordanian village and refugee camp at Karameh. On 24 March the Security Council unanimously adopted resolution 248 (1968) —

The Security Council . . . Observing that the military action by the armed forces of Israel on the territory of Jordan was of a large-scale and carefully planned nature,

Considering that all violent incidents and other violations of the cease-fire should be prevented and not overlooking past incidents, Recalling further resolution 237 (1967) which called upon the Government of Israel to ensure the safety, welfare and security of the inhabitants of the areas where military operations have taken place.

(1) Deplores the loss of life and heavy damage to property;
(2) Condemns the military action launched by Israel in flagrant violation of the United Nations Charter and the cease-fire resolutions;
(3) Deplores all violent incidents in violation of the cease-fire and declares that such actions of military reprisal and other grave violations of the cease-fire cannot be tolerated and that the Security Council would have to consider further and more effective steps as envisaged in the Charter to ensure against repetition of such acts;
(4) Calls upon Israel to desist from acts or activities in contravention of resolution 237 (1967); . . .

The next Security Council vote came on 27 April. Adopted unanimously, resolution 250 (1968) said —

376

The Security Council . . . Considering that the holding of a military parade in Jerusalem will aggravate tensions in the area and will have an adverse effect on a peaceful settlement of the problems in the area.

Calls upon Israel to refrain from holding the military parade in Jerusalem which is contemplated for 2 May 1968 . . .

The parade was, nevertheless, held and resolution 251 (1968) of 2 May put Israel's defiance on record . . .

The Security Council . . . Deeply deplores the holding of the military parade in Jerusalem on 2 May 1968 in disregard of the unanimous decision adopted by the Council on 27 April 1968 . . .

On 21 May the Security Council adopted the extremely important resolution 252 (1968) on the status of Jerusalem. The voting was 13-0, with the United States and Canada abstaining —

The Security Council

Recalling General Assembly resolutions 2253 and 2254 of 4 and 14 July 1967,

Having considered the letter of the Permanent Representative of Jordan on the situation in Jerusalem and the report of the Secretary-General,

Having heard the statements made before the Council,

Noting that since the adoption of the above mentioned resolutions, Israel has taken further measures and actions in contravention of those resolutions,

Bearing in mind the need to work for a just and lasting peace,

Reaffirming that the acquisition of territory by military conquest is inadmissible,

(1) Deplores the failure of Israel to comply with the General Assembly resolutions mentioned above;
(2) Considers that all legislative and administrative measures and actions taken by Israel, including expropriation of land and properties thereon, which tend to change the legal status of Jerusalem are invalid and cannot change that status;
(3) Urgently calls upon Israel to rescind all such measures already taken and to desist forthwith from taking any further action which tends to change the status of Jerusalem . . .

Meanwhile, Dr. Jarring, based on Nicosia, was travelling almost incessantly between Cairo, Amman, Jerusalem and Beirut, all through April and the first half of May. He then returned to U.N. Headquarters and, for five weeks, had frequent contacts with the permanent representatives of those involved in the problem. On a "vacation trip" to Europe at the end of June and early July he met the Foreign Ministers of the United Arab Republic, Israel and Jordan in Stockholm, The Hague and London respectively. U Thant reported to the

Security Council on 29 July—

> ... In the light of his most recent discussions, Ambassador Jarring has
> arrived at the conclusion, which I fully endorse, that it will be important
> and advisable for him to pursue further his efforts to promote agreement
> among the parties. In the near future, he will return to the Middle East for
> renewed contacts with the parties concerned.
>
> Ambassador Jarring is due great credit for the patience, persistence and
> statesmanship he has demonstrated in carrying out his extremely vital
> mission. He has applied to this task qualities of dedication, wisdom and
> tact which he has in rare degree.

The Secretary-General was more informative in the introduction to his
Annual Report to the General Assembly, published on 26 September —

> ... The basic situation in the Middle East in relation even to the
> beginnings of a settlement remains much the same as it was eight months
> ago. Until now, the one clear point of agreement among all concerned has
> been that Ambassador Jarring should continue his efforts.
>
> One party has insisted upon 'direct negotiations' by which is meant,
> apparently, a face to face confrontation of the two sides; the other side
> has rejected, initially at any rate, the direct procedure, but has been willing
> to carry on substantive talks concerning the implementation of the
> resolution indirectly, with Ambassador Jarring as the intermediary. All of
> his efforts will be unavailing unless he is able to carry on some form of
> dialogue with the two sides involving matters of substance ...

When the General Assembly opened Dr. Jarring was back in New York after
yet another round of visits in the Middle East to the Governments concerned.
On 3 December U Thant's fifth report to the Security Council contained the
following—

> ... With the arrival of foreign ministers of the parties for the twenty-third
> session of the General Assembly, Ambassador Jarring began a series of
> frequent meetings with them individually, which were at first mainly of an
> informal nature, but which, following the delivery by the foreign ministers
> of their speeches in the general debate, assumed a more formal character
> and concluded with written communications from the foreign ministers of
> Israel and of the United Arab Republic restating the positions of their
> respective Governments. In November, the foreign ministers returned to
> their countries. Before departing they repeated the readiness of their
> Governments to continue to co-operate with Ambassador Jarring and to
> enter into further discussions with him when he may deem it appropriate.

The "written communications" mentioned by U Thant were the subject of
a UPI message carried by The Financial Times datelined New York, October 23—

> Egypt has formally declared that Israel's withdrawal from captured Arab
> territory and agreement to settle the refugee problem 'would lead to the
> achievement of peace in the Middle East,' it was learned to-day. The
> declaration is contained in a two-page memorandum sent ... to the UN's
> Middle East peace envoy, Dr. Gunnar Jarring, by the Egyptian Foreign

Minister Mahmoud Riad. Its delivery followed by several days a memorandum on the Israeli position sent to Dr. Jarring by the Israeli Foreign Minister, Abba Eban . . . Riad's letter asked Dr. Jarring to 'clarify' Israel's position on two points — her readiness to implement the November 1967, Security Council resolution and to withdraw her forces from all Arab territory captured during the June war.

Some information about Dr. Mahmoud Riad's contacts with Dr. Jarring had been given a little earlier, in a despatch dated May 16, by The Times New York Correspondent—

A spokesman for the Egyptian delegation quoted a letter from Mahmoud Riad, the Egyptian Foreign Minister, to Dr. Jarring . . . The letter said that the United Arab Republic was ready to continue the contacts which Dr. Jarring had been conducting with the parties and that it would welcome a time-table presented by him for carrying out the Security Council resolution . . .

As 1968 drew to a close the lack of progress towards a settlement was all too apparent and the world's anxiety was growing ever more acute. Thoughtful journalists as well as political leaders were thinking more and more in terms of some sort of action by the Four Powers, as the following from The Observer of 15 December shows—

The Middle East remains the most dangerous area in the world. Like the Balkans before 1914, it is the place where old-fashioned national conflicts between local States could most easily drag Great Powers into war. Recently military action by Israel and the Arabs has been escalating at an alarming rate, while the efforts to bring about a political settlement of the 1967 war through the United Nations mediator, Dr. Jarring, have produced scarcely any progress.

Increasing violence makes the need for peace-making more urgent, but also more difficult. It undermines the position of those on both sides who are genuinely seeking a peaceful solution. It strengthens those who believe that force is the only answer — a desperate fight to a finish or a Spartan fortress existence.

On the Arab side, the military escalation has been accompanied by a significant political phenomenon: a Palestine Arab resistance movement has emerged, offering new leadership to the Palestinians and in Jordan. Its power and influence is increasing throughout the Arab countries, especially among the young, and at the same time a sense of Palestinian nationhood is growing. It will become increasingly difficult for Arab Governments to agree to peace terms which the Palestinian guerrillas reject, and the guerrillas' terms are of the most radical kind: not merely the withdrawal of Israel from the territories she occupied in June 1967 but also the replacement of the Jewish State of Israel by a multi-racial Palestinian State severed from the international Zionist movement.

For the time being the Egyptian and Jordanian Governments still declare themselves ready to accept the implementation of the Security Council resolution of November last year, which has been the basis of Dr. Jarring's mediation. Israel has also continued talks on the basis of this resolution. But the talks have made little or no progress, because each side puts its own interpretation on the resolution and is hampered by domestic divisions of opinion. Israel is trying to get a permanent peace treaty, without giving back all the territory she conquered. The Arabs are trying to get a complete Israel withdrawal, with an agreement less definitive than a final peace treaty.

The Security Council resolution, being a diplomatic compromise, is ambiguously or vaguely worded here and there. But the spirit of it is quite clear and reflects unmistakably the view of the majority of the UN as shown in the previous debates of the General Assembly. The majority of the international community was concerned with the maintenance of four basic principles, implicit and explicit in the UN Charter, that disputes between member States must be settled peacefully and not by force; that a member State cannot make territorial gains from another member State by conquest; that no member State should try to destroy or threaten the existence of another member State; that there should be freedom of innocent passage through international waterways.

The plain sense of this was that most members of the UN believed that Israel should withdraw completely from her conquests; that the Arabs should conclude a permanent and complete peace; and that outstanding questions, such as the refugees or the international status of the Gulf of Aqaba, should be settled by negotiations carried out not under duress by either side.

A settlement on these lines, with direct physical guarantees by the Great Powers, must surely still be the only sensible aim of international diplomacy. But the pressure and encouragement of the Great Powers are essential to overcome the misgivings and distrust on both sides and the real domestic problems which the Israel and Arab Governments have to deal with. It is still possible that with such backing Egypt and Jordan might be able to ensure acceptance of a definitive peace treaty — one which brought the complete withdrawal of Israel's forces from the occupied territories, while the Israel Government could also accept a similar exchange if the safeguards were powerful enough. But time is running out. In Jordan, already, this might involve a civil war to crush the guerrilla organisations as the Irish Government had to deal with IRA extremists after the settlement in Britain.

One way to avoid such a clash or to limit its scale would be to find some method of giving the Palestinians for the first time an opportunity to express their views freely on their own future. For unless a settlement is accepted by them it is unlikely to last, even if King Hussein and his Army, with the agreement of President Nasser, are strong enough to impose it temporarily.

Although the UN is still the proper instrument for seeking a settlement, the main responsibility for making it work in the Middle East, as elsewhere, lies with the Great Powers. The longer the Great Powers wait to exert their full influence, the more difficult it will be for them to make that influence effective. What could be done by joint persuasion now might involve a hazardous military intervention in a few years' time — with the formidable risk of their finding themselves on opposite sides.

The Soviet Government took the first initiative by circulating on 2 January 1969 to the Governments of Britain, France and the United States detailed proposals for the implementation of the Security Council's resolution of 22

November 1967. The following text is as published in The Times on February 28—

Israel and Israel's Arab neighbour-countries who will be ready to take part in the implementation of such a plan, shall confirm their agreement with the resolution of the Security Council of November 22, 1967, and shall state their readiness to implement all of its provisions.

In doing so they agree that by means of contacts through Dr. Jarring a time schedule and procedure for the withdrawal of Israel troops from the territories occupied during the conflict in 1967 will be established, and at the same time an agreed plan for the fulfilment by the parties of the other provisions of the Security Council resolution will be outlined, bearing in mind the establishment of a just and lasting peace in the Middle East, with which each state in this area can live in security.

The purpose of these contacts could be agreement upon concrete measures for implementing the said Security Council resolution.

1. Agreement shall be reached on simultaneous statements by the Government of Israel and the Governments of Israel's Arab neighbour-countries, who will take part in the implementation of this plan: on their readiness to proceed to a cessation of the state of war between them and to achieve a peaceful settlement after withdrawal of Israel troops from the occupied Arab territories.

In this connexion Israel shall state its willingness to start the withdrawal of its troops from the Arab territories occupied as a result of the conflict during the summer of 1967 on the date specified.

2. On the day the withdrawal of Israel troops begins, carried out by stages under the supervision of United Nations representatives, the said Arab countries as well as Israel shall deposit with the United Nations the appropriate documents concerning the cessation of the state of war, respect and recognition of the sovereignty, territorial integrity and political independence of each state in this area and their right to live in peace, within secure and recognized boundaries, that is in accordance with the said resolution of the Security Council.

In accordance with the understanding which shall be reached through Dr. Jarring, provisions shall also be agreed upon which concern secure and recognized boundaries (with corresponding maps attached), the safeguarding of freedom of navigation in the international waterways in this area, just settlement of the refugee problem, safeguarding of the territorial inviolability and political independence of each state in this area (possibly with the aid of measures which include the establishment of demilitarized zones).

It is intended that this understanding be regarded in accordance with the Security Council resolution as one whole entity, pertaining to all aspects of the settlement in the whole area of the Middle East, as a "package".

3. During the course of the succeeding month (or as agreed) Israel troops shall withdraw from a part of the Arab territories to certain intermediate lines on the Sinai peninsula, on the west bank of the Jordan river (as well as from Syrian territory, from the El Quneitra area).

On the day when Israel troops reach the intermediate lines in the peninsula agreed to in advance (for example, 30 to 40 km. from the Suez canal) the Government of the United Arab Republic will bring troops into the Suez canal area and begin the clean-up of the canal for resumption of navigation.

4. During the course of the second month (or as agreed) the Israel troops shall withdraw to the line they held prior to June 5, 1967, after which the administration of the corresponding Arab country shall be completely restored in the vacated territories and its troops and police forces be introduced.

On the day when the second stage of Israel troop withdrawal begins, the United Arab Republic and Israel (or the United Arab Republic only, in the event that its government agrees) shall state their consent to the stationing of United Nations troops near the line prior to June 5, 1967, on the Sinai peninsula, at Sharm-Ash-Shaikh and in the Gaza strip: that is, the situation in this area which existed in May 1967, shall be restored.

The Security Council shall adopt a decision on sending United Nations troops in accordance with the United Nations Charter and affirm the principle of freedom of navigation through the Straits of Tiran and in the gulf of Aqaba for the vessels of all countries.

5. After completion of the Israel troops' withdrawal to the lines of interstate demarcation, either through the mediation or the signing of a multilateral document, the documents of the Arab states and Israel deposited earlier shall finally enter into effect.

The Security Council, basing itself upon provisions of the United Nations Charter, shall adopt a decision on guarantees for the Arab-Israel boundaries (the possibility of guarantees by the Four Powers — permanent Security Council members — is also not to be excluded).

The Israeli reaction was prompt. "Israel Rejects Soviet Appeal", said one of the headlines to a story datelined Jerusalem January 5 which appeared in the Guardian—

Israel has told the United States and Britain that the latest Soviet proposals for peace in the Middle East cannot be regarded as a basis of a framework for discussion . . . The Israeli position was discussed today at a weekly Cabinet meeting, when Mr. Aba Eban, the Foreign Minister, told his colleagues that the Soviet proposals did not amount to a specific peace plan . . . Mr. Eban explained that the Russian proposals demanded a Israeli withdrawal without peace or secure borders. They did not include provision for free navigation and did not envisage the foundation of Israeli-Arab relations on a firm contractual basis.

The firm proposal that the Big Four representatives in the Security Council should meet to discuss peace efforts in the Middle East came from a spokesman of the French Foreign Ministry on January 17. A release from the UN Press Services the next day gave U Thant's reaction—

Asked whether a meeting of the Big Four would give the needed impetus to the efforts of Ambassador Gunnar Jarring, U Thant said: 'From my point of view, what is important is that their endeavours either collectively or separately to contribute to peace in the Middle East must be only within the context of the Security Council resolution of 22 November 1967. Only within the United Nations context . . . that is most important.'

Asked whether he still believed, as he had stated in his letter of 7 October to the Foreign Ministers of France, Soviet Union, United Kingdom and United States, that a meeting of the Big Four would be useful in giving guidance to the Jarring mission, the Secretary-General said 'Definitely'. . . .

President-Elect Nixon had given high priority to the Arab-Israel problem, sending Mr. William Scranton, former Governor of Pennsylvania, to the Middle East on a mission of inquiry. During his tour Mr. Scranton made some outspoken comments. In Tel Aviv for instance, he said that he could not understand Israel's insistence on direct peace talks with the Arabs as distinct from contact through a mediator. Mr. Scranton got back to New York on December 11, and the next day Mr. Adam Raphael cabled to The Guardian—

> Though Mr. Nixon has stressed that he places a high priority on achieving stability in the Middle East, his foreign policy advisers have been puzzled by some of Mr. Scranton's more outspoken remarks. In particular, they are at some pains to dissociate the new Administration from a statement made by Mr. Scranton in Jordan that the United States would now adopt 'a more even-handed American policy in the region', a comment that has caused apprehension in Israel.
>
> 'His remarks are Scranton remarks, not Nixon remarks', said Mr. Ron Zeigler, the President-elect's Press spokesman . . .
>
> Mr. Scranton, questioned on his return at Kennedy Airport about what he meant by a more even-handed policy, said: "The impression in the Middle East is widespread that the US is interested only in Israel's point. I don't think this is true of the present Adminstration or of Americans. I think we have other interests . . .

One of President Nixon's first big decisions after taking office concerned the Four Power talks idea. On 5 February The Times reported—

> The United States is ready to take part in four-power talks with the Soviet Union, Britain and France to promote a settlement in the Middle East within the framework of the United Nations. President Nixon yesterday met his National Security Council for a review of the situation and has apparently given approval to the French request for the 'big four' meeting. Washington sources emphasized, however, that the Nixon Administration has no desire to impose a solution on Israel and Arab leaders. Its object is to strengthen the United Nations approach.

The Four Power talks did not start till early April, being preceded by many bilateral contacts. Meanwhile, Israel's dislike of the idea of any sort of Four Power intervention to help Dr. Jarring was made very plain. For instance, Mr. John Wallis of The Daily Telegraph, in a despatch published on 31 March—

> The Israeli Government yesterday firmly declared its opposition to the

plan for a four-Power meeting to discuss a Middle East settlement. In its strongest statement yet on the subject, it added that Israel would not accept any recommendation from the meeting contrary to her interests . . .

There was no let-up in Israeli opposition to the Four Power talks. When the Israeli Prime Minister visited London in June The Guardian headlined its Diplomatic Correspondent's report of her Press conference, "Mrs. Meir Scornful of Big Power Talks". Mr. Terence Prittie wrote, on June 18—

> The Israeli Premier, Mrs. Golda Meir . . . was as apprehensive as ever about the Four Power talks . . .
> Israel remained unalterably opposed to 'others talking to others about our problems and the problems of the Arabs. Her Government did not know when the Four were likely to reach agreement, and she did not think that the Four knew either . . .
> The Israeli view, in fact, remains that the Four Power talks are weighted against Israel and that direct Arab-Israeli talks should take place instead. Mrs. Meir has not, however, convinced the British Government, which is still relying on a successful outcome to the Four Power talks.

Towards the end of March there was a foreign affairs debate in the House of Commons. Both the Leader of the Opposition and the Foreign Secretary devoted important passages in their speeches to the Middle Eastern situation and the prospects for the Four Power consultations. From Hansard—

> MR. EDWARD HEATH (BEXLEY) . . . Perhaps the Foreign Secretary could report on the progress of the Four Power approach to the problem. It seems to me that there are now several considerations which might work in favour of a settlement, although this may take a long time. Perhaps there are some signs that President Nasser recognises that it is in his interest to regain somewhat greater independence and certainly that it is in the interest of the United Arab Republic and the other Arab States which are providing the resources to make up the deficit on Canal dues.
> It must be in the long-term interest of Israel to reach a settlement of these disputes. It is in the immediate as well as the long-term interest of the super-Powers, the Soviet Union and the United States, not to be dragged into war by a further outbreak of conflict in this inflammable area. It is in the Soviet Union's interest, perhaps even more than that of America, to have the Canal open, since the Soviet Union wishes to use its influence in the Gulf and in the Indian Ocean by both political and military means. It is a British interest generally to achieve stability in the area from the point of view of our trade and, in particular, our oil supplies.
> The United Nations resolution, which was sponsored by Her Majesty's Government after the six-day war, is in itself ambiguous. Whether it was designedly so or not, I do not know, but the fact of its ambiguity does nevertheless give scope for negotiation between the parties about the various aspects of it. Dr. Jarring has not been able to achieve a settlement or even to bring the two sides round the table. Perhaps it is right to accept that they will not come to the same table. It is really this which led to the proposal for a Four Power attempt to reach a settlement.
> In my view, the Four Powers are not likely to be able to impose a settlement, though for political reasons those concerned may wish it to

appear so and be able to claim it as so in order to have a settlement which they can tell their people was imposed against their will but which they think it advisable to accept. However, that does not alter the principle that any settlement, if it is to last, must be agreed and accepted by those concerned. If it were to be imposed by the Four Powers there are many small Powers today which would be gravely apprehensive at the idea of the Four Powers imposing their view on particular disturbed parts of the world.

This matter requires intense diplomatic activity now, to deal sector by sector with the problems revealed by the United Nations resolution, the acceptance and timing of each depending on acceptance of the whole package when it has been completed. Sinai, the Gaza Strip, the Syrian Heights, the West Bank, Jerusalem, refugees, access through the Canal and the Gulf of Aqaba, recognition, in the case of Israel, and security, the international use of forces in some areas — all these must be dealt with as particular aspects of the problem. Merely to list them shows the formidable nature of the effort to reach a settlement.

There is no need for us in this country or the House to be violently partisan on either side. Ours is a general interest in a settlement of the problem and in peace and stability in the area. I hope that the Foreign Secretary will let us know what the Government is going to do in concert with other Powers in order to obtain a fair and just solution.

THE SECRETARY OF STATE FOR FOREIGN AND COMMONWEALTH AFFAIRS (MR. MICHAEL STEWART) . . . I must turn now to the last subject with which the right hon. Gentleman dealt — perhaps, adding together size and urgency and potential danger, the greatest of the lot — the situation in the Middle East. There is here an urgent need for settlement because with each day that goes by there is the risk of another incident, killing innocent people, inflaming tempers, making a final settlement more difficult. The tragedy of this is that it ought not to be too difficult to take the United Nations Security Council Resolution and spell it out in the form of a workable calendar, timetable, package — call it what you like. I believe there are a considerable number of well-informed and well-intentioned people in the world who could write out such a package or calendar which all the parties to the dispute, although they would probably complain about bits of it, would know would be better for them than letting the thing drift on as it now is.

Why then does it drift on? I believe because there are two balancing suspicions — the Arab suspicion that Israel has no intention of withdrawing at all from the territory she occupies, and the Israeli suspicion that whatever she does or signs or agrees to, the Arabs will not abandon the idea of one day destroying the State of Israel. I am not saying for one moment that either of those suspicions is justified — indeed, I do not believe they are — but it is a tragic fact that those suspicions are held on both sides.

Both sides could do something to reduce that burden of suspicion. If Israel would say, without cavil or qualification, that she not only accepts but will carry out the whole Resolution, this would reduce some of the suspicion. If the Arab countries would put it clearly beyond doubt that if a settlement is reached on the basis of the whole Resolution, they accept the words "just and lasting peace" in the Resolution without qualification and that any idea of destroying the State of Israel which may have been held in the past is permanently abandoned, this seems to me to be an early first step. This requires no more than saying explicitly what I think both parties know they must agree to in the end, if there is to be any settlement — saying it explicitly and saying it early. We have urged this on them for some time. I trust the counsel will in time be taken.

Beyond that — for this is only the beginning of the matter — we have to recognise that the United Nations Resolution, is I believe, now the essential basis of a settlement. It is the one fixed point in the argument. We may take some pride in the fact that it was my right hon. Friend the Member for Belper (Mr. George Brown) whose initiative caused this Resolution to be accepted. The Resolution having been passed, we felt it was certainly right to give Dr. Jarring a chance to turn it, by consultations with the parties, from a Resolution into a practicable detailed plan. Unhappily, despite his best efforts, he has been unable to do so, I believe basically because of these two suspicions one on each side that I mentioned. It is for that reason that I think it is necessary for the Four Powers to act.

In May of last year I agreed with Mr. Gromyko that we and the Russians must consult together about this, and there have been already a number of bilateral consultations between the various pairs that one can pick out of the Four. So the time has not been lost. But I must say that I regret that I am not able to tell the House today that the Four Powers talks have actually begun. However, I do not believe they will now be long delayed. When they do meet, our view is that they must meet without conditions and without limitations of agenda.

I know it is sometimes said: Will this get us anywhere? Have not Israel and her Arab neighbours got to sit down round a table themselves if there is to be any hope? I think the refusal of Arab countries to enter into direct talks is one that is extremely difficult for people in this country to understand. We are so used to the concept — and it is a very sensible concept — that if there is a dispute — the parties, whatever they think of each other, should at least sit down to discuss it. On the other hand, I am bound to say that I do not think it is reasonable for Israel to say that certain parts of the problem — Jerusalem, for instance — are not negotiable.

It seems to me in this situation that we cannot expect direct talks at present. This, again, reinforces the need for the Four to come in. What will they have to do? Certainly they will get in touch with the parties concerned — Israel and the Arab States. They will continue to urge certain courses of action on them. They will encourage them in particular to go to Dr. Jarring with suggestions on the substance of the dispute, which in effect they have not yet done.

But, for my own part, I do not believe the work of the Four can stop there. I think the Four will have to start on the job of actually making the package, time table or calendar, which is the heart of the matter, and making that will mean that both Israel and her Arab neighbours will have to make some concessions to the other side's point of view. The Four, or anyone who tries to make such a timetable or package, will have to interpret some of the phrases in the Resolution which are not yet defined and, indeed, could not be defined. For example, there is reference to the refugees. The Resolution does not say exactly what ought to be done about them. I believe that it is incumbent on Israel to be rather more forthcoming on this problem than she has so far been. But if Arab countries want her to do it is all the more important that they make it clear beyond any doubt that the idea of destroying or waging future war on Israel is abandoned. It is one thing for Israel to admit people on humanitarian grounds. It is another to ask to admit people who she fears may be a deadly peril to her security in the future.

There is another matter on which it may be necessary to interpret the Resolution. When one deals with the reference to boundaries there may well be a need for a United Nations Force. If there is, I believe that it will be necessary to make it clear that it is not a Force that can be withdrawn at the request of one side alone.

Finally, the question of whether there can be a solution imposed by the Four Powers has been raised. If by 'impose' one means something that both sides, or even one side, bitterly hated but were told they must accept, I do not think that such a solution would work. Even if one made it work to begin with, it would not last, and no one would be prepared to guarantee it. On the other hand, there is clearly the necessity to have some degree of very urgent persuasion by the Four Powers, because if that were not necessary a settlement would have been reached long ago. The real solution, therefore, stands somewhere between 100 per cent free acceptance by the parties concerned, which, if it could be achieved, would have been achieved already, and 100 per cent imposition, which is impossible.

What one can hope for, with patience, is a settlement that in the end will be accepted by the parties concerned with a certain limited amount of grumbling all round, and a situation in which, therefore, some of the Governments concerned will be able to tell their populations that the responsibility for the bits of the settlement they do not like lies on the backs of the Four. The shoulders of the Four must be big enough to bear that, provided that the degree of dissatisfaction is quite moderate. I think that one could draw up such a settlement, about which every party to the dispute would say 'This is not all we hoped for', but would know quite certainly that it was infinitely better than allowing the struggle to continue. Such a settlement could be found. The Four will try to find it, but the parties concerned are not thereby stripped of their responsibility to help in finding it.

When we consider the situation in the Middle East now, with the waste of that great earning asset, the Canal; with the constant killing and border incidents; with the dread in which the whole of that part of the world lives; I should have thought that if there is any wisdom or compassion in the countries concerned they will all make up their minds that some concessions must be made. If the talks of the Four can be the channel through which that is done, and a settlement is achieved, it will be a great advance for humanity and a great boon to the people of that region.

On April 10, when the Four Power talks were in their early stages, King Hussein addressed the National Press Club in Washington. His speech ended with his six points—

1. The end of all Belligerency.
2. Respect for and acknowledgement of the Sovereignty, territorial integrity and political independence of all States in the area.

3. Recognition of the right of all to live in Peace within secure and recognised boundaries free from threats or acts of war.

4. Guaranteeing for all the freedom of navigation through the Gulf of Aqaba and the Suez Canal.

5. Guaranteeing the territorial inviolability of all States in the Area through whatever measures necessary including the establishment of Demilitarized Zones.

6. Accepting a just settlement of the Refugee problem.

In return for these considerations our sole demand upon Israel is the withdrawal of its armed forces from all territories occupied in the June '67 war, and the implementation of all the other provisions of the Security Council Resolution. The challenge that these principles present is that Israel may have either peace or territory, but she can never have both.

The Guardian Foreign Staff described the Israeli reaction on April 12 under the headline "Israelis scoff at Hussein's Offer"—

King Hussein of Jordan's six-point plan for peace in the Middle East . . . was given a sceptical reception yesterday in official circles in Tel Aviv . . . It was pointed out that . . . it demanded complete withdrawal of all Israeli forces from all occupied territories, including Jerusalem. This, according to some comments, was not an offer Israel could treat earnestly . . . In London, however, it was thought that Hussein's apparent offer to recognise Israel and to support the right of free passage for Israeli ships through the Suez Canal represents the clearest reaffirmation so far of the principles laid down by the 1967 Security Council resolution. His statement has, therefore, been readily welcomed in London . . .

Some time later the Jordan Government had to bring Israeli policy and actions in Jerusalem once again to the attention of the Security Council. The Council on 3 July, unanimously adopted a second resolution on the status of Jerusalem — Resolution 267 (1969), reaffirming resolution 252 and the inadmissibility of the acquisition of territory by military conquest, and censuring in the strongest terms all the measures taken by Israel to change the status of the City. The resolution carried unanimously, but the United States abstained on a separate vote on the paragraph calling on Israel to rescind all measures tending to change the status of Jerusalem.

The Security Council,

Recalling its resolution 252 of 21 May 1968 and the earlier General Assembly resolutions 2253 and 2254 of 4 and 14 July 1967 respectively concerning measures and actions by Israel affecting the status of the City of Jerusalem . . .

Having heard the statement of parties concerned in the question,

Noting that since the adoption of the above-mentioned resolutions Israel has taken further measures tending to change the status of the City of Jerusalem,

Reaffirming the established principle that acquisition of territory by military conquest is inadmissible,

(1) Reaffirms its resolution 252 (1968);

(2) Deplores the failure of Israel to show any regard for the General Assembly and Security Council resolutions mentioned above;

(3) Censures in the strongest terms all measures taken to change the status of the City of Jerusalem;

(4) Confirms that all legislative and administrative measures and actions by Israel which purport to alter the status of Jerusalem, including expropriation of land and properties thereon, are invalid and cannot change that status;

(5) Urgently calls once more upon Israel to rescind forthwith all measures taken by it which may tend to change the status of the City of Jerusalem, and in future to refrain from all actions likely to have such an effect;

(6) Requests Israel to inform the Security Council without any further delay of its intentions with regard to the implementation of the provisions of this resolution;

(7) Determines that in the event of a negative response or no response from Israel, the Security Council shall reconvene without further delay to consider what further action should be taken in this matter.

(8) Requests the Secretary-General to report to the Security Council on the implementation of this resolution.

But to return to Dr. Jarring. He had paid yet another visit to the Middle East early in the year but, when the Four Power representatives began to meet, the temporary suspension of his work was announced. Reuter reported from UN Headquarters on 9 April—

Dr. Jarring is interrupting his mission to resume his post as Swedish Ambassador to the Soviet Union. A UN spokesman said that Dr. Jarring was relinquishing his Middle East post 'for the time being' . . . The spokesman added that Dr. Jarring would be 'immediately available for any renewed effort in connection with his mission in the Middle East whenever developments may require it'.

The Four Power representatives held fifteen meetings in thirteen weeks, and adjourned on 1 July. From UN Headquarters, The Financial Times Correspondent wrote—

A brief Press statement, issued following the 15th session of the talks — which lasted barely an hour — said that 'because of important consultations on the Middle East taking place among the four Governments, the date of the next meeting of permanent representatives will be set at a later time.

Meanwhile, the Ambassadors entrusted a working group of their deputies with the task of continuing the consultations. But informed sources said that no top level meetings should now be expected until late August. The Ambassadors' deputies, meanwhile, would probably mark time until some positive results came out of the Middle East bilateral discussions between Russia and the US in Washington.

But diplomatic circles here expressed the fear that the talks might just die out if the Americans and Russians cannot reach a compromise or if events in the area overtake diplomatic manoeuvres . . .

So hopes of breathing new life into the Jarring Mission seem to depend on American-Soviet exchanges and upon the work that can be done in the General Assembly of the United Nations. In July the Security Council was preoccupied, not only with Israeli behaviour in Jerusalem but also with cease-fire infringement along the Suez Canal. In that context a letter from Mr. Abdullah el-Erian, the Acting-Representative of the U.A.R. at the United Nations, was addressed on 17 July to the president of the Security Council—

> . . . Israel has adopted an obstructive attitude against all of the efforts exerted to reach a peaceful settlement in accordance with Security Council resolution 242; efforts carried out by Ambassador Jarring, as well as those actually undertaken by the Four Powers to achieve a peaceful settlement of the Middle East crisis. In taking such an attitude, Israel is seeking to impose its own terms and realize its expansionist aims in utter disregard of the dangers that threaten peace in the area.
>
> In the meantime, the United Arab Republic has always exerted all efforts in a positive and practical way for the success of Ambassador Jarring's mission. It has, moreover, supported all international efforts for achieving a peaceful and just settlement in the Middle East.
>
> The United Arab Republic has accepted the Security Council resolution 242, it has declared its readiness to implement its provisions. Furthermore, and in contrast to Israel's policy, it has supported international efforts as long as they aim at the implementation of the Security Council resolution, being convinced that the continuation of the Israeli policy in the area will definitely lead to an explosive situation which would endanger peace in the area.
>
> Israel, however, has persistently rejected the resolutions of the Security Council and the General Assembly of the United Nations. It is to be noted in this respect that Israel rejected the Security Council resolution on Jerusalem adopted unanimously on 3 July 1969 and that the campaign she launched against the Council itself is a clear attack against the United Nations Organizaton and its organs and an evidence of Israel's disregard of the will of the world community . . .

In his annual report to the 24th General Assembly of the United Nations Secretary-General U Thant has issued a sombre warning about the Middle Eastern situation. He wrote, "It is no exaggeration to say that, failing some early progress towards a settlement, there is a very real danger that this great and historical region, the cradle of civilization and of three world religions, will recede steadily into a new dark age of violence, disruption and destruction". It was against this background that the Four Powers resumed their efforts, at Foreign Minister's level, to help Dr. Jarring in his immensely important task.

INTERNATIONAL GUARANTEES
AND
INTERNATIONAL POLICE FORCES

Ministry of Foreign Affairs
(Jerusalem)

In theory, all member-States of the United Nations enjoy international guarantees for their borders, under the Charter. The experience of the twenty-six years since the establishment of the UN has not shown these guarantees to be effective. This may be the reason why many member-States have formed separate organizations providing mutual guarantees for their borders. NATO, the Warsaw Pact and SEATO are such organizations. These organizations are more effective than the UN as a whole, because the interests common to the members of them are greater than those which unite members of the UN as a whole. (At times these organizations may be altogether too efficient. It was in the name of what was later promulgated as the Brezhnev Doctrine that the Warsaw Pact nations threatened Czechoslovakia and invaded it.)

The function of the organizations is to provide a joint defence against a specific potential enemy, and they serve as political-military instruments in the inter-bloc conflict. Because of this, there has never been an instance of guarantees, or mutual defence organizations, cutting across the inter-bloc lines, nor ever a case when a country was given the combined guarantees of both the US and the USSR. When both these great Powers are interested in preserving the independence and boundaries of a particular nation, it is no longer in any real danger, and it becomes unnecessary to sign pacts and set up defence organizations.

The conflict in the Middle East represents in some of its aspects the conflict between the two Great Powers. So long as these hold different positions and support rival sides in the conflict, it is unlikely that they could act in concert to guarantee the peace or the boundaries of an involved State. Such guarantees, therefore, however solemnly proclaimed, would remain empty promises.

SUPPOSING THERE WERE GUARANTEES
For the purpose of analysing this hypothesis, let us imagine the following situation. The Great Powers have persuaded the two sides to accept an arrangement wherein Israel would withdraw from the areas that it occupied in

June 1967. Peace agreements between Israel and the Arabs have not been signed, because of Arab opposition. There are no political or economic relations between the sides. Instead, the Great Powers have guaranteed the borders between Israel and the Arab States. A year or two later a revolution breaks out in one of the Arab States and the new ruler begins to threaten Israel with ideological-nationalist slogans and warnings against "Israeli expansionist attempts". The ruler concentrates military forces along the border with Israel.

What would the great powers do? In all probability they would do nothing at all — because they would be unable to agree on the facts, much less on concrete steps. Not because they are too weak, but because they are too powerful and know that a conflict between them endangers world peace, they would be extremely cautious. Unable jointly to implement the guarantees, they would not attempt to do so separately. Regardless of Great Power attempts to influence their respective friends in the Middle East, if Governments in the region wanted an escalation, the effect of the influence would be limited. Thus the Great Powers, joint guarantors of the peace in the Middle East, would have to follow the lead of extremists in small countries in threatening the peace of the region and of the world. If this sounds fanciful, it is no more than a faithful reproduction of the events of 1967. The rulers of Egypt and Syria began a series of manoeuvres which threatened the peace. Their great ally, the USSR, was unable, or unwilling, to hinder them in this course of action. The result was war. (A similar process took place in Vietnam, in several stages.)

Diplomatic guarantees, therefore, provide no security. If there is a genuine desire for peace, they are unnecessary. If there is no such desire, not only are such guarantees ineffective, but they may actually intensify the danger by involving the Great Powers in the conflict.

What about an inter-power police force? The establishment of an inter-Power Police Force would only aggravate the situation further, in that the involvement of the Great Powers would be wider and deeper to begin with. Their troops would be stationed on the firing line. A shot fired across the border might strike an American or a Russian soldier and create a dangerous international incident, since the prestige of the Great Powers would thus be involved, in addition to their political and economic interests in the region. It is not a coincidence that the Great Powers have never yet succeeded between them in establishing a functioning UN force.

When the UN Organization was first established, it was agreed to include in its Charter certain provisions for placing combined armed forces of the Great Powers at the disposal of the UN. But, in the twenty-six years of the UN's existence, such a force has never been organized, because political realities made it impossible. Whenever a conflict arose which required, in theory, the deployment of such a force, at least one of the Powers was involved and another Power generally had opposing interests in the conflict. This state of affairs made it impossible to establish an emergency force combining troops of the Great Powers. It was the USSR which opposed the 33 Nation Committee's proposal for such a force, and yet it is the USSR which today actively supports the establishment of one in the Middle East. Why assume that here, in the most dangerous conflict in the world, the first attempt at establishing such a force will be successful?

THE EXPERIENCE OF UN FORCES

There have been several attempts in the past to deploy United Nations forces in various parts of the world. There have even been military and police

Cyprus. An analysis of these experiences may indicate the conditions under which a UN force can prevent a war, as well as the conditions under which the presence of a UN force is a lamentable farce, sharply illustrating the impotence of the international community, or the exploitation of the UN in the interest of every Power.

There has been only one occasion when UN forces were able to stop bloodshed, and that was in Cyprus. On the other hand, the UN has never been able to compel India — a member-State — to comply with its resolution on Kashmir. India continues to rule this territory, the subject of a prolonged conflict, despite a number of solemn Resolutions.

In the Congo, the UN was used to force unity upon a new State. This interference in the internal affairs of one nation was carried out in the name of the international community. Without going into a thorough historical analysis of that conflict, it is plain that, behind the sides directly involved, stood non-African nations. Events there transpired according to the relative strength of those nations and the degree of their involvement in the conflict.

A UN Police Force, consisting of hundreds of thousands of US and US-allied troops, was deployed in Korea. This force repelled aggression at the cost of hundreds of thousands of lives, military and civilian, and the massive destruction of the two States in Korea. That the UN flag could have been flown over this operation was due to the fact that the United States was able to utilise a diplomatic mistake of the USSR, which was at that time boycotting the UN debates. The United States put through a Resolution in the Security Council which provided UN authorisation for what was in fact a unilateral United States action.

But it is Israel's experience of the operations of UN police forces and emergency forces which best illuminates the ineffectuality of these instruments.

WHEN IS A UN FORCE SUCCESSFUL?

In contrast with its various failures, the deployment of UN forces in Cyprus stands out as a relative success. There it was able to bring a halt to the civil war between Greek and Turkish Cypriots. Perhaps from this success it might be possible to learn when such a force can be effective, at least temporarily. Several conditions must exist:

None of the Powers was directly involved. In the case of Cyprus, none of the Great Powers was involved in the conflict between the two communities in this small country. While the Powers had some interests and sympathies in the conflict, none was unequivocally associated with either side.

The rivals belonged to the same bloc. Turkey and Greece supported their respective communities in the Cypriot conflict. The two States are both members of NATO and allies of the United States, which was able to exert its influence upon them, and through them on the rival factions in Cyprus itself.

The military forces involved were relatively small. The number of combatants in Cyprus was small, the arms at their disposal were meagre, and the area of the conflict was limited. In such circumstances a relatively small UN Emergency Force can effectively supervise a cease-fire.

The forces were roughly equal. In Cyprus neither side had an overwhelming numerical superiority which would enable it to "solve the problem" quickly, before the slow-moving diplomatic apparatus could be activated. The UN had time to debate the issue, determine a course of action and carry it out. The presence of a substantial air force, missiles and heavy artillery might have escalated the conflict rapidly before effective intervention could have been time to debate the issue, determine a course of action and carry it out. The presence of a substantial air force, missiles and heavy artillery might have escalated the conflict rapidly before effective intervention could have been brought to bear.

The aims of the rival factions were not acutely polarised. Neither side in the Cyprus conflict wished to annihilate the other in the modern style of genocide. The conflict was an expression of a long-standing struggle between two traditionally hostile communities. The style of fighting was also "traditional".

Both sides wanted to end the conflict and searched for an honourable solution. There was a point when the rival factions in Cyprus knew — as did their supporters across the Mediterranean — that the bloodshed had to stop. The arrival of an UN Emergency Force was an honourable way to achieve this.

Despite all these favourable conditions, the struggle in Cyprus continues to simmer, though on a much lower level. In the Middle East none of these conditions exists. Israel's experience with UN Emergency Forces was highly unsatisfactory, even when the conflict was less acute. What are the chances, now that the conflict has been intensified, that such a force would be successful in its mission?

ISRAEL AND THE UN EMERGENCY FORCE

Israel, which has had more dealings than any other State with UN Emergency Forces, has had a very bad experience with them. UN observers entered the area immediately after the establishment of the State of Israel, but they were unable to stop the war. When the hostilities did end, it was through armistice agreements negotiated by the two sides, mainly in Rhodes and partly in secret meetings between Israeli and Jordanian representatives.

UN forces were stationed along the Arab-Israel borders until 1956, but were helpless to prevent acts of terror and sabotage against Israeli soldiers and civilians. These acts were carried out by irregular organizatons and largely supported by regular Arab armed forces. The UN apparatus was not only unable to prevent these acts from taking place, but evolved into a sort of corporate referee to adjudicate a series of cease-fire violations on both sides — taking care to distribute the blame even-handedly, out of political considerations. This attitude was a natural consequence of the political character of the UN, in which the Arab States carry a good deal of weight.

The situation in the Middle East was aggravated by the advent of another Big Power involvement, which turned the region into an inter-Power arena. It is characteristic that the new presence expressed itself first of all in the despatch of additional arms into the area. These were the developments which intensified the conflict and led to the Sinai campaign of 1956.

The imposed arrangement of 1957, which brought about the complete Israeli withdrawal from Sinai, did not lead to peace. It did restore a UN force to the borders. Once again, this force was unable to prevent acts of sabotage, terror and regular Arab military operations against Israel. On the contrary — it shielded these activities and minimised their aggressive nature by the studied "neutrality" of its observations.

The worst crisis was in May 1967. Never was the impotence of the UN more obvious. The Emergency Force was withdrawn at the very moment when the situation had worsened and the risk of war was imminent. The withdrawal was the result of political pressures on the UN, and revealed the UN force to be "an umbrella, which is removed at the moment when it begins to rain."

It is, of course, impossible to declare with any certainty what would have happened if a UN force had not been present along the Israel-Arab borders. It is a reasonable assumption, however, that this force, which "supervised the armistice", obviated any Arab movement toward peace. The presence of the force enabled the Arab Governments to hide under the political mantle of the UN and avoid the need for a peace settlement, a need which would have been much more clearly felt if the Arab nations had had to face Israel directly. Thus, while the UN force perhaps prevented a great conflagration, it certainly kept the conflict "on the boil". On the basis of this experience, Israel believes that a UN Force does not promote the cause of peace, but, at best, prevents progress towards a genuine peace.

A FOUR-POWER EMERGENCY FORCE

Another type of emergency force is a Four-Power one, such as that which has policed Berlin since its occupation in 1945. This example, which has been mentioned in connection with the Middle East conflict, emphasises the ineffectuality — and risk to world peace — entailed in such a solution.

From the very beginning, the Four-Power Berlin Police Force was a technical fiction. Berlin was divided into four sectors, each policed by a different Power. The three Western Powers unified their sectors, while the Soviet sector remained separate, and was in effect annexed to East Germany. The city was cut in two, with a border running across it. There was constant tension along this border, and much suffering ensued for the inhabitants. The presence of armed forces of the two Great Powers intensified the danger to the world whenever tension mounted in Berlin. The two best-remembered crises were the Berlin Blockade in 1948 and the erection of the Berlin Wall in 1962.

In 1948, the USSR imposed a blockade on West Berlin and severed its overland communications with West Germany. It was a symbolic move in the inter-bloc struggle, with the inhabitants of Berlin serving as pawns in the global chess-game. The presence in West Berlin of several thousand American troops only served to increase the tension. The US faced the dilemma whether to succumb to the Soviet pressure or to escalate the conflict dangerously. It then decided to stand on its rights and began the air-lift, a decision which undoubtedly stemmed from its direct involvement in the dispute. The sharp confrontation between the two Great Powers made this decision a highly hazardous one for the entire world. A similar situation arose when the USSR and its client-State, East Germany, decided to erect the Berlin Wall. Once again, the direct involvement of the two Super-Powers brought the world to the brink of war. The inescapable conclusion from this analysis is that the direct presence of the Great Powers not only does not lead to peace, but rather aggravates any crisis in which they are involved.

In the Middle East conflict the fact that one of the Super-Powers is directly involved in it through the presence of its "advisors" has accentuated the crisis. Would the direct involvement of US military forces serve to alleviate the tension, or to intensify it? So long as the two Super-Powers continue in their rivalry, any area in which they are both militarily present becomes a threat to world peace — and not the reverse.

WHY DO THE EGYPTIANS WANT A FOUR-POWER FORCE?

In view of this experience it may seem strange that anyone should propose the stationing of a Four-Power Force along the Israel-Arab borders. The propaganda basis for this proposal has already been discussed. Such a proposal can serve to create the impression that a Police Force of this type guarantees peace along the borders, eliminating the need both for a genuine, negotiated peace agreement which would commit both sides and for truly defensible boundaries.

The Israelis are not so naive as to believe that a peace agreement between them and the Arabs would in itself be a guarantee of peace. They do believe that the explicit willingness to sign a peace agreement would represent a psychological change in the Arab world, showing that it is willing to contemplate peaceful co-existence with the State of Israel. The fact that the Arab leadership remains unwilling to discuss, openly and unequivocally, a peace agreement with Israel, but is willing only to propound a variety of substitutes for it, proves that this psychological change has not yet taken place. Israel believes that a peace agreement will not produce a willingness to live in peace, but, rather the contrary — that the willingness to live in peace would lead to such an agreement. On the other hand, unwillingness to sign such an agreement surely demonstrates an unwillingness to live in peace.

But the proposal for a Four-Power Force has a political dimension beyond that of propaganda. The establishment of a UN military force, including Soviet troops, would serve to legitimise a Soviet military presence in the region. Today, there are in fact military personnel of one of the Powers on the soil of one of the nations of the Middle East, viz. the Soviet "technical advisors" in Egypt. The UN military force would make their presence legal and official.

Once this political objective had been attained, the Soviets could intervene, or threaten to intervene directly whenever it suited them. Such long and unquiet borders would always provide them with some real or imaginary incident which they could utilise to make political and military demands upon Israel. Their military presence would enable them to use force, or to threaten the use of force, so as to achieve compliance with their demands. The presence of other US, British or French troops could not prevent such incidents or their exploitation for military or political purposes. On the contrary, it would serve to turn a minor incident into a grave inter-Power crisis, or might produce Western concessions to the USSR and Egypt at Israel's expense, so as to avoid a confrontation.

Even if the Police Force consisted of troops not of the Great Powers but of smaller nations, it would always be possible for the USSR to demand that soldiers of Soviet-bloc States be included in it. There have been several instances where the Czechs or Hungarians acted on behalf of the USSR, and Israel has been well aware of this fact since the Soviets first supplied Egypt with arms in 1955, under the guise of a "Czech arms deal". The USSR has also intervened in several conflicts in Africa in this manner. A UN and Four-Power legitimation of a Soviet military intervention — or the threat of such an intervention — is, therefore, the chief danger to the peace of Israel and of the entire world.

WHAT DOES ISRAEL WANT?

Israel's position, which rejects international guarantees and police forces, has been misunderstood by those unfamiliar with the situation. It can be summed up in the following statements:

Israel wants a genuine peace — not a substitute.

Whoever wants peace is willing to sign a peace-agreement. Whoever refuses to sign a peace agreement does not want peace.

Declarations of a desire for peace are no substitute for a real peace.

Rival Powers cannot jointly guarantee peace.

If there is a genuine desire for peace, then international guarantees are unnecessary; if there is no such desire, international involvement is dangerous.

Too many wars have been conducted in the name of Peace Forces.

The way to peace in the Middle East is the removal of Great Power forces, not the introduction of more of them.

An Emergency Force was unable to prevent war in 1967 — can it do so in 1971?

There are already too many armed forces in the Middle East; it is not necessary to bring in more.

XIII. Negotiations and Peace

INTRODUCTION

The Arab-Israeli conflict differs from other world tensions because of its complexity. The major issue is not merely ideological, religious, ethnic, economic or territorial. Yet despite the many facets of the conflict, the question of Israel's very right to exist in the Middle East remains fundamental.

The Arab position has demanded elimination or dismemberment of Israel either by "the liquidation of all traces of aggression" of 1948 and 1967, or by "deZionization," or by the establishment of a "Palestinian state" where Moslems, Christians, and Jews will live in peace. This policy is consistent with recent Arab resolutions advocating "no recognition of Israel, no negotiation with Israel, no peace with Israel" and adherence to the rights of the Palestinians to their country. Although in February, 1971, Egypt for the first time announced its willingness to make peace with Israel, it has insisted on the withdrawal of enemy forces to the pre-June 1967 lines before any negotiations could take place. This pre-condition has been unacceptable to Israel and has resulted in a deadlock.

Israel, on the other hand, asserts that Arab unwillingness to negotiate with her directly and without preconditions are reflections of Arab unreadiness to let Israel coexist in the area. Without a direct dialogue between the parties primarily involved in the conflict, the likelihood for peace, the Israelis believe, is extremely remote. They insist on their right to a negotiated peace treaty and reject demands for a withdrawal of forces to the 1967 boundaries without permanent peace. Such peace would include Israel's recognition, by the Arabs, an end to warfare by regular or irregular armies, a stop to the propaganda warfare, the granting of freedom of passage in the Gulf of Aqaba and the Suez Canal, the promotion of commercial relations and the development of diplomatic links.

Several aspects of peace-making are analyzed in this chapter. The first selection, "Israel and Negotiation," was published in Beirut by the Palestine Liberation Organization Research Center in July, 1970. The author, Ibrahim Al-Abid, seeks to expose the "falseness" of Israel's desire for accommodation and peace. The second selection is an excerpt from an undated pamphlet published in Tel-Aviv by the Association for Peace, a voluntary private group engaged in encouraging dialogue on the resolution of the conflict. While four solutions based on totally different premises are presented, the authors believe that only the recognition of an Arab Palestine and a Jewish Israel as separate states will offer a feasible answer to the lingering problem.

ISRAEL
AND
NEGOTIATIONS

Ibrahim Al-Abid

Since the June 1967 War, Israel has been wont to declare its belief that the only way to establish permanent peace in the area is through direct negotiations between it and the Arab States. This plea for negotiations seems, at first sight, to be innocent, logical and to reflect a positive, realistic and peaceful policy. However, a glance at the background of the conflict in the area and at the pattern of the Israeli political and military conduct from 1948 to the present time, will be sufficient to expose the falseness of this plea and its remoteness from any desire for a just and permanent peace in this part of the world.

Israel has been established on the ruins of another entity, Palestine. Its people are individuals gathered from other countries, occupying the lands of the original inhabitants of Palestine, who have been made to disperse in dozens of countries. The soil on which Israel stands is occupied territory, not land owned or bought by the present occupiers. Israel exists because Palestine does not exist. The Israelis are there because the Palestinians are not where they ought to be, in the land of their fathers and forefathers. The mere existence of Israel is a condition which leads to the non-existence, to the abolition, of Palestine and its original inhabitants. The mere existence of Israel means non-recognition and non-acceptance of the Palestinian Arab people and its natural right to live in its homeland and to enjoy its right to self-determination. The Arabs' non-recognition of Israel becomes, then, a negative response to Israel's positive non-recognition of Palestine and the Palestinians, to its expulsion of the Palestinian Arabs, to its usurpation of their public and private property, and to their displacement by aliens from different parts of the world.

Here lies the root of the Palestine Question. The Palestine problem, in fact, is a conflict between the Palestinian Arab people and the Zionist Movement allied with imperialism in its old and new forms, with its old and new leaders. From this, also stems the Palestinian rejection of direct negotiations with Israel. For this call involves basically a recognition of Israel, i.e. a guarantee for it to continue enjoying its gains. The principal Zionist political end for the establishment of a State has been reached. Most, not all, of Israel's avowed territorial

399

aims have been realized. The greatest part possible in the present circumstances of its demographic task, to decrease the number of the original Palestinian inhabitants under its rule to a size easily manageable, while substituting for them about two sixths of World Jewry, has been achieved. By calling for immediate negotiations, Israel desires to invest with legality these acts, which have been realized through the use of force. In other words, Israel intends by its plea, to legalize and perpetuate its act of forcibly uprooting and dispossessing the Palestinian people.

Represented by its fighting vanguard, the Arab Palestinian people rejects any call or project which will invest with legality the Zionist colonialist presence on the soil of Palestine. This rejection applies as well to the Security Council Resolution of November 22, 1967. In this, the Palestinian rejection concurs with the Israeli rejection, but for different reasons.

While Israel rejects the Security Council Resolution because it desires to retain the gains it acquired during the June 1967 aggression and to consecrate its occupation of additional Arab territories, the Palestinian rejection is based on the rejection of the Zionist colonialist phenomenon and of any attempt at investing it with legality and continuity. This rejection emanates from an absolute faith in the necessity of the reign of justice and peace in this part of the world.

Instead of the lame solutions proposed to end the Middle East crisis, the Palestinian Revolution proposes a positive solution for this crisis which goes beyond its seemingly negative stand based on the rejection of negotiations and the Security Council Resolution. This stand is summarized by the call for the establishment of a democratic Palestinian state in which Muslim, Christian and Jewish citizens shall enjoy equal rights and duties and where there will be no trace of discrimination in any form.

The only solution in which the Arab Palestinian people have faith is the liberation of Palestine from Zionist colonialism in alliance with world imperialism, and the establishment of a democratic state in Palestine which shall guarantee for all, Muslims, Christians and Jews, equal rights and duties. The Arab Palestinian people, which is engaged in an armed struggle for the sake of this aim, considers this solution to be the only just, acceptable and lasting one, not only from its own viewpoint but also from that of the Jewish inhabitants of Palestine.

Four conditions must obtain in any solution of the Palestine Question. These points and the following analysis occurred in a speech by Professor Yusif Sayegh, Director General of Palestine Liberation Organization Planning Center, delivered at the Joint Middle East Churches and World Council of Churches Convention, Nicosia, Cyprus, September 29-October 4, 1969. The four conditions are:

1. The solution should equally satisfy and be beneficial to both Arab and Jew.

2. It should be centered on the substance of the problem not the details.

3. It should be based on justice.

4. It should be a final solution not temporary and palliative.

The solution proposed by the Arab Palestinian people fulfills these four conditions:

1. The proposed Democratic State of Palestine entails permitting the Jewish community in Palestine to live in peace and stability for the first time since the Balfour Declaration. The avowed aim of Jewish immigration into and settlement in Palestine was to provide a haven for Jews. This has been striven for against the

will of the Arab Palestinian people. A truly peaceful haven for Jewish citizens, not for their powerful army and governing institutions, cannot be attained without an entente with the Palestinian Arabs. The democratic state based on the principle of partnership is the only form acceptable to the Arabs of Palestine, if they are to turn over a new leaf and pay no further attention to the injustice and sufferings they were subjected to during the long years of dispersion and deprivation.

2. The solution in which the Palestinian Revolution has faith is a fair one as regards the Jewish community in Palestine. It entails permitting Jews to remain in Palestine although they occupied it by force without recourse to law, and without the consent of its original inhabitants. The Arab Palestinian people is willing to waive any claims of redress for the great calamity that has befallen it, shattering its unity and identity as a community and menacing its very physical existence, if the Palestine Jews are willing to free themselves from Zionism and all the expansion, colonization, bigotry and racism it contains.

3. The solution which the Palestinians support has the quality of being durable, not temporary, for it returns the problem to its origin, to the point at which the wrong started, not to the derivatives of the error. All the proposed solutions, including the one proposed by the Security Council (November 22, 1967) deal with side effects, never with the essential problem. But the establishment of a democratic state in Palestine provides all parties with a permanent solution to their major problems and creates a tolerant, stable and peaceful climate in which they can coexist, free from coercion and belligerence, striving towards cultural and scientific achievement.

4. Finally, this call for the establishment of a democratic state in Palestine is completely realistic. Israel's military superiority over the Arab States is a temporary matter, no matter how long it lasts. The Arab States have potentialities that exceed, in the long run, Israel's potentialities, a condition which will eventually give the Arab States the opportunity to inflict on Israel a smashing defeat. The acceptance on the part of the Palestine Jews, of the Democratic State of Palestine, which shall rise on the ruins of the Zionist State and its political, military, economic and intellectual institutions, is the only solution which leads not to the inevitable Zionist defeat, but to a tolerant and peaceful society.

The Palestinian Arabs today carry arms to make Jewish citizens in Israel recover from the blinding ecstasy of the military victories which the Zionist army and world imperialism have realized for them, and to make them listen to the Palestinian voice calling for a permanent, just and acceptable solution for Jews and Arabs alike.

SOLUTIONS
TO THE PALESTINIAN PROBLEM

Association for Peace

The destruction of Israel is the solution proposed by Fatah, and by all other Palestinian organizations. It calls for the conduct of a violent struggle against Israel, with the objective of destroying the independence of Israel. Only when Israel ceases to exist as an independent state — so runs Fatah's argument — can the Palestinian problem be really solved.

ADVANTAGES OF THIS SOLUTION
1. The destruction of the independence of Israel appears to many Arabs as a just and honourable solution.
2. It gives full satisfaction to the Palestinian Arabs.
3. By defining a negative objective (the destruction of Israel) this solution evades indefinitely the crucial Arab problem: What are the positive political objectives of the Palestinians? What is the political framework to which they aspire? What are the boundaries they seek? And what will be their relationship with other Arab States?

DISADVANTAGES OF THIS SOLUTION
1. Such a solution cannot possibly be acceptable to Israelis. Therefore to propose such a solution means in effect to conduct a protracted conflict against Israel.
2. Those who suffer most from a protracted conflict are the Palestinians and not the Israelis because protracted conflict postpones indefinitely the solution of the Palestinian problem, while it does not affect the independence and survival of Israel. Protracted conflict further postpones the settlement of the human problem of the Palestinian refugees, who await the solution of the conflict since 1948. Finally, protracted conflict has already caused immense suffering to Arab civilian population along the cease-fire lines of the Jordan and the Suez Canal. Since Arab fidayun made the Jordan Valley a base of their operations against Israel, more than 70,000 Arab farmers have fled from the Jordanian side of the Valley. (On the Israeli side not a single farm has been evacuated and not a single

402

field has been abandoned.) When the UAR Government decided to replace the cease-fire on the Suez front with warlike operations, it evacuated more than half a million people from Port Said, Suez and other towns.

3. Arab policy of conducting a protracted conflict has the following effects on Israel: Israel cannot negotiate with Palestinian organizations whose objective is to put an end to Israel's independence. In any case, all those organizations are violently opposed to any negotiations with Israel. Israel cannot return to the Arabs territory which will serve as a base to such organizations and will only bring them closer to the heart of Israel. A Palestinian struggle for "national liberation" which seeks the destruction of the independence of Israel becomes for Israel a struggle for national independence and for national survival.

4. The destruction of Israel as a solution serves only the extremists in both camps. It obliges Arab Governments to refuse any negotiations with Israel on the solution of the Palestinian problem. It persuades Israelis that they have no alternative but to stay at the present cease-fire lines which best assure their security, their survival and their independence as long as the protracted conflict lasts.

IS THIS SOLUTION AT ALL POSSIBLE?

1. The destruction of the independence of Israel could be a realistic objective, if it were conceivable that the Arabs could destroy Israel's military capability, her economy, and her morale. To what extent are these targets realistically possible?

2. The Six Day War has proved that the destruction of Israel by sheer Arab military force is not a realistic objective. Since the war, this objective has become even less feasible. The cease-fire lines have given Israel additional strategic dimensions for her defence which she lacked before 1967. Israel has since doubled her defence effort and her army is now stronger than it was in 1967. Small guerilla-type actions conducted by Palestinian fidayun along the cease-fire lines cannot substantially affect the military balance of power.

3. Fatah says its aim is "to destroy the political, economic and intellectual institutions of Israel" (Fatah pamphlet of August 1967). How far has this aim been achieved since June 1967?

Israel's economy is prospering. GNP rose in 1968 by 12%. Tourism to Israel which Fatah says it seeks to disrupt, rose by 48% in 1968, when 432,272 tourists visited Israel. In 1968 the El Al company, three times the target of Palestinian attacks, carried a record number of 466,668 passengers. Immigration to Israel which Fatah seeks to stop, rose by 70% in 1968 and reached a total of 31,570 persons, most of whom are professional people with academic or technical training.

4. Israelis can withstand a protracted conflict indefinitely because after waiting 1900 years to regain their independence, they will resist any attempt to deprive them of independence. Israelis realize that if they lose their independence, their survival will once again be at the mercy of others. The lessons of Czechoslovakia in 1938 and 1968, the lessons of Ethiopia in 1935, of Biafra today, and their own bitter memory, have taught Israelis never again to entrust their survival to foreign hands. They will therefore persistently fight against all those who attempt to suppress their independence. Compared with the losses their nation suffered when it was deprived of independence, their present losses are infinitesimal. Between 1939 and 1945 they lost 6 million of their kin. In their war of independence in 1948 they lost 6000 people. In 1968 in all hostile actions initiated by Arabs, both regular and irregular, Israel lost 224 dead. (In

the same year 408 Israelis were killed in traffic accidents).

Long-term predictions (Sources: SCIENCE JOURNAL, London, October 1967; Bell, TOWARDS THE YEAR 2000. Beacon Press, Boston, 1969) indicate a growing, not diminishing, technological gap between Israel and the Arabs, in favour of Israel. According to those predictions in the year 2000 Israel will belong to a group of post-industrial countries which will include the United Kingdom, the Soviet Union, East Germany and Australia. National income per capita will be between 4000 dollars and 10,000 dollars. At the same time Arab countries will belong to groups of countries with income per capita ranging from 600 to 1500 dollars (Iraq and Lebanon), 200 to 600 dollars (UAR) and 50 to 200 dollars (other Arab countries).

Protracted conflict has increased the rate of Israel's technological development, because of her urgent need to become self-sufficient in sophisticated arms. In consequence, Israel is making a rapid advance in aircraft production, electronics, armaments and other industrial fields.

TO SUM UP:

The destruction of Israel by Arab military force, regular or irregular, is not a realistic objective, neither at present, nor in the foreseeable future.

Israel's economic and technological potential is growing, not diminishing. Protracted conflict helps to quicken this process rather than retard it. The Israeli nation can withstand protracted conflict, with human losses, indefinitely, because Israelis prefer their independence to any other form of existence, and the losses they incur are infinitesimal compared with the persecution and genocide they suffered in the past.

ANOTHER SOLUTION

Most solutions proposed for the Palestinian problem result in further conflict, instead of resolving the conflict. This is so, because those solutions implicitly deny the separate national indentity either of the Israelis or of the Palestinians.

Any enduring solution of the conflict must be based on the recognition of the separate national identities of Israel and of the Palestinian Arabs. Israel is an independent nation which cannot be destroyed and which will resist all attempts to deprive it of its independence, and the Palestinian Arabs are a nation and are entitled to live as they choose, in agreement among themselves and in agreement with Arab governments and with Israel.

Therefore, the solution of the Palestinian problem should consist of the following steps.

Palestinians should evolve a political framework which is both representative and authoritative. As long as such a framework does not exist any solution of the problem will be an outside solution and therefore not durable. Palestinians should seek their national and political fulfilment within an Arab context and not by seeking the destruction of Israel, which is anyhow an impossible goal. This implies that Palestinians must be persuaded to accept and recognize the existence and independence of Israel as a necessary step towards the settlement of the Palestinian problem.

Once the Palestinians have constituted a representative authority, with realistic political objectives, they should call upon Israel to start formal negotiations on the solution of their problem. As for Israel, it has been waiting since 1948 for the emergence of an Arab authority, both capable and willing to conclude a settlement of this problem.

ADVANTAGES OF THIS SOLUTION
1. This is a solution which seeks to resolve the conflict instead of prolonging it.

2. It is a solution which should enable Israelis and Palestinians to maintain their separate identities and so prevents further conflict.

3. It is a solution based on mutual recognition of each other's different reality and on direct negotiations which follow from such recognition. This should enable Israelis and Palestinians to replace a relationship based on conflict by a relationship based on coexistence and cooperation.

4. It is a solution which may at last settle the problem of the Palestinian refugees.

DISADVANTAGES OF THIS SOLUTION
1. It is at present extremely unpopular to suggest such a solution in any Arab country.

2. The Palestinians are still fragmented. Extremist organizations may sabotage any attempt to resolve the conflict along these lines.

3. There are 14 Arab Governments, and at any time some of them may support and encourage the view of extremists — who oppose any solution based on mutual recognition and on direct negotiations.

4. With the passage of time and in face of persistent Arab animosity, Israelis may grow less and less inclined to give up the security of the present cease-fire lines and to risk any recognition of the Palestinians.

IS THIS SOLUTION AT ALL POSSIBLE?
1. It requires the fulfilment of many conditions, each of which is extremely difficult to implement.

2. When and if these difficulties are surmounted, this is the only solution which may really resolve the conflict and settle the Palestinian problem on a durable basis.

MULTILATERAL, BILATERAL
AND
UNILATERAL DOCUMENTS

CONVENTION BETWEEN GREAT BRITAIN, GERMANY, AUSTRIA-HUNGARY, SPAIN, FRANCE, ITALY, THE NETHERLANDS, RUSSIA, AND TURKEY, RESPECTING THE FREE NAVIGATION OF THE SUEZ MARITIME CANAL

Signed at Constantinople, 29 October 1888

ARTICLE I

The Suez Maritime Canal shall always be free and open, in time of war as in time of peace, to every vessel of commerce or of war, without distinction of flag.

Consequently, the High Contracting Parties agree not in any way to interfere with the free use of the Canal, in time of war as in time of peace.

The Canal shall never be subjected to the exercise of the right of blockade.

ARTICLE II

The High Contracting Parties, recognising that the Fresh-Water Canal is indispensable to the Maritime Canal, take note of the engagements of His Highness the Khedive towards the Universal Suez Canal Company as regards the Fresh-Water Canal; which engagements are stipulated in a Convention bearing the date of 18th March, 1863, containing an exposé and four Articles.

They undertake not to interfere in any way with the security of that Canal and its branches, the working of which shall not be exposed to any attempt at obstruction.

ARTICLE III

The High Contracting Parties likewise undertake to respect the plant, establishments, buildings, and works of the Maritime Canal and of the Fresh-Water Canal.

ARTICLE IV

The Maritime Canal remaining open in time of war as a free passage, even to the ships of war of belligerents, according to the terms of Article I of the present Treaty, the High Contracting Parties agree that no right of war, no act of hostility, nor any act having for its object to obstruct the free navigation of the Canal shall be committed in the Canal and its ports of access, as well as within a radius of three marine miles from those parts, even though the Ottoman Empire should be one of the belligerent Powers.

Vessels of war of belligerents shall not revictual or take in stores in the Canal and its ports of access, except in so far as may be strictly necessary. The transit of the aforesaid vessels through the Canal shall be effected with the least possible delay, in accordance with the Regulations in force, and without any other intermission than that resulting from the necessities of the service.

Their stay at Port Said and in the roadstead of Suez shall not exceed twenty-four hours, except in cases of distress. In such case they shall be bound to leave as soon as possible. An interval of twenty-four hours shall always elapse between the sailing of a belligerent ship from one of the ports of access and the departure of a ship belonging to the hostile Power.

ARTICLE V

In time of war belligerent Powers shall not disembark nor embark within the Canal and its ports of access either troops, munitions, or materials of war. But in case of an accidental hindrance in the Canal, men may be embarked or disembarked at the ports of access by detachments not exceeding 1,000 men, with a corresponding amount of war material.

ARTICLE VI

Prizes shall be subjected, in all respects, to the same rules as the vessels of war of belligerents.

ARTICLE VII

The Powers shall not keep any vessel of war in the waters of the Canal (including Lake Timsah and the Bitter Lakes).

Nevertheless, they may station vessels of war in the ports of access of Port Said and Suez, the number of which shall not exceed two for each Power.

This right shall not be exercised by belligerents.

ARTICLE VIII

The Agents in Egypt of the Signatory Powers of the present Treaty shall be charged to watch over its execution. In case of any event threatening the security of the free passage of the Canal, they shall meet on the summons of three of their number under the presidency of their Doyen, in order to proceed to the necessary verifications. They shall inform the Khedivial Government of the danger which they may have perceived, in order that that Government may take proper steps to insure the protection and the free use of the Canal. Under any circumstances, they shall meet once a year to take note of the due execution of the Treaty.

The last-mentioned meetings shall take place under the presidency of a Special Commissioner nominated for that purpose by the Imperial Ottoman Government. A Commissioner of the Khedive may also take part in the meeting, and may preside over it in case of the absence of the Ottoman Commissioner.

They shall especially demand the suppression of any work or the dispersion of any assemblage on either bank of the Canal, the object or effect of which might be to interfere with the liberty and the entire security of the navigation.

ARTICLE IX

The Egyptian Government shall, within the limits of its powers resulting from the Firmans, and under the conditions provided for in the present Treaty, take the necessary measures for insuring the execution of the said Treaty.

In case the Egyptian Government shall not have sufficient means at its disposal, it shall call upon the Imperial Ottoman Government, which shall take the necessary measures to respond to such appeal; shall give notice thereof to the Signatory Powers of the Declaration of London of the 17th March, 1885; and shall, if necessary, concert with them on the subject.

The provisions of Articles IV, V, VII, and VIII shall not interfere with the measures which shall be taken in virtue of the present Article.

ARTICLE X

Similarly, the provisons of Articles IV, V, VII, and VIII shall not interfere with the measures which His Majesty the Sultan and His Highness the Khedive, in the name of His Imperial Majesty, and within the limits of the Firmans granted, might find it necessary to take for securing by their own forces the defence of Egypt and the maintenance of public order.

In case His Imperial Majesty the Sultan, or His Highness the Khedive, should find it necessary to avail themselves of the exception for which this Article provides, the Signatory Powers of the Declaration of London shall be notified thereof by the Imperial Ottoman Government.

It is likewise understood that the provisions of the four Articles aforesaid shall in no case occasion any obstacle to the measures which the Imperial Ottoman Government may think it necessary to take in order to insure by its own forces the defence of its other possessions situated on the eastern coast of the Red Sea.

ARTICLE XI

The measures which shall be taken in the cases provided for by Articles IX and X of the present Treaty shall not interfere with the free use of the Canal. In the same cases, the erection of permanent fortifications contrary to the provisions of Article VIII is prohibited.

ARTICLE XII

The High Contracting Parties, by application of the principle of equality as regards the free use of the Canal, a principle which forms one of the bases of the present Treaty, agree that none of them shall endeavour to obtain with respect to the Canal territorial or commercial advantages or privileges in any international arrangements which may be concluded. Moreover, the rights of Turkey as the territorial Power are reserved.

ARTICLE XIII

With the exception of the obligations expressly provided by the clauses of the present Treaty, the sovereign rights of His Imperial Majesty the Sultan and the rights and immunities of His Highness the Khedive, resulting from the Firmans, are in no way affected.

ARTICLE XIV

The High Contracting Parties agree that the engagements resulting from the present Treaty shall not be limited by the duration of the Acts of Concession of the Universal Suez Canal Company.

ARTICLE XV

The stipulations of the present Treaty shall not interfere with the sanitary measures in force in Egypt.

ARTICLE XVI

The High Contracting Parties undertake to bring the present Treaty to the knowledge of the States which have not signed it, inviting them to accede to it.

ARTICLE XVII

The present Treaty shall be ratified, and the ratifications shall be exchanged at Constantinople within the space of one month, or sooner if possible.

In faith of which the respective Plenipotentiaries have signed the present Treaty, and have affixed to it the seal of their arms.

Done at Constantinople the
29th day of the month of
October of the year 1888.

LEAGUE OF NATIONS MANDATE FOR PALESTINE

The Council of the League of Nations:

Whereas the Principal Allied Powers have agreed, for the purpose of giving effect to the provisions of Article 22 of the Covenant of the League of Nations, to entrust to a Mandatory selected by the said Powers the administration of the territory of Palestine, which formerly belonged to the Turkish Empire, within such boundaries as may be fixed by them; and

Whereas the Principal Allied Powers have also agreed that the Mandatory should be responsible for putting into effect the declaration originally made on November 2nd, 1917, by the Government of His Britannic Majesty, and adopted by the said Powers, in favour of the establishment in Palestine of a national home for the Jewish people, it being clearly understood that nothing should be done which might prejudice the civil and religious rights of existing non-Jewish communities in Palestine, or the rights and political status enjoyed by Jews in any other country; and

Whereas recognition has thereby been given to the historical connection of the Jewish people with Palestine and to the grounds for reconstituting their national home in that country; and

Whereas the Principal Allied Powers have selected His Britannic Majesty as the Mandatory for Palestine; and

Whereas the mandate in respect of Palestine has been formulated in the following terms and submitted to the Council of the League for approval; and

Whereas His Britannic Majesty has accepted the mandate in respect of Palestine and undertaken to exercise it on behalf of the League of Nations in conformity with the following provisions; and

Whereas by the afore-mentioned Article 22 (paragraph 8), it is provided that the degree of authority, control or administration to be exercised by the Mandatory, not having been previously agreed upon by the Members of the League, shall be explicitly defined by the Council of the League of Nations;

Confirming the said mandate, defines its terms as follows:

413

ARTICLE 1.

The Mandatory shall have full powers of legislation and of administration, save as they may be limited by the terms of this mandate.

ARTICLE 2.

The Mandatory shall be responsible for placing the country under such political, administrative and economic conditions as will secure the establishment of the Jewish national home, as laid down in the preamble, and the development of self-governing institutions, and also for safeguarding the civil and religious rights of all the inhabitants of Palestine, irrespective of race and religion.

ARTICLE 3.

The Mandatory shall, so far as circumstances permit, encourage local autonomy.

ARTICLE 4.

An appropriate Jewish agency shall be recognized as a public body for the purpose of advising and co-operating with the Administration of Palestine in such economic, social and other matters as may affect the establishment of the Jewish National home and the interests of the Jewish population in Palestine, and, subject always to the control of the Administration, to assist and take part in the development of the country.

The Zionist organisation, so long as its organisation and constitution are in the opinion of the Mandatory appropriate, shall be recognised as such agency. It shall take steps in consultation with His Britannic Majesty's Government to secure the co-operation of all Jews who are willing to assist in the establishment of the Jewish national home.

ARTICLE 5.

The Mandatory shall be responsible for seeing that no Palestine territory shall be ceded or leased to, or in any way placed under the control of, the Government of any foreign Power.

ARTICLE 6.

The Administration of Palestine, while ensuring that the rights and position of other sections of the population are not prejudiced, shall facilitate Jewish immigration under suitable conditions and shall encourage, in co-operation with the Jewish agency referred to in Article 4, close settlement by Jews on the land, including State lands and waste lands not required for public purposes.

ARTICLE 7.

The Administration of Palestine shall be responsible for enacting a nationality law. There shall be included in this law provisions framed so as to facilitate the acquisition of Palestinian citizenship by Jews who take up their permanent residence in Palestine.

ARTICLE 8.

The privileges and immunities of foreigners, including the benefits of consular jurisdiction and protection as formerly enjoyed by Capitulation or usage in the Ottoman Empire, shall not be applicable in Palestine.

Unless the Powers whose nationals enjoyed the afore-mentioned privileges and immunities on August 1st, 1914, shall have previously renounced the right to their re-establishment, or shall have agreed to their non-application for a specified period, these privileges and immunities shall, at the expiration of the mandate, be immediately re-established in their entirety or with such modifications as may have been agreed upon between the Powers concerned.

ARTICLE 9.

The Mandatory shall be responsible for seeing that the judicial system established in Palestine shall assure to foreigners, as well as to natives, a complete guarantee of their rights.

Respect for the personal status of the various peoples and communities and for their religious interests shall be fully guaranteed. In particular, the control and administration of Wakfs shall be exercised in accordance with religious law and the dispositions of the founders.

ARTICLE 10.

Pending the making of special extradition agreements relating to Palestine, the extradition treaties in force between the Mandatory and other foreign Powers shall apply to Palestine.

ARTICLE 11.

The Administration of Palestine shall take all necessary measures to safeguard the interests of the community in connection with the development of the country, and, subject to any international obligations accepted by the Mandatory, shall have full power to provide for public ownership or control of any of the natural resources of the country or of the public works, services and utilities established or to be established therein. It shall introduce a land system appropriate to the needs of the country, having regard, among other things, to the desirability of promoting the close settlement and intensive cultivation of the land.

The Administration may arrange with the Jewish agency mentioned in Article 4 to construct or operate, upon fair and equitable terms, any public works, services and utilities, and to develop any of the natural resources of the country, in so far as these matters are not directly undertaken by the Administration. Any such arrangements shall provide that no profits distributed by such agency, directly or indirectly, shall exceed a reasonable rate of interest on the capital, and any further profits shall be utilised by it for the benefit of the country in a manner approved by the Administration.

ARTICLE 12.

The Mandatory shall be entrusted with the control of the foreign relations of Palestine and the right to issue exequaturs to consuls appointed by foreign Powers. He shall also be entitled to afford diplomatic and consular protection to citizens of Palestine when outside its territorial limits.

ARTICLE 13.

All responsibility in connection with the Holy Places and religious buildings or sites in Palestine, including that of preserving existing rights and of securing free access to the Holy Places, religious buildings and sites and the free exercise of worship, while ensuring the requirements of public order and decorum, is assumed by the Mandatory, who shall be responsible solely to the League of Nations in all matters connected herewith, provided that nothing in this article shall prevent the Mandatory from entering into such arrangements as he may deem reasonable with the Administration for the purpose of carrying the provisions of this article into effect; and provided also that nothing in this mandate shall be construed as conferring upon the Mandatory authority to interfere with the fabric or the management of purely Moslem sacred shrines, the immunities of which are guaranteed.

ARTICLE 14.

A special Commission shall be appointed by the Mandatory to study, define and determine the rights and claims in connection with the Holy Places and the rights and claims relating to the different religious communities in Palestine. The method of nomination, the composition and the functions of this Commission shall be submitted to the Council of the League for its approval, and the Commission shall not be appointed or enter upon its functions without the approval of the Council.

ARTICLE 15.

The Mandatory shall see that complete freedom of conscience and the free exercise of all forms of worship, subject only to the maintenance of public order and morals, are ensured to all. No discrimination of any kind shall be made between the inhabitants of Palestine on the ground of race, religion or language. No person shall be excluded from Palestine on the sole ground of his religious belief.

The right of each community to maintain its own schools for the education of its own members in its own language, while conforming to such educational requirements of a general nature as the Administration may impose, shall not be denied or impaired.

ARTICLE 16.

The Mandatory shall be responsible for exercising such supervision over religious or eleemosynary bodies of all faiths in Palestine as may be required for the maintenance of public order and good government. Subject to such supervision, no measures shall be taken in Palestine to obstruct or interfere with the enterprise of such bodies or to discriminate against any representative or member of them on the ground of his religion or nationality.

ARTICLE 17.

The Administration of Palestine may organise on a voluntary basis the forces necessary for the preservation of peace and order, and also for the defence of the country, subject, however, to the supervision of the Mandatory, but shall not use them for purposes other than those above specified save with the consent of the Mandatory. Except for such purposes, no military, naval or air forces shall be raised or maintained by the Administration of Palestine.

Nothing in this article shall preclude the Administration of Palestine from contributing to the cost of the maintenance of the forces of the Mandatory in Palestine.

The Mandatory shall be entitled at all times to use the roads, railways and ports of Palestine for the movement of armed forces and the carriage of fuel and supplies.

ARTICLE 18.

The Mandatory shall see that there is no discrimination in Palestine against the nationals of any State Member of the League of Nations (including companies incorporated under its laws) as compared with those of the Mandatory or of any foreign State in matters concerning taxation, commerce or navigation, the exercise of industries or professions, or in the treatment of merchant vessels or civil aircraft. Similarly, there shall be no discrimination in Palestine against goods originating in or destined for any of the said States, and there shall be freedom of transit under equitable conditions across the mandated area.

Subject as aforesaid and to the other provisions of this mandate, the Administration of Palestine may, on the advice of the Mandatory, impose such taxes and customs duties as it may consider necessary, and take such steps as it may think best to promote the development of the natural resources of the country and to safeguard the interests of the population. It may also, on the advice of the Mandatory, conclude a special customs agreement with any State the territory of which in 1914 was wholly included in Asiatic Turkey or Arabia.

ARTICLE 19.

The Mandatory shall adhere on behalf of the Administration of Palestine to any general international conventions already existing, or which may be concluded hereafter with the approval of the League of Nations, respecting the slave traffic, the traffic in arms and ammunition, or the traffic in drugs, or relating to commercial equality, freedom of transit and navigation, aerial navigation and postal, telegraphic and wireless communication or literary, artistic or industrial property.

ARTICLE 20.

The Mandatory shall co-operate on behalf of the Administration of Palestine, so far as religious, social and other conditions may permit, in the execution of any common policy adopted by the League of Nations for preventing and combating disease, including diseases of plants and animals.

ARTICLE 21.

The Mandatory shall secure the enactment within twelve months from this date, and shall ensure the execution of a Law of Antiquities based on the following rules. This law shall ensure equality of treatment in the matter of excavations and archaeological research to the nations of all States Members of the League of Nations.

(1)

"Antiquity" means any construction or any product of human activity earlier than the year A.D. 1700.

(2)

The law for the protection of antiquities shall proceed by encouragement rather than by threat.

Any person who, having discovered an antiquity without being furnished with the authorisation referred to in paragraph 5, reports the same to an official of the competent Department, shall be rewarded according to the value of the discovery.

(3)

No antiquity may be disposed of except to the competent Department, unless this Department renounces the acquisition of any such antiquity.

No antiquity may leave the country without an export licence from the said Department.

(4)

Any person who maliciously or negligently destroys or damages an antiquity shall be liable to a penalty to be fixed.

(5)

No clearing of ground or digging with the object of finding antiquities shall be permitted, under penalty of fine, except to persons authorised by the competent Department.

(6)

Equitable terms shall be fixed for expropriation, temporary or permanent, of lands which might be of historical or archaeological interest.

(7)

Authorisation to excavate shall only be granted to persons who show sufficient guarantees of archaeological experience. The Administration of Palestine shall not, in granting these authorisations, act in such a way as to exclude scholars of any nation without good grounds.

(8)

The proceeds of excavations may be divided between the excavator and the competent Department in a proportion fixed by that Department. If division seems impossible for scientific reasons, the excavator shall receive a fair indemnity in lieu of a part of the find.

ARTICLE 22.

English, Arabic and Hebrew shall be the official languages of Palestine. Any statement or inscription in Arabic on stamps or money in Palestine shall be repeated in Hebrew, and any statement or inscription in Hebrew shall be repeated in Arabic.

ARTICLE 23.

The Administration of Palestine shall recognise the holy days of the respective communities in Palestine as legal days of rest for the members of such communities.

ARTICLE 24.

The Mandatory shall make to the Council of the League of Nations an annual report to the satisfaction of the Council as to the measures taken during the year to carry out the provisions of the mandate. Copies of all laws and regulations promulgated or issued during the year shall be communicated with the report.

ARTICLE 25.

In the territories lying between the Jordan and the eastern boundary of Palestine as ultimately determined, the Mandatory shall be entitled, with the consent of the Council of the League of Nations, to postpone or withhold application of such provisions of this mandate as he may consider inapplicable to the existing local conditions, and to make such provision for the administration of the territories as he may consider suitable to those conditions, provided that no action shall be taken which is inconsistent with the provisions of Articles 15, 16 and 18.

ARTICLE 26.

The Mandatory agrees that, if any dispute whatever should arise between the Mandatory and another Member of the League of Nations relating to the interpretation or the application of the provisions of the mandate, such dispute, if it cannot be settled by negotiation, shall be submitted to the Permanent Court of International Justice provided for by Article 14 of the Covenant of the League of Nations.

ARTICLE 27.

The consent of the Council of the League of Nations is required for any modification of the terms of this mandate.

ARTICLE 28.

In the event of the termination of the mandate hereby conferred upon the Mandatory, the Council of the League of Nations shall make such arrangements as may be deemed necessary for safeguarding in perpetuity, under guarantee of the League, the rights secured by Articles 13 and 14, and shall use its influence for securing, under the guarantee of the League, that the Government of Palestine will fully honour the financial obligations legitimately incurred by the Administration of Palestine during the period of the mandate, including the rights of public servants to pensions or gratuities.

The present instrument shall be deposited in original in the archives of the League of Nations and certified copies shall be forwarded by the Secretary-General of the League of Nations to all Members of the League.

Done at London the twenty-fourth day of July, one thousand nine hundred and twenty-two.

Certified true copy:

For the Secretary-General,
RAPPARD,
Director of the Mandates Section.

Multilateral Document No. 3

UNITED NATIONS RESOLUTION
181 (II) of 29 NOVEMBER 1947 —
PARTITION OF PALESTINE

The General Assembly,

Having met in special session at the request of the mandatory Power to constitute and instruct a Special Committee to prepare for the consideration of the question of the future Government of Palestine at the second regular session;

Having constituted a Special Committee and instructed it to investigate all questions and issues relevant to the problem of Palestine, and to prepare proposals for the solution of the problem, and

Having received and examined the report of the Special Committee (document A/364) including a number of unanimous recommendations and a plan of partition with economic union approved by the majority of the Special Committee,

Considers that the present situation in Palestine is one which is likely to impair the general welfare and friendly relations among nations;

Takes note of the declaration by the mandatory Power that it plans to complete its evacuation of Palestine by 1 August 1948;

Recommends to the United Kingdom, as the mandatory Power for Palestine, and to all other Members of the United Nations the adoption and implementation, with regard to the future Government of Palestine, of the Plan of Partition with Economic Union set out below;

Requests that:
a) The Security Council take the necessary measures as provided for in the plan for its implementation;
b) The Security Council consider, if circumstances during the transitional

period require such consideration, whether the situation in Palestine constitutes a threat to the peace. If it decides that such a threat exists, and in order to maintain international peace and security, the Security Council should supplement the authorization of the General Assembly by taking measures, under Articles 39 and 41 of the Charter, to empower the United Nations Commission, as provided in this resolution, to exercise in Palestine the functions which are assigned to it by this resolution;

c) The Security Council determine as a threat to the peace, breach of the peace or act of aggression, in accordance with Article 39 of the Charter, any attempt to alter by force the settlement envisaged by this resolution;

d) The Trusteeship Council be informed of the responsibilities envisaged for it in this plan;

Calls upon the inhabitants of Palestine to take such steps as may be necessary on their part to put this plan into effect;

Appeals to all Governments and all peoples to refrain from taking any action which might hamper or delay the carrying out of these recommendations, and

Authorizes the Secretary-General to reimburse travel and subsistence expenses of the members of the Commission referred to in Part I, Section B, Paragraph 1 below, on such basis and in such form as he may determine most appropriate in the circumstances, and to provide the Commission with the necessary staff to assist in carrying out the functions assigned to the Commission by the General Assembly.

Multilateral Document No. 4

RESOLUTION ADOPTED BY THE GENERAL ASSEMBLY,
11 DECEMBER 1948.
(A/RES/194-111)

The General Assembly,
Having considered further the situation in Palestine,

1. Expresses its deep appreciation of the progress achieved through the good offices of the late United Nations Mediator in promoting a peaceful adjustment of the future situation of Palestine, for which cause he sacrificed his life; and

Extends its thanks to the Acting Mediator and his staff for their continued efforts and devotion to duty in Palestine;

2. Establishes a Conciliation Commission consisting of three States Members of the United Nations which shall have the following functions:

a) To assume, in so far as it considers necessary in existing circumstances, the functions given to the United Nations Mediator on Palestine by resolution 186 (S-2) of the General Assembly of 14 May 1948;

b) To carry out the specific functions and directives given to it by the present resolution and such additional functions and directives as may be given to it by the General Assembly or by the Security Council;

c) To undertake, upon the request of the Security Council, any of the functions now assigned to the United Nations Mediator on Palestine or to the United Nations Truce Commission by resolutions of the Security Council; upon such request to the Conciliation Commission by the Security Council with respect to all the remaining functions of the United Nations Mediator on Palestine under Security Council resolutions, the office of the Mediator shall be terminated;

3. Decides that a Committee of the Assembly, consisting of China, France, the Union of Soviet Socialist Republics, the United Kingdom and the United States of America, shall present, before the end of the first part of the present session of the General Assembly, for the approval of the Assembly, a proposal concerning the names of the three States which will constitute the Conciliation

Commission;

4. Requests the Commission to begin its functions at once, with a view to the establishment of contact between the parties themselves and the Commission at the earliest possible date;

5. Calls upon the Government and authorities concerned to extend the scope of the negotiations provided for in the Security Council's resolution of 16 November 1948 and to seek agreement by negotiations conducted either with the Conciliation Commission or directly, with a view to the final settlement of all questions outstanding between them;

6. Instructs the Conciliation Commission to take steps to assist the Governments and authorities concerned to achieve a final settlement of all questions outstanding between them;

7. Resolves that the Holy Places — including Nazareth — religious buildings and sites in Palestine should be protected and free access to them assured, in accordance with existing rights and historical practice; that arrangements to this end should be under effective United Nations supervision; that the United Nations Conciliation Commission, in presenting to the fourth regular session of the General Assembly its detailed proposals for a permanent international regime for the territory of Jerusalem, should include recommendations concerning the Holy Places in that territory; that with regard to the Holy Places in the rest of Palestine the Commission should call upon the political authorities of the areas concerned to give appropriate formal guarantees as to the protection of the Holy Places and access to them; and that these undertakings should be presented to the General Assembly for approval;

8. Resolves that, in view of its association with three world religions, the Jerusalem area, including the present municipality of Jerusalem *plus* the surrounding villages and towns, the most eastern of which shall be Abu Dis; the most southern, Bethlehem; the most western, Ein Karim (including also the built-up area of Motsa); and the most northern, Shu'fat, should be accorded special and separate treatment from the rest of Palestine and should be placed under effective United Nations control;

Requests the Security Council to take further steps to ensure the demilitarization of Jerusalem at the earliest possible date;

Instructs the Conciliation Commission to present to the fourth regular session of the General Assembly detailed proposals for a permanent international regime for the Jerusalem area which will provide for the maximum local autonomy for distinctive groups consistent with the special international status of the Jerusalem area;

The Conciliation Commission is authorized to appoint a United Nations representative, who shall cooperate with the local authorities with respect to the interim administration of the Jerusalem area;

9. Resolves that, pending agreement on more detailed arrangements among the Governments and authorities concerned, the freest possible access to Jerusalem by road, rail or air should be accorded to all inhabitants of Palestine;

Instructs the Conciliation Commission to report immediately to the Security Council, for appropriate action that organ, any attempt by any party to impede such access;

10. Instructs the Conciliation Commission to seek arrangements among the Governments and authorities concerned which will facilitate the economic development of the area, including arrangements for access to ports and airfields and the use of transportation and communication facilities;

11. Resolves that the refugees wishing to return to their homes and live in peace with their neighbours should be permitted to do so at the earliest practicable date, and that compensation should be paid for the property of those choosing not to return and for loss of or damage to property which, under principles of international law or in equity, should be made good by the Governments or authorities responsible;

Instructs the Conciliation Commission to facilitate the repatriation, resettlement and economic and social rehabilitation of the refugees and the payment of compensation, and to maintain close relations with the Director of the United Nations Relief for Palestine Refugees and, through him, with the appropriate organs and agencies of the United Nations;

12. Authorizes the Conciliation Commission to appoint such subsidiary bodies and to employ such technical experts, acting under its authority, as it may find necessary for the effective discharge of its functions and responsibilities under the present resolution;

The Conciliation Commission will have its official headquarters at Jerusalem. The authorities responsible for maintaining order in Jerusalem will be responsible for taking all measures necessary to ensure the security of the Commission. The Secretary-General will provide a limited number of guards for the protection of the staff and premises of the Commission;

13. Instructs the Conciliation Commission to render progress reports periodically to the Secretary-General for transmission to the Security Council and to the Members of the United Nations;

14. Calls upon all Governments and authorities concerned to co-operate with the Conciliation Commission and to take all possible steps to assist in the implementation of the present resolution;

15. Requests the Secretary-General to provide the necessary staff and facilities and to make appropriate arrangements to provide the necessary funds required in carrying out the terms of the present resolution.

RESOLUTION ADOPTED BY THE UN SECURITY COUNCIL, 1 SEPTEMBER 1951 (S/2322)

The Security Council,

1. Recalling that in its resolution of 11 August 1949 relating to the conclusion of Armistice Agreements between Israel and the neighboring Arab States it drew attention to the pledges in these Agreements against further acts of hostility between the parties;

2. Recalling further that in its resolution of 17 November 1950 it reminded the States concerned that the Armistice Agreements to which they are parties contemplate the return to permanent peace in Palestine, and therefore urged them and other States in the area to take all such steps as will lead to the settlement of the issues between them;

3. Noting the report of the Chief of Staff of the Truce Supervision Organization to the Security Council of 12 June 1951;

4. Further noting that the Chief of Staff of the Truce Supervision Organization recalled the statement of the senior Egyptian delegate in Rhodes on 13 January 1949, to the effect that his delegation was inspired with every spirit of cooperation, conciliation, and a sincere desire to restore peace in Palestine, and that the Egyptian Government have not complied with the earnest plea of the Chief of Staff made to the Egyptian delegate on 12 June 1951, that they desist from the present practice of intering with the passage through the Suez Canal of goods destined for Israel;

5. Considering that since the Armistice regime which has been in existence for nearly two and a half years is of a permanent character, neither party can reasonably assert that it is actively a belligerent or requires to exercise the right of visit, search, and seizure for any legitimate purpose of self-defense;

425

6. Finds that the maintenance of the practice mentioned in paragraph 4 above is inconsistent with the objectives of a peaceful settlement between the parties and the establishment of a permanent peace in Palestine set forth in the Armistice Agreement.

7. Further finds that such practice is an abuse of the exercise of the right of visit, search and seizure;

8. Further finds that practice cannot in the prevailing circumstances be justified on the grounds that it is necessary for self-defense;

9. And further noting that the restrictions on the passage of goods through the Suez Canal to Israeli ports are denying to nations at no time connected with the conflict in Palestine valuable supplies required for their economic reconstruction, and that these restrictions together with sanctions applied to Egypt to certain ships which have visited Israeli ports represent unjustified interference with the rights of nations to navigate the seas and to trade freely with one another, including the Arab States and Israel;

10. Calls upon Egypt to terminate the restrictions on the passage of international commercial shipping and goods through the Suez Canal wherever bound and to cease all interference with such shipping beyond that essential to the safety of shipping in the Canal itself and to the observance of the international conventions in force.

ARAB SUMMIT CONFERENCE IN KHARTOUM
29 AUGUST TO 1 SEPTEMBER 1967

A. JOINT COMMUNIQUE ISSUED AT CLOSE OF CONFERENCE
The summit conference held its closing session at 1815 hours in the Legislative Assembly building in Khartoum. At the beginning of the session, the Chairman of the Sudan Sovereign Council, Azhari, read out the following joint communiqué:

In accordance with the invitation of the Government of Sudan for a conference of Arab Heads of State to assemble in Khartoum from 29 August to 1 September 1967 to discuss the present Arab situation and to outline a joint Arab programme to eliminate the consequences of the aggression, a summit meeting was held in Khartoum, attended by the Heads of State or of Government of the Arab League members and the head of the Palestine Liberation Organization.

The representatives at the conference sessions shared in the common awareness of the magnitude of the historic responsibility facing the Arab peoples at the present decisive and delicate stage of their struggle. They stressed their firm determination to stand together as one man in face of the challenges which would determine their destiny, responsibility to meet which was incumbent on the Arab peoples. The Heads of State discussed the consequences of the aggression that the Arab States were faced with on 5 June 1967. They decided that elimination from Arab soil of the consequences of the aggression is a joint responsibility incumbent on all the Arab States, calling for mobilization of all Arab resources, in complete confidence that these resources constitute a sufficient guarantee that the effects of the aggression will be eliminated and that the setback suffered by the Arab peoples must serve as a powerful motive for closing the ranks and strengthening joint Arab action.

On the basis of this evaluation, the Heads of State agreed on effective steps to be taken to ensure elimination of the consequences of the aggression, amongst other things, strengthening those States whose economic resources had been directly affected as a result of the aggression, in order to enable those States to stand firm against economic pressures.

The Heads of State voiced their firm belief in and their absolute determination regarding continued Arab action for the preservation of the sacred right of the Palestinian people in its homeland. The Arab leaders call on the peoples and Governments of the world to support this just right by taking up an active attitude towards the forces of Zionist imperialism that are the obstacle to the Palestinian people's exercise of their rights.

The Heads of State reviewed the relations between the Arab States in all their aspects and agreed to take the necessary steps to strengthen their ties with each other in accordance with the Charter of Arab Solidarity. Thus they will realise the Arab nation's aspirations for progress and prosperity.

They also expressed their appreciation of the initiative taken by the Government of the Sudan, which called for the holding of this historic meeting. They also expressed their heartfelt gratitude for the enthusiastic welcome which they received from the Sudanese people.

B. RESOLUTIONS ADOPTED BY THE ARAB HEADS OF STATE

1. The conference has affirmed the unity of Arab ranks, the unity of joint action and the need for co-ordination and for the elimination of all differences. The Kings, Presidents and representatives of the other Arab Heads of State at the conference have affirmed their countries' stand by and implementation of the Charter of Arab Solidarity which was signed at the third Arab summit conference in Casablanca.

2. The conference has agreed on the need to consolidate all efforts to eliminate the effects of the aggression on the basis that the occupied lands are Arab lands and that the burden of regaining these lands falls on all the Arab States.

3. The Arab Heads of State have agreed to unite their political efforts on the international and diplomatic level to eliminate the effects of the aggression and to ensure the withdrawal of the aggressive Israeli forces from the Arab lands which have been occupied since the aggression of 5 June. This will be done within the framework of the main principles by which the Arab States abide, namely, no peace with Israel, no recognition of Israel, no negotiations with it, and insistence on the rights of the Palestinian people in their own country.

4. The conference of Arab Ministers of Finance, Economy and Oil recommended that suspension of oil pumping be used as a weapon in the battle. However, after thoroughly studying the matter, the summit conference has come to the conclusion that the pumping of oil can itself be used as a positive weapon, since oil is an Arab resource that can be used in the service of Arab ends. It can contribute to the efforts to enable those Arab States which were exposed to the aggression and thereby lost economic resources to stand firm in the face of any economic pressure.

5. The participants in the conference have approved the plan proposed by

Kuwait to set up an Arab Economic and Social Development Fund on the basis of the recommendation of the Baghdad conference of Arab Ministers of Finance, Economy and Oil.

6. The participants have agreed on the need to adopt the necessary measures to strengthen military preparation to face all eventualities.

7. The conference has decided to expedite the elimination of foreign bases in the Arab States.

C. RESOLUTION ON ANNUAL PAYMENTS
   BY SAUDI ARABIA, KUWAIT AND LIBYA
   Resolution adopted by the Arab Heads of State who participated in the Khartoum conference from 29 August to 1 September 1967:

The Kingdom of Saudi Arabia, the State of Kuwait and the Kingdom of Libya have each agreed to pay the following annual amounts, which are to be paid in advance every three months, beginning from October, until the effects of the aggression are eliminated: Saudi Arabia, £50,000,000, Kuwait, £55,000,000, Libya, £30,000,000. In this way, the Arab nation ensures that it will be able to carry on this battle, without any weakening, until the effects of aggression are eliminated.

Multilateral Document No. 7

UNITED NATIONS SECURITY COUNCIL
RESOLUTION OF 22 NOVEMBER 1967

The Security Council,

Expressing its continuing concern with the grave situation in the Middle East,

Emphasizing the inadmissibility of the acquisition of territory by war and the need to work for a just and lasting peace in which every State in the area can live in security,

Emphasizing further that all Member States in their acceptance of the Charter of the United Nations have undertaken a commitment to act in accordance with Article 2 of the Charter,

1. Affirms that the fulfillment of the establishment of a just and lasting peace in the Middle East which should include the application of both the following principles:

   (i) withdrawal of Israeli armed forces from territories occupied in the recent conflict;

   (ii) termination of all claims or states of belligerency and respect for and acknowledgement of the sovereignty, territorial integrity and political independence of every State in the area and their right to live in peace within secure and recognized boundaries free from threats or acts of force;

2. Affirms further the necessity

   (a) for guaranteeing freedom of navigation through international waterways in the area;

   (b) for achieving a just settlement of the refugee problem;

(c) for guaranteeing the territorial inviolability and political independence of every State in the area, through measures including the establishment of demilitarized zones;

3. Requests the Secretary General to designate a Special Representative to proceed to the Middle East to establish and maintain contacts with the States concerned in order to promote agreement and assist efforts to achieve a peaceful and accepted settlement in accordance with the provisions and principles in this resolution;

4. Requests the Secretary General to report to the Security Council on the progress of the efforts of the Special Representative as soon as possible.

THE HUSAYN-McMAHON CORRESPONDENCE
14 JULY 1915 — 10 MARCH 1916

1. FROM SHARIF HUSAYN, 14 JULY 1915

Whereas the whole of the Arab nation without any exception have decided in these last years to live, and to accomplish their freedom, and grasp the reins of their administration both in theory and practice; and whereas they have found and felt that it is to the interest of the Government of Great Britain to support them and aid them to the attainment of their firm and lawful intentions (which are based upon the maintenance of the honour and dignity of their life) without any ulterior motives whatsoever unconnected with this object;

And whereas it is to their (the Arabs') interest also to prefer the assistance of the Government of Great Britain in consideration of their geographical position and economic interests, and also of the attitude of the above-mentioned Government, which is known to both nations and therefore need not be emphasized;

For these reasons the Arab nation see fit to limit themselves, as time is short, to asking the Government of Great Britain, if it should think fit, for the approval, through her deputy or representative, of the following fundamental propositions, leaving out all things considered secondary in comparison with these, so that it may prepare all means necessary for attaining this noble purpose, until such time as it finds occasion for making the actual ne-gotiations:—

Firstly — England to acknowledge the independence of the Arab countries, bounded on the north by Mersina and Adana up to the 37° of latitude, on which degree fall Birijik, Urfa, Mardin, Midiat, Jezirat (Ibn Umar), Amadia, up to the border of Persia; on the east by the borders of Persia up to the Gulf of Basra; on the south by the Indian Ocean, with the exception of the position of Aden to remain as it is; on the west by the Red Sea, the Mediterranean Sea up to Mersina, England to approve of the proclamation of an Arab Khalifate of Islam.

Secondly— The Arab Government of the Sherif to acknowledge that England shall have the preference in all economic enterprises in the Arab countries whenever conditions of enterprises are otherwise equal.

Thirdly — For the security of this Arab independence and the certainty of such preference of economic enterprises, both high contracting parties to offer mutual assistance, to the best ability of their military and naval forces, to face any foreign Power which may attack either party. Peace not to be decided without agreement of both parties.

Fourthly — If one of the parties enters upon an aggressive conflict, the other party to assume a neutral attitude, and in case of such party wishing the other to join forces, both to meet and discuss the conditions.

Fifthly — England to acknowledge the abolition of foreign privileges in the Arab countries, and to assist the Government of the Sherif in an International Convention for confirming such abolition.

Sixthly — Articles 3 and 4 of this treaty to remain in vigour for fifteen years, and, if either wishes it to be renewed, one year's notice before lapse of treaty to be given.

Consequently, and as the whole of the Arab nation have (praise be to God) agreed and united for the attainment, at all costs and finally, of this noble object, they beg the Government of Great Britain to answer them positively or negatively in a period of thirty days after receiving this intimation; and if this period should lapse before they receive an answer, they reserve to themselves complete freedom of action. Moreover, we (the Sherif's family) will consider ourselves free in word and deed from the bonds of our previous declaration which we made through Ali Effendi.

2. FROM SIR HENRY McMAHON, 24 OCTOBER 1915

I have received your letter ... with much pleasure and your expressions of friendliness and sincerity have given me the greatest satisfaction.

I regret that you should have received from my last letter the impression that I regarded the question of the limits and boundaries with coldness and hesitation; such was not the case, but it appeared to me that the time had not yet come when the question could be discussed in a conclusive manner.

I have realised, however, from your last letter, that you regard this question as one of vital and urgent importance. I have therefore lost no time in informing the Government of Great Britain of the contents of your letter, and it is with great pleasure that I communicate to you on their behalf the following statement which, I am confident, you will receive with satisfaction:—

The two districts of Mersina and Alexandretta and the portions of Syria lying to the west of the districts of Damascus, Homs, Hama and Aleppo cannot be said to be purely Arab, and should be excluded from the limits demanded.

With the above modification, and without prejudice to our existing treaties with Arab chiefs, we accept those limits.

As for those regions lying within those frontiers wherein Great Britain is free to act without detriment to the interests of her ally, France, I am empowered in the name of the Government of Great Britain to give the following assurances and make the following reply to your letter: —

1. Subject to the above modifications, Great Britain is prepared to recognise and support the independence of the Arabs in all the regions within the limits demanded by the Sherif of Mecca.

2. Great Britain will guarantee the Holy Places against all external aggression and will recognise their inviolability.

3. When the situation admits, Great Britain will give to the Arabs her advice and will assist them to establish what may appear to be the most suitable forms of government in those various territories.

4. On the other hand, it is understood that the Arabs have decided to seek the advice and guidance of Great Britain only, and that such European advisers and officials as may be required for the formation of a sound form of administration will be British.

5. With regard to the vilayets of Bagdad and Basra, the Arabs will recognise that the established position and interests of Great Britain necessitate special administrative arrangements in order to secure these territories from foreign aggression, to promote the welfare of the local populations and to safeguard our mutual economic interests.

I am convinced that this declaration will assure you beyond all possible doubt of the sympathy of Great Britain towards the aspirations of her friends, the Arabs, and will result in a firm and lasting alliance, the immediate results of which will be the expulsion of the Turks from the Arab countries and the freeing of the Arab peoples from the Turkish yoke which, for so many years, has pressed heavily upon them . . .

3. FROM SHARIF HUSAYN, 1 JANUARY 1916

We received from the bearer your letter, dated the 9th Safar (the 14th December, 1915), with great respect and honour, and I have understood its contents, which caused me the greatest pleasure and satisfaction, as it removed that which had made me uneasy.

Your honour will have realised, after the arrival of Mohammed (Faroki) Sherif and his interview with you, that all our procedure up to the present was of no personal inclination or the like, which would have been wholly unintelligible, but that everything was the result of the decisions and desires of our peoples, and that we are but transmitters and executants of such decisions and desires in the position they (our people) have pressed upon us.

These truths are, in my opinion, very important and deserve your honour's special attention and consideration.

With regard to what had been stated in your honoured communication concerning El Iraq as to the matter of compensation for the period of occupation, we, in order to strengthen the confidence of Great Britain in our attitude and in our words and actions, really and veritably, and in order to give her evidence of our certainty and assurance in trusting her glorious Government, leave the determination of the amount to the perception of her wisdom and justice.

As regards the northern parts and their coasts, we have already stated in our previous letter what were the utmost possible modifications, and all this was only done so to fulfil those aspirations whose attainment is desired by the will of the Blessed and Supreme God. It is this same feeling and desire which impelled us to avoid what may possibly injure the alliance of Great Britain and France and the agreement made between them during the present wars and calamities; yet we find it our duty that the eminent minister should be sure that, at the first opportunity after this war is finished, we shall ask you (what we avert our eyes from to-day) for what we now leave to France in Beirut and its coasts.

I do not find it necessary to draw your attention to the fact that our plan is of greater security to the interests and protection of the rights of Great Britain than it is to us, and will necessarily be so whatever may happen, so that Great Britain may finally see her friends in that contentment and advancement which she is endeavouring to establish for them now, especially as her Allies being neighbours to us will be the germ of difficulties and discussion with which there will be no peaceful conditions. In addition to which the citizens of Beirut will decidedly never accept such dismemberment, and they may oblige us to undertake new measures which may exercise Great Britain, certainly not less than her present troubles, because of our belief and certainty in the reciprocity and indeed the identity of our interests, which is the only cause that caused us never to care to negotiate with any other Power but you. Consequently, it is impossible to allow any derogation that gives France, or any other Power, a span of land in those regions.

I declare this, and I have a strong belief, which the living will inherit from the dead, in the declarations which you gave in the conclusion of your honoured letter. Therefore, the honourable and eminent Minister should believe and be sure, together with Great Britain, that we still remain firm to our resolution, which Storrs learnt from us two years ago, for which we await the opportunity suitable to our situation, especially in view of that action the time of which has now come near and which destiny drives towards us with great haste and clearness, so that we and those who are of our opinion may have reasons for such action against any criticisms or responsibilities imposed upon us in future.

Your expression "we do not want to push you to any hasty action which might jeopardise the success of your aim" does not need any more explanation except what we may ask for, when necessary, such as arms, ammunition, etc.

I deem this sufficient, as I have occupied much of your Honour's time. I beg to offer you my great veneration and respect.

4. FROM SIR HENRY McMAHON, 25 JANUARY 1916.
We have received with great pleasure and satisfaction your letter of the 25th Safar (the 1st January) at the hands of your trusty messenger, who has also transmitted to us your verbal messages.

We fully realise and entirely appreciate the motives which guide you in this important question, and we know well that you are acting entirely in the interests of the Arab peoples and with no thought beyond their welfare.

We take note of your remarks concerning the vilayet of Bagdad, and will take the question into careful consideration when the enemy has been defeated and the time for peaceful settlement arrives.

As regards the northern parts, we note with satisfaction your desire to avoid anything which might possibly injure the alliance of Great Britain and France. It is, as you know, our fixed determination that nothing shall be permitted to interfere in the slightest degree with our united prosecution of this war to a victorious conclusion. Moreover, when the victory has been won, the friendship of Great Britain and France will become yet more firm and enduring, cemented by the blood of Englishmen and Frenchmen who have died side by side fighting for the cause of right and liberty.

In this great cause Arabia is now associated, and God grant that the result of our mutual efforts and co-operation will bind us in a lasting friendship to the mutual welfare and happiness of us all.

We are greatly pleased to hear of the action you are taking to win all the Arabs over to our joint cause, and to dissuade them from giving any assistance to our enemies, and we leave it to your discretion to seize the most favourable moment for further and more decided measures.

You will doubtless inform us by the bearer of this letter of any manner in which we can assist you and your requests will always receive our immediate consideration.

You will have heard how El Sayed Ahmed el Sherif el Senussi has been beguiled by evil advice into hostile action, and it will be a great grief to you to know that he has been so far forgetful of the interests of the Arabs as to throw in his lot with our enemies. Misfortune has now overtaken him and we trust that this will show him his error and lead him to peace for the sake of his poor misguided followers.

We are sending this letter by the hand of your good messenger, who will also bring to you all our news.

ARAB-JEWISH AGREEMENTS
RELATIVE TO PALESTINE

A. AGREEMENT BETWEEN EMIR FEISAL AND DR. WEIZMANN. JANUARY 3, 1919.

His Royal Highness the Emir Feisal, representing and acting on behalf of the Arab Kingdom of Hedjaz, and Dr. Chaim Weizmann, representing and acting on behalf of the Zionist Organisation, mindful of the racial kinship and ancient bonds existing between the Arabs and the Jewish people, and realising that the surest means of working out the consummation of their national aspirations is through the closest possible collaboration in the development of the Arab State and Palestine, and being desirous further of confirming the good understanding which exists between them, have agreed upon the following Articles:

ARTICLE I
The Arab State and Palestine in all their relations and undertakings shall be controlled by the most cordial goodwill and understanding, and to this end Arab and Jewish duly accredited agents shall be established and maintained in the respective territories.

ARTICLE II
Immediately following the completion of the deliberations of the Peace Conference, the definite boundaries between the Arab State and Palestine shall be determined by a Commission to be agreed upon by the parties hereto.

ARTICLE III
In the establishment of the Constitution and Administration of Palestine all such measures shall be adopted as will afford the fullest guarantees for carrying into effect the British Government's Declaration of the 2d of November, 1917.

ARTICLE IV
All necessary measures shall be taken to encourage and stimulate immigration of Jews into Palestine on a large scale, and as quickly as possible to settle

437

Jewish immigrants upon the land through closer settlement and intensive cultivation of the soil. In taking such measures the Arab peasant and tenant farmers shall be protected in their rights, and shall be assisted in forwarding their economic development.

ARTICLE V
No regulation nor law shall be made prohibiting or interfering in any way with the free exercise of religion; and further the free exercise and enjoyment of religious profession and worship without discrimination or preference shall forever be allowed. No religious test shall ever be required for the exercise of civil or political rights.

ARTICLE VI
The Mohammedan Holy Places shall be under Mohammedan control.

ARTICLE VII
The Zionist Organisation proposes to send to Palestine a Commission of experts to make a survey of the economic possibilities of the country, and to report upon the best means for its development. The Zionist Organisation will place the aforementioned Commission at the disposal of the Arab State for the purpose of a survey of the economic possibilities of the Arab State and to report upon the best means for its development. The Zionist Organisation will use its best efforts to assist the Arab State in providing the means for developing the natural resources and economic possibilities thereof.

ARTICLE VIII
The parties hereto agree to act in complete accord and harmony on all matters embraced herein before the Peace Congress.

ARTICLE IX
Any matters of dispute which may arise between the contracting parties shall be referred to the British Government for arbitration.

Given under our hand at London, England, the third day of January, one thousand nine hundred and nineteen.

Chaim Weizmann.
Feisal Ibn-Hussein.

RESERVATION BY THE EMIR FEISAL
If the Arabs are established as I have asked in my manifesto of January 4th addressed to the British Secretary of State for Foreign Affairs, I will carry out what is written in this agreement. If changes are made, I cannot be answerable for failing to carry out this agreement.

Feisal Ibn-Hussein.

B. FEISAL-FRANKFURTER CORRESPONDENCE
Delegation Hedjazienne, Paris, March 3, 1919.
Dear Mr. Frankfurter: I want to take this opportunity of my first contact with American Zionists to tell you what I have often been able to say to Dr. Weizmann in Arabia and Europe.
We feel that the Arabs and Jews are cousins in race, having suffered similar

oppressions at the hands of powers stronger than themselves, and by a happy coincidence have been able to take the first step towards the attainment of their national ideals together.

We Arabs, especially the educated among us, look with the deepest sympathy on the Zionist movement. Our deputation here in Paris is fully acquainted with the proposals submitted yesterday by the Zionist Organization to the Peace Conference, and we regard them as moderate and proper. We will do our best, in so far as we are concerned, to help them through: we will wish the Jews a most hearty welcome home.

With the chiefs of your movement, especially with Dr. Weizmann, we have had and continue to have the closest relations. He has been a great helper of our cause, and I hope the Arabs may soon be in a position to make the Jews some return for their kindness. We are working together for a reformed and revived Near East, and our two movements complete one another. The Jewish movement is national and not imperialist. Our movement is national and not imperialist, and there is room in Syria for us both. Indeed I think that neither can be a real success without the other.

People less informed and less responsible than our leaders and yours, ignoring the need for cooperation of the Arabs and Zionists have been trying to exploit the local difficulties that must necessarily arise in Palestine in the early stages of our movements. Some of them have, I am afraid, misrepresented your aims to the Arab peasantry, and our aims to the Jewish peasantry, with the result that interested parties have been able to make capital out of what they call our differences.

I wish to give you my firm conviction that these differences are not on questions of principle, but on matters of detail such as must inevitably occur in every contact of neighbouring peoples, and as are easily adjusted by mutual goodwill. Indeed nearly all of them will disappear with fuller knowledge.

I look forward, and my people with me look forward, to a future in which we will help you and you will help us, so that the countries in which we are mutually interested may once again take their places in the community of civilised peoples of the world.

Believe me,
Yours sincerely,

(Sgd.) Feisal.
5th March, 1919.

Royal Highness:

Allow me, on behalf of the Zionist Organisation, to acknowledge your recent letter with deep appreciation.

Those of us who come from the United States have already been gratified by the friendly relations and the active cooperation maintained between you and the Zionist leaders, particularly Dr. Weizmann. We knew it could not be otherwise; we knew that the aspirations of the Arab and the Jewish peoples were parallel, that each aspired to reestablish its nationality in its own homeland, each making its own distinctive contribution to civilisation, each seeking its own peaceful mode of life.

The Zionist leaders and the Jewish people for whom they speak have watched with satisfaction the spiritual vigour of the Arab movement. Themselves seeking justice, they are anxious that the just national aims of the Arab people be confirmed and safeguarded by the Peace Conference.

We knew from your acts and your past utterances that the Zionist movement — in other words the national aims of the Jewish people — had your support and the support of the Arab people for whom you speak. These aims are now before the Peace Conference as definite proposals by the Zionist Organisation. We are happy indeed that you consider these proposals "moderate and proper," and that we have in you a staunch supporter for their realisation. For both the Arab and the Jewish peoples there are difficulties ahead — difficulties that challenge the united statesmanship of Arab and Jewish leaders. For it is no easy task to rebuild two great civilisations that have been suffering oppression and misrule for centuries. We each have our difficulties we shall work out as friends, friends who are animated by similar purposes, seeking a free and full development for the two neighbouring peoples. The Arabs and Jews are neighbours in territory; we cannot but live side by side as friends.

Very respectfully,

(Sgd.) Felix Frankfurter.

His Royal Highness Prince Feisal.

ISRAEL-LEBANESE GENERAL ARMISTICE AGREEMENT

PREAMBLE

The parties to the present Agreement,

Responding to the Security Council Resolution of 16 November 1948, calling upon them, as a further provisional measure under Article 40 of the Charter of the United Nations and in order to facilitate the transition from the present truce to permanent peace in Palestine, to negotiate an armistice;

Having decided to enter into negotiations under United Nations Chairmanship concerning the implementation of the Security Council Resolution of 16 November 1948; and having appointed representatives empowered to negotiate and conclude an Armistice Agreement;

The undersigned representatives, having exchanged their full powers found to be in good and proper form, have agreed upon the following provisions:

ARTICLE I

With a view to promoting the return of permanent peace in Palestine and in recognition of the importance in this regard of mutual assurances concerning the future military operations of the Parties, the following principles, which shall be fully observed by both Parties during the armistice, are hereby affirmed:

1. The injunction of the Security Council against resort to military force in the settlement of the Palestine question shall henceforth be scrupulously respected by both Parties.
2. No aggressive action by the armed forces — land, sea or air of either Party shall be undertaken, planned or threatened against the people or the armed forces of the other; it being understood that the use of the term "planned" in this context has no bearing on normal staff planning as generally practised in military organisations.
3. The right of each Party to its security and freedom from fear of attack by the armed forces of the other shall be fully respected.
4. The establishment of an armistice between the armed forces of the two parties is accepted as an indispensable step toward the liquidation of

441

armed conflict and the restoration of peace in Palestine.

ARTICLE II

With a specific view to the implementation of the Resolution of the Security Council of 16 November 1948, the following principles and purposes are affirmed:

1. The principle that no military or political advantage should be gained under the truce ordered by the Security Council is recognized.
2. It is also recognized that no provision of this Agreement shall in any way prejudice the rights, claims and positions of either Party hereto in the ultimate peaceful settlement of the Palestine question, the provisions of this Agreement being dictated exclusively by military considerations.

ARTICLE III

1. In pursuance of the foregoing principles and of the Resolution of the Security Council of 16 November 1948, a general armistice between the armed forces of the two Parties — land, sea, and air — is hereby established.

2. No element of the land, sea or air military or para-military forces of either Party, including non-regular forces, shall commit any warlike or hostile act against the military or para-military forces of the other Party, or against civilians in territory under the control of that Party; or shall advance beyond or pass over for any purpose whatsoever the Armistice Demarcation Line set forth in Article V of this Agreement; or enter into or pass through the air space of the other Party or through the waters within three miles of the coastline of the other Party.

3. No warlike act or act of hostility shall be conducted from territory controlled by one of the Parties to this Agreement against the other Party.

ARTICLE IV

1. The line described in Article V of this Agreement shall be designated as the Armistice Demarcation Line and is delined in pursuance of the purpose and intent of the Resolution of the Security Council of 16 November 1948.

2. The basic purpose of the Armistice Demarcation Line is to delineate the line beyond which the armed forces of the respective Parties shall not move.

3. Rules and regulations of the armed forces of the Parties, which prohibit civilians from crossing the fighting lines or entering the area between the lines, shall remain in effect after the signing of this Agreement with application to the Armistice Demarcation Line defined in Article V.

ARTICLE V

1. The Armistice Demarcation Line shall follow the international boundary between the Lebanon and Palestine.

2. In the region of the Armistice Demarcation Line the military forces of the Parties shall consist of defensive forces only as is defined in the Annex to this Agreement.

3. Withdrawal of forces to the Armistice Demarcation Line and their reduction to defensive strength in accordance with the preceding paragraph shall be completed within ten days of the signing of this Agreement. In the same way the removal of mines from mined roads and areas evacuated by either Party, and the transmission of plans showing the location of such minefields to the other Party shall be completed within the same period.

ARTICLE VI

All prisoners of war detained by either Party to this Agreement and belonging to the armed forces, regular or irregular, of the other Party, shall be exchanged as follows:

1. The exchange of prisoners of war shall be under United Nations supervision and control throughout. The exchange shall take place at Ras En Naqoura within twenty-four hours of the signing of this Agreement.
2. Prisoners of war against whom a penal prosecution may be pending, as well as those sentenced for crime or other offence, shall be included in this exchange of prisoners.
3. All articles of personal use, valuables, letters, documents, identification marks, and other personal effects of whatever nature, belonging to prisoners of war who are being exchanged, shall be returned to them, or, if they have escaped or died, to the Party to whose armed forces they belonged.
4. All matters not specifically regulated in this Agreement shall be decided in accordance with the principles laid down in the International Convention relating to the Treatment of Prisoners of War, signed at Geneva on 27 July 1929.
5. The Mixed Armistice Commission established in Article VII of this Agreement, shall assume responsibility for locating missing persons, whether military or civilian, within the areas controlled by each Party, to facilitate their expeditious exchange, Each Party undertakes to extend to the Commission full co-operation and assistance in the discharge of this function.

ARTICLE VII

1. The execution of the provisions of this Agreement shall be supervised by a Mixed Armistice Commission composed of five members, of whom each Party to this Agreement shall designate two, and whose Chairman shall be the United Nations Chief of Staff of the Truce Supervision Organisation or a senior officer from the Observer personnel of that Organisation designated by him following consultation with both Parties to this Agreement.

2. The Mixed Armistice Commission shall maintain its headquarters at the Frontier Post north of Metullah and at the Lebanese Frontier Post at En Naqoura, and shall hold its meetings at such places and at such times as it may deem necessary for the effective conduct of its work.

3. The Mixed Armistice Commission shall be convened in its first meeting by the United Nations Chief of Staff of the Truce Supervision Organisation not later than one week following the signing of this Agreement.

4. Decisions of the Mixed Armistice Commission, to the extent possible, shall be based on the principle of unanimity. In the absence of unanimity, decisions shall be taken by majority vote of the members of the Commission present and voting.

5. The Mixed Armistice Commission shall formulate its own rules of procedure. Meetings shall be held only after due notice to the members by the Chairman. The quorum for its meetings shall be a majority of its members.

6. The Commission shall be empowered to employ Observers, who may be from among the military organisations of the Parties or from the military personnel of the United Nations Truce Supervision Organisation, or from both, in such numbers as may be considered essential to the performance of its functions. In the event United Nations Observers should be so employed, they

shall remain under the command of the United Nations Chief of Staff of the Truce Supervision Organisation, Assignments of a general or special nature given to United Nations Observers attached to the Mixed Armistice Commission shall be subject to approval by the United Nations Chief of Staff or his designated representative on the Commission, whichever is serving as Chairman.

7. Claims or complaints presented by either Party relating to the application of this Agreement shall be referred immediately to the Mixed Armistice Commission through its Chairman. The Commission shall take such action on all such claims or complaints by means of its observation and investigation machinery as it may deem appropriate, with a view to equitable and mutually satisfactory settlement.

8. Where interpretation of the meaning of a particular provision of this Agreement, other than the Preamble and Articles I and II, is at issue, the Commission's interpretation shall prevail. The Commission, in its discretion and as the need arises, may from time to time recommend to the Parties modifications in the provisions of this Agreement.

9. The Mixed Armistice Commission shall submit to both Parties reports on its activities as frequently as it may consider necessary. A copy of each such report shall be presented to the Secretary-General of the United Nations for transmission to the appropriate organ or agency of the United Nations.

10. Members of the Commission and its Observers shall be accorded such freedom of movement and access in the area covered by this Agreement as the Commission may determine to be necessary, provided that when such decisions of the Commission are reached by a majority vote United Nations Observers only shall be employed.

11. The expenses of the Commission, other than those relating to United Nations Observers, shall be apportioned in equal shares between the two Parties to this Agreement.

ARTICLE VIII

1. The present Agreement is not subject to ratification and shall come into force immediately upon being signed.

2. This Agreement, having been negotiated and concluded in pursuance of the Resolution of the Security Council of 16 November 1948 calling for the establishment of an armistice in order to eliminate the threat to the peace in Palestine and to facilitate the transition from the present truce to permanent peace in Palestine, shall remain in force until a peaceful settlement between the Parties is achieved, except as provided in paragraph 3 of this Article.

3. The Parties to this Agreement may, by mutual consent, revise this Agreement or any of its provisions, or may suspend its application, other than Articles I and III, at any time. In the absence of mutual agreement and after this Agreement has been in effect for one year from the date of its signing, either of the Parties may call upon the Secretary-General of the United Nations to convoke a conference of representatives of the two Parties for the purpose of reviewing, revising or suspending any of the provisions of this Agreement other than Articles I and III. Participation in such conference shall be obligatory upon the Parties.

4. If the conference provided for in paragraph 3 of this Article does not result in an agreed solution of a point in dispute, either Party may bring the matter before the Security Council of the United Nations for the relief sought on the grounds that this Agreement has been concluded in pursuance of Security Council action toward the end of achieving peace in Palestine.

5. This Agreement is signed in quintuplicate, of which one copy shall be retained by each Party, two copies communicated to the Secretary-General of the United Nations for transmission to the Security Council and to the United Nations Conciliation Commission on Palestine, and one copy to the Acting Mediator on Palestine.

Done at Ras en Naqoura on the twenty-third of March nineteen forty-nine, in the presence of the Personal Deputy of the United Nations Acting Mediator on Palestine and the United Nations Chief of Staff of the Truce Supervision Organisation.

<table>
<tr><td>For and on behalf of the
Government of Israel
(Signatures)</td><td>For and on behalf of the
Government of the Lebanon
(Signatures)</td></tr>
</table>

ANNEX: DEFINITION OF DEFENSIVE FORCES

I. The Military Defensive Forces referred to in Article V, paragraph 2, shall not exceed:

  1. In the case of the Lebanon:

    (i) Two battalions and two companies of Lebanese Regular Army Infantry, one field battery of 4 guns and one company of 12 light armoured cars armed with machine guns and 6 light tanks armed with light guns (20 vehicles). Total 1500 officers and enlisted men.

    (ii) No other military forces, than those mentioned in (i) above, shall be employed south of the general line El Qasmiye — Nabatiye Ett Tahta — Hasbaiya.

  2. In the case of Israel:

    (i) One infantry battalion, one support company with six mortars and six machine guns, one reconnaissance company with six armoured cars and six armoured jeeps, one battery of field artillery with four guns, one platoon of field engineers and service units as Quartermaster and Ordnance, total not to exceed fifteen hundred officers and enlisted men.

    (ii) No other military forces, than those mentioned in 2 (i) above shall be employed north of the general line Nahariya — Tarshiha — Jish — Marus.

II. There shall be no restriction of movement imposed on either side in connexion with the supply and/or movement of these defensive forces behind the demarcation line.

Unilateral Document No. 1

THE BALFOUR DECLARATION.

Foreign Office,
November 2nd, 1917.

Dear Lord Rothschild,

I have much pleasure in conveying to you, on behalf of His Majesty's Government, the following declaration of sympathy with Jewish Zionist aspirations which has been submitted to, and approved by, the Cabinet.

"His Majesty's Government view with favour the establishment in Palestine of a national home for the Jewish people, and will use their best endeavours to facilitate the achievement of this object, it being clearly understood that nothing shall be done which may prejudice the civil and religious rights of existing non-Jewish communities in Palestine, or the rights and political status enjoyed by Jews in any other country"

I should be grateful if you would bring this declaration to the knowledge of the Zionist Federation.

Arthur James Balfour

THE PALESTINIAN NATIONAL CHARTER

DECISIONS OF THE NATIONAL CONGRESS OF THE PALESTINE LIBERA-
TION ORGANIZATION HELD IN CAIRO FROM 1-17 JULY 1968.

Article 1: Palestine is the homeland of the Arab Palestinian people; it is an indivisible part of the Arab homeland, and the Palestinian people are an integral part of the Arab nation.

Article 2: Palestine, with the boundaries it had during the British mandate, is an indivisible territorial unit.

Article 3: The Palestinian Arab people possess the legal right to their homeland and have the right to determine their destiny after achieving the liberation of their country in accordance with their wishes and entirely of their own accord and will.

Article 4: The Palestinian identity is a genuine, essential and inherent characteristic; it is transmitted from parents to children. The Zionist occupation and the dispersal of the Palestinian Arab people, through the disasters which befell them, do not make them lose their Palestinian identity and their membership of the Palestinian community, nor do they negate them.

Article 5: The Palestinians are those Arab nationals who, until 1947, normally resided in Palestine regardless of whether they were evicted from it or have stayed there. Anyone born, after that date, of a Palestinian father — whether inside Palestine or outside it — is also a Palestinian.

Article 6: The Jews who had normally resided in Palestine until the beginning of the Zionist invasion will be considered Palestinians.

Article 7: That there is a Palestinian community and that it has material,

447

spiritual and historical connection with Palestine are indisputable facts. It is a national duty to bring up individual Palestinians in an Arab revolutionary manner. All means of information and education must be adopted in order to acquaint the Palestinian with his country in the most profound manner, both spiritual and material, that is possible. He must be prepared for the armed struggle and ready to sacrifice his wealth and his life in order to win back his homeland and bring about its liberation.

Article 8: The phase in their history, through which the Palestinian people are now living, is that of national struggle for the liberation of Palestine. Thus the conflicts among the Palestinian national forces are secondary, and should be ended for the sake of the basic conflict that exists between the forces of Zionism and of imperialism on the one hand, and the Palestinian Arab people on the other. On this basis the Palestinian masses, regardless of whether they are residing in the national homeland or in diaspora, constitute — both their organizations and the individuals — one national front working for the retrieval of Palestine and its liberation through armed struggle.

Article 9: Armed struggle is the only way to liberate Palestine. Thus it is the overall strategy, not merely a tactical phase. The Palestinian Arab people assert their absolute determination and firm resolution to continue their armed struggle and to work for an armed popular revolution for the liberation of their country and their return to it. They also assert their right to normal life in Palestine and to exercise their right to self-determination and sovereignty over it.

Article 10: Commando action constitutes the nucleus of the Palestinian popular liberation war. This requires its escalation, comprehensiveness and the mobilization of all the Palestinian popular and educational efforts and their organization and involvement in the armed Palestinian revolution. It also requires the achieving of unity for the national struggle among the different groupings of the Palestinian people, and between the Palestinian people and the Arab masses so as to secure the continuation of the revolution, its escalation and victory.

Article 11: The Palestinians will have three mottoes: national unity, national mobilization and liberation.

Article 12: The Palestinian people believe in Arab unity. In order to contribute their share towards the attainment of that objective, however, they must, at the present stage of their struggle, safeguard their Palestinian identity and develop their consciousness of that identity, and oppose any plan that may dissolve or impair it.

Article 13: Arab unity and the liberation of Palestine are two complementary objectives, the attainment of either of which facilitates the attainment of the other. Thus, Arab unity leads to the liberation of Palestine; the liberation of Palestine leads to Arab unity; and work towards the realization of one objective proceeds side by side with work towards the realization of the other.

Article 14: The destiny of the Arab nation, and indeed Arab existence itself, depends upon the destiny of the Palestine cause. From this interdependence springs the Arab nation's pursuit of, and striving for, the liberation of Palestine.

The people of Palestine play the role of the vanguard in the realization of this sacred national goal.

Article 15: The liberation of Palestine, from an Arab viewpoint, is a national duty and it attempts to repel the Zionist and imperialist aggression against the Arab homeland, and aims at the elimination of Zionism in Palestine. Absolute responsibility for this falls upon the Arab nation — peoples and governments — with the Arab people of Palestine in the vanguard. Accordingly the Arab nation must mobilize all its military, human, moral and spiritual capabilities to participate actively with the Palestinian people in the liberation of Palestine. It must, particularly in the phase of the armed Palestinian revolution, offer and furnish the Palestinian people with all possible help, and material and human support, and make available to them the means and opportunities that will enable them to continue to carry out their leading role in the armed revolution, until they liberate their homeland.

Article 16: The liberation of Palestine, from a spiritual point of view, will provide the Holy Land with an atmosphere of safety and tranquillity, which in turn will safeguard the country's religious sanctuaries and guarantee freedom of worship and of visit to all, without discrimination of race, color, language, or religion. Accordingly, the people of Palestine look to all spiritual forces in the world for support.

Article 17: The liberation of Palestine, from a human point of view, will restore to the Palestinian individual his dignity, pride and freedom. Accordingly the Palestinian Arab people look forward to the support of all those who believe in the dignity of man and his freedom in the world.

Article 18: The liberation of Palestine, from an international point of view, is a defensive action necessitated by the demands of self-defence. Accordingly, the Palestinian people, desirous as they are of the friendship of all people, look to freedom-loving, justice-loving and peace-loving states for support in order to restore their legitimate rights in Palestine, to re-establish peace and security in the country, and to enable its people to exercise national sovereignty and freedom.

Article 19: The partition of Palestine in 1947 and the establishment of the state of Israel are entirely illegal, regardless of the passage of time, because they were contrary to the will of the Palestinian people and to their natural right in their homeland, and inconsistent with the principles embodied in the Charter of the United Nations, particularly the right to self-determination.

Article 20: The Balfour Declaration, the mandate for Palestine and everything that has been based upon them, are deemed null and void. Claims of historical or religious ties of Jews with Palestine are incompatible with the facts of history and the true conception of what constitutes statehood. Judaism, being a religion, is not an independent nationality. Nor do Jews constitute a single nation with an identity of its own; they are citizens of the states to which they belong.

Article 21: The Arab Palestinian people, expressing themselves by the armed Palestinian revolution, reject all solutions which are substitutes for the total

449

liberation of Palestine and reject all proposals aiming at the liquidation of the Palestinian problem, or its internationalization.

Article 22: Zionism is a political movement organically associated with international imperialism and antagonistic to all action for liberation and to progressive movements in the world. It is racist and fanatic in its nature, aggressive, expansionist and colonial in its aims, and fascist in its methods. Israel is the instrument of the Zionist movement, and a geographical base for world imperialism placed strategically in the midst of the Arab homeland to combat the hopes of the Arab nation for liberation, unity and progress. Israel is a constant source of threat vis-a-vis peace in the Middle East and the whole world. Since the liberation of Palestine will destroy the Zionist and imperialist presence and will contribute to the establishment of peace in the Middle East, the Palestinian people look for the support of all the progressive and peaceful forces and urge them all, irrespective of their affiliations and beliefs, to offer the Palestinian people all aid and support in their just struggle for the liberation of their homeland.

Article 23: The demands of security and peace, as well as the demands of right and justice, require all states to consider Zionism an illegitimate movement, to outlaw its existence, and to ban its operations, in order that friendly relations among peoples may be preserved, and the loyalty of citizens to their respective homelands safeguarded.

Article 24: The Palestinian people believe in the principles of justice, freedom, sovereignty, self-determination, human dignity, and in the right of all peoples to exercise them.

Article 25: For the realization of the goals of this Charter and its principles, the Palestine Liberation Organization will perform its role in the liberation of Palestine in accordance with the Constitution of this Organization.

Article 26: The Palestine Liberation Organization, representative of the Palestinian revolutionary forces, is responsible for the Palestinian Arab people's movement in its struggle — to retrieve its homeland, liberate and return to it and exercise the right to self-determination in it — in all military, political and financial fields and also for whatever may be required by the Palestine case on the inter-Arab and international levels.

Article 27: The Palestine Liberation Organization shall cooperate with all Arab states, each according to its potentialities; and will adopt a neutral policy among them in the light of the requirements of the war of liberation; and on this basis it shall not interfere in the internal affairs of any Arab state.

Article 28: The Palestinian Arab people assert the genuineness and independence of their national revolution and reject all forms of intervention, trusteeship and subordination.

Article 29: The Palestinian people possess the fundamental and genuine legal right to liberate and retrieve their homeland. The Palestinian people determine their attitude towards all states and forces on the basis of the stands they adopt vis-a-vis the Palestinian case and the extent of the support they offer to the

Palestinian revolution to fulfill the aims of the Palestinian people.

Article 30: Fighters and carriers of arms in the war of liberation are the nucleus of the popular army which will be the protective force for the gains of the Palestinian Arab people.

Article 31: The Organization shall have a flag, an oath of allegiance and an anthem. All this shall be decided upon in accordance with a special regulation.

Article 32: Regulations, which shall be known as the Constitution of the Palestine Liberation Organization, shall be annexed to this Charter. It shall lay down the manner in which the Organization, and its organs and institutions, shall be constituted; the respective competence of each; and the requirements of its obligations under the Charter.

Article 33: This Charter shall not be amended save by (vote of) a majority of two-thirds of the total membership of the National Congress of the Palestine Liberation Organization (taken) at a special session convened for that purpose.

DECLARATION OF
THE ESTABLISHMENT
OF THE STATE OF ISRAEL

Eretz-Israel was the birthplace of the Jewish people. Here their spiritual, religious and political identity was shaped. Here they first attained to statehood, created cultural values of national and universal significance and gave to the world the eternal Book of Books.

After being forcibly exiled from their land, the people kept faith with it throughout their Dispersion and never ceased to pray and hope for their return to it and for the restoration in it of their political freedom.

Impelled by this historic and traditional attachment, Jews strove in every successive generation to re-establish themselves in their ancient homeland. In recent decades they returned in their masses. Pioneers, *ma'pilim* and defenders, they made deserts bloom, revived the Hebrew language, built villages and towns, and created a thriving community, controlling its own economy and culture, loving peace but knowing how to defend itself, bringing the blessings of progress to all the country's inhabitants, and aspiring towards independent nationhood.

In the year 5657 (1897), at the summons of the spiritual father of the Jewish State, Theodor Herzl, the First Zionist Congress convened and proclaimed the right of the Jewish people to national rebirth in its own country.

This right was recognized in the Balfour Declaration of the 2nd November, 1917, and re-affirmed in the Mandate of the League of Nations which, in particular, gave international sanction to the historic connection between the Jewish people and Eretz-Israel and to the right of the Jewish people to rebuild its National Home.

The catastrophe which recently befell the Jewish people — the massacre of millions of Jews in Europe — was another clear demonstration of the urgency of solving the problem of its homelessness by re-establishing in Eretz-Israel the

Jewish State, which would open the gates of the homeland wide to every Jew and confer upon the Jewish people the status of a fully-privileged member of the comity of nations.

Survivors of the Nazi holocaust in Europe, as well as Jews from other parts of the world, continued to migrate to Eretz-Israel, undaunted by difficulties, restrictions and dangers, and never ceased to assert their right to a life of dignity, freedoms and honest toil in their national homeland.

In the Second World War, the Jewish community of this country contributed its full share of the struggle of the freedom — and peace — loving nations against the forces of Nazi wickedness and, by the blood of its soldiers and its war effort, gained the right to be reckoned among the people who founded the United Nations.

On the 29th November, 1947, the United Nations General Assembly passed a resolution calling for the establishment of a Jewish State in Eretz-Israel; the General Assembly required the inhabitants of Eretz-Israel to take such steps as were necessary on their part for the implementation of that resolution. This recognition by the United Nations of the right of the Jewish people to establish their State is irrevocable.

This right is the natural right of the Jewish people to be masters of their own fate, like all other nations, in their own sovereign State.

Accordingly We, Members of the People's Council, Representatives of the Jewish Community of Eretz-Israel and of the Zionist Movement, Are Here Assembled on the Day of the Termination of the British Mandate Over Eretz-Israel and, by Virtue of Our Natural and Historic Right and on the Strength of the Resolution of the United Nations General Assembly, Hereby Declare the Establishment of a Jewish State in Eretz-Israel, to be Known as the State of Israel.

We Declare that, with effect from the moment of the termination of the Mandate, being tonight, the eve of Sabbath, the 6th Iyar 5708 (15th May, 1948), until the establishment of the elected, regular authorities of the State in accordance with the Constitution which shall be adopted by the Elected Constituent Assembly not later than the 1st October, 1948, the People's Council shall act as a Provisional Council of State, and its executive organ, the People's Administration, shall be the Provisional Government of the Jewish State, to be called "Israel".

The State of Israel will be open for Jewish immigration and for the Ingathering of the Exiles; it will foster the development of the country for the benefit of all inhabitants; it will be based on freedom, justice and peace as envisaged by the prophets of Israel; it will ensure complete equality of social and political rights to all its inhabitants irrespective of religion, race or sex; it will guarantee freedom of religion, conscience, language, education and culture; it will safeguard the Holy Places of all religions; and it will be faithful to the principles of the Charter of the United Nations.

The State of Israel is prepared to cooperate with the agencies and representa-

453

tives of the United Nations in implementing the resolution of the General Assembly of the 29th November, 1947, and will take steps to bring about the economic union of the whole of Eretz-Israel.

We Appeal to the United Nations to assist the Jewish people in the building-up of its State and to receive the State of Israel into the comity of nations.

We Appeal — in the very midst of the onslaught launched against us now for months — to the Arab inhabitants of the State of Israel to preserve peace and participate in the upbuilding of the State on the basis of full and equal citizenship and due representation in all its provisional and permanent institutions.

We Extend our hand to all neighbouring states and their peoples in an offer of peace and good neighbourliness, and appeal to them to establish bonds of cooperation and mutual help with the sovereign Jewish people settled in its own land. The State of Israel is prepared to do its share in common effort for the advancement of the entire Middle East.

We Appeal to the Jewish people throughout the Diaspora to rally round the Jews of Eretz-Israel in the tasks of immigration and upbuilding and to stand by them in the great struggle for realization of the age-old dream — the redemption of Israel.

Placing Our Trust in the Almighty, We Affix Our Signatures to This Proclamation at This Session of the Provisional Council of State, on the Soil of the Homeland, in the City of Tel-Aviv, on This Sabbath Eve, the 5th Day of Iyar, 5708 (14th May, 1948).

DAVID BEN-GURION

DANIEL AUSTER	ZVI LURIA
MORDEKHAI BENTOV	GOLDA MYERSON
YITZCHAK BEN-ZVI	NACHUM NIR
ELIYAHU BERLIGNE	ZVI SEGAL
FRITZ BERNSTEIN	RABBI YEHUDA LEIB
RABBI WOLF GOLD	HACOHEN FISHMAN
NEIR GRABOVSKY	DAVID ZVI PINKAS
YITZCHAK GRUENBAUM	AHARON ZISLING
Dr. ABRAHAM GRANOVSKY	MOSHE KOLODNY
ELIYAHU DOBKIN	ELIEZER KAPLAN
MEIR WILNER-KOVNER	ABRAHAM KATZNELSON
ZERACH WAHRHAFTIC	FELIX ROSENBLUETH
HERZL VARDI	DAVID REMEZ
RACHEL COHEN	BERL REPETUR
RABBI KALMAN KAHANA	MORDEKHAI SHATTNER
SAADIA KOBASHI	BEN-ZION STERNBERG
RABBI YITZCHAK	BEKHOR SHITREET
RABBI MEIR LEVIN	MOSHE SHAPIRA
MEIR DAVID LOEWENSTEIN	MOSHE SHERTOK

LAW OF RETURN
(5710 — 1950)

1. Every Jew has the right to come to this country as an *oleh*.

2. (a) *Aliyah* shall be by *oleh*'s visa.
   (b) An *oleh*'s visa shall be granted to every Jew who has expressed his desire to settle in Israel, unless the Minister of Immigration is satisfied that the applicant:
   (1) is engaged in an activity directed against the Jewish people; or
   (2) is likely to endanger public health or the security of the State.

3. (a) A Jew who has come to Israel and subsequent to his arrival has expressed his desire to settle in Israel, while still in Israel, receive an *oleh*'s certificate.
   (b) The restrictions specified in section 2(b) shall apply also to the grant of an *oleh*'s certificate, but a person shall not be regarded as endangering public health on account of an illness contracted after his arrival in Israel.

4. Every Jew who has immigrated into this country before the coming into force of this Law, and every Jew who was born in this country, whether before or after the coming into force of this Law, shall be deemed to be a person who has come to this country as an *oleh* under this Law.

5. The Minister of Immigration is charged with the implementation of this Law and may make regulations as to any matter relating to such implementation and also as to the grant of *oleh*'s visas and *oleh*'s certificates to minors up to the age of 18 years.

MAPS

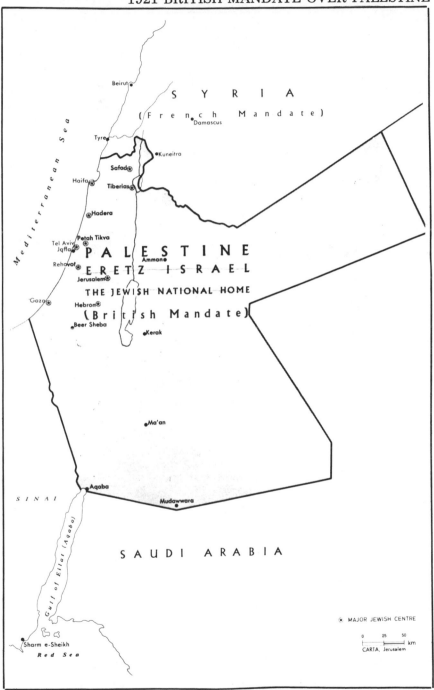

SYRIA

(French Mandate)

Beirut

Damascus

Tyre

Kuneitra

Safad

Haifa

Tiberias

Hadera

Mediterranean Sea

Petah Tikva

Tel Aviv

Jqfla

PALESTINE

Rehovot

ERETZ ISRAEL

Amman

Jerusalem

THE JEWISH NATIONAL HOME

Gaza

Hebron

(British Mandate)

Beer Sheba

Kerak

Ma'an

SINAI

Aqaba

Mudawwara

Gulf of Eilat (Aqaba)

SAUDI ARABIA

Sharm e-Sheikh

Red Sea

⊛ MAJOR JEWISH CENTRE

0   25   50
|——————| km
CARTA, Jerusalem

MAJOR
JEWISH CENTRE

JEWISH STATE

ARAB STATE

INTERNATIONAL
ZONE

0   25   50
                km
CARTA, Jerusalem

1949 ARMISTICE AGREEMENTS BOUNDARIES

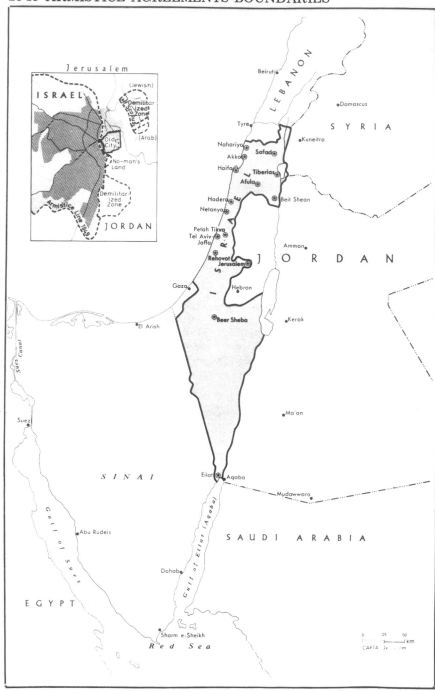

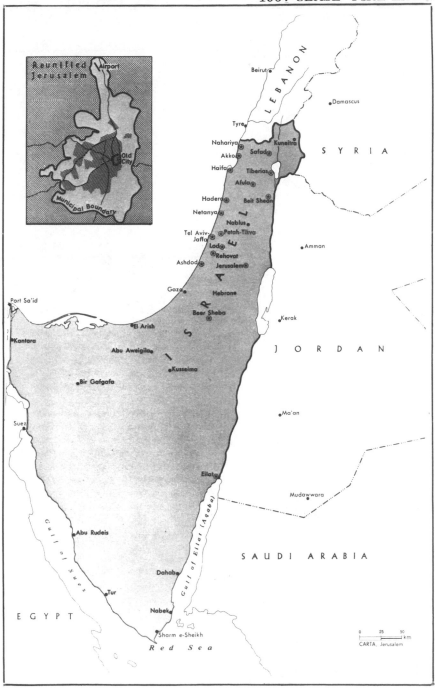

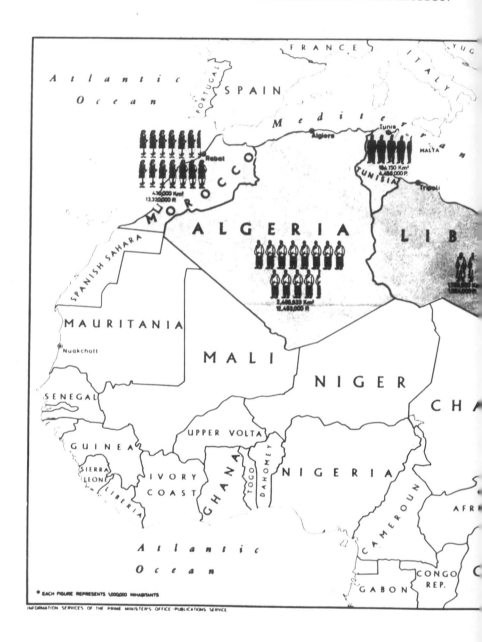

Israel Citizens | Jews 2,345,000 | Non Jews 392,000
Others | | 300,000

BASED MAINLY ON THE STATESMAN'S YEAR BOOK 1968-1969
FIGURES ON ISRAEL REFER TO THE CEASE FIRE LINES JUNE 1967

CARTA, Jerusalem

SELECTED
BIBLIOGRAPHY

SELECTED BIBLIOGRAPHY

THE ARAB-ISRAELI CONFLICT: GENERAL

King Abdallah. trans. H. W. Glidden. MY MEMOIRS COMPLETED. Washington, D. C.: American Council of Learned Studies, 1954.

Alami, M., "The Lesson of Palestine," MIDDLE EAST JOURNAL, Vol. 3 (Autumn 1949), p. 373.

Avnery, U. ISRAEL WITIIOUT ZIONISTS: A PLEA FOR PEACE IN THE MIDDLE EAST. New York: Macmillan, 1968.

American Professors for Peace in the Middle East. THE ARABS NEED AND WANT PEACE, BUT . . . . New York: American Professors for Peace in the Middle East, 1968.

THE ANATOMY OF PEACE IN THE MIDDLE EAST. New York: American Academic Association for Peace in the Middle East, 1969.

THE ARAB-ISRAELI CONFLICT. (Documents and Comments). New Delhi: The Indian Society of International Law, 1967.

Baehr, K. IN SEARCH OF BROTHERHOOD IN THE HOLY LAND. New York: Interfaith and University Committee, 1970.

Be'eri, E. ARMY OFFICERS IN ARAB POLITICS AND SOCIETY. New York: Praeger, 1970.

Bell, J. THE LONG WAR: ISRAEL AND THE ARABS SINCE 1946. Englewood Cliffs, New Jersey: Prentice Hall, 1969.

Ben Gurion, D. ISRAEL: YEARS OF CHALLENGE. New York: Holt, Rinehart & Winston, 1963.

Berger, E. THE COVENANT AND THE SWORD: ARAB-ISRAELI RELATIONS, 1948-56. London: Routledge and Kegan Paul, 1956.

Brecher, M. THE FOREIGN POLICY SYSTEM OF ISRAEL: SETTING, IMAGES, PROCESS. New Haven, Connecticut: Yale University Press, 1972.

Burdett, W. ENCOUNTER WITH THE MIDDLE EAST: AN INTIMATE REPORT ON WHAT LIES BEHIND THE ARAB-ISRAELI CONFLICT. New York: Atheneum, 1969.

Cattan, H. PALESTINE, THE ARABS AND ISRAEL — THE SEARCH FOR JUSTICE. London: Longmans, 1969.

Cohen, A. ISRAEL AND THE ARAB WORLD. London: W. H. Allen, 1970.

Copeland, M. THE GAME OF NATIONS: THE AMORALITY OF POWER POLITICS. London: Weidenfeld and Nicolson, 1969.

Davis, J. THE EVASIVE PEACE. London: John Murray, 1968.

Dekmejian, H. EGYPT UNDER NASIR: A STUDY IN POLITICAL DY-NAMICS. Albany: State University of New York Press, 1971.

Dodd, C. H. and Sales, M. E. ISRAEL AND THE ARAB WORLD. London: Routledge and Kegan Paul, 1970.

Elon, A. THE ISRAELIS: FOUNDERS AND SONS. New York: Holt, Rinehart & Winston, 1971.

ESCO, Foundation for Palestine. PALESTINE: A STUDY OF JEWISH, ARAB AND BRITISH POLICIES, 2 vols. New Haven, Connecticut: Yale University Press, 1947.

Eytan, W. THE FIRST TEN YEARS: A DIPLOMATIC HISTORY OF ISRAEL. New York: Simon and Schuster, 1958.

Feinberg, N. THE ARAB-ISRAELI CONFLICT IN INTERNATIONAL LAW. Jerusalem: Magnes Press, 1970.

Frankenstein, E. PALESTINE IN THE LIGHT OF INTERNATIONAL LAW. New York: 1947.

Goitein, S. D. JEWS AND ARABS. New York: Schocken, 1955.

Hadawi, S. BITTER HARVEST: PALESTINE, 1914-67. New York: New World Press, 1967.

Halderman, J. W. ed. THE MIDDLE EAST CRISIS: TEST OF INTER-NATIONAL LAW. Dobbs Ferry, New York: Oceana Publications, 1969.

Harkabi, Y. ARAB ATTITUDES TO ISRAEL. trans. by Misha Louvish. Jerusalem: Israel Universities Press, 1972.

Higgins, R. THE MIDDLE EAST. London: Oxford University Press, 1969.

Hurewitz, J. C. THE STRUGGLE FOR PALESTINE. New York: Greenwood Press, 1968.

IMPERIALISM AND THE MIDDLE EAST CONFLICT: SOME LEFT-WING VIEWPOINTS. London: Ad Hoc Committee for Peace in the Middle East, N. D. (Pamphlet Series).

INTERNATIONAL LAW AND THE MIDDLE EAST CRISIS: A SYMPOSIUM. New Orleans, La.: Tulane Studies in Political Science, 1957.

John, R. and Hadawi, S. THE PALESTINE DIARY. 2 vols. Beirut: The Palestine Research Center, 1970.

Johnson, J. E. "Arabs vs. Israel: A Persistent Challenge," MIDDLE EAST JOURNAL. Vol. 18 (Winter 1964), p. 1.

Khadduri, M. D. ed. THE ARAB-ISRAELI IMPASSE. Washington, D. C.: Robert B. Luce, Inc., 1968.

Khouri, F. J. THE ARAB-ISRAELI DILEMMA. Syracuse, New York: Syracuse University Press, 1968.

Kimche, J. THE SECOND ARAB AWAKENING. London: Thames and Hudson, 1970.

Kimche, D. and D. Bawly. THE SANDSTORM: THE ARAB-ISRAELI WAR OF 1967 — PRELUDE AND AFTERMATH. London: Secker and Warburg, 1968.

Lall, A. THE U. N. AND THE MIDDLE EAST CRISIS, 1967. Rev. ed. New York: Columbia University Press, 1970.

Landau, J. ISRAEL AND THE ARABS. Jerusalem: Israel Communications, 1972.

Laqueur, W. THE ISRAEL-ARAB READER. New York: Bantam Books, 1969.

_____ . THE ROAD TO WAR 1967: THE ORIGINS FOR THE ARAB-ISRAEL CONFLICT. London, Weidenfeld and Nicolson, 1968.

Lilienthal, A. M. THE OTHER SIDE OF THE COIN. New York: Devin-Adair, 1965.

Mehdi, M. T. PEACE IN THE MIDDLE EAST. New York: New World, 1967.

THE MIDDLE EAST: PROSPECTS FOR PEACE. Dobbs Ferry, New York: Oceana Publications, 1969.

MYTHS AND FACTS: BACKGROUND TO THE ARAB-ISRAEL WAR. Washington: Near East Report, 1967.

PALESTINE: A SYMPOSIUM. New Delhi: The League of Arab States Mission, July, 1969.

Perlmutter, A. MILITARY AND POLITICS IN ISRAEL: NATION BUILDING AND ROLE EXPANSION. New York: Praeger, 1969.

Prittie, T. ESHKOL: THE MAN AND THE NATION. New York: Pitman Publishing Corp., 1969.

Rubin, J. A. TRUE FALSE ABOUT . . . ISRAEL. New York: Herzl, 1972.

Safran, N. FROM WAR TO WAR: THE ARAB-ISRAELI CONFRONTATION, 1948-1967. New York: Pegasus, 1969.

Sayegh, F. A. THE ZIONIST DIPLOMACY. Beirut: Palestine Liberation Organization Research Center, June 1969.

SEMINAR OF ARAB JURISTS ON PALESTINE, ALGIERS, 22-27 JULY 1967 — THE PALESTINE QUESTION. trans. from French by E. Rizk. Beirut: Institute for Palestine Studies, 1968.

Sharabi, H. PALESTINE AND ISRAEL: THE LETHAL DILEMMA. New York: Pegasus, 1969.

Soustelle, J. THE LONG MARCH OF ISRAEL. New York: American Heritage Press, 1969.

Syrkin, M. GOLDA MEIR. Rev. ed. New York: G. P. Putnam's Sons, 1969.

TO MAKE WAR TO MAKE PEACE: A SYMPOSIUM ON THE MIDDLE EAST. Tel Aviv: Ben Hur Press, 1969.

Wahby, M. ARAB QUEST FOR PEACE. Madras: Orient Longman, 1971.

Weizmann, C. TRIAL AND ERROR: AUTOBIOGRAPHY. New York: Harper & Brothers, 1949.

I. NATIONALISM AND STATEHOOD

AlRoy, G. C. ed. ATTITUDES TOWARD JEWISH STATEHOOD IN THE ARAB WORLD. New York: American Academic Association for Peace in the Middle East, 1971.

Antonius, G. THE ARAB AWAKENING. Philadelphia: Lippincott, 1938.

Arnoni, M. S. ARAB NATIONALISM AND THE NAZIS. Tel-Aviv: World Labour Zionist Movement, August 1970.

Avineri, Shlomo. ed. ISRAEL AND THE PALESTINIANS: REFLECTIONS ON THE CLASH OF TWO NATIONAL MOVEMENTS. New York: St. Martin's Press, 1971.

Balfour, A. J. SPEECHES ON ZIONISM. London: Arrowsmith, 1928.

Bavly D. and F. David. ISRAEL AND THE PALESTINIANS. London: Anglo-Israel Association, January 1971.

Cattan, H. TO WHOM DOES PALESTINE BELONG? Beirut: The Institute for Palestine Studies, 1967.

Eban, A. THE TIDE OF NATIONALISM. New York: Horizon Press, 1959.

Feinberg, N. ON AN ARAB JURIST'S APPROACH TO ZIONISM AND THE STATE OF ISRAEL. Jerusalem: The Magnes Press, 1971.

_____ . "The Recognition of the Jewish People in International Law," JEWISH YEARBOOK OF INTERNATIONAL LAW. (1948). p. 1.

Finer, H. "Reflections on the Nature of Arab Nationalism," MIDDLE EASTERN AFFAIRS, Vol. 9 (October 1958), p. 302.

Haim, S. Ed. ARAB NATIONALISM: AN ANTHOLOGY. Berkeley & Los Angeles: University of California, 1962.

Halpern, B. THE IDEA OF THE JEWISH STATE. Cambridge, Massachusetts: Harvard University Press, 1969.

Herzberg, A. THE ZIONIST IDEA: A HISTORICAL ANALYSIS AND READER. New York: Atheneum, 1970.

Khalidi, W. FROM HAVEN TO CONQUEST: READINGS IN ZIONISM AND THE PALESTINE PROBLEM UNTIL 1948. Beirut: Institute for Palestine Studies, 1970.

Mallison, W. T., Jr. "The Zionist-Israel Judicial Claims to Constitute The Jewish People Nationality Entity and to Confer Membership in It: Appraisal in Public International Law," GEORGE WASHINGTON LAW REVIEW. Vol. 32 (1964), p. 983.

Patai, R. Ed. ENCYCLOPEDIA OF ZIONISM AND ISRAEL. 2 vols. New York: Herzl Press, 1972.

Peretz, D., E. M. Wilson & R. J. Ward. A PALESTINE ENTITY? Washington, D. C.: The Middle East Institute, 1970.

Stone, J. "Peace and Palestinians," NEW YORK UNIVERSITY JOURNAL OF INTERNATIONAL LAW AND POLITICS. Vol. 3 (1970), p. 247.

_____ . SELF DETERMINATION AND THE PALESTINIAN ARABS. Jerusalem: Truman Research Institute, 1970.

Sakran, F. C. PALESTINE DILEMMA: ARAB RIGHTS VERSUS ZIONIST ASPIRATIONS. Washington, D. C.: Public Affairs Press, 1948.

II. RELIGIOUS AND ETHNICAL CONFLICTS

Alexander, Y. "A Christian Church in the Search of Peace in the Middle East," INTERNATIONAL PROBLEMS, Vol. X (June 1971), p. 41.

CHRISTIANS, ZIONISM AND PALESTINE. Beirut: The Institute for Palestine Studies, 1970.

Cohn, N. WARRANT FOR GENOCIDE: THE MYTH OF THE JEWISH WORLD CONSPIRACY AND THE PROTOCOLS OF ZION. London: Eyre & Spottiswoode, 1967.

Eckhardt, A. R. ELDER AND YOUNGER BROTHERS: THE ENCOUNTER OF JEWS AND CHRISTIANS. New York: Charles Scribner, 1967.

Flannery, E. H. THE ANGUISH OF THE JEWS: TWENTY-THREE CENTURIES OF ANTI-SEMITISM. New York: Macmillan, 1965.

Green, D. F. Ed. ARAB THEOLOGIANS ON JEWS AND ISRAEL. Geneve: Editions de l'Avenir, 1971.

Hadawi, S. WHO BENEFITS FROM ANTI-SEMITISM? New York: Arab Information Center, 1961.

Haim, S., "Arabic Antisemitic Literature," JEWISH SOCIAL STUDIES, Vol. 17 (1955), p. 307.

HATRED IS SACRED: EXTRACTS FROM ARAB SCHOOL TEXTS. Jerusalem: Ministry for Foreign Affairs, 1968.

Lerner, N. "The U. N. Debate on Antisemitism and Zionism," INTERNATIONAL PROBLEMS, Vol. 1 (1966). p. 10.

Parkes, J. ANTISEMITISM. London: Vallentine Mitchell, 1963.

Rosenblatt, S., "The Jews in Islam" in Pinson, K. S. Ed. ESSAYS ON ANTISEMITISM, 2nd Ed. New York: Jewish Social Studies, 1960, p. 111.

Rosenthal, E. I. J. JUDAISM AND ISLAM. London: Yoseloff, 1961.

Sa'ab, H. ZIONISM AND RACISM, Beirut: Palestine Liberation Organization Research Center, December 1965.

Smith, W. D. ISLAM IN MODERN HISTORY. Princeton, New Jersey: Princeton University Press, 1957.

Werblowsky, R. J. Z. and G. Wigoder, Eds. ENCYCLOPEDIA OF THE JEWISH RELIGION. New York: Holt, Rinehart and Winston, 1966.

Zander, W. ISRAEL AND THE HOLY PLACES OF CHRISTENDOM. London: Weidenfeld and Nicolson, 1971.

III. MINORITY AND HUMAN RIGHTS

"The Administered Territories" (Background, Highlights, Legalities), MIDDLE EAST INFORMATION SERIES, (October 1969).

Al-Abid, I. HUMAN RIGHTS IN THE OCCUPIED TERRITORIES. Beirut: Palestine Liberation Organization Research Center, September, 1970.

_____ . ISRAEL AND HUMAN RIGHTS. Beirut: Palestine Liberation Organization Research Center, November 1969.

ARABS IN ISRAEL. Jerusalem: Ministry for Foreign Affairs, 1961.

THE ISRAELI ADMINISTRATION IN JUDAEA, SAMARIA AND GAZA: A RECORD OF PROGRESS. Tel Aviv: Ministry of Defense, 1968.

THE JEWISH EXODUS FROM THE ARAB COUNTRIES AND THE ARAB REFUGEES. Jerusalem: Israel Ministry for Foreign Affairs, N.D.

LAW AND COURTS IN THE ISRAEL-HELD AREAS. Jerusalem: Faculty of Law, Hebrew University, 1970.

Landau, J. M. THE ARABS IN ISRAEL: A POLITICAL STUDY. London: Oxford University Press, 1969.

Peretz, D. ISRAEL AND THE PALESTINE ARABS. Washington, D. C.: The Middle East Institute, 1958.

Raphaeli, N., "The West Bank: Governing Without Administration," PUBLIC ADMINISTRATION IN ISRAEL AND ABROAD. No. 10 (1970), p. 27.

Rejwan, N., "Israel's Arab Citizens," MIDSTREAM Vol. 8 (December 1962), p. 34.

Sayegh, F. A. DISCRIMINATION IN EDUCATION AGAINST THE ARABS IN ISRAEL. Beirut: Palestine Liberation Organization Research Center, September 1966.

Schechtman, J. B. ON THE WINGS OF EAGLES: THE PLIGHT, EXODUS, AND HOMECOMING OF ORIENTAL JEWRY. New York: Thomas Yoseloff, 1961.

Schwartz, W. THE ARABS IN ISRAEL. London: Faber, 1959.

Stock, E. FROM CONFLICT TO UNDERSTANDING: RELATIONS BETWEEN JEWS AND ARABS IN ISRAEL SINCE 1948. New York: Institute of Human Relations Press, 1968.

Teveth, S. THE CURSED BLESSING. London: Weidenfeld and Nicolson, 1969.

Tuma, E. H., "The Arabs of Israel: An Impasse," NEW OUTLOOK Vol. 9 (March-April 1966), p. 39.

VIOLATIONS OF HUMAN RIGHTS IN ISRAEL. New York: Arab Information Center, 1961.

Weigert, G. FACT AND FICTION: HUMAN RIGHTS IN THE ISRAELI ADMINISTERED TERRITORIES. Jerusalem: Israel Communications, 1971.

WHERE JEWS AND ARABS MEET. New York: Israel Information Services, 1968.

IV. ARAB REFUGEES

"The Arab Refugees," THE MIDDLE EAST RECORD, Vol. 11 (1961), p. 228.

Dodd, P. and H. Barakat. RIVER WITHOUT BRIDGES: A STUDY OF THE EXODUS OF THE 1967 PALESTINIAN ARAB REFUGEES. Beirut: The Institute for Palestine Studies, 1969.

Gabbay, R. THE POLITICAL STUDY OF THE ARAB-JEWISH CONFLICT: THE ARAB REFUGEE PROBLEM. (A Case Study). Geneva: Librairie Droz, 1959.

Holborn, L. W., "The Palestine Arab Refugee Problem," INTERNATIONAL JOURNAL, Vol. 23 (1968), p. 82.

Kaplan, D. THE ARAB REFUGEES. Jerusalem: Rubin Mass, 1959.

THE PALESTINE REFUGEE PROBLEM: A NEW APPROACH AND A PLAN FOR A SOLUTION. New York: Institute for Mediterranean Affairs, 1959.

Peretz, D., "The Arab Refugee: A Changing Problem," FOREIGN AFFAIRS, Vol. 41 (April 1963), p. 558.

_____ ., "Israel's Administration and Arab Refugees," FOREIGN AFFAIRS, Vol. 46 (1968), p. 336.

Pinner, W. HOW MANY REFUGEES? London: Macgibbon & Kee, 1959.

_____ . THE LEGEND OF THE ARAB REFUGEES. Tel Aviv: Economic and Social Research Institute, 1967.

Syrkin, M., "The Arab Refugees: A Zionist View," COMMENTARY, Vol. 41, (January 1966), p. 23.

Schechtman, J. B. THE ARAB REFUGEE PROBLEM. New York: Philosophical Library, 1952.

Tomeh, G. J., "Legal Status of Arab Refugees," LAW AND CONTEMPORARY PROBLEMS, Vol. 33 (1968), p. 110.

V. EXPANSIONISM AND BOUNDARY DISPUTES

Bar-Yaacov, N. THE ISRAEL-SYRIAN ARMISTICE: PROBLEMS OF IMPLEMENTATION. Jerusalem: Magnes Press, 1967.

Blum, Y. Z., "The Missing Reversioner: Reflections on the Status of Judea and Samaria," ISRAEL LAW REVIEW. Vol. 3 (1968), p. 279.

Blum, Y. Z. SECURE BOUNDARIES AND MIDDLE EAST PEACE. Jerusalem: The Hebrew University, Faculty of Law, 1971.

Elaraby, N., "Some Legal Implications of the 1947 Partition Resolution and the 1949 Armistice Agreements," LAW AND CONTEMPORARY PROBLEMS Vol. 33 (1968), p. 97.

Hurewitz, J. C., "The Israeli-Syrian Crisis in the Light of the Arab-Israel Armistice System," INTERNATIONAL ORGANIZATION, Vol. 5 (1951), p. 459.

Kishtainy, K. WHITHER ISRAEL? A STUDY OF ZIONIST EXPANSIONISM. Beirut: Palestine Liberation Organization Research Center, July, 1970.

Meron, T., "The Demilitarization of Mount Scopus: A Regime that Was," ISRAEL LAW REVIEW Vol. 3 (1968), p. 501.

Rossenne, S. ISRAEL'S ARMISTICE AGREEMENTS WITH THE ARAB STATES. Tel Aviv: Blumstein, 1951.

Secure and Recognized Boundaries: Israel's Right to Live in Peace Within Defensible Frontiers. Jerusalem: Carta, 1971.

VI. THE STATUS OF JERUSALEM

Aumann, M. JERUSALEM. Jerusalem: Israel Digest, 1968.

Borman, S., "Territorial Acquisition by Conquest in International Law and the Unification of Jerusalem," INTERNATIONAL PROBLEMS. Vol. VII No. 1-2 (May 1968), p. 11.

Bernadotte, F. TO JERUSALEM. London: Hodder and Stoughton, 1951.

Collins, L. and D. Lapierre. O JERUSALEM. New York: Simon and Schuster, 1972.

Davis, H. E. THE JERUSALEM QUESTION, 1917—1968. Hoover, 1971.

Hollis, C. and Brownrigg, R. HOLY PLACES: JEWISH, CHRISTIAN, AND

MUSLIM MONUMENTS IN THE HOLY LAND. Tel Aviv: Steimatzky, 1969.

JERUSALEM: A COLLECTION OF UNITED NATIONS DOCUMENTS. Beirut: The Institute for Palestine Studies, 1970.

Jones, S. S. "The Status of Jerusalem: Some National and International Aspects," LAW AND CONTEMPORARY PROBLEMS, Vol. 33 (1968), p. 169.

Joseph, B. THE FAITHFUL CITY: THE SIEGE OF JERUSALEM, 1948. New York: Simon and Schuster, 1960.

Kollek, T. JERUSALEM: ONCE AGAIN Jerusalem: Ministry for Foreign Affairs, Spring, 1968.

Kollek, T. and Pearlman, M. JERUSALEM: A HISTORY OF FORTY CENTURIES. New York: Random House, 1968.

Laqueur, W. THE ROAD TO JERUSALEM. New York: Macmillan Co., 1968.

Lauterpacht, E. JERUSALEM AND THE HOLY PLACES. London: Anglo-Israel Association, 1968.

Levin, H. JERUSALEM EMBATTLED. London: Gollancz, 1950.

Meron, T., "The Demilitarization of Mount Scopus: A Regime That Was," ISRAEL LAW REVIEW, Vol. 3 (1968), p. 501.

Mohn, P., "Jerusalem and the United Nations," INTERNATIONAL CON-CILIATION, No. 464 (October, 1950).

Pfaff, R. H. JERUSALEM: KEYSTONE OF AN ARAB-ISRAELI SETTLE-MENT. Washington, D. C.: American Enterprise Institute, August, 1969.

Rachauskas, C. THE INTERNATIONALIZATION OF JERUSALEM. Washington, D. C.: Catholic Association for International Peace, 1954.

Rousan, M. PALESTINE AND THE INTERNATIONALIZATION OF JERUSALEM. Baghdad: Ministry of Culture and Guidance, 1965.

VII. THE JORDAN RIVER

COMMENTARY ON WATER DEVELOPMENT IN THE JORDAN VAL-LEY REGION. Beirut: Arab Palestine Office, 1954.

Doherty, K. B. "Jordan Waters Conflict," INTERNATIONAL CONCILIA-TION, No. 553 (May 1965), p. 26.

THE JORDAN WATER PROBLEM. Washington: American Friends of the Middle East, 1964.

Rizk, E. THE RIVER JORDAN. New York: Arab Information Center, 1964.

Rosenne, S. SOME LEGAL ASPECTS OF ISRAEL'S LAKE KINNERET-NEGEV WATER PROJECT. Jerusalem: Ministry for Foreign Affairs, 1964.

Saliba, S. N. THE JORDAN RIVER DISPUTE. The Hague: Nijhoff, 1968.

Stevens, G. JORDAN RIVER PARTITION. Stanford, California: The Hoover Institute, 1965.

VIII. FREEDOM OF NAVIGATION

Babovic, B., "The International Legal Position of the Suez Canal and Nationalization," INTERNATIONAL PROBLEMS (Belgrade), Vol. I (1960), p. 191.

Badr, G. M., "Israel and the Suez Canal — A New Approach," REVUE EGYPTIENNE DE DROIT INTERNATIONAL, Vol. 23 (1967), p. 63.

Bloomfield, L. M. EGYPT, ISRAEL AND THE GULF OF AQABA IN INTERNATIONAL LAW. Toronto: Carswell, 1957.

Brown, T. D. "World War Prize Law Applied in a Limited War Situation: Egyptian Restrictions on Neutral Shipping with Israel," MINNESOTA LAW REVIEW, Vol. 50 (1966), p. 849.

Carmichael, J. "On Again, Off Again: Egypt's Blockade of the Suez Canal," MIDSTREAM, Vol. 6 (Summer 1960), p. 56.

Dinitz, S., "The Legal Aspects of the Egyptian Blockade of the Suez Canal," GEORGETOWN LAW REVIEW, Vol. 45 (1956/57), p. 169.

El Khatib, M. F. and O. Z. Ghobashy. THE SUEZ CANAL, SAFE AND FREE PASSAGE. New York: Arab Information Center, 1960.

El-Oteifi, G., "The Gulf of Aqaba and Israel," REVIEW OF INTERNATIONAL AFFAIRS. Vol. 18 (July 1967), p. 5.

Ghobashy, O. Z., "The Gulf of Aqaba and the Straits of Tiran," ISLAMIC REVIEW Vol. 45 (1957), p. 31.

_____ . "Tiran and Aqaba," EGYPTIAN ECONOMIC AND POLITICAL REVUE Vol. 3 (January 1959), p. 18.

Gross, L., "The Geneva Conference on the Law of the Sea and the Right of Innocent Passage Through the Gulf of Aqaba," AMERICAN JOURNAL OF INTERNATIONAL LAW, Vol. 53 (July 1959), p. 564.

_____ . "Passage Through the Suez Canal of Israel-Bound Cargo and Israel Ships," AMERICAN JOURNAL OF INTERNATIONAL LAW Vol. 51 (1957), p. 530.

Hammad, M. B. W. "Right of Passage in the Gulf of Aqaba," REVUE INTERNATIONAL EGYPTIENNE DROIT INTERNATIONAL PUBLIQUE Vol. 15 (1959), p. 118.

Huang, T. "Some International and Legal Aspects of the Suez Canal Questions, AMERICAN JOURNAL OF INTERNATIONAL LAW, Vol. 51 (1957), p. 277.

Johnson, D. H. N., "Some Legal Problems of International Waterways, with Particular Reference to the Straits of Tiran and the Suez Canal," MODERN LAW REVIEW Vol. 31 (1968), p. 153.

Khadduri, M., "Closure of the Suez Canal to Israeli Shipping," LAW AND CONTEMPORARY PROBLEMS Vol. 33 (1968), p. 147.

Lauterpacht, E. ed. THE SUEZ CANAL SETTLEMENT: A SELECTION OF DOCUMENTS (OCTOBER 1956 — MARCH 1959). New York: Praeger, 1960.

Nurti, B. S. N., "The Legal Status of the Gulf of Aqaba," INDIAN JOURNAL OF INTERNATIONAL LAW, Vol. III (1967), p. 201.

Meir, F. THE U. N. CHARTER OUTLAWS WAR: FREEDOM OF SHIPPING IS INDIVISIBLE. New York: Israel Office of Information, 1959.

Obieta, J. A. THE INTERNATIONAL STATUS OF THE SUEZ CANAL. The Hague: M. Nijhoff, 1960.

Porter, P. THE GULF OF AQABA: AN INTERNATIONAL WATERWAY. Washington, D. C.: Public Affairs Press, 1957.

Selak, C. B., "A Consideration of the Legal Status of the Gulf of Aqaba," AMERICAN JOURNAL OF INTERNATIONAL LAW, Vol. 52 (October 1958), p. 660.

A SELECTION OF DOCUMENTS RELATING TO THE INTERNATIONAL STATUS IN THE SUEZ AND THE POSITION OF THE SUEZ CANAL COMPANY. London: Society of Comparative Legislation and International Law, 1956.

Shukairy, A. TERRITORIAL AND HISTORICAL WATERS IN INTERNATIONAL LAW. Beirut: Palestine Liberation Organization, 1967.

Slonim, S., "The Right of Innocent Passage and the 1958 Geneva Conference on the Law of the Sea," COLUMBIA JOURNAL OF TRANSNATIONAL LAW, Vol. 5 (1966), p. 96.

IX. AGGRESSION AND SELF DEFENSE

Alexander, Y. and M. L. Sweet, "The 'Just War' Concept and Its Application to the 1967 Arab-Israeli War," INTERNATIONAL PROBLEMS, Vol. 9 (November 1970), p. 34.

"The Arab-Israeli War and International Law," HARVARD INTERNATIONAL LAW JOURNAL, Vol. 9 (1968), p. 232.

Blum, Y., "The Beirut Raid and the International Double Standard," AMERICAN JOURNAL OF INTERNATIONAL LAW, Vol. 64 (1970), p. 73.

Dayan, M. DIARY OF THE SINAI CAMPAIGN. New York: Harper and Row, 1966.

Dinstein, Y., "The Legal Issues of Para-War and Peace in the Middle East," ST. JOHN'S LAW REVIEW, Vol. 44 (1970), p. 466.

Draper, T. ISRAEL AND WORLD POLITICS: ROOTS OF THE THIRD ARAB-ISRAELI WAR. New York: Viking Press, 1968.

Falk, R. A., "The Beirut Raid and the International Law of Retaliation," AMERICAN JOURNAL OF INTERNATIONAL LAW, Vol. 63 (1969), p. 415.

Goodhart, A. L. ISRAEL, THE UNITED NATIONS AND AGGRESSION. London: Anglo-Israel Association, 1968.

Feinberg, N. THE LEGALITY OF A "STATE OF WAR" AFTER THE CESSATION OF HOSTILITIES UNDER THE CHARTER OF THE UNITED NATIONS AND THE COVENANT OF THE LEAGUE OF NATIONS. Jerusalem: Magnes Press, 1961.

JORDANIAN BELLIGERENCY. New York: Israel Information Services, 1967.

Laqueur, W. THE ROAD TO WAR — THE ORIGIN AND AFTERMATH OF THE ARAB ISRAELI CONFLICT 1967-68. London: Weidenfeld & Nicolson, 1968.

Malawer, S. S., "Anticipatory Self-Defense Under Article 51 of the United Nations Charter and the Arab-Israeli War 1967," INTERNATIONAL PROBLEMS (Tel Aviv), Vol. 1 (1970), p. 14.

Mushkat, M., "Some Legal and Political Problems of the Arab War Against Israel," INTERNATIONAL PROBLEMS (Tel Aviv), Vol. 4 (1967), p. 51.

O'Brien, V. W., "International Law and the Outbreak of War in the Middle East, 1967," ORBIS, Vol. 11 (1967), p. 692.

Higgins, R., "The June War: The United Nations and Legal Background," JOURNAL OF CONTEMPORARY HISTORY, Vol. 3 (1968), p. 253.

Schwebel, S. M., "What Weight to Conquest?," AMERICAN JOURNAL OF INTERNATIONAL LAW, Vol. 64 (1970), p. 344.

Shapira, A., "The Six-Day War and the Right of Self-Defense," ISRAEL LAW REVIEW, Vol. 6 (1971), p. 65.

Stock, E. ISRAEL ON THE ROAD TO SINAI, 1949—1956, with a sequel on THE SIX-DAY WAR. Ithaca, New York: Cornell University Press, 1967.

Stone, J. THE MIDDLE EAST UNDER CEASE-FIRE. Sydney: A Bridge Publication, 1967.

Wright, Q., "Legal Aspects of the Middle East Situation," LAW AND CONTEMPORARY PROBLEMS, Vol. 33 (1968), p. 5.

X. ECONOMIC WARFARE

Ben-Horin, E., "The Arab Boycott and Arab Anti-Semitism" RECON-STRUCTIONIST, Vol. 30 (April 3, 1964), p. 12.

Kimche, J. "The Arab Boycott Against Israel: New Aspects," MIDSTREAM, Vol. 10 (September 1964), p. 14.

Levine, S., "The Arab Boycott Involves Americans in the War Against Israel: A Special Survey," NEAR EAST REPORT, May 1965.

Remba, O., "The Arab Boycott: A Study in Total Economic Warfare," MIDSTREAM, Vol. 6 (Summer 1960), p. 40.

Sharif, A. A. A STATISTICAL STUDY ON THE ARAB BOYCOTT OF ISRAEL. Beirut: The Institute for Palestine Studies, 1970.

Shefer, M., "The Effect of the Arab-Israel Rupture on the Economy of the Arab Countries," NEW OUTLOOK, Vol. 7 (November-December 1964), p. 16.

Vitta, E., "The Boycott of 'Zionist Goods' by the Arab League," JEWISH YEARBOOK OF INTERNATIONAL LAW, (1948), p. 253.

"The United States Against the Arab Boycott," NEAR EAST REPORT, October, 1965.

XI. GUERRILLA ACTIVITIES

"Arab Terrorism." Jerusalem: Ministry for Foreign Affairs, December, 1969.

Bell, B. J., "Arafat's Man in the Mirror: The Myth of the Fedayeen," NEW MIDDLE EAST, Vol. 19 (April 1970), p. 19.

Harkabi, Y. FEDAYEEN ACTION AND ARAB STRATEGY. London: Institute for Strategic Studies, December 1968.

Meron, T. SOME LEGAL ASPECTS OF ARAB TERRORISTS' CLAIMS TO PRIVILEGED COMBATANCY. New York: Sabra Books, 1970.

Rejwan, N., "Lebanon and the Guerrillas," MIDSTREAM (December 1969), p. 15.

Schechtman, J. B. ARAB TERROR: BLUEPRINT FOR POLITICAL MURDER. New York: Zionist Organization of America, 1969.

Sharabi, H. PALESTINE GUERRILLAS: THEIR CREDIBILITY AND EFFECTIVENESS. Beirut: The Institute for Palestine Studies, 1970.

"Support of Terrorist Units: A Case of Aggression." Jerusalem: Ministry for Foreign Affairs, April, 1969.

Yahalom, Y. ARAB TERROR. Tel Aviv: Labor Zionist Movement, 1969.

XII. THE ROLE OF THE UNITED NATIONS AND THE BIG POWERS

Afifi, M. THE ARABS AND THE U. N. London: Longmans, 1964.

Akzin, B., "The United Nations and Palestine," JEWISH YEAR BOOK OF INTERNATIONAL LAW (1948), p. 87.

Anabtawi, S. N., "The United Nations and the Middle East Conflict of 1967," THE ARAB WORLD, Vol. 14 (1968), p. 53.

Badeau, J. S. THE AMERICAN APPROACH TO THE ARAB WORLD. New York: Harper and Row, 1968.

Burns, E. L. M., "The Withdrawal of UNEF and the Future of Peace-keeping," INTERNATIONAL JOURNAL, Vol. 23 (1968), p. 1.

Campbell, J. C., "The Arab-Israeli Conflict: An American Policy," FOREIGN AFFAIRS, Vol. 49 (1970), p. 51.

Dagan, A. MOSCOW AND JERUSALEM. London: Abelard-Schuman, 1970.

Elaraby, N., "United Nations Peacekeeping by Consent: A Case Study of the Withdrawal of the United Nations Emergency Force," NEW YORK UNIVERSITY JOURNAL OF INTERNATIONAL LAW AND POLITICS, Vol. 1 (1968), p. 149.

El-Farra, M. H., "The Role of the United Nations Vis-a-vis the Palestine Question," LAW AND CONTEMPORARY PROBLEMS, Vol. 33 (1968), p. 68.

Finer, H. DULLES OVER SUEZ. Chicago: Quadrangle Books, 1964.

Golan, G. THE SOVIET INVOLVEMENT IN THE MIDDLE EAST. Jerusalem: The Hebrew University, Soviet and East European Research Center, 1971.

Goldberg, A., "A Basic Mideast Document — Its Meaning Today," INTERNATIONAL PROBLEMS, Vol. 1 (1970), p. 10.

Goodrich, L. M. and G. E. Rosner, "The UNEF," INTERNATIONAL ORGANIZATION, Vol. 11 (1957), p. 413.

Hadawi, S., ed. PALESTINE BEFORE THE UNITED NATIONS. Beirut: Institute for Palestine Studies, 1966.

_____ ., ed. UNITED NATIONS RESOLUTIONS ON PALESTINE 1947—1966. Beirut: Institute for Palestine Studies, 1967.

Higgins, R. UNITED NATIONS PEACEKEEPING, 1946—1967: DOCUMENTS AND COMMENTARY I, The Middle East. London: Oxford University Press, 1969.

Hurewitz, J. C., Ed. SOVIET-AMERICAN RIVALRY IN THE MIDDLE EAST. New York: Frederick A. Praeger, 1969.

ISRAEL AND THE UNITED NATIONS. New York: Carnegie Endowment for International Peace, 1956.

Jansen, M. E. THE UNITED STATES AND THE PALESTINIAN PEOPLE. Beirut: The Institute for Palestine Studies, 1970.

Lall, A. THE U. N. AND THE MIDDLE EAST CRISIS. New York: Columbia University Press, 1968.

Laqueur, W. THE STRUGGLE FOR THE MIDDLE EAST: THE SOVIET UNION AND THE MIDDLE EAST, 1958-68. London: Routledge and Kegan, 1969.

Lapidoth, R., "The Security Council in the May 1967 Crisis: A Study in Frustration," ISRAEL LAW REVIEW, Vol. 4 (1969), p. 534.

Lauterpacht, E., Ed. THE UNITED NATIONS EMERGENCY FORCE: BASIC DOCUMENTS. London: Stevens, 1960.

Merlin, S., Ed. THE BIG POWERS AND THE PRESENT CRISIS IN THE MIDDLE EAST. Teaneck, New Jersey: Farleigh Dickinson University Press, 1968.

Nevakivi, J. BRITAIN, FRANCE AND THE ARAB MIDDLE EAST. London: Athlone Press, 1969.

Pranger, R. J. AMERICAN POLICY FOR PEACE IN THE MIDDLE EAST, 1969—1971. Washington, D. C.: American Enterprise Institute for Public Policy Research, 1971.

Ra'anan, U. THE U.S.S.R. ARMS TO THE THIRD WORLD. Cambridge, Massachusetts: M.I.T. Press, 1969.

Robinson, J. PALESTINE AND THE UNITED NATIONS: PRELUDE TO SOLUTION. Washington, D. C.: Public Affairs Press, 1947.

Rosner, G. THE UNITED NATIONS EMERGENCY FORCE. New York: Columbia University Press, 1963.

Safran, N. THE UNITED STATES AND ISRAEL. Cambridge, Massachusetts: Harvard, 1963.

Sayegh, F. A. THE RECORD OF ISRAEL AT THE UNITED NATIONS. New York: Arab Information Center, 1957.

Shapira, A., "The Security Council Resolution of November 22, 1967 — Its Legal Nature and Implications," ISRAEL LAW REVIEW, Vol. 4 (1969), p. 229.

Tannous, I. FAILURES OF THE U. N. IN THE PALESTINE TRAGEDY. New York: Palestine Arab Refugee Office, 1959.

UNITED NATIONS RESOLUTIONS ON PALESTINE. Beirut: Institute for Palestine Studies, 1966.

Von Horn, C. SOLDIERING FOR PEACE. New York: David McKay, 1967.

XIII. NEGOTIATIONS AND PEACE

Lord Caradon, "A Plan for Middle East Peace," WAR/PEACE REPORT, Vol. 10 (December 1970), p. 7.

Comay, M., "Peace in the Middle East," INTERNATIONAL PROBLEMS, Vol. 9 (November 1970), p. 14.

Eban, A. FOR PEACE AND SECURITY. New York: Israel Office of Information, 1954.

_____ . FROM A STATE OF WAR TO A STATE OF PEACE. New York: Israel Information Services, 1967.

_____ . NOT BACKWARD TO BELLIGERENCY BUT FORWARD TO PEACE. New York: Israel Information Services, 1967.

Goldman, N., "The Future of Israel," FOREIGN AFFAIRS, Vol. 48 (1970), p. 442.

ISRAEL'S PEACE OFFERS TO THE ARAB STATES, 1948—1963. Jerusalem: Ministry for Foreign Affairs, 1963.

ISRAEL'S STRUGGLE FOR PEACE. New York: Israel Office of Information, 1960.

Majus, J. STRUGGLING FOR A PEACEFUL SOLUTION. Tel Aviv: Middle East Peace Institute, 1970.

Mehdi, M. T. PEACE IN THE MIDDLE EAST. New York: New World Press, 1967.

Peretz, D., "A Binational Approach to the Palestine Conflict," LAW AND CONTEMPORARY PROBLEMS, Vol. 33 (1968), p. 32.

Rosenne, S., "Directions for a Middle East Settlement — Some Underlying Legal Problems," LAW AND CONTEMPORARY PROBLEMS, Vol. 33 (1948), p. 44.

Rostow, E. V., "Legal Aspects of the Search for Peace in the Middle East," 1970 PROCEEDINGS OF THE AMERICAN SOCIETY OF INTERNATIONAL LAW, p. 64.

Stone, J., "Peace and the Palestinians," NEW YORK UNIVERSITY JOURNAL OF INTERNATIONAL LAW AND POLITICS, Vol. III, No. 2 (Winter, 1970), p. 248.

Wright, Q., "The Middle East Problem," AMERICAN JOURNAL OF INTERNATIONAL LAW, Vol. 64 (1970), p. 270.

A Note about This Book

The text of this book was set on an IBM Selectric Composer System in the type face, Century. The book was composed by dcmj typesetting, New York and was printed and bound by Thomson-Shore, Dexter, Michigan. Production supervision by diz and Roger Hudson. The cover for the paperback edition and the jacket for the clothbound edition was designed by Donald Mowbray.